Acclaim for
Inhuman Bondage: The Rise and Fall of Slavery in the New World

"David Brion Davis, our greatest historian of slavery and abolition, weaves together here one of the central stories of modern world history—and does so with a power, authority, and grace that is his alone."—Edward L. Ayers, author of *In the Presence of Mine Enemies: War in the Heart of America, 1859–1863*

"A tour de force. . . . Could not be more welcome. . . . Davis follows the large story of slavery into all corners of the Atlantic world, demonstrating that hardly anyone or anything was untouched by it. He is particularly interested in the way ideas shaped slavery's development. But 'Inhuman Bondage' is not a history without people. Princes, merchants and reformers of all sorts play their role, though Davis gives pride of place to the men and women who suffered bondage. Drawing on some of the best recent studies, he not only adjudicates between the arguments, but also provides dozens of new insights, large and small, into events as familiar as the revolt on Saint-Domingue (now Haiti) and the American Civil War. . . . An invaluable guide to explaining what has made slavery's consequences so much a part of contemporary American culture and politics."—Ira Berlin, *The New York Times Book Review*

"David Brion Davis has been the preeminent historian of ideas about slavery in the Western world since the early modern period. . . . Davis, a leading practitioner of intellectual and cultural history, has now gone far beyond the history of ideas and attempted to study New World slavery in all its ramifications, social, economic, and political, as well as intellectual and cultural. . . . He convincingly demonstrates that slavery was central to the history of the New World."—George M. Fredrickson, *The New York Review of Books*

"Ranging from ancient Babylonia to the modern Western Hemisphere, David Brion Davis offers a concise history of slavery and its abolition that once again reminds us why he is the foremost scholar of international slavery. There is no more up-to-date account of this pivotal aspect of the world's history."—Eric Foner, author of *Reconstruction: America's Unfinished Revolution, 1863–1877*

"In this gracefully fashioned masterpiece, David Brion Davis draws on a lifetime of scrupulous scholarship in order to trace the sources and highlight the distinctiveness of America's central paradox by situating it in both its New World and Western contexts. His powerful narrative is enhanced and deepened by persuasively rendered details. For students of slavery, and of American history more generally, it is simply indispensable. With all the makings of a classic, *Inhuman Bondage* is the glorious culmination of the definitive series of studies on slavery by one of America's greatest living historians."—Orlando Patterson, author of *Rituals of Blood: Consequences of Slavery in Two American Centuries*

"Impressive and sprawling. . . . Davis's account is rich in detail, and his voice is clear enough to coax even casual readers through this dense history."—*Publishers Weekly*

"A magisterial achievement, a model of comparative and interdisciplinary scholarship, and the best study we have of American slavery within the broader context of the New World. It is also a powerful and moving story, told by one of America's greatest historians."—John Stauffer, author of *The Black Hearts of Men: Radical Abolitionists and the Transformation of Race*

"Lives up to what readers expect from Davis: it is engagingly written and impressively broad in its scope and analysis."—Laurent Dubois, *American Historical Review*

Also by David Brion Davis

Challenging the Boundaries of Slavery

In the Image of God: Religion, Moral Values and
Our Heritage of Slavery

From Homicide to Slavery: Studies in American Culture

Revolutions: Reflections on American Equality
and Foreign Liberations

Slavery and Human Progress

The Problem of Slavery in the Age of Revolution, 1770–1823

The Slave Power Conspiracy and the Paranoid Style

The Problem of Slavery in Western Culture

Homicide in American Fiction, 1789–1859:
A Study in Social Values

INHUMAN BONDAGE

The RISE and FALL of SLAVERY in the NEW WORLD

DAVID BRION DAVIS

OXFORD
UNIVERSITY PRESS

Contents

Maps   ix

A Selective Calendar of Events   xi

Prologue   1

1   The *Amistad* Test of Law and Justice   12

2   The Ancient Foundations of Modern Slavery   27

3   The Origins of Antiblack Racism in the New World   48

4   How Africans Became Integral to New World History   77

5   The Atlantic Slave System: Brazil and the Caribbean   103

6   Slavery in Colonial North America   124

7   The Problem of Slavery in the American Revolution   141

8   The Impact of the French and Haitian Revolutions   157

9   Slavery in the Nineteenth-Century South, I:
     From Contradiction to Defense   175

10 Slavery in the Nineteenth-Century South, II:
    From Slaveholder Treatment and the Nature of Labor to
    Slave Culture, Sex and Religion, and Free Blacks   193

11 Some Nineteenth-Century Slave Conspiracies and Revolts   205

12 Explanations of British Abolitionism   231

13 Abolitionism in America   250

14 The Politics of Slavery in the United States   268

15 The Civil War and Slave Emancipation   297

    Epilogue   323

    Notes   333

    Acknowledgments   415

    Index   419

Illustrations follow page 174.

Maps

Map 1   Routes of the *Amistad* Story: From Slavery to Freedom   25

Map 2   Late Medieval Prototypes of Sugar and Slaves   83

Map 3   Sugar Plantations on the Atlantic Islands   85

Map 4   Some Major Sources of African Slaves   101

Map 5   Origins and Destinations of African Slaves, 1500–1870   105

Map 6   Slave Origins and Destinations: Another Estimate   106

Map 7   The Caribbean Center of New World Slavery   113

Map 8   America's Internal Slave Trade, by Land and Sea,
1790–1860   182

A Selective Calendar of Events

71–73 B.C.E. (Before the Common Era): Tens of thousands of Roman slaves revolt, led by Thracian gladiator Spartacus. Thousands then crucified along Appian Way.

869–883 C.E.: Massive revolt of *Zanj*, black African slaves, in Basra region of present-day Iraq.

1444: Gomes Eannes de Zurara observes sale of 235 captured Africans, some of them black, near Lagos in southern Portugal; during following decades, Portugal continues to import black slaves.

1495: Columbus transports some five hundred enslaved Native Americans eastward across the Atlantic to Seville.

1501: Enslaved black Africans brought to New World; some perhaps even earlier.

1518: Bartolomé de Las Casas, an ardent defender of Indian rights, calls for large importations of African slaves in order to help save Native Americans.

1542: Spain outlaws enslavement of Native Americans.

1619: Twenty blacks brought by Dutch ship to Virginia; some blacks had arrived even earlier.

1799: New York State adopts a law for gradual emancipation.

1800: Gabriel's slave rebellion in Virginia.

1803: The Louisiana Purchase doubles the territory of the United States and ultimately leads to intense debate over the expansion of slavery into regions like Missouri; South Carolina responds by opening the way to importation of thirty-eight thousand slaves before 1808.

1804: New Jersey adopts a law for gradual emancipation.

1808: Britain and the United States both outlaw participation in the African slave trade.

1811: Slave uprising in Louisiana.

1816: Major slave rebellion in British Barbados.
        In the United States, the American Colonization Society is formed to promote the colonization of free blacks in Africa.

1817: New York State adopts a law that frees all remaining slaves in 1827.

1818–21: The Missouri Crisis, followed by the Compromise of 1820 and further debate over Missouri's constitution, which restricts entry of free blacks and mulattoes.

1822: Denmark Vesey's alleged conspiracy in South Carolina.
        Brazil wins independence from Portugal.

1823: Large slave rebellion in British colony of Demerara.
        In Britain, the Society for the Amelioration and Gradual Abolition of Slavery is founded, and the House of Commons approves George Canning's resolutions for "amelioration" of colonial slavery.

1831: Immense slave revolt ("Baptist War") in Jamaica.

1833: The American Anti-Slavery Society is founded.
        Britain emancipates nearly eight hundred thousand colonial slaves, paying twenty million pounds sterling to owners or their creditors.

1835: In Brazil, a Muslim-led slave revolt in Bahia.

1845: The United States annexes the large new slave state of Texas.

1846: Slaves emancipated in Sweden's New World colonies. Bay of Tunis, under pressure from Britain, rules that any slave who requests freedom will be given it.

1846–48: The Mexican War leads to the annexation of much Western territory, including California, thereby igniting much controversy over the expansion of slavery.

1848: Revolution in Europe leads France and Denmark to abolish slavery in their colonies.

1850: Brazil, under British pressure, stops African slave imports.
   In the United States, the Compromise of 1850 includes the Fugitive Slave Law, much hated in the North since any white citizen can be enlisted in the hunt and arrest of alleged runaway slaves.

1851–52: *Uncle Tom's Cabin*, by Harriet Beecher Stowe, appears, first in serial form in the *National Era*; in book form, it sells over three hundred thousand copies in the first year.

1854: Stephen Douglas succeeds in passing the Kansas-Nebraska Act, overruling the Missouri Compromise, rekindling sectional controversy over slavery, and leading to the birth of the Republican Party and then "Bloody Kansas."

1857: In the United States, the Dred Scott decision denies citizenship to blacks and denies Congress the right to legislate regarding slavery in the territories.

1858: Lincoln-Douglas debates in Illinois.

1859: John Brown's raid on Harpers Ferry, Virginia, followed by his execution.

1860: Abraham Lincoln is elected president; South Carolina leads the way to secession.

1861: Jefferson Davis begins his term as president of the Confederate States of America, whose constitution gave recognition and protection to "the institution of negro slavery." Firing on Fort Sumter brings on the Civil War.

1862: The bloody battle at Antietam, Maryland, between Generals Robert E. Lee and George B. McClellan gives Lincoln encouragement to issue Preliminary Emancipation Proclamation.

1863: Emancipation Proclamation; enlistment of blacks into Union army and navy. Lee's invasion of the North is checked at Gettysburg, but the Union suffers many other defeats. Draft riots lead to lynching of blacks in New York City.

1864: Lincoln is reelected president over the Democrat McClellan.

1865: Lee gives up Petersburg; black Union troops free slaves in Richmond, the Confederate capital; Lee surrenders at Appomattox. Lincoln is assassinated; Andrew Johnson becomes president. The Thirteenth Amendment, permanently abolishing all slavery, is ratified.

1866–76: Reconstruction in U.S. South, including Fourteenth and Fifteenth amendments; but final abandonment of cause of racial equality.

1868: Start of Cuban Ten Years' War for independence; enlistment and freeing of many slaves on both sides.
   Liberal revolution in Spain.

1870: Spain passes a gradual emancipation act.

1873–76: Puerto Rico frees slaves and then ex-slave apprentices.

1871: Brazil passes the Rio Branco Act, freeing all children of slaves at age twenty-one.

1883–84: Slaves are freed, usually by philanthropic purchase, in northeast Brazil. The Brazilian abolitionist movement gains strength.

1888: Brazil celebrates immediate, uncompensated emancipation of all remaining slaves. There is no attempt, as in the United States, at "reconstruction."

1948: The United Nations' Universal Declaration of Human Rights, which sets common goals for all nations and all peoples, declares in Article 4: "No one shall be held in slavery or servitude; slavery and the slave trade shall be prohibited in all their forms."

INHUMAN
BONDAGE

Prologue

In 1770, on the eve of the American Revolution, African American slavery was legal and almost unquestioned throughout the New World. The ghastly slave trade from Africa was still expanding and for many decades had been shipping five Africans across the Atlantic for every European immigrant to the Americas. An imaginary "hemispheric traveler" would have seen black slaves in every colony from Canada and New England all the way south to Spanish Peru and Chile. In the incomparably rich colonies of the Caribbean, they often constituted population majorities of 90 percent or more. But in 1888, one hundred and eighteen years later, when Brazil finally freed all its slaves, the institution had been outlawed throughout the Western Hemisphere.

This final act of liberation, building on Abraham Lincoln's emancipation achievement in the American Civil War, took place only a century after the creation of the first antislavery societies in human history—initially small groups in such places as Philadelphia, London, Manchester, and New York.[1] The abolition of New World slavery depended in large measure on a major transformation in moral perception—on the emergence of writers, speakers, and reformers, beginning in the mid-eighteenth century, who were willing to condemn an institution that had been sanctioned for thousands of years and who also strove to make human society something more than an endless contest of greed and power.[2]

In this current age of globalization, which has expanded our comprehension of earlier international connections and dependencies, American slavery can no longer be understood in parochial terms or simply as a chapter in the history of the U.S. South. The peoples of West Africa, as well as those of every maritime nation in western Europe and every colony in the New World, played a part in the creation of the world's first system of multinational production for what emerged as a mass market—a market for slave-produced sugar, tobacco, coffee, chocolate, dye-stuffs, rice, hemp, and cotton. For four centuries, beginning in the 1400s with Iberian plantation agriculture in the Atlantic sugar islands off the African coast, the African slave trade was an integral and indispensable part of European expansion and the settlement of the Americas. The demand for labor was especially acute in the tropical and semitropical zones that produced the staples and thus the wealth most desired by Europeans. By the mid-1700s the value of exports to Britain from the British West Indies was more than ten times that of exports from colonies north of Virginia and Maryland. And the economy of the Northern colonies depended in large part on Caribbean markets, which depended in turn on the continuing importation of African labor to replenish an oppressed population that could not sustain itself by natural increase.

Inhuman Bondage is designed to illuminate our understanding of American slavery by placing this subject within the much larger contexts of the Atlantic Slave System and the rise and fall of slavery in the New World. It is not a comprehensive or encyclopedic survey of slavery in every New World colony, but rather an exploration of America's greatest historical problem and contradiction, which deeply involved such disparate places as Britain, Spain, Haiti, and ancient Rome.

For me the term "inhuman" has two connotations with respect to our subject. After first considering the title of W. Somerset Maugham's famous novel of 1915, *Of Human Bondage*, and discussing the issue with friends and family, it occurred to me that chattel slavery is the most extreme example we have not only of domination and oppression but of human attempts to *dehumanize* other people. When the Spiritans, a French Catholic missionary group, published in 1999 a special study of the Church and slavery, they chose the title "*L'esclavage négation de l'humain*—Slavery, the negation of the human."[3] Under Roman law as well as in the United States, slaves were deprived of legally recognized spouses or families and of genuine property ownership. As with most domestic animals, their lowly status was enforced by the threat of almost unlimited physical punishment. As Frederick Douglass put it, after describing the ways that the "slave breaker" Mr. Covey had "tamed" him: "I was broken in body, soul, and spirit. My natural elasticity was crushed, my intellect languished, the disposition to read departed, the cheerful spark that lingered about my eye died; the dark night of slavery closed in upon me; and behold a man transformed into a brute!"[4]

In an earlier essay on this subject, I have theorized that, given the repeated comparisons of slaves to domestic animals throughout history (and Aristotle wrote that the ox was "a poor man's slave"), the initial enslavement and "bestialization" of prisoners of war may well have been modeled on the successful techniques of taming and domesticating wild animals.[5]

But some animals could never be domesticated, and even those slaves who at times felt themselves transformed, like Douglass, into "brutes" did not lose their essential humanity, a fact that repeatedly underscored the preeminent contradiction of "inhuman bondage." Indeed, one of the central and inspiring truths of African American history, a truth dramatized by fugitives like Frederick Douglass, was the way slaves succeeded in asserting their humanity and reinventing their diverse cultures, despite being torn away from their natal African families and societies, despite being continuously humiliated, bought and sold, and often subjected to torture and the threat of death. Thus the word "inhuman," in this book's title, refers to the unconscionable and *unsuccessful* goal of bestializing (in the form of pets as well as beasts of burden) a class of human beings. This is not meant to deny, as much slave testimony indicates, that some slaves suffered recurrent psychological as well as physical damage.

The second aspect of "inhuman," when linked with bondage, refers to the special harshness of New World slavery, which white colonists almost always confined, from the very beginning, to Native Americans and then overwhelmingly to black Africans—in both cases to people who were strikingly different in physical appearance as well as in cultural background. Though I do not believe that various historical examples of slavery can be ranked on a scale of severity, there can be no doubt that racial slavery in the Americas widened the gap between slaves and the descendants of slaves, in one castelike group, and nonslave populations that, despite their internal hierarchies, now appeared to be forever "free." I should add that racial distinctions became more ambiguous as a result of sexual exploitation and intermixture, which meant that slaves like Frederick Douglass were one-half "white."

In addition to this racist element, most slaves in the New World became chained to a mercantilist or capitalist system that intensified labor in order to maximize production for distant, international markets. And after about 1815, the slave system in the United States became distinctive by virtually closing off the possibility of manumission, which in many societies had been at least a theoretical check on dehumanization, since it showed that a slave *was* capable of becoming a free person. Despite exceptions, personified by various kinds of highly privileged slaves, American slavery thus became the ultimate form of inhuman bondage.

This book originated in an intensive two-week summer seminar I began teaching in 1994 for high school teachers, mostly from New York City.[6] My scholarly work on slavery began decades earlier, but I taught university courses on very different subjects, since slavery was not yet considered a topic worth an entire semester's course. Still, I was extremely fortunate that my books on what I termed "the problem of slavery" reached an international academic audience and even nonacademic readers. Then, by the 1990s, when there were signs of a new public interest in the subject, we historians began to realize that our scholarly debates, along with the vast number of exciting new discoveries made since the 1960s, were virtually unknown in the nation's schoolrooms and even among most college students. The same could also be said of the general public, despite the prevalence of national historic sites with connections to slavery. This point became especially clear to me in 1988–89, when as president of the Organization of American Historians I witnessed altogether new efforts by college and university professors to reach out, include, and communicate with public historians.

During the decade before my retirement from teaching at Yale (2001), nothing seemed more important than the attempt to synthesize and translate the findings of historians and economists regarding American slavery, viewed from a global perspective. The high school teachers I taught for nearly a decade—with the invaluable help of Professor Steven Mintz—turned out to be extraordinarily excited, appreciative, and highly motivated. Some members of each year's class let me know how they had incorporated slavery and abolition into their high school curricula. I therefore eagerly expanded my teaching notes into a new large lecture course on New World slavery for Yale undergraduates.

The extent of public interest (as well as ignorance) became strikingly evident in 2001, when the *New York Times* asked me to write an article about the realities of American slavery that would begin on the front page of their Sunday "Week in Review," an article that evoked an amazing response from some major public figures as well from descendants of both slaves and masters.

Inhuman Bondage is the product of this cumulative experience.[7] Since lectures for teachers and college students include no footnotes, even when based on considerable research, it has taken a good bit of time and effort to create this book's extensive endnotes, which are intended to serve, for some readers, as a guide to further learning. I have included more citations and sources for certain broad, complex subjects—subjects that I have tried to approach from an original perspective, such as the long-term origins of anti-black racism and New World slavery, nineteenth-century slave conspiracies and revolts, and the Civil War and slave emancipation.

The book begins with the dramatic *Amistad* case in 1839–41, which highlights the multinational character of the Atlantic Slave System, from Sierra Leone to Cuba and Connecticut, as well as the involvement of the American judiciary, the presidency (and a former president), the media, and both black and white abolitionists.

The difficulties of defining and comprehending the meaning of slavery, given the diversity of historical examples, then take us in Chapter Two to the Bible, to ancient Babylonia, and to ancient Greco-Roman models, which were especially meaningful in an American age fascinated with neo-classical architecture, the Roman idea of a "Senate," and ancient slaves as diverse as Aesop, Spartacus, and the biblical Joseph. Many of the more literate Southern planters also stressed that the ancient Greeks had combined slaveholding with the invention of democracy; some planters saw themselves as modern Roman Catos and found a guide for training and managing slaves in Columella's *De Re Rustica*, a Roman work still widely used in the Middle Ages and known in later centuries to people who had received a common classical education.

In Chapter Three the graphic testimony of an American free black, concerning the grim meaning of racism in 1836, leads us back to the complex ancient and medieval origins of such prejudice. Recent scholarship has immensely enriched our knowledge of medieval European stereotypes of the supposedly black-skinned serfs and peasants (who were darkened by dirt and by labor in the sun); of early Arab stereotypes of black African slaves (millions of whom were transported from East Africa to the Near East); and of the story of the biblical Noah, whose curse subjected all the descendants of Canaan, the son of Noah's own misbehaving son Ham, to the lowliest form of eternal bondage. This confusing biblical passage became for many centuries a major justification for black slavery. But my discussion of antiblack prejudice also considers the very ambivalent messages conveyed by European art and sculpture and culminates with the "modern" forms of antiblack racism that appear in the writings of such figures of the Enlightenment as David Hume, Thomas Jefferson, and Immanuel Kant and then reach a symbolic climax in the 1911 *Encyclopædia Britannica*.

Chapter Four, "How Africans Became Integral to New World History," rejects various economic deterministic theories and emphasizes the contingent ways in which greed and a desire for profit became fused with issues of religion and ethnic identity—as in the early eighteenth-century anthem: "Rule, Britannia! Britannia rules the waves . . . Britons never will be slaves!" (written at a time when thousands of Britons were in fact being enslaved by Muslim Barbary corsairs, who raided England's and continental Europe's coastlines and also seized captives from countless European ships).

Before turning to African slave dealers and Euro-African negotiations on the West African coast, the reader will learn about changing sources of slave labor in the late medieval Mediterranean, as well as the Italian and German bankers and merchants who ultimately provided a capitalist foundation for the later Atlantic Slave System and its production of sugar, coffee, rice, and tobacco—some of which created, by the mid-1700s, the first mass consumer markets in the world. Along with offering vivid descriptions of the atrocious overpacking and dehydration on slave ships crossing the Atlantic, I argue that racial slavery became an intrinsic and indispensable part of New World settlement, not an accident or a marginal shortcoming of the American experience. We must face the ultimate contradiction that our free and democratic society was made possible by massive slave labor.

Chapter Five considers the Portuguese colony of Brazil and then the Caribbean as the true centers of the Atlantic Slave System, which concentrated on the production of sugar (and later, molasses and rum). Chapter Six then moves on to the spread of racial slavery to colonial North America, which, surprisingly, received only 5 to 6 percent of the African slaves shipped across the Atlantic, but whose slaves developed an almost unique natural and rapid rate of population growth, freeing the later United States from a need for further African imports.

While slave labor has often been seen as economically backward and almost feudalistic, I stress the fact that plantation agriculture, even in Brazil, resembled factories in the field and, with its carefully structured gang labor, anticipated in many ways the assembly lines and agribusinesses of the future. Planters, particularly in Brazil but also in the United States, adopted a façade of patriarchal paternalism that helped them reconcile precapitalist traditions with the inherent brutality and attempts at dehumanization symbolized by what I term "inhuman bondage."

I also devote attention to the ways that blacks created their own Afro–New World cultures and devised means for continuing negotiation with their owners and drivers. It was this negotiation that sustained slave productivity and allowed the system to work and even prosper for many centuries, despite slave resistance. The opportunity to negotiate in no way mitigates the intrinsic oppression of slavery. But slaves often did win slightly more land and time for growing their own provisions, or managed their own market exchanges and conducted their own marriages and burials. Urban slave women, in such cities as Rio de Janeiro and Charleston, South Carolina, achieved remarkable "freedom" to run outdoor public markets, where they sold all kinds of food and handicrafts for the profit of their owners.

It soon becomes clear that in a single colony the differences between urban slaves, plantation workers, privileged slave artisans, and household servants could be as significant as any differences between separate colonies or New World regions. Some slaves in Connecticut or Brazil would have eagerly changed places with some of those in Virginia or South Carolina, and of course the reverse would also be true. Yet as Chapters Five and Six make clear, there were enormous differences between slavery in colonial New York and Virginia (and in 1770 there were more black slaves in New York than in

Georgia), to say nothing of the difference between having patriarchs in Brazil and absentee English owners and hired professional managers in most of the British West Indies.

Chapters Seven and Eight consider "The Problem of Slavery in the American Revolution" and then the very different "Impact of the French and Haitian Revolutions," both within a broad international context that begins with the French defeat in the Seven Years' War and ends with the Napoleonic Wars (including Napoleon's restoration of slavery) and the Latin American Wars of Independence. Few historians of the American Revolution have recognized the central role of slavery—a subject that ranges from the issue of freeing and arming slave soldiers to the escape of many thousands of slaves behind British lines, as well as the glaring ideological contradiction that led slaves in the Northern states to petition for their freedom, using the same natural-rights language that the whites employed against so-called British tyranny. It was this contradiction that helped reformers in the North to pass laws for very gradual slave emancipation, thus pushing the new Northern states in the direction of "free soil."

It is also true that few historians have recognized that John Adams's administration gave crucial secret aid to Toussaint Louverture and the blacks' cause of Haitian independence from France.

Chapter Eight begins with the famous former slave and abolitionist Frederick Douglass proclaiming in 1893 that the brave "sons of Haiti" "struck for the freedom of every black man in the world." But I also stress that for a later age "obsessed with the problems of freedom and order," the Haitian Revolution suggested "the unleashing of pure id." The Haitian blacks' defeat of the best armies of the British, the Spanish, and the French inspired black rebels in Virginia, Cuba, Barbados, South Carolina, and Venezuela and hovered like a weapon of mass destruction in the minds of slaveholders as late as the American Civil War.

Having viewed this extremely broad and crucial context, we move in Chapters Nine and Ten to the heart of the book, "Slavery in the Nineteenth-Century South." Drawing on the vast scholarship of recent decades, we begin with the perceptions of foreign travelers and then consider the thesis that this institution of extreme inequality made it possible for white Americans to perceive their other relationships, among whites of different social classes, as being relatively equal.

These chapters give serious attention to such diverse subjects as black slaveholding planters; the rise of the Cotton Kingdom; the daily life of ordinary slaves; the highly destructive *internal*, long-distance slave trade, often by ship around the Florida Keys to New Orleans; proslavery thought; the sexual exploitation of slaves; the emergence of an African American culture, in which oral traditions became "a sanctuary of human dignity"; the testimony of slaves (dramatically symbolized by the letter of a literate slave wife, written to her husband as she and their child are about to be sold away); and the declining status and persecution of free blacks as an ominous weathervane with respect to a postemancipation America.

After such detailed exposure to the appalling inhumanity of the system, the reader should welcome Chapter Eleven, "Some Nineteenth-Century Slave Conspiracies and Revolts." This is a subject that calls out for careful comparisons. We therefore place several American conspiracies and revolts next to the three huge slave insurrections in the British West Indies: Barbados in 1816, Demerara in 1823, and Jamaica in 1831.

Since thousands of slaves were involved in these events, what seems most incredible, especially when compared with the massacres of Nat Turner in Virginia and the bloodshed of eighteenth-century Caribbean uprisings, is the fact that hardly any whites were killed! Clearly the slave leaders in the British West Indies exercised great restraint and discipline—putting planters in the "stocks," for example, that had once been used to punish slaves—because they were aware of a growing and powerful antislavery sentiment in the British mother country, a sympathetic public that would be alienated by any vengeful slaughter of whites.

The open cursing and growling of West Indian whites, who were livid and almost paranoid over news of the British antislavery movement, conveyed much information to the kind of privileged head slaves who led these insurrections. The role of white missionaries was also extremely important in Demerara and Jamaica. I use these examples as a way to account for the infrequency and counterproductive effects of slave conspiracies in America, which, unlike those in the British Caribbean, could not really address a powerful central government that was sensitive to a large and influential abolitionist public. But ironically, white Southerners ignored the restraint of the British West Indian slave rebels and interpreted the massive insurrections as the inevitable result of abolitionist agitation.

My thesis regarding British Caribbean revolts merges naturally into Chapter Twelve, "Explanations of British Abolitionism." Although general readers are understandably uninterested in most debates carried on by historians, the story of British abolitionism is exceptional because it raises profound and universal questions about the nature and possibility of collective moral actions in human history. If, as most experts now agree, it was highly contrary to Britain's economic self-interest to peacefully emancipate eight hundred thousand colonial slaves in the 1830s and pay a staggering sum of taxpayers' money as compensation to the slaves' owners (or creditors), how can we explain the success of this pioneering "do good" movement for radical social reform?

As contemporary foreign critics and later historians remind us, Britain's moral record with respect to workers in the Industrial Revolution, to say nothing of Britain's exploitation of India and Ireland and response to the latter's disastrous famine in the 1840s, hardly conveys the image of a benevolent or sinless society. Therefore, after presenting a concise summary of the history of the British antislavery movement from the 1780s to the 1830s, I have felt it necessary to discuss the debates among historians and then highlight the importance of religious changes beginning with the Quakers, the rise of various philanthropic movements, and the need to uplift and dignify the concept of free wage labor.

Abolitionism in Britain leads logically in Chapter Thirteen to "Abolitionism in America." Here, despite much crucial transatlantic influence and exchange, one must focus on a different religious phenomenon—the "Second Great Awakening" of the early nineteenth century and its generation of various movements for moral reform. After noting the relevance of rapid socioeconomic change—the so-called Market Revolution and the Transportation Revolution—I underscore the leadership of free blacks in opposing the movement for black colonization, which was long fused with whites' attacks on slavery, as well as the quest for human perfectibility by "redeeming man from the dominion of man."

American abolitionism was always confined to a small minority, in contrast to the British movement, and I suggest that William Lloyd Garrison's eccentricities and extremist rhetoric may have deterred many potential converts. But ultimately the "invasion" of the North by Southern owners and agents, who as a result of the infamous Fugitive Slave Law of 1850 could draft any white males into a posse in order to capture an alleged runaway slave, increased the opponents of the now "peculiar institution." The Christian passion aroused by the vision of slavery as the essence of sin can be seen in the famous lines of "The Battle Hymn of the Republic": "As he died to make men holy, let us die to make men free." A similar but more universalized sense of slavery, guilt, and death appears in the immortal words of Lincoln's Second Inaugural Address, with which I conclude this chapter.

"The Politics of Slavery in the United States," the subject of Chapter Fourteen, is so vast, complex, and underappreciated that I must be highly selective and avoid a numbing clutter of facts. I do take account of the wider international context, beginning with the Napoleonic Wars and the collapse of most of Spain's empire in the Americas, which undermined slavery from Mexico to Chile (but had the reverse effect on Cuba). A succession of American administrations was determined to prevent France or especially Britain, still seen as America's "natural enemy," from acquiring territories in the former Spanish world. America's expansion into Louisiana, Florida, and Texas involved the expansion and consolidation of slavery and provided enormous markets for some of the "excess" numbers of blacks in the East, especially Virginia.

Partly because of the clause in the Constitution that gave the South added political representation for three-fifths of its slave population, Southern leaders increasingly challenged restrictions on the westward expansion of slavery and the creation of new slave states. Southern slaveholding presidents governed the nation for fifty of the seventy-two years between the inaugurations of Washington and Lincoln, and before Lincoln none of the Northern presidents challenged the slaveholding interests. Since slaveholders also tended to dominate the Senate and Supreme Court, it is not surprising that America long had a proslavery foreign policy, typified by the case of the slave ship *Creole*, or that the succession of major political compromises, beginning with the Missouri Crisis of 1819–21, largely favored the South. This chapter gives a detailed examination of the Missouri Crisis; the effects of British abolition on the Southern tendency to overreact to the supposed danger of Northern reformers, the Lincoln-Douglas debates, and the reasons for Southern secession after Lincoln's election in 1860.

Chapter Fifteen, "The Civil War and Slave Emancipation," proceeds in a somewhat unorthodox way. Beginning with the Union capture of the Confederate capital of Richmond, in April 1865, and with the way that black Union troops freed a bevy of slaves in a Richmond jail, I emphasize the truly "revolutionary" meaning of the Civil War—reinforced by the fact that the Union confiscated without compensation a hitherto legally accepted form of property that was worth an estimated $3.5 billion in 1860 dollars (about $68.4 billion in 2003 dollars). (Most of the other emancipations of slaves in the Western Hemisphere provided slaveholders with some compensation, often in the form of unpaid labor from the "free-born" children of slaves who were required to work until age eighteen or a good bit older, or a period of unpaid apprenticeship for former slaves; even Haiti had to pay France a staggering sum of "compensation" in order to gain diplomatic recognition and the right to trade.)

I then move on to the way this revolutionary meaning of the Civil War was repressed and transformed from the 1880s to the late 1950s (before I turn to the story of President Lincoln and slave emancipation). I believe that most readers will more deeply appreciate the issue of fugitive slave "contrabands," the centrality of the slaveholding border states, and the fortuitous series of events that led to the Battle of Antietam and to Lincoln's Emancipation Proclamation, if they first know how racism and the goal of national reconciliation later led to a romanticized view of the antebellum South and an interpretation of the Civil War as a great military Super Bowl contest between Blue and Gray heroes. As my colleague David Blight has compellingly shown in his prizewinning book *Race and Reunion*, this was a "memory" in which race and slavery were never mentioned. Fortunately, this tradition of denial never wiped out an "emancipationist" tradition, kept alive by such black writers as W.E.B. Du Bois, which helped inspire the civil rights movement in the 1960s and which transformed at least our academic understanding of the rise and fall of racial slavery. This book, I hope, will join the small shelf of works that have begun to convey our academic understandings to a wider public.

In the Epilogue I first consider the influence of the American Civil War on the slave emancipations in Cuba and Brazil in the 1880s. After describing the highly distinctive ways in which slavery was abolished in these last two bastions of plantation agriculture, I briefly survey the persistence in the twentieth century and beyond of various forms of coerced labor. Above all, I conclude, we should consider the meaning, in the early twenty-first century, of the historically unique antislavery movements that succeeded in overthrowing, within the space of a century, systems of inhuman bondage that extended throughout the hemisphere—systems that were still highly profitable as well as productive. But this positive message of willed moral achievement must also be linked with the need to recognize the heavy and complex legacies of America's greatest historical contradiction.

1

The *Amistad* Test of Law and Justice

ALTHOUGH THE STORY of the Cuban ship *La Amistad* was long ignored in American history textbooks and standard works on slavery and antislavery, it received enormous publicity in 1997 as a result of Steven Spielberg's somewhat inaccurate but powerful film, *Amistad*. I have chosen to begin with this historical narrative because it presents a concrete test of American law and justice and also dramatically illustrates the multinational character of the Atlantic Slave System.[1] Indeed, if the American courts had reached a different decision, one can well imagine England imposing a naval blockade on Cuba and even a war exploding between Britain and the United States and perhaps Spain. The *Amistad* case involved American politics, the judiciary, and foreign relations at the highest levels. It also epitomized slavery's deepest contradictions, both legal and philosophical.

Early in 1839, in the Mende region of Sierra Leone, the twenty-five-year-old Joseph Cinqué (whose real Mendean name was Sengbeh) was seized by four black strangers from his own tribe or clan while he was working on a road between two villages. Chained by the neck to other blacks, Cinqué was marched like a prisoner of war three days to Lomboko, on the Sierra Leone coast. Having no way to get word to his wife and three children, Cinqué suspected that he had been seized to pay a debt he owed to a business associate. For nearly four centuries West Africans had been devising techniques, including war, to enslave other Africans—usually members of other lineage or ethnic groups—to sell to European and American traders on the coast and thus meet the continuing and generally rising demand for the cheapest and most exploitable form of drudge labor. One should note that African slave traders almost always sold their captives some distance from where the captives had lived. Today many readers are shocked to learn that virtually all of the enslavement of Africans was carried out by other Africans, but as the African American historian Nathan Huggins pointed out long ago, the concept of an African "race" was the invention of Western rationalists, and most African merchants "saw themselves as selling people other than their own."[2]

On the coast, after being sold to Portuguese merchants working for the Cuban house of Martínez, in Havana, Cinqué and some five hundred other Africans, mostly women and children, were loaded on the slave ship *Teçora*. During the two-month voyage to northern Cuba, over one-third of the slaves died from disease and dehydration, a staggeringly high and atypical proportion for the nineteenth century. Then, as the ship approached the Cuban coast, the captain had the captives unchained and brought up on deck, where as valuable property they were bathed, better fed, and given clean clothing. Since the slave trade to Cuba had been illegal since 1820, the Portuguese traders smuggled Cinqué and the other slaves at night in small boats to a deserted beach and then into warehouses in a tropical forest. There they recuperated for two weeks before being marched to the roofless, oblong barracks that stood as part of the slave market in Havana.

While crossing the Atlantic from Sierra Leone to Cuba, the *Teçora* always faced the danger of being intercepted by an armed British cruiser. After outlawing its own gigantic slave trade in 1808 (the same year in which the United States took similar action), Britain adopted a long-range policy of pressuring and bribing other maritime powers, even at the cost of millions of pounds, to say nothing of decades of diplomacy and the expansion of anti-slave-trade naval patrols, with the goal of stopping the flow of African slaves into both the Atlantic and Indian oceans. According to an Anglo-Spanish treaty of 1817, reinforced by Spanish positive law, any Africans imported into Cuba after May 1820 were supposed to be legally free. The African slave trade to Cuba was not only illegal; as with piracy, violators of the law were subject to the death penalty.

Unfortunately, the Spanish government never took these measures seriously. In Cuba the laws were not considered to be "in force," especially after new shipments of Africans had been successfully landed. Partly as a result of the Haitian Revolution of 1791–1804, which devastated the world's major producer of sugar and coffee, the nineteenth-century Spanish government reaped enormous profits from Cuba's relatively sudden emergence as the world's greatest producer of sugar. (By 1856 Cuba was producing over four times as much sugar as Brazil, though slave-grown sugar was still Brazil's major export.)

Moreover, by 1839, at the end of a decade when Cuba illegally imported around 181,600 slaves from Africa, this supply of labor was becoming even more valuable for Spain. When Britain emancipated its own colonial slaves in 1834 and then abolished the coercive system of "apprenticeship" in 1838, the production of British sugar and other slave-grown staples plummeted, thus opening an even larger global market for the slave societies of Cuba and Brazil. And since Spain had lost Mexico and her South and Central American colonies in the wars of liberation, the Spanish government was extremely anxious to preserve the surviving bonds with Cuba and Puerto Rico. Both planters and Spanish leaders viewed the slave system as the central link in maintaining the loyalty of the two Caribbean colonies.

In June 1839 two Spaniards joined the throng of shoppers at Havana's barracoons. Everyone understood that when newly imported slaves were sold, officials, often bribed, would issue fraudulent passports certifying that the slaves were not *bozales*, illegally imported from Africa, but *ladinos*, who could speak Spanish and who had either been born in Cuba or legally imported before May 1820. Though only twenty-four, José Ruiz, the first Spaniard, was an experienced slave merchant. He examined the bodies and teeth of the recent involuntary immigrants and bought Cinqué and forty-eight other adult males for $450 apiece. Pedro Montes, who was fifty-eight, bought four young Mendean children, three girls and a boy, and joined Ruiz in chartering *La Amistad*—a sleek black schooner built in Cuba on a Baltimore model for coastal trading. The following people boarded the vessel: the fifty-three Africans; an enslaved *ladino* mulatto cook, Celestino; the captain's sixteen-year-old slave cabin boy, Antonio; and six whites, including Montes, Ruiz, two sailors, and the captain and shipowner, Ramón Ferrer. That done, *La Amistad* set out at midnight for Puerto Príncipe, about three hundred miles east of Havana.

On July 1, following three nights at sea, Cinqué determined to lead a revolt after Celestino indicated by sign language that the blacks would be killed, cut into pieces, salted, and eaten. (There was a widespread African belief that whites were cannibals, just as many Euro-Americans believed that Africans were cannibals.) With a nail, Cinqué picked the locks on his own and others' iron collars. The captives then found boxes filled with sugarcane knives. Within minutes, they killed Captain Ferrer and his cook; the two sailors disappeared, probably overboard; and the rebels wounded and captured Ruiz and Montes, their supposed owners.[3] Discovering in some way that Montes was a former sea captain, Cinqué ordered him to sail the ship into the morning sun until they returned to Africa. Secretly, the two Spaniards devised a plan of heading north at night, hoping to be rescued by a British cruiser or to land at a Southern slaveholding port in the United States.

La Amistad encountered a number of other ships, which usually fled at the sight of blacks on deck with long knives, though Burnah, a Mendean who spoke some English, succeeded in obtaining a keg of water and some apples from one captain. Ten of the Africans died, mostly from drinking dangerous medications to quench their terrible thirst. Finally, in late August, an American revenue cutter seized *La Amistad* near the tip of Long Island, after Cinqué had anchored the ship and gone ashore with a small group to find provisions.

At first the American officers suspected that the blacks were pirates, but then Montes and Ruiz dropped to their knees and pleaded for liberation. (Ruiz could speak some English, and Lieutenant Richard Meade could understand Spanish.) Having heard the Spaniards' story, Lieutenant Thomas Gedney, commander of the revenue vessel, towed *La Amistad* to New London, Connecticut. He had no warrant or legal authority to do this, as former president John Quincy Adams later pointed out, but he probably knew that slavery was still legal in Connecticut. (It would not be outlawed until 1848, twenty-one years after New York took such action in accordance with a law of 1817.) Gedney planned to file a claim in admiralty court for salvage, hoping to win the value of the ship and its cargo, including the "slaves."

AT THIS POINT it is helpful to glance at the state of New World slavery and antislavery in 1839–42, "the *Amistad* period." Largely as a result of the American Revolution, from 1777 to 1804 the states from Vermont to New Jersey had either abolished slavery or enacted laws that freed all children of slaves sometime in their twenties (in Rhode Island, at age eighteen for females). A similar pattern followed the Spanish-American wars of independence, and slavery gradually disappeared as the older generations died off. Thus by 1840 slavery had been outlawed in Mexico, Central America, and Chile and only small numbers of aging slaves remained in Venezuela, Colombia, and Peru. Though racial slavery had been legal throughout the Western Hemisphere in 1775, by 1840 it flourished only in Brazil, the southern United States, Cuba, and Puerto Rico (and to a certain degree in the French and Dutch Caribbean).

Britain, from 1680 to 1808 the major carrier of African slaves across the Atlantic, had taken the lead in abolishing its own slave trade and then in curtailing and attempting to suppress the slave trade of other nations. While the French, the Spanish, and many Americans saw such policies as a hypocritical instrument of British imperialism, in 1834 Britain freed nearly eight hundred thousand of its own colonial slaves (including those in South Africa and the Indian Ocean) and in 1838 ended the institution of West Indian apprenticeship. (In the revolutions of 1848, France and Denmark would emancipate their own colonial slaves, including the African slaves in the French plantation colony of Réunion, in the Indian Ocean east of Madagascar.)

Yet despite these encouraging trends, by 1839 American abolitionists had failed in their concerted efforts at "moral suasion"—that is, in convincing significant numbers of Southern Christians that every minute they kept their slaves in bondage they were compounding the guilt of the original act of enslavement. Although they were highly successful in utilizing new steam-driven technology for printing and distributing mountains of pamphlets and pictures that Southerners said were "calculated to rouse and inflame the passions of the slaves against their masters," the abolitionists were wholly unprepared for the Southern fury they aroused. They were even more shocked by the Northern racist backlash that took the form of violent mobs, usually organized by "gentlemen of property and standing," who at best pelted black and white abolitionist speakers with rotten eggs and stones.[4]

Thus by 1839, two years after an Illinois mob shot and killed Elijah P. Lovejoy, an abolitionist martyr who was trying to defend his fourth printing press from destruction, antislavery leaders were desperately searching for ways to challenge any national authorization of slavery. They mobilized vast petitioning campaigns against slave markets in the nation's capital; against the growing interstate slave trade to the lower Mississippi Valley, and against the settling of slaves in the publicly owned and federally governed Western territories. All three of these demands seemed to fall within the constitutional powers of Congress.

It was in this context that Americans read the news that federal Judge Andrew T. Judson, having examined *La Amistad*'s papers and having heard the testimony of Montes, Ruiz, and Antonio, a *ladino* slave who made it clear that the others had recently arrived in Cuba from Africa, had asked a grand jury of the U.S. circuit court in Hartford to decide if American treaties with Spain applied to this case, and if the African captives should be tried for mutiny and murder. Judson, a Jacksonian Democrat with a notorious record of antiblack racism, had also ordered the federal marshal to take all the blacks to jail without bond in New Haven, an unthinkable action if the ship *La Amistad* (meaning "friendship" in English) had been in control of whites who had freed themselves from pirates or kidnappers.

Once the circuit court trial had determined in September that the captives' legal status fell under the jurisdiction of the federal judiciary, abolitionists saw the coming trial before the U.S. district court as a providential opportunity to dramatize the illegal violence in which all slaveholding originated. The central issue, for key leaders like Lewis Tappan, the wealthy silk merchant who with his brother, Arthur, largely financed the American Anti-Slavery Society, was the glaring discrepancy between American positive law—that is, the explicitly enacted statutes that recognized slaves as legitimate private property—and the fundamental doctrine of natural rights embodied in the Declaration of Independence.

By September 1839 President Martin Van Buren's mind focused on one issue, an issue that seems almost glued to the high office he held: reelection! And even in 1839, news spread quickly from New London and Hartford to the nation's capital. Lacking the popularity of his predecessor and mentor, Andrew Jackson, Van Buren had been weakened politically by a disastrous economic receession. Because he faced an uphill struggle for reelection in 1840, any prolonged controversy involving slavery could bring acute embarrassment to the reigning Democratic Party, whose power depended on appeasing the increasingly volatile and aggressive South. From Jefferson onward, slaveholding Southern Democrats owed much of their power to the "three-fifths" clause in the Constitution, which counted three-fifths of the slave population in apportioning presidential electors and congressmen; it is probable that neither Jefferson nor Jackson would have been elected president without taking count of nonvoting slaves, a fact that greatly embittered New England Federalists. For almost twenty years Van Buren had been obsessed with the need to suppress sectional discord. Van Buren was a New Yorker who came from an old Dutch slaveholding family; his supporters had taken the lead in antiabolition riots and demonstrations intended to reassure the South that the northern public would not tolerate abolitionist "fanatics."

Thus the president and his Southern, proslavery secretary of state, John Forsyth, were prepared to bypass the judicial system, if necessary, to prevent the abolitionists from exploiting the *Amistad* affair. Van Buren and Forsyth relied heavily on treaties made with Spain in 1795 and 1819, which contained detailed provisions for the return of ships and other property rescued from pirates or robbers. The Spanish government demanded that the ship, cargo, and "slaves" be immediately delivered to the Spanish consul in Boston, in order to be returned to Cuba for trial. When it became apparent that the Mendeans' status as slaves was in doubt, Spain insisted on their return as "assassins."

The American government, some of whose leaders had long looked on Cuba as a rich island that should be annexed sometime in the future,[5] was eager to support Spain's ties with Cuba and thus head off any British plans to intervene or even seize Cuba, on the pretext of gross slave-trade treaty violations. Aside from unpaid debts, from 1834 to 1845 Spain was shaken by the Carlist civil war and successive uprisings that raised the threat of British or French intervention. Unlike Britain, the United States had never signed a treaty with Spain for suppressing the slave trade; in fact, in 1825 John Marshall, chief justice of the U.S. Supreme Court, had even ruled that the slave trade, though outlawed by most nations, was sanctioned by international law. Moreover, American courts had no jurisdiction over Spanish subjects or over crimes, aside from piracy, committed on Spanish ships. And since slavery was legal in both Cuba and the United States, it appeared to Spain and to the Van Buren

administration that American courts had no right to question the ship's papers, which falsely affirmed that the blacks were *ladinos*, or bona fide slaves,
not *bozales* from Africa. On September 11, 1839, Secretary of State Forsyth
ordered the federal district attorney in Connecticut, William S. Holabird, to
make sure that no judicial proceedings permitted the cargo and "SLAVES"
to go "beyond the control of the Federal Executive."

Van Buren felt so strongly about returning the blacks to Cuba and avoid-
ing the publicity of a long trial that he was willing to subvert the federal
judicial system and deprive the captives of the right of due process. In the
United States the rights of even free blacks were still an unsettled question,
interpreted differently in different states. When the trial began in the federal
district court in New Haven, in the extremely cold January of 1840, the president diverted a small naval vessel, the USS *Grampus*, to New Haven harbor.
He issued secret orders to the district attorney to have the captives smuggled
to the ship, presumably in the wholly expected event of a court decision favorable to the president and to Spain.[6] Such action would immediately cut
off any right of an appeal to the Supreme Court. But as John Quincy Adams,
the seventy-three-year-old congressman, former president, and defender of
the Africans, would later point out to the Supreme Court, Van Buren's order
was "not conditional, to be executed only in the event of a decision by the
court against the Africans, but positive and unqualified to deliver up all the
Africans in his custody . . . while the trial was pending." Speaking as a former
president, Adams added that Van Buren had also violated his oath to protect and defend the Constitution by treating all thirty-six persons "in a
mass," totally ignoring the supreme point that the right of personal liberty
is individual.[7]

Moreover, because of the *Grampus*'s limited space below deck, Cinqué,
Grabeau, Fabanna, and many of the others would have been chained to the
deck in icy winter weather. Those who survived and landed in Cuba would
almost certainly have been executed for murder. This point was confirmed
by the testimony of Dr. Richard Madden, the English veteran of the Anglo-
Spanish Mixed Commission in Cuba, who on his return to Britain came a
thousand miles out of his way to testify in New Haven. Later, the Van Buren
administration obstructed every effort of the defense to obtain copies of treaties
and other official documents, and was probably responsible for what Adams
called a "scandalous mistranslation" of Spanish words which, if undetected,
might well have destroyed the entire case of the defense.[8]

To avoid confusion, it may be helpful here to summarize the sequence of
Amistad trials: After Judge Judson examined the ship's papers on the American revenue brig in New London harbor, the federal circuit court tried the
captives in Hartford; then the federal district court trial began briefly in
Hartford but moved to New Haven; after Judge Judson ruled that the cap-

tives were free and should be returned by the president to Africa, the federal government appealed the case first to the circuit court and finally to the Supreme Court in Washington.

At the first federal circuit court trial, before a packed courtroom in Hartford, the four Mendean children "appeared to be in great affliction, and wept exceedingly." The *Colored American*, the leading African American newspaper in New York City, continued: "Public opinion is decidedly in favor of [the Africans'] liberation, in as much as they have committed no crime, either legal nor moral, notwithstanding which they are held as prisoners."[9] Associate Justice Smith Thompson, on circuit from the U.S. Supreme Court, denied even the three girls' release on a writ of habeas corpus, but ruled that the Africans would not stand trial in the United States for murder or piracy. The issues regarding their status, the treaties with Spain, and claims for salvage were referred to the federal district court, with specific provision for appeal. These procedural decisions allowed Lewis Tappan to enable the Mendeans to sue Ruiz and Montes, who were arrested and temporarily jailed in New York City on charges of assault and battery and false imprisonment, a development that evoked outrage in the South, as Tappan had intended.

Meanwhile, for a period of some eighteen months, until the Supreme Court in March 1841 upheld Judge Andrew T. Judson's startling decision to free everyone except Antonio, who was a true *ladino*, the surviving thirty-six African men were imprisoned in or just outside New Haven. John Quincy Adams told of seeing them confined in a thirty-by-twenty-foot room while the four children lived with the jailer and his wife. Thousands of visitors paid twelve and a half cents for the sight of these "African Savages."

On the other hand, the New Haven district court allowed the blacks, when weather permitted, to exercise and do gymnastics on the New Haven "Green," or central park. Onlookers were amazed by the Africans' graceful agility. Lewis Tappan paid for their religious instruction from members of the Yale faculty, an exercise in learning that was clearly a two-way street. Given the realities of power, one must emphasize that without the religiously motivated aid of Lewis Tappan, Joshua Leavitt, Simeon Jocelyn, and other abolitionist members of the "*Amistad* Committee," who skillfully cooperated with outstanding nonabolitionist attorneys like Roger Sherman Baldwin and John Quincy Adams, the Africans would surely have been shipped back to Cuba and executed.[10] As I have suggested, that outcome, which Spain and President Van Buren demanded, might well have provoked a British blockade or even seizure of Cuba, and the United States threatened military intervention in response to any such action. (The United States and Britain, having already fought two wars, were now in sharp conflict over unrelated incidents along the Canadian border.)

What made the *Amistad* case so distinctive was the fact that the slave trade to Cuba was illegal after 1820, a violation of Spanish law as well as treaties. Thus Cinqué and his fellow prisoners were not slaves even by any positive law (unless one recognized local African law from Sierra Leone), and if no positive law applied, there was room for an appeal to natural law. In the New Haven district court, Judge Judson overcame some of his racial prejudices and ruled that a mutiny by men who were wrongfully enslaved was not "cognizable," that is, capable of being recognized as a crime in an American court. Since there was no Spanish or American law that authorized the slavery of the *Amistad* blacks, they were entitled to fall back on natural law even if that meant revolution.

After the Van Buren administration appealed the case to the Supreme Court, John Quincy Adams used the Declaration of Independence to assert the "natural right" to revolution:

> I know of no law . . . no code, no treaty, applicable to the proceedings of the Executive or the Judiciary, except that law [pointing to the copy of the Declaration of Independence, hanging against one of the pillars of the courtroom], that law, two copies of which are ever before the eyes of your Honors. I know of no other law that reaches the case of my clients, but the law of Nature and of Nature's God on which our fathers placed our own national existence. The circumstances are so peculiar, that no code or treaty has provided for such a case. That law, in its application to my clients, I trust will be the law on which the case will be decided by this Court.[11]

Adams seems to have meant that nature's law, which he "was not at liberty to argue," applied because no other law was in effect. The abolitionists went much further and cited the famous English *Somerset* case (1772) as proof that local laws allowing slavery were confined to a specific territory and could not extend out to sea. They also asked why, if it was a capital crime to transport an African captive to the New World, it was legitimate to buy or sell a captive or her descendants who by chance had arrived in Cuba before 1820 or in the United States before 1808. The Spanish at least gave the appearance of consistency when they thumbed their noses at what they saw as an externally imposed law intended to prevent them from reaping the profits that the English and Americans had reaped from the Atlantic slave trade from the seventeenth century to the early nineteenth. In the United States, as the *Amistad* case demonstrated, slavery was indeed becoming, given its coexistence with the belief in equal human rights, a "peculiar institution." And the key to that American dilemma was "race."

THE *AMISTAD* TRIALS evoked grotesque outbursts of racism: The *New York Herald* depicted the captives as "blubber-lipped" savages with "baboon-like expressions." Critics ridiculed Lewis Tappan as a fanatic when he compared Cinqué to Othello. Even in the North there were deep fears of racial inter-mixture, disunion, or national suicide sparked by the abolitionists. But the *Amistad* trials also confirmed the strength of America's Revolutionary ideals.

John Quincy Adams, born in 1767, was the last surviving American leader with strong ties to America's founding: As a young diplomat he had been praised and respected by Washington, Jefferson, and Madison; under President Monroe he had been one of America's greatest secretaries of state (perhaps the greatest). Though party politics had undermined the goals of his own presidency, as an aging congressman he led the ultimately successful nine-year battle against Southerners to defeat the House of Representatives' "gag rule" against the reception of antislavery petitions. In the midst of this battle, Adams served as the key legal adviser to Roger Sherman Baldwin, before becoming the senior defense attorney in the *Amistad* trial before the U.S. Supreme Court.[12]

At ages seventy-three and seventy-four, as Adams fought slavery on two fronts, he exemplified the noblest meaning of the Revolutionary heritage. As he told William Jay, the abolitionist son of the first chief justice, John Jay, the blacks had "vindicated their own right to liberty" by "executing the justice of Heaven" upon a "pirate murderer, their tyrant and oppressor." Adams's view that the Africans had freed themselves by "self-emancipation" won surprising support from the Northern press. (The Southern press gave the issue slight coverage, and the Cuban press was mostly silent.)[13] The Africans' mutiny "was a better rising than Bunker Hill or Lexington," according to the *Herald of Freedom*, a white abolitionist paper reprinted in the *Colored American*. The courts, according to this writer, Nathaniel P. Rogers, would not dare to acquit the blacks since that would be seen as "sanctioning of negro insurrection, and the [Southern] chivalry would not sleep again." This, Rogers extravagantly predicted, would turn Nat Turner into a Sir William Wallace, the Scots hero who died for liberty.[14] Yet even Andrew T. Judson, the racist and antiabolitionist federal district court judge, affirmed that the blacks had revolted against illegal bondage only out of the "desire of winning their liberty & returning to their families & kindred."

The abolitionists feared the decision of Roger Taney's Southern-dominated Supreme Court and made plans to defy the law and enable the blacks to escape to Canada. But it turned out that Van Buren blundered by appealing Judson's ruling, which would in fact have kept the blacks under the president's control while being returned to Africa. The captives' case was brilliantly argued before the Supreme Court by Roger Baldwin and especially by John Quincy Adams. Adams's two-day oration juxtaposed the ideal of justice, defined by the ancient Justinian Code as "the constant and perpetual will to secure to every one his own right," with the federal government's racial prejudice, or what Adams termed the "sympathy" for the two white slave traders. For Adams, the case had been governed from the beginning by "sympathy with the white, antipathy to the black," which precluded any possibility of justice.[15]

With withering irony and sarcasm Adams also exploited the Spaniards' assumption that the American president could act like a dictator and dominate the judicial system. He made much of the Spanish minister's claim that the Spanish public's demand for "vengeance" had not been satisfied. Chevalier Argaiz, the Spanish minister to the United States, did not seem to realize that American law was not based on a popular cry for vengeance.[16] On the other hand, the Senate had earlier given unanimous approval to a resolution presented by John C. Calhoun that in effect affirmed that only Spain had jurisdiction over a ship like La Amistad, sailing on a "lawful voyage" in peacetime.

All the same, Associate Justice Joseph Story ruled for the Supreme Court that the captives had exercised their basic right of self-defense, since they had been kidnapped in Africa (by Africans) and unlawfully transported to Cuba. They were not legally slaves and therefore should be allowed to go free. The single exception was Antonio; he was supposed to be returned to Cuba, but the abolitionists succeeded in smuggling him to Montreal.

This verdict undercut the emerging Southern view that black Africans were naturally suited to be slaves and that even free blacks had no rights of due process. Even so, Justice Story had no intention of inviting slaves to rebel. Both Judson and Story were scrupulously careful to uphold the positive laws that sanctioned black slavery, which helps explain why all the Southern Supreme Court justices supported Story's decision. Judson and Story restricted the application of natural law to those rare situations in which no positive law applied. Thus if the African captives had been imported into Cuba as small children in 1819 and had then revolted in 1839 while being shipped from Havana to Puerto Príncipe, they undoubtedly would have been returned to Cuba. Still, if the abolitionists failed to win full judicial approval for their "higher-law doctrines," the arguments of Baldwin and Adams before the courts exposed the irreconcilable contradictions between American slavery and the principles of America's Revolutionary heritage.

Furthermore, in 1840, at the very moment when the American abolitionist movement was splintering into fragments, Lewis Tappan and other non-Garrisonians showed rare skill as tacticians, effectively publicizing the Amistad case while keeping themselves in the background. American free blacks, led by the Reverend James W. C. Pennington, also joined white abolitionists in efforts to raise money, organize missionary support, and communicate with the Amistad captives.[17]

The main proof that the captives were not *ladinos*, as the ship's documents claimed, was their inability to speak or understand Spanish. It was on the key issue of language that some of Yale's faculty came to the rescue. Josiah Willard Gibbs, the distinguished Orientalist and philologist, and father of the physicist and mathematician of same name, first learned the names for numbers in the Africans' languages (mainly Mende). He then searched the waterfronts of New York and New Haven, hoping to find a native African who could understand the captives. In New York, Gibbs discovered on a British warship two African sailors: James Covey, a former slave from Sierra Leone, and Charles Pratt, a Mendean like Cinqué, who had been seized by a Spanish slaver seven years earlier.[18]

Gibbs took both Africans to New Haven, where, according to the *Colored American* and the *New Haven Record*, "as soon as one of the newcomers addressed them in their native tongue, there was an instant explosion of feeling—they leaped and shouted and clapped their hands, and their joy seemed absolutely uncontrollable."[19] Thanks to Professor Gibbs, who learned Mende from Covey and conversed with twenty or more of the captives, it was possible for Cinqué and other Africans to give testimony and depositions at the New Haven trial. Professor Gibbs also testified on the significance of language and of Mendean personal names. Another Yale professor, George E. Day, also learned some Mende from one of the sailors and testified on behalf of the captives, much to the government's annoyance.[20]

At the district court in New Haven, beginning in January 1840, Yale students, especially from the Law School and the Theological Seminary, crowded in, eager to hear blacks testify. Cinqué was the last to be called to the stand. Tall, wrapped in a blanket, he seemed magisterial in his bearing as Covey interpreted his words. When telling of the voyage from Africa, Cinqué sat on the floor and held his hands and feet together to show how he had been chained. He then gave a vivid description of how Ruiz had inspected him at the Havana slave market and of the slaves' whippings during the coastal voyage before the mutiny.

When the Supreme Court finally ruled in 1841 that the *Amistad* captives were free, Cinqué replied to the news from Washington: "Me glad—me thank the American men—me glad." Asked if he wanted to return to Africa, he replied, surprisingly, "I don't know. I think one or two days—then say—we all talk—think of it—then me say." Unlike Judson, the Supreme Court did not order the president to return the blacks to Africa. The *Amistad* Committee was relieved that the Mendeans were free from any control by Van Buren, who might conceivably have shipped them to Cuba instead of Sierra Leone. But there was a serious problem of what to do with the Africans in a deeply racist society, especially given the end of any government support for their maintenance.

The diary of the abolitionist John Pitkin Norton gives fascinating glimpses of the Mendeans' experiences after they were removed for safety in mid-March 1841 to Norton's small village of Farmington, Connecticut, to the west of Hartford.[21] In New Haven, Norton noted, circus proprietors and managers of theaters swooped in "like so many sharks," hoping to exploit the blacks in exhibits. As white reformers scrambled in Farmington to put up bunks and berths, and to transport the blacks over snow in a dozen sleighs, the question arose whether Africans undressed at night! Norton soon became much more familiar with an alien culture as he and others became involved in teaching the Africans in daily classes. Even while riding with a group of the blacks in a sleigh, where the men shivered despite many blankets and buffalo skins, Norton exclaimed: "They have not yet learned the contempt felt for their race here & consequenty have the looks & actions of men. I brought seven of them & to my surprise found that I could easily talk with them. They talked to each other in their own language constantly & laughed frequently, evidently having a good many jokes among themselves."[22]

By March 23 Norton could write: "Teaching them is a perfect pleasure. Some of them read very well indeed. Kennah with fluency." Cinqué, despite having caught a bad cold, exhibited a "truly noble" countenance.[23] Yet by April Norton was shocked to see that Kennah, in response to his treatment by whites, "probably has already learned to feel the inferiority of his race. It is melancholy to see such a mind as his feel the iron of oppression and prejudice."[24]

The cutting edge of this prejudice became apparent on the night of September 3, when four local Farmington "toughs," led by one Henry Hart, assaulted Grabeau. Cinqué then led about half of the Mendeans up the street to protect any of their brethren who were still outdoors. Norton wrote that, according to Cinqué, "they came into a rascally gang in front of Phelps & were with great difficulty restrained from making an attack upon them. As it was, Noble Andrus struck Cinqué." In response, Andrus "got pretty well flogged" and "if the Africans had not been restrained [by Cinqué] they would have routed the whole crew & most probably have killed some of them. The general feeling of the town is one of deep indignation against Hart & his comrades."[25]

In some ways the Mendeans fit in surprisingly well at Farmington. In a great farewell meeting at the local church, after funds had been raised by the African-American Union Missionary Society in Hartford, and in England, to help the blacks return to Sierra Leone, the minister preached a sermon to an immense crowd, according to Norton, "which pretty completely demolished the rationality of the prejudice against color." The Mendeans then sang and danced with great skill, and Cinqué delivered what seemed to be an eloquent speech in Mende.[26] It was generally agreed that the former captives should

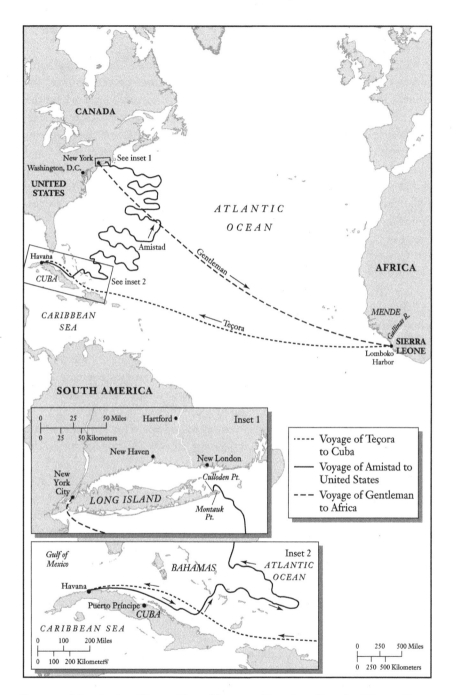

Routes of the *Amistad* Story: From Slavery to Freedom. Based on Howard Jones, *Mutiny on the* Amistad: *The Saga of a Slave Revolt and Its Impact on American Abolition, Law, and Diplomacy* (New York: Oxford University Press, 1987), ii.

be returned to Sierra Leone, though Margru, one of three young girls, would later return from Africa to attend Oberlin College.[27]

"On November 27, 1841," as Howard Jones writes, "thirty-five black survivors (two others had died) of the initial fifty-three on the *Amistad*, including the three girls, along with James Covey, departed New York on the barque *Gentleman*."[28] The ship also carried five white missionaries and teachers. Because of the danger of a Spanish attack or attempts at reenslavement, the British naval patrol along the African coast was put on alert. The freed captives landed in Sierra Leone in January 1842, nearly three years after they had been forced to leave their homeland. Some of the group remained in the small British colony of Sierra Leone and worked with Christian missionaries. Cinqué and the majority returned to their Mende homeland, and as Howard Jones has pointed out, "there is no justification for the oft-made assertion that [Cinqué] himself engaged in the slave trade on his return home."[29]

Until the Civil War, the U.S. government was plagued by continuing disputes over Spanish claims and demands for monetary compensation. The *Amistad* affair underscored the interrelationships within the Atlantic Slave System, from a ship built on an American model and a treaty between Britain and Spain to an 1844 House of Representatives committee report that attacked the Supreme Court's decision and called for payment of indemnity to Spain, an action that reflected the South's growing interest in acquiring Cuba. Similar moves for indemnity payment were made in the Senate, and President Polk, in his address to the nation of December 9, 1847, in the midst of the Mexican War, called for appropriations to pay Spain for the value of the *Amistad* "slaves" as the only way of restoring friendly relations between the two nations.[30]

The trials clearly represented a crucial test of the American judicial system. The two courts' affirmation of freedom may well have helped to motivate Chief Justice Roger Taney to issue his later defense of slavery and official racism in his infamous *Dred Scott* decision of 1857. One can only speculate whether the abolitionists, if their national movement had not been seriously divided in 1840, might have built on and further exploited the courts' limited but still significant affirmation of freedom. Certainly anyone who reads the full text of Adams's powerful indictment of slavery can understand why he became in all likelihood the statesman who passed on to Abraham Lincoln, via Charles Sumner, the conviction that a president, as commander in chief during a war or civil war, had the power to emancipate America's slaves.

2

The Ancient Foundations of Modern Slavery

To GIVE SOME IDEA of the difficulty and complexity of finding a workable definition of slavery, I will begin by considering two examples of premodern bondage: the first from Neo-Babylonia in the sixth century before the Common Era (B.C.E.); the second from the Tupinamba, an aboriginal tribe living along the coast of Brazil from the Amazon south at the time of the first European contact.

Though the Babylonian slave Madanu-bel-usur lived over 2,500 years ago, we have an astonishing amount of factual information regarding his activities and way of life for a period of forty-three years.[1] A highly privileged slave, Madanu-bel-usur lived for a time in Babylon and its suburbs with a family of his own. He owned considerable property, including a house, cattle, sheep, grain, dates, and other produce he used in trade. (While some later North American slaves also owned, traded, and even inherited property,[2] they had no legal rights of ownership.) Madanu-bel-usur also leased fields and paid rent in the form of dates. He acted as an agent for his masters and carried out assignments of a business kind, managing his master's property, paying taxes, and even lending out food and money. In total contrast to modern New World slavery, Madanu-bel-usur became involved in a successful lawsuit with a free man and succeeded in getting an insolvent debtor arrested.

Yet if Madanu-bel-usur's wealth made him the envy of many free Babylonians, he himself was sold at least five times. For example, he, his wife, and his six children were sold in the year 508, in the fourteenth year of the reign of Darius I, to Marduk-nasir-apli, and then again in 506 by Marduk-nasir-apli's wife, Amat-Bau, for twenty-four minas of silver. Amat-Bau's husband had transferred ownership of the slave family to her as compensation for her dowry, which he had squandered. While this sale in 506 was later canceled because the buyer refused for some reason to pay the silver, Madanu-bel-usur could be sold at the whim of an owner and even killed with relative impunity. (At worst, his killer would be required to pay his price to his owner, as if he were livestock.) It seems likely that Madanu-bel-usur was even branded with his owners' names, like many other Babylonian slaves. Even so, there are no records of antislavery protest or even of slave rebellions in the ancient Near East.

Crossing the Atlantic to preconquest Brazil, we find that the Tupinamba, like many primitive slaveholding peoples, had no economic need for slave labor.[3] Food was abundant as a result of the hunting done by males and the gathering as well as slash-and-burn planting and harvesting done by women. Nevertheless, the men, who had much time on their hands when not hunting, seemed to be perpetually at war with their neighbors, and the wars gave much cultural and symbolic importance to the large numbers of enslaved captives, who were eventually killed in ritualistic vengeance and then eaten. Orlando Patterson, a preeminent expert on global slavery, underscores the difference of such practices from the norm in primitive warfare throughout the world. In general, hunting-and-gathering peoples immediately killed male captives, who were considered too dangerous to keep, and either killed or temporarily enslaved female captives, who were then absorbed and assimilated into the conquering society, especially as the need grew for women's agricultural labor.

The Tupinamba gave the appearance of treating their slaves surprisingly well, though everyone knew they would eventually be murdered in an elaborate ritual. The captives were given food, clothing, and sometimes even temporary Tupinamba wives for the male slaves, an indication of the status of women among these particular Indians. As the foreign slaves lived and worked with their captors, they were constantly required to humble themselves and show respect to their conquerors. Thus the function of slavery, as in many societies, was to make the Tupinamba feel honored, superior, or almost godlike as they defined themselves as "nonslaves." It was only in ancient Greece and Rome that "nonslave" began to mean "free" in our individualistic sense; in Africa and most other premodern societies, the opposite of being a slave has traditionally been defined as being a member of a specific tribe, chiefdom, or clan, with close ties to both ancestors and descendants.

Before the final stage of murder and cannibalism, the Tupinamba humiliated their slaves, denouncing and reviling their tribes of origin. The

Tupinamba also engaged in cat-and-mouse games, allowing a frantic slave to escape before being recaptured. It is crucial to realize that such slaves were being treated essentially as animals, a fact symbolized by their ritualistic slaughter and the final cannibal feast. This behavior dramatizes the point that, wholly apart from later economic functions, slaves from the very beginning were perceived as dehumanized humans—humans deprived of precisely those traits and faculties that are prerequisites for human dignity, respect, and honor. By a depraved but all too human logic, this freedom to degrade, dishonor, enslave, and even kill and eat gave the Tupinamba not only solidarity but a sense of superiority and transcendence—of rising above the constraints and material conditions of life.[4]

That modern Americans have not been so far removed from the Tupinamba in a moral or even ritualistic sense can be seen in the enthusiasm for lynching former slaves and their descendants a century ago. American lynch mobs did not eat the blacks whom Rebecca Felton called "ravening human beasts" who should be lynched by the thousand every week. (Felton, a prominent Southern feminist and journalist, was the first woman to become a U.S. senator.) We are told, however, that Southern whites eagerly gathered as souvenirs the lynched victims' fingers, toes, bones, ears, and teeth.[5] In Paris, Texas, for example, some ten thousand whites came in 1893 to participate in the lynching of Henry Smith, an insane former slave accused of raping and killing a three-year-old white girl "in the mad wantonness of gorilla ferocity." High on a platform, so the men, women, and children could see the torture of Smith, the father and brother of the dead girl applied white-hot irons to Smith's bare feet and tongue before burning out his eyes. One observer recalled "a cry that echoed over the prairie like the wail of a wild animal." There was even a primitive gramophone to make a recording of Smith's ghastly cries. After the platform had been soaked with oil and set ablaze, cremating what was left of Smith, people raked the ashes to acquire "nigger" buttons, bones, and teeth to keep as relics. As with the Tupinamba, we find a ritual sacrifice, consecrated by fire, designed to purge society of the ultimate domestic enemy.[6]

WE NOW FACE a momentous question: Can Madanu-bel-usur and other privileged slaves, including elite military slaves like the Egyptian Mamluks and the chief eunuch agents of Chinese and Byzantine emperors (whom Patterson labels "the ultimate slaves"), be lumped together with the captives of the Tupinamba, to say nothing of the millions of African American slaves from colonial Brazil to the pre–Civil War South? Can we exclude from such a broad category of "slavery" the so-called free Negroes like Henry Smith in the 1890s; or Chinese contract laborers who in the late nineteenth century were transported across the Pacific to Peru and Ecuador, where they typically died within a year or two from the lethal effects of mining and shoveling sea-bird manure for the world's fertilizer markets?

I do not want to get deeply involved in the controversies over definition, but a book of this kind should give some attention both to the concept of slavery and to various examples and social embodiments of bondage, in part because most people assume they know what slavery is and never give much thought to what our Thirteenth Amendment means when it affirms that "Neither slavery [this is the first and only time the word is used in the Constitution][7] nor involuntary servitude, except as a punishment for crime whereof the party shall have been duly convicted, shall exist within the United States, or any place subject to their jurisdiction." The "except" clause allowed states in the post-Reconstruction South to send blacks to prison or "prison farms" on trifling or trumped-up charges and to lease slavelike convict labor to large private farms and mines.[8]

Traditional definitions of slavery have stressed that the slave's person is the chattel property of another man or woman, and thus subject to sale and other forms of transfer; that the slave's will is subject to the owner's authority; that the slave's labor or services are obtained through coercion, meaning that the owner's authority is always backed up by the whip or other instruments for inflicting pain; and that the master-slave relationship is "beyond the limits of family relations," thus differentiating it from the slavelike subordination of women and children in a patriarchal family.

As we will see a bit later, slavery may well have been modeled on the domestication of animals, especially livestock and beasts of burden (i.e., "chattel," from the medieval Latin *capitale* [and Latin *capitalis*], which was the root for both "cattle" and "capital"). The domestication of livestock began around 8000 B.C.E.,[9] and as the laws governing chattel property evolved in the Mideastern Fertile Crescent and then in other food-producing societies, it was almost universally agreed that a slave could be bought, sold, bequested, inherited, traded, leased, mortgaged, presented as a gift, pledged for a debt, included in a dowry, freed, or seized in a bankruptcy. These legal points generally applied even to privileged slaves in ancient Mideastern civilizations and for the Western world were much later codified in Roman law.

Orlando Patterson has surprisingly argued that defining humans as property is of secondary importance and is not an essential constituent of slavery. He defines slavery as "the permanent, violent, and personal domination of natally alienated and generally dishonored persons." One must read his now classic book, *Slavery and Social Death*, to fully understand this tightly packed sentence. In brief, his first point stresses that slavery is always an extreme form of personal domination, so even a privileged slave like Madanu-bel-usur lived under the direct power of his owner, a power that often extended to life and death (though we should note that a father could legally kill or sell a rebellious son in some patriarchal societies).

Patterson's second point holds that the slave, whether a foreign captive or a degraded and dehumanized member of the master's ethnic group, is always "an excommunicated person," lacking an independent social existence. This condition of "social death" was clearly recognized in Greco-Roman antiquity and even in medieval Jewish rabbinic sources.[10] By stressing the slave's "natal alienation," Patterson means that the captive and his or her descendants are torn away and uprooted from an original family, clan, ancestors, and even legal descendants (since his or her children become the property of the mother's owner). At least in theory and in law, the slave has no legitimate, independent being, no place in the cosmos except as an instrument of her or his master's will.

While this Aristotelian view of the slave's condition would not apply to traditionally dependent but "free" wives and children, it could and did symbolize an ideal of religious allegiance and total dependency. For example, in the Hebrew Bible Moses is pictured as God's slave (often translated as "servant"), and early Christians were exhorted in the New Testament to become the slaves (or servants) of Jesus and even to free themselves of all family ties. The Hebrew *'eved*, the Greek *doulos*, the Latin *servus*, and the Arabic *'abd* were all used to signify total dependence on God along with meaning "slave" (a word, as we shall see in Chapter Three, derived from the medieval Latin *sclavus*, meaning "Slav").

Patterson's third constituent is the slave's perpetual condition of dishonor. All slaves, he argues, are like the captives of the Tupinamba in the sense that they provided a master class with a resource for parasitic and psychological exploitation. Even when slaves were purchased primarily for economic reasons, their degradation gave their masters a sense of honor, prestige, and superior identity. One can see this mechanism in embryonic form in sibling rivalry, when one brother or sister achieves a sense of pride and superiority from the humiliation of a usually younger sibling. More profound forces were at work in the master-slave relationship, as the German philosopher Hegel demonstrated in his classic account of slavery emerging from a struggle of my self-consciousness to gain recognition from your self-consciousness, your sense of being the center of the universe.[11] Hegel's paradigm of slavery is far too complex to analyze here,[12] but it is worth noting that there are deep philosophic and psychological aspects to the dishonoring, humiliating, or dehumanizing of slaves, a process that nourished what we now call "racism"—epitomized in extreme form in the Texas mob's response to the lynching of Henry Smith.

I would modify Patterson's view of slavery in two ways. First, I would restore the crucial element of chattel property, which is closely related to Patterson's "natal alienation" and "generalized dishonor."[13] The key to this relationship, as I have suggested, lies in the "animalization" or "bestialization" of slaves. This is not to say that masters literally saw slaves as "only animals," or as an entirely different species, except in extreme cases or in response to the scientific racism that emerged in the mid-nineteenth century. To give an example of one such extreme case, when in 1856 the northern traveler Frederick Law Olmsted exclaimed to a white overseer that it must be disagreeable to punish slaves the way he did, the overseer replied, "Why, sir, I wouldn't mind killing a nigger more than I would a dog."[14] For the most part, though, viewing slaves as "human animals" meant focusing on and exaggerating the so-called animal traits that all humans share and fear, while denying the redeeming rational and spiritual qualities that give humans a sense of pride, of being made in the image of God, of being only a little lower than angels. According to the philosopher Nietzsche, "Man didn't even want to be an 'animal.'"[15]

IT MAY BE HELPFUL at this point to distinguish the idea or concept of slavery from various historical varieties of servitude and bondage. From the first written records in ancient Sumer, the concept of slavery has been a way of classifying and categorizing the most debased social class. In the ancient Near East, as in Asia, Africa, and the Americas, various forms of slavery arose long before they were systemized by laws, such as the Hammurabi Code of the eighteenth century B.C.E.

The first documents revealing the existence of slavery come from Sumer as early as 2000 B.C.E., but some six thousand years earlier Mesopotamia led the world in the revolutionary shift from a hunting-and-gathering society to an agricultural one with urban centers. Although men and domesticated dogs had already been hunting together for two millennia, it was only with the Neolithic Revolution (some ten thousand years ago) that sheep, cattle, pigs, horses, goats, and other social animals were domesticated, consequently undergoing an evolutionary process called neoteny, or progressive juvenilization. In other words, the domesticated animals became more submissive than their wild counterparts, less fearful of strangers and less aggressive. Far from being fortuitous, these changes in biology and behavior were closely geared to human needs in farming. To control such beasts, humans not only branded them but devised collars, chains, prods, and whips and also castrated and subjected certain animals to specific breeding patterns. Though one cannot move beyond speculation, the continual comparison of slaves to domestic animals suggests that as formal wars developed between more densely populated societies, similar techniques of control were imposed on captives. No doubt for a time most male captives were considered too dangerous to enslave and were thus killed, while women were often raped and taken as concubines. Then, with an increasing need for agricultural labor and public works, victors devised better methods of branding, marking off, and controlling male prisoners, whose foreign speech would sometimes have made them seem more like animals than men. We can see why Aristotle said that the ox was the poor man's slave. And Xenophon, like many other writers on incentives for slaves, "compared the teaching of slaves, unlike that of free workers, with the training of wild animals."[16]

Despite widespread attempts to equate human captives with domestic animals and even to market them and price them the same way—as the Portuguese, for example, dealt with African captives taken to Lisbon in the mid-fifteenth century—slaves were fortunately never held long enough in a distinctive group to undergo genetic neoteny (and as Jared Diamond makes clear, many mammals, such as zebras, successfully resisted domestication).[17] Yet a kind of neoteny was clearly the goal of many slaveholders, even if they lacked a scientific understanding of how domestication changed the nature and behavior of animals. Aristotle's ideal of the "natural slave" was very close to what a human being would be like if subjected to a genetic change similar to that of domesticated plants and animals. The same point can be seen in the later stereotype of the slave "Sambo."

In actuality, however, the animal species *Homo sapiens* exhibits remarkably little genetic variation, compared, for example, to gorillas, and also shares an amazing capacity for self-transcendence and rational analysis—for viewing ourselves from a vantage point outside the self and for imagining what it would be like to be someone else. We also have the capacity to analyze our own genome and the nature of the cosmos surrounding it. And since humans can imagine abstract states of perfection, they very early imagined a perfect form of subordination. Thus Plato compared the slave to the human body and the master to the body's rational soul; slaves supposedly incarnated the irrationality and chaos of the material universe, as distinct from the masterlike force of creation and shaping the world. The natural slave, according to Aristotle, could have no will or interests of his own; he or she was merely a tool or instrument, the extension of the owner's physical nature. In an important passage that deserves to be quoted in full, Aristotle made explicit the parallel between the slave and the domesticated beast:

> Tame animals are naturally better than wild animals, yet for all tame animals there is an advantage in being under human control, as this secures their survival. . . . By analogy, the same must necessarily apply to mankind as a whole. Therefore all men who differ from one another by as much as the soul differs from the body or man from a wild beast (and that is the state of those who work by using their bodies, and for whom that is the best

they can do)—these people are slaves by nature, and it is better for them to be subject to this kind of control, as it is better for the other creatures I've mentioned. . . . [A]ssistance regarding the necessities of life is provided by both groups, by slaves and by domestic animals. Nature must therefore have intended to make the bodies of free men and of slaves different also; slaves' bodies strong for the services they have to do, those of free men upright and not much use for that kind of work, but instead useful for community life."[18]

While even Aristotle admitted that sometimes "slaves can have the bodies of free men" and that free men could have "only the souls and not the bodies of free men," he could nevertheless conclude, in an argument that would have immeasurable influence in Western culture, that "it is clear that there are certain people who are free and certain who are slaves by nature, and it is both to their advantage, and just, for them to be slaves." While slaves in antiquity could usually be recognized by clothing, branding, collars, and other symbols, the millennia-long search for ways to identify "natural slaves" would eventually be solved by the physical characteristics of sub-Saharan Africans.

After quoting Cato, Varro, and Columella, all famous Roman writers, on the similar treatment of slaves and animals, the ancient historian Keith Bradley notes that Aristotle also stated "that the slave was as appropriate a target of hunting as the wild animal" and concludes that "the ease of association between slave and animal . . . was a staple aspect of ancient mentality, and one that stretched back to a very early period: the common Greek term for 'slave,' andrapodon, 'man-footed creature,' was built on the foundation of a common term for cattle, namely, tetrapodon, 'four-footed creature.'"[19]

Yet a few ancient Greek writers, especially Cynics and Stoics, saw a fundamental contradiction in trying to reduce even foreign human beings to a petlike or animal status. They saw that a master's identity depended on having a slave who recognized him as master and owner, and that this in turn required an independent consciousness. Contrary to Aristotle, the master/slave roles could be reversed, a phenomenon that actually occurred in ancient Rome as well as in such regions as the nineteenth-century Kongo.[20] When pirates captured the early Cynic Diogenes of Sinope and took him to a slave market, he supposedly pointed to a spectator wearing purple robes and said, "Sell me to this man; he needs a master."[21]

The only surviving all-out attack in antiquity on the enslavement of human beings, by Gregory of Nyssa in the late fourth century, makes much of the animal parallel. Complaining that slaveholders set themselves up as masters of creatures who had been made "in the image of God," Gregory wrote: "You have forgotten the limits of your authority, and that your rule is confined to control over things without reason. . . . Surely human beings have not been produced from your cattle? Surely cows have not conceived human stock? Irrational beasts are the only slaves of mankind." Despite language like that of abolitionists fourteen centuries later, however, Gregory's repudiation of slavery, as Peter Garnsey has shown, was part of a more general attack on the "love of money, usury, drunkenness, love of pleasure," and he never called for actions that would weaken or eliminate what he clearly saw as "inhuman" bondage, that is, the treatment of humans as nonhuman beasts of burden.[22]

This paradox of trying to reduce a human being to salable chattel is what I have termed the basic "problem of slavery," arising from the irreducible human dignity of the slave. Although a slave is supposed to be treated like a dog, horse, or ox, as reflected in all the laws that define the slave as a chattel or thing, the same laws have had to recognize that slaves run away, rebel, murder, rape, steal, divulge revolts, and help protect the state from external danger. (Virtually every slaveholding state has had to arm slaves, no matter how reluctantly, in times of crisis.)[23]

No masters or lawmakers, whether in ancient Rome, medieval Tuscany, or seventeenth-century Brazil, could forget that the most obsequious servant might also be what Renaissance Italians termed a "domestic enemy," bent on theft, poisoning, or arson. Throughout history it has been said that slaves, if occasionally as loyal and faithful as good dogs, were for the most part lazy, irresponsible, cunning, rebellious, untrustworthy, and sexually promiscuous. This central contradiction was underscored in Roman law, especially the fifth-century Code of Justinian, which ruled that slavery was the single institution contrary to the law of nature but sanctioned by the law of nations, or international law. (We have seen how American courts dealt with this contradiction in the *Amistad* case.) Hence bondage came in the Western world to symbolize the brutal world as it is—to represent the compromises man must make with the sinful world of Adam's fall, with reality.[24]

As one might expect, there was much divergence between the legalistic or philosophical concept of slavery and the actual systems of servitude and forced labor that arose in various societies around the world. Still, the concept has guided judges and legislators who at times have tried to shape bondage according to biblical or classical models. It is of inestimable importance that the classical and biblical traditions linked slavery with original sin, punishment, Noah's curse of Canaan (often confused with Ham), and the irremediable realities of human life, including, in the post-Edenic world, the grim or even tortuous need of most humans to toil, as the Bible puts it, "by the sweat of your brow" in order to get enough bread to eat and live. By the same token, the later abolition of slavery became tied with personal and collective freedom, with the redemption from sin, with the romanticizing of many forms of labor, and with the ultimate salvation of humankind. These associations and symbols lie at the core of our Western cultural heritage and are echoed in some other cultural traditions as well.[25]

This point is dramatically illustrated by the Exodus theme in the Bible, which, as we will later see, encouraged and inspired many slaves. Although bondage was sanctioned and taken for granted in the Old Testament, the central message and dynamic of the Hebrew Bible involves an *escape* from slavery and a forty-year struggle to find the meaning of freedom. (This was why in 1777 Benjamin Franklin proposed to the Continental Congress a depiction of Moses leading Israel's liberation from slavery for the reverse side of the Great Seal of the United States.) The historian Michael Walzer has documented the many ways in which the biblical Exodus story has been used to justify movements of liberation.[26]

One can imagine a spectrum of states of freedom and dependency or powerlessness, with various types of serfdom and peonage shading off into actual slavery. Within the category of slavery itself, we can also imagine a spectrum of slave systems beginning with those that accord slaves a variety of protections and rights. Orlando Patterson has analyzed sixty-six slaveholding systems, ranging from the Bella Coola of British Columbia to the Taureg and Ashanti of Africa and "the ultimate slave," or chief eunuch agents of emperors from Turkey to China. Patterson has been far more concerned with the dynamics of power and the relation of masters and slaves to the rest of society than with questions of harshness or leniency. Accordingly, his comparisons reveal much complexity.

It is clear that some forms of contract and prison labor have been harsher and more lethal than most examples of slavery. The same point can be made concerning the coerced labor in totalitarian states, such as Hitler's Germany, Stalin's Russia, and Mao's China. If the laboring prisoners in the Nazi death camps and in Russia's gulag were not legally defined as owned chattel property, they were thereby completely made expendable and could be starved or frozen to death or simply shot, without any recognized loss. In terms of material standard of living, the slaves in the nineteenth-century American South were clearly far better off than most slaves and forced labor in history; yet they were victims of one of the most oppressive slave systems ever known in terms of the rate of manumission, racial discrimination, and psychological oppression, or what Patterson terms "generalized dishonor."

As Patterson shows, some slave systems with high rates of manumission and the purchase of freedom were among the most brutal and oppressive regimes in other ways. Some societies enacted impressive-sounding laws intended to protect slaves, but then we discover that these laws were hardly ever enforced. Similarly, while laws in the U.S. South deprived slaves of legal marriage, nineteenth-century planters and ministers did much to encourage slave marriages and families, in part for self-interested reasons. Patterson's work thus far has focused largely on premodern slavery and on psychological and social functions that transcended economic motives. Yet it is crucial to remember that the central quality of a given kind of slavery was usually defined by the nature of the work required: whether this meant cutting sugarcane or working in a sweltering boiler room of a sugar mill in the tropical West Indies (where the climate contributed to high mortality); or serving as a sex object in a Persian harem; or wearing fine linens and driving white people in a coach in Virginia; or performing as an acrobat, dancer, soldier, doctor, or bureaucrat in Rome.

It is also important to remember that in most societies, even the most privileged slave—the wealthy farm agent in Babylon, the Greek poet or teacher in Rome, the black driver, musician, blacksmith, or boat captain in Mississippi—could be quickly sold, or stripped and whipped, or raped, or sometimes even killed at the whim of an owner. All slave systems shared this radical uncertainty and unpredictability. The slave, even the Mamluk army officer or powerful eunuch issuing orders in the emperor's name, was deprived of any supportive family or clan, any continuity with a genuine history. Whatever privileges she or he may have gained could be taken away in a flash—leaving the slave as naked as an animal at an auction. This absence of a past and a future, of a place in history and society from which to grow in small increments, made each slave totally vulnerable. This may be the very essence of dehumanization.

Since New World slavery was affected by significant but often neglected continuities and influences that extended back to the ancient Near East, the Bible, and Greece and Rome, it is important to take a number of snapshots of the nature of bondage in those times and regions. Slavery did appear in a number of primitive hunting-and-gathering societies, such as the Tupinamba, but it acquired a more central role when people learned to exploit the muscle power of animals, developed extensive agriculture, and built urban civilizations with complex social stratification. In ancient China, for example, where many criminals as well as foreign captives were enslaved, bondsmen were viewed as subhuman and were tattooed for identification, and captive Turks and Indonesians were often referred to as "blacks." As in parts of the ancient Near East, mutilation and death awaited any slave who had sex with a free person.[27]

From Sumeria and Babylonia on to Egypt, the economies of ancient societies were not truly based on slave labor as in later Athens and Rome. In Mesopotamia a wide range of statuses, with varying degrees of dependency, stretched between slaves and godly rulers. Nor was there any status resembling the later Greek and Roman concept of individual freedom. Indeed, in the eyes of later Greeks, all Persians or other Asian subjects of authoritarian kings were essentially slaves, a term easily extended to the subjects of any authoritarian rule. (Similarly, in eighteenth-century England it often seemed that most other Europeans were "enslaved" to authoritarian kings, in contrast to the "free" English, and by the 1770s most white North Americans claimed that the English were determined to "enslave" them.)

The first and primary source of slaves in many societies was foreign prisoners of war and victims of piracy and kidnapping. Orlando Patterson has described the "social death" of such captives as "intrusive," since they were brought into a society where they were seen as strange, alien objects of contempt and dishonor. The Greek word for "barbarians" (*barbaroi*), whom the Greeks much preferred as slaves, referred to foreigners like Scythians and Thracians who spoke a different language and who were thus "ignorant of the political institutions and cultural characteristics of the city."[28] Thus, like an ox or an ass, a barbarian was unable to communicate with her or his captors. Gerda Lerner has argued persuasively that the archetypal slave was a woman and that the status of slaves as inferior dependents was closely modeled on the status of women in patriarchal societies.[29] Certainly we see in both Homeric and biblical literature that the males defeated in wars were usually slaughtered while foreign women were enslaved and used for household service as well as for sex and heavy labor.

In Mesopotamia by the second millennium B.C.E. (i.e., 2000 to 1000), civilizations had become sufficiently developed to absorb large numbers of male prisoners, especially as temple slaves, or slaves of a state who were not individually owned. Such men lived together in work houses near temples and performed heavy work digging canals for irrigation and transport. In Sumer, public slaves were referred to as *iginu'du*, meaning "not raising their eyes," which apparently they were forbidden to do as a symbol of their degradation and social death—and probably to prevent their eyes from looking at nonslave women. Some slaves were branded with the same mark as livestock. In Babylon, their hair was cut short in front to reveal the brand on their forehead; in the Neo-Babylonian period, slaves often had their owner's name branded on the back of their hand.[30]

Although the Hebrew Bible tells us to give shelter to a fugitive slave, this compassion was doubtless meant only for a Hebrew slave of a non-Hebrew owner. The Hammurabi Code of the eighteenth century B.C.E. prescribed death for anyone who sheltered a fugitive or helped a slave escape. When recaptured, a fugitive was to be branded with an additional identifying mark on his face for all to see. In theory at least, ancient Hebrews limited the servitude of their own people, who would have mostly been debt slaves, to six years, and when a slave was set free, the master must not "let him go empty-handed: furnish him out of the flock, threshing floor, and vat, with which the Lord your God has blessed you. Bear in mind that you were slaves in the land of Egypt and the Lord your God redeemed you." Other Hebrew slaves were to be emancipated at the Jubilee, every fifty years.[31] This meant confining perpetual chattel slavery to the Israelites' enemies—especially the Canaanites, a "white" Semitic people and a label many Jews later applied to all gentile slaves.

As later Christians searched the Old Testament for proslavery sanctions, they also found, in Leviticus:

> Such male and female slaves as you may have—it is from the nations ["heathen" in King James Bible] round about you that you may acquire male and female slaves. You may also buy them from among the children of aliens ["strangers" in King James Bible] resident with you, or from their families that are among you, whom they begot in your land. These shall become your property: you may keep them as a possession for your children after you, for them to inherit as property for all time. Such you may treat as slaves. But as for your Israelite brothers, no one shall rule ruthlessly over the other.[32]

This portentous if very human distinction between people like us and the Outsiders not only validated perpetual slavery but even seemed to imply that non-Hebrew slaves could be ruled ruthlessly or "with rigor."[33] Yet Leviticus and Exodus also proclaim versions of the Golden Rule, "Love your fellow [or neighbor] as yourself," and "You shall not oppress a stranger, for you know the feelings of the stranger, having yourselves been strangers, in the land of Egypt."[34] Both Jews and Christians have long struggled to reconcile these oppressive and compassionate passages and precepts. (Some later captains of slave ships claimed that their treatment of Africans conformed to the Golden Rule.)[35]

Though Egyptians in the New Kingdom (c. 1575–1075 B.C.E.) used many war-captive slaves for heavy labor on temples, obelisks, and other public works, it appears that most slaves in Mesopotamia were not captured in war or slaving raids. (Both the Hammurabi Code and Hebrew Bible prescribed death as the penalty for kidnapping minors.) Orlando Patterson uses "extrusive" to refer to internal or domestic sources of slaves. He speaks of the forcible expulsion of people within an in-group from the status and privileges enjoyed by nonslaves. One clear example would be the early modern Russian slaves and later serfs who were degraded and dehumanized by masters of the same ethnicity. Yet the Old Testament describes a ritual for Hebrew slaves who chose to remain with a master instead of being freed and perhaps starving or having to leave a wife and children at the end of six years of service. Such a slave would be brought to a doorpost where "his master shall bore his ear through with an awl; and he shall serve him forever."[36] Presumably the bored hole would hold an earring or clay tag of some kind with the master's logo.

One major source of extrusive slaves throughout the ancient world was the thousands of unwanted babies who were abandoned and exposed to the elements. This was the main form of birth control throughout antiquity. There were no foundling centers or hospitals, as in medieval Europe. Hence numerous documents speak of infants being placed "in the mouth of a dog" or "crow" or "in a pit," which could mean a symbolic descent to animal status as infants were deprived of human protection. Most of these children, abandoned at wells or on the street, died of hunger and cold (and their corpses might well have been fed upon by dogs and crows). Of those who were rescued, some were adopted as free children, but most were raised as slaves. Some parents even sold their own small children into slavery.

Desperate poverty and indebtedness were other common sources of extrusive slaves, especially in the second millennium in the eastern Mediterranean and much later among various African and Asian peoples. Yet debt slaves were increasingly elevated above chattel slaves in the ancient Near East; they were also apparently of declining importance from the seventh to the fourth century B.C.E. According to Plutarch, Solon, the great Greek lawgiver and reformer of the late sixth century, totally abolished debt bondage because "all the common people were in debt to the rich."

IN BABYLONIA, EGYPT, and the ancient world in general, the number of slaves never approached 50 percent of the population. Most agricultural work was done by tenant farmers; free workers dominated most of the craft industries, though in the Neo-Babylonian period slaves appeared as artisans, agents, tenant farmers, merchants, and even bankers. Apart from the public temple slaves, private household slaves became an important symbol of wealth and power, as in later Greece and Rome. The richest families might own over one hundred slaves and use them in a variety of ways. For thousands of years slavery was simply taken for granted in ancient Babylonia and Egypt (as in India, China, and the Americas). Manumissions were exceedingly rare, in contrast to later Rome. If someone killed a slave, he was not guilty of murder but simply required to pay the slave's market price to the master, as if he had killed a horse or cow. In the Neo-Babylonian kingdom, from 626 to 538 B.C.E., it was still not a crime to kill a slave, in contrast to fifth-century B.C.E. Athens and the nineteenth-century C.E. American South.[37]

Victor Hanson has recently pointed to an agricultural revolution that began in ancient Greece around 750 B.C.E., in which small numbers of slaves were associated with family farms producing a mix of crops. Aided by as few as one or two slaves, small-scale farmers succeeded in producing sufficient food to maintain a democratic polis, or city-state. Thus slavery became economically important as soon as farmers began producing a surplus of grain, olives, fruit, and wine that could be sold or exchanged.[38] As in the much later North American colonies, freedom and slavery advanced together. Indeed, Greece was probably the first genuine "slave society"—that is, a collection of states totally dependent on slave labor, as distinct from the many societies that simply possessed slaves.[39]

If the ancient Greeks hold the distinction of having created democracy, they also came to see slave labor as absolutely central to their entire economy and way of life. Along with a growing emphasis on individual and political liberty, Greek free citizens came to disdain all types of manual labor. Within the city-state, at least, the free male Greek citizen needed time and leisure to participate in civic society and make use of his rational thought and creative powers. "The condition of the free man," said Aristotle, "is that he does not live under the constraint of another." As a noted British classicist puts it:

> [The Greeks] could imagine no alternative [to slave labor]; the life of the citizens in the polis, the only form of civilized organization they knew or could imagine, would have been impossible without that leisure they prized so highly, leisure to haunt the gymnasium, the roofed porches where men congregated for conversation and dispute, the theater, the assembly, the courts, and all the varied, time-consuming duties and pleasures of the free male citizen.[40]

Of course there were many pronouncements from Athens and other cities against enslaving any Greek peoples, even when defeated in war. Yet Greeks continued to war against and enslave fellow Greeks, and often looked upon such a sparing of life as an act of mercy. Greeks also accepted the right to enslave infant foundlings who had been abandoned by a parent. As the demand for slaves grew, merchants increasingly purchased slaves as part of long-distance seaborne commerce; in other words, the trade in such commodities as ceramics and olive oil opened up distant markets for human labor. From the sixth century B.C.E. onward, merchants followed armies in the field and bought up prisoners of war who were then transported with other goods to such commercial centers as Athens, Corinth, Aegina, and Chios. It is estimated that in such cities slaves made up at least one-third of the population and were even more widely dispersed among slaveowners than in the later U.S. South.

As in the later Roman world, this linkage of slavery with long-distance commerce by sea served to separate the urban centers of culture and learning from the violent origins of enslavement. A respected urban master might have little mental picture of the bloody battlefields or terrifying raids of a pirate ship that had furnished him with servants. Moreover, from the sixth century on, the gulf continued to widen between slaves and free citizens, in contrast to the much earlier Homeric slaves, who ate, drank, and worked side by side with their nonwealthy masters. It should be added, however, that there were many manumitted slaves in Greek society, some of them citizens, and that Athens freed most male slaves of military age in 406 B.C.E. so they could serve in the Peloponnesian War.[41]

While Greek slaves worked as nurses, prostitutes, urban artisans, and domestic servants, we should not forget the less visible and far more miserable slaves in the mines. Diodorus Siculus described the miners in Ptolemaic Egypt:

> No leniency or respite of any kind is given to any man who is sick, or maimed, or aged, or in the case of a woman for her weakness, but all without exception are compelled by blows to persevere in their labors, until through ill-treatment they die in the midst of their tortures. Consequently, the poor unfortunates believe, because their punishment is so excessively severe, that the future will always be more terrible than the present and they therefore look forward to death as more to be desired than life.[42]

In modern times the eminent classicist Bernard Knox climbed into the mine shaft at Laurion, in Attica, the main source of revenue and coinage for Athens, where the supposedly virtuous statesman Nicias owned one thousand of the slaves who extracted silver. Knox found that the shafts down which one descended by ladders 130 meters into the earth measured 2 meters by 1.3 meters. At the bottom, miners were forced to crawl into dark galleries or tunnels, 1 meter high and from 0.6 to 0.9 meters wide. Knox badly scratched his knees and hands, frayed his shirt and trousers, and then got stuck in a dark bend as he tried to crawl out backward. Yet thousands of slave miners worked in such a hellish environment, with crude oil lamps, ten hours on and ten hours off.[43]

SIMILAR CONDITIONS were perpetuated and extended by the Romans—for example, in the notorious silver mines in Spain—and it was Rome that bequeathed to Christian Europe the juridical and philosophical foundations for modern slavery. As the legal scholar Alan Watson has written, "it is not going too far to suggest that Southern [U.S.] slave law, when it did not adopt Roman rules, preferred others because of the power of racism." Watson adds that "nonracist slavery is very different but may be no less horrifying in many respects than racist slavery." Perhaps the most crucial point of influence is "the principal distinction in the law of persons ... [A]ll men are either free or slaves—there is no third, intermediate, category in Roman law.[44]

Through many centuries of time, learned lawyers, judges, and professors passed on a kind of culture of law, concerning the uses of power and the regulation of slavery, based on the mid-sixth-century C.E. Institutes of Justinian, which was revived at the end of the eleventh century and especially influential in Spain, France, and Portugal. Despite the striking differences in the English common-law tradition, educated American Southerners, as Watson observes, were very familiar with Roman law, and well-informed travelers in the American South exclaimed over the similarities between Roman slave law and the laws of Southern states. This is not to deny some significant differences, often stemming from the racial character of American slavery, including restrictions on manumissions and rules governing the *peculium*, or property entrusted to slaves but still legally owned by a master. And even the harshest Southern lawmakers in the United States did not copy Roman laws allowing naked slaves to be put in an arena to fight hungry lions or ruling that if a slave raped a free virgin, molten lead was to be poured down his throat.

Still, as matters developed, many antebellum Southern leaders, writers, and journalists were very familiar with classical Roman texts.[45] From the late eighteenth century well into the first half of the nineteenth, Americans fixated on classical models, from architecture to prose (producing, for instance, a Latin and therefore "eternal" biography of George Washington) on to republican theories of government and a "Senate," as in ancient Rome. Thus eminent slaveholders, having absorbed some classics in Southern academies and colleges, could think of themselves as modern Catos or Columellas. In addition to such leaps over time, which were also stimulated by the growing popular familiarity with the Bible (one of the themes of this book), there was a genuine continuity of slave-trading and slaveholding from ancient Greece to Rome and from the late Roman Empire to the Byzantine and Arab worlds, from the medieval shipment of slaves from the Balkans, the Black Sea, and Caucasia to Muslim and Christian Mediterranean markets, and from there to the beginnings in the fifteenth century of an African slave trade to Portugal and Spain, and then to the Atlantic Islands and New World. As we shall see in subsequent chapters, this crucial continuity in no way diminishes the importance of changing contexts, ethnicities, and economic needs and markets.

It is probably a mistake, however, to picture the entire Roman Empire as a massive collection of slave societies. My colleague Ramsay MacMullen has argued that if we could travel during the late Roman Empire in a great circle from Gaul to Britain, Germany, Dalmatia and the Balkans, Palestine, Egypt, northern Africa, and Spain, we would see most of the agricultural work being performed by free peasants. Slaves, of course, would appear everywhere, but mostly as urban and household servants, weaving, fetching water, cleaning stables and latrines, cutting wood, assisting women in childbirth and nursing, dressing and transporting wealthy owners. At the same time, Keith Bradley, the leading expert on the subject, stresses that slavery was an integral part of the social order throughout the Roman world. An estimated million house slaves obeyed the orders of the richest 5 percent of Italy's population. Some of the wealthiest families possessed and paraded many hundreds of slave-servants; indeed, a man with no more than two or three slaves was "an object of pity."[46]

The great exception, where slaves were concentrated in large-scale agriculture, serving as a prototype for New World plantations, were the latifundia of southern Italy and Sicily. As Roman armies conquered region after region in the two centuries before the Common Era, an immense flow of captives, many of them transported by merchant slave traders, were channeled to the farmlands of Italy and Sicily to produce grain, wine, wool, and olive oil. Large landlords repeatedly evicted the small farmers of these regions, who migrated as a jobless proletariat to Rome and other cities. The inflow of war captives was supplemented by a growing number of slaves by birth.[47]

Except for the highly productive latifundia, along with some factories producing fine pottery, swords, shields, and other products, most Roman slaves were to be found in towns and cities. Even so, estimates range from two to three million slaves in Italy at the time of Augustus, alongside a free population of four to five million. Taking account of the uncertainty of such statistics, "the proportion of slaves in the Roman population was very close to that at the heyday of American slavery, some 30 percent."[48] Contrary to much scholarly opinion, MacMullen thinks that the number of slaves may not have changed much from the time of Augustus, at the beginning of the Common Era, to the reign of Alaric, in 410.

The Roman adoption of Christianity, in the fourth century, had little effect on slave law, though it doubtless made manumission much easier and more widely approved. While the Romans, as Watson observes, showed little interest in an "ideal law," Justinian's Institutes proclaimed (following the mid-second century jurist Florentinus) that "slavery is an institution of the law of nations (*ius gentium*) by which, contrary to nature, a person is subjected to the dominion of another."[49] This was the only instance in which a rule of international law was said to be contrary to the law of nature, but Augustine and other church fathers had already provided an answer by drawing a profound and influential connection between slavery and original sin. While Augustine urged masters to treat slaves as their brothers in Christ, he interpreted society's need for slaves as part of a universal human depravity, as the way the world is and must be accepted, as distinguished from the City of God. This dualistic view of slavery as a product of sin represented a significant departure from the Romans, who not only accepted inhuman bondage (in the sense that slaves were not fully human) but simply took it for granted.[50]

In the Roman world of reality, it was not problematic to burn alive a slave criminal or to join huge audiences in watching the ritual death of slave gladiators. The law provided that if a slave murdered his master, all the slaves in the household must be questioned under torture and then executed. The jurist Ulpian explained the rationale: "Since otherwise no home can be safe, unless slaves at the risk of their own lives are compelled to guard their masters as much from members of the household as from outsiders." When, in 61 C.E., a slave murdered the senatorial prefect of Rome, Pedanius Secundas, in his own home, the Roman Senate plunged into a heated debate whether to carry out this law and execute all four hundred slaves, including women and children, in the victim's household. Such an action would deprive the master's heirs of a great fortune. Yet as Gaius Cassius told the Senate, "Whom will the number of his slaves protect when four hundred did not protect Pedanius Secundus?" In the end, the issue of security prevailed. All four hundred were crucified, though the Emperor Nero had to call out troops against a crowd wielding firebrands and stones, wanting to stop the executions. Afterward, other rich slaveholders could presumably sleep more soundly.[51]

Relations between Roman slaves and their owners, both male and female, were the subject of much study and even advice manuals, written almost in the spirit of scientific management. Columella's *De Re Rustica*, well known to some nineteenth-century American masters (it had even been cited by Milton), emphasized the need for positive incentives and inducements that would encourage slaves to compete and become more productive. Columella wrote that he even loved to jest with his slaves and engage in friendly conversations. He even stressed that it was wise to consult with some slaves on the best ways to tackle new work. It is also worth noting that beginning in the second century C.E., many masters stopped the practice of branding ordinary slaves and substituted metal collars bearing the name of the owner.

On the other hand, Keith Bradley points out that Roman slavery was always based on physical and psychological terror, and it was never a disgrace to burn alive a slave accused of some crime. Bradley most vividly illustrates the Roman slave's status of animality in an analysis of Apuleius' mid-second-century C.E. novel, *The Golden Ass, or Metamorphoses*. In this story a prosperous, well-born, and well-educated young man, Lucius, becomes suddenly transformed into a four-footed ass or donkey—"a paradigmatic illustration of the animalization of the slave in real life." Since Lucius retains his rational human identity but is unable to speak or complain as he is flogged, "set to the drudgery of turning a mill," and even sexually exploited, he symbolizes the plight of the dehumanized human, yearning for ways to resist but also learning that "once slaves were set on the level of beasts all need to cater to their human sensibilities was removed." Ironically, the author Apuleius was himself a slaveowner, and his account of one man's temporary bestialization was meant as comedy, not a call for abolitionist action.[52]

Relations between slaves and their owners became the subject of much literary satire, fable, and comedy, which provides insight into the fears, tensions, and desires of the Roman slaveholding society. Though slaves were sometimes portrayed as grateful, loyal, and obsequious, it was difficult to forget the Roman proverb "All slaves are enemies." Especially revealing is the *Life of Aesop*, a fictional slave biography from Roman Egypt in the first century C.E. Since slaves had long and commonly been likened to animals, it is significant that the slave Aesop, supposedly living in the sixth century B.C.E., constructed famous animal fables (like later African American slaves) that served as an indirect way of communicating the slaves' view of their masters' world.

One of the main themes of Aesop's biography, like the biblical story of the slave Joseph and Potiphar's wife, involves sexual relations between male slaves and the wife of the master, who is portrayed as a "sex-crazed slut," on a lascivious lookout for a "young, handsome, athletic, good-looking blond slave." As Keith Hopkins puts it, "the baths, cleanliness, heat and lust were a heady mixture; and the close association between powerful female mistresses and their male slave attendants in public and in private stimulated the anxieties of husbands . . . and later of Christian moralizers."[53] Aesop himself, who begins by severely rebuking his new mistress for her immorality, ends up by seducing her, in revenge for his master's ingratitude.

Apart from lurid sexual details centering on Aesop's frightening potency, Hopkins makes two important points: First, humor camouflages "unceasing guerrilla warfare between master and slave," especially the slaves who help to bathe, dress, and feed their masters, and who thus know every point of weakness and vulnerability. Second, a comedy like the *Life of Aesop* provides a way of dealing with the humanity of a slave, even if at the end he is put to death. By inverting normality, with a picture of the wise, shrewd slave protagonist, the story finally moves on to restore normality by putting the slave "in his place." Disorder implies order. Thus the Roman festival of Saturnalia, by allowing slaves to act like masters for one day, reinforced the basic structures of authority.[54] Colonial and early national Americans would experiment with similar rituals, but racial distinctions made rituals more complex and threatening.

Nothing in the Roman world was really like the racial slavery that came to pervade the Western Hemisphere. Romans imported slaves from countless countries and all directions, including blond, blue-eyed slaves from northern Europe, highly educated and professional slaves from Greece and northern Africa, and even a few black slaves from south of the Sahara. In addition, especially in the period of relative peace after the empire had been firmly established, increasing numbers of slaves were obtained from "breeding," piracy, and the exposure of infants. The public did associate some ethnic stereotypes with slavery. Because slaves in certain regions included a disproportionate number of red-haired Thracians, actors playing the part of slaves sometimes wore red wigs, as an identifying symbol.

Indeed, Spartacus, the famous leader of the third major slave revolt in southern Italy and Sicily was a Thracian. Trained as a swordsman at a school for gladiators, Spartacus led from 73 to 71 B.C.E. a slave army that grew to some seventy thousand. The Romans finally crushed the rebellion and crucified Spartacus and some six thousand other survivors. Thus along with the precedent and sanction for slave plantation agriculture, the Roman era also passed on a heroic precedent for slave resistance (even if the lesson, confirmed scores of times in the New World, was that slave revolts are suicidal).

In 1770, a classic work partially written and edited by the radical French historian and writer the Abbé Raynal, condemned New World slavery and called for "a black Spartacus" who would be a vehicle for nature asserting her rights against the blind avarice of Europeans and American colonists.[55] In the 1790s, Toussaint Louverture, the leader of the rebellious blacks in the Haitian Revolution, was hailed as the long-awaited black Spartacus, especially by the French general Etienne Laveaux, who called him "the black Spartacus, the Negro predicted by Raynal who would avenge the outrages done to his race."[56]

3

The Origins of Antiblack Racism
in the New World

THE WORD "RACISM" was apparently not used in America until 1936, but the reality to which the word refers loomed like a fatal and contagious disease in the eyes of free African Americans one hundred years earlier. For black abolitionists like Theodore S. Wright, such racial prejudice was the central evil to be overcome, even more than slavery. A Presbyterian minister in New York City, a graduate of Princeton Seminary, and a founding member of the American Anti-Slavery Society, Wright was physically assaulted by a Southern student when he visited his alma mater in September 1836. The attacker who seized and kicked him yelled, "Out with the nigger—out with the nigger."

The next month, at the annual meeting of the New York State Anti-Slavery Society, Wright defended a resolution that equated such prejudice with "the very spirit of slavery": "This is serious business, sir," Wright proclaimed. "The prejudice which exists against the colored man, the freeman, is like the atmosphere everywhere felt by him." Though it was true, Wright acknowledged, that the "free" colored men of the North were not whipped nor "liable to have their wives and infants torn from them[,] . . . [s]ir, still we are slaves—everywhere we feel the chain galling us. . . . This spirit [of prejudice] is withering all our hopes, and oft times causes the colored parent as he looks upon his child, to wish he had never been born." Wright suggested that if whites understood what we now term racism as well as they understood slavery, he would not need to explain the subtle difference. As things were, "this influence cuts us off from every thing; it follows us up from child-hood to manhood; it excludes us from all stations of profit, usefulness and honor; takes away from us all motive for pressing forward in enterprises, useful and important to the world and to ourselves." [1]

Historians and social scientists still debate definitions of racism, and since we will be considering some ancient forms of "proto-racism," there can be no doubt that Wright was describing a form of racism "fully developed."[2] Wright and other black reformers recognized that this humiliating prejudice was related to slavery and could be self-reinforcing in the sense that such contempt and denial of hope could lead to despair and patterns of behavior that provoked more prejudice. Yet even in the Northern states, black educa-tion, upward mobility, and middle-class behavior seemed to stimulate in-creasing white violence—as the old saying went, "Negroes" had to be "kept in their place," meaning in the most degraded, castelike class to prevent "amal-gamation" with whites.

But why, we must ask, did slavery and prejudice become linked to a par-ticular people, to dark-skinned descendants of Africans? Did antiblack rac-ism lead to the choice of African slaves to supply the immense demand for physical labor in the New World, or was such racism the consequence of long-term interaction with black slaves, as some historians have claimed? Long before 1836, American slavery had become almost entirely limited to people classified as "Negroes"—even though many "Negroes" had large per-centages of European and/or Indian ancestry. Yet the English word "slave" and its western European counterparts—such as *esclave* in French, *esclavo* in Spanish, and *sklave* in German—stemmed from the Latin *sclavus*, meaning a "Slav," or person of Slavic descent. In the early Middle Ages *sclavus* replaced the nonethnic and traditional Latin words for owned bondspeople, *servus* and *mancipium*.[3] And from the early thirteenth to the late fifteenth century, Italian merchants participated in a booming long-distance seaborne trade that transported tens of thousands of "white" Armenian, Bulgarian, Circassian, Mingrelian, and Georgian slaves from regions around the Black Sea and Sea of Azov to Mediterranean markets extending from Muslim Egypt and Syria to Christian Crete, Cyprus, Sicily and eastern Spain (hence the widespread Western equation of bondage with so-called Slavs). Such slave labor was increasingly used for the production of sugar. As a remnant of this white slave trade, in 1600 there were a few Greek and Slavic slaves in Spanish Havana, and in the 1580s, when conducting his famous naval raids, Sir Francis Drake found and freed Turks, North African Moors, and even Frenchmen and Germans among the Spanish galley slaves in Santo Domingo and Carta-gena, the great center of trade and transshipment of slaves in what is today Colombia.[4]

The ultimate choice of black Africans and the related evolution of anti-black racism were not the results of a simple linear progression of events. Since a chronological narrative cannot capture the complexity of the subject, this chapter will consider such seemingly unrelated issues as the fairly universal stereotypes of slaves and peasants; color symbolism; the significance of Islamic and then Christian geographic expansion and conflict; changing interpretations of the biblical "Curse of Ham" (really Canaan), connections between Spanish fears of having their blood "contaminated" by intermixture with Jewish converts and then by blacks, and, briefly, some telling examples of "scientific" racism in the eighteenth and nineteenth centuries.

As we saw in Chapter Two, various historians have shown that from antiquity onward, slaves have been subjected to certain common stereotypes regardless of race, ethnicity, or time period. Since most slaves have been foreigners, part of this degrading vision arose from xenophobia and a fairly universal contempt that self-defined "superior" chiefdoms or states have shown toward neighbors seen as "inferior." In both the ancient and medieval worlds, there was a strong inclination to equate slaves with ugliness and dark skin, wholly apart from the reality of their appearance. Thus various interpreters over the ages claimed that the biblical Joseph, sold by his brothers to slave traders, did not "look like a slave," since he was so handsome and light-skinned.[5]

In the second and first millennia B.C.E., the North Chinese tended to view even the South Chinese as barbarians, to say nothing of the dark-skinned "wild tribes" farther south and west. Much later on, in the T'ang Dynasty (618–907 C.E.), the Chinese had no compunction about enslaving Koreans, Turks, Persians, and Indonesians and thought that enslavement was especially appropriate for the "black" barbarians of the southern islands, whose supposed inferiority was proved by their nakedness and primitive customs.[6] In ancient India, slavery was initially linked with dark-skinned Dravidian people conquered by Aryan invaders from the north. And from at least as early as the fifth century B.C.E., many Greek writers dehumanized non-Greeks as "barbarians" (without any relation to color) and argued that enslavement should be limited to these supposedly inferior peoples.[7]

Yet even when slaves and slavelike serfs belonged to the same ethnic group as their masters, as in eighteenth- and nineteenth-century Russia, they were said to be intrinsically lazy, childlike, licentious, and incapable of life without authoritative direction. Some Russian noblemen reinvented a supposedly separate historical origin of Russian serfs and even claimed that they had black bones! The historian Paul Freedman has also shown that in medieval western Europe, serfs and peasants were commonly depicted as subhuman and even "black," as a result of their constant exposure to the sun, soil, and manure. But because peasants were an indispensable, food-producing majority of the population, writers often balanced the serfs' or rustics' alleged filth, stupidity, and bestiality with occasional tributes to their piety, simplicity, and closeness to God. [8]

The contempt that medieval writers showed for supposedly "dark-skinned" serfs and slaves, even in Scandinavia, was an extreme example of a far more universal construction of class-consciousness.[9] From early antiquity and in various parts of the globe, the elites who lived indoors and sheltered themselves from the sun sharply differentiated themselves from the field workers who were darkened by dirt as well as exposure to the sun—a striking physical distinction that above all enhanced the appeal and honor of light-skinned, privileged women.[10] It would be hard to overemphasize the importance of this linkage between low social class and the physical markers of menial labor, especially when we have long lived in an age of admiration for tanned skin and of wealthy entertainers and politicians who pose as ranchers and splitters of wood.

Moreover, at a time when occupations are commonly seen as stages in lifetime routes toward success, happiness, and "self-fulfillment," and when we even allocate a day in September to honor "Labor," it is difficult to understand that through much of Western history the upper classes and literate classes viewed physical work "as a chore best left to slaves" (or peasants and household servants). Saint Augustine spoke for many Christians in future times when he saw the pain of slave labor as part of the "wretchedness of man's condition." [11]

Orlando Patterson, the historical sociologist introduced in Chapter Two, who ranks among the world's leading authorities on slavery, argues that the "Sambo" stereotype, as defined in 1959 by the historian Stanley Elkins, has been universal from the most primitive to the most advanced systems of slavery—as a *stereotype* (not applied, of course, to all slaves). Thus while Patterson is well aware of the exceptional depictions of defiant slaves such as the rebel leader Spartacus, or princelike slaves such as those in the highly privileged households of the early Roman emperors, or the palatine eunuch slaves of Byzantium and imperial China, he insists that as a result of the ultimate power of masters, "the degraded man-child" stereotype was "an ideological imperative of all systems of slavery." As Elkins summarizes this totally dishonored character:

> Sambo, the typical plantation slave, was docile but irresponsible, loyal but lazy, humble but chronically given to lying and stealing; his behavior was full of infantile silliness and his talk inflated with childish exaggeration. His relationship with his master was one of utter dependence and childlike attachment: it was indeed this childlike quality that was the very key to his being.

Unlike Elkins, Patterson stresses that

> the Sambo ideology . . . is no more realistic a description of how slaves
> actually thought and behaved than was the inflated conception of honor
> and sense of freedom an accurate description of their masters. What was
> real was the *sense* of honor held by the master, its denial to the slave, its
> enhancement through the degradation of the slave, and possibly the slave's
> own feeling of being dishonored and degraded.[12]

As we will see in later chapters, American slaves bore little resemblance
to Elkins's exaggerated stereotype, even if some adopted a similar mask as
they played different roles. It is also important to recall that the great Frederick
Douglass spoke of himself being "broken in body, soul, and spirit. . . . [T]he
dark night of slavery closed in upon me; and behold a man transformed into
a brute!"[13] Douglass's self-definition as a "brute," which was clearly not meant
to imply any lasting mental damage, brings us back to the complex connections between slavery and animalization that we discussed in Chapter Two.
Indeed, the infant or child metaphor was often a variant on the animal
metaphor—remembering that animals can be petted, cuddled, and endear-
ing, or made to perform tricks as well as much of the labor and energy humans needed for millennia of time. Children in many cultures have been
referred to and treated like animals, in both loving and degrading ways.[14] In
general, however, when adults are likened to animals, it is an insult (he, she,
or they are "dogs, bitches, pigs, swine, snakes in the grass, vermin, rats, lice,"
etc.; in Christian Europe, even Christianized Jews moved from the Spanish
label for swine [*Marranos*] to the Nazi designations for lice, bloodsuckers, or
vampires [*Ungeziefer, Blutsauger*]).

As Europeans continued to discover more "primitive" peoples on the
planet, countless observers echoed the sixteenth-century English voyagers
who described sub-Saharan Africans as "beastly savage people," "wilde men,"
and "brutish blacke people." An early French explorer wrote that Australian
aborigines, who unlike the West Africans were still hunter-gatherers, were
"the most miserable people in the world, and the human beings who approach closest to brute beasts."[15] With respect to the links between bestiality
and slavery, from the earliest Sumerian tablets and other records dating from
the mid-third millennium B.C.E., captive slaves have been equated with domesticated animals in pricing, status, and the way they have been described.
In Chapter Two I suggested that the early enslavement and treatment of
prisoners of war may have been modeled on the domestication of beasts of
burden; and according to the great anthropologist Claude Lévi-Strauss, the
main function of the first ancient writing was "to facilitate the enslavement
of other human beings," not to enable individuals to write poetry.[16]

It is thus of immense importance that slaves, regardless of origin or ethnicity, were seen to carry the marks of childlike and animalistic inferiority later ascribed to such supposedly inferior peoples as Australians and sub-Saharan Africans. That said, we should remember that various forms of proto-racism and even genocidal racism are not necessarily linked with slavery. For example, the Nazis' elaborate program to exterminate all Jews seemed to have nothing to do with slavery, except for the slavelike, dehumanizing treatment given to Jews, whether in factories or death camps.[17] And the fact that Jews were always the archetypal Other living within Christian Europe should remind us that while medieval European elites perceived many slave-like traits in their own serfs and peasants, the distinctions were sharper, as in ancient Greece, when the archetypal slaves were foreigners or "barbarians." Thus long before the eighteenth-century invention of "race" as a way of classifying humankind, a different phenotype or physical appearance made the dehumanization of enslavement much easier. Despite the remarkable genetic uniformity of all human beings (given our common origin and our relatively brief existence on this planet), empathy is more immediate and easily expressed toward family members, clans, tribes, and the people who most closely resemble us—though the biblical Joseph, unfortunately, would not be the last person to be sold to slave traders by his brothers or other family members.

Throughout the ancient Euro-Asian world as well as in the preconquest Western Hemisphere, slaves were commonly marked off by identifying symbols or icons, such as brands, tattoos, collars, hairstyles, or clothing. Clearly such emblems would have been less necessary if all slaves had shared distinctive physical characteristics that quickly differentiated them from all nonslaves. Since so many Jews could not be physically distinguished from non-Jewish Europeans, for example, medieval Christians found it necessary to require all Jews to wear special clothing or a yellow spot on their clothes—largely to prevent intermixture of various kinds.[18] Thus in one sense, people with very dark skin, closely twisted black hair, and broad lips and noses were "made to order" for Mesopotamians and Europeans who struggled for centuries to find markers that would help justify class polarities and also help to identify, at some distance, people who could be classified as "natural slaves."

But this kind of "logic" did not shape the flow of history. As early as the year 869 C.E. there were enough black African slaves to launch a massive revolt in the marshlands of today's southern Iraq, threatening even Baghdad and the Abbasid Empire until 883.[19] It is difficult if not impossible to know whether this war served as a disincentive, at least for Arabs using African slaves in large-scale agriculture. In any event, and partly because of western Europe's long isolation in what used to be called "the Dark Ages," it took six more centuries before the Portuguese and Spaniards began to import a significant number of slaves from sub-Saharan Africa and two more centuries before western Europe began to become dependent on the equation of slavery with black Africans in the settlement of the New World. One should note, however, that from the seventh to the eleventh century, the eastern Europeans in the Byzantine Empire both enslaved many Muslims and were themselves enslaved by Muslims as the rapidly expanding Islamic states transformed the heritage of slavery from the late Roman era.[20]

Little in human history is inevitable, and the European approach to racial slavery was unplanned, haphazard, and long barred by the formidable Islamic control of North Africa, by the vast Sahara desert, and by the availability of diverse populations of white or tan "infidel" slaves (including some Eastern Christians as well as Muslims). Since Europeans in every region were enslaved in Roman and early medieval times (to say nothing of Asia and Africa), and since Barbary corsairs continued to enslave white Europeans and Americans well into the nineteenth century, it seems highly probable that if we could go back far enough in time, we would discover that all of us reading these words are the descendants of both slaves and masters in some part of the world. It was not until the seventeenth century that even New World slavery began to be overwhelmingly associated with people of black African descent—as opposed to Native Americans.

In theory, at least, the Judeo-Christian tradition of a monotheistic God presiding over a relatively homogeneous species, made in His *own* image, presented a certain barrier to the division of society into wholly opposite classes of the enslaved and the free. Despite legends of wild men and animal-headed people, there was a broad Judeo-Christian consensus regarding at the very least a common human origin. Of course, this belief turned out to be scientifically true, in contrast to the popular nineteenth- and early twentieth-century "scientific" claims of polygenesis and racial differences so deep that they approached or crossed the boundary of species. Christians also believed in a common or universal propensity to sin, and many also believed in a compelling need to baptize and "save" as much of humanity as possible.

This genuine compassion, however, when combined with a sharp division between an all-important eternal heaven and a finite sinful world, provided a way to combine postponed love and virtue with pragmatic needs of the present. Thus a succession of popes in the mid-1400s, confronted by the threatening expansion of Islam, saw enslavement as an instrument for Christian conversion and gave religious approval to the Portuguese ventures along the western coast of Africa, including the shipment of African slaves back to Europe.[21] Aside from seeing the enslavement of infidels and pagans as a means of conversion, the recovery of classical texts, especially Aristotle, by Muslims, Jews, and finally Christians provided some writers in the Near East and Europe with a conceptual basis for regarding even baptized slaves as inherently deficient in reason, analysis, and judgment.

For Aristotle, as we have seen, the relationship between master and slave was as natural as the relationship of soul to body, husband to wife, or humans to domesticated animals. "From the hour of their birth," Aristotle proclaimed, "some are marked out for subjection, others for rule." Slavery was truly good for the slave, who lacked the necessary mental capacity to make decisions and exercise forethought for himself. Furthermore, as Plato had earlier maintained, the division between master and slave was part of a vast cosmic scheme in which irrational nature was ordered and controlled by an intelligent and purposeful authority. Some thirteen centuries later the Muslim Aristotelian Avicenna (980–1037) could even assert that "God in his providential wisdom had placed, in regions of great heat or great cold, peoples who were by their very nature slaves, and incapable of higher things—for there must be masters and slaves."[22]

Paradoxically, in the 1200s, at the very time when chattel slavery was disappearing from northwestern Europe, Christian theologians revived and made extensive use of many of Aristotle's propositions. Though banned for a time by the Church, Aristotle shaped Saint Thomas Aquinas's view of the slave as the physical instrument of his owner, who had full claim to everything the slave possessed or produced, including children. Noting that Saint Gregory and others had ruled, like the Justinian Code, that slavery was contrary to nature, Aquinas emphasized that the institution was contrary only to the first intention of nature, but not to the second intention, which was adjusted to man's limited capacities in a sinful world. Aquinas still thought of slavery as occasioned by sin, but he made it seem more natural and tolerable by identifying it with the rational structure of being, which required each individual to accept, along with old age and death, the necessity of subordination to higher authority. While Aquinas avoided Aristotle's views on natural inferiority, some of his followers, such as Ptolemy of Lucca and the famous and prestigious philosopher Egidius Colonna, appeared to accept the Aristotelian belief that some men were slaves by their very nature.[23]

It is significant that Aristotle's theory of slavery formed the framework for the momentous debate in Spain, in 1550–51, between Juan Ginés Sepúlveda and Bartolomé de Las Casas, on whether American Indians had been created to be natural slaves (with Las Casas attacking that conclusion but not Aristotle's basic premises). Fifty-two years earlier, the great Jewish philosopher and statesman Isaac ben Abravanel, having seen many black slaves both in his native Portugal and in Spain, merged Aristotle's theory of natural slaves with the belief that the biblical Noah had cursed and condemned to slavery both his son Ham and his young grandson Canaan. Abravanel concluded that the servitude of animalistic black Africans should be perpetual.[24] And while it would be absurd to blame Aristotle for all the uses to which his writings have been put, he did eventually provide the conceptual basis for much nineteenth-century Southern proslavery ideology and scientific theories of racial inferiority.

It is important to recognize that Aristotle was responding to a Greek opponent, and that even the Aristotelian "natural slave" was not literally seen as an animal but as a subhuman who lacks the higher powers of reason and imaginative judgment to govern and balance such animalistic functions as eating, sleeping, defecating, and, above all, mating—the things we share with animals, often with a touch of embarrassment and with a strong counterdrive to "elevate" and "civilize" our behavior and that of people around us. Hence in the classical Greek tradition, the slavish person would be ideally suited to perform all the menial, unpleasant, and degrading labor that made the civilized state possible, providing "citizens" with the freedom and leisure needed for the so-called good life.

This view of slavery tied in, as I have already suggested, with more general assumptions about the meaning of most human labor, which is described in the Book of Genesis as one of the curses that God inflicted on Adam and Eve and their descendants. The Bible also repeatedly links the lowliest forms of labor with the "curse" of slavery, as when Joshua tells the Gibeonites, "There is a curse upon you for this [occupying the Israelites' land]: for all time you shall provide us with slaves, to chop wood and draw water for the house of my God."[25] While many artisans and professionals long took pride in their work, it was not until writers in the Enlightenment and early nineteenth century began to ennoble free labor, even equating work with the individual's quest for achievement, self-expression, and happiness, that it became possible to launch a popular attack on slavery as a backward and inhuman institution that stigmatized and dishonored the very essence of labor. It was precisely such free labor, as the nineteenth and twentieth centuries progressed, that became the idealized and supposedly voluntary route—as an alternative to aristocratic birth—to both individual success and respected identity.[26]

As WE TURN TO THE MORE SPECIFIC ORIGINS of antiblack racism and its relationship to Africa's long exportation of slaves, there seems to be a consensus among historians concerning the lack of such racism, at least in any clear-cut or widely accepted sense, in Greco-Roman or early Jewish antiquity.[27]

In many ways this is a surprise, since the biblical Hebrews as well as the Greeks and Romans expressed at times considerable hostility and prejudice toward such peoples as the Egyptians, Canaanites, Persians, Phoenicians, Syrians, and even each other. The Greeks and Romans, judging at least by their surviving literature, strongly favored certain facial and bodily features, including lighter skin; they frowned on ethnic sexual intermixture and also believed that the physical features of some peoples signified mental and be-havioral inferiority even if these supposedly hereditary traits could originally be ascribed to different climates and geography. In short, as the ancient his-torian Benjamin Isaac has recently demonstrated, forms of proto-racism flour-ished in the ancient Greco-Roman world.[28]

Moreover, with respect to likely preconditions for antiblack racism, nu-merous scholars have shown that the color black (really an absence of color) has evoked highly negative symbolism not only in antiquity and in Western culture in general but also among various Asian, Native American, and even sub-Saharan African peoples. We have already taken note of the widespread mention of black or dark skin as a stigmatizing trait that distinguished slaves, serfs, and peasants even when they were born with light skin. Given humanity's universal need for sunlight, and fear or mistrust of darkness, the moral and aesthetic "power of blackness" seems first to emerge in the Bible when God brings light into the dark void and divides day from night, and then contin-ues as the Children of Light struggle with the Children of Darkness and as the ancient Persian Zoroastrian forces of Ormazd (or Ahura Mazda), that is, light, confront the forces of Ahriman, darkness and evil.

In 1837 the French painter and theorist Jacques-Nicolas Paillot de Monta-bert reminded other artists that while white "is the symbol of Divinity or God," black "is the symbol of darkness and darkness expresses all evils," add-ing that black signifies chaos, ugliness, vice, guilt, sin, and misfortune. Simi-lar themes pervade the Bible, especially the New Testament's revelation that Jesus is "the light of the world" and that "God is light and in him there is no darkness at all." If black became the color of death, hunger, melan-cholic bodily fluids, and the River Styx, the Qur'ān affirms that hellfire black-ens the skin.[29]

Yet given the complexities of the human mind, it would be simplistic to assume that the negative associations evoked by the abstract absence of color were automatically applied to specific people who happened to have black or near black skin. Even with respect to abstract color, Herman Melville was hardly alone when he observed that while white, the color of purity and ho-liness, gave the Europeans "ideal mastership over every dusky tribe," there "lurks an elusive something in the innermost idea of this hue [white], which strikes more panic to the soul than that redness which affrights in blood." A black Moby-Dick or a white Othello would lose all meaning.

According to Edmund Burke, blackness was a prime source of the sub-lime, as custom teaches us "to transmute our fear of dark things into feelings of awe, melancholy, and fascination." If Paillot de Montabert had lived forty more years, he could have learned far more exciting, imaginative, and subtle meanings of the color black from the great French master Edouard Manet, whose paintings use black in ways that thrill and dazzle the viewer. Over two centuries earlier, Velázquez had portrayed the warm flesh tones of a black woman servant (or slave), whose resigned expression only heightened her great beauty and dignity—the kind of dignity and individuality that were also captured in the portraits of blacks painted by such great artists as Memling, Rubens, Bosch, and Rembrandt. Even some European slave-ship captains commented with wonder on the agility, the gracefulness, and the physical beauty of enslaved Africans! In short, despite the extremely negative symbolism of the color black, despite beliefs in the Greco-Roman era in the congenital inferiority of some nonblack ethnic groups, and despite the point I have made that African blacks, because of their distinctive physiognomy and high "visibility," seemed "made to order" for the classification of natural slaves, there is no evidence in antiquity or even in medieval and Renaissance Europe of the kind of fully developed racist society that the Reverend Theodore Wright confronted in the American North in 1836.[30]

It is true that ancient Egyptian and Greco-Roman art presents many caricatures of thick-lipped, black-faced Africans, most of them presumably slaves—images that seem hardly distinguishable from the racist caricatures of nineteenth-century America. But there are also ancient caricatures of the more frequently enslaved Greeks and Thracians, and there is always a danger of projecting modern meanings and assumptions into the more distant past. Ancient Western art also displays more realistic portraits of blacks as dancers, musicians, actors, acrobats, jugglers, charioteers, and soldiers. This tradition extended onward, for example, to the German painter and sculptor Erasmus Grasser's attractive *Moorish Dancer* of the late 1400s. In view of later antiblack stereotypes, it is striking that ancient Roman writing often mocked and sneered at the physical appearance of black African slaves, who were sometimes seen as physically repulsive, cowardly, and sexually dangerous (from the viewpoint of white husbands), but who were said to be endowed with sharp intelligence—a judgment apparently not noticed centuries later by that lover of classical literature, Thomas Jefferson.[31]

Though one can always find examples of xenophobic prejudice, the crucial points concern the relative scarcity of black Africans in the ancient Greco-Roman world; the vulnerability of all peoples, including learned Greek scholars, to the bad luck of becoming enslaved; and the isolation of sub-Saharan Africa until the rapid expansion of Islam, beginning in the seventh and eighth centuries. It was this latter momentous event that led to the first massive export of black African slaves, a disastrous loss that extended well into the twentieth century.

Before examining the effects of large-scale black enslavement on Arab and Persian views of black Africans, we should look briefly at the ambivalent or even contradictory images of blacks in medieval Europe, where the presence of sub-Saharan Africans must have been exceedingly rare.

On the positive side, European artists in the late Middle Ages tended to picture Egyptians as at least dark or black-skinned and to include recognizable Africans in scenes from the Old Testament. There was also the favorable portrayal of the wealthy black king of Mali, based on thirteenth-century accounts of Mansā Mūsā's pilgrimage to Mecca, laden with much gold and accompanied by black slaves. The Catalan Atlas noted that Mansā Mūsā was "the richest and noblest king in all the land." In addition to gold, which was long one of Africa's major attractions for European travelers and traders, the sub-Saharan regions were famous for legendary amounts of salt and copper. With respect to religion, news filtered northward of Ethiopian Christians, and by the early fifteenth century European artists had gradually accepted the idea of a black African magus, or wise man, in scenes of the Nativity.[32]

Even earlier, we encounter the curious popularity of an armored black knight with distinctive and realistic African features—the heroic leader Saint Maurice. While the legendary Saint Maurice was supposedly from Thebes, by the mid-thirteenth century he had become a black man in armor, a black African leader of the Teutonic Knights! The remarkable sculptures and paintings of Saint Maurice that appear in churches and cathedrals in Germany and Switzerland represented one of the supposed Christian leaders of the Holy Roman Empire's crusade against the pagan Slavs to the east. The black Saint Maurice was rivaled only by depictions of the black Queen of Sheba—and the black Virgin Mary.[33]

There was, however, another representation of black Africans constantly on view for even the illiterate masses of Christian Europe. From the twelfth to the mid-fourteenth century, the iconography of western European churches became stocked with the images of unmistakable black Africans as torturers, tempters, and executioners, often in scenes of the Passion of Christ. It thus seems probable that most Europeans received their first subliminal impressions of so-called Negroes in a local church or cathedral—the image of black death squads serving the devil, or of the devil himself portrayed as an animalistic black man (usually without any African features).

In mid-sixteenth-century Spain one could find another far more ambiguous example, whose symbolism forecast in no doubt unconscious ways the settlement of the Americas. I refer to a painting of the "Miracle of the Black Leg," in Valladolid, in which two white saints replace the gangrenous leg of a white man with the amputated limb of a dying black man, whose face is contorted with pain. Today, at least, the message seems to be "An African's sacrifice is a European saved," a message that conveys much of the meaning of New World slavery.[34]

WHILE A FEW SUB-SAHARAN BLACK SLAVES mixed with other slaves in the ancient world, the Arabs and their Muslim converts were the first people to make use of literally millions of blacks from sub-Saharan Africa and to begin associating black Africans with the lowliest forms of bondage. This is not to say that Arabs ever limited bondage to people of sub-Saharan ancestry or practiced the kind of systematic racial oppression that later appeared in white South Africa and most of the New World. Indeed, as we have already seen, the initial expansion of Islam led to the enslavement of many Byzantine Christians (and to the Christian enslavement of Muslims) and later to a regular flow of Caucasian slaves to Egypt and the Mideast. Christian Europeans long associated "Africa" with their Muslim enemies, with Barbary corsairs capturing their ships and conducting naval or military raids on their own coasts, and with the threat of their own enslavement.

Yet with respect to African slaves, we have mentioned the massive slave revolt that began in 869 C.E. in the marshlands of the Tigris-Euphrates delta, in modern Iraq. Those thousands of slaves were blacks, called *Zanj* by the Arabs, and most had originally been transported by sea from East Africa. Worked in regimented gangs, they had been draining and reclaiming wasteland for cultivation—probably of sugarcane and cotton. Though the *Zanj* revolt must be understood within an Islamic social and political context (it was led by Ali ibn Muhammad), the Arabs, the Berbers, and their Muslim allies were the first people to develop a specialized, long-distance slave trade, by ships and desert caravans, from sub-Saharan Africa.[35]

In the early Middle Ages, as Christians began their slow reconquest of Spain and Portugal from the Muslims, light-skinned Arabs and Berbers began exploring and mapping sub-Saharan Africa. Drawing on the Greeks and Romans, the Arabs really "invented" Africa as a continent, along with a black-skinned "African people," at a time when Europeans themselves were still being classified by Arabs as barbarians. For centuries to come, the highly diverse African ethnic groups would have no sense of sharing a common or "continental identity."[36]

Like Judaism and Christianity, Islam emerged at a time when chattel slavery was as universally accepted as human warfare. All three religions sought to regulate and ameliorate slavery. The Hebrew Bible, in Deuteronomy, even demands giving shelter to and not returning escaped slaves belonging to foreign masters. The prophet Jeremiah condemned ancient Israelites who had reenslaved fellow Jewish slaves after first freeing them. Yet in Leviticus, as we have seen in Chapter Two, God tells Moses that since the Hebrews should not sell their own brethren or rule over them "with rigor," they should buy their slaves "of the nations that are round about you."[37] Islam, which emerged in the 620s and 630s, long after Christianity and Judaism, was most explicit in its conviction that freedom, not hereditary slavery, is the natural and presumed status of mankind. On the other hand, Islamic law, while prohibiting the forcible enslavement of fellow Muslims, gave religious sanction to the enslavement of infidels and to holding even Islamic converts as inheritable slaves, a perpetual status unless a master chose to manumit a particular person. These rules provided a special incentive to obtain slaves from the regions north and west of Turkey and from infidels in sub-Saharan Africa. Yet the records also show that even after their conversion to Islam, large numbers of black Africans, in both the east and west, continued to be enslaved and transported to the Mediterranean lands and the Middle East.[38]

By 740 C.E. the spectacular Muslim conquests had created a vast intercontinental world extending from modern Pakistan westward across the Mideast and northern Africa to Spain and southern France. These revolutionized geographic boundaries produced an immense flow of slaves for employment as servants, soldiers, members of harems, eunuch chaperons, and bureaucrats. Thanks to such earlier innovations as the North Arabian saddle and camel caravans, Arabs, Berbers, and their converts made deep inroads into sub-Saharan Africa, thus tapping, through purchase or capture, an unprecedented pool of slave labor. According to some scholarship, this importation of black slaves into Islamic lands from Spain to India constituted a continuous, large-scale migration—by caravan and sea over a period of more than twelve centuries, beginning in the 600s—that may have equaled in total number all the African slaves transported to the New World. The absence of large populations descended from these millions of African slaves—and there are small communities of blacks in India and the Mideast—can be explained by the assimilation of blacks over the lapse of many centuries and by the fact that few slave societies have ever been capable of natural growth, especially when there has been a large sexual imbalance. Many of the males transported to Muslim lands had been castrated (legally only by non-Muslims), and there was a much larger demand for females.[39]

We should also note that little trace remains today of the large African slave populations in sixteenth- and early seventeenth-century Mexico and Peru. Black slaves once constituted over half the population of both Mexico City and Lima. Yet the region that became the United States, which received less than 4 percent of the slaves shipped to the New World, was highly unusual in having a slave population that increased rapidly by natural means, and thus contained by 1850 over 30 percent of the African New World diaspora.[40]

Because the Arab literary sources focus on life in the towns and administrative centers, we know very little about the nature of mining and agriculture in the Islamic world, though we do have descriptions of black slaves working in underground copper mines in Islamic North Africa. It is clear that the explosive expansion of Islam did not lead to capitalist markets and

investment, to dramatic economic growth, or to a widespread system of plantation production as in the New World. Moreover, the Qur'ān and Islamic
law, like the earlier Hebrew and Christian Bibles, show no trace or even
awareness of what we would term racism. And from the early 1500s to the
early 1800s, when Moorish corsairs captured European and American ships
and raided coastal regions to capture Christians from Italy to Iceland, they
showed no compunction about enslaving over a million people we would
regard as "white."[41]

Yet it is also clear that regardless of their continuing enslavement and
purchase of white Christian infidels, medieval Arabs and Persians came to
associate the most degrading forms of labor with black slaves—especially with
the so-called *Zanj*, who, according to Jahiz of Basra, "are the least intelligent
and the least discerning of mankind, and the least capable of understanding
the consequences of their actions." Most Muslim writers ranked Nubians
and especially Ethiopians a bit higher than the despised *Zanj*, a vague term
applied to Bantu-speaking laborers from East Africa and, as we have seen, to
the slave rebels in what is now Iraq.[42]

This connection between dehumanizing labor and people with a highly
distinctive physical appearance led Muslim writers in increasing numbers to
describe blacks in terms that fit Aristotle's image of natural slaves (whether
they had heard of Aristotle or not). In fact, the Arabic word for slave, *'abd*,
came in time to mean only a *black* slave and in some regions referred to any
black whether slave or free—surely not a sign that black slaves were considered capable of genuine freedom. Many Arab writers echoed the racial contempt typified by the famous fourteenth-century Tunisian historian Ibn
Khaldūn when he wrote that black people were "characterized by levity, ex-
citability, and great emotionalism" and were "as a whole submissive to slavery, because Negroes have little that is essentially human and have attributes
that are quite similar to those of dumb animals."[43] The historian Gernot
Rotter shows that Arab and Persian writers frequently associated blacks with
apes; a thirteenth-century Persian concluded that the *Zanj* differed from animals only because "their two hands are lifted above the ground" and reported
that "many have observed that the ape is more teachable and more intelligent than the *Zanji*."[44]

There can be no doubt that the increasing purchase or capture of sub-
Saharan African slaves, usually for the most degrading kinds of labor, generated an early form of racism as well as an Islamic literature *defending* the
humanity and equality of blacks by explaining the supposed environmental
origins of their physical difference.

The prevalence of antiblack prejudice is revealed by the outcries from
poets and other writers of African or mixed African and Arabic parentage
(called "the ravens of the Arabs"): "Though my hair is woolly and my skin

coal-black,/ My hand is open and my honor bright." "My color is pitch-black, my hair is woolly, my appearance repulsive." "I am a black man," a famous singer and musician wrote in Damascus: "Some of you may find me offensive. I shall therefore sit and eat apart." Many African Americans of the nineteenth century, such as the now famous escaped slave Harriet Jacobs, would have understood the pain and dilemma these captive Africans faced eight or more centuries earlier, as well as the need to devise methods of negotiation and ways to preserve self-esteem.[45]

For many medieval Arabs, as for later Europeans, the blackness of Africans suggested sin, damnation, and the devil. Despite the protests of free black writers themselves, some medieval Muslims continued to describe the *Zanj* as being ugly, stupid, dishonest, frivolous, lighthearted, and foul-smelling but gifted with a sense of musical rhythm and dominated by unbridled sexual lust (symbolized by the males' supposedly large penis).[46] Point by point, these stereotypes of medieval Muslim writers resemble those of the later Spaniards, Portuguese, English, and Americans. I should stress that Muslim jurists and theologians continued to reject the popular idea that black Africans were designed by nature to be slaves and insisted that human beings were divided only by faith: All infidels or pagans, regardless of skin color or ethnic origin, could lawfully be enslaved in a jihad.[47]

On the other hand, Arab antiblack racism has been flagrantly revealed in recent years in the persecution and enslavement of black Africans in southern Sudan, along with their genocide in Darfur, which was long a major export center of the Arab trans-Saharan slave trade as well as a site for farms that bred black slaves for sale like cattle or sheep. As late as 1960, Lord Shackleton reported to the House of Lords that African Muslims on pilgrimages to Mecca still sold slaves upon arrival, "using them as living traveller's cheques."[48] Since we will turn in a moment to the biblical "Curse of Ham," it should also be noted that while medieval and early modern Arab and Persian writers usually attributed the blacks' physical traits to climatic and environmental forces, they increasingly invoked the biblical curse to explain why the "sons of Ham" had been blackened and degraded to the status of natural slaves as punishment for their ancestor's sin. Still, there were voices like the Muslim jurist Ahmad Baba of Timbuktu, who exclaimed that "even assuming that Ham was the ancestor of the blacks, God is too merciful to punish millions of people for the sin of a single individual."[49]

Though much further research is needed, it seems highly probable that racial stereotypes were transmitted, along with black slavery itself—to say nothing of algebra and a knowledge of the ancient Greek classics—as Christians traded and fought with Muslims from the first Islamic challenges to the Byzantine Empire, in the seventh and eighth centuries, through the era of the crusades. This interchange became especially important, with respect to

African slaves, as Christian Europeans slowly pushed the Moors out of that melting pot of religions and cultures, the Iberian Peninsula. As Professor James H. Sweet has emphasized, "by the fifteenth century, many Iberian Christians had internalized the racist attitudes of the Muslims and were applying them to the increasing flow of African slaves to their part of the world." Sweet then adds the truly crucial point: "Iberian racism was a necessary precondition for the system of human bondage that would develop in the Americas during the sixteenth century and beyond."[50]

THIS EMPHASIS ON THE EXPANSION, conflict, and borrowings of Islam and Christianity brings us to a seeming digression concerning a text we have already mentioned, a text that was familiar as the word of God to medieval Muslims as well as to Christians and Jews. This text would become absolutely central in the history of antiblack racism. No other passage in the Bible has had such a disastrous influence through human history as Genesis 9:18–27. This story of Noah's curse of slavery comes soon after God succeeds in using a catastrophic flood, lasting just over a year, to "blot out from the face of the earth" all land and air life (or "flesh"), except for the animals and eight humans who were allowed to board Noah's ark. The human survivors, whom God orders "to be fruitful and multiply," were Noah, his three sons, and their four wives.[51]

Here is the relevant text:

> The sons of Noah who came out of the ark were Shem, Ham, and Japheth— Ham being the father of Canaan. These three were the sons of Noah, and from these the whole world branched out.
>
> Noah, the tiller of the soil, was the first to plant a vineyard. He drank of the wine and became drunk, and he uncovered himself within his tent. Ham, the father of Canaan, saw his father's nakedness and told his two brothers outside. But Shem and Japheth took a cloth, placed it against both their backs and, walking backwards, they covered their father's nakedness. When Noah woke up from his wine and learned what his youngest son had done to him, he said, "Cursed be Canaan;/ The lowest of slaves/ [literally "the slave of slaves"] Shall he be to his brothers." And he said, "Blessed be the Lord/ the God of Shem;/ Let Canaan be a slave to them./ May God enlarge Japheth,/ And let him dwell in the tents of Shem;/ and let Canaan be a slave to them.[52]

These biblical words immediately raise two major problems that were bound to intrigue and concern generations of Jewish, Christian, and Muslim interpreters of the text. First, the punishment of eternal slavery seems very excessive for Ham's vaguely described crime. And it is noteworthy that at this near beginning of human history, according to the Bible, hereditary slavery is seen as a severe *penalty* inflicted by a curse. Saint Augustine stressed that the word for "slave" does not appear in the Bible until Noah branded the sin of his son with this name and condition—proving that slavery is the result of human sin, including, for Augustine, the "just wars" that produce legitimate slaves.[53]

As for the sin committed, according to two traditions, found in the Jewish midrashic literature, Ham had either castrated his naked father, to humiliate him and prevent the future conception of any further siblings, or, as another third-century Talmudic debater speculated, Ham had sodomized his unconscious father. (In the laws of Leviticus 18, which also prohibit male homosexuality, "uncovering nakedness" is a euphemism for sexual intercourse.) Yet on a far less extreme level, the scrupulous care shown by Shem and Japheth to cover Noah without glimpsing his naked body suggests that simply staring at him would have then been regarded as an egregious offense. It has been argued that in ancient Mesopotamia, "looking at another's genitals" was seen as a way of obtaining illegitimate "mastery and control," for which slavery, or "losing all mastery and control," would be an appropriate punishment. Ham supposedly worsened this sin by laughing contemptuously, in front of his brothers, after he had viewed his father's body.[54]

The obvious second problem arises from the fact that Noah does not curse Ham, the offender, but rather Ham's son and Noah's grandson, Canaan. For well over two thousand years Jews and then Christians and Muslims wrestled with this anomaly, sometimes arguing that Ham could not be directly cursed since he had been blessed by God, or that Ham and the youthful Canaan (whose birth and age are not mentioned) had both gazed on Noah. The immensely influential Jewish philosopher Philo of Alexandria (born c. 25 B.C.E.) devised an ingenious "allegorical" explanation in which Ham symbolizes mind or thought, Canaan represents action, and Noah's curse of Canaan "virtually" curses Ham.

The often ignored biblical "Table of Nations," which immediately follows the story of "the Curse" and provides genealogical lists of Noah's descendants, makes no reference to race, skin color, or even Israel and seems arbitrary enough to allow many diverse interpretations. The descendants of Japheth include the peoples to the north and west of the ancient Near East, such as the Scythians, "the maritime nations," and the ancestors of the Greeks and other eastern Europeans. Shem bequeathed not only the Arabs and Assyrians but a line of descent that later leads to the Hebrew Abraham and Sarah and thus to the future "great nation" of Israelites, to whom God promises the land already occupied by the Canaanites, or descendants of Canaan. The latter, like the Egyptians, Philistines, Babylonians, and other future enemies of Israel, were the offspring of Ham, the sinner. But so was Cush (or Kush, to use the Hebrew term), who occupied the African lands south of Egypt including Nubia (or Ethiopia in later Greek), and despite later attempts to extend the curse of slavery to black-skinned Kushites—including the claim that Kush was the son of Canaan instead of Ham—the Bible tells us that "Kush also begot Nimrod," who was the first great king on earth, and "was a mighty hunter by the grace of the Lord" (Genesis 10:8–9). The Bible, then, is by no means clear on how the curse of eternal slavery affected the descendants of Canaan—let alone other offspring of Ham, such as the Kushites of Africa.[55]

Yet the "Curse of Ham" was repeatedly used as the most authoritative justification for "Negro slavery" by nineteenth-century Southern Christians, by many Northern Christians, and even by a few Jews, such as the Stockholm-born Orthodox rabbi Morris Jacob Raphall of New York City, who, as a sign of his prestige, was the first Jew to open a session of the U.S. House of Representatives. Raphall's 1861 sermon and booklet *The Bible View of Slavery* was perhaps the most authoritative religious defense of black slavery ever written.[56] In 1862 Alexander Crummell, a distinguished and well-educated free African American, hardly exaggerated when he declared that "the opinion that the sufferings and the slavery of the Negro race are the consequence of the curse of Noah [is a] general, almost universal, opinion in the Christian world." This opinion, Crummell added,

> is found in books written by learned men; and it is repeated in lectures, speeches, sermons, and common conversation. So strong and tenacious is the hold which it has taken upon the mind of Christendom, that it seems almost impossible to uproot it. Indeed, it is an almost foregone conclusion, that the Negro race is an accursed race, weighed down, even to the present, beneath the burden of an ancestral malediction.[57]

The puzzling story of Noah, Ham, and Canaan provided a way of remaining faithful to the biblical account of a common human origin while also giving divine authority for the enslavement and subordination of African blacks and their descendants. Acceptance of "the Curse," even by many blacks, continued well into the twentieth century and has surely not disappeared among Christian and probably even Jewish and Muslim literalists.[58] Although the racist argument was circular—in David Goldenberg's words, "it must have been black Ham who was cursed with slavery because the Blacks are all enslaved"[59]—this circularity points to an actual causal sequence in the origins of antiblack racism: The very presence of increasing numbers of black African slaves, first in the Islamic world, fused the ancient stereotypes of slaves (regardless of ethnicity), and the negative symbolism of "blackness," with the physical features of sub-Saharan Africans. Given this emerging precondition, ingenious reinterpretations of "the Curse" provided divine sanction and justification to an emerging or existing social order for well over a thousand years. Thus as we shall find, it was not an originally racist biblical script that led to the enslavement of "Ham's black descendants," but rather the increasing enslavement of blacks that transformed biblical interpretation.[60]

As we have seen, the actual biblical account of "the Curse" includes no hint or implication regarding race or color, but Noah (allegedly with God's approval) clearly intended to punish some of his descendants with the lowliest form of eternal slavery and to reward other descendants with this cheap, humiliating, and involuntary labor. As David Goldenberg insightfully demonstrates, countless biblical commentators throughout the ages simply and conveniently forgot the actual wording of the story and passed on a revised text or declaration in which Canaan virtually disappears and Noah curses Ham, the obvious offender, and his descendants. Even Saint Augustine overlooked the distinction between Ham and Canaan. In countless Jewish, Christian, and especially Muslim sources, from the eighth and ninth centuries to the present, including even some writings of nineteenth-century American abolitionists, "it was not Canaan whom Noah cursed with slavery, but Ham[,] instead of or in addition to Canaan."[61] This "solution" to the problem became easier when Ham's claimed descendants no longer included medieval European serfs or Asian Mongolian invaders but were wholly identified with sub-Saharan Africans. As the historian Benjamin Braude has shown, medieval and Renaissance writers often identified Ham with Asia; his "Curse" was also used to justify European serfdom and the medieval enslavement of Slavs, Turks, and other peoples.[62]

It is most unfortunate that blame for a racist "Curse"—that is, for singling out blacks as the only people the Bible condemns with slavery—has been linked in modern times with a series of anti-Semitic mythologies that have also wrongly pictured Jews as the main traders in slaves across medieval Europe and then as the dominant force behind the transatlantic African slave trade to the New World.[63] David Goldenberg and other scholars have now made it clear that interpretations of the curse of slavery and the supposed curse of blackness had separate origins and long had separate histories. Contrary to the claims of a number of earlier reputable historians, who unintentionally fed the needs of an anti-Semitic tradition, there is nothing in the Talmud or other early post-biblical Jewish writing that relates blackness of skin to the curse of perpetual slavery. This distortion of evidence has been made easier by a long series of scribal errors, mistranslations, misinterpretations, and confusion over such Jewish sources as the Babylonian Talmud, the Palestinian Talmud, and the midrashic Tanhuma. To give one small linguistic example, Goldenberg's exhaustive etymological research now shows that, contrary to long-standing belief, the original Hebrew name "Ham" did not derive from a root meaning "dark," "black," or "hot."[64] While this misinterpretation of the meaning of "Ham" helped later Christian, Muslim, and

Jewish writers to link Noah's son with sub-Saharan Africans and eventually contributed to justifications for racial slavery, the early rabbinic explanations for Ham's allegedly dark skin were not connected to the curse of slavery, which Jewish writers still associated with their light-skinned Canaanite foes.

Moreover, in biblical and early antiquity, when human bondage carried no racial implications, Hebrews and other peoples often took a somewhat positive view of black Africans, despite the negative symbolism of abstract "blackness." Hebrew literature described black Africans as being tall, smooth of skin, extremely formidable in their use of long bows and arrows, and by far the fastest runners in the world. Though most of the ancient Egyptians had quite different facial features from sub-Saharan Africans, the black Kushites,[65] from the regions south of Aswan, invaded and conquered Egypt, taking command of the nation in the Twenty-fifth Dynasty (often called "the Ethiopian Dynasty") from approximately 760 to 660 B.C.E.[66] The Hebrew Bible repeatedly shows respect for the military strength of these Kushites (called Nubians or Ethiopians by others) and, like the great Greek historian Herodotus, reports that Egypt imported an immense flow of gold from the peoples to the south.[67] As Goldenberg makes clear, skin color was simply not an issue in the Bible or early rabbinic midrash, even after the name "Ham" was incorrectly understood to mean "black" or "dark." Jews accepted Kushi, who was almost certainly black, as being the father of the prophet Zephaniah, and those who thought that Moses' wife had been a black African raised no objections to miscegenation (even if some complained that he had married a non-Israelite).

Nevertheless, by the third century c.e., Rabbi Hiyya, writing in Israel, interpreted black skin as a punishment and passed on a tradition that ultimately became a standard Jewish explanation of the origin of black or dark skin, an account that appeared even in some later Islamic texts. As Goldenberg concludes after carefully analyzing an early medieval Jewish version of Ham's punishment for staring at his naked father, which actually avoids mention of skin color, "given the fact that the physical features detailed by Tanhuma—red eyes, thick lips, tightly curled hair, nakedness, and a large phallus—are commonly given by pagan, Christian, and Muslim writers over many centuries to describe the black African, we may conclude that the Tanhuma text is similarly meant to depict the black African."[68]

According to a different Jewish legend, God had pragmatically prohibited Noah and all the humans and animals on the ark from having sex during the great flood. After all, they lived in very limited space and had no room for progeny. Nevertheless, three creatures supposedly broke this law. The punishments that God inflicted on the dog and the raven are not relevant to this discussion. For his part, Ham, who had had intercourse on the ark with his wife, found that his skin had been "blackened." In a still different version of this "penalty," Ham himself was not transformed but his wife gave birth to a black child, Kush, the ancestor of all black Africans (in other traditions, Ham's wife gave birth on the ark to Canaan, or to a fourth son called Yonton or Yoniton).[69] The main point, however, is that this interest in the origins of all dark-skinned peoples was not yet explicitly tied with slavery.

Having clarified early Jewish views on black Africans and slavery, it is crucially important not to project blame to Islamic writers, who from the seventh century onward did establish strong precedents for linking blackness with slavery, often reinforced by references to Noah having simultaneously cursed his son Ham with both slavery and black skin.[70] If Jews or Christians had been in the Arabs' place, actively enslaving, purchasing, and transporting sub-Saharan Africans, they would surely have generated their own justifying ideology. In fact, as early as the twelfth century, Ibn Ezra, a Jewish writer within the Islamic world, noted that "some say that the Blacks are slaves because of Noah's curse on Ham," and in the fourteenth and fifteenth centuries Jewish authors were directly "incorporating the Curse of Ham into their writings."[71] In later periods, extending on into the nineteenth century, many Jews and Christians seem to have had few qualms about adopting or constructing such ideologies—and a few Jews were involved in the Atlantic slave trade and in owning and selling black slaves from Dutch Brazil and the Caribbean to North America. Indeed, some proto-racist themes began to appear in Jewish and Christian writings after the seventh- and eighth-century Islamic conquests in Africa, which, as we have seen, greatly increased the number of black slaves in Islamic lands from Iraq and Arabia to Spain. Christian use of the biblical curse became more important as a defense of the sixteenth-, seventeenth-, and eighteenth-century African slave trade, though for many Europeans it was sufficient to argue that the black Africans were infidels, pagans, or savages who would actually be "civilized" by enslavement in Iberia or the New World.

Some European writers, especially beginning in the seventeenth century, even devised an alternative biblical defense of racial slavery, going back further than Noah's flood. They argued that the mysterious biblical "mark" that God had imprinted on Adam and Eve's son Cain, whose murder of his brother Abel was clearly far worse a crime than gazing at a naked father, was in fact a blackened skin. Hence in antebellum America the Mormon Church ruled that "the seed of Cain were black and had not place among [the seed of Adam]," and Brigham Young taught his fellow Mormons that blacks would "continue to be the servant of servants until the curse is removed." Much earlier, the African American poet Phillis Wheatley assumed that Cain was a Negro.[72]

Turning back now to transitions and influences in Iberia, some five hundred years before Brigham Young, the most famous example of the transmission of "the Curse" from Islamic to Christian Europe came when Portugal's official royal chronicler, Gomes Eannes de Zurara, who stressed that black Africans "lived like beasts,"[73] included a reference to Ham (spelled Cham or Cam) in his 1453 account of the earlier Portuguese "discovery" and conquest of Guinea (following the expulsion of the Moors from Portugal and the Portuguese capture in 1415 Ceuta, on the northwest African mainland). In describing the arrival and sale in Portugal of the first group of captured African slaves, Zurara drew a distinction between the light-skinned Moors and the blacks who had been enslaved by the Moors and then used as a ransom, in Jonathan Schorsch's words, "for a Muslim nobleman whom the Portuguese had earlier captured." Drawing on some alleged Jewish sources as well as a Catholic archbishop, and anticipating a long Christian tradition to come, Zurara wrote:

> And here you must note that these blacks, though they were Moors [Muslims] like the others, were nonetheless slaves [servos] of these by ancient custom, which I believe to be by the curse which after the flood Noé threw on his son Cam, by which he cursed him, that the descendants should be subject to all the other peoples of the world, from whom [Cam] these [Blacks] descend.[74]

In one of history's bitter ironies, it was the Spanish and Portuguese treatment of Jews, whose Torah had now been misinterpreted to fuse slavery with "Negritude," that provided the final seedbed for Christian Negrophobic racism, including the desire to make use of black labor while protecting the "purity" of white blood. I refer particularly to the Jews and their descendants who had converted to Christianity. In other words, there is much evidence that the Christians' growing fears and anxiety over the mass conversion and intermixture of Jews in late medieval Spain gave rise to a more general concern over "purity of blood"—*limpieza de sangre* in Spanish—and thus to an early conception of biological race.[75]

For centuries, Portugal and especially Spain, which became fully "liberated" from Moorish "occupation" only in 1492, were multicultural centers as well as battlegrounds for large numbers of Muslims, Christians, and Jews. The Spanish transition from tolerance to persecution was a complex one: Christians and Jews enjoyed surprising autonomy under Muslim rule. Even under Christian rule, Spanish kings relied on Jewish financiers, doctors, and advisers. Sometimes Jews served as godfathers and godmothers at baptismal rites of Christian friends, and Christians similarly attended the circumcision ceremonies of Jewish friends. Some Christians went to hear the sermons of noted rabbis, Jews listened to the sermons of eloquent priests, and according to Léon Poliakov, before the fourteenth century the conversion of a Jew was a rather "exceptional event."[76]

But long before Portugal began in the 1440s to import significant numbers of sub-Saharan black slaves, who were later sold in Spain as well as Portugal, Christians launched a great crusade to convert and assimilate Jews. After extremely bloody anti-Semitic riots in 1391, many thousands of Jews either were forced to convert or felt a need to do so for self-preservation or self-interest. This seeming Christian triumph in solving "the Jewish problem"— and it has been estimated that by 1492 at least one-half of Spain's Jews had become *Conversos*—began to be seen by some Spaniards, and eventually by the Inquisition, as an exacerbation of the problem. As Yosef Hayim Yerushalmi puts it: "A critical juncture had been reached. The traditional distrust of the Jew as outsider now gave way to an even more alarming fear of the Converso as insider." One anti-Semitic text even alleged that the chief rabbi of Constantinople had urged Spanish Jews to convert in order to destroy Christianity from within. [77]

The growing presence of large communities of *Conversos*—that is, Jewish converts and any Christians with Jewish ancestry, now often referred to as *Marranos*, or "swine"—raised concerns about the "essential *immutability*" of Jewishness, epitomized by Jewish "blood," and thus the false motives that had led to conversion. According to the Inquisition and earlier champions of *limpieza de sangre*, many of these "New Christians" continued to practice Judaism in secret. Hence issues of religious and ethnic identity could easily lead to an artificial construction of something like the more modern concept of race.[78]

The fifteenth century, the century that brought the European "discovery" of a real Africa and then of a New World, and thus revolutionary new understandings of the earth and its peoples, was also a time of much religious excitement and uncertainty. As many Jews awaited the Coming of the Messiah and as Christians looked to the Second Coming of Jesus, a surprising number of Spanish Jews and *Conversos* moved upward in the professions, especially medicine, but also within the Church itself. It has even been claimed that Fray Tomás de Torquemada, the founder of the unified Spanish Inquisition, Queen Isabella's Catholic confessor, and the most powerful persecutor of the Jews, did everything possible to hide the fact that his grandmother was a *Converso*. The historian Henry Kamen makes the crucial point that precisely because *Conversos* were so successful and so many members of the nobility and aristocracy acquired some Jewish ancestry, the *limpieza* movement appealed to demagogues of lowly backgrounds, who celebrated their own purity of blood while revealing the contamination of the elite. This issue of social class helped to check and qualify efforts to enact and enforce *limpieza* laws, and by the end of the sixteenth century "there was widespread unease about *limpieza* in the upper levels of society."[79]

Still, along with growing public suspicion, fear, and jealousy of professed Christians with Jewish ancestry, the Inquisition led a notorious campaign, much like a witch-hunt, to spy on, torture, and burn at the stake thousands of *Conversos*, ferreting out evidence, for example, that seemingly Christian families had prohibited the use of lights on Saturday, the Jewish Sabbath, or had circumcised male children. Some *Conversos*, it was charged, had entered the priesthood for the sole purpose of listening to the confessions of genuine Christians in order to gain knowledge of their "secret sins." This fear of religious heresy and of Jews "polluting and staining the pure blood" of Castilians became translated by the later 1400s into racial terms—with near paranoid depictions of Christians who, tainted by Jewish blood and ancestry, engaged in subtle deals and machinations to gain control of both church and state. Much is yet to be learned about the ways in which Christian anti-Semitism developed into a racist ideology which long led to laws excluding *Conversos* from certain privileges and professions, as well as to the expulsion of Jews from Spain in 1492 (and from Portugal in 1497, unless they immediately converted to Christianity).[80]

The relevance of such actions to the growing antiblack racism, especially in Spain, can be seen in the following text of 1604 by Fray Prudencio de Sandoval, the biographer of Spain's Holy Roman Emperor, Charles V:

> Who can deny that in the descendants of Jews there persists and endures the evil inclination of their ancient ingratitude and lack of understanding, just as in the Negroes [there persists] the inseparability of their blackness. For if the latter should unite themselves a thousand times with white women, the children are born with the dark color of the father. Similarly, it is not enough for the Jew to be three parts aristocrat of Old Christian, for one family line [that is, one Jewish ancestor] alone defiles and corrupts him.[81]

It seems highly probable that as the Spaniards and Portuguese became familiar with Muslim writings concerning black slaves, they began to transfer to the newly imported blacks the kind of racial concerns originally ignited by the Jews who had converted and then intermixed with Christians. The Sandoval quotation employs as a metaphor the exaggerated surprise and alarm that nonblacks have expressed for millennia over the effects of the dominant genes governing such black physical traits as hair and skin color—effects that would long be used in the Western world to oppose racial intermixture.[82] As for the actual treatment of blacks, in 1515 King Manuel I made note of the growing number of dead Africans lying in the streets of Lisbon, some of them eaten by dogs and many eventually "thrown in the dung heap."[83]

By 1516 and 1518, when Bartolomé de Las Casas called for the massive importation of African slaves into the New World, to spare the Indians from the kind of annihilation he was already viewing, antiblack racist stereotypes had already become embedded in Iberian societies, where large numbers of African slaves had already been transported, usually to engage in the lowliest and least desirable kinds of work. In Chapter Five we will examine some of the reasons that enslaved Indians were replaced by Africans in regions like Brazil. Here it is sufficient to note that while it was not until the late 1700s that white North Americans totally repudiated Indian slavery and limited chattel servitude to people of African descent, a papal bull of 1537 declared that "Indians are by no means to be deprived of their liberty, nor should they be any way enslaved; should the contrary happen, it should be null and void." In 1542 Spain did outlaw the enslavement of Native Americans, though the practice long continued in the Spanish New World.[84]

Historians have explained this moral exemption from slavery by pointing to such factors as the Indians' supposed "innocence," to their appalling rates of mortality, to their ineptitude as agricultural laborers, and to their possible status as "the Lost Tribes of Israel" (hence their foreshadowing the millennium). Surely, though, the contrast between red and black also owes something to Noah's "Curse," coupled with the long-term stereotypes of black slaves we have been discussing.

Whatever borrowings occurred between cultures, it is clear that by the time the Spanish and Portuguese began to conquer and settle the New World, chattel slavery had taken on deep racial connotations. And the dishonor, contempt, and dehumanization always associated with human bondage were now being transferred to the scores of African ethnic groups that Arabs and Europeans had begun to perceive as a single race.

THE HISTORIAN James H. Sweet has convincingly argued that "though the pseudoscientific classification of persons based on race in the eighteenth and nineteenth centuries gave greater legitimacy to racism, this new science merely reinforced old ideological notions." Imanuel Geiss presents a similar argument.[85] While I do not wish to minimize the importance of pseudoscientific racism, especially for the post-emancipation, "Social Darwinist" period and the twentieth century, I have chosen to focus on the less well known "old ideological notions" and will conclude by devoting only a few pages to some examples of a perverted and highly damaging form of science.

Winthrop D. Jordan, in his classic study of early British and American racism, *White Over Black*, makes the important point that the English discovery of the chimpanzee (then called "orang-outang") coincided in time with northern Europe's involvement with the African slave trade and first significant encounter with sub-Saharan West Africans, some of whom came from roughly the same region as the chimpanzees.[86] At a time when many educated people were moving away from (or had never been exposed to) biblical literalism, there was widespread astonishment that animals like chimpanzees could be so intelligent and communicative. Consequently, beginning in the late 1600s, there was much pre-Darwinian speculation on the relationship between Africans and apes (this was anticipated, as we have seen, in some medieval Islamic literature).

As matters developed, there were many precedents, in the century before he wrote, for Thomas Jefferson's notorious lines, in his *Notes on the State of Virginia*, about blacks themselves preferring whites, "as uniformly as is the preference of the Oranootan [*sic*] for the black woman over those of his own species." One must always balance this appalling claim that black women had sexual relations with orang-outangs (chimpanzees) with Jefferson's contradictory reassurance that blacks were equal to whites in their innate "moral sense," even if they were inferior to whites "in the endowments both of body and mind" and were more crudely "ardent after their female." (Of course, we now know that Jefferson himself was almost certainly "ardent" after one African-American female.) Jefferson did not go as far as the earlier Jamaican historian Edward Long, who declared, "I do not think that an orang-outang husband would be any dishonour to an Hottentot female," and asserted that the animal "has in form a much nearer resemblance to the Negroe race, than the latter bear to White men."[87]

Jordan also points out that during the eighteenth-century Enlightenment, the theory of a "Great Chain of Being," with infinite gradations from stones and snails up through a hierarchy of animals to apes and finally to "types of mankind," and then perhaps on up to angels and God, became increasingly popular. This paradigm challenged and endangered the orthodox Judeo-Christian view that all humans created in the image of God and that all descended from two common ancestors, Adam and Eve. Thus from the Renaissance onward, contrary to the more simplistic view of a progressive secular Enlightenment, the worst early ventures in racism were expounded by eccentrics, heretics, and "free thinkers." Much later, scientific racism blossomed in France in the aftermath of the French Revolution, whereas in England and America the mainstream Christians vehemently defended the biblical account of the unity of mankind, leaving less room than in France for insinuations that blacks constituted a separate species.[88]

While Jefferson's racist views have attracted some attention in recent times, few readers have any inkling of the racist statements made by many of the leading figures of the European Enlightenment. For example, David Hume, Britain's most respected philosopher in the twentieth century, wrote in 1748:

I am apt to suspect the Negroes, and in general all other species of men, to be naturally inferior to the whites. There never was any civilized nation of any other complection [*sic*] than white. . . . No ingenious manufactures among them, no arts, no sciences. . . . Such a uniform and constant difference could not happen, in so many countries and ages, if nature had not made an original distinction between these breeds of men (from "Essays: Moral, Political and Literary").

And here is Voltaire, writing in 1756:

Their round eyes, their flat nose, their lips which are always thick, their differently shaped ears, the wool on their head, the measure even of their intelligence establishes between them and other species of men prodigious differences (from *"Essai sur les moeurs"*).

And Immanuel Kant, writing in 1764:

The Negroes of Africa have received from nature no intelligence that rises above the foolish. The difference between the two races is thus a substantial one: it appears to be just as great in respect to the faculties of the mind as in color. . . . Hume invites anyone to quote a single example of a Negro who has exhibited talents (from "Observations on the Feeling of the Beautiful and the Sublime").[89]

The list can be greatly extended, but it is important to put these statements into a European context in which most information about black Africans came from distant America and concerned only black slaves. We should also remember that this was the beginning of a pre-Darwinian realization, as revolutionary as the discovery that the sun and universe do not encircle the earth, that humans are really part of the animal world, as well as the fact that such white philosophers and other writers had no knowledge of the long-term effects of such speculations. I should add that such Enlightenment figures as Francis Hutcheson, Montesquieu, and Condorcet not only attacked slavery but insisted on human equality. Even the anti-Semitic Voltaire added, in a phrase that is especially meaningful in the twenty-first century, that "one needs time for everything." While I think that George Fredrickson, one of the world's leading authorities on racism, is too generous in his treatment of such figures as Voltaire, he makes the crucial point that "the scientific thought of the Enlightenment was a precondition for the growth of a modern racism based on physical typology."[90]

Though certainly not guilty of racism, the great Swedish botanist Carl Linnaeus and the German zoologist Johann Friedrich Blumenbach led the way in the 1700s in devising extremely influential classifications of the human species within the primate genus. Thus Blumenbach affirmed the essential unity of the human species while differentiating Caucasians, Mongolians, Ethiopians, American Indians, and Malays. The last five groups had supposedly diverged or degenerated from the original form set by the Caucasians, who were named for the supposed beauty of the people living in the mountainous region between the Black and Caspian seas.

Without any intention of doing so, Linnaeus, Blumenbach, and other pioneering scientists had put their disciplines on a road that led by the later nineteenth century to a kind of official racism in Western culture. It is extremely important to add that this "road" was anything but straight and unbroken, especially in Britain. Despite the prejudice of Hume and some other eighteenth-century writers, and in striking contrast to post-Revolutionary France, most British scientists of the earlier 1800s, exemplified by James Cowles Prichard, insisted on the unity and even perfectibility of all human groups. The historian Seymour Drescher makes the extraordinary point that in the parliamentary debates over slave emancipation in 1833, not a single M.P. spoke of any alleged incapacity of the Negroes. But by the 1850s African American visitors in Britain, like Frederick Douglass, sensed a deeply troubling change in attitude even from the mid-1840s (symbolized by Thomas Carlyle's 1853 *Occasional Discourses on the Nigger Question*).[91]

From today's perspective, this racism soon won shockingly wide acceptance and professional authority. Two examples will suffice. In 1865 Dr. James Hunt, who cofounded the Anthropological Society in London and whose work helped to legitimate anthropology in various British and American universities, gave a paper at the British Association in which he argued that Negroes were a distinct and irredeemably inferior species. He also maintained that there is a far greater difference in intelligence between a Negro and a European than between a gorilla and a chimpanzee.

Forty-six years later, the long article on "Negro," in the masterful eleventh edition of the *Encyclopædia Britannica*, asserted:

> Mentally the negro is inferior to the white. The remark of F. Manetta, made after a long study of the negro in America, may be taken as generally true of the whole negro race: "the negro children were sharp, intelligent and full of vivacity, but on approaching the adult period a gradual change set in. The intellect seemed to become clouded, animation giving place to a sort of lethargy, briskness yielding to indolence. . . . [T]he arrest or even deterioration in mental development is no doubt very largely due to the fact that after puberty sexual matters take the first place in the negro's life and thoughts.[92]

4

How Africans Became Integral
to New World History

In THE PAST, many historians, including Marxists, accepted a model of "economic determinism" when discussing the origins of New World slavery and the restriction of enslavement to Native Americans and then almost exclusively to sub-Saharan Africans and their descendants. Presenting racial slavery as an economically backward but inevitable and temporary stage in historical development, given the shortage of labor and the almost limitless expanses of land in the Americas, they tended to ignore or underestimate cultural and ideological factors, especially religion.

Yet there is now a broad consensus that plantation slavery, far from being archaic, was not only highly productive but anticipated much of the efficiency, organization, and global interconnectedness of industrial capitalism. The economic historian David Eltis has also argued that if only economic forces had prevailed, western Europeans would have revived white slavery, since it would have been much cheaper to enslave and transport white vagabonds, criminals, and prisoners of war to the New World than to sail all the way to West Africa and purchase increasingly expensive slaves in such a distant region. But the first option, Eltis stresses, was negated by whatever cultural forces had brought a sense of unity and freedom to Christians of western Europe, thus blocking the possibility of any significant revival of white slavery.[1]

Turning to the influence of religions, the long struggles between Christianity and Islam and the cultures they generated have seldom been given sufficient attention with respect to the changing sources of slave labor. For well over a millennium, the ultimate division between "Us" and "Them," or "the Other," a paradigm for the polarity between masters and slaves, was nourished by the Muslim invasions of eastern and western Europe; by the Christian crusades into Muslim territories; by the Christian reconquest of Portugal, Spain, and the Mediterranean islands; and by the Muslim enslavement, from the 1500s to the early 1800s of well over a million western Europeans from Italy, France, Spain, Portugal, Holland, and Britain.[2]

Some of these whites, who had been seized at sea or taken in larger numbers along the European coasts from Italy to England and even Iceland, were ransomed by Europeans and publicly celebrated as symbols of the inherent freedom and "non-enslaveability" of Christian whites—a concept that began to develop in Byzantium in the early Middle Ages, when enslavement and ransoming first became linked with religious identity.[3] In England especially, this ceremonial liberation of English captives—who often appeared in urban parades wearing their chains and tattered slave clothing—coincided in the eighteenth century with a growing desire to dignify "free labor," along with the kind of new nationalism signified in the early eighteenth century by James Thompson's famous lines that would become a kind of national anthem: "Rule, Britannia! Britannia rules the waves . . . Britons never will be slaves."[4]

As can be seen in their almost continuous wars, especially the ferocious Thirty Years' War from 1618 to 1648, western Europeans had few qualms about slaughtering and torturing one another, or even about exterminating civilians. Yet their own convicts, vagabonds, and prisoners of war were exempt from the kind of enslavement that seemed appropriate for Moors and then for what the English termed "Blackamoors."[5]

I do not mean to minimize the importance of greed, economic self-interest, and an increasing desire for greater productivity and profit, all of which lay at the heart of early modern and modern slavery. But these economic desires were also fused with issues of identity, ideology, and power.

In Chapter Three we considered at least four cultural preconditions for the antiblack racism that dominated the white settlement and development of the Americas, especially from the late seventeenth century onward.

First (and I will not follow the exact order of topics in Chapter Three), there were the strong sanctions for slavery in the West's religious and philosophical heritage extending back to the Hebrew and Christian Bibles and to the classical literature of the Greco-Roman era. Thus chattel slavery remained an acceptable institution even after it had disappeared from northwest Europe and after the Barbary corsairs underscored the belief that Christians from western Europe could not be legitimately enslaved.

Ironically, the revival and rediscovery of classical learning—supposedly a liberating step toward progress—gave new support for slavery in the Renaissance. But whereas Roman slaves had included virtually all the ethnic groups then available, the emerging modern world would be more influenced by the ancient Israelite distinction between Hebrew and enemy Canaanite slaves, and by the Islamic laws against forcibly enslaving free Muslims. This need to enslave "outsiders," except in Russia and parts of eastern Europe, which differed in demography and cultural traditions, also tied in with the ancient Greco-Roman conviction that external facial and physical traits correlated with internal mental and characterological strengths and weaknesses that were hereditary even if originally derived from climate and geography.[6]

The second precondition we considered was the medieval Arab precedent of enslaving and transporting by ship or caravan enormous numbers of black Africans, who came to be seen as especially suited for the most degrading forms of work. In marked contrast to the enslaved Europeans in North Africa, hardly any of these black slaves were redeemed by their own people, though many were converted to Islam and some were freed by their owners.

Third, there is evidence suggesting that racist stereotypes as well as a racist interpretation of the biblical "Curse of Ham" were transmitted by Iberian Muslims to Christians, who by the 1400s were already becoming obsessed with the alleged danger that Jews and New Christians posed to their own "purity of blood." This incipient racism was then magnified in the fifteenth century when the Portuguese imported increasing numbers of West African slaves, who were auctioned in Lisbon or shipped to Spanish cities from Seville to Valencia. Still, unlike England, which deported its small Jewish population in 1290 and attempted to deport its small number of blacks in the late 1500s, Spain and Portugal absorbed much Jewish and especially Moorish culture. Despite Spain's expulsion of Jews and then Moriscos (converted Moors), Iberians became accustomed to the coexistence of a range of skin colors from black to white—a fact of life that would lead to a greater acceptance of racial intermixture in their future colonies in the New World.

This point, particularly when we take account of the much lighter-skinned people of northwestern Europe, brings us back to a fourth and final precondition: the negative connotations and symbolism of the "color" black. Having briefly considered the mixed and complex imagery associated with "black" in medieval Europe, it is sufficient to note that the deeply imprinted visual memories derived from depictions of black demons, devils, and torturers could and no doubt did reinforce other factors in creating a perception of the ultimate Outsiders, even more alien than Arabs and Jews, as the blacks from distant and pagan Africa. If some popes could welcome delegations of black Christians from Jerusalem and Ethiopia, Portugal's "discovery" of West Africa brought papal approval of black slavery and even the shipment of some black slaves as gifts to popes and their friends in Rome.

BY 1750, when the British Crown finally sanctioned African American slavery in the English colony of Georgia, any informed observer would have had grounds for concluding that, from the very beginning, the Western Hemisphere could not have been colonized and settled without the importation of staggering amounts of African slave labor. In 1735 slavery had been excluded by a special law "for rendering the Colony of Georgia more Defencible [*sic*]" from Spanish Florida. This goal complemented the initial desire to create just south of slave-populous Carolina an economically productive refuge for orphans, debtors who had been imprisoned, and European refugees. But the law excluding slaves proved to be impossible to enforce.[7]

In 1750 black slaves could be seen in an uninterrupted succession of colonies from French Canada and New England all the way south to the Spanish settlements in Chile and Argentina. In the Caribbean they constituted up to 90 percent or more of the population of the richest colonies in the world. And the demand for such productive slaves continued to rise in one colony after another.

In retrospect, it appears that the entire New World enterprise depended on the enormous and expandable flow of slave labor from Africa. Though in 1495 Columbus transported some five hundred Native American slaves to Seville, and dreamed of a profitable slave trade of American "Indians" to Iberia, Italy, Sicily, and the Atlantic islands, some African slaves arrived in the Caribbean at least as early as 1501. By 1820 nearly 10.1 million slaves had departed from Africa for the New World, as opposed to only 2.6 million whites, many of them convicts or indentured servants, who had left Europe. Thus by 1820 African slaves constituted almost 80 percent of the enormous population that had sailed toward the Americas, and from 1760 to 1820 this emigrating flow included 8.4 African slaves for every European. From 1820 to 1880 the African slave trade, most of it now illegal, continued to ship off from Africa over 2.3 million more slaves, mainly to Brazil and Cuba. In other words, there can be no doubt that black slave labor was essential in creating and developing the "original" New World that began by the 1840s to attract so many millions of European immigrants.[8]

By the early 1700s most English merchants and political leaders agreed with the eminent economist Malachy Postlethwayt: "The Negroe-Trade and the natural Consequences resulting from it, may be justly esteemed an inexhaustible Fund of Wealth and Naval Power to this Nation."[9] For Josiah Child, Charles Davenant, and other influential political economists who thought in terms of global strategy and the development of a self-sufficient, mercantilist, and imperial economy, the African trade had those characteristics of a divinely contrived system, the kind of system that greatly appealed to the eighteenth-century mind, in France as well as England.[10]

It was now argued that the slave trade to the British colonies prevented the emigration of large numbers of white laborers that would deprive England not only of workers but of consumers, and the African markets for the goods that were exchanged for slaves stimulated both shipping and manufacturing. (We will later specify the kind of imports that induced Africans to sell so many slaves to Europeans and Americans.) British defenders of their relatively new Atlantic Slave System emphasized the way it stimulated domestic jobs for iron manufacturers, gunmakers, shipbuilders, refiners, ropemakers, sailmakers, weavers, and scores of other trades—just as exports to the West Indies had become vital to the prosperity of New England and the Middle Colonies.

Moreover, the slave trade helped to provide Britain with a favorable balance of trade, and surplus blacks could be illegally sold to the Spanish colonies in exchange for gold and silver. Even the slaves should benefit, it was claimed, since they were rescued from being killed, starved, or cannibalized in primitive Africa and were taken to Christian lands where they were well fed (supposedly in their owners' self-interest), where they had their own garden plots, and where they at least had a chance of becoming gradually "civilized." Jean Barbot, a French slave-ship captain, claimed that he conducted the trade according to the Golden Rule and argued that other European traders and owners should treat blacks as they themselves would want to be treated if they had the misfortune of being captured by the Algerian corsairs from North Africa.[11]

In the beginning, however, the European maritime nations, from Spain and Portugal in the 1500s to France and England in the 1600s, did not undertake New World colonization with the intent of relying on African slaves (South Carolina is arguably an exception). Despite the importance of the preconditions we have considered, the New World of 1750 emerged from a long series of fortuitous, haphazard, and even catastrophic events, especially as the Mediterranean patterns of piracy, banditry, plunder, cruelty, and ruthless reprisals were transferred to the Caribbean. In Central America, for example, where the conquistadores were disappointed by the absence of tribute in comparison with Mexico, they found some compensation by branding Indian slaves on the face and shipping some sixty-seven thousand to Panama, Peru, and the Caribbean.[12] In the sixteenth and seventeenth centuries the colonizing powers relied heavily on Indian labor, and in the seventeenth century the British in Barbados and Virginia depended for many decades on a large flow of white indentured servants, who long outnumbered black slaves.

MOVING BACK AGAIN TO ORIGINS, Venetian and Genoese merchants were at the forefront in developing conquered Arab sugar-producing regions in the Mediterranean, in supplying non-African slaves for a variety of economic needs in addition to sugar production, and finally in extending the system for slave-grown sugar to the so-called Atlantic islands of Madeira, the Canaries, the Cape Verdes, and São Tomé, off the west coast of Africa. Here, in order to grasp a more global picture, we should mention again the changing sources of slave labor from the 1200s to the late 1400s, a subject that highlights shifting boundaries and provides perspective on the ultimate choice of Africans.

Following the Western capture of Constantinople, in the Fourth Crusade (1204), Italian merchants participated in a booming long-distance seaborne trade that transported tens of thousands of "white" Armenian, Bulgarian, Circassian, Mingrelian, and Georgian slaves from regions around the Black Sea and the Sea of Azov to Mediterranean markets extending from Muslim Egypt and Syria to Christian Crete, Cyprus, Sicily, and eastern Spain. The slaves were used for the production of sugar as well as for numerous other services. What needs to be stressed is that the Tatars and other slave traders north of the Black Sea were as eager as their later African counterparts to march streams of captives, in this case mostly "white" captives, to shoreline markets where they could be exchanged for coveted goods.

Between 1414 and 1423 no fewer than ten thousand bondsmen (mostly bondswomen, to meet the demand for household servants) were sold in Florence alone. In the early 1400s this white slave trade from the Black Sea foreshadowed almost every aspect of the African slave trade, which was about to begin, including complex organization, permanent posts or forts for trade, and long-distance shipment by sea to multinational markets. In fact, although the Portuguese began importing black African slaves in the 1440s, the region between the Black and Caspian seas might conceivably have been a significant source of slaves for New World settlements after 1492 (and we have noted that a very few white "Eastern" slaves were shipped to Hispanic America).[13]

But in 1453 the Ottoman Turks captured Constantinople and thus the entrance from the Mediterranean into the Black Sea. The Turks soon diverted the flow of Black Sea and Balkan captives solely to Islamic markets. Turkish expansion brought an end to Italian colonization efforts in the eastern Mediterranean and sharply reduced Europe's supply of sugar. The Turks also cut off Christian Europe from its major source of slaves, and for most potential buyers the price of slaves became prohibitive. Aside from captured Muslims, the only alternative to the Crimea and the steppes of western Asia (given the understood prohibition against enslaving western Europeans) was sub-Saharan Africa. For a time, this new demand stimulated the Arab caravan trade across the Sahara. Hence a very few black slaves taken to the shores of Libya and Tunisia were dispersed to Sicily, Naples, Majorca, southern France, and Mediterranean Spain. (In Sicily a notary recording in Latin referred to *sclavi negri*, literally "black Slavs," who outnumbered white slaves by the 1490s.)[14]

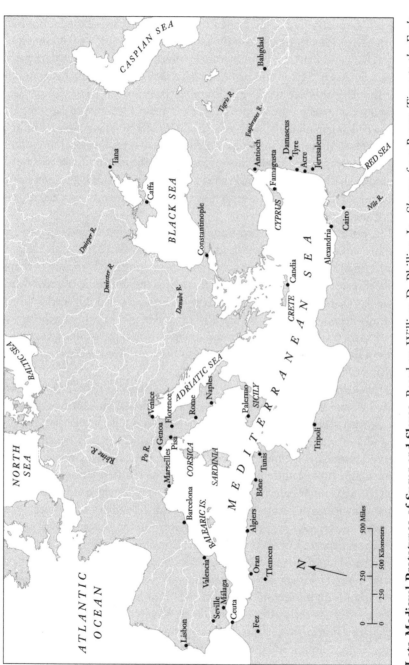

Late Medieval Prototypes of Sugar and Slaves. Based on William D. Phillips, Jr., *Slavery from Roman Times to the Early Transatlantic Trade* (Minneapolis: University of Minnesota Press, 1985), 98.

At the same time, Genoese capital and technology had strengthened Portuguese sea power, and Portugal's harbors had proved to be ideal for the small ships, mostly owned by Italian merchants, that carried commodities from the Near East to England and western Europe. Some of the same Italian merchant and banking families long involved in the Black Sea slave trade now sent agents to Seville and Lisbon, where they became pioneers in developing the African slave trade. For example, Bartolomeo Marchionni, who represented one such family, moved in 1470 from Florence to Lisbon. He soon owned sugar plantations in Madeira, worked by black slaves, and the king of Portugal granted him a monopoly for slave trading on the Guinea coast. There could hardly be a clearer example of the continuity between the late medieval Black Sea–Mediterranean slave networks and the emerging Atlantic Slave System, both energized by the expansion and westward movement of sugar cultivation.[15]

The Portuguese naval expeditions to West Africa in the mid-1400s were originally intended to find wheat and barley, to outflank the Arab caravan trade, to find the rich sources of gold and pepper south of Mali, and perhaps to find "Prester John," a legendary Christian ruler somewhere beyond the Islamic world. In the event, Prince Henry's voyagers also initiated a direct slave trade between West Africa and Lisbon and began to colonize the uninhabited Madeira Islands, at first using as slaves the light-skinned Guanche natives of the Canary Islands, who had also been enslaved and massacred by the Spaniards.[16]

By the time of Columbus's first American voyage, in 1492, Madeira had already become a wealthy sugar colony mainly dependent on the labor of black African slaves. The Atlantic islands had originally been bases for pirates and sources for water and supplies for mariners; partly because they presented less risk of tropical diseases than the African mainland, they then became major sites of agricultural production. As the first true colony committed to sugar monoculture and increasingly to black slave labor, Madeira was the transitional prototype for later mercantilist ideals of empire. Madeira soon outstripped the entire Mediterranean in the production of sugar, which was reexported by the late 1490s to England, France, Italy, and even the eastern Mediterranean. Columbus, who had lived for over ten years on an island near Madeira, had the foresight to take sugarcane from the Spanish Canary Islands on his second voyage to the "Indies" in 1493.[17]

Meanwhile, as early as 1495, São Tomé, situated much farther south, in the Gulf of Guinea, was shipping slave-grown sugar directly to Antwerp, long the major refining and distributing center for Europe. For the next half-century São Tomé would import more African slaves than Europe, the Americas, or the other Atlantic islands combined. Some wealthy Africans in Angola actually invested in sugar plantations on São Tomé, which also became a

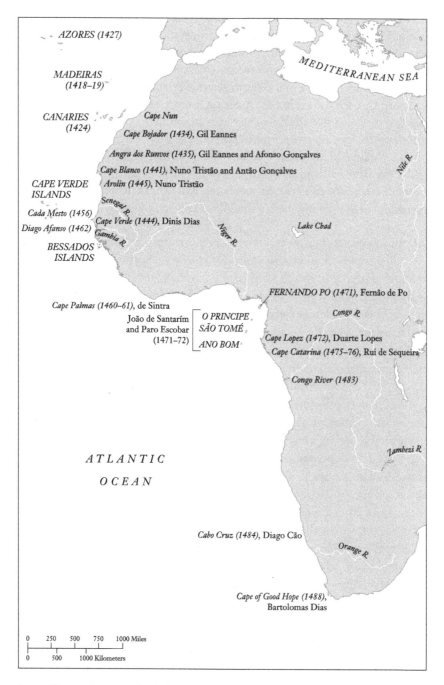

AZORES (1427)

MADEIRAS
(1418–19)

CANARIES
(1424)

Cape Nun

Cape Bojador (1434), Gil Eannes

Angra dos Runvos (1435), Gil Eannes and Afonso Gonçalves

Cape Blanco (1441), Nuno Tristão and Antão Gonçalves

CAPE VERDE   Arolin (1445), Nuno Tristão
ISLANDS

Senegal R.

Cada Mesto (1456)

Diago Afanso (1462)   Cape Verde (1444), Dinis Dias

Gambia R.

BESSADOS
ISLANDS

MEDITERRANEAN SEA

Nile R.

Niger R.

Lake Chad

Cape Palmas (1460–61), de Sintra

João de Santarím
and Paro Escobar
(1471–72)

O PRINCIPE
SÃO TOMÉ

ANO BOM

FERNANDO PO (1471), Fernão de Po

Congo R.

Cape Lopez (1472), Duarte Lopes

Cape Catarina (1475–76), Rui de Sequeira

Congo River (1483)

Zambezi R.

ATLANTIC

OCEAN

Cabo Cruz (1484), Diago Cão

Orange R.

Cape of Good Hope (1488),
Bartolomas Dias

0   250   500   750   1000 Miles

0   500   1000 Kilometers

Sugar Plantations on the Atlantic Islands. Based on Clayborne Carson, Emma J. Lapsansky-Werner, and Gary B. Nash, *African American Lives: The Struggle for Freedom* (New York: Pearson/Longman, 2005), 30.

gathering place for slaves whom the Portuguese then sold *to* Africans in exchange for gold, or later shipped westward to the Americas. By 1507 there
were about two thousand slaves working on São Tomé's sugar plantations
and another five to six thousand awaiting reexport.[18]

In summary, then, while African slaves were not part of original European blueprints for colonizing the Americas (except for South Carolina), spatial
boundaries had shifted even by the 1490s in a way that would easily enable
Europeans to draw on an enormous potential supply of African slave labor—
aided, I should add, by the favorable system of Atlantic winds and currents,
and by the later cultivation in Africa of such highly nutritious New World
crops as manioc (or cassava), corn (maize), and squash, which had the long-
term effect of greatly increasing the West African population.[19]

COLUMBUS'S ONCE CELEBRATED VOYAGE of 1492 was anything but an isolated
event. It was part of an almost explosive cluster of Spanish and Portuguese
explorations that discovered and mastered in the space of a decade the major
ocean currents and wind systems of the north and south Atlantic which had
kept the Western Hemisphere protected from earlier invasions and also isolated from many of the diseases of Eurasia and Africa. These Atlantic winds
and currents suddenly became the means, beginning in the 1490s, of major
intercontinental contact that would have, as we shall see, catastrophic consequences for both Amerindian and African populations.[20]

This first step toward globalization was made possible by several engineering or technological innovations. One of them was the caravel, a fast,
maneuverable sailing vessel with lateen and triangular sails for sailing close
to the wind, a ship adapted from an earlier Arab model. The Portuguese
caravels and larger Spanish *navios* could sail to almost any point in the world's
oceans and return. No less important was the compass, which probably came
via the Arabs from China, and such navigational instruments as the astrolabe
and quadrant, which allowed accurate readings of the "heavenly bodies" and
enabled sailors to plot a ship's latitude at sea. For some instruments as well as
charts and maps, navigators owed much to Jewish cosmographers in Portugal and Majorca.[21]

In 1488, when Bartolomeu Dias ran into contrary winds and currents
along the southwestern African coast, he swung out in a wide circle and
rounded the Cape of Good Hope, proving that it was possible to sail from
the Atlantic into the Indian Ocean. In 1497 Vasco da Gama followed a wide
arc of wind systems in the south Atlantic. For ninety-three days he was out of
sight of land—compared to the thirty-three days of Columbus's first voyage;
but once in the Indian Ocean, where da Gama drew on Arab sailing experience, he succeeded in reaching India. By the 1550s Japanese screen paintings

depicted the arrival of tall, long-nosed Portuguese traders, closely followed and fanned in the heat by barefoot black African slaves.[22]

The Portuguese thus accomplished what Columbus had claimed to have done: reaching Asia by sea. From their accidental discovery of Brazil in 1500 to their interactions with Southeast Asia and China in 1513, the Portuguese were the first to grasp the strategic meaning of world geography and to achieve dominion of the major seas and oceans. This meant that they soon displaced the Venetians in importing spices from Asia and gaining hegemony over trade in gold, spices, and slaves from Africa. By 1565, when the Portuguese had been trading with the Japanese for thirty years, the rapidity of change was also symbolized by a Spanish galleon that sailed east across the Pacific from the Philippines, finally unloading a cargo of cinnamon in Mexico![23]

I would also underscore the multinational character of the imperial ventures that created an Atlantic Slave System for the production of sugar, coffee, rice, tobacco, and other New World products. Columbus himself, a seaman from Genoa, was part of a larger picture that included colonies of Italian traders, bankers, and sailors in Lisbon, Seville, and other Atlantic ports, men who soon became deeply involved with West African trade. The connections extended to the great Italian merchant-banking families who were skilled at raising capital, selling insurance, and handling bills of credit and exchange—all of which became essential for lengthy voyages that delayed any return of profits for several years.

Moreover, some Italian bankers and moneylenders were also linked with great German merchant capitalist families such as the Fuggers and Welsers of Augsburg. The Fuggers, descended from a Bavarian weaver, moved from banking and providing loans to popes and kings, such as Emperor Charles V, to leasing mines in Spain and Hungary that produced especially copper, a commodity much desired in sub-Saharan Africa as well as Europe. Many of these rich merchant-bankers first concentrated on importing spices from India and silver from Spanish America, at a time when Europe had few major exports. Silver was even more valued in India than in Europe. Soon, however, the merchant-bankers also turned to sugar. And it is no exaggeration to say that the sugar colonies in the Atlantic islands, followed by those in Brazil and the Caribbean, were made possible by investment capital from merchant-bankers who then reaped enormous profits by marketing sugar and other slave-grown produce throughout Europe.[24]

Even in its early stages, the Atlantic Slave System foreshadowed certain features of our modern global economy. One sees international investment of capital in distant colonial regions, where the slave trade resulted in extremely low labor costs to produce goods for a transatlantic market. With respect to consumerism, it is now clear that slave-produced sugar, rum, coffee, tobacco, and chocolate greatly altered the European diet. Apart from their damaging effects, ranging from sugar-induced tooth decay to lung cancer, these luxuries helped to shape by the late eighteenth century a consumer mentality among the masses, especially in England, so that workers became more pliant and willing to accept factory discipline in order to afford their luxury stimulants.[25]

FIFTEENTH-CENTURY PORTUGUESE LEADERS, such as Prince Henry "the Navigator," initially saw the country's southward voyages along the West African coast as a continuation of their long struggle to defeat and expel the Moors from Portugal, culminating in 1415 with their invasion of the northwest tip of Africa and capture of Ceuta and Casablanca, in Morocco. Yet when the Portuguese attacked some African blacks south of the River Senegal, they were badly defeated. Even by the mid-1400s it became clear that given the distances involved, to say nothing of the Africans' military power, peaceful cooperation and trade with the coastal peoples was the only way to obtain slaves as well as gold, malaguetta pepper (called "grains of paradise"), and other desired goods. Unfortunately, slaves eventually superseded all other exports.

As the historian John Thornton has vividly shown, European slave traders dealt with Africans as equals, at least from the mid-fifteenth to the end of the seventeenth century. If West Africans lacked ships that could sail on the high seas, their numerous vessels were fast, maneuverable, and filled with skillful archers and javelin-men (and the quality of West African iron and steel at least equaled that of European). West Africans could and did attack and even sink some European ships, and the rulers of Kongo, Benin, and some other regions succeeded at times in temporarily stopping the trade in slaves.[26] Yet it is crucially important to recognize that Europeans profited from the total lack of any "pan-African consciousness." Similarity in skin color and other bodily traits (as Europeans viewed them) brought no sense of a common African identity.

But if Africans were themselves divided into many ethnic groups—or, above all, into family or clan lineages, based on highly respected ancestors— they quickly learned how to play off one group of Europeans against another and how to maximize the inflow of European goods. Portuguese ship captains and other Europeans soon learned the need to present ceremonial gifts to African rulers and to pay fees and taxes even to anchor and to engage in trade. In addition, the whites were often required to pay for butlers, messengers, trunk keepers, and washerwomen, among others. And they very seldom gained access to the Africans' actual networks and procedures for producing gold and slaves. As late as 1721, after a half-century of transporting slaves across the Atlantic, the British Royal African Company asked its agents in Africa to investigate modes of enslavement in the interior and find out whether there was any source besides "that of being taken Prisoners in War time"—a striking example of the limitations of European knowledge and control.[27]

In the 1400s, as in many preceding centuries, indigenous slavery and slave trading were very widespread in West Africa. But Europeans had no better understanding of the nature of African slavery than Africans had of the emerging New World plantation system to which the slaves they sold would be sent. (When black slaves boarded the European slave ships, many, like the *Amistad* captives we discussed in Chapter One, assumed they would be taken to some place where they would be killed and eaten.) European elites exercised power over the European masses by means of private, revenue-producing land—exemplified in the landlord-tenant relationship. By contrast, as John Thornton puts it, "slavery was widespread in Atlantic Africa because slaves were the only form of private, revenue-producing property recognized in African law." In West Africa, land was "owned by the state as a corporation," and thus the main symbols of *private* wealth and success were large numbers of slaves (and wives, in accordance with socially accepted polygyny). And while many slaves were treated much like peasant farmers, and some served as administrators, soldiers, and even royal advisers, others labored in mines or were ritually used for human sacrifice. Despite the huge cultural differences, the African and European forms of slavery were, in Thornton's words, "legally indistinguishable," and the African "political and economic elites" were eager "to sell large numbers of slaves to whoever would pay and thus fueled the Atlantic slave trade." The words "would pay" take on appalling significance when we note that in the period between 1680 and 1830—when the trade had its most devastating effects on Africa—the price paid for slaves (in Senegambia) rose by 1,031 percent.[28]

When in 1482 the Portuguese built their famous fortress at São Jorge da Mina (Elmina), in present-day Ghana, it was intended to protect their newly purchased gold from European interlopers, not from Africans. And Elmina (captured by the Dutch in the mid-seventeenth century) would soon become a major base for collecting and housing slaves awaiting shipment.

Much later, when some inexperienced and freelance white traders did occasionally seize and enslave black coastal people, as the British slave-trading Royal African Company complained, they invited harsh African retaliation. Such anarchy also threatened the elaborate mercantile network that enabled European traders to deal with African princes, kings, and merchants who sold slaves for textiles (often Asian), liquor, hardware, bars of iron, guns and gunpowder, tools or utensils of various kinds, and cowry seashells (widely used as currency and brought from the distant Maldive Islands).[29]

There has long been a widespread mythology claiming that Europeans were the ones who physically enslaved Africans—as if small groups of sailors, who were highly vulnerable to tropical diseases and who had no supply lines to their homelands, could kidnap some eleven to twelve million Africans. In actuality, from 1482 to the 1530s the Portuguese even purchased gold in the Elmina section of the Gold Coast in exchange for large numbers of black slaves whom they had purchased farther east and southward, where slaves were cheaper. Africans in the Elmina region and elsewhere expressed a growing demand for slaves who could be used as porters to carry European goods into the interior. Eventually, King John III of Portugal futilely declared that this sale of slaves to "infidels" was immoral and should be stopped, an edict that the king could hardly enforce.

Most Portuguese ships carried black interpreters, trained in Portugal or São Tomé, who went ashore with the captain to haggle and bargain with local rulers over the price of slaves. On some slave ships, especially Portuguese, at least a few black seamen worked alongside whites. Some were slaves, who were required to turn over most of their earnings to their owners; others were free blacks. Men of mixed descent even commanded Brazilian and Portuguese slave ships, and one African slave trader sailed all the way to Barbados, where he sold his slaves before returning to Africa.[30]

As the island of São Tomé became a gathering point for slaves, some working on local plantations before being sent to America, there was increasing intermixture between whites and blacks. By 1550 some of the daughters of rich black planters had married Portuguese settlers. A scattering of Portuguese adventurers, including New Christians or the descendants of Jews, even braved the risks of malaria and other diseases and settled on the African mainland. (In the early nineteenth century the annual death rates for British troops on the Gold Coast was as high as 668 per 1,000.) Called *tangomãos* or *lançados*, they lived like Africans, left many mulatto descendants, and often served as intermediaries for the selling and buying of slaves.[31]

In the sixteenth century Portugal issued licenses, which were usually then sold or subcontracted, for acquiring and transporting African slaves. Spain was officially barred from Africa by Pope Alexander VI's 1493 Treaty of Tordesillas, which drew a longitudinal line dividing the Atlantic into Portuguese and Spanish zones of influence (Spain gaining the mostly unexplored New World except for the as yet undiscovered Brazil, which extended eastward into Portugal's domain). Spain nevertheless became increasingly determined to use exclusive contracts, called *asientos*, to monopolize and control the supply of slave labor to its American colonies. But not only were *asientos* sold and subcontracted, privateers and interlopers from various European countries continued to break any meaningful monopoly. By the mid-seventeenth century the Dutch had gained a major share of the African slave trade, and leadership then passed to England and, to a lesser degree, France, until the early nineteenth century. From 1650 to 1810 the British, who won Spain's *asiento* in 1713, transported the greatest number of Africans to the New World, though they and the Americans outlawed their own slave trading in 1808. Because the Portuguese took the lead before 1650 and after 1810, they ultimately carried the most Africans to the Americas.[32]

In the early 1500s Portugal's King Manuel I recognized the African king of Kongo, Afonso I, as a brother and ally who would aid Portugal's efforts to Christianize the vast region to the north and south of the Congo River. Also known as Nzinga Mbemba, Afonzo became Kongo's second Christian king. With the aid of knowledgeable clerks, he carried on an extensive correspondence with Portugal's ruler. Historians have often quoted lines from Afonzo's amazing letter dated July 6, 1526, in which he pleads for help in curbing the terrible damages inflicted by the slave trade:

> Merchants are taking every day our natives, sons of the land and sons of our noblemen and vassals and our relatives because the [African] thieves and men of bad conscience grab them wishing to have the things and wares of this Kingdom. . . . [S]o great, Sir, is the corruption and licentiousness that our country is being completely depopulated. . . . [I]t is our will that in these Kingdoms there should not be any trade of slaves nor outlet for them.

John Thornton, who has studied the entire correspondence, warns that these bitter words can easily be misinterpreted. At this moment, Afonso deplored the unofficial aid that some Portuguese had given the ruler of rival Ndongo, which had led to the capture and sale of Afonso's subjects and even nobles. Yet Afonso personally participated in the slave trade, along with his nobles, and he soon wrote a quite different letter describing a new policy of appointing his own inspectors to ensure that the people sold as slaves had been legally enslaved.

But if Afonso accepted both slavery and the export of slaves, he fervently believed in lawful regulation and in 1525 had even seized a French ship and its crew because they were trading illegally, without royal permission. Thornton stresses that Afonso and his immediate successors were successful not only in curbing internal robbery and limiting the export of slaves but also in spreading Christianity and literacy and maintaining profitable contacts with Portugal and the Vatican. As a result, Portuguese slave traders soon moved south and focused their attention on Angola, where they established a permanent settlement as well as military alliances and interactions in local conflicts.[33]

IN THE FIFTEENTH AND SIXTEENTH CENTURIES the Portuguese established many of the practices for transporting slaves by ship, such as the total separation of the sexes, which the other maritime nations would adopt in the centuries to come. The conditions on transatlantic slave ships, which David Eltis has termed "the purest form of domination in the history of slavery," were probably too horrible to fully convey in human words. The density of packing slaves in the decks between a ship's bottom hold and main deck far exceeded the crowding of indentured servants or even Irish prisoners shipped to the British Caribbean. The males, especially, had to lie like spoons locked together, with no real standing room above them, surrounded by urine and feces, with little air to breathe. One would need to turn to the suffering of slaves in ancient Greek silver mines or to the victims of Nazi death camps to find worse or roughly equivalent examples of what Eltis calls "sheer awfulness."

Matters hardly improved in the nineteenth century. The illegal slave ships captured by the British between 1839 and 1852 had an average of *four* square feet for each slave, compared with the twelve square feet required by British law for contemporary North Atlantic immigrant ships—the same space, roughly, given to modern economy fare passengers on a Boeing 747. As David Eltis puts it, "the occupant of the typical slave ship could neither lie full length nor stand upright for five weeks except for the limited time spent above deck each day."[34]

Consider some of the eyewitness testimony given in 1790 and 1791 to a select committee of the British House of Commons:

> After meals they are made to jump in their irons [up on the deck]. This is called dancing by the slave-dealers. In every ship he [the witness] has been desired to flog such as would not jump. He had generally a cat of nine tails in his hand. . . . In his ship even those who had the flux, scurvy, and such edematous swellings in their legs as made it painful to them to move at all, were compelled to dance by the cat. . . . The captain ordered them to sing, and they sung songs of sorrow.
>
> When the scuttles are obliged to be shut, the gratings are not sufficient for airing the rooms. He [Dr. Trotter, a ship's surgeon] never himself could breathe freely, unless immediately under the hatchway. He has seen the slaves drawing their breath with all those laborious and anxious efforts for life, which are observed in expiring animals, subjected by experiment to foul air. . . .
>
> Mr. [Alexander] Falconbridge also states on this head, that when employed in stowing the slaves he made the most of the room and wedged them in. They had not so much room as a man in his coffin either in length or breadth. It was impossible for them to turn or shift with any degree of ease. He had often occasion to go from one side of their rooms to the other, in which case he always took off his shoes, but could not avoid pinching them; he has the marks on his feet where they bit and scratched him. . . . He says he cannot conceive any situation so dreadful and disgusting as that of the slaves when ill of the flux: in the [ship] *Alexander*, the deck was covered with blood and mucus, and resembled a slaughter-house. The stench and foul air were intolerable.[35]

Captains of slave ships faced a difficult dilemma. They longed to maximize profits by maximizing the number of slaves taken on each voyage, yet they feared both lethal slave revolts and an increase in slave mortality that would reduce their own share of the total New World sales. Unlike most planters, they had virtually no personal contact with the slaves; they felt no constraints on ordering the most sadistic public punishments in order to terrify "the cargo."

A Portuguese caravel could carry as many as 150 slaves, and a three-masted *navio* could hold as many as 400 as well as provisions for a long voyage. By the eighteenth century a typical French slaver would transport as many as 400 slaves, but British ships were much smaller. Because of the danger of revolt, ships had to carry much larger crews than on ordinary voyages. In the 1500s an average Middle Passage voyage took from two to three months. By the late 1700s such transatlantic trips lasted about a month, but of course much depended on weather and the distance to the New World destination.[36]

From the time of the first voyages to the Americas, male slaves were bound by chains, manacles, neck rings, and padlocks, though when out of sight of land and when weather permitted, crew members brought them to the deck for exercise (including forced "dancing," as we have seen) and some coerced labor. Slave mortality, most of it from dehydration (including dysentery, or "the flux"), averaged around 15 percent, but could easily range from as low as 5 percent to 33 percent or even more. Mortality decreased somewhat by the nineteenth century.

A major motive for separating the women was the fear that they would encourage the males to revolt (but the separation of sexes also made it far easier for members of the crew to rape black women, a very common occurrence). In actuality, slaves did rebel on approximately 10 percent of all slave ships, usually when still near the African coast. This resistance significantly increased the cost of the African slave trade—in terms of added crew, guns, and insurance—and thus prevented still more African slaves from being shipped to the New World.[37]

IT IS IMPORTANT TO REMEMBER that in the beginning, African slaves were not taken to the Americas but rather to Iberia and the Atlantic islands. Brazil only began importing a significant number of black slaves in the late 1500s, approximately 140 years after they were first brought into Portugal. It took another century before the truly hemispheric slave trade began to rise to wholly new levels, peaking in the late eighteenth century. From 1700 to 1880 an estimated 10.7 million slaves were deported from Africa, or about 86.3 percent of the total transatlantic slave migration (not counting shipboard mortality). Yet as early as 1550 black slaves constituted 10 percent of Lisbon's population of about 100,000.[38]

When the Africans arrived in Portugal, merchants divided them into lots according to age, sex, and physical condition. They were then paraded stark naked for inspection by prospective buyers, and sold by brokers who dealt with them as livestock, as if they had been horses or cattle. (The same procedure became almost universal when the slaves were first sold to European buyers.) Upon each sale, a white man would brand the slave, usually on a cheek, sometimes on both cheeks. The price of such chattel more than doubled during the first half of the sixteenth century, especially as they were reexported to Spain and the Mediterranean.

Like Moors and Jews, blacks were often called "dogs" or "bitches," and there is considerable evidence that most Portuguese whites regarded blacks as inherently inferior or even as a separate species, displaying the color of the devil. Since various popes authorized the buying of slaves who had supposedly been taken in a "just war," for a "just cause," it was generally agreed that these terms applied to people who were guilty of cannibalism, sodomy, incest, or simply living naked like beasts, in ignorance of the civilized standards of life.[39]

Even so, since the Church insisted that all human beings possessed immortal souls, popes and clerics demanded that the slaves be Christianized. In a letter of 1513 to the pope, Portugal's King Manuel I conveyed much concern over the fact that many blacks from Guinea had died at sea, before they could receive baptism. He ordered all masters to be sure that all black adults had been baptized within six months of landing. While complaints persisted for decades that many slaves had still not been baptized, the Portuguese, in marked contrast to later English colonists in the Caribbean and North America, encouraged blacks to form their own segregated religious confraternities, dedicated to the cult of Our Lady of the Rosary.

No less striking, the Portuguese loved the Africans' music and enlisted the slaves to perform at plays and other types of public entertainment, even at royal functions. (Little could the later British slave-ship captains, who forced slaves for exercise to dance on deck to the sound of bagpipes, dream that these Africans' descendants would revolutionize popular music on a global level in the twentieth century!) In Portugal the Africans were much less feared than Moorish slaves, who had much greater possibilities for escape or ransom. The historian Debra Blumenthal presents much evidence to show that in Spain, "fifteenth-century Valencians could not conceive of anyone more 'base' or 'vile' than a black male slave." Yet precisely because black African slaves were so far removed from their places of origin, they were truly "natally alienated," to use Orlando Patterson's term, and just as whites in colonial South Carolina relied for many decades on arming their black slaves to beat off Indian and Spanish attacks, so wealthy Valencians armed trusted black slaves and used them to insult rivals or enemies and to protect their masters and especially their masters' honor.[40]

Moreover, in Portugal black slaves were soon owned by whites and even free blacks of almost all social classes, including laborers, sailors, and even prostitutes, who were legally prohibited from having free servants. Despite the widespread antiblack racism in Portugal and Spain, blacks won a significant degree of acceptance among poor Portuguese whites (in sharp contrast to nineteenth-century America).[41] Socialization led to some interracial marriages, almost always between white men and mulatto women. As in later Latin America (and less formally and less universally in the United States), mulattoes acquired a much higher status than blacks.[42]

BY THE LATE 1500s, then, the central elements of an Atlantic Slave System had already emerged. When we take account of the increasing flow of Africans to Brazil and to the Spanish-American colonies, along with the rise of great sugar refining and distributing centers in Antwerp and then in Amsterdam, one wonders why the emergence of such a slave-driven economy evoked so little protest—especially in view of the disappearance of slavery several centuries earlier in western Europe and the rhetorical unease or even repudiation of domestic slavery in such countries as France, Holland, and especially England. (This latter is best symbolized, perhaps, by the use of such words as "servant" or "handmaiden" when translating the biblical Greek and Latin words for "slave" in the first Bibles to reach a truly wide audience.)[43]

It is true that in August 1444, at the first public auction of African slaves in Portugal (near Lagos, on the southern coast), many of the common people, enraged by the cries and moans prompted by the separation of slave families, temporarily interrupted the proceeding. Even Gomes Eannes de Zurara, the official chronicler for the Portuguese king, whom I quoted in Chapter Three, expressed sorrow and sympathy for the slaves' "sufferings." But the Portuguese, like diverse African peoples, had long been familiar with slavery in a variety of forms and accepted hierarchical societies headed by authoritarian or even "divinely chosen" kings.[44]

Today it also requires an imaginative leap to picture the state of human life in even supposedly "advanced" nations in the fifteenth and sixteenth centuries. When life expectancy at birth rose only to the low twenties, everyone was accustomed to ghastly rates of death from disease, especially in towns and cities, where epidemics killed up to 20 percent of the people every twenty-five or thirty years. Moreover, much of the population always remained on the verge of starvation, and officials left decomposing corpses in open pits, like the offal of butchered animals in the streets of London. In Lisbon, after numerous complaints over the public ubiquity of black people's corpses, the city constructed a special and segregated pit. If the stench of death lessened as one moved outside urban Europe, other odors did not: Partly because

bathhouses had long been associated with the sexual profligacy of late Roman times, Europeans bathed very seldom if at all. Indeed, there is repeated
testimony that West Africans, who did bathe and oil their skin, were revolted
by the strong odor of white sailors—and were even more shocked by the
whites' undisguised flatulence. That said, thieves and robbers infested the
countryside. In Genoa, the homeless poor sold themselves as galley slaves
every winter.

Throughout Europe, authorities pursued and burned at the stake thousands of women and men accused of witchcraft. In the Saint Bartholomew
Massacre of 1572, Catholics slaughtered fifty thousand Protestant (Hugue-
not) men, women, and children; their body parts were sold openly in the
streets, and Pope Gregory XIII ordered bonfires to be kindled in celebration
of this Catholic triumph. In short, New World slavery emerged at a time
when most people took it for granted that this world was a very cruel, sinful,
and brutal place. Until the late eighteenth century (with its own French Reign
of Terror), the European public was not only insensitive but rushed to witness the most terrible spectacles of torture, dismemberment, and death.[45]

In view of this cold-blooded culture, it is perhaps remarkable that the
emerging African slave trade drew as much courageous fire as it did. While
he never condemned slavery in principle, the great Spanish and Jesuit theologian and moralist Luis de Molina delivered scathing attacks on the ways in
which Africans were being enslaved. Tomás de Mercado, of Seville, was only
one of several Spanish jurists who correctly stressed that the high prices Europeans offered for slaves in Africa encouraged every form of trickery, fraud,
and violence: Slave hunters raided villages, judges accepted trumped-up
charges in order to sentence people to slavery, and fathers even sold their
own children for the slightest disobedience. Mercado's description of the
stench and overcrowding of slave ships in 1571 was as horrifying as the testimony presented by British abolitionists in the late 1780s and early 1790s.
Bartolomé Frías de Albornoz, a great Spanish lawyer living in Mexico, even
denied that Christianity could justify the violence of the slave trade and was
radical enough in his sometimes sarcastic attack on African slavery to have
his work condemned by the Inquisition.[46]

But in 1573 the world was hardly ready for an abolitionist movement.
The critics focused on the abusive methods of African enslavement, not on
the principle of slavery itself. Even so, they had no influence on political or
clerical policy. Nevertheless, we have noted that Europeans transported relatively few African slaves to the New World until the late 1500s. The slave
trade's effects on Africa would have been very limited if the major markets
for slave labor had continued to be Europe and the Atlantic islands. Why,
then, did the Americas become so dependent on an almost limitless flow of
slave labor from Africa?

THE CARIBBEAN'S so-called Greater Antilles—Hispaniola (later divided between French Saint-Domingue and Spanish Santo Domingo), Jamaica, Cuba, and Puerto Rico—were densely populated with millions of indigenous peoples. Yet in marked contrast with Portugal's long recognition of the West Africans' power and sovereignty, and with the attempts of the Portuguese and other Europeans to negotiate trade with various African groups, the Spaniards became intoxicated by prospects of sudden wealth, soon symbolized by rivers rich with gold. With guns and attack dogs they seized much land from the relatively passive Arawak/Taino Indians (and generally passed by the smaller islands in the Lesser Antilles, which were defended by fierce Carib Indians).

After some early efforts to enslave indigenous peoples in the Americas, which were later condemned by Spain and the papacy, the Spaniards relied on the *encomienda*, a semifeudal system of tributary labor first applied to the conquered Moors in Spain.[47] Since in theory the main justification for ruling the Indians was to convert them to Christianity and a Christian way of life, the system supposedly required a Spanish master, or *encomendero*, to protect and slowly Christianize a small community of Indians in exchange for tribute. The tribute could be in the form of crops, personal service, or work in underground mines. In actuality, not only did the Spaniards continue to enslave some Indians, but *encomenderos* made large fortunes by exploiting Indian workers as if they were worthless slaves who could not be sold or purchased. If the Indians had certain freedoms that were usually denied slaves, they hardly represented "free labor" in any meaningful sense. And as the *encomienda* system helped to destroy native populations in the Caribbean, it spread, with some modifications, from New Spain (Mexico) to Central and South America.

To make matters worse, the Arawak/Taino agriculture had been productive but depended on a fragile ecology—for example, high earth mounds for yucca, beans, maize, and other crops. These mounds were rapidly destroyed by the Spaniards' cattle and especially hogs, which quickly multiplied and in time severely damaged the base of the Indians' food supply.

Moreover, as we have already noted, the Amerindians throughout the hemisphere had little capacity for resisting imported diseases, both temperate and tropical pathogens, including smallpox, malaria, yellow fever, influenza, typhus, and the plague. Given the previous isolation of the Western Hemisphere, this disaster has been called a "virgin soil pandemic." Even whites suffered heavy mortality—of the twenty-five hundred colonists who arrived in Hispaniola in 1502, one thousand died in a fairly in short period of time—but the Spaniards were bewildered and some even horrified as the Indian populations seemed to evaporate before their eyes. Because these diseases struck all age groups, there was little possibility of mitigating the mortality with an increased birthrate.

While specialists differ with respect to numbers, which are necessarily somewhat speculative, we are clearly considering the greatest known population loss in human history—that is, mortality as a percentage of population. The population of central Mexico may well have fallen by almost 90 percent in seventy-five years. Estimates for Peru and Chile, where the diseases spread well before the arrival of Europeans, are almost as high. The death rate was even worse in the Caribbean, where pestilence coincided with the *encomienda* system and much mass slaughter. Estimates of Hispaniola's pre-Columbian Arawak/Taino Indian population range from about three hundred thousand to half a million; by the 1540s there were fewer than five hundred survivors.[48]

Though the word "genocide" has been recently used, the Spaniards clearly had no plan or motive for the systematic extermination of most Native Americans. On the contrary, the colonial entrepreneurs wanted to seize and exploit as many laborers as possible. Back in Castile, Queen Isabella and King Ferdinand became increasingly concerned over the flow of reports documenting the appalling mortality and cruel treatment of Native Americans. Drawing on his extensive experience in the Caribbean, the great Catholic bishop Bartolomé de Las Casas led the way in condemning the injustices of the *encomienda* system and publicizing the crimes committed against the Indians, who were worked all day and night, he reported, to enrich the *encomenderos*. Spain's famous New Laws of 1542, influenced by Las Casas, sought in various ways to protect the Indians' rights, allowing them to own property, for example, and forbidding the Spaniards from working them in mines. These and other reforms were difficult if not impossible to enforce, but over a period of three centuries the Spanish and Portuguese created a vast body of legislation intended to segregate and protect Native Americans from the exploitive forces of colonization.

The immense tragedy, however, was the slow but almost universal replacement of Indian slaves with black Africans. As early as 1516 two of the most humane and sensitive witnesses to the horrors of the New World, Licenciado Zuazo and Bartolomé de Las Casas, "protectors of the Indians," called for the sparing of Indian lives, especially in the mines, by importing many more African slaves. For twenty-five years Las Casas saw the importation of black slaves as the "solution" for the Spaniards' oppression of Indians.[49] This substitution of Africans for Indians became a common pattern. The great Jesuit pioneer Manuel da Nobrega arrived in Brazil in 1549 and courageously denounced the settlers for their mistreatment of Indians and later helped to restrict the enslavement of Indians. Yet Nobrega, like Las Casas, appealed for the importation of more black slaves, both for the colony and for his own religious order. Nobrega claimed that the legality of black slavery had been carefully weighed in the consciences of the people.[50]

There were also more compelling and pragmatic reasons for this racial replacement: Throughout the New World, colonists agreed that the labor of one black was worth that of several Indians. Unlike the Native Americans, most West Africans were familiar with large-scale agriculture, labor discipline, and making iron or even steel tools. They also shared with Europeans some resistance to Old World diseases.

Still, it seems quite possible that if the Caribbean Indians had not been so susceptible to Old World pathogens, and if their food base had not been destroyed, they might have provided a significant labor force for Caribbean sugar plantations once the small gold supplies had been exhausted. The near extermination of native populations created an immense vacuum, easing the seizure of fertile land from Hispaniola to Peru by the Spaniards and in Brazil by the Portuguese, but in many regions this invasion left only a skeletal native population that could be coerced to perform heavy labor.

Cortés made it clear that he and other conquistadores had no intention of pushing a plow, and the same could be said with respect to other Europeans who freely and voluntarily traveled to the Americas in search of a fortune. Western Europe contained no uprooted or "surplus" population willing to volunteer for heavy agricultural labor in the tropics—at least not until the seventeenth century, when England shipped tens of thousands of indentured servants and convicts to the Chesapeake and the Caribbean, especially Barbados. In time this labor supply proved to be wholly inadequate and the indentured servants were replaced by far larger numbers of African slaves.

In short, while Europeans settled each New World colony in a special and often fortuitous way, we can also see a more general pattern being repeated from Hispaniola and Brazil in the sixteenth century to Virginia and Carolina in the seventeenth. First, we note a strongly human element of greed, a desire for instant wealth from gold and silver, whether stolen from Indians, seized from the Spaniards by Dutch, British, or French pirate ships, or gained from forcing Indians to work in the mines for mineral wealth.

In a second and usually later alternative, colonial leaders turned to cash crops, such as tobacco and especially sugar, produced by slaves imported from Africa after initial experiments with Indian labor. For reasons we will later examine, the African workers could never come close to reproducing their numbers (except in the Chesapeake by the 1720s, and in South Carolina a half-century later); hence the need for a continuing and growing stream of labor from Africa to make up for slave mortality and to clear new land and found new colonies for cultivation. Much of the New World, then, came to resemble the Death Furnace of the ancient god Moloch—consuming African slaves so increasing numbers of Europeans (and later, white Americans) could consume sugar, coffee, rice, and tobacco.

And what about Africa? Historians still debate the long-term effects of four centuries of slave exports on Africa itself. The fairly recent emphasis on the equality of Euro-African trade negotiations has undermined any simplistic model of victimization, but a few key points need to be kept in mind.[51]

Clearly the increasing *external* demand for slave labor led to the death of enormous numbers of Africans killed in wars of enslavement and driven like cattle, often bound by the neck, from interior locations to the coast. Many more died, or longed for death, as they were jammed into open barracoons or stone forts and then packed into the white men's slave ships, where mortality even before departure equaled that of Europe's fourteenth-century Black Death. Since both Africans and Europeans favored the sale of males, the resulting preponderance of women in many West African societies helped to increase polygyny and more rapid reproduction. (Overall, about two-thirds of the captives shipped from Africa to the New World were male.)[52]

In the more decentralized societies, this same external demand encouraged kidnapping, as we saw in Chapter One with the capture in Sierra Leone of Cinqué, the future leader of the *Amistad* revolt. Over the centuries village after village became the targets of surprise raids by bands of armed men. As the African historian Robert Harms comments, "it was as if each [such African] person walked around with a price on his or her head." No less important was the rise of predatory states, such as Futa Jallon, Dahomey, Asante, Kasanje, and the Lunda Empire, which found it financially profitable to wage war on neighbors and sell prisoners to the Portuguese, Dutch, English, French, Danes, or Americans. These Africans mainly sold slaves for luxury goods, such as Asian and European textiles, rum and brandy, metal goods, bars of iron, tobacco, and personal ornaments such as beads, copper armlets, and anklets. After about 1690, with the growing perfection of European firearms, the enslaving states became increasingly powerful as they exchanged slaves for gunpowder and the latest weapons.

A relatively few African rulers, government officials, military officers, and merchants acquired symbols of wealth and status in exchange for the massive export of labor, but the slave trade did not stimulate an internal African economy. Indeed, when the European demand suddenly ended in the 1850s and 1860s, the African slave-making mechanisms continued to operate, flooding various regions with nonexportable slaves. There seemed to be no economic alternative.[53]

Finally, we should note that the geographic sources of slaves shifted over time. The Atlantic slave trade drew captives from a vast area stretching thirty-five hundred miles along the West and West Central African coast, from present-day Senegal in the north to the Kalahari Desert in Angola in the south, and from five hundred to even a thousand miles inland. During the fifteenth century many captives came from Senegambia—the region that now encompasses Senegal, Gambia, northern Guinea, southern Mali, southern

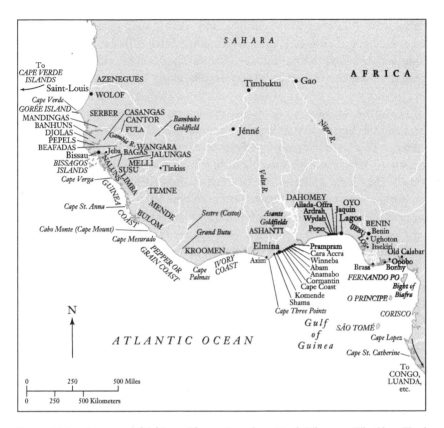

Some Major Sources of African Slaves. Based on Hugh Thomas, *The Slave Trade: The Story of the Atlantic Slave Trade* (New York: Simon & Schuster, 1997), 317–18.

Mauritania, and Guinea-Bissau. By the early sixteenth century, West Central Africa (including present-day Congo and Angola) had begun to export significant numbers of slaves; it would ultimately provide about 44 percent of all the slaves shipped out of Africa. But beginning in the 1670s, with the emergence of British dominance of the trade, the Bight of Benin (western Nigeria and southeast Niger, then known as the Slave Coast) and the Gold Coast (present-day Ghana, Burkina Faso, eastern Ivory Coast, and southern Niger) became the major slave-exporting regions. During the mid-eighteenth century the Bight of Biafra (an area that included western Cameroon and eastern Nigeria) and Sierra Leone also grew to be major sources of slaves.[54]

Africans from particular regions also tended to concentrate in particular parts of the New World. Thus slaveholders in the Carolinas and Georgia purchased many slaves from West Central Africa and many from Senegambia and Sierra Leone, who were sought for their rice-cultivation skills. Virginians imported large numbers of Igbos and other peoples from the Bight of

Biafra, as well as many Senegambian and Akan slaves. It seems clear that large numbers of enslaved Africans, from Muslims in Brazil to Angolans in Louisiana, retained their ethnic identities in the New World and organized social rituals, such as funerals and even revolts, along ethnic or national lines.[55]

THIS CHAPTER is meant to underscore the central truth that black slavery was basic and integral to the entire phenomenon we call "America." This often hidden or disguised truth ultimately involves the profound contradiction of a free society that was made possible by black slave labor. Until the late 1700s, none of the "slave societies" or "societies with slaves"[56] spread out around the world had committed themselves to the twin ideals of liberty and equality, grounded in a dream or vision of historical progress. As I have tried to suggest, it was the larger Atlantic Slave System, including North America's trade with the West Indies and the export of Southern rice, tobacco, indigo, and finally cotton, that prepared the way for everything America was to become. Thus vital links developed between the profit motive, which led to inhuman efforts to dehumanize African slaves, and the conception of the New World as an environment of liberation, opportunity, and upward mobility.

Racial slavery became an intrinsic and indispensable part of New World settlement, not an accident or an unfortunate shortcoming on the margins of the American experience. From the very beginnings, America was part black, and indebted to the appalling sacrifices of millions of individual blacks who cleared the forests and tilled the soil. Yet even the ardent opponents of slaveholding could seldom if ever acknowledge this basic fact. To balance the soaring aspirations released by the American Revolution and by evangelical religion, in the First and Second Great Awakenings, slavery became the dark underside of the American dream—the great exception to our pretensions of perfection, the single barrier blocking our way to the millennium, the single manifestation of national sin. The tragic result of this formulation was to identify the so-called Negro—and the historically negative connotations of the word are crucial for an understanding of my point—as the GREAT AMERICAN PROBLEM. The road would be clear, everything would be perfect, if it were not for his or her presence.

Such assumptions tainted some white and even black abolitionist writing, and lay behind the numerous projects and proposals for deporting or colonizing the black population outside the United States. Hence the victims of the great sin of slavery became, in this subtle psychological inversion, the embodiment of sin, exemplified in the Negro's alleged and sometimes "comic" failings, indignities, and mistakes. For some two hundred years African Americans have struggled against accepting or above all internalizing this prescribed identity, this psychological curse.

5

The Atlantic Slave System:
Brazil and the Caribbean

IN THE MID-TO-LATE 1500s the Portuguese gradually transferred the system of sugar plantations worked by slaves from their Atlantic islands such as Madeira, São Tomé, and Principe to northeastern Brazil. The plantation system involved everything from long-term capital investment and the African slave trade to the technology and economic organization for cultivating and harvesting sugarcane and then manufacturing sugar and eventually molasses and rum. It was largely because of the expanding international market for sugar, molasses, syrup, and rum that regions south of what became the United States imported some 95 percent of the African slaves brought to the New World.

During the first decades of the sixteenth century the small Portuguese settlements in Brazil exported little more than brazilwood, parrots, and monkeys, at a time when the Portuguese islands of São Tomé and Madeira produced much of Europe's sugar, which was still a rare luxury and traditional medication.[1] But Portugal became increasingly alarmed by French and British gestures toward founding settlements in Brazil, and in the 1530s and 1540s Portuguese expeditions attempted to chase off foreign ships and then succeeded in establishing sugar plantations or *engenhos* in northeastern Brazil. By the late 1500s sugar mills had multiplied, African slaves were replacing forced Indian labor, and Brazil was producing more sugar than the Atlantic islands combined with regions like the Algarve, in southern Portugal. These developments represented the first stage of the unforeseen and unprecedented expansion of economic and cultural boundaries initiated by New World slavery.

The sugar mill and surrounding plantation land came to epitomize New World slavery and "inhuman bondage" in its most extreme form. Sugar plantations also gave rise to the central problem of reconciling traditional European and African cultures with a highly modern, systematized, and profitable form of labor exploitation. In many ways it was sugar that shaped the destination of slave ships and the very nature of the Atlantic Slave System. In the long era from 1500 to 1870, according to a recent estimate, it was sugar-producing Brazil that absorbed over 45 percent of all African slaves and the sugar-producing British, French, Dutch, Danish, and Spanish Caribbean that imported nearly 46 percent more. The Spanish mainland in South America took just over 5 percent of the Africans brought into the Americas, and the British mainland in North America less than 4 percent—despite the later millions of African Americans who appeared as a result of unprecedented natural population growth.[2]

As sugar mills and slavery moved gradually from the late medieval Mediterranean to the Spanish Canary Islands and the Portuguese islands of Madeira and São Tomé, and then to the Caribbean and northeastern Brazil, they increasingly became prototypes of modern assembly-line production. Even the cultivation, weeding, and cutting of sugarcane resembled "factories in the field" as drivers wielding whips sought to maximize the annual work of carefully organized and regimented gangs of slaves. Since slave labor represented an investment in a special kind of property, owners were economically motivated to maximize the productivity of workers who could not simply be fired or have their wages lowered.

Much later, with respect to the point about prototypes, even Thomas Jefferson took pleasure in personally supervising the movements and productivity of his young teenage male slaves in a small nail factory at Monticello, suggesting that he would have welcomed the time-and-motion studies of Frederick Winslow Taylor, the champion of "scientific management" in the late nineteenth and early twentieth centuries.[3] Yet despite this seeming obsession with efficient industrial production, Jefferson presented himself as a traditional agrarian republican, dedicated to yeoman farming and repelled by the thought of cities and industrialization.

There were various ways in which Caribbean, Brazilian, and North American planters sought to counteract or disguise the purely economic connotations of racial slavery in the New World. In the British West Indies many successful planters were able to escape back to Britain and purchase aristocratic status and land. Though Portugal was more reluctant to ennoble Brazilian sugar magnates, some of whom could be identified as New Christians who had thus inherited "tainted Jewish blood," the leading planters succeeded in creating a façade of patriarchal paternalism or a network of protective boundaries, a subject we will turn to later in this chapter. For now it is sufficient to

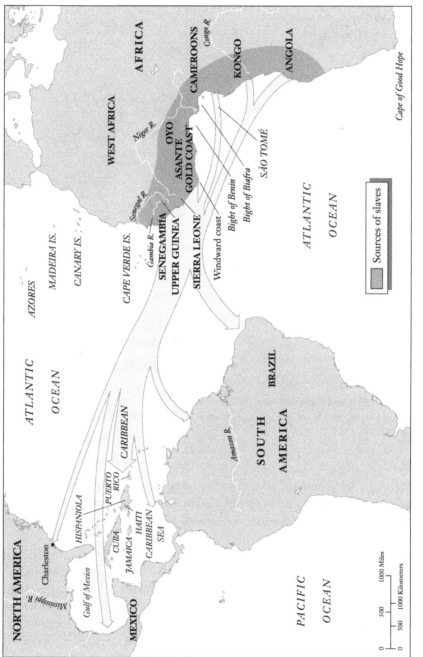

Origins and Destinations of African Slaves, 1500–1870. Based on Joe Trotter, Jr., *Origins and Destinations of Africans Enslaved in the New World* (Westport: Greenwood, 2000), 30.

Slave Origins and Destinations: Another Estimate. Based on Darlene Clark Hine, William Hine, and Stanley Harrold, *African-American Odyssey* (New York: Prentice Hall, 2006), 34.

note that a self-ennobled seigneur who owned a sugar mill and often dealt with slaves indirectly, through deferential slave-owning sugar farmers, or *lavradores de cana*, could give the appearance of reconciling traditional Christian principles with the inherent brutality of slavery.

Moreover, in all parts of the hemisphere, slaveholders *eventually* benefited, at least ideologically, from a growing consensus that defined slave labor as a "backward" and anachronistic institution necessitated by the need to Christianize and civilize a "savage people" from Africa. This last answer to "the problem of slavery," emphasizing the economically archaic, retrograde, premodern, but essentially humane character of racial "servitude," prevailed in much of America long after the emancipation of slaves and even after the Second World War.[4] Indeed, many historians initially attacked the economic historians' discovery that Southern slavery, despite its ghastly evils, was more efficient, productive, and profitable than free-labor farming in the North. For several decades historians also engaged in heated debates over whether the master-slave relationship in the South or in Brazil was "semifeudal," "seigneurial," or "paternalistic." There can be no doubt that many slaveholders endeavored to convey such impressions. Yet the compatibility of unbounded forced labor with modern life has been dramatized by the millions of "state slaves" exploited by Nazi Germany, the Soviet Union, and Communist China, to say nothing of the black penal laborers in the Jim Crow South and the sexual slaves and other coerced workers in various parts of the world today. For the rulers of such modern slaves there has been no need for even a pretense of paternalism.

Since sugar gradually became one of the first luxuries consumed by the masses in Western societies (along with slave-produced coffee, tobacco, and eventually chocolate), it also became the principal incentive for transporting millions of Africans to the New World.[5] At the outset, therefore, we should look briefly at the nature of the labor required for sugar production, which differed little from one colony to another, though of course the lives of slaves were affected by differences in topography, demography, climate, the relative ease of escape, and economic activities apart from sugar.[6]

From the very beginning, sugar production came closer to resembling a modern agribusiness than the kind of farming done in feudal Europe. In the autumn and also sometimes in the spring, slaves used hoes to dig trenches or large numbers of holes, roughly a foot deep and three feet square, often in heavy soils baked hard by the sun (ploughs were seldom used even in the eighteenth century).

The next step required the coordinated planting of shoots or cuttings of cane, which took up to a year and a half to mature. As planters learned more about soil erosion and the need for fertilizer, at least in the Caribbean, slaves had to carry on their heads baskets of manure, sometimes as heavy as eighty pounds, to fertilize the shoots. Along with arduous weeding, this was the labor slaves hated the most, especially when they had to trudge up steep hillsides, as was often the case in the Caribbean.[7] In the British colony of St. Christopher, for example, an aristocratic Englishwoman described drivers with whips following such slaves as they carried heavy manure: "They go up at a trot, and return at a gallop, and did you not know the cruel necessity of this alertness, you would believe them the merriest people in the world."[8]

Except for Sundays and some religious holidays in Catholic colonies, the slaves' work day on sugar plantations generally began around 5:00 A.M., later followed by a half-hour for breakfast and an hour or two for a midday meal. They would return to their cabins at dusk, except when the milling and boiling of cane required them to work around the clock, often with sleep only on every other night.[9] In Brazil the harvest season lasted for some nine months and planting for another two or more months; clerics continually complained that relief from work on saints' days was not strictly observed.[10]

Because of the perishability of the crop, everything depended on speed and perfect timing: cutting the roughly six-foot-long cane in the dry season, between January and May in the Caribbean, and then crushing, boiling, and curing the liquid before the hurricane season from midsummer to early October. If the cane was not crushed within a day of cutting, the treasured juice could go sour. In Brazil the crucial harvest and milling began in early August, and slaves labored for most of a year in order to produce a "clayed" or more finely grained white sugar that was seldom seen in the Caribbean. Small sugar mills were typically driven by moving oxen or horses; some mills were water-powered, though this equipment was more expensive. Prosperous planters in Barbados and other colonies later made use of windmills, and steam power appeared on nineteenth-century sugar plantations especially in Cuba.

Slaves also devoted much time to caring for livestock and cutting trees to provide firewood for the sweltering boiler houses. In regions where timber had been exhausted, slaves collected and dried the residue, or "trash," from pressed cane, which when burned would provide the needed heat and was also used as litter for cattle pens. It took roughly a ton of cane to produce one hundred pounds of grain sugar.

Particularly after technological improvements appeared in the early 1600s, the sugarcane plantation became an industrial enterprise, anticipating assembly lines and time-and-motion regimentation. Unlike various kinds of Euro-American farmers and artisans, the coerced sugar worker had no claim to the tools and technology that he or she learned to master; as with the later globalized economy, thousands of miles of distance separated production from the consuming public. The plantation enterprise also depended on highly skilled as well as semiskilled slave labor.[11]

After sugarcane had been cut, slaves brought it to the mill where seven or eight or sometimes as many as thirty slave men and women worked. Some passed it by hand, piece by piece, through three vertical rollers to squeeze out the juice. Others conducted the liquid through a series of heated vats and cauldrons until repeated skimming purified a substance that could be poured into molds and eventually dried and crated as sugar. When slaves were working shifts of sixteen to eighteen hours, usually with inadequate diets, there was considerable danger, especially at night, of a worker catching his or her fingers in the vertical rollers: "A hatchet was kept in readiness to sever the arm, which in such cases was always drawn in; and this no doubt explains the number of maimed watchmen." In northeastern Brazil slave women with a missing arm were a common sight.[12]

The tremendous work pressure during the sugar harvest far exceeded anything that slaves encountered when cultivating tobacco, cotton, rice, or indigo (for dyes). Some planters as well as travelers described the terrible heat as slaves "night and day stand in great Boyling Houses, where there are Six or Seven large Coppers or Furnaces kept perpetually Boyling; and from which with heavy Ladles and Scummers they Skim off the excrementitious parts of the Canes, till it comes to its perfection and cleanness."[13]

The final steps included the drying and curing of sugar "heads," the draining of molasses and the distillation of rum, and the boxing of white sugar, especially in Brazil, or in the West Indies a coarser and darker "muscovado" that could be refined in Holland or Britain.

Though a larger market for sugar and sucrose-sweetened foods and drinks began to develop only in the late 1600s, the known profits from selling sugar had stimulated an interest in such investments even before the first European settlements in the Americas. In Chapter Four we examined the European colonists' transition from using Native American slaves to their increasing transport and purchase of Africans. Portuguese Brazil, in which this process took a half-century, became after 1575 the largest slave-importing region in the New World, and by 1600 Brazilian sugar was bringing Portugal even greater profits than the fabled Asian spice trade.

It is therefore still something of a mystery why the Spaniards were not more successful in producing this treasured commodity, since they started to cultivate sugar in the Caribbean decades before the Portuguese began to do so in Brazil. Moreover, as later history would show, islands like Santo Domingo (also called Hispaniola and, when the French took over the western part, Saint-Domingue), Jamaica, and Cuba contained ideal environments for sugar production, and the Spaniards also experimented with sugar in coastal regions of mainland South and Central America.

Columbus himself took sugarcane shoots to the Caribbean on his second voyage. Cortés, in a letter to Emperor Charles V (who had earlier been King Charles I of Spain), asked that sugarcane, along with other seeds and cuttings of European plants, be sent to Mexico. Despite the Spanish focus on gold and silver, Charles V actually encouraged sugar production in Santo Domingo, sending experts on sugar-making, or "sugar masters," from the Spanish Canary Islands. Genoese merchants in Seville, who along with other Italian entrepreneurs were active in transferring sugar and black slaves from the Mediterranean and Atlantic islands to the New World, helped raise capital for Spanish-American sugar production. By 1600 there were over forty licensed sugar mills in Mexico and many even in Peru.[14]

Somehow these promising early initiatives never led to a major sugar industry in the Spanish colonies. Most of the Caribbean remained open to later Dutch, English, French, and even Danish economic development. The standard explanation points to the Spaniards' obsession with precious metals, which led many acquisitive whites to rush from the Caribbean islands to

Mexico and Peru, and also diverted many African slaves to the mines and cities on the mainland.

No less important, northeastern Brazil jutted out relatively close to the large supplies of labor in West Africa, labor that would long be nearly monopolized by the Portuguese. The ferocious Carib Indians presented a barrier on some of the islands, though the rapid death and near extinction of the Arawak/Taino Indians also deprived the Spaniards of the cheapest labor force on Santo Domingo, a large island that would later become one of the major producers of sugar in the world.[15] In addition, some historians have pointed to the Spaniards' possible lack of access to markets and to the absence of private entrepreneurs, given the Spanish government's authoritarian control of the American conquest. Still, more information is needed to explain why Brazilian planters, unlike their Spanish counterparts, profited so much from African slaves and sugar production from the 1570s to the 1620s.[16]

Portuguese Brazil even became very lucrative for privateers from France, England, and Holland. While such famous privateers as Francis Drake and Sir Walter Raleigh were seizing fortunes in silver, gold, indigo, and other goods from Spanish ships, in the 1560s John Hawkins and John Lovell captured dozens of Portuguese ships filled with sugar. Between 1588 and 1591 English ships captured thirty-four such vessels.[17] By 1591 a Spanish spy could report that "English booty in West India [American] produce is so great that sugar is cheaper in London than it is in Lisbon or the Indies themselves."[18]

The English also took delight in illicitly selling African slaves to the Spanish colonists and in scheming to enlist fugitive slaves in Central America in founding a colony that could prey on the Spaniards. From the mid-1500s on through the 1600s a consensus developed in Europe that the West Indies "lay beyond the line," or in other words beyond the boundaries of treaties and international law. In the Caribbean there were to be no limits on robbery, massacre, rape, alcoholism, or the defiance of conventions, including dress. This sense of moving beyond all social and moral boundaries was clearly related to the emerging Atlantic Slave System.[19]

Of course, European sugar prices fluctuated in response to changing supply and markets. As matters developed, the plantations in the state of Pernambuco, at the extreme eastern tip of Brazil, as well as in the state of Bahia,[20] a bit southwestward, surpassed all competitors until the turn of the eighteenth century. But by 1700 the British colonies of Barbados and Jamaica, together with the Leeward Islands, supplied nearly half the sugar consumed in western Europe, and the value of sugar arriving in England was double that of tobacco (though Bahia had about the same output of sugar as Jamaica until the 1730s).[21]

The history of slavery in the Caribbean and in the New World in general was profoundly affected by Holland's long struggle for independence from Spain and the Catholic House of Hapsburg. The mostly Protestant Dutch struggled for their freedom from 1568 to 1648, with a twelve-year truce beginning in 1609. Portugal and Spain were united under a single Hapsburg monarchy for the sixty years from 1580 to 1640. Thus especially from 1621 onward, all the global empires of Spain and Portugal were open to Dutch attack and even conquest by the Dutch East India Company, founded in 1602, and the Dutch West India Company, created in 1621. In Asia the Dutch captured Ceylon and much of Indonesia; in 1652 they established a base at the Cape of Good Hope, in South Africa, having earlier seized the major Portuguese slave-trading centers of El Mina (now in Ghana) and Luanda (in Angola) on the West African coast.

In the later 1500s the Portuguese had hired Dutch ships to carry much of the produce from Brazil to Europe. But with the end of the truce in 1621 and an intensification of the Hollanders' war against Hapsburg Spain and Portugal, the Dutch temporarily captured Salvador (Brazil's capital), disrupted the Bahian economy, and in 1630 seized Brazil's largest sugar-producing region, Pernambuco. This complex and continuing war led to the destruction of many sugar mills and plantations, to the death and escape of many slaves, and to the steep decline in Pernambuco's sugar production. Although the Portuguese finally expelled the Dutch from Brazil in 1654, the Dutch had already founded colonies in the Caribbean, such as St. Eustace and Curaçao (to say nothing of New Amsterdam—later New York—in North America), and had taught British colonists in the Caribbean how to grow and process sugar. The Dutch, who had achieved naval dominance in the Caribbean, even supplied the British with African slaves, at bargain prices, and refined and marketed British-grown sugar in Amsterdam.

There were thus various ways in which the decades of Dutch warfare and occupation of northeastern Brazil led to the creation of extremely prosperous English and French "sugar islands" in the West Indies, which long posed a competitive threat to Brazil. First, and perhaps most important, the warfare and destruction of many Brazilian *engenhos* reduced the supply and thus escalated the price of sugar in Europe. This provided the English, Dutch, French, and even Portuguese Bahians with a growing incentive to invest in sugar production, especially as the market demand increased spectacularly from the mid-seventeenth to the eighteenth century. Second, the Dutch disseminated the necessary technological knowledge, especially when refugees fled from Brazil to the Caribbean. At this time Holland also acquired temporary dominance of the African slave trade.[22]

Given the way history is taught, few educated Americans realize that when the English were beginning to grow tobacco in Jamestown and Pilgrims were imposing order at Plymouth by cutting down a Maypole, other Englishmen were beginning to settle in St. Christopher (St. Kitts) (1624),

Barbados (1627), Nevis (1628), and Montserrat and Antigua (1630s). They were closely followed by the French, who actually joined the English on St. Christopher in a surprise night attack on native Indians. The French proved more willing than the English to combat and push back the fierce Carib Indians on Guadeloupe and Martinique, though they took somewhat longer to turn to sugar. By 1655 England was ruled by Oliver Cromwell, who sent a large army to join pirates in seizing Jamaica from the Spaniards. A few years later the French occupied the western third of Santo Domingo, now named Saint-Domingue (later Haiti). Cromwell's expedition had tried but had failed to capture any part of Santo Domingo.[23]

This acquisition of island territories would have been of little economic significance if only tobacco and food crops had continued to be raised by grungy, ill-disciplined, and hard-drinking white servants. In time, however, thanks to the exploitation of tens of thousands of African slaves, the British planters in the Caribbean became far richer than their cousins in the North American wilderness. From 1713 to 1822 the British West Indies continued to win a larger share of total British trade than did all of North America (or, for that matter, Latin America, Asia, or Africa).[24] As the British and then French Caribbean began producing sugar, molasses, rum, and coffee for an international mass market, the West Indies became the true economic center of the New World, a point confirmed by the fact that imperial powers immediately sent their navies to protect or capture Caribbean colonies upon the outbreak of a war. The American and French victory at Yorktown in 1781, which ensured American independence, depended on the arrival from the Caribbean of a French fleet.)

By the eighteenth century the West Indies had also become the crucial market for exports from New England and the Middle Colonies of North America. It was the sugar islands that purchased the dried fish, corn, grain, barreled meat, flour, beer, lumber, staves for sugar hogsheads, ironware, shoes, and other supplies on which the economy of the largely free-labor Northeastern colonies depended. New England, New York, and Pennsylvania were not only oriented toward the British West Indies but became the major if illegal suppliers of the French, especially in Saint-Domingue.

By the mid-eighteenth century Britain also looked to the West Indies as a market for selling luxury goods as well as provisions, and by 1850 the English working class was consuming more sugar per capita than the aristocracy. Along with all the other foods containing sucrose, slave-grown sugar in one's tea was a necessity that virtually every English person took for granted. It has even been suggested that these extra calories, together with the need for money to satisfy the desire for sweetness, contributed to a more disciplined labor force in early industrial Britain.[25]

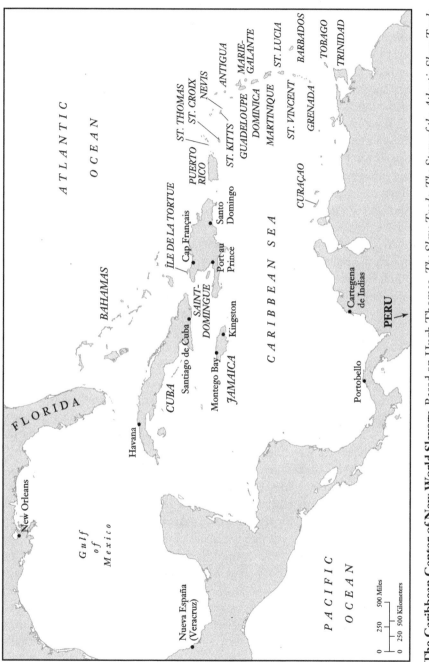

The Caribbean Center of New World Slavery. Based on Hugh Thomas, *The Slave Trade: The Story of the Atlantic Slave Trade* (New York: Simon & Schuster, 1997), 88.

Barbados led the way in this economic and dietary revolution, and the first momentous change occurred in only three years, from 1640 to 1643. There is a profound historical irony, or some might say evidence of God's design, in the fact that the birth of Britain's slave plantation economy in the West Indies coincided in time with Britain's domestic civil war of the 1640s, in which radical religious groups challenged all forms of oppression and privilege, including private property, and established the theological foundation for the much later antislavery movements.[26]

By 1640 leading planters recognized that Barbados stood in desperate need of a new crop; tobacco and even cotton brought little profit. As we have seen, Brazil had maintained a virtual monopoly on sugar production for Europe, but warfare and rebellion severely disrupted both Portuguese and Dutch efforts to meet the rising demand down to 1654, when the Portuguese finally expelled the Dutch. Although the Barbadian soil and climate were ideal for sugar cultivation, the English had no experience in producing such a commodity. Barbadian planters quickly learned the techniques from Hollanders, though the precise story is unclear. Some sugarcanes were brought in from Dutch Pernambuco, which a few English Barbadians had also visited, and according to one account, a planter named James Drax, of Anglo-Dutch background, brought a model of a sugar mill to Barbados from Holland.[27]

However the transfer was accomplished, Barbadians were producing sugar for Europe by 1643, and within seven years there was a tenfold increase in the value of plantation land. Dutch traders had a continuing partnership with the English in Barbados, acting as middlemen and offering in Holland the best refineries in Europe. When Dutch exiles arrived in the Caribbean from Brazil, they brought additional skills, experience, and capital for sugar production. The exodus from Brazil in 1654 also included thousands of Sephardic Jews, who had enjoyed relative religious freedom in Dutch Brazil as in Holland itself. Many of these Jews settled in such new Dutch colonies as Curaçao and Suriname. By 1680 there were even fifty-four Jewish households in Bridgetown, the only true urban center in Barbados, with a population of almost three thousand. Mostly urban merchants, these Jews, unlike their brethren in Suriname, never became members of the wealthy planter elite.[28]

Before long, about two hundred British sugar planters, with plantation units averaging two hundred acres, obtained the best of the limited acreage in Barbados. As a result, less successful proprietors, even those who purchased a few slaves, found themselves pushed onto small plots of marginal land, and in time increasing numbers of white farmers and servants began to emigrate from Barbados as the soaring demand for black slave labor totally transformed the island's demography.[29]

By 1680, a time when Virginia was just beginning to turn to African slave labor on a large scale, Barbadian society had become extremely hierarchical. From a broad base of nearly 40,000 black slaves the pyramid moved upward to 2,300 white servants, 1,000 small planters, and 175 big planters at the top. The population of Barbados still included some 20,000 whites, more than any British-American colony except Virginia and Massachusetts. But the small planter elite, in the words of the historian Richard S. Dunn, "held the best land, sold the most sugar, and monopolized the best offices. In only one generation these planters had turned their small island into an amazingly effective sugar-production machine and had built a social structure to rival the tradition-encrusted hierarchy of old England."[30]

As Dunn adds, these increasingly wealthy planters had also "made their tropical paradise almost uninhabitable. . . .Those who had money squandered it by overdressing, overeating, and overdrinking and by living in ornate English-style houses unsuited to the climate." Because the white elite hated and feared the masses of black captives they had surrounded themselves with, the goal of most successful planters was to escape from the West Indies and retire in England. Dunn concludes by saying sunny Barbados had become "the richest and yet in human terms the least successful colony in English America."[31] The slave colony of Barbados had lost most of the reassuring social and psychological boundaries of traditional societies.

Nevis, St. Christopher, Antigua, and other Leeward Islands to the north followed a similar pattern to that of Barbados, as did Jamaica, somewhat belatedly, a thousand miles to the west. Through the eighteenth and early nineteenth centuries an increasing number of plantation owners became "absentees," living and spending in Britain, where a few Barbados planters were knighted or received baronetcies. They hired professional "book-keepers" (managers) and overseers to manage their estates, men who were intent on maximizing plantation output and making a nest egg that would enable them to leave the tropics forever. Still, one should add that despite a significant white emigration from Barbados to North America, where Barbadians played a decisive role in founding South Carolina in 1679–80, that island had fewer absentee planters and a more settled English community than any of the other British West Indian colonies. Even in the late twentieth century one could see the effects of this enduring English culture and even find in the interior of the island descendants of "red-legs," or Scotch-Irish indentured servants, who were named for their sunburned legs below their clothed knees.

Although British Caribbean planters initially borrowed their sugar-making technology from Dutch and Portuguese Brazilians, the political culture of their slave plantations differed markedly from that in Brazil, where the wealthiest mill owners at least posed as patriarchs and community leaders, even though they too desired to make profits. British planters made little effort to conceal the fact that they were entrepreneurs whose primary goal in life was to make money, not to become resident seigneurs. The British sugar plantation became a purely capitalistic enterprise, not a quasi-seigneurial community with religious and social services that stimulated a surrounding economy. British planters were always on the lookout for cost-saving devices, such as partnerships and plantations that shared a common sugar-works.[32]

This business mentality eventually worked to the slaves' benefit in the late 1700s and early 1800s. British planters and their agents discovered that slave productivity could be greatly increased by eliminating the most cruel and grisly punishments and by offering various positive incentives, such as extra time for the slaves' own gardening and food production as well as local Sunday markets. British planters also tried to encourage more slave births and longevity, especially in response to the mounting English political pressure to abolish the Atlantic slave trade, followed from 1791 to 1804 by the terrifying Haitian Revolution. There is a danger, however, in exaggerating the humanitarian effects of the so-called amelioration policy in the British colonies that was supposed to follow the abolition in 1808 of further slave imports from Africa. Slavery was still slavery, even if some reformers proposed calling slaves "assistant planters."[33]

The early nineteenth century did witness dramatic increases in British West Indian slave productivity and, especially on smaller islands like Barbados, an impressive decline in the rates of slave mortality and a corresponding increase in slave fertility, caused in part by a decrease in the percentage of African-born slaves. In fact, in striking contrast to Cuba and Brazil, the slave populations of a very few British colonies like Barbados and the Bahamas actually achieved a natural positive growth rate just before emancipation in 1834 (well over a century after a positive growth rate began among slaves in Virginia). A similar transformation occurred more gradually among the creole, or Caribbean-born, slaves in Jamaica.[34]

In 1682 a Capuchin missionary reported that Brazilian planters considered a slave who lasted seven years to have lived very long.[35] While that estimate is misleading, it is true that a Brazilian sugar planter could double his investment if an adult slave lived and worked for only five years.[36] Similar cynical statements about the short life spans of African slaves became common in the late-seventeenth- and eighteenth-century British and French Caribbean, where planters often affirmed that it was much cheaper to work slaves to death and buy replacements from Africa than to "breed" new generations of slaves from infancy. Charles Pennell, the British consul at Salvador, reported in 1827 that Brazilian sugar planters calculated that it was cheaper to buy imported African slaves than to pay the costs of raising black children to adulthood. Such conditions provided little incentive to take on the risks and costs of raising Brazilian-born slaves for fourteen or more years before they became productive workers.[37]

Demographic historians have convincingly objected that some of this rhetoric distorts the actual shift toward higher fertility and lower mortality among creole (plantation-born) slaves, as opposed to slaves imported from Africa, who were more vulnerable to a new disease environment. Throughout the New World, slaves' life expectancy was a good bit longer than seven years, though in Brazil and much of the Caribbean, unlike the United States and earlier British North American colonies, slaves never achieved a positive growth rate that would have lessened the system's dependence on continuing importations from Africa. In northeastern Brazil, in the late eighteenth century, a slave's life expectancy at birth was approximately twenty-three years, or twelve years less than that of an American slave in 1850.[38]

Historians have long debated the reasons for this high slave mortality and low level of births in different New World colonies. The issue is highly complex because there are so many variables, from the sex ratio (sometimes two or even three males for every female on Brazilian sugar plantations) and age structure of the slave population to the incidence of tetanus when the infants' umbilical cords were cut with instruments contaminated by the manure of oxen or horses that were unknown in sub-Saharan Africa (because the disease was spread elsewhere among livestock by the tsetse fly). Yet aside from such technical medical issues, including diet, diseases, lowland or swampy locations, and possible male infertility, it seems clear that the hard-pressed gang labor used in sugar cultivation and milling was not conducive to long life spans.[39]

Certainly the high slave mortality in Brazil and Cuba persisted on through most of the nineteenth century, and slave life expectancy was markedly lower than in the United States. As we have seen, an illegal but massive slave trade from Africa to Brazil came to an end only in 1850, after decades of British bribes, naval blockades, and other coercion, and the illegal slave trade from Africa to the sugar plantations of Cuba persisted for another seventeen years.

Though planters in northeastern Brazil were no less eager for profits than were British planters in the Caribbean, they adopted something of the style of feudal lords living nobly in a Big House and presiding over a paternalistic community with many retainers as well as a church or chapel, court, and police force, to say nothing of wage-earning carpenters, blacksmiths, and even a doctor or lawyer. Like their Portuguese predecessors in the Atlantic islands, Brazilian sugar planters typically leased small units of their cane fields to tenant farmers, known as *lavradores de cana*.[40] Each *lavrador* supervised and usually owned a squad of slaves, ranging in number from a single digit to as many as thirty, and sent his harvested cane to his landlord's sugar works, eventually receiving a variable share of the output, fluctuating from one-third to as little as one-twentieth.[41]

These sugar farmers often thought of themselves as proto-planters and sometimes were even relatives of rich landlords who owned the *engenhos*, or plantations with sugar mills. The class of *lavradores* included wealthy widows and priests as well as poorer sharecroppers. Despite some evidence of upward mobility, the latter had little chance of becoming landed mill-owners. Until the late eighteenth century, *lavradores de cana* were exclusively white. Eventually, small numbers of free mulattoes, often slaveholders, became sugar farmers linked to *engenhos*, but in the nineteenth century the class and status of *lavradores* suffered an irreversible decline.

In one sense the very existence of such sugar farmers as dependent intermediaries between seigneurial planters and a slave labor force perpetuated the complex boundaries of medieval European society. Such continuities are also symbolized by the historian Stuart B. Schwartz's description of the ritual that preceded the beginning of the sugar harvest in early August each year:

> At the mill itself, slaves and free persons gathered to hear the prayers and observe the sprinkling of holy water on the mill. With a signal, the mill was set in motion, and the [parish] priest and the owner passed the first canes through the rollers. The slaves took the matter no less seriously than their masters. Slaves refused to work if the mill was not blessed, and during the ceremony they often pressed forward to receive some drops of holy water on their bodies.[42]

Yet Schwartz also emphasizes that despite these traditions of paternalistic patronage, fealty, and religious observance, "such attitudes did not mean that slaveholders in Brazil were kinder in their treatment of bondsmen than were 'capitalistic' slaveholders of nineteenth-century Mississippi."[43] As we have already seen, and as Schwartz reaffirms, the drive for profit and the methods of sugar production led to a process that "closely resembled the modern industrial assembly line.... The labor was exhausting.... The nighttime scenes of boiling cauldrons, the whirring mill, and the sweating bodies caused more than one observer to evoke the image of hell." Numerous travelers and commentators stressed the lack of restraint or interference with the savage punishment of Brazilian slaves, who (reminding us of the treatment of slaves in ancient Rome) "were burned or scorched with hot wax, branded on face or chest, tortured with hot irons, had their ears or noses lopped off, or suffered sexually related barbarities as the result of jealousy." That said, in contrast to slavery in North America and in most Caribbean colonies, the extreme exploitation of slaves "was set in an ideological context in which the metaphors of family, obligation, fealty, and clientage predominated."[44]

Brazil's immense size, like that of the United States, reveals the extraordinary diversity and adaptability of racial slavery in the New World. The ordeal slaves endured on the sugar plantations of Bahia and Pernambuco bore little resemblance to the life of urban slaves in such expanding nineteenth-century cities as Rio de Janeiro. Urban household slaves shared some of the status of their wealthy or poor owners. Others worked in factories or as boatmen, fishermen, porters, craftsmen, carpenters, midwives, and musicians. A very few slaves became the owners of their own slaves and other property, but many urban slaves were not spared from public whippings, chain gangs, or sale at large public markets.[45]

The adaptability of slave labor is also dramatized by Brazil's great gold rush, which began in 1693 when large gold deposits were discovered in Minas Gerais, some two hundred miles inland and north of Rio de Janeiro. The urgent need for the use of slave labor in placer mining brought in some eighty thousand black bondspeople and stimulated a major increase in the price of slaves even in the northeast. Given the disorder of a mining boom, some slaves were able to obtain their own gold, buy their freedom, and even become rich. Yet in Minas Gerais the heads of fugitive slaves were posted along the roadsides.

In the last third of the eighteenth century a particularly harsh and semi-industrial form of slavery began to develop in Brazil's southernmost states, Rio Grande do Sul and Santa Catarina. In this region a grazing and ranching economy led to the large-scale production of leather and jerked beef. While a negative and stereotyped view of people of African descent pervaded all of Brazil (and all of the slave societies of the New World), a virulent form of racism emerged in the nineteenth century in this southern part of the nation.[46]

The nineteenth century brought a still different use and form of black slavery as a great coffee boom exploded in the inland valleys of south-central Brazil. A growing international demand for coffee triggered a new demand for slave labor, leading to the involuntary movement of tens of thousands of Afro-Brazilians from the northeast to inland regions extending from the province of Rio de Janeiro and Minas Gerais to Rio Claro, northwest of São Paulo, and even farther south. This internal slave trade became especially large after the ending in 1850 of the importation of slaves from Africa. Some of these highly priced coffee workers came from sugar plantations in the northeast. Because of the great distance of their travel, many were transported by ship—just as even larger numbers of North American slaves were shipped by sea from eastern coastal regions around the tip of Florida and then northwestward to New Orleans and the Old Southwest. Like the vast internal slave trade in the United States, the sales and forced transport in Brazil resulted in the breakup of black families and conditions of travel that matched the horrors of the original passage from Africa.

By the 1880s the four major coffee provinces held some 65 percent of Brazil's slaves. Though black slaves worked at a variety of occupations throughout Brazil, and sugar remained the most valuable export until the mid-nineteenth century, it was the southwestward-moving coffee boom that kept reinvigorating a tradition-bound institution.[47]

Compared to the British, French, Dutch, and especially Cuban nineteenth-century competition, the Brazilian sugar industry appeared increasingly stagnant and inefficient. While Brazilian sugar accounted for some 80 percent of all sugar sold in London in the 1630s, by 1690, when the market had become much larger, Brazilian sugar had fallen to only 10 percent of London's sales. Like that of the competitive British West Indies, Brazil's sugar industry received an enormous boost from the Haitian Revolution's destruction of the plantation economy of Saint-Domingue. Then Brazil may have profited even more from Britain's decision to emancipate nearly eight hundred thousand slaves, an action that brought a fatal drop after 1838 in the output of the British sugar colonies. The same events helped to stimulate a thriving and expanding slave economy in Spanish Cuba. By the mid-nineteenth century most of the world's cane sugar flowed from the coerced labor of black slaves in Cuba. Yet by that time European beet sugar, supplemented by cane sugar from Asian countries, was beginning to increase the overall supply, a fact that pointed to a critical long-term decline in the price of sugar during the later nineteenth century.[48]

Beginning in the 1960s, historians have demolished the myths that Brazilian slavery was benign or humane and that Brazil was relatively free from racism. It is true that partly because of the shortage of white women, coupled with the Moorish-Christian heritage of the Iberian Peninsula, racial intermixture was much more widely and openly accepted than in North America. Despite the Spanish and Portuguese early expulsion of Jews and Moriscos, and despite the Inquisition's obsession with purity of blood, Iberians, unlike the English, had lived for many centuries with a kind of multiculturalism and even with the domestic presence of many black slaves. It is therefore not surprising that in Brazil male slaveowners were much more likely than their North American counterparts to free black or especially mulatto lovers as well as their own colored children.

Nevertheless, most free colored people had been born free, and few slaves working on rural plantations had a chance of gaining freedom, even after a law of 1871 provided for the eventual emancipation of the children of slaves, who were to remain in a state of semibondage until age twenty-one.[49] Certainly slave revolts and escapes to *quilombos*, or hidden settlements of fugitive slaves, had been more common than in North America (a subject we shall turn to in Chapter Eleven). As I have suggested, Brazilian historians have also documented, especially in southern Brazil, extreme forms of racial prejudice coupled with the view that slaves were mere instruments of production, mostly lacking in human personality. As in other New World slave societies, Brazil's culture and institutions were geared to the maintenance of a highly exploitative system of labor, to the preservation of public security, and to the perpetuation of power in the hands of a white ruling caste.[50]

Some historians would argue that the dehumanization of slavery reached its most extreme form in the British, French, and Dutch Caribbean, a conclusion I will soon question. It is surely true that when the proportion of slaves in a given colony could rise to 90 percent or more, the usual boundaries of human society evaporated as the whole society became oriented to the twin goals of lowering production costs and increasing output. In most of the Caribbean there were no sectors of society that were truly independent from sugar production—no countervailing or moderating pressures, at least within the white "free world." Even within the growing society of "free coloreds," mostly children or descendants of white planters, there were many who aspired to enter the class of landowners and even slave-owning planters. In French Saint-Domingue, in 1789, free colored planters may well have owned as many as one hundred thousand, or one-quarter, of the colony's slaves.[51]

Moreover, the political structure of the older British colonies removed the slaves and their owners even further from the mother country's surveillance or control. As in Virginia, the power of a royal governor, usually close to the planter elite, was balanced by a locally elected assembly dominated by the planter class. In England itself, the planters' and slave merchants' interests were long protected by agents or lobbyists who could exert considerable influence in Parliament. Especially after imperial interference triggered the American Revolution and the loss of the United States, Britain became extremely cautious about various forms of colonial intervention, a point reinforced by West Indian threats of secession when Parliament began to consider the possibility of abolishing the African slave trade.

For us today, it is almost incomprehensible that a few whites could control tens or even hundreds of thousands of black slaves in the rural areas of small, isolated islands—an environment that seems even less secure than having a handful of white sailors controlling two hundred or three hundred African slaves chained below the deck of a slave ship. Try to imagine yourself, whatever your identity and skills, being given orders to supervise a hundred and fifty or even fifty black slaves, to ensure that they weed and fertilize long rows of sugar plants, working as hard as possible, without letup, in an orderly and regimented way. Would you use a whip? Would you try to delegate enforcement to a "driver"?

When, in 1945, I was an eighteen-year-old soldier on a troopship, I was given a billy club and ordered to descend into the lower depths of the ship, where for four hours I was to keep the "Negroes" (a worse word was probably used) from gambling. Until then I had not even known there were any black troops aboard (the army was, of course, "segregated"). When I at last arrived in what seemed like the lowest hold of a slave ship, one of the many crap shooters asked, "What you doin' down here, white boy?" I finally found a shadow in which to hide.[52]

This memory suggests another mental exercise. Imagine that you are a middle-aged slave artisan, long inured to the surrounding whites who think of themselves as a super-race. You detest the dehumanizing pressures of bondage and a world in which you, stamped with alleged inferiority, are continually being given orders. You empathize with the field hands who are flogged by drivers as they work long hours, but you have also learned how to flatter and even manipulate whites in various ways. If you learned that some of the slaves you hardly knew were planning an escape, or a revolt, and if you knew that you would be rewarded with freedom and a small artisan's shop if you unveiled the plot, would you consider such a choice? Aside from such a betrayal, would you try to improve your life through attempts at negotiation, resistance, building solidarity with fellow slaves, or acting alone?

In the Caribbean colonies black slaves were anything but docile or passive creatures; and when they outnumbered whites nine to one, they clearly possessed considerable power, even if they recognized, most of time, that armed rebellion was suicidal. Slavery has always depended, ultimately, on physical power, and Caribbean planters, no matter how small their numbers, could always summon armed troops who had no compunctions about mass slaughter.

Recent historiography has moved beyond the two simplistic views that blacks must either have been brainwashed, passive victims, stunned into happily obeying whatever whites commanded; or, more popular after the mid-1960s, revolutionaries constantly plotting to overthrow an intolerably oppressive system. It is easy for us to forget that throughout thousands of years of history, the great majority of human beings were essentially forced to do hard, menial labor and to accept unscalable hierarchies of power. No less relevant is the "mystery" of control and discipline in armies and navies throughout history. Soldiers and sailors have often been treated like slaves, and many have been coerced, duped, or drafted into service. Yet revolts and even desertion have been relatively rare; the majority of such men have obeyed orders and have even been willing to risk their lives for their comrades or to fight for a variety of "causes."

Whatever can be learned from such examples, there is abundant evidence that in the Caribbean especially, where slaves formed a decisive majority, they engaged in continuing negotiations, testing the multiple boundaries between field and household slaves, drivers, overseers, and the master class. The goals sought in such bargaining had little to do with the issue of abstract freedom. Slaves sought more land for growing their own provisions, or more time free from plantation labor, or monetary rewards for special service, or freedom to run and manage their own market exchanges, or the right to conduct their own burials, marriages, and religious services (especially in Virginia following the Great Awakenings of the mid-eighteenth and early nineteenth centuries).

Though West Indian slaves knew all too well that they lived and worked in societies based on violence and torture, they found surprising room for maneuver and for the creation of rich African-Caribbean cultures.[53] With this in mind, and remembering that blacks sometimes outnumbered whites by as much as nine to one, it is easy to understand why slave insurrections were much more frequent in the Caribbean than in North America,[54] and why, if an African slave had been given an informed choice of location, he or she might well have preferred Jamaica to most parts of North America. In Jamaica such a slave would be surrounded by his or her own people, would share in their developing culture, and might even have an opportunity to escape to a protected maroon community. In North America the same African would be outnumbered by whites and placed under their constant supervision, care, and control.

6

Slavery in Colonial North America

ALTHOUGH HISTORIES OF SLAVERY in North America have usually begun with the famous sale in 1619 of twenty "negars" by a Dutch ship captain to some English settlers in Jamestown, Virginia, we now know that some blacks had arrived in Jamestown even earlier and that African slaves had appeared in Spanish Florida as early as the 1560s. Even more telling, by the mid-1600s, when the sugar revolution was beginning to transform the important English colony of Barbados, the Dutch in New Netherland, which was to become England's New York in 1664, were far more dependent on black slave labor than were the English in Virginia and Maryland![1] Racial slavery became embedded in the Americas in diverse and unpredictable ways.

Because human life is so extraordinarily complex, any overview of American slavery must move beyond official restrictive laws and leave some room for slaves who rented out their labor, slaves who employed white workers as they transported cargoes on Mississippi River boats, and even slave doctors and midwives who treated upper-class white patients.[2] Thanks to the enormous scholarly research of the past two or three decades, one can find exceptions to virtually any generalization made about slave occupations, treatment, families, resistance, population growth, and many other matters. Nevertheless, slavery was always slavery in the sense of defining and selling human beings as salable property; privileges of any sort could and often did disappear as fast as a flash of lightning. Much of the diversity and complexity stems from the all-important paradox that, as the historian Philip D. Morgan has eloquently put it, slaves actively participated in their destiny *and* were victims of a brutal, dehumanizing system. Subject to grinding daily exploitation, caught in the grip of powerful forces that were often beyond their power to control, slaves nevertheless strove to create order in their lives, to preserve their humanity, to achieve dignity, and to sustain dreams of a better future.[3]

Since almost two-thirds of the history of North American slavery occurred before the American Revolution, not even counting Spanish Florida, it is highly misleading to think of all slavery in America in terms of cotton plantations in Mississippi in the 1850s. In this chapter we will examine in some detail the evolution of slavery in three of the following four geographic colonial regions.

First is the often ignored North, where slaves worked in agricultural and urban employments from the Delaware River to the Canadian Maritime Provinces, but where a true plantation system failed to develop. Second is land facing and encircling Chesapeake Bay and extending into Virginia's piedmont. By the time of America's War of Independence, Virginia and Maryland contained over one-half of the nation's slaves and nearly one-third of the total colonial population. Thus by 1775 two out of every five Virginians was a black slave.[4] Though the original demand for slave labor focused on the production of tobacco, a decline in profits from tobacco led in the eighteenth century to the increasing use of slave labor, especially in inland farming, for the planting, care, and harvesting of corn and grains. As urban centers like Richmond and Baltimore grew in the post-Revolutionary era, owners also made profitable use of slave labor in iron manufacture, shipbuilding, mining, and other industries.

In the third distinct region, the Carolina and Georgia lowcountry, plantations originally modeled on the Caribbean prospered by producing rice and, for a briefer period, indigo, for the dying of textiles. By the late eighteenth century many planters turned to high-grade "Sea Island cotton" along the coast. Then the perfection of the cotton gin and screw press gave a tremendous stimulus to the cultivation of short-staple cotton, which revolutionized the British and American textile industries and eventually spread westward from inland Georgia and South Carolina to Alabama, Mississippi, Louisiana, Arkansas, and Texas.

The fourth region, Spanish Florida and French Louisiana, was of minor economic importance until those territories were annexed to the United States in the nineteenth century and will thus be only mentioned here. Spanish Florida, which fell under British rule from 1763 to 1783, was especially notable for its raids against its northern neighbors and its role as a refuge for fugitive slaves from South Carolina and Georgia. French Louisiana, which was ruled by Spain from 1763 to 1800, moved toward the development of a plantation system, but this goal was impeded by a combination of slave insurrection and Native American attacks.

To turn, then, to the history of colonies north of the Chesapeake, we should first observe that no British founders of North American colonies, except for South Carolina, intended to create slave societies. By the 1600s Britain had been relatively free from slavery for four centuries, and in New England, despite the enslavement of hostile Indians, many of whom were shipped to the West Indies and even exchanged for black slaves, there was some resistance to the entry of slaves from Africa. In 1646 Puritan magistrates in Massachusetts were shocked to discover that some New Englanders had raided an African village and seized two Africans by treachery and violence and had then brought them across the Atlantic for sale in Massachusetts. The General Court condemned this "haynos and crying sinn of man stealing" and ordered the two blacks to be returned to their native land. Six years later, Rhode Island passed a law condemning the practice of enslaving Negroes for life and ordered that any slaves brought "within the liberties of this Collonie" be set free after a term of ten years, "as the manner is with the English servants." But the law was not enforced, and by the 1690s New England laws were beginning to regulate the conduct of black slaves.[5]

Despite the rarity and novelty of moral repudiations of slavery before the mid-eighteenth century, two early antislavery documents serve as examples of the misgivings felt by a few Northern colonists before racial slavery became both widely accepted and deeply entrenched. In 1688, at a time when English and American Quakers were becoming increasingly involved as the owners and traders of slaves in the Atlantic Slave System, four Dutch-speaking Quaker immigrants in Germantown, Pennsylvania, signed and sent a strongly worded antislavery petition to their local Quaker Monthly Meeting, which then referred it to higher governing groups, which quietly buried it. The Germantown Quakers condemned the purchase of African slaves as the equivalent of purchasing stolen goods and asserted that the blacks had a perfect right to liberty since slaveholding was based on sheer physical force and thus violated divine law.

The authors stressed the hypocrisy of a model Quaker colony robbing and selling men against their will. As refugees from Europe's religious intolerance, these radical Quakers compared those who were "oppressed for conscience sake" with "these oppressed who are a black colour." It was highly disturbing, they stressed, to think that countries in Europe would hear that Quakers in Pennsylvania "doe here handle men as they handle there the cattle."[6] Unfortunately, this early document was unknown to such later Quaker abolitionists as John Woolman and Anthony Benezet and was not rediscovered until the nineteenth century.[7]

A second revealing example is the pamphlet *The Selling of Joseph*, written by the prominent Massachusetts jurist Samuel Sewall and published in 1700, a time when Boston was receiving a sudden influx of African slaves. Sewall had recently and publicly asked for forgiveness for his sins in helping in 1692 to condemn to death the so-called witches in Salem. In 1700, after he had upheld a young male slave's claim to freedom, Sewall was plunged into a long and bitter debate with the slave's former owner, a prosperous merchant and landowner who had served as a judge himself. While Sewall's tract displayed some doubts and uncertainty, and asserted that freed blacks could never "embody with us, and grow up into orderly Families, to the Peopling of the land: but [must] still remain in our Body Politick as a kind of extravasat Blood," he did attack the injustice of enslaving fellow humans who, like the Puritans, were also the descendants of Adam and Eve. This break with the traditional Christian acceptance of slavery as a necessary part of a sinful world would help to inspire such later radical opponents of slavery as the apocalyptic Quaker Benjamin Lay.[8]

Unlike the Puritan founders of New England, the Dutch who began settling Manhattan and the larger New Netherland in the early seventeenth century could not rely on the immigration of thousands of their native people. There were no Dutch Puritans eager to escape religious persecution and to found model societies. The influx of black slaves—and by 1630 there were free blacks as well as slaves in white settlements on both sides of the Hudson River—can be seen as a part of an almost cosmic movement of Africans to virtually every New World colony as European proprietors compared the promising wealth to be derived from almost infinite amounts of fertile land with the dire shortage of productive labor. But the fact that black slaves would constitute about 20 percent of the population of New Amsterdam by the end of Dutch rule in 1664 was also related to such fortuitous events as Holland's long war for independence from Spain, which led to the capture of many slaves on Spanish and Portuguese ships and to Holland's temporary dominance of the Atlantic slave trade, following the Dutch capture of Elmina and other slave-trading centers on the West African coast. Governor Peter Stuyvesant and local Dutch merchants even sold many slaves to Virginia and Maryland.[9]

While New Amsterdam's small population included settlers from various European nations, the colony failed to attract many indentured servants to do the heaviest and least desirable kinds of work. It is thus revealing that the Dutch West India Company, which ran the colony, tried over a period of thirty years to attract prosperous farmers from Holland by promising to import and sell African slaves as a means of ensuring a cheap supply of labor. As it happened, the lives of white workers who did emigrate, and who were typically bound to work for a master for seven years, were not significantly different from the lives of most slaves, whose status under the Dutch was more ambiguous than it would be under the English in the later seventeenth and the eighteenth centuries. Many of the slaves, having lived in the West Indies, the Spanish colonies, or the Atlantic islands, were multilingual, familiar with Christian cultures, and adept at acquiring privileges and negotiating for their freedom or "half-freedom."[10] When the English acquired New Amsterdam (renamed New York) in 1664, 75 of the city's 375 blacks were free. Partly owing to Dutch uncertainties over the effects of baptism (and the Dutch ended religious conversions by 1655), blacks had come to see Christian conversion as a means of appealing for liberation.[11] Hair and skin color had not yet become a symbol of inherent degradation and a screen to obscure the realities of economic dependence and exploitation.

The discovery in 1991 of the underground burial site of some twenty thousand African Americans in lower Manhattan underscored the central economic importance of black slavery in Northern cities as well as in many rural areas. It is highly misleading to look only at the small percentage of slaves in eighteenth-century colony-wide populations—for example, 8 percent in New Jersey or under 4 percent in Connecticut. In the mid-eighteenth century black slaves performed at least one-third of all physical labor in New York City.[12] By 1750 slaves made up 34 percent of the population of Kings County (Brooklyn) and 18 percent of New York County. Rural slaves, who were indispensable in supplying the towns and cities with food, were concentrated in highly productive farms on Long Island, in northern New Jersey, and in the great manors and estates along the Hudson Valley. Even the more prosperous white *tenant* farmers owned slaves on the great manors of families like the Livingstons, the Van Rensselaers, and the Schuylers (somewhat analogous to the *lavradores de cana* in Brazil, though on a much smaller scale).

Sojourner Truth, the famous nineteenth-century black abolitionist and feminist, had been born a slave on such a manor in Ulster County, New York, a state in which slavery persisted until 1827. Connecticut, which outlawed slavery only in 1848, contained an estimated 5,698 blacks, most of them slaves, in 1770, compared to 25 in Vermont, 4,754 in Massachusetts, 10,460 in New Jersey, and 19,062 in New York.[13] Connecticut even contained a large slave plantation-like farm in New London County. Neighboring Rhode Islanders, who dominated the eighteenth-century Northern slave trade with Africa, used many slaves in a horse-breeding industry that also led to great estates modeled on those of West India planters. Amazingly, in 1770 there were more black slaves in the colony of New York than in Georgia.[14]

What mainly distinguished Northern "societies with slaves" from Southern, West Indian, and Brazilian "slave societies" was the lack of staple crops for export, such as tobacco, sugar, and rice, and thus the fact that their economies were not truly based on slave labor. Yet the whites in charge of much

Northern farming, stock-raising, and rural industry, including tanneries, salt works, and iron furnaces, employed many slaves and also shipped their products to West Indian markets.

In eighteenth-century New York and East Jersey, slaves could be found working at virtually every kind of job from building roads, clearing land, cutting timber for firewood, and herding cattle and pigs in the countryside to such urban skilled occupations as carpentry, shoemaking, blacksmithing, stoneworking, butchering, milling, weaving, and even goldsmithing. Moreover, slaves and free blacks were especially evident as dockworkers, boat pilots, and sailors. Slaves not only worked alongside white laborers but were often leased out by their owners or even allowed to hire out their labor and skills at considerable profit for their owners. Above all, ownership of black slaves as household servants became almost universal among the white elite and even the prosperous middle class from Boston to Baltimore. In British Manhattan, some 40 percent of white households owned slaves. By the 1760s black slaves constituted three-quarters of Philadelphia's servant population.[15]

Blacks of both sexes, living in back rooms, lofts, attics, or alley shacks, were engaged throughout the North in cooking their owners' meals, housecleaning, caring for children, tending gardens and stables, and running errands. There was thus far less racial segregation by residence in the mid-eighteenth century than in the early twenty-first century. One should also stress that in the North most labor was performed by whites, including apprentices and bound servants, and that very few whites were exempt from work. This meant that slaves often worked alongside white farmers. There were no planters, as in the Caribbean, lolling in hammocks while guzzling rum and giving orders to black stewards. Nor, as in Brazil, were there squads of slaves transporting privileged whites in sedan chairs.

Some travelers were shocked when they discovered that American families were "too familiar" with their slaves. Madam Sarah Kemble Knight, for example, was filled with disgust at the sight of a Connecticut family that allowed their slaves to sit and eat with them at the family table, "(as they say to save time) and into the [same] dish goes the black hoof as freely as the white hand."[16] Yet evidence from the Manhattan African Burial Ground also suggests a level of strenuous overwork for black children as well as adults.

The social heterogeneity of New York and East Jersey helps to explain many of the surprising aspects of racial slavery from the time when the Dutch used slaves as the executioners of white criminals and as soldiers to fight off Indian attacks to the early English period when at least thirty free blacks had become independent landowners in Manhattan. A large cultural gap separated the many acculturated or semiacculturated slaves who drank, gambled, and danced with lower-class whites at various taverns and alehouses, or who were persuaded to become serious members of the white Lutheran or

Moravian churches, from the slaves who after 1712 began arriving in increasing numbers directly from Africa. Yet the white decision to import more Africans and to reduce the number of slaves, especially Spanish-speaking slaves, from the tumultuous West Indies was in part a response to the threat of slave unity and violent resistance signified by the New York conspiracies of 1712 and 1741. Many whites considered Africans less dangerous than blacks from the Caribbean.[17]

Ironically, though two Spanish-speaking slaves were involved in the insurrection of 1712, most of the rebels, who set fire to a building and then ambushed and killed nine of the whites who rushed to extinguish the fire, were "Koromantine" and "Pawpaw" Africans (whites used such labels, often connected with the original African point of departure). The much larger 1741 conspiracy not only included a group of Spanish blacks recently captured by a British ship in the Caribbean but coincided with a major English war with Spain and France and with news of a succession of slave insurrections in the West Indies. When the plot was suddenly uncovered, implicating Irish, French, Dutch, and even English conspirators, the whites could thus be seen and punished as traitors who were guilty of a criminal attempt to aid the Spanish and French Catholic cause by plotting with African and American-born slaves to burn down the city of New York. As the hysteria mounted, nearly two hundred slaves were arrested and interrogated, and thirteen blacks were burned at the stake and seventeen were hanged. The number of executions exceeded those at the Salem witchcraft debacle, and seventy blacks were deported to the Caribbean.[18]

Strangely enough, while convicted slaves were being hanged and burned at the stake (and hanging corpses were allowed to rot in the summer heat), the transatlantic wars, which included many Native Americans on different sides, created a drastic labor shortage in the Middle Colonies and thus a greater demand for slave labor directly from Africa. The arrival of increasing numbers of Africans renewed among slaves a knowledge of West African traditions and cultures. This development helps to explain the use of the word "African" as free blacks in the late eighteenth century began to name their first churches and fraternal societies. And both slaves and free blacks injected African elements into their celebration of such Christian rituals as Pinkster, originally the Dutch version of Pentecost, the time when Christ's apostles received the Holy Spirit, a holy day that some slaves had known in Africa as a result of the teachings of Catholic missionaries. On such occasions in New Amsterdam blacks and whites had drunk wine together and had danced to African as well as Dutch music. There was also racial mixing and partying in the merry celebration of the later "Negro Election Day," which included symbolic role reversals—typified by parades in which blacks dressed in their masters' clothing and rode their masters' horses—as well as the election of black kings and judges.[19]

Despite such events and the racial mingling at cockfights and fairs, white workers increasingly resented the competition from slave workers and the way that slavery degraded most forms of labor. Skilled workers were especially sensitive to this kind of stigma by the mid-1700s, a time when Northerners began a long quest to ennoble physical labor. (As I will argue in Chapter Twelve, this growing desire helped prepare the way for antislavery movements.) In urban centers like Boston, New York, and Philadelphia, this gradual reevaluation of white "ambition," leading to the birth of what would later be termed "the American dream," helped to weaken the foundations of slavery. It also intensified the fumes of racism.

We seem to find an opposite climate of opinion when we move to the Chesapeake in the mid-seventeenth century. Many decades ago historians were astonished to discover relative racial tolerance and flexibility, especially in Virginia's Northampton County, on the eastern shore of Chesapeake Bay. For example, among various examples of self-purchase, the owner of the slave Francis Payne agreed in 1643 to give him full control over the crops he grew in exchange for delivery at the end of the season of a stipulated amount of tobacco and corn. Then the owner signed a contract allowing Payne to buy his freedom by using his profits to purchase for his owner three white male servants. Over a period of thirteen years Payne succeeded not only in buying white indentured servants but in paying for his own freedom as well as that of his wife and children. Moreover, Payne's wife may even have been white. Other black slaves, such as Anthony Johnson, bought their own freedom, acquired sizable estates of land, conducted business with white planters and merchants, and even purchased their own slaves or white servants.[20]

No one knows how typical or atypical Northampton County may have been, since we lack such detailed records for other parts of Virginia and Maryland. Nevertheless, there is evidence to support the conclusion of the historian Ira Berlin: "Throughout the seventeenth and into the first decades of the eighteenth century, black and white servants ran away together, slept together, and upon occasion, stood shoulder to shoulder against . . . established authority."[21] Since class divisions were then more meaningful than race, it appears that in the mid-1600s one-quarter to one-third of the illegitimate children born to white females, mostly indentured servants, were mulattoes.[22] In both Virginia and Maryland the legislatures became increasingly alarmed by this sexual intermixture and passed laws against racial intermarriage as well as punishments for white women who gave birth to mulatto children—"that abominable mixture and spurious issue," as the Virginia Assembly put it. Nothing was said about black women who gave birth to the mulatto children of white fathers. Even though laws beginning in the 1660s imposed increasing restrictions on black slaves and by 1691 prohibited Virginian masters from manumitting their slaves unless they paid for the expulsion of such freedpeople from the colony, it is clear that in the earlier period blacks had become acculturated and even integrated to a degree in the Chesapeake societies.[23]

To understand this anomaly and the later shift to a sharp and almost unbridgeable separation between black slaves and poor whites, one must look at Anglo-American demography and the changing sources of the Chesapeake region's labor supply from the founding of Jamestown in 1607. During the 1500s and early 1600s England's population grew far more rapidly than the economy did. Given the resulting shortage of jobs, the roads became crowded with so-called vagabonds in search of work, food, or things to steal. The government's enclosure policy greatly exacerbated this problem by seizing public lands and evicting whole villages of people. One of the motives for New World colonization was the desire of authorities to rid England of the so-called dangerous classes while also discovering precious metals and producing the kinds of commodities England had been forced to import from foreign countries.

Despite the arrival of a handful of black slaves, English indentured servants more than met the demand for labor stimulated by Virginia's great tobacco boom of 1620s. With contracts covering from five to seven years, or longer for minors, such white servants could be sold and resold; their conditions of life were closer to those of a slave than to a servant in England. Some indentured servants did later manage to acquire farms and even servants of their own, but, given their appalling mortality from disease in the early decades, such servants had only a fifty-fifty chance of surviving a five-year term and collecting their "freedom dues," a small cash payment or a piece of land. Until the last third of the seventeenth century, there were enough English teenagers, farm laborers, and artisans who were deluded by the colonizers' propaganda to meet the Chesapeake colonies' expanding demand for labor. The flow of such voluntary immigrants was supplemented by the deportation of petty criminals, including debtors, as well as Irish prisoners and rebellious Scots.

This picture began to change dramatically when the English birthrate fell, especially during the Civil War of the 1640s, when wages rose in England, and when the city of London needed rebuilding after the disastrous fire of 1666. Moreover, many English migrants or potential migrants found such new colonies as Pennsylvania, New York, and South Carolina more promising. Thus, beginning in the mid-1670s, large landowners in Virginia and Maryland, many of whom said they would prefer white indentured servants, turned to the purchase of slaves directly from Africa. In the late 1670s white servants still outnumbered black slaves four to one, but by the early

1690s slaves outnumbered white servants nearly four to one. The slave ships would drop anchor near the houses of great planters along shores of the York, Rappahannock, or Potomac rivers. Wealthy planters, like Robert "King" Carter, who owned the local iron foundry, flour mill, and blacksmith shop, would then board a ship, examine slaves, and agree for a 10 percent commission to sell the captive Africans to his neighbors.

In time most of the Africans, who were disproportionately male, would be sent to more distant inland quarters where they could more easily be supervised and controlled as they performed heavy labor in clearing forests and new land before the planting of tobacco. Planters tended to view Africans as strange and bestial savages who needed to be confined in sex-segregated barracks and stripped of any family or ethnic identity. But while planters and overseers subjected such slaves to much whipping and other violence, and required them to work in regimented gangs following the pace of the fastest laborer, it also became essential for the slaves to acquire certain skills. It should be stressed that the cultivation of tobacco required careful, painstaking effort, which included care in worming and topping each plant, in cutting the stalks, and then in curing the leaves in tobacco houses. Slaves also devoted much time to raising livestock and growing edible crops.

A small number of native-born blacks, or Creoles, had much greater opportunities of entering various artisan trades. Some became carpenters, wheelwrights, tanners, tailors, blacksmiths, masons, architects, silversmiths, and furniture makers; a few others appeared as household servants or even managers of estates, familiar with their masters' language and mores, which they could often turn to their own advantage. This creation of a slave hierarchy helped to counteract any sense of effective black unity. (While it is true that conspiracies were often led by privileged slaves, they were also usually revealed by privileged slaves.) In colonial Virginia masters were especially inclined to encourage slave skills and also, when labor demands diminished, to "hire out" some slaves for wages that would increase the owners' profits.[24]

A few slaves, particularly Africans, escaped at least temporarily to Virginia's swamps, but such maronage was not nearly as successful as the maroon settlements in the Caribbean, Brazil, and even Florida. Partly for demographic and geographic reasons, whites in the Chesapeake could exercise much stricter racial control than whites in the West Indies or South Carolina.

Of course, many slaves became fugitives, as in all slave-owning regions, but the posted advertisements often suggested a paternalistic desire on the part of owners to negotiate with such slaves, who may often have absconded precisely for such bargaining. Some masters advertised, in effect, "Jack, if you return home, you'll be free to choose a new owner!" Or an owner would promise forgiveness or, in order to avoid a capital loss, would promise "to return you to your former beloved owner." Masters also expressed outrage over the "insolence" or the "saucy and impudent tongue" of a given runaway. Ads often repeated the charge that a slave had been "ungrateful," or had run away "without any cause." We also find the complaint that "he has great notions of freedom." It is clear that African-born slaves were more quickly spotted and apprehended, but the ads show a special concern over light-skinned slaves who might "pass" as whites, and over literate blacks who forged passes and were "quick talking" or "fluent and skilled." Fugitives often headed for towns where they might blend into a community of free blacks, but when habitual runaways were apprehended, they faced severe punishment and often sale to an unsuspecting buyer. Robert "King" Carter bragged about curing a fugitive slave by cutting off his toes.[25]

In the colonial Chesapeake such brutal punishments (and there were worse dismemberments) coexisted with a kind of white paternalism that was rare in regions farther south. Masters supervised and intervened in most areas of black life, giving their slaves orders, advice, instruction, and all kinds of attention. This involvement was partly the result of demography. Even in tidewater Virginia, in the 1730s, only about 30 percent of adult slaves lived on plantations with ten or more slaves, and another 30 percent lived on units with only one or two slaves. This low density could sometimes lead to very close ties between slaves and white families, as can be seen in the nineteenth century in letters sent back to Virginia from slaves who had been freed and sent to Liberia. Philip D. Morgan has even found a case in the late 1780s in which a fugitive slave named Peter "was in cahoots with his former master to defraud would-be owners of slaves."[26]

In Virginia, in contrast to slave societies farther south and to most examples of slavery in human history, the slave population began by the 1720s to increase rapidly by natural means. While the reasons for this natural expansion are complex— and the positive growth rate would soon distinguish North American slavery in general— most Virginia planters were eager to encourage this result, which brought them significant capital gains on their investments. They promoted slave marriages and often showed sympathy to the slaves' appeals to allow husbands and wives to reside on the same plantation. For a time there may have been a conscious effort to import more female slaves in order to achieve a balanced sex ratio. By the 1760s this rapid growth enabled Virginia's leaders to take a seemingly high moral ground against the Atlantic slave trade. Their efforts to restrict or even halt further importations from Africa were disallowed by the Crown.

One must also add that many Virginia planters and political leaders were becoming by the 1760s increasingly terrified by the rapid growth of the slave population at time when no one could foresee the vast future markets for slaves in Kentucky and the Southwest. Like some white Cubans in the nineteenth century, many Virginians expressed alarm over the growing density of blacks in eastern counties and over the danger, as the famous Virginian William Byrd had earlier put it, that their colony would "some time or other be confirmd [*sic*] by the Name of New Guinea."[27]

This understanding that Virginia should be thought of and preserved as a colony for *whites* helps to explain a fundamental difference from South Carolina or especially such Caribbean societies as the French colony of Saint-Domingue, where whites allied themselves with a large free colored class, which enjoyed privileges denied to blacks. In the Chesapeake, *all* people of African ancestry were increasingly seen and defined as "Negro." This arbitrary racial classification gradually became the norm for most of the United States. And this basic dualism or division between whites and Negroes, between the free and the slave, leads to the argument of the historian Edmund S. Morgan that Virginia's slavery and racism became, paradoxically, the social and ideological basis for America's dedication to freedom and equality.

One should remember that Virginia, which in the 1770s had a larger population than New York and Pennsylvania combined, produced the leaders who wrote the Declaration of Independence and the first state constitution, who led in winning the war against Britain, and who did the most in drafting the Constitution and setting in motion the new federal government. Morgan's thesis in *American Slavery, American Freedom* is best summarized by his own words and is important enough to deserve a long and vivid quotation:

> Racism thus absorbed in Virginia the fear and contempt that men in England, whether Whig or Tory, monarchist or republican, felt for the inarticulate lower classes. Racism made it possible for white Virginians to develop a devotion to the equality that English republicans had declared to be the soul of liberty. There were too few free poor on hand to matter. And by lumping Indians, mulattoes, and Negroes in a single pariah class, Virginians had paved the way for a similar lumping of small and large planters in a single master class.
>
> Virginians knew that the members of this class were not in fact equal, either in property or in virtue, just as they knew that Negroes, mulattoes, and Indians were not one and the same. But the forces which dictated that Virginians see Negroes, mulattoes, and Indians as one also dictated that they see large and small planters as one. Racism became an essential, if unacknowledged, ingredient of the republican ideology that enabled Virginians to lead the nation.[28]

Thus it was the collective degradation of "outsider people" that enabled Virginians to free white Americans from the traditional constraints of class conflict and pursue the dream of a new era of liberty and equality.

The far more conservative culture of the Deep South centered in South Carolina, which by 1690 had been partly settled by whites and black slaves from Barbados and in that year instituted a slave code adapted from Barbados. Though North Carolina imported some slaves directly from Africa in the 1680s, the colony had a much slower development than South Carolina as a result of its treacherous coastline and lack of harbors. Even by 1730 North Carolina contained no more than six thousand settlers.

Georgia, only founded in the 1730s, was originally intended to be an asylum for poor whites, orphans, and debtors. Some pragmatic English philanthropists and statesmen envisioned a colony that would enable members of the unproductive classes to supply England with silk, wine, and other products for which England had long depended on Catholic Europe. No less important, Georgia would be a buffer state between South Carolina and Spanish Florida. Since there was a fear that the presence of slaves would deter the immigration of white workers and also present the Spanish in Florida with an opportunity to incite insurrections, a special law of 1735 "for rendering the Colony of George more Defencible" prohibited slavery. James Oglethorpe, the main founder and original governor of Georgia, owned slaves on a Carolina plantation and was also a high officer of the slave-trading Royal African Company. Nevertheless, he and some of the first settlers struggled to maintain Georgia as the only free-soil region in the Western Hemisphere. By 1749, however, so many slaves had been smuggled into the colony and so many settlers had come to see the necessity of slave labor that the trustees decided to ask for a repeal of the "antislavery" law. Despite some futile attempts at imperial regulation, Georgia finally emerged as a slave society in which, like South Carolina, blacks outnumbered whites along the coast and in the islands just off the coast.[29]

Any foreign visitor to the colony of South Carolina would have been amazed by the differences between the lowcountry plantation districts producing rice and indigo, and urban Charlestown (later Charleston), which happened to be the port of entry for 40 percent of all African slaves imported into North America before 1808. Few whites could have understood the Gullah language, which for hundreds of years enabled the coastal plantation slaves to communicate with one another. This creole mixture of Elizabethan English and such African languages as Fante, Igbo, Yoruba, Ewe, and Mandinka developed through trial and error and was part of a rich evolving culture of music, art, food, and storytellers. Individual Gullah words (*buh*, brother; *sabe*, save; *bress*, bless; *attuh*, after) might have been easier for a visitor to understand than the spoken flow of cadence and accents. Such creole languages with distinctive grammatical forms were common in the Caribbean and Brazil.[30]

In Charlestown, on the other hand, slaves tended to be highly acculturated and skilled at interacting with colonial whites and their institutions. Slave women, for example, dominated Charlestown's central market, selling beef, pork, fish, and vegetables. No other townspeople handled so much cash, a large percentage of which went to their owners. Some slaves lived on their own, apart from their masters, and hired out their own time or even opened shops, paying a portion of their earnings for this de facto freedom. In Charlestown one could also find slaves who had become tailors, carpenters, cabinetmakers, shipwrights, and barrelmakers, often earning and keeping or hiding impressive profits. Others worked as butchers, fishermen, and porters.[31]

Tenuous privileges and initiatives were not limited to towns and to American-born slaves. Some white planters seem to have known that they could greatly benefit from the skills of African-born slaves who were familiar with the flora and fauna of semitropical coastal regions, and above all with the techniques of rice cultivation. As the historian Peter H. Wood has observed, "literally hundreds of black immigrants were more familiar with the planting, hoeing, processing, and cooking of rice than were the European settlers who purchased them." During the pioneering period of settlement, a few former Africans even acquired managerial positions as they showed whites how to develop a lowland cattle industry and helped plan as well as construct dikes to control the irrigation of low-lying rice fields.[32] It should be added that despite some unenforced laws, many rural slaves supplemented their diet by regular hunting, fishing, and gardening.

Despite constant complaints from whites about the independence of black slaves, for the first half-century of South Carolina's history black soldiers proved to be indispensable in repelling attacks from the west by Indians and from the south by the Spanish. When white colonists recognized that their "Province is in Danger of being Lost & our Lives are Threatened," they saw the necessity of giving slaves lances and guns as well as drums to beat in order to communicate and arouse a will to fight. One planter who noted that the militia included "a considerable Number of active, able Negro Slaves" added that any slave "who in the Time of an Invasion, kills an Enemy" would be freed and his master recompensed. While only a few slaves seem to have been liberated, hundreds fought the powerful Indian attacks in the Tuscarora War of 1711–12 and the Yemasee War of 1715. If some blacks deserted and joined the enemy, others were captured and tortured along with the white prisoners.[33]

Too little attention has been given to the long and extremely complex relationship between blacks and Indians, especially in the South. Indians long helped whites track down fugitive slaves hidden in forests and swamps and also helped suppress slave uprisings. Some Indians profited from stealing and selling slaves, actions encouraged by the British in the American Revolution. In 1783, for example, Alexander McGillivray, a mixed-blood Indian chief, sent stolen slaves to Pensacola, Florida, for shipment to Jamaica. Whites kept reminding slaves of such hazards and used blacks as troops when raiding

Indian camps. In general, the major Southern tribes accepted racial slavery, acquired and traded many black slaves, adopted laws based on those of the Southern states, and even transported slaves westward when the Indians were forced to move to what became Oklahoma. Yet despite the Indians' racist laws, there was much intermixture, and large numbers of African Americans eventually became proud of their Indian ancestry.

To return to the remarkable disorder and fluidity of South Carolina's early pioneering period, before the truly massive importation of Africans began, one can often learn much from protests and grievances, as in the following complaint of some white petitioners in 1706: "For at this last election, Jews, Strangers, Sailors, Servants, Negroes & almost every French Man in Craven & Berkly County came down to elect, & their votes were taken." In other words, a region that would ultimately become the most ardently proslavery and racist center in America seems at one time to have allowed blacks, perhaps even slaves, to vote, along with a motley assortment of settlers.[34]

If some slaves willingly joined backwoods expeditions against the Cherokees, others appeared in frontier gangs of banditti or escaped to Spanish Florida, where many found refuge among the Seminoles. It was not until the 1760s that a "Regulator Movement" emerged to combat frontier crime and employ force to capture a labor force for farmers in the upcountry who aspired to become planters.

Much earlier, blacks in the lowcountry had suffered a dramatic change of status after a few white planters made spectacular fortunes from growing and exporting rice and indigo. As the eighteenth century progressed, rich planters congregated in Charlestown or traveled to the North during the malaria season, entrusting their estates to stewards, overseers, and black drivers. This success led South Carolina planters to invest in massive purchases of slaves from Africa, mostly males, in order to maximize production. Increasing slave mortality (the result of a higher percentage of Africans), coupled with the imbalanced sex ratio, helps to explain why South Carolina's black population—unlike that in the Chesapeake—did not achieve a positive growth rate until shortly before the American Revolution.

In one respect South Carolina's slaveholders were more integrated with their blacks than were their Virginian counterparts: They were far more inclined to acknowledge their sexual relations with black women and sometimes freed their own mulatto offspring. Thus a somewhat privileged caste emerged, as in the Caribbean, though on a much smaller scale, made up of light-skinned people of color. Eventually, local courts even bestowed the status of "white" on some families who were visibly colored but known to be "of good character." Since there were also people of color who unofficially "passed" into the racially elite white category, an unknown number of later "white" South Carolinians actually had some African ancestry.[35]

While the great majority of South Carolina's slaves were subjected to a harsh regimen of labor, they had far more social and cultural autonomy in the colonial period than slaves in the Chesapeake. According to Philip D. Morgan, this flexibility and relative lack of restraint probably gave the owners of urban slaves greater rather than less physical security: "The ability of slaves to visit a relative, or go underground probably siphoned off as much potential disorder as it created. . . . [S]lavery in Charleston [where the majority of slaves were women] was more, not less, secure than it was in the surrounding countryside."[36]

On the lowcountry plantations, in striking contrast to other parts of the South, the "task system" became the norm. Each day an overseer or some other authority would call for a precise work objective: so many rows of rice to sow, so much grain to thresh. In practice, this system gave most slaves the incentive to work hard and complete the "task" by early afternoon, allowing them to leave the fields, return home, and tend their own gardens and livestock. Surprisingly, it was common for masters and other whites to buy from slaves such produce as melons, corn, peas, potatoes, fish, poultry and even the slaves' own-grown rice and small livestock.[37] This measure of control over their own lives also enabled lowland slaves, at least those who remained in coastal South Carolina, to accumulate a good bit of personal property. Despite the absence of legal title, some slave families passed on to their descendants household goods, linens, glassware, china, cows, pigs, ducks, guns, saddles, horses, and at least in one case, a personal slave named Tom.[38]

Such liberal-sounding customs were more than counterbalanced by the workings of positive law regarding human property and debt. As increasing numbers of slaveholders in the South took out mortgages on their slave property or faced bankruptcy, it became more and more common to see the spectacle of slaves being auctioned on courthouse steps. The multiplication of creditors with claims against the bankrupt and the deceased, to say nothing of the rising demand for slaves as settlement spread westward, meant that slave families were constantly broken and divided by greed as well as the workings of the law.

In the long era before the American Revolution, the greatest trial of the slave regime in the Deep South came in 1739, a time when blacks in South Carolina outnumbered whites almost two to one and when news of war between England and Spain meant that the Spanish in Florida would offer liberty to Carolinian slaves who could escape to the south. In what would be known as the Stono Rebellion, about twenty slaves broke into a store by the Stono River, seized arms, and killed two white storekeepers, whose heads were left on the store's front steps.

At this point a slave named Jemmy led the band southward to the beat of drums. While burning plantations, killing whites, and enlarging the rebel group to at least sixty, the rebels came close to capturing South Carolina's lieutenant governor. But accounts of this uprising often fail to mention that over thirty slaves were later rewarded for protecting their masters and fighting and killing some of the insurgents. The latter apparently included Africans, whereas the loyal slaves were more likely to be assimilated Creoles. Eventually, mounted and well-armed planters headed off and defeated the rebels. Scores of blacks were then executed.[39]

In 1740, partly as a result of the Stono uprising, South Carolina adopted a new, harsher slave code and cut back temporarily on importing slaves from Africa. In the Deep South, we must conclude, slavery was successful; as an economic system, "it worked." Yet with or without rebellions, the system always involved brutal treatment and exploitation as well as a continual testing of limits.

7

The Problem of Slavery
in the American Revolution

MUCH AS SLAVERY in the United States was part of a larger Atlantic Slave System, so America's War of Independence was an outgrowth of Europe's Seven Years' War—from 1756 to 1763—and also a precursor or harbinger of the French and Haitian revolutions and of the subsequent Latin American wars for independence from Spain. Those foreign upheavals, really beginning with British and French fighting on the American frontier in 1755, had tremendous political, ideological, and territorial consequences for the future United States.

The Anglo-American defeat of the French in 1763, followed by the winning of American independence in 1783, opened the trans-Appalachian West to American settlement and to the rapid expansion of slavery into such regions as Kentucky and Tennessee. And the independence of the United States could not have been achieved without France's decisive intervention in the Revolutionary War, followed by Spain and Holland. It is noteworthy that all these European maritime powers owned slave colonies in the New World and had been deeply involved in both the Atlantic slave trade and the Atlantic Slave System. But the wars and revolutions led to wholly new boundaries that separated regimes dependent on slavery from regions that later became identified as "free soil."

Although the wars and revolutions during the fifty years from 1775 to 1825 had an immense impact on New World slavery, it is still debatable whether they put the institution on the path toward "ultimate extinction," to

use Lincoln's later phrase.[1] The French Revolution, beginning in 1789, ignited the almost continuous global and naval wars of the long period from
1793 to 1815, which ranged from India and Russia to the Caribbean, and
which then led to the Latin American wars of independence. Spain had been
an ally of France in the Seven Years' War and as a result had lost Florida, a
sparsely populated slave colony, to Britain, but Spain was on the winning
side in the American War of Independence, and thus regained Florida.[2] Yet
after this victory, Spain began a period of great decline, especially as a satel-
lite of Napoleonic France (Napoleon's brother Joseph became king of Spain
in 1807), culminating with its own internal revolution in 1820 and a French
invasion in 1823.

Following abortive insurrections from 1809 to 1816, today's nations of
Argentina, Paraguay, Uruguay, Chile, Peru, Bolivia, Ecuador, Venezuela,
Colombia, Mexico, and Central America had all achieved independence from
Spain by 1825. Brazil also declared its independence from Portugal in 1822.
As a consequence, by 1825 France, Spain, and Portugal had been removed as
major contenders in New World imperial rivalry (though Spain and France
still had important slaveholding colonies in the Caribbean, such as Cuba and
Martinique); moreover, America's Monroe Doctrine, informally backed by
the British navy, stood as a warning against any further intervention by European powers (including the so-called Holy Alliance or Quintuple Alliance).[3]

In 1775, at the start of the American Revolution, racial slavery, meaning
the slavery of Africans and people of African descent, was a legal institution
from Canada to Chile, and there were no restrictions on the expanding slave
trade from Africa to most parts of the New World, but by 1825 Britain and
the United States had outlawed their Atlantic slave trades (a commerce even
declared to be piracy by the United States). Britain had also negotiated treaties with France, Holland, Spain, and Portugal, with the effect that the only
remaining *legal* Atlantic slave trade involved ships sailing south of the equa-
tor, transporting slaves to Brazil, a commerce that was supposed to end in
1830. Unfortunately, as we have already seen with the case of the *Amistad*, in
Chapter One, an illegal slave trade was already flourishing and would continue for decades to deliver hundreds of thousands of African slaves to both
Brazil and Spanish Cuba.[4]

Yet by 1830 slavery itself had become illegal in Haiti, where by 1804
rebellious slaves had in effect freed themselves and terrified slaveholders
throughout the Hemisphere (as we shall see in Chapter Eight). Slaves had
also been freed in Central America. Mexico outlawed the institution in 1829.
Freedom also reigned in Maine, Massachusetts, New York, Ohio, Indiana,
and Illinois. By 1830 gradual emancipation laws had eroded the number of
slaves in Rhode Island (17), Connecticut (25), Pennsylvania (403), and New
Jersey (2,254)—as well as in most of Hispanic South America.[5]

In the British, French, Dutch, and Danish West Indies, slave labor was still highly productive, but especially in the British colonies the institution had been weakened by the decline of the slave population occasioned by the ending of British slave imports from Africa. Thus in 1830 slavery was a vital and thriving institution only in Brazil, Cuba, and the southern United States (as well as in the vast Islamic world, parts of India, and most of Africa). But despite all of this, from 1775 to 1825 the number of slaves in the New World had more than doubled, having tripled in the United States and increased sevenfold in Cuba.[6]

All of the New World slave societies had been highly vulnerable in wartime. Imagine trying to repel an enemy raid or invasion if you were living with what even medieval Italians termed "an enemy within," potential rebels not only in the fields but within your very households and bedrooms. Wise slaveholders knew that apparently loyal servants could become dangerous if the discipline and mystique of power and authority were weakened. Warfare always presented slaves with opportunities for escape, sometimes to maroon communities or behind enemy lines, though as valuable property slaves were also likely to be carried off by an invader and sold.

Warfare also raised the momentous issue of enlisting and even arming slaves when there was a desperate need for manpower. Though avoided by the Romans except in emergencies, this practice had long been universal in Muslim societies without undermining slavery and usually without toppling a given regime.[7] During the first five decades of South Carolina's history, as we have already noted, whites relied on the arming of trusted black slaves to beat off attacks by both Indians and Spaniards.[8] Beginning in 1795, despite the fears and opposition of planters and other Caribbean whites, the British increasingly and effectively resorted to black West Indian regiments to save their colonies as the Napoleonic war intensified in the Caribbean and as appalling numbers of white soldiers died of disease.

Black troops in British red coats, some of them veterans of the American Revolution and many of them enlisted soon after they disembarked from slave ships, did much to save the British regime of plantation slavery in the Caribbean.[9] Yet a few years later, in the South American wars of independence, the crucial need for black soldiers on both the Spanish and rebel sides ultimately undermined slavery in Venezuela and some other parts of Hispanic America.[10]

One crucial variable appears to be ideology—a system of beliefs, assumptions, values, and aspirations: in this case, the ideals of liberty and equality associated with secular republican principles as well as with the evangelical religious emphasis on every person's ability to triumph over sin, thanks to a capacity to receive divine grace based on the image of God within each human being. No such ideologies of liberty and equality were present in seventeenth-century Brazil when the warfare between the Dutch and Portuguese resulted in the flight and freedom of many slaves. Even major slave revolts from the time of Spartacus in republican Rome to the uprising of thousands of black slaves from 868 to 883 in what is now southern Iraq were not so far as we know directed against slavery in *principle*.

By the time of the American Revolution, however, the French, English, and Scottish Enlightenments, new forms of religious revivalism, and Anglo-American popular culture, typified in countless poems, essays and editorials, and even plays, had helped to push slavery in many Anglo-American minds beyond the boundaries of accepted exploitation.[11] As the white American colonists rose in revolt against what they perceived as a British effort to "enslave" them, many, especially in the North, could not escape from recognizing the "contradiction" of actually owning slaves. Meanwhile, though slaves throughout history had yearned for their *own* liberation (without questioning the institution of bondage), the American rhetoric and ideology of freedom brought a wholly new perspective to blacks whose ears—and whose understanding of contradictions—were at least as sensitive as those of their masters. If most slaves were illiterate, white leaders knew or soon discovered that the slaves' networks of communication passed on every kind of news almost as quickly as horses could gallop.[12]

Take, for example, a slave named Prince, who accompanied and cared for his master, Captain William Whipple, of Portsmouth, New Hampshire. Prince, who had seen combat and had overheard much revolutionary rhetoric, was one of the oarsmen who had rowed George Washington and his small party across the icy Delaware River in a sleet storm on Christmas night of 1776. The following summer, according to one account, Captain Whipple asked Prince why he was so moody and depressed. Prince responded, "Master, *you* are going to fight for your *liberty*, but I have none to fight for." At this point Whipple realized he would have to free Prince without delay.[13]

Obviously blacks could not rely on such individual motives and goodwill in response to Samuel Johnson's famous jibe at Americans: "How is it that we hear the loudest *yelps* for liberty among the drivers of negroes?" Yet owners manumitted a surprisingly large number of slaves during the Revolution or soon after. Even James Madison, after one of his slaves had been captured when escaping toward the British lines, could affirm that the young man had desired only "that liberty for which we have paid the price of so much blood, and have proclaimed so often to be [the] right, and worthy pursuit of every human being." Madison also concluded, as he promptly freed this man, that the would-be fugitive might "corrupt" other slaves if he were returned to the plantation. When another eminent Virginian first read the Declaration of

Independence, he interpreted it to mean that he would have to manumit all his slaves.[14]

As it happened, however, the connections between slavery and the white American leaders' ideals of freedom and independence were extremely complex, as the above example of Madison suggests. We have already taken note (in Chapter Six) of Edmund S. Morgan's brilliant thesis that in colonial Virginia slavery and racism became the social and ideological *basis* for America's dedication to freedom and equality for all whites. According to Morgan, racial slavery enabled Virginia's planter class to co-opt the poorer whites and thus perpetuate a highly exploitative and unequal society under the banner of republican liberty.[15]

This tradition helps to explain the paradox of a revolution that seemed to challenge slavery but in fact entrenched and strengthened it. As one historian has written, "in those Chesapeake districts where most blacks lived, slavery was more deeply rooted when Jefferson stepped down from the presidency [1809] than when he composed the Declaration of Independence [1776]."[16] The freeing of unprecedented numbers of slaves seemed to evoke a more pervasive and heightened prejudice against blacks, in the North as well as the South. Another historian has summed up the growing pattern of segregation:

> Shortly after the Revolution, Americans began haphazardly but with detectable acceleration to legislate Negroes into an ever-shrinking corner of the American community. . . .For ten years after the war there were some signs of relaxation, but then came a trend which included tighter restrictions upon slaves and especially free Negroes, separation of the races at places of social gathering, and the founding of all-Negro churches. The American interracial mold was hardening into its familiar ante-bellum shape.[17]

Yet from the very beginning of colonial protests against British imperial policies, antislavery writers drew parallels between the grievances of whites and those of blacks. Numerous pamphlets and sermons posed the central question: If Americans feared "enslavement" by encroaching British power, on what possible grounds could they justify keeping blacks as slaves? In the late 1760s Benjamin Rush, the noted physician and reformer, wrote to a French correspondent, "It would be useless for us to denounce the servitude to which the *Parliament of Great Britain* wishes to reduce us, while we continue to keep our fellow creatures in slavery just because their color is different from ours."[18]

While humans have always shown a remarkable capacity to accept glaring inconsistencies, especially in times of crisis, even Jefferson himself played with vehement antislavery rhetoric in his famous clause of the Declaration of

Independence that Congress suppressed. Jefferson even ties together the British enslavement of Africans with British oppression of colonial whites, charging that King George "has waged cruel war against human nature itself, violating the most sacred rights of life & liberty in the persons of a distant people [i.e., Africans] who never offended him, captivating & carrying them into slavery in another hemisphere, or to incur miserable death in their transportation thither." Jefferson then accuses the king of prostituting his veto power by disallowing all American legislative attempts to prohibit or restrain "this execrable commerce," since King George was "determined to keep open a market where MEN should be bought & sold."[19]

By 1773, a year that marked a record number of early antislavery pamphlets and sermons in America, a slave named Felix sent a petition on behalf of many slaves in Boston and the surrounding province to the governor and legislature of Massachusetts. Though he worded it with extreme deference and respect, Felix expressed the key point that slaves were embittered by the intolerable thought that no matter how well they behaved, "neither they, nor their Children to all Generations, shall ever be able to do, or to possess and enjoy any Thing, no, not even *Life itself*, but in a Manner as the *Beasts that perish*." Legally deprived of property, wives, children, a city, a country, slaves according to this petition were defined essentially as animals with no afterlife. Hence even a form of "relief" that would bring no "Wrong or Injury" to their masters would be "to us . . . as Life from the dead."[20]

As slaves and their supporters wrote increasing numbers of such petitions, the contradiction between the principles of the American Revolution and any defense of the dehumanizing institution of slavery became harder to evade, especially when slaves themselves began speaking the language of natural rights! This language had not been available even to the most rebellious slaves from Roman times to mid-eighteenth century Jamaica. But now, from Massachusetts to South Carolina, slaves heard whites shouting indignantly about British threats to liberty and the urgent need for resistance to prevent colonists from becoming "enslaved."

As early as the Stamp Act crisis of 1765, slaves in Charleston, South Carolina, watched white crowds parade around the homes of stamp officers, chanting, "Liberty! Liberty! and stamp'd paper." Soon a group of the city's slaves followed this model and began shouting, "Liberty! Liberty!"—a demonstration that evoked panic among some whites.[21] Nevertheless, as late as 1788 Robert Goodloe Harper, a young lawyer who had graduated from Princeton and would later join the Charleston Jacobin Club, could deliver a speech in the South Carolina backcountry asserting that slavery was a sin and that blacks were by nature equal to whites and even calling for Negro education. Though Harper stressed the temporary "necessity" of slavery on purely pragmatic grounds, his rejection of racial inequality might well have led in a later time to his being lynched. But in 1794 the backcountry South Carolinians elected him to Congress.[22]

When slaves in New England petitioned for emancipation they shrewdly emphasized their Christian faith, praised the whites for resisting British tyranny, and then appealed to the same natural rights as well as "the divine spirit of *freedom* [that] seems to fire every human breast on this continent." One group of Massachusetts slaves promised to wait patiently for their award of freedom, after which they would "from our joynt labours procure money to transport ourselves to some part of the Coast of *Africa*, where we propose a settlement," making no claims for compensation for past wrongs.[23] Though such blacks disavowed the violent means whites were using to resist the British, white Americans became increasingly aware of the danger of a revolution within the Revolution. And since only a minority of colonists actively supported the American Revolution, the manpower shortage highlighted the advantages if not the necessity of enlisting blacks as troops.

Blacks had fought or been used as support troops in many of the previous colonial wars, and some blacks appeared among the rebellious New Englanders at the battles of Lexington, Concord, and Bunker Hill.[24] But because of their fear of black insurrection, combined illogically with a racist stereotype of black cowardice, both George Washington, the slaveholding commander in chief of the Continental army, and Southerners within the Continental Congress initially opposed the enlistment of African Americans whether slave or free.[25] By 1777, however, the manpower shortage led various northern towns and states to enroll blacks in order to fill the troop quotas imposed by Congress. Rhode Island and Connecticut both formed all-black military units, and Rhode Island even enlisted 250 slaves with the promise of freedom in exchange for service. Some states even approved mixed biracial regiments. Later on, when France joined the war, a Black Brigade arrived from Saint-Domingue. It included a number of young men who would later become leaders in the Haitian Revolution.[26]

A critical turning point came late in 1778, when the British invaded Georgia in an all-out effort to enlist Loyalists and conquer the Southern states. Faced with this crisis, Isaac Huger, a wealthy brigadier general from South Carolina, proposed that the Continental Congress free and arm three thousand slaves in Georgia and South Carolina, a plan strongly endorsed and promoted by Henry Laurens, a South Carolinian member and former president of the Congress.

In mid-March 1779 Alexander Hamilton wrote to John Jay, president of the Continental Congress, eagerly recommending Laurens's young son, Colonel John Laurens, who was on his way to Congress and then to his native South Carolina, where he hoped to take command of the black battalions. Hamilton foresaw "much opposition from prejudice and self-interest":

The contempt we have been taught to entertain for the blacks, makes us fancy many things that are founded neither in reason nor experience; and an unwillingness to part with property of so valuable a kind will furnish a thousand arguments to show the impracticability or pernicious tendency of a scheme which requires such a sacrifice. But it should be considered, that if we do not make use of them [the slaves] in this way, the enemy probably will. . . . An essential part of the plan is to give them freedom with their muskets. This will secure their fidelity, animate their courage, and I believe will have a good influence upon those who remain, by opening a door to their emancipation.[27]

Upon the recommendation of a committee, Congress unanimously approved enlisting and arming some three thousand slave troops in South Carolina and Georgia. Congress agreed to compensate the slaves' owners, and at the war's end each slave who had served "well and faithfully" would be emancipated, would return his arms, and would receive fifty dollars as a bonus. Given the hopes Hamilton expressed to Jay, South Carolina's legislators may well have been right when they predicted that if this plan were carried out, the example of collective emancipation would undermine slavery in the Deep South. We should note that these two states, Georgia and South Carolina, later won momentous sanctions and protections for slavery in the Constitutional Convention and in the first federal Congress.

Despite the continuing lobbying of Henry Laurens's idealistic son, the South Carolina legislature kept rejecting the proposal, subordinating military needs to the protection of the slave labor system. Despite the precedents of arming slaves in early colonial times, for many of the Carolinians defeat and a return to British rule were preferable to a dependence on African or African American soldiers.[28]

Ironically, some British commanders came away from this bitter warfare in the South with precisely the opposite conclusion. Their willingness to rely on black soldiers in the American Revolution would later help them "save" the British slave colonies in the Caribbean by enlisting black West India regiments.

Yet Southern slavery might have disintegrated if the British government had approved the proposal by Lord Dunmore, the royal governor of Virginia, to conquer the South with an army of ten thousand blacks. Even earlier, in January 1775, an M.P. in the House of Commons had called for "humbling the high aristocratic spirit of Virginia and the southern colonies" by declaring a general emancipation of slaves. But England greatly feared the effects of any such move on its own West Indies, where Americans had already aroused alarm over a possible threat to incite slave insurrections. The British elites also understood that an all-out attack on one form of property could easily lead to an assault on all boundaries of privilege and social order, as envisioned by radical religious sects in Britain's seventeenth-century civil wars.

Moreover, Britain still led the world in its dominance of the African slave trade. The powerful British merchant community would never have tolerated any military measures such as Lieutenant Colonel Archibald Campbell's proposal to enlist, arm, and transport at least fourteen hundred West Indian slaves to the mainland colonies, where their very presence, according to Campbell, would induce 90 percent of America's slaves to desert their masters and destroy the economy.[29] British merchants knew that such an "insane plot" would mean an end to the production of rice, indigo, tobacco, and other commodities for Britain while wiping out the American market for British exports.

Again, one must stress that the revolutionary ideology of the later eighteenth century cast a wholly new perspective on such issues as the arming of slaves and slave revolts. Imagine how white listeners felt when one of the captured conspirators in Gabriel's planned slave insurrection of 1800, in Virginia, asserted that "I have nothing more to offer than what General Washington would have had to offer, had he been taken by the British and put on trial. I have adventured my life in endeavoring to obtain the liberty of my countrymen [i.e., African Americans], and am a willing sacrifice in their cause."[30] Clearly the idea of natural rights could not be monopolized by white Americans.

That said, we can only speculate on the outcome of the American Revolution if the situation had been similar to that in South America in the early nineteenth century, when Spain discovered that black troops were indispensable for crushing the first independence movements. In response, this meant that in Venezuela and Peru, in 1812 and 1814, the rebels were willing to promise freedom to any slave who would fight the Spaniards for ten years. Yet even in most of these emerging nations, in which the proportion of slaves was no greater than in the Northern states at the time of the American Revolution, the process of *gradual* emancipation took approximately as long as in New York State—that is, about thirty years (in New York from 1799 to 1827; in Venezuela [Gran Colombia] and Peru from the 1820s to the 1850s).[31]

Britain, when confronted by the rebellious American colonists, hoped to exploit their *fear* of slave revolts while also reassuring the large number of slaveholding Loyalists and wealthy Caribbean planters and merchants that *their* slave property would be secure. Despite this contradictory approach, which could be as self-defeating as the Patriot desire to resist British "enslavement" while defending racial slavery, the majority of American blacks probably hoped for a British victory. Such hopes were clearly nourished as word spread in late 1775 that Lord Dunmore, the royal governor of Virginia, had actually promised freedom to all blacks and indentured servants owned by rebels if they were "able and willing to bear Arms" and fled from their masters in order to join His Majesty's troops. (The fate of women and children was unclear.)

The beleaguered and desperate Dunmore was acting on his own initiative and had no intention of triggering a slave insurrection. Perhaps as many as a thousand blacks made their way to Dunmore's small army, stealing food, clothes, and jewelry before reaching his ships in Norfolk harbor. Although Dunmore's black and white troops were soon defeated at the Battle of Great Bridge, the response of American Patriots, especially in the South, was little short of hysterical.

The contradictions persisted. British military leaders tried to be sensitive to the interests of slaveholding Loyalists, who were actually given large numbers of slaves confiscated from the rebels. Nevertheless, in 1779, when Sir Henry Clinton was still at his headquarters in Philipsburg, New York, and about to launch his southern campaign, he made an offer of freedom somewhat similar to that of Dunmore's: All slaves captured while they were serving the rebels were to be sold for the benefit of their captors; but all slaves who deserted the rebels were given an assurance that was hardly clear: "full security to follow within these Lines, any Occupation which [they] shall think proper."

Clinton intended this Philipsburg proclamation to counteract the Patriots' military use of slaves and to provide needed labor for the British forces in the South, but many slaves interpreted it as an emancipation measure. In Georgia alone, some five thousand slaves, or one-third of the prewar slave population, escaped, leaving the economy in ruins and much of the black population without food. (Clinton actually attempted to stop this deluge of fugitives and ordered the return of many runaways to their owners.)[32]

The British eventually evacuated about ten thousand fugitives from Savannah and Charleston, and according to one estimate, South Carolina lost as many as twenty-five thousand slaves either through escape or death. As the historian Sylvia Frey puts it, "without meaning to do so, the British army had thus made the revolutionary war in Georgia a war about slavery."[33] This had the ironic effect of infuriating even Loyalist whites, intensifying white solidarity, and thus contributing to British defeats and to the ultimate collapse of the British cause in America.

The British invasion, occupation, and final withdrawal from the Southern states led to an estimated net loss of eighty thousand to one hundred thousand black slaves. Between four thousand and five thousand bedraggled blacks of all ages followed General Cornwallis's army across Virginia to the unexpected defeat at Yorktown. Even thirty of Thomas Jefferson's slaves joined the throng, and most white families along the way lost not only slaves but silk breeches, fancy jackets and shirts, silk corsets, and hats of all kinds worn by the slaves, some of whom thought they were heading to the Promised Land. In the Bible, the ancient Israelites also stripped the Egyptians of gold, silver, and clothing before heading for freedom in the Promised Land. The Egyptians supposedly consented to this restitution, since they were so eager to have the Jews leave and avoid further divine punishment; the British officers, on the contrary, fearing that their black "allies" would exhaust scarce provisions, used force to drive away "freed" slaves, many of whom died. But some blacks continued to fight. Years after the Revolution, black troops calling themselves "King of England Soldiers" continued to harass planters in South Carolina and Georgia.[34]

A large number of African Americans who were taken by the British ended up as slaves in the Bahamas, where they trebled the black population and initiated a new era of cotton production, though some freed blacks also founded communities in the same islands. Thousands of others, including slaves of Loyalists and the veterans of some black military units, found themselves enslaved in the British Caribbean. The British shipped the largest group of freed slaves to Nova Scotia. Given the poorest land on which to farm, most of these black colonists soon became sharecroppers or tenants, disdained and persecuted by the local white population.[35] John Clarkson, brother of the famous British abolitionist Thomas Clarkson and Britain's first governor of Sierra Leone, eventually secured a fleet of fifteen ships to transport over a thousand of these Nova Scotian (and New Brunswick) blacks to the supposedly free soil of Sierra Leone. Despite heavy mortality, these migrants created a coherent community united by American evangelical Christianity and Revolutionary ideology.

Meanwhile, by 1786 some twelve hundred other African American refugees struggled to find a means of living in London, a city that offered them little in the way of employment. Since the black immigrants did not qualify for any kind of welfare governed by a geographic parish, they were reduced to begging and became increasingly destitute. A "Committee to Aid the Black Poor," partly headed by the pioneer abolitionist Granville Sharp, provided some food and medical care and then in 1787 led the way in creating the African colony of Sierra Leone, which was planned by humanitarians as a model community that would provide a refuge as well as an economic alternative to the slave trade. When Sharp learned of the disastrous mortality of the first shipments of blacks from England to Sierra Leone, he blamed the losses on "the intemperance of the people, and their enervating indolence in consequence of it."[36]

Britain's removal of thousands of slaves or former slaves had the effect of committing the newly independent government of the United States to a defense and sanctioning of racial slavery as a consequence of its newly won "freedom." Since slaves were legally a form of property, the government felt compelled, in its earliest Anglo-American diplomacy, to demand either a return of the slaves or monetary compensation.[37] Moreover, the loss of so many slaves from the Deep South led to calls for reopening the slave trade from Africa. Georgia led the way in resuming such slave imports until 1798, when the Haitian Revolution underscored fears of acquiring too dense populations of black slaves.

Yet the American Revolution had the effect of committing the Northern states to eventual emancipation and thus to the beginning of an ominous division of "sections": slaveholding versus free soil. In eighteenth-century France and Britain, courts had gradually created models of free soil by depriving citizens of any legal grounds for forcibly retaining slaves brought in from abroad. While these legal decisions validated a long-existing longitudinal boundary between slavery and freedom drawn somewhere in the Atlantic, similar to the later latitudinal Mason-Dixon line within the United States, they did not affect British or French slave trading, or the legality of slavery in the colonies. "Free soil" regions meant something different in the United States since states were contiguous and not separated by thousands of miles of sea.

In 1777, early in the war, Vermont became the first region in the New World to outlaw slavery, in this instance by constitutional mandate. Massachusetts achieved almost "immediate emancipation" in the early 1780s by judicial decision, and New Hampshire followed suit. In 1780, when the outcome of the war was still uncertain, the Pennsylvania legislature became the first to adopt a law for the gradual emancipation of the newborn children and descendants of slaves. Though it became illegal to sell slaves outside the state, Pennsylvania's newspapers continued to run advertisements for the sale of slaves as late as 1820, and as we have seen, there were still some four hundred slaves in the state according to the census of 1830. In 1784 Connecticut and Rhode Island adopted similar measures. (During the war Connecticut's upper house had defeated a far more radical bill.) Slavery was more deeply entrenched in New York and New Jersey, in which even gradual abolition bills failed until 1799, in New York, and 1804, in New Jersey. Similar measures never passed the legislatures of Delaware and Maryland, though both states witnessed a drastic decline in the number of slaves and a related increase in the number of free blacks.

Although slavery was not of *central* importance to the Northern economy, as it was in most of the South, the institution did not decline or disappear in the North because it was uneconomical, unproductive, or a burden on the economy. Yet the methods adopted for abolition brought little if any economic sacrifice. Since only *future* generations were freed in the five states with the most to lose, and since the children of slaves were compelled to work for their mothers' owners until the children were in their twenties, the owners in effect received handsome compensation for the "loss" of this form of property. The economists Robert William Fogel and Stanley L. Engerman, in an elegant study of the Northern emancipation acts, concluded that they represented "philanthropy at bargain prices."[38]

Nevertheless, one should not dismiss the idealistic motives of early, mostly unrecognized abolitionists or the enduring effects of Revolutionary ideology. Though in Britain there was much continuity between the early, cautious, gradualist foes of slavery and the radical "immediatists" of the early 1830s, Americans, including later historians, largely ignored the early reformers and legislators who overcame formidable opposition, especially in New York and New Jersey. Much of this hostility to emancipation in any form arose from the widespread white fear that if blacks were released from the surveillance of bondage, their crime rate would soar and the costs of their maintenance would be transferred from their owners to the taxpayers responsible for what we would call local welfare.

Today we can see that such fears were based on a profound but unacknowledged racism that made the white fear of black crime and economic dependence almost universal. White authorities tended to exaggerate the number of serious black crimes and ignore the fact that most of the blacks housed in prisons, jails, and work houses had been convicted of petty theft. In actuality, "larger percentages of white prisoners were incarcerated for such violent crimes as murder (by a margin of about 5:3) and aggravated assault (by about 5:4)."[39] Negrophobic racism increased dramatically after the 1780s, which meant that white society in the North barred freed blacks from most occupations and professions, to say nothing of most schools and churches, except for a few segregated ones.[40]

There were, of course, some examples of extraordinary success, such as Philadelphia's black sailmaker James Forten, who acquired considerable wealth and helped to finance William Lloyd Garrison's *Liberator* and the antislavery movement of the 1830s, and the Massachusetts sailor Paul Cuffe, who became a successful shipowner.[41] African Americans in the North made remarkable progress in forming what they usually termed "African" churches and benevolent societies, but as free blacks migrated overwhelmingly into the cities of the North, they found themselves, in the words of one historian, "huddled in rotten shacks, crammed into narrow menial occupations; excluded from much of the city's life and activity; harassed and assaulted; mired in perpetual poverty and often unrelieved want."[42] They also faced continuing and increasing competition for jobs with such immigrant groups as the Irish.

Since racial exclusion also interacted with the rural slaves' lack of needed skills, "emancipation" and movement to a less oppressive urban environment meant, as another historian has put it, "stevedoring on the city's busy docks; digging graves, wells, and house foundations; and toiling as chimneysweeps,

ashmen, porters, waiters, bootblacks, and in the case of women, clothes wash-
ers. Many young men, perhaps as many as one of every four, made their
living at sea for at least a few years."[43] There was also the continuing danger
of being kidnapped and transported for sale in the South or even the Caribbean, something that urban abolitionist societies tried to prevent.[44]

Before leaving the Revolutionary and early national periods in the United
States, we should at least touch on the momentous question of "lost opportunities" and what I have termed elsewhere "the perishability of Revolutionary
time."[45] No one can doubt that the 1780s witnessed a great upsurge of antislavery fervor, in the Upper South as well as in the North, in Britain, and
even in parts of France. In the United States, with the exception of Georgia
and South Carolina, there was a broad commitment to end slave imports
from Africa. Though many planters in the Deep South were deeply concerned over their declining rice economy and their loss of slaves to the British, Americans in general expected that the federal government would outlaw
the slave trade in 1808, following the twenty-year restraint imposed by the
Constitution. Virginians, to be sure, were partly motivated by their own shift
toward the cultivation of corn, wheat, and other grains, and by their wish to
sell some of their growing surplus of slaves to the Deep South or Southwest.
Still, in 1782 Virginia passed a law that eased and even encouraged private
manumissions.

In 1784 the Continental Congress came within one vote of passing Jefferson's bill that purported to exclude slavery from the *entire* trans-Appalachian
territory—that is, from the territory that would become Alabama and Mississippi as well as from Kentucky and Ohio. While we should not exaggerate
the practical effectiveness of that measure, the vote would have been inconceivable twenty years later. And the Northwest Ordinance of 1787 did exclude the future entry of slaves into the western territory *north* of the Ohio
River, though, as future events would show, blacks would be brought in as de
facto slaves and struggles would be required to keep Indiana and especially
Illinois from becoming slave states.

No less significant is the fact that many national leaders including Washington, Franklin, Jefferson, Madison, Hamilton, John Adams, John Jay,
Gouverneur Morris, and Rufus King saw American slavery as an immense
problem, a curse, a blight, or a national disease. If the degree of their revul-
sion varied, they agreed that the nation would be much safer, purer, happier,
and better off without the racial slavery that they had inherited from previous generations and, some of them would emphasize, from *England*. Most of
them also believed that America would be an infinitely better and less complicated place without the African American population, which most white
leaders associated with all the defects, mistakes, sins, shortcomings, and animality of an otherwise almost perfect nation.

Nevertheless, as can be seen in Hamilton's 1779 letter to Jay, there was some genuine interest in laying a foundation for future emancipation. But even foundations can mean postponement. As Jefferson put it, at age forty-three, "we must await with patience the workings of an overruling providence, and hope that that is preparing deliverance of these our suffering brethren." Having failed to gain approval for an emancipation measure in his native Virginia, Jefferson felt that the time was simply "not ripe" for decisive action.[46] And as momentum grew in the economically troubled 1780s for a stronger and more centralized government, it became crystal clear that no Union would be possible unless the Northern states were prepared to sanction and even protect the South's most vulnerable institution.

Thus any serious push for even an eventual end to slavery would mean, by the loss of Union, that the Founding Fathers could take no immediate and effective actions to secure America's borders, or strengthen the nation's shaky credit, or attract foreign investment and diversify the economy. And though the Framers of the Constitution were determined to avoid the words "slave" and "slavery," which had long carried extremely negative connotations, they finally proved willing to meet most of the Southerners' demands.[47]

The fury and outrage with which Georgian and South Carolinian representatives in the First Congress, in 1790, reacted to respectful and cautiously worded antislavery petitions from Quakers and from the Pennsylvania Abolition Society were like a weathervane pointing toward the storms to come. The petition from the Pennsylvania Abolition Society, signed by its president, the elderly Benjamin Franklin, called on Congress to "step to the very verge of the power vested in you" for discouraging the slave trade and "to countenance the restoration of liberty to those unhappy men, who alone, in this land of freedom are degraded into perpetual bondage."

Congressman Thomas Tucker of South Carolina warned that any attempt to free Southern slaves by law would lead to civil war, and James Jackson of Georgia asserted that slavery was not only allowed by the Savior but positively commended by the Bible.[48] In reply, Franklin, shortly before his death, wrote a satirical letter to the *Federal Gazette*, putting parts of Jackson's speech in the mouth of a Muslim Algerian ruler defending the enslavement of Christians.

To plunge for a moment into the realm of the hypothetical: In 1860 and 1861 Virginia and the Upper South in general were very slow in following the Deep South in seceding from the Union, following Lincoln's election in 1860. In many ways the slaveholding states were not truly united. Therefore, one can only wonder what the United States might have been like if Georgia and South Carolina had joined the Caribbean colonies in *not* rebelling in the 1770s and in remaining part of the British Empire. This would surely have deepened the difficulties for British abolitionists but might possibly have saved the United States from a Civil War.

We can summarize the gains of the American Revolutionary period as follows: the immediate abolition of slavery in Massachusetts and northern New England, where the African American population was small but not insignificant; a commitment to gradual emancipation in the other Northern states and adjacent territories moving west from Ohio to the Mississippi River. This meant that opponents of slavery could reasonably count on a large expanse of free soil in future decades, presenting a potential peril to a South now marked off as a slaveholding land that might begin to shrink even further if Maryland, Delaware, Kentucky, or even Virginia were to follow the path of Pennsylvania, New York, and New Jersey (and, as we have seen, in parts of the North the percentage of slaves had been similar to that in parts of the Upper South).

Moreover, by 1798, when Georgia finally took action, all the Atlantic seaboard states had prohibited the importation of slaves from Africa or the Caribbean. This encouraging development was somewhat undermined by South Carolina five years later. Largely in response to the Louisiana Purchase of 1803 and to the expected demand for slaves in the West, South Carolina threw open its ports at the end of that year. By January 1, 1808, when the federal government finally outlawed the African slave trade, the state had imported some thirty-eight thousand slaves—more than in any previous decade. Still, the nation as a whole was shocked and angered by South Carolina's action (in part because whites did not want a nation with more and more blacks, enslaved or free).

Finally, and most important in the long run, was the Revolution's legacy of ideology—the popularization among blacks as well as whites of a belief in individual freedom and inalienable natural rights. The period from 1765 to the early 1790s produced countless numbers of tracts, pamphlets, broadsides, sermons, speeches, and editorials that challenged the basic core of slavery: the belief that human beings could be "animalized," that they could be degraded to the level of chattel property.

In some ways this Revolutionary ideology, epitomized by the opening lines of the Declaration of Independence, showed that the very idea of slavery is a fiction or fraud, since liberty and equality are fundamental rights that no one can legitimately lose. This mode of thinking would have as great an influence on the free black David Walker's *Appeal to the Coloured Citizens of the World* (1829) as on Abraham Lincoln's Gettysburg Address.[49] As nineteenth-century abolitionists and feminists would show, these values of the Revolutionary era were open to very radical interpretations and applications. They would be extraordinarily inspiring to some privileged slaves, to many free blacks, and to white abolitionists who fused religious zeal with a sense of irrevocable human equality.

8

The Impact of the French
and Haitian Revolutions

O~N~ JANUARY 2, 1893, the aging Frederick Douglass delivered an eloquent speech dedicating the Haitian Pavilion at the Chicago World's Fair, or "Columbian Exposition."[1] As a recent United States minister and consul general to Haiti and as an Exposition Commissioner of the Haitian government, Douglass had helped to plan the exhibits of the pavilion, which he called, following the Puritan John Winthrop (and, from the New Testament, Matthew 5:14) "a city set upon a hill." If few white Americans associated Haiti with a beacon of hope and salvation, it was a stroke of brilliance for the world's most famous former slave to reverse popular imagery regarding a famous part of the islands Columbus had "discovered" four centuries earlier.[2]

After discrediting the common stereotype that Haitians were lazy barbarians who devoted their time to voodoo and child sacrifice, Douglass looked back on the previous century of slave emancipation. Born a slave himself in 1818, he had won international fame as an abolitionist orator and writer and had become the most prominent black spokesman and statesman in the New World. Speaking, as he said, "for the Negro," Douglass had no difficulty in identifying the central event in the entire history of emancipation:

> We should not forget that the freedom you and I enjoy to-day; that the freedom that eight hundred thousand colored people enjoy in the British West Indies; the freedom that has come to the colored race the world over, is largely due to the brave stand taken by the black sons of Haiti ninety

years ago. When they struck for freedom . . . they struck for the freedom of every black man in the world.

Douglass acknowledged that blacks owed much to the American and British abolitionists and to the antislavery societies in various countries of the world, "but," he said, "we owe incomparably more to Haiti than to them all," for Haiti was "the original pioneer emancipator of the nineteenth century." It had been Haiti's mission to teach the world the dangers of slavery and the latent powers and capabilities of the black race. After the former slaves of Saint-Domingue had defeated fifty thousand of Napoleon's veteran troops and had established their own independent nation, the white world could never be the same. Until Haiti spoke, Douglass pointed out, "no Christian nation had abolished Negro slavery. . . . Until she spoke, the slave trade was sanctioned by all the Christian nations of the world, and our land of liberty and light included. . . . Until Haiti spoke, the church was silent, and the pulpit dumb."[3]

Douglass knew that history was more complex than that; he knew that if whites had seen Haiti as "a very hell of horrors" whose "very name was pronounced with a shudder," as he noted at the beginning of his speech, the revolution had inevitably had contradictory effects. As an abolitionist from the time he first began reading William Lloyd Garrison's *Liberator*, soon after escaping from slavery, Douglass had hardly mentioned the Haitian Revolution in his public speeches, debates, and interviews.[4] For numerous whites the Haitian Revolution reinforced the conviction that emancipation in any form would lead to economic ruin and to the indiscriminate massacre of white populations.

But Douglass's address of 1893 contained a profound truth. The Haitian Revolution was indeed a turning point in history. Like the Hiroshima bomb, its meaning could be rationalized or repressed but never really forgotten since it demonstrated the possible fate of every slaveholding society in the New World. The Haitian Revolution impinged in one way or another on the entire emancipation debate from the British parliamentary move in 1792 to outlaw the African slave trade to Brazil's final abolition of slavery ninety-six years later. Like the Exodus narrative in the Bible, the Haitian Revolution showed blacks that liberation was a possibility in historical time. Their condition was not an inescapable fate.

In the 1780s the French colony of Saint-Domingue, the western third of Hispaniola (or Santo Domingo) was the centerpiece of the Atlantic Slave System. It produced over half the world's coffee, mainly on smaller slave plantations in the south owned by free colored farmers, or lighter-skinned "*gens de couleur*." White planters owned and controlled the much larger sugar plantations in the North Province, and in 1787 Saint-Domingue exported almost as much sugar as Jamaica, Cuba, and Brazil combined.

Then the French Revolution ignited a massive slave insurrection and civil war, which from 1791 to 1804 destroyed this highly exploitative "pearl of the Antilles." The slaves and free descendants of slaves defeated not only their masters but the most formidable armies of Spain, Britain, and France. As Douglass put it, Haiti's freedom "was not given as a boon, but conquered as a right! Her people fought for it. They suffered for it, and thousands of them endured the most horrible tortures, and perished for it." Whereas the American Revolution had been led by what Douglass termed "the ruling race of the world," who "had the knowledge and character naturally inherited from long years of personal and political freedom," the Haitian rebels repre-sented a race that "stood before the world as the most abject, helpless, and degraded of mankind."[5]

This heroic achievement evoked little applause from whites, even those who rejoiced over European and Latin American movements of national liberation. Two notable exceptions deserve mention. When the revolution began, Abraham Bishop and Theodore Dwight were both young recent gradu-ates of Yale College, but Bishop was a Jeffersonian Republican while Dwight was a conservative Federalist and brother of the more famous Timothy Dwight, who later became president of Yale. As it happened, both Bishop and Theodore Dwight affirmed that the black slaves of Saint-Domingue were fighting for the same cause and principles that Americans had fought for in their own Revolution. Both men urged Americans to aid the black rebels.[6] But President Washington's administration was so convinced that the black revolution threatened vital American interests that it advanced the white colo-nists $726,000 for the purchase of arms, munitions, and supplies.[7]

In general, the Haitian Revolution reinforced the conviction (of slaveholders especially) that slave emancipation in any form would lead to economic disaster as well as the slaughter of whites. The waves of fear trav-eled even faster than the thousands of Dominguan refugees who streamed westward to Cuba and Jamaica and northward to Spanish Louisiana and the port cities and towns of the United States. Throughout the Americas plant-ers and government officials learned in the 1790s to live in a state of alert. The very words "Santo Domingo," which English-speakers used to refer to the doomed French colony Saint-Domingue, evoked at least a moment of alarm and terror in the minds of slaveholders throughout the hemisphere.

Sometimes this example of self-liberation was dismissed as the freakish result of French legislative and military blunders exacerbated by the subver-sive ideology of abolitionism and the tropical diseases that decimated British and French armies. Abolitionists, both contemporary and in later decades, vacillated between a policy of ignoring the explosive subject of Haiti and warning that insurrections and racial war would be inevitable unless the slaves were *peacefully* emancipated and converted into grateful free peasants.

Whether the Haitian Revolution hastened or delayed the numerous emancipations of the following century, imagery of the great upheaval hovered over the antislavery debates like a bloodstained ghost. No Internet was required to distribute the British West Indian Bryan Edwards's unforgettable descriptions of a white infant impaled on a stake, of white women being repeatedly raped on the corpses of their husbands and fathers, or of the fate of Madame Sejourné:

> This unfortunate woman (my hand trembles while I write) was far advanced in her pregnancy. The monsters, whose prisoner she was, having first murdered her husband in her presence, ripped her up alive, and threw the infant to the hogs.   —They then (how shall I relate it) sewed up the head of her murdered husband in ——!!!   —Such are thy triumphs, Philanthropy![8]

Similar imagery moved back and forth from the printed page to oral traditions. And both French and English publications made repeated use of animal imagery: When once aroused, blacks were savage, tigerlike men or ferocious beasts gorged with blood.

In human life, though, fear seldom overcomes greed. Planters in Cuba, Brazil, Jamaica, Trinidad, and South Carolina clamored for *more* African slaves who could help make up the deficit in the world's production of sugar and coffee left by the devastation of Saint-Domingue. The destruction of slavery in Saint-Domingue gave an immense stimulus to plantation slavery from neighboring Cuba and the British West Indies to far-off Brazil. Moreover, as we just briefly noted, in December 1803, just after the disease-ridden French army had finally capitulated to Jean-Jacques Dessalines's former slaves, South Carolina reopened the slave trade and in the next four years imported some thirty-eight thousand Africans. As Charleston's merchants well knew, the defeat of Napoleon's New World ambitions had opened the way for the Louisiana Purchase. This momentous event, combined with the productivity of the new cotton gin, ensured that American slavery could expand westward without foreign interference.[9]

Nevertheless, even Cuba, South Carolina, and other slave-importing regions sought to exclude bondsmen from those colonies in which blacks had been exposed to revolutionary ideas, such as Saint-Domingue, Guadeloupe, and Martinique. Although slave insurrections had usually been associated with a labor force containing a high proportion of recently imported Africans, white leaders now became far more fearful of blacks who had been contaminated by French or abolitionist conceptions of liberty. Yet many of the French refugees who escaped from Saint-Domingue took at least some household slaves with them.

In Britain and the United States, abolitionists argued that slavery itself was the obvious cause of slave revolts. Early in 1792 the British abolitionist leader Thomas Clarkson insisted that while the French Revolution had presented the slaves with an opportunity to vindicate their humanity, the insurrection in Saint-Domingue could be attributed only to the brutal slave trade and the oppressive system it produced. Far from being an argument against Britain's petitions against the slave trade, Clarkson contended, the events in Saint-Domingue showed that it was sheer madness for the British to continue transporting Africans, who, having "the passions of men," would sooner or later avenge their wrongs.[10]

Such reasoning was clearly influential in the United States, where planters could rely on a rapid natural increase in the slave population and where opposition to further slave importation had won sanction from the War of Independence.[11] The nation as a whole was outraged and alarmed by South Carolina's reopening of the slave trade in 1803. The Haitian Revolution thus strengthened the political argument for pressing Congress to outlaw the American slave trade in 1807, the earliest date allowed by the Constitution. The Haitian example, reinforced in 1800 and 1802 by major slave conspiracies in Virginia, also led to laws restricting manumission and nourished interest in deporting free blacks to some distant colony.[12]

But what led in the first place to the conflagration in Saint-Domingue? For many decades the colony had seemed far more stable than neighboring Jamaica. With respect to the French Revolution, it is a fairly self-evident principle that when a nation is absorbed with a major domestic crisis, especially a crisis that explodes into revolution, little attention will be given to foreign policy or the management of distant colonies. As the French Estates General gave way to the Constituent Assembly, in the spring of 1789, domestic issues inevitably pushed colonial affairs to the extreme margins of concern.

Nevertheless, responsible leaders could hardly forget that the French government, whose bankruptcy ignited the revolutionary crisis, drew crucial revenue from its slave colonies. In addition, millions of French jobs, especially in port cities like Bordeaux, depended on the Atlantic slave trade and the stability of the slave system. Saint-Domingue alone, with some 465,000 slaves by 1789, accounted for about 40 percent of the total value of France's foreign trade and was responsible for the livelihood of many thousands of French workers.[13] Finally, as tensions and conflicts arose between colonial governments and the metropolis, some leaders feared that France, having lost Canada in 1763, might find that its far richer Caribbean colonies would follow the example of the British colonies immediately south of Canada and secede.

These basic economic and political realities help to explain why, despite all the radical rhetoric and radical actions in France, the Constituent Assembly— in power from the spring of 1789 to September 30, 1791—refused to consider petitions against the slave trade submitted by the abolitionist society, the Société des Amis des Noirs. By the same token, the French slave trade continued to receive an official subsidy until 1793, that is, even after the abolition of the monarchy and the execution of Louis XVI, and two years after the start of the massive slave insurrection in Saint-Domingue![14]

From the outset, French colonial issues were complicated by the contested status of free blacks and *gens de couleur*. (The freed population included some people of pure African descent, like Toussaint Louverture.) In Saint-Domingue the number of these free coloreds approximated the number of whites; they greatly outnumbered whites in the South and West provinces and included many slave-owning coffee planters.

In the West Indies, free blacks and coloreds generally supported the slave regime (as had the freed slaves in Rome, some of whom became slaveowners, and in the premodern world in general). In Saint-Domingue's North Province many people of color had become indispensable as managers of sugar estates. As members of the militia and especially the rural police, they provided security forces that captured runaway slaves, kept the maroons at bay, and preserved the colony's peace. A few of the free coloreds became quite wealthy; as a group, they owned at least one hundred thousand slaves. The elite free blacks and coloreds generally sent their children to France for education. Enough of them remained in France to form a significant community, symbolized by their Société des Colons Américains (the word "American" being reserved for colonists of mixed blood, as distinct from "Europeans" or "Africans").[15]

Understandably, the free coloreds in Saint-Domingue deeply resented the indignities and discriminations that were part of white efforts to reduce them to the position of an undercaste. From their first organized protests in Saint-Domingue, freedmen demanded an equal right to participate in the system, so that wealth rather than race would be the criterion of status. Yet local laws, based on what the Jamaican Assembly termed the "corruption of blood," tried to prohibit them from wearing European dress, from taking the title of "monsieur" or "madame," from sitting with whites at meals or in church and the theater, or from entering the professions and prestigious trades. Though many such restrictions were not strictly enforced, the free coloreds felt an increasing rage and resentment over institutional racism, along with a special hostility toward lower-class whites, who loved to flaunt their racial superiority over coloreds who were both wealthier and better educated than themselves.[16]

At the start of the French Revolution, free coloreds, especially in France, were greatly encouraged by the Declaration of the Rights of Man and the egalitarian rhetoric of 1789. A group of mulattoes, led by Julien Raimond, a distinguished Parisian lawyer, appeared before the bar of the Constituent Assembly in October, petitioning to be seated as West Indian deputies. Their cause of racial equality became unintentionally fused with antislavery when they received strong support from the elite white Amis des Noirs.

The Amis were quickly shouted down and accused of being tools of an English conspiracy to destroy the French colonies. (American abolitionists would face similar accusations of being agents of England some forty-five years later.) The white procolonial faction was very strong in France and continued to outmaneuver the abolitionists. While some of the wealthy white colonial leaders saw political and social advantages in granting equality to the free coloreds, they felt a compelling fear that concessions on the color line would lead to white rebellion in the West Indies and then to the loss of the colonies. Yet as matters developed, it was precisely this issue of rights and representation for free coloreds that opened the way for slaves in Saint-Domingue to free themselves.[17]

At first, the assembly toyed with the possibility of granting suffrage to *all* persons over twenty-five who owned a certain amount of property or paid taxes, thus co-opting wealthy mulattoes. Then, in 1790, one of the mulatto leaders in France, Vincent Ogé, received funds from British abolitionists before sailing to the United States, where he obtained arms. After finally landing in Saint-Domingue, he demanded elections and suffrage for all free males, on the basis of existing French law. Ogé and his followers professed full support for the slave system, but they soon became involved in an armed rebellion, which French officials crushed. After fleeing eastward to Spanish Santo Domingo, Ogé was extradited, broken on a wheel, and killed.[18] At this point the French assembly promised never to interfere with "the status of persons," meaning persons of African descent, in the colonies.

In the colonies, however, growing turmoil erupted in response to belated news from France. White communities dissolved into clashing factions of royalists, Jacobins, secessionists, and French officials. By the spring of 1791, the French assembly was finally willing to hear testimony from mulattoes on the evils of racial discrimination. Julien Raimond now assured the delegates that *only* the free coloreds could keep the slaves subdued and avoid a destructive uprising. Yet as part of the increasing radicalism of the Revolution, the radical Jacobin leader Maximilien Robespierre delivered a flaming oration intended to expose the national disgrace of officially sanctioning slavery. On May 15 a compromise amendment timidly breached the color wall when the assembly proclaimed, in highly legalistic and confusing language, that no law would be passed on the status of "persons not free, other than those born of free mothers and fathers." In other words, the revolutionary assembly tried to reassure planters that it would pass no law regarding slaves or even the descendants of slaves unless both parents of an individual had been free at the time of birth. It has often been assumed that the number of such people was small, but Julien Raimond claimed that the new law would apply to the vast majority of people of African descent.[19]

The decree sent to colonies was intended to reassure the whites, supposedly reaffirming the white colonists' autonomy in defining the status
both of slaves and the majority of freedpeople, contrary to Raimond. Yet
the assembly had insisted that the children of two free parents, regardless
of color, should enjoy the full rights of citizenship. This was exactly the
kind of "Trojan Horse legislation" that South Carolinians had sought to
permanently prevent, four years earlier, in the American Constitutional Convention. And in 1791 white French colonists saw the decree as a betrayal of
the assembly's earlier promise never to interfere with "the status of persons
in the colonies." When some white colonists predicted that the measure
would inevitably lead to slave emancipation, there was increasing talk of
secession and an alliance with England.[20] For the Western world, Saint-
Domingue faced the crucial test of reform—of the possibility of elevating
freedmen to the status of citizens without jeopardizing the richest plantation regime the world had yet seen.

This was the stormy context in which slaves in Saint-Domingue's North
Province rose in a well-planned and massive insurrection in August 1791. As
the historian Laurent Dubois describes it:

> A troop of nearly 2,000 slaves went from plantation to plantation, killing
> whites, burning houses, and setting cane fields alight. . . . Much of the
> northern plain was soon engulfed by the rebellion. "The fire, which they
> spread to the sugarcane, to all the buildings, to their houses . . . covered the
> sky with churning clouds of smoke during the day, and at night lit up the
> horizon with aurora borealis that projected far away the reflection of so
> many volcanoes, and gave all objects a livid tint of blood."[21]

News reached Britain, still at peace with revolutionary France, that over
one hundred thousand French slaves had risen in revolt and that hundreds of
great plantation houses were now in ashes.[22] Though most white colonists
recognized their dependence on the support of the free colored population
in suppressing the rebellious slaves, and though mulattoes agreed to an alliance with the wealthier whites, the outgoing Constituent Assembly in Paris
panicked and backtracked once again, in part because of the long delay in
receiving news.

The assembly now renounced jurisdiction over all race relations and over
the status of persons in the colonies. When received, this news infuriated
many mulattoes, who felt betrayed and who now launched their own war of
racial vengeance. To further complicate matters, the beleaguered and outnumbered whites in the South Province armed their slaves to fight free mulattoes. And in Paris, on April 4, 1792, the new Legislative Assembly decreed
full equal rights for all free blacks and mulattoes in the French colonies. This
act, granting full racial equality as a matter of law, was one of the truly great

achievements of the French Revolution, but it has seldom been noticed in history textbooks.

With anarchy spreading in Saint-Domingue, the Legislative Assembly sent an army of some six thousand troops, headed by three civil commissioners, to end civil war in the colony. The commissioners, especially Léger-Felicité Sonthonax, a radical Jacobin, were deeply committed to the egalitarian ideology of the French Revolution. The military need to enlist more soldiers kept eroding racial barriers, especially after France declared war on England and Spain. But it is a mistake to think of all the colony's slaves united in a single revolt. Alliances kept shifting and differed dramatically from one local region to another. When the Spanish invaded Saint-Domingue from the east, Toussaint Louverture and some other future Haitian leaders fought on their side. Confusion increased even further in September 1793 when a large English expeditionary force landed from Jamaica. By April 1794 the British had gained temporary control not only of French Martinique, Guadeloupe, and Saint Lucia but of roughly one-third of Saint-Domingue.

Meanwhile, when Sonthonax had in 1793 faced a pressing need to gain the military support of slaves against the Spanish and conservative French whites, he had moved from a limited to a more general emancipation proclamation. Then, on February 4, 1794, the French National Convention outlawed slavery in all the French colonies and guaranteed the rights of citizenship to all men regardless of color. Such a manifesto would have been inconceivable during the first years of the Revolution, and it may have been instrumental in persuading Toussaint Louverture to abandon the Spanish, who were intent on preserving slavery, and to take a decisive leadership of the republican army.[23]

Sir Adam Williamson, the leader of the British forces, was confident that with the support of the free coloreds he could easily conquer the colony and pacify the slaves. But such support, he informed London, would depend on his authority to abolish legal distinctions of color. In Britain, however, racial dogma took precedence over military strategy. Refugee French royalists and proprietors, along with British West India planters, convinced the British government that the color line was an indispensable foundation of the slave system. If equality of color were granted in Saint-Domingue, how could it be avoided in neighboring Jamaica?

Accordingly, the official measures Britain adopted for governing the occupation of foreign West Indian colonies specified that all free coloreds would have the same status as the free coloreds in the British colonies. In Saint-Domingue the *affranchis*, or freed slaves, refused to accept this provision in the capitulation agreements, and British commanders promised for a time to maintain equal rights. But by the summer of 1794 British policy had encouraged white racism as well as growing discrimination in the occupied zones.

Some whites talked openly of exterminating the free coloreds or of deporting them to Botany Bay (in Australia). Dismayed by this turn of events, the *gens de couleur* plotted rebellions and wavered uneasily between the British and French sides. Though Toussaint deeply mistrusted the *gens de couleur*, he succeeded in skillfully undermining their alliance with the British.[24]

Free coloreds throughout the West Indies had tried to keep their aspirations distinct from those of slaves, but events in Saint-Domingue suggested that demands for racial equality could provide slaves and freedmen with a common enemy and destroy the wealthiest slave regime in the Americas. For planters in other countries it made little difference that the slaves had revolted well *before* the *gens de couleur* were granted equal rights, or that the British might well have subdued Saint-Domingue if they had reaffirmed this French policy and had mobilized the free colored forces. Most slaveholders simply believed that black slavery would be untenable if free blacks and coloreds were accorded equal status with whites.

In the eyes of British leaders, Jacobin and abolitionist principles threatened by 1795 to subvert the entire West Indian world. In Saint-Domingue, Toussaint's ex-slaves had won brilliant victories and were closing in on Britain's disease-ridden troops; armies of former slaves and free coloreds had expelled the British from Guadeloupe and Saint Lucia; racial warfare raged in Grenada and Saint Vincent; French free colored agents were blamed for inciting a Maroon War in Jamaica.

By 1798 the British had lost nearly thirty-five thousand soldiers and perhaps half that many sailors in the Caribbean.[25] Edmund Burke wrote caustically of "recruits to the West Indian grave" and of fighting to conquer a cemetery. The British responded by recruiting their own slave troops with promises of eventual freedom, and sometimes enlisted Africans who had only recently disembarked from slave ships. In Saint-Domingue thousands of blacks fought for the British and thus for the maintenance of the slave regime until 1798, when some joined whites in the British evacuation to Jamaica. It is significant that Sir Adam Williamson defended the recruiting and freeing of male slaves on the ground that they would mostly die or reenlist and would not add to the long-term growth of the freed population. David Geggus, in the most exhaustive study of the British occupation, concludes that British intervention weakened the *gens de couleur*, contributed to the growing power of the blacks, and helped to destroy the French slave regime the British were trying to preserve.[26]

The defeat of the Spanish, British, and eventually French armies is especially remarkable in view of the persistent division between blacks and mulattoes, which continued to dominate the long history of an independent Haiti. The distinction of color partially overlapped the distinction between the *anciens libres*, the people who owed their freedom to pre-revolutionary acts of manumission, and the *nouveaux libres,* or recently emancipated slaves. Color and the timing of freedom both symbolized the degree by which a person was removed from the degradation and humiliation of bondage. The *anciens libres* included large landholders who had owned slaves themselves. Their interests and outlook were often at odds with those of the black military elite associated with Toussaint Louverture. Toussaint did not win mastery of Saint-Domingue until he had crushed mulatto resistance and defeated the pro-French mulatto general, André Rigaud.

On the other hand, Toussaint himself was an *ancien libre* who had owned land and at least one slave; he was also highly intelligent, a Catholic, and surprisingly well educated.[27] His ex-slave lieutenants, Henri Christophe and Jean-Jacques Dessalines, made fortunes from Toussaint's reinstitution—without formal slavery—of the plantation system.[28] Black and mulatto leaders shared a common interest in encouraging exports that could pay for the arms and supplies, mostly imported from the United States, needed for the island's defense. Their experiences with white oppression also gave them the sense of sharing a common African heritage. Although Toussaint was willing to acknowledge nominal French sovereignty and even tried to induce refugee white planters to return to Saint-Domingue, he and his black and mulatto followers were determined to prevent the restoration of either slavery or the color line. Toussaint's constitution of 1801 abolished slavery forever, prohibited distinctions according to color, and affirmed equal protection of the law—measures that were appended to the U.S. Constitution in compromised form only *after* the Civil War.[29]

General Charles Victor Emmanuel Leclerc, whom Napoleon dispatched early in 1802 with an initial force of some sixteen thousand troops to subjugate Saint-Domingue, knew he would have to pledge support for these high principles. Yet Napoleon, who expected that the forthcoming Treaty of Amiens would ensure at least the temporary pacification of Europe, had secretly resolved to restore colonial slavery, the African slave trade, and white supremacy, as part of the reconstruction of a new French colonial empire in the Caribbean and North America.

Leclerc, who happened to be Napoleon's brother-in-law, hoped to deceive and divide the blacks and mulattoes while wooing their leaders, pacifying the countryside, and reestablishing French sovereignty. Leclerc was wholly unprepared for the skillful and heroic resistance he encountered, but the French succeeded after incredibly bloody warfare in enlisting the services of Christophe and Dessalines, promising them amnesty and a policy of freedom and racial equality. Christophe even entrusted his nine-year-old son to the French and provided funds for his education in France. (The boy was thrown into an orphan asylum in Paris, where he died from neglect and want.) Leclerc then succeeded in seizing Toussaint Louverture by a ruse, after first negotiating a deceptive surrender. After being shipped to France, as Napoleon had ordered, Toussaint died in a freezing fortress high in the Jura mountains. Still Leclerc's army, now reinforced by over thirty thousand men, could not subdue the black guerrillas in the hills.[30]

In the summer of 1802, when Napoleon's veterans were being decimated by yellow fever and malaria, news arrived that slavery had been restored in Guadeloupe. Leclerc complained in frantic letters to Napoleon and the minister of marine (really a secretary of state) that "the moral force I had obtained here is destroyed. I can do nothing by persuasion." Just when a political settlement seemed in sight, Leclerc wrote, his work was undermined by the revelation of French intentions and by the return from exile of planters and merchants who talked only of slavery and the slave trade. As blacks took up arms to defend their freedom, Leclerc reported to Napoleon that "these men die with an incredible fanaticism; they laugh at death; it is the same with the women."

Thousands of mulattoes joined the rebel forces when they learned that the French had reestablished the color line in Guadeloupe. The defectors included Alexandre Pétion, a mulatto officer and future president of southern Haiti, who had fought Toussaint and had then joined Leclerc's expedition in France. In the fall of 1802, when Leclerc died of yellow fever while pleading to Napoleon for more troops, Christophe and Dessalines deserted the French. Leclerc's successor, General Rochambeau, then resorted to a policy of at least partial genocide. The French concluded that Saint-Domingue could be pacified only by exterminating most of the existing black and mulatto population, which could later be replaced by African slaves.[31]

The racial war of 1802–3 carried profound implications for every black and mulatto in the New World. Napoleon's reversal of French policy showed that a white nation could reinstitute slavery, strip the free descendants of slaves of their rights, and kill even children of the stigmatized race if their families had been contaminated with ideas of liberty. The rebels' response showed that blacks and mulattoes could unite and defeat a professional European army. White commentators insisted that the army had really been defeated by disease and by the naval blockade the British imposed when war resumed in 1803. It was difficult to deny, however, that the blacks had won battles and knew how to make the most of the yellow fever and the British blockade. The blacks turned the entire white cosmos upside down when they forced the French to evacuate Saint-Domingue in late 1803, when Dessalines proclaimed the independence of Haiti on January 1, 1804, and then in 1805 ordered the massacre of most of the remaining whites. Every New World society was familiar with slave rebellions; some maroon communities had resisted conquest for many decades and had even negotiated treaties, as in

Jamaica, with colonial authorities. But no slaves in history had ever expelled their former masters and established their own nation-state.

The very existence of Haiti challenged every slaveholding regime in the New World (and for that matter in the Cape Colony of South Africa and in the French and English colonies in the Indian Ocean). As the London *Times* put it, "a Black State in the Western Archipelago is utterly incompatible with the system of all European colonisation."[32] Hoping to allay white fears and ease the way for diplomatic recognition, Dessalines and his successors disavowed any interest in interfering with the domestic institutions of neighboring countries. Except for invading and annexing Spanish Santo Domingo, the eastern part of the island from which various enemies could threaten Haitian independence, Haiti posed no direct military danger to foreign slaveholders.[33] Despite temporary panic over reports of Haitian agents inciting slaves in the Caribbean colonies and the Southern United States, slave revolts were not as frequent after 1804 as in previous centuries. There is fragmentary evidence, however, that slaves in many localities were well aware of the Haitian Revolution and of the possibility of actually destroying the system to which they were violently subjected. Even in 1791 Jamaican slaves sang songs about the Saint-Domingue insurrection within a month after the uprising began.[34]

After the great Barbadian insurrection of 1816, which we will discuss in Chapter Eleven and which resulted in the execution of over two hundred blacks, some of the slave testimony pointed to Haiti as a model. Nanny Grigg, a literate house servant who apparently concluded from news of the parliamentary debates over slave registration that Britain intended to emancipate colonial slaves on New Year's Day 1816, urged her brethren to fight for the freedom their owners had withheld and to set fires, "as that was the way they did in Saint Domingo." Whites also found evidence of the Dominguan influence on slave revolts or conspiracies in such far-flung spots as Maracaibo, in Venezuela; Cartagena, in Colombia; and Pointe Coupée, in Spanish Louisiana.

In view of Louisiana's heavy influx of white, free colored, and slave refugees from Saint-Domingue, it seems almost certain that knowledge of the revolution had spread among the hundreds of slaves who in 1811 rose in rebellion and marched to within eighteen miles of New Orleans before being defeated by an American militia. In this instance Governor William Claiborne shrewdly enlisted as militiamen free colored refugees who had recently fled from revolutionary destruction in the French colonies.[35]

Caribbean planters and government officials were accustomed to risk and expected Haitian-inspired subversion. They were also convinced that their fortunes or livelihood depended on a labor force that would soon die off unless replenished by continuous imports from Africa. The catastrophe in Saint-Domingue, they claimed, showed the dangers of abolitionist agitation, not of a labor supply on which the Caribbean colonies had always depended. Planters therefore did all they could to suppress information that might undermine the official doctrine that black slaves, unless aroused by outsiders, were helpless, degraded beings whose servitude was as natural as the force of gravity. It is therefore extremely difficult to assess the actual influence of the Haitian Revolution on the behavior of slaves and freedpeople.

For example, the arrival in Virginia of a motley assortment of French colonists and their slaves may well have led to increasing white complaints about black "insolence" and unrecoverable runaway slaves. But little can be said with certainty about the sources of the great Gabriel slave conspiracy of 1800, except that court testimony indicated that the insurgents planned to spare the lives of Frenchmen and that the *Virginia Argus* opined that the insurrection had been organized "on the true French plan."[36]

The Haitian inspiration was much clearer in Cuba, where in 1812 José Antonio Aponte and his rebel followers, including some whites, flew the Haitian colors and wore Haitian hats before being defeated, tortured, and put to death. Like Cuba, Jamaica simmered with rumors of conspiracy as refugees streamed in from Saint-Domingue and as Jamaican slaves escaped to Haiti. In 1815 an assembly committee reported that young blacks had vowed to kill off the white population if they were not granted their freedom. As late as 1835 there were clear marks of Haitian influence when hundreds of Brazilian slaves and freedmen joined the Mâle revolt in the city of Salvador, even though this major uprising was largely Muslim inspired and took place during Ramadan.

Although the Jamaican free coloreds generally supported the slave system, they began by 1823 to address their appeals for civil rights to influential Englishmen who were already calling for the gradual abolition of slavery. This reprise of Dominguan events of 1789–93 alarmed Jamaican officials. Significantly, they arrested two colored merchants, Louis Lecesne and Edward Escoffery, whose white fathers had much earlier fled to Jamaica from Saint-Domingue. Lecesne and Escoffery were charged with arming and training slaves for a general insurrection, and both men were deported without a trial to Haiti. For white Jamaicans this move proved to be counterproductive since the blatant racial hysteria played into the hands of British reformers. In 1830 Lecesne and Escoffery were repatriated and financially compensated for their losses, a reversal that was part of Britain's general extension of civil liberties to the colonial free colored.[37]

Denmark Vesey, the free black leader of the supposedly momentous 1822 slave conspiracy in Charleston, South Carolina (also discussed in Chapter Eleven), had worked as a slave in Saint-Domingue in the early 1780s. After winning an extraordinary $1,500 in a Charleston lottery and buying his freedom in 1800, Vesey took a lively interest in the Haitian Revolution. In the trials following the exposure of the alleged massive plot, one black testified that Vesey, also known as Telemaque, "was in the habit of reading to me all the passages in the newspapers that related to S[ain]t Doming[ue]," as well as "every pamphlet he could lay his hands on, that had any connection with slavery."[38]

Other slave testimony referred to letters to Haiti requesting aid and to one of Vesey's followers promising "that St. Domingo and Africa would come over and cut up the white people if we only made the motion here first." The evidence suggested that Vesey may have hoped to gain assistance from Haiti and the North and to sail to Haiti after exterminating the whites and destroying Charleston. Henry William Desaussure, South Carolina's leading jurist, spoke of the rebels' appealing to the Haitians "as their natural allies." He predictably used the history of Haiti as an example of the destructive civil wars that would inevitably follow any move toward slave emancipation.[39]

While the Haitian example inspired a few violent conspiracies, it had a deeper and more enduring impact on the self-image and nascent national identity of free blacks, especially in the northern United States. From the outset, the Haitian Revolution stirred the free black community of Philadelphia, a port city long involved in West Indian commerce. What impressed a black leader like James Forten, a prosperous sailmaker and entrepreneur, was not the violence that could be attributed to war and to slavery itself. It was rather the providential message that the black people "would become a great nation" and "could not always be detained in their present bondage." By the 1820s, when blacks in various Northern cities began celebrating the anniversary of Haitian independence, the revolution became a symbolic negation of everything slavery represented. As William Watkins, an African Methodist Episcopal minister in Baltimore, put it in 1825, Haiti had become "an irrefutable argument to prove . . . that the descendants of Africa never were designed by their Creator to sustain an inferiority, or even a mediocrity, in the chain of being; but they are as capable of intellectual improvement as Europeans, or any other nation upon the face of the earth."

In his revolutionary *Appeal to the Coloured Citizens of the World* (1829), Boston's David Walker, a free black dealer in used clothes, urged his brethren to read the history of Haiti, which he termed "the glory of the blacks and terror of tyrants." A decade earlier, Robert Wedderburn, a Jamaican mulatto who had emigrated to London, merged the cause of blacks with the cause of Britain's working class. A member of Thomas Spence's circle of ultra-radicals, Wedderburn appealed to the precedent of Haiti when he called on West Indian blacks to "slay man, woman and child" and exhorted English wage-slaves to revolt against their oppressors.[40]

Yet as a model of liberation, the Haitian Revolution suffered from in-herent liabilities. One clue to this no-win dilemma can be seen in the white response to the freed slaves' military performance. In popular imagery the blacks were either cowards or fiends, excited barbarians who panicked when hard-pressed or demons capable of unthinkable atrocities. Though Wordsworth paid famous tribute to Toussaint Louverture in 1802—"There's not a breathing of the common wind/ That will forget thee; thou has great allies"—Toussaint's sudden capitulation in 1802 evoked some scorn for the blacks and confident reassurances that in normal circumstances white disci-pline could always overcome, as young Henry Brougham put it, "the vast numbers and ferocious strength of a savage people."[41]

Racial stereotypes of "savagery" reinforced the fear and contempt that slaves had always aroused among nonslaves. When the French were finally defeated, even abolitionists found it difficult to acknowledge that the de-graded blacks of Saint-Domingue had vindicated their honor in a way com-parable to the American patriots of 1776 (or the patriots of the later Latin American or Greek struggles for independence).

It is true that in the late 1790s American Federalists became so fearful of the infidel French that they not only praised Toussaint but the Adams ad-ministration provided his army with indispensable supplies and even naval support.[42] After Britain resumed war against Napoleon in 1803, various writ-ers tried to portray the Haitians as heroic allies in a common struggle for freedom. Toussaint, once he had perished in Napoleon's prison, became a legitimate martyr and even a man of honor, largely because he could serve as a foil to Napoleon as the treacherous "Enslaver of Nations." But since Brit-ain had a compelling self-interest to protect Haitian independence, what seems really striking is the relative absence of popular sympathy for the Haitians as a people when compared, let us say, to Napoleon's Continental subjects or to the Greeks in their later War of Independence. The enduring memory of the Haitian Revolution was not simply the isolated Toussaint as a tragic hero but also Dessalines, the butcher of whites. For an age obsessed with the prob-lem of freedom and order, the Haitian Revolution suggested the unleashing of pure id.[43]

Haiti faced a similar double check in the field of political economy. When black leaders beginning with Toussaint sought to revive the export economy by resorting to forced labor on the plantations, they were accused of reinsti-tuting slavery. When they accommodated the peasants' desires for small plots of land and acquiesced in a sharp decline in exports and the dominance of subsistence farming and local markets, the world perceived Haiti as regress-ing to savagery. The seeming alternatives of regimented labor or tropical indolence were hailed by proslavery writers as proof of two irrepressible truths: that blacks would not work unless coerced, and that in tropical climates slavery was indispensable for progress. Few commentators questioned the desirability of the plantation system itself.

British abolitionists were eager to celebrate Haiti's material and moral progress as proof of the blacks' capability for freedom and civilization. The very fact that the new nation could be burdened with such momentous expectations meant that the issue of capability was in doubt, that the Haitians' friends had put them before the bench of world opinion as the defendants of their race. It would have been alien to the age, however, to propose economic aid for a region devastated by thirteen years of civil war. Indeed, beginning with Jefferson's presidency, the United States quarantined Haiti as a potential source of racial subversion; England postponed even partial recognition of Haitian independence until 1825, when France finally gave up hope of reconquering the rebellious colony.

Even after Napoleon's fall, Haiti's leaders faced a genuine danger of French invasion or less direct forms of conquest. In 1825 Haiti's President Jean-Pierre Boyer finally won French recognition only by agreeing to a staggering indemnity of 150 million francs and to reduced customs charges for French ships, concessions that made the republic fatally dependent on foreign credit and foreign economic control.[44]

During the first third of the nineteenth century Haiti stood as the single decisive example of mass emancipation. Britain had established a small colony of freed blacks at Sierra Leone, which helped to inspire the later American settlement of Liberia, but it was difficult to extrapolate any general principles from these faltering experiments. The seaboard states from New Jersey to New Hampshire might have presented more suitable laboratories if the freedpeople had not confronted immense white majorities and an enveloping racism that deprived them of the most elemental rights and opportunities, beginning with good schools. Abolitionists in both England and America made remarkably few references to the Northern states' emancipation acts and their consequences. For a time, however, abolitionists did pin their hopes on Haiti.[45]

In most respects the very existence of Haiti was a godsend for the abolitionists' opponents. Sanguine predictions of the moral and educational advance of the people, of economic enterprise that would soon lead to thriving towns and to Haitian ships entering the harbors of the world, increasingly gave way to reports of political upheaval and hopeless poverty. The tacit comparison with the fruits of *North American* independence locked the abolitionists into a defensive posture. It became necessary to explain why Henri Christophe's Anglophilic northern kingdom collapsed, why President Boyer imposed a draconian labor code, why exports plummeted, why the economy stagnated, why the mulattoes and blacks contested for power, why the Haitians should be compared to the British barbarians of Roman times, as some apologists argued, rather than to peoples who had benefited from centuries of progress.[46] While it is impossible to measure public opinion on such matters, the negative images of Haiti—hardly ever accompanied by historical analyses and explanations—probably reinforced the conviction, especially among American whites, that free blacks were incapable of governing themselves in a civilized state.

As we have already seen, however, the Haitian Revolution conveyed a different message to free blacks and to a few white abolitionists. For them it was not simply a matter of black power and capability, though the ex-slaves' creation and governance of an independent nation, however poor and unstable, clearly contradicted the worst stereotypes of black inferiority. The birth of Haiti was also an unprecedented and unforeseen historical event, a revelation of God's will and a harbinger of universal emancipation.

Pompée Valentin Vastey, Henri Christophe's publicist and adviser, wrote of a global liberation in which "five hundred million men, black, yellow, and brown," would reclaim their natural rights and privileges.[47] The constitution of Alexandre Pétion's southern republic in Haiti invited the black and colored populations of other New World countries to a kind of aliyah (the immigration of Jews to Israel) that would in effect convert Haiti into a black Israel. In the 1820s President Boyer's appeal for African American immigrants stirred the free black communities of the northern American states. Although thousands who emigrated to Haiti became quickly disillusioned and many returned to the United States, Haiti remained a symbol of hope and a historical reassurance, long embedded in African American consciousness. As Frederick Douglass proclaimed in 1893, Haiti proved that human bondage was not an inevitable or eternal fate.

A black slave in ancient Egypt (from 1560 to 1314 B.C.E.).
Bas relief fragment. *St. Louis Art Museum.*

An ancient Greek depiction of an elderly African man (from
600 to 550 B.C.E.). Kantharos (drinking cup). *Boston Museum
of Fine Arts.*

Trial of the *Amistad* captives at the federal district court in New Haven, Connecticut. Oil on canvas by Hale Woodruff, c. 1940. *The New Haven Colony Historical Society.*

Above, left   Balthazar, the black king (or Magus), who is joining the two white Magi in honoring the Christ Child. Detail from "The Adoration of the Magi" by Hieronymus Bosch, in Holland, c. 1490–1510. *Scala / Art Resource, NY.*

Above, right   The heroic Saint Maurice, who allegedly led a German army against the Slavs to the east. Sandstone sculpture, St. Mauritius Cathedral, Madgeburg, Germany, c. 1240–50 C.E.

A mural by the famous Italian painter Giotto, in Padua, of "a black man raising a stick to beat Christ, as white Jews mock and denounce him," c. 1304–05. This portrayal draws on a long tradition of black devils and torturers. *Scala / Art Resource, NY.*

Left Branding slaves on the coast of Africa, after their sale to whites. By C. E. Wagstaff (1844). *Massachusetts Historical Society.*

Below Famous illustration of "packing" on the slave ship *Brookes*, 1789. Used in Parliamentary hearings. *Library of Congress.*

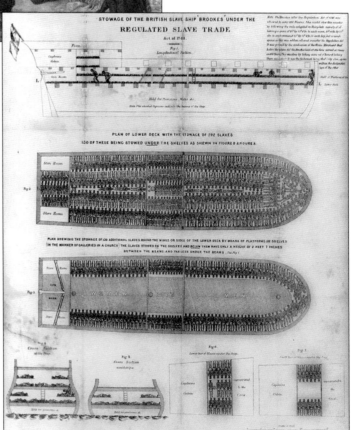

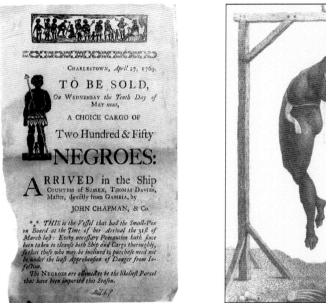

Above, left A 1769 broadside advertising the sale of 250 slaves in Charleston, South Carolina.

Above, right "A Negro hung alive by the ribs to the gallows" in the Dutch colony of Suriname. An engraving by the famous artist and poet William Blake for the book *Narrative, of a Five Years' Expedition, against the Revolted Negroes of Surinam* by John Gabriel Stedman (1796).

"An Overseer Doing His Duty." Sketched from life near Fredericksburg, Virginia, by Benjamin Henry Latrobe, 1798. *The Maryland Historical Society.*

Above, left The famous jasperware medallion of a slave, "Am I Not a Man and a Brother?," designed by one of Josiah Wedgwood's craftsmen in 1787 for the British Society for Effecting the Abolition of the Slave Trade. First used as a seal for stamping the wax to close envelopes, the image was reproduced in many forms in Britain and the United States. *Courtesy of the Wedgwood Museum Trust, Staffordshire (England).*

Above, right William Wilberforce, as a young M.P. For more than three decades Wilberforce led the abolitionist movement in Parliament. *Library of Congress.*

Toussaint Louverture, the former slave and then slaveowner who became the leader of the Haitian Revolution; hailed as "the Black Spartacus." *Snark / Art Resource, NY.*

A portrait of John Quincy Adams, the former President of the United States who as a congressman led a heroic assault on the "gag law" barring the reception of all antislavery petitions. As a lawyer, Adams also helped persuade the Supreme Court to free the *Amistad* captives. *Library of Congress.*

"Revenge taken by the black Army [in the Haitian Revolution] for Cruelties practiced on them by the French." From Marcus Rainsford, *A Historical Account of the Black Empire of Hayti* (London, 1805). *Library of Congress.*

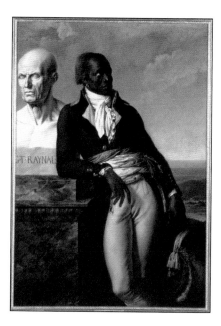

Portrait of Jean-Baptiste Belley, 1797, who was one of the six elected deputies sent in 1793 from Saint-Domingue to the French Convention in Paris. Originally from Senegal, Belley was transported to Saint-Domingue as a slave. He was present at the French Convention in 1794 when it proclaimed the emancipation of all colonial slaves. Belley is pictured next to a statue of the recently deceased Abbé Raynal, who had condemned colonial slavery and called for a "Black Spartacus."Oil painting by Anne Louis Girodet de Roussy-Trioson, Chateau de Versailles et de Trianon, Versailles, France. *Réunion des Musées Nationaux / Art Resource, NY.*

Above, left William Lloyd Garrison, who became the principal leader of the American abolitionist movement from 1831 to 1865. *Library of Congress.*

Above, right An 1852 daguerrotype by Samuel J. Miller of Frederick Douglass, the escaped slave, at age thirty-four. Douglass became the most famous black leader of the nineteenth century. *The Art Institute of Chicago.*

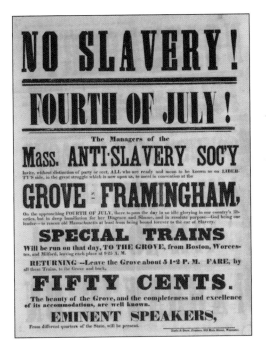

A broadside advertising a huge antislavery rally in 1854, in Framingham, Massachusetts. Along with presenting speeches from eminent figures such as Henry David Thoreau, Garrison burned copies of the Fugitive Slave Law and the U.S. Constitution. *The Massachusetts Historical Society.*

9

Slavery in the Nineteenth-Century South, I:
From Contradiction to Defense

T HE STRONGEST CARD in the hands of American abolitionists was their ability to indict the entire American nation for what appeared to be the most hypocritical contradiction in all human history: A nation conceived in liberty and dedicated to the proposition "that all men are created equal" happened also to be the nation, by the mid-nineteenth century, with the largest number of slaves in the Western Hemisphere—a nation whose most valuable exports, particularly cotton, were produced by slaves.

Indeed, far from being a marginal misfortune, African American slavery pulsated at the heart of the national economy and thus at the core of American political culture. If by the 1850s the North seemed well launched on an alternative road of industrial capitalism, the two sections were closely linked in terms of trade, finance, insurance, family bonds, and even the slave-grown cotton, rice, hemp, tobacco, and sugar that Northerners consumed in exchange for all the products they sold in the South. By the 1850s, too, following the annexation of Texas and California, the high confidence of some slaveholding Southerners emerged in dreams of annexing an expanding tropical empire ranging from Cuba to Nicaragua. Of course, Northerners and Southerners clashed over such issues as extending slavery to California and Kansas, and the very presence and increasing public support of abolitionists can be interpreted as evidence that Revolutionary ideals of liberty and equality were acquiring new life and might make a difference in shaping the future of a nation that had more than tripled in size since the beginning of the century.

As Americans argued over their momentous contradiction, British travelers, who began arriving in increasing numbers in the 1820s, took delight in exposing and ridiculing the extraordinary inconsistency of a freedom-touting democracy based on slave labor.[1] The English also loved to lampoon the Americans' boorishness, greed, arrogance, and terrible inns and roads, to say nothing of the Americans' filthy habit of spitting tobacco in all directions. As England took the leadership in trying to suppress the international slave trade and began debating whether to emancipate all the slaves in its own colonies, English travelers and writers were able to expose a much deeper and more vulnerable American evil.

Morris Birkbeck, an English immigrant who left Virginia for Illinois because he did not want to degrade himself and corrupt his children by living in a slave state, described in 1818, in a widely read book, what it was like to watch the sale of two slave women and their children on a Virginia street: "I could hardly bear to see them handled and examined like cattle; and when I heard their sobs, and saw the big tears roll down their cheeks at the thought of being separated, I could not refrain from weeping with them."[2]

Isaac Holmes, another English critic, was also appalled by the vice and corruption he saw when traveling through the South in 1823, following the explosive debates in Congress over admitting Missouri as a slave state:

> The Americans may boast of the rights of man, the great law of nature, as being the basis of their constitution; they may declaim against tyranny and oppression; yet every man who becomes a slave-holder in Missouri is a tyrant of their creation.... The effects of slavery are truly appalling. Where slavery exists, virtue and morality are swept away as with a flood of corruption.[3]

Of course, Holmes's England, with its exceptionally hierarchical system of social classes, was hardly free from tyranny and hypocrisy. Even many decades later, an English wage laborer who on his own prompting quit his job or moved to a new employer could easily be imprisoned for breaking a highly coercive "contract."[4] Holmes was writing at a time when British women and small children still worked on their hands and knees in unbelievably oppressive British mines. Apart from the noxious conditions in British factories and mines, there were also psychological aspects to the judgments of Britons when they thought of Americans "winning independence" from a former "mother country"—when they thought of a rebellious, English-speaking people who in the 1770s had committed a verbal and symbolic form of "regicide." By the same token, the emergence in America of so-called Jacksonian democracy presented a direct threat, similar in some ways to the Communism of the twentieth century, of bringing on class warfare in Britain and the toppling of royal and aristocratic privilege.

Frances Trollope (mother of the well-known novelist Anthony Trollope), in her famous *Domestic Manners of the Americans* (1832), remarked that

> they inveigh against the governments of Europe; because, as they say, they favor the powerful and oppress the weak. You may hear this declaimed in every drawing-room, satirized [*sic*] upon the stage, nay, even anathematised from the pulpit: listen to it, and then look at them at home; you will see them with one hand hoisting the cap of liberty, and with the other flogging their slaves.[5]

British critics also used attacks on slavery in America as a vehicle for exposing such supposedly "democratic manners" as bragging, a proclivity to violence, and a refusal on the part of whites to take servile jobs. Thus Frances Trollope commented on the fact that "it is more than petty treason to the Republic to call a free citizen a *servant*": Thanks to the understood presence of racial slaves, Americans could show off their egalitarianism by referring hypocritically to white servants as their "help" instead. White Americans not only disliked the word "servant" but refused to be treated the way English servants had been treated for centuries. According to Trollope, young white women were even taught that the "most abject poverty is preferable to domestic service."[6]

Another Englishman, who took his male servant with him on a visit to America's "Western Country," was shocked to find that his boots had not been cleaned for two days; the servant, when questioned, replied that "it was negroes' work to clean boots." It appeared that this English servant was quickly learning how to become "Americanized." In this probably exaggerated tale, the servant then refused at dinner to stand *behind* his master's chair, as was customary in England. Instead, the servant sat at the table *beside* his master, announcing that this was a land of "liberty and equality"![7]

Even if apocryphal, this parody of democracy highlights the process by which the ever-present dichotomy between slave and free could erode or disguise class differences among whites. In Chapter Six we have already taken note of the historian Edmund Morgan's thesis that in the seventeenth- and eighteenth-century Chesapeake, black slavery became the necessary basis for white freedom and equality. Moving on to 1820, Secretary of State John Quincy Adams, who had spent much of his youth in Europe, expressed surprise and shock when John C. Calhoun, a fellow cabinet member, confided to Adams that one of the major benefits of racial slavery was its effect on lower-class whites, who could now take pride in their skin color and feel equal to the wealthiest and most powerful whites. Thus slavery, in Calhoun's eyes, defused class conflict. Precisely because slavery was the most extreme instance of inequality, it helped to make other relationships seem relatively equal.[8]

We should also consider the example of an Englishman like Thomas Cooper, who totally acculturated himself to the Southern slaveholding world. In England Cooper had been an eminent scientist, lawyer, and political radical, who supported the French Jacobins and even called for the abolition of the slave trade. Then in America he became a close friend of Thomas Jefferson, taught for a while at the University of Pennsylvania, received an honorary M.D. degree from the University of New York, and in 1820 became a professor of chemistry and then president of South Carolina College. Having moved increasingly toward ultra-conservative politics, Cooper late in life emerged as a brilliant defender of slavery and states' rights. Proslavery ideology, to which we will later turn, did not require a nurturing from childhood in a slave society.[9]

For their part, America's defenders of slavery could point to other forms of hypocritical contradiction. The moralistic abolitionists in New England and especially old England seldom acknowledged the great fortunes amassed by slave-trading families in Rhode Island or in Liverpool, Bristol, and London. From the late seventeenth century onward, Britain had been by far the greatest transporter of African slaves to the New World, stopping only in 1808. In subsequent decades, despite all the antislavery rhetoric, private British firms continued to supply ships, chains, manacles, insurance, and trading goods for both legal and illegal foreign slave traders.

Moreover, the British abolitionists and petition signers, who had no need to face the social consequences of emancipating hundreds of thousands of slaves, were hardly demanding a massive migration of freed blacks to join the British proletariat. Nor should it be forgotten, many Southerners added, that the entire British cotton textile industry depended on slave-grown cotton, some 70 percent of which came from the American South. And by the 1840s, when the British Caribbean's plummeting plantation production and land values confirmed the worst predictions on the economic consequences of slave emancipation, England turned after much debate to a new policy of free trade and thus benefited enormously from the productivity of the foreign slave systems in Cuba, Brazil, and the United States—nations that had to take the *political* responsibilities for maintaining the cheapest and therefore most exploitative labor system.[10]

That said, abolitionists were committed to the distinctively modern view that the status quo and legacies from the past need not be tolerated, that no beneficial ends or economic benefits could justify a system in which one human being treats another like a domesticated animal or a salable tool or instrument. With respect to our initial theme of contradictions, abolitionists seized upon the central contradiction at the very heart of slavery.[11]

Even ancient Roman writers like Seneca wrestled with the conviction that slaves were in some sense equal and capable of true virtue, much as early

Christians declared that a slave could be a saint and his master a sinner.[12] Yet what made slavery so appealing and seductive, especially in the long era before self-powered appliances, engines, and other labor-saving devices, was the freedom it brought for slaveholders. Thus slave labor gave Aristotle the time to contemplate the nature of man and worldly existence, much as it freed Washington to lead the American Revolution and Jefferson to compose the Declaration of Independence. And from earliest antiquity writers drew parallels between both the treatment and behavior of slaves and those of domestic animals, often implying that the dehumanization or bestialization of slaves could serve the psychological function of elevating the oppressor and even generating the illusion of something approaching divine power.

Frederick Douglass, who escaped from slavery, well understood and articulated both the process and effects of dehumanization; he knew all too well what it was like to be treated as an animal. It bears repeating to note that when young Douglass was sent to be psychologically "conditioned" by the slavebreaker Edward Covey, Douglass's "intellect languished," and he had no desire to read: "The dark night of slavery closed in upon me; and behold a man transformed into a brute!" Douglass goes on to report that he spent Sundays, his only leisure time, in a "beast-like stupor." When he did read and learned the truth about Africans being stolen from their homes, "I would at times feel that learning to read had been a curse rather than a blessing. . . . It opened my eyes to the horrible pit, but to no ladder upon which to get out. . . . I envied my fellow-slaves for their stupidity. I have often wished myself a beast."[13]

It was only after Douglass resorted to physical force and overcame Covey that he could feel himself to be truly a man: "It was a glorious resurrection, from the tomb of slavery, to the heaven of freedom." He now resolved that however long he might remain a slave in *form*, he would never again be a slave in fact, that is, in his own sense of self-identity. Douglass's account illuminates the heroic efforts on the part of many enslaved African Americans to resist attempts at dehumanization. Harriet Jacobs, in her *Incidents in the Life of a Slave Girl*, reiterates the theme of internal resistance to degradation—in her case, sexual degradation: "When he told me that I was made for his use[,] . . . [t]hat I was nothing but a slave, whose will must and should surrender to his, never before had my puny arm felt half so strong. . . . My master had power and law on his side; I had a determined will. There is might in each." These accounts reflect a certain heroism but also suggest that the very worst effect of bondage occurred when men and women internalized their masters' desires and perceived themselves as slaves not only in outward form but in inward *fact*.[14]

Scholars have done much to recognize and recover the heroic efforts of enslaved men and women to resist dehumanization. But to assume a homogeneity of nineteenth-century black experience, or to assume a uniform selfless political solidarity, is to lose sight of our shared humanity, not only our triumphal possibilities but also our profound limitations. This point leads to the final example of contradictions within contradictions: the slave who eventually becomes a master and an owner of slaves.

In parts of Africa, where the dangers of being enslaved were even greater than the chances of being freed, some slaveholders actually became the slaves of their former slaves.[15] In the Caribbean, sharp distinctions of color made it much easier than in the United States for some emancipated slaves or their descendants to become owners of slaves. We have already noted that in Saint-Domingue, *gens de couleur* owned as many as one hundred thousand slaves. With respect to color, colonies like Jamaica gave informal recognition to a hierarchy ranging upward from free blacks and sambos (the offspring of a black and a mulatto) to mulattoes, quadroons, mustees, and persons deemed white because of being four generations or more removed from a black ancestor.

While freedmen were divided among themselves by color, wealth, occupation, and town or rural residence, they shared a common quest for equality with whites and an orientation to white values. They were "eager for honor," to use the words of a Spanish priest referring to the free colored in Puerto Rico, and were quick to take affront if anyone implied they were darker in color than their own self-image.[16] Since Jamaican society openly sanctioned informal conjugal unions between white men and black women, some of the most respectable and refined colored women thought it more honorable to be the mistress of a white man, and bear children who might be considered white or near-white, than to marry a colored husband. This general pattern prevailed through much of the Caribbean and Latin America, where white males greatly outnumbered white females and where generations of intermixture had produced a large class of free coloreds.

Somewhat similar racial distinctions appeared in parts of the Lower South, especially in Louisiana, which became a haven for French West Indian refugees and which had also acquired under French and Spanish rule a tradition of open racial intermixture. At least until the later antebellum period, the Lower South remained relatively flexible in its treatment of freedmen and their descendants. Despite strict restrictions on manumission, Louisiana and even South Carolina made room for a small number of privileged free coloreds, some of whom became slaveholding planters.

William Ellison, for example, was born a slave in 1790 in upcountry South Carolina. As a young mulatto apprentice he learned the new and highly prized craft of making and repairing cotton gins. After apparently purchasing his own freedom in 1816, Ellison changed his name from "April" to "William," bought freedom for his de facto wife and daughter, and shrewdly won the respect of his white clients and neighbors. Almost immediately he purchased slaves to work in his gin shop, building "the economic foundation of his freedom on slave labor," and eventually became a major cotton planter and owner of sixty-three slaves. He even won a lawsuit against a white man who refused to pay his bills. By 1860 Ellison's property holdings placed him among the richest 10 percent in South Carolina's wealthy Sumter District. He owned more slaves than 97 percent of South Carolina's other slaveholders![17] In Louisiana there were colored planters who possessed more slaves and were even richer than Ellison.

To turn from contradictions and paradoxes to the actual rise of the "Cotton Kingdom," Southern planters beginning about 1820 benefited from three economic advantages unavailable in the North. First, the climate and soil of large parts of the South were ideally suited for growing short-staple cotton, the indispensable raw material for the early Industrial Revolution. The South thus produced an exportable product for which there was an international demand. The perfection of the cotton gin and screw press, devices for extracting cotton from the plant and compressing it into bales, gave Southerners benefits of technological innovation that Northerner farmers did not begin to approximate until the late 1850s (and even by 1860 over 80 percent of the American population lived in rural regions). In contrast to Northern family farms, the larger Southern plantations were more like the agribusinesses of the later twentieth century in terms of size, efficiency, and complex organization.

A second Southern advantage can be seen in the rapid improvement and widespread use of steamboats that opened the way to *upriver* navigation of the Mississippi, to say nothing of other boat travel along the rich network of Southern rivers from the Savannah and Potomac to the Arkansas. Such rivers outdid even Northern canals in lowering transportation costs.

Third, and most important in purely economic terms, Southern agriculture could exploit the coerced labor of black slaves, especially in field gangs in which slaves were forced to work at maximum speed and efficiency by black drivers who positioned workers according to their relative strength and speed of labor—in some ways, as we have seen, foreshadowing the "time and motion" studies of the early twentieth century.

Scholars still dispute some questions relating to the economics of American slavery, but during the past thirty years a broad consensus has confirmed the arguments of Stanley L. Engerman and the Nobel laureate Robert William Fogel concerning the extraordinary efficiency and productivity of plantation slave labor, which in no way implies that the system was less harsh or even less criminal.[18] The historian Seymour Drescher has also shown that most of the British and French political economists of the early decades of the nineteenth century rejected Adam Smith's overconfident assertion in 1776, in *The Wealth of Nations*, that because of its incentives, free labor was always cheaper and more efficient and productive than slave labor.[19] Wholly apart from these issues, no one could question the fact that America's shortage of white labor, in relation to available land, was a crucial condition affecting both Northern and Southern agriculture. Since land was generally accessible as a result of the death or removal of Indians, especially in the West, it was difficult for farmers to hire nonfamily labor in order to specialize, expand production, and take advantage of the rising demand for cash crops, such as wheat, cotton, and corn.

In the North this labor shortage led in time to improved transportation, labor-saving machinery, and promotional schemes to attract immigrants, but in the South black slaves provided a highly mobile and flexible supply of labor. Even without significant illegal imports from Africa or the West Indies, the number of American slaves increased from 1.5 million in 1820 to nearly 4 million in 1860. This unprecedented natural increase of the slave population enabled white Southerners to clear and settle the vast Cotton Kingdom, extending from inland South Carolina and Georgia across Alabama and Mississippi to Louisiana, Arkansas, and eventually eastern Texas.

America's Internal Slave Trade, by Land and Sea, 1790–1860. Based on Clayborne Carson, Emma J. Lapsansky-Werner, and Gary B. Nash, *African American Lives: The Struggle for Freedom* (New York: Pearson/Longman, 2005), 166.

Far too often slavery in the American South has been pictured as a fixed and static institution, almost frozen in time. In reality, an immense domestic or internal slave trade transported close to one million slaves from the Chesapeake and other Atlantic coastal regions to the "Old Southwest," centering on the lower Mississippi Valley. While some slaves accompanied their mobile owners as they moved westward, most were sent by slave ships around the Florida Keys to ports like New Orleans or were sold at auctions and to professional traders who marched them in shackles hundreds of miles, sometimes for as long as seven or eight weeks, to the most profitable markets.[20]

Because slaves rightly dreaded such agonies, as well as being separated from spouses, parents, or children, masters continually used the threat of sale as a means of discipline and control.[21] One former slave recalled that his master "come . . . down to the quarters," determined to stop the slaves from making noise and disturbing him on Sundays. The angry master picked out "de fam'ly dat got de most chillun an' say, 'Fo' God, nigger, I'm goin' to sell all dem chillun o' your'n lessen you keep 'em quiet.' Dat threat was worsen prospects of a lickin'. Ev'ybody sho' keep quiet arter dat."[22]

Whether slave sales were used for discipline or profit, their impact on African American families was disastrous. In 1852 Maria Perkins, a literate slave in Virginia, wrote a probably final letter to her husband, referring first to the sale of their son:

> Dear Husband   I write you a letter to let you know my distress my master has sold albert to a trader on Monday court day and myself and other child is for sale also and I want you to let [me] hear from you very soon before next cort if you can I don't know when . . . I want you to tell dr Hamelton and your master if either will buy me they can attend to it [now] and then I can go afterwards. I don't want a trader to get me . . . I don't expect to meet with the luck to get that way till I am quite heartsick nothing more   I am and ever will be your kind wife   Maria Perkins.[23]

Large planters and speculators could quickly transport an army of involuntary workers to clear rich Western land or could sell slaves to meet the labor demands of expanding areas. Some owners moved many slaves from urban centers out to the fields and then back to urban employment as cotton prices rose or fell.[24] Even prospering family farmers could buy or rent a few slaves to increase their output of cotton or other cash crops. The renting of slave labor was widespread. The flexibility of the system also enabled planters to allocate needed labor to raising livestock and growing foodstuffs for domestic consumption. When market conditions improved, slaveholders could increase the proportion of work time devoted to cotton or other cash crops. In contrast to the free population, slaves began working as children and were burdened with orders and assignments even if they survived to old age.

These various advantages meant that slaves became the major form of Southern wealth (aside from land), and slaveholding became the means to prosperity. Southern investment flowed mainly into the purchase of slaves, whose soaring price reflected an apparently limitless demand, despite major fluctuations in the price of cotton. The large planters soon ranked among America's richest men. Indeed, by 1860 two-thirds of the wealthiest Americans lived in the South—a fact that became difficult to believe after the devastation of the Civil War and the full industrialization of the North.[25] As late as 1863, well after Lincoln's Emancipation Proclamation, the president of a North Carolina railroad could assure his stockholders that although slave prices were very high now, slaves were worth probably only one-half what they would be at the end of the war! This is only one of many examples of the strength and confidence of the slaveholding South.

The later impoverishment of the South nourished the myth that the slave economy had always been historically "backward," stagnating, and unproductive. We now know that investment in slaves brought a considerable profit and that the Southern economy grew rapidly throughout the pre–Civil War decades. It is true, however, that the system depended largely on the international demand for cotton as the world entered the age of industrialization, led by the British textile industry. There was an increasing demand for clothing that was cheaper than linen and not as hot and heavy as wool. At times the South's production of cotton exceeded international demand, and cotton prices fell sharply in the economic recessions that followed the panics of 1819 and 1837, but until the Civil War, the world market for cotton textiles grew at such a phenomenal rate that both Southern planters and British manufacturers thought only of infinite expansion.

By 1840 the South grew more than 60 percent of the world's cotton and supplied not only Britain and New England but also the rising industries of continental Europe, including Russia. Throughout the antebellum period cotton accounted for over half the value of all American exports, and thus it paid for the major share of the nation's imports and investment capital. A stimulant to Northern industry, cotton also contributed to the growth of New York City as a distributing and exporting center that drew income from commissions, freight charges, interest, insurance, and other services connected with the marketing of America's number-one commodity.

Though the South continued to export large quantities of rice, tobacco, and other cash crops, Southern business conventions unsuccessfully called for a more balanced economy. Except for the bustling port of New Orleans, and a few small cities like Richmond and Mobile, great urban centers failed to appear. Internal markets failed to grow. Most European immigrants, including Germans, German Jews, and Irish, had no wish to compete with slave labor. Immigrants generally shunned the region, though there are a few examples of Irish laborers who allied themselves with slaves (and some Irish railroad workers in Texas were regarded by white Southerners as even more lowly and degraded than slaves). The greatest single peril to the Southern slavocracy was the possible disaffection of nonslaveholding farmers and workers followed by an alliance with blacks, both slave and free. This point underscores the crucial function of racism and racial identity, which succeeded in maintaining much unity among whites.

For all its shortcomings, the slave economy was anything but inflexible. In Louisiana, wealthy sugar growers expanded production by using the newest technology for the processing of cane. Some Southerners effectively applied slave labor to the cultivation of corn, grain, and hemp (for making rope and twine), to mining and lumbering, to building canals and railroads, and even to the manufacture of textiles, iron, and other industrial products.[26]

Nevertheless, no other American region contained so many white farmers who merely subsisted on their own produce. The "typical" white Southerner was not a slaveholding planter but a small farmer who tried, often without success, to achieve both relative self-sufficiency and a steady income from marketable cash crops. In no other American region had agriculture become so speculative and commercial—for small cotton farmers who could not afford slaves, as well as for the planter elite. Like some of the later Third World regions where involuntary labor produced raw materials for industrial nations, the South was intimately connected with industrial capitalism and yet cut off for various reasons from its liberalizing and diversifying influences.[27]

From the time of the Revolution, a cautious, genteel distaste for slavery had been fashionable among some of the planters of the Upper South. This Jeffersonian tradition persisted even after the tiny number of true abolitionists had been driven from the land and after Methodist and Baptist leaders had backtracked on various resolutions encouraging gradual emancipation. The desire to find some way of ridding the South of its "burden," "blight," or "curse," as the Jeffersonian reformers called it, was kept alive by some of the sons of affluent plantation owners who went to the North or to Europe to study. Moreover, in some regions possessing very few slaves, such as western North Carolina and eastern Tennessee, small numbers of Quakers and Baptists continued to sustain antislavery societies.[28]

Even in the 1830s and 1840s the hope of removing the South's burden won support from a few broadminded plantation owners, mostly Whigs, who were troubled by the economic decline of the tobacco regions of eastern Virginia and Maryland and by the continuing loss of population to the Old Southwest. In 1832 the belief that slavery was "ruinous to the whites" received unexpected support in the Virginia legislature from *nonslaveholders* who lived west of the Blue Ridge Mountains and in the region that later become West Virginia.

Nat Turner's bloody slave revolt of 1831 alarmed many of Virginia's women as well as men and led to a momentous and unprecedented legislative debate over the possibility of slave emancipation. In 1832 the representatives from western Virginia had various motives for condemning slavery and challenging the political control of tidewater planters, but in the end, their arguments demonstrated the pervasive power of white racism. Even the nonslaveholding radicals acknowledged that bondage was beneficial for blacks and that its destructive effects on white society could be ended only by gradually freeing and deporting the entire black population. Emancipation seemed inconceivable unless coupled with the colonization of freed slaves, a view shared even much later by Northern leaders like Lincoln and by virtually all whites except the small group of radical abolitionists. In the Virginia legislature the antislavery delegates failed even to carry a resolution that would have branded slavery as an evil to be dealt with at some future time.[29]

In response to this legislative debate, Thomas R. Dew, a professor of law, history, and political economy at the College of William and Mary, wrote a book that became a famous turning point in the Southern defense of slavery as a rational and superior form of labor management. Looking to the long-range future, Dew even predicted that "in 1929, our police would be much more efficient than now, if the two castes [races] preserve anything like the same relative numbers."[30] Though some moral doubts over slavery persisted in the Upper South, the gradualists tended to abandon the impractical notion of colonization and began to rely on what they termed "diffusion"—the hope that the slave population would slowly move southwestward toward Texas, Mexico, and tropical regions for which black people were supposedly suited.[31]

But after the 1830s Southern intellectuals, clergymen, editors, and other professionals became increasingly determined to overcome the moral and self-interested doubts of the nonslaveholding majority. The aggressive antislavery assault from the North, and indirectly from Britain, actually made it easier to instill the conviction that emancipation in any form would be a disaster, for blacks as well as for whites. On the one hand, some Southerners channeled their moral concerns into dedicated efforts to reform, improve, and humanize the so-called peculiar institution. On the other hand, while the South remained highly diverse and divided on some issues, political statesmen like Virginia's Senator William C. Rives, President Andrew Jackson's cosmopolitan envoy to Paris, warned that "for people of non-slaveholding States to discuss the question of Slavery at all, is to attack the foundation of the Union itself."[32]

Most of the arguments used to defend slavery were neither of Southern nor of nineteenth-century origin. As soon as Judge Samuel Sewell published a rare antislavery pamphlet in Boston in the year 1700, John Saffin launched a proslavery counterattack. Later in the century, when a burst of English pamphlets and sermons depicted the evils of the British slave trade, the wealthy West India interest sponsored a swarm of pamphlets defending both slavery and the slave trade with arguments ranging from the Bible to national interest.

One of the primal sources for proslavery thought regardless of time or place was, of course, the Bible. In the Old Testament God tells Moses that the ancient Israelites should take their male and female slaves "from the nations round about you. . . .You may also buy them from among the children of aliens resident among you. . . . These shall become your property: you may keep them as a possession for your children after you, for them to inherit as property for all time."[33] And as we have seen in Chapter Three, Jews, Christians, and Muslims came up with various important interpretations of Noah's curse of Ham's youngest son: "Cursed be Canaan; the lowest of slaves shall he be to his brothers [and their descendants]."[34]

A few historians have erroneously minimized the importance of the "Curse of Ham" as a means for white Southerners to justify the slavery of African Americans. As Thomas Virgil Peterson has shown, drawing on the anthropological theories of Clifford Geertz and Claude Lévi-Strauss, the biblical story sustained a worldview for Southern Presbyterians, Baptists, and Methodists by bringing together their "racial stereotypes, political theories, religious beliefs and economic realities." Above all, since most Southern Christians fervently believed in the descent of all humans from Adam and Eve, and could not accept the new theories of polygenesis (to which we will soon turn), Ham's sinful contempt for his father provided a way for distinguishing the animal-like "Canaanite race" from the superior descendants of the "fair and comely" Japheth—and even from the red or brown progeny of Shem. The curse of slavery was even "good" for the Canaanite race, since masters had a duty to Christianize their slaves and, according to one prominent agricultural reformer, "the excesses of his [Negro's] animality are kept in restraint and he is compelled to lead an industrious, sober life, and certainly a more happy one than he would if he was left to the free indulgences of his indolent savage nature." For some Southern Christians the biblical story fit into a larger defense of patriarchy (Noah being the first patriarch), as the only means of controlling mankind's natural inclination to evil—though by the 1850s some abolitionists were developing sophisticated and compelling arguments against patriarchies of many kinds. Still, the Noachic myth's power and longevity emerged in the 1950s when white Southern Christians revived "the Curse" as a biblical defense of racial segregation.[35]

Moreover, the Hebrew Bible makes it clear that Abraham and many of the prophets owned slaves as a matter of course. In the New Testament Jesus never speaks to a slave or criticizes the slaveholding that surrounded him, and key passages in Peter, Timothy, Titus, and Luke (some printed in Chapter Two) exhort slaves to obey their masters and even justify the flogging of slaves. While the Bible also contains words that abolitionists could seize upon, the total absence of antislavery in antiquity gave comfort to religious planters, especially when abolitionists denounced every instant of slaveholding as a heinous sin.[36]

As for a second source, Aristotle set a long-lived precedent for defending bondage on natural and empirical grounds, by pointing to the actual inequalities in human physical strength and intelligence, by arguing that some people are simply born to serve, and by emphasizing the social and political benefits flowing from the slaveowners' free leisure time.[37]

When considering the slavery debates, one should note that in 1850, 17.2 percent of Southern native white adults were illiterate, compared with 4.12 percent in the free states.[38] Nevertheless, a relatively large number of young Southern men attended college, some traveling abroad and many more to the North, especially to Princeton and Yale. Others made South Carolina College, in Columbia, a hotbed of Southern nationalism and radical proslavery thought.[39] By the 1840s, some highly talented young intellectuals and writers had become determined to defend slavery while improving the level of Southern life and defining a distinctive Southern culture. Though outraged by abolitionist attacks, this "Sacred Circle," as one group called itself, was less interested in a Northern audience than in unifying, spiritualizing, and revitalizing their society—much as Transcendentalists and moral reformers were trying to do for the North.[40]

From Aristotle, Edmund Burke, and European romantic reactions against the French Revolution and Enlightenment, these Southerners derived theories of the organic cohesiveness of society, the inevitability of inequalities, and the danger of applying abstract principles to human relationships—such as the slogan "all men are created equal." While attracted by images of feudalism and the cult of chivalric honor, they were also committed, like most Southern clergy, to a belief in science, the wonders of technology, and historical progress.

That said, figures like James Henry Hammond, the young governor of South Carolina, and George Frederick Holmes, a professor of history and literature at the University of Virginia, were deeply troubled by the threat of an individualistic, acquisitive society based on the capitalist wage system. According to the Sacred Circle, racial slavery was the labor system most conducive to the elevation of the intellect, since it protected some men from the allurements of greed and gave leisure to a master class that could cultivate "mental improvement and refinement of manners." This was essentially a reworking of Aristotle's classic argument, but Aristotle was never able to identify "the natural slave," and he admitted that men born to be free were sometimes wrongfully enslaved by sheer force.

For Southerners, a white skin was the distinguishing badge of mind and intellect. Black skin was the sign that a given people had been providentially designed to serve as menial laborers, as what Hammond called the "mud-sill" class necessary to support every society. In his famous "Cotton is King" speech to the U.S. Senate, in 1858, Hammond affirmed that

> in all social systems there must be a class to do the menial duties, to perform the drudgery of life. . . . Its requisites are vigor, docility, fidelity. Such a class you must have, or you would not have that other class which leads progress, civilization, and refinement. It constitutes the very mud-sill of society and political government, and you might as well attempt to build a house in the air, as to build either the one or the other, except on this mud-sill.[41]

Hammond and other Southern leaders considered themselves exceptionally fortunate in having found a race that had been created to be a mud-sill. Like early New England Puritans, they had a mission to teach the world. Most proslavery theorists eagerly embraced at least part of the new science of ethnology. Its theories of racial inequalities promised to reconcile religion with empirical science.

Holmes, for example, turned to the classic racialist work of the Frenchman Joseph de Gobineau, whose four-volume *The Moral and Intellectual Diversity of Races* (1856) helped to disseminate the doctrine of Negro inferiority through much of the Western world.[42] Hammond also became close to Josiah C. Nott, a Southern physician who called his research "the nigger business" and who drew on the scientific racism of Samuel Morton, George Gliddon, and Louis Agassiz.[43]

The latter, a distinguished Harvard professor originally from Switzerland, preached the doctrine of polygenesis—arguing that Africans were a separately created and inferior species. Since Southern culture was so deeply oriented to orthodox interpretations of the Bible, including the primacy of Adam and Eve, this theory of separate origins was far too radical for most Christians to accept. (Ironically, Darwin's science helped to restore the belief in a common human origin, today substantiated by both African archeology and genetics.)

Men like Governor Hammond shied away from polygenesis. In 1845, in his famous two long public letters to the eighty-five-year-old British abolitionist Thomas Clarkson, Hammond simply declared that "the African, if not a distinct, is an inferior, race, and never will effect, as it never has effected, as much in any other condition as in that of Slavery."[44]

For Hammond it was a stroke of genius, which won acclaim throughout the South, to respectfully address Clarkson, arguably the great Founding Father of all abolitionism, an Englishman no less, and then to demolish point by point the entire intellectual edifice on which Clarkson had based his life's work. Hammond disarmingly admitted at the outset that he had no wish to defend the African slave trade, which Clarkson had devoted almost a half-century of sustained effort to suppress, but then Hammond correctly observed that an illegal slave trade from Africa was still thriving and apparently could not be abolished by force (though the trade to Brazil would be stopped in five more years).[45]

Hammond's letters devoted much space to comparisons of Southern slavery with British industrialism. He admitted that one could find *some* evil and suffering in every society, but from the *Reports of Commissioners* appointed by Parliament, he quoted descriptions of English boys eight to twelve years of age crawling on all fours in mine shafts, dragging barrows of one hundred pounds of coal. He cited verified instances of children as young as four and five working in mines and factories, twelve hours a day, for $2.50 to $7.50 a month. There was much further evidence on English labor exploitation and on Irish famine and destitution. (The great Irish potato famine, for which England was at least partly responsible, had just begun.)

Apart from the British abolitionists' hypocrisy and inconsistencies, Hammond argued that if their premises were logically extended to all property and authority, the result would be a complete disorganization of society, reducing man to a state of nature, "red with blood, and shrouded once more in barbaric ignorance." What Hammond called "our patriarchal scheme of domestic servitude," in contrast, stimulated the finer feelings of human nature, as opposed to your "*artificial money power system.*"

According to Hammond, abolitionists simply did not recognize what they were doing. Clarkson and his followers were striking at the very core of social unity and were really disregarding what Hammond called the Negro's "elemental humanity"—since after emancipation the blacks would be cut off from all bonds with paternalistic and caring whites, abandoned to progressive decline and decay (a scenario supposedly verified in the mid-nineteenth century by the history of Haiti and Sierra Leone). Such decline and decay, Hammond claimed, was already starkly apparent in the British West Indies after only seven years of "freedom"—a view, as we shall see in Chapter Twelve, that was winning increasing support in Britain. If Clarkson and other abolitionists objected to keeping men in bondage by the law of force, Hammond asked, in what country do you see human affairs regulated merely by the law of love?

If Hammond were to get a glimpse of the world in modern times, he would no doubt be shocked by the nearly universal moral condemnation of slavery. But he might well feel vindicated by the research of a respected sociologist who shows that in our allegedly free world many millions of contract and indebted laborers in the so-called developing nations are physically forced like slaves to do the dirtiest work, often by labor contractors for multinational corporations. And Hammond would quickly point out that these modern "slaves" have no "caring owners," as in the antebellum South, whose self-interest coincides with the good health and longevity of their "servants" and their "servants' " children.[46] I am by no means implying any acceptance of Hammond's proslavery views, but it is often sobering to momentarily borrow the perspective of such critics.

Hammond concluded by saying to Clarkson, "May God forgive you." He pictured the abolitionist, in other words, as a do-good dupe, whose reforms had brought far more harm than good to the world. In a later speech in the U.S. Senate, Hammond asserted: "Your whole hireling class of manual laborers and 'operatives,' as you call them, are essentially slaves. The difference between us is, that our slaves are hired for life and well compensated."[47]

As Hammond's letters and speeches demonstrate, the most striking part of the Southern proslavery ideology was its indictment of liberalism and capitalism—its well-documented charge that the prevailing rule in so-called free societies, as George Fitzhugh put it, was "every man for himself, and Devil take the hindmost." In his *Sociology for the South* (1854) and *Cannibals All!* (1857), Fitzhugh sharply criticized the philosophic premises of an individualistic, egalitarian society. When all men are considered equal, he pointed out, all aspire to the highest honors and largest possessions: "In a free society none but the selfish virtues are in repute, because none other help a man in the race of competition."[48]

Fitzhugh also examined the destructive historical consequences of dissolving the social and psychological networks that had once given human beings a sense of place and purpose. While successful men in Britain and the North deluded themselves into thinking that their social system was fair and just, and congratulated themselves for their own affluence, the whole "weight" of society, Fitzhugh claimed, was thrown upon its poorest and weakest members, who were then condemned for failure. Fitzhugh, in some ways the most rigorous and consistent proslavery theorist, presented the master-slave relation as the only alternative to a world in which unlimited self-interest had subjected workers without property to the impersonal exploitation of "wage-slavery." Ironically, Fitzhugh carried on a fascinating correspondence with the radical abolitionist Gerrit Smith, who had married Fitzhugh's cousin. Characterizing himself as a reformer, Fitzhugh told Smith that his views of slavery as benign apprenticeship were not that different from Smith's abolitionism.[49]

For some years Fitzhugh was consistent enough to renounce racial justifications for actual slavery and to propose that the benefits of the institution he boasted of be extended to white workers. As Abraham Lincoln pointed out, when with some alarm he read Fitzhugh's *Sociology for the South*, if enslavement were to be determined by intellectual superiority or skin color, one could be enslaved by anyone who was smarter or fairer in complexion.[50]

But Fitzhugh's arguments, however interesting theoretically, only showed how far he had moved from social reality. Virulent racism lay at the heart of the South's extremely shaky unity. The enslavement of whites was politically unthinkable, and in the 1850s the South even rejected proposals for expelling or reenslaving a quarter-million free blacks. In the 1850s Southern legislatures also rejected extremist but powerful moves to reopen the African slave trade in order to enable more middle-class whites to join the elite ranks of slaveowners.[51]

The great mission of proslavery theorists was to convince and command the loyalty of non-slaveholding whites, who constituted a growing majority. In an early version of the American dream, writers also stressed the goal of upward mobility and the possibility of joining the slaveholding class. Whatever moral doubts about slavery persisted, at least in the Upper South, they were more than counterbalanced by the growing conviction that emancipation in any form would be a disaster, for blacks as well as for whites.

A few Southerners channeled their moral concern into efforts to reform and improve the system—thus in the 1850s some clergy led a futile movement to legalize and protect slave marriage—but as the Southern states seceded and began to fight for their independence, proslavery ideology permeated schoolbooks, newspapers, speeches, and sermons. It was the mission of the Confederacy, ordinary whites were told, to carry out God's design for an inferior and dependent race. Slaveholders claimed that owning slaves always entailed a duty and a burden—a duty and burden that defined the moral superiority of the South. And this duty and burden was respected by millions of nonslaveholding whites, who were prepared to defend it with their lives. That, perhaps, was the ultimate meaning of a "slave society."

10

Slavery in the Nineteenth-Century South, II: From Slaveholder Treatment and the Nature of Labor to Slave Culture, Sex and Religion, and Free Blacks

I<small>N</small> THEORY, the Southern slaveholder possessed all the power of any owner of living chattel property, such as horses, sheep, cows, or oxen. We have seen that Aristotle referred to the ox "as the poor man's slave"; "the chattel principle" was probably best defined by the American fugitive slave James W. C. Pennington:

> The being of slavery, its soul and its body, lives and moves in the chattel principle, the property principle, the bill of sale principle; the cart-whip, starvation, and nakedness, are its inevitable consequences. . . . You cannot constitute slavery without the chattel principle—and with the chattel principle you cannot save it from these results. Talk not about kind and Christian masters. They are not masters of the system. The system is master of them.[1]

The system did include state laws that were partly designed to limit the power of masters, but such laws were difficult to enforce, especially in sparsely populated rural states where slaveowners monopolized political power. By the nineteenth century state laws were supposed to protect slaves from murder and mutilation. They set minimal standards for food, clothing, and shelter. They also prohibited masters from teaching slaves to read or from allowing slaves to carry firearms or roam about the countryside. They increasingly restricted or in effect prohibited manumission. These slave codes acknowledged that bondsmen were human beings who were capable of plotting, stealing, fleeing, or rebelling, and who were likely to be a less "troublesome property" if well cared for under a program of strict discipline. Yet as in ancient Rome and even Babylonia, the laws also insisted that the slave was a piece of property that could be sold, traded, rented, mortgaged, and inherited. In contrast to some other slave societies, the laws did not recognize the interests and institutions of the slave community, or the slave's right to marry, to hold property, or to testify in court.[2]

In practice it proved impossible to treat human beings as no more than possessions or as the mere instruments of an owner's will, though attempts to do so were often made, as many former slaves recounted. Today, following a long but revolutionary shift in moral perception that has stigmatized slavery as a crime, it is extremely difficult to see the world through slaveholders' eyes. Most masters were primarily motivated by the desire for income and profit, supplemented by a desire for personal power that could be mitigated by a desire to be thought of, especially by fellow planters, as good Christians and decent fellows—values that could change abruptly when there was an alarm or sudden panic or a need to get really tough. Still, one can neither overlook nor exaggerate many instances when whites expressed genuine admiration and even affection for individual slaves.

In economic terms, owners wanted to maximize their slaves' productivity while protecting the value of their capital investment, a value that kept rising with the generally escalating trend in slave prices. Accordingly, it made sense to provide a material standard of living that would promote good health and a natural increase in the size of slave families, and thus increase capital gains. It also made sense to keep the slaves' morale as high as possible and to encourage them to do willingly and even cheerfully the work they would be forced to do in the last resort. Convinced of the moral legitimacy of the system, most slaveowners sincerely believed that their own best interests were identical with their slaves' best interests, though most masters admitted that the system, like any institution, was capable of being abused.

Still, like marriage, slavery could supposedly be made to work to everyone's advantage. Planters therefore sought to convince the slaves of the essential justice of slavery. Like their Roman predecessors, they also expected gratitude for their acts of kindness, indulgence, and generosity, and even for their restraint in inflicting physical punishment.

The countless ads for runaway slaves reveal an almost pathetic faith that a given slave, who was said at times to have been very friendly and wanting to please, would accept an offer of forgiveness and "come home" like an errant son. Most masters desperately sought a consensual element, a sign of consent and gratitude on the part of at least some slaves. This is what some historians have meant by "paternalism," which should never be understood as implying that slavery was less cruel or exploitative than the abolitionists claimed.[3]

Clearly most slaves were not passive, agreeable puppets who could be manipulated at will, though in every group such people probably exist. As human beings, most slaves had one overriding objective: self-preservation at a minimal cost of degradation and loss of self-respect. For most, the goal of "freedom" was simply unrealistic, especially after the sharp decline in manumissions, except under highly unusual circumstances.

To avoid punishment and win rewards, slaves carried out their owners' demands with varying degrees of thoroughness. It is impossible for us to deny that they *did* work hard or that they *were* productive, but black slaves became cunningly expert at testing their masters' will. They learned how to mock while seeming to flatter; how to lighten unending work with moments of spontaneity, song, intimacy, and relaxation; how to exploit the whites' dependence on black field drivers and household servants; and especially how to play on the conflicts between their masters and white overseers.[4] Even at slave markets they learned how body language, feigned illness, unruliness, and saying what traders or buyers wanted to hear could influence their sale. In short, they learned through constant experiment and struggle how to preserve a core of dignity and self-respect.[5]

In certain personal situations a slave could also gain extraordinary power. Sarah Gayle, the young wife of an Alabama governor, recorded in her diary the frustrations she felt over what she called the "insubordination" of a household slave named Hampton:

> I never saw such a negro in all my life before—he did not even pretend to regard a command of mine, and treated me, and what I said, with the utmost contempt. He has often laughed in my face and told me that I was the only mistress he ever failed to please, on my saying he should try another soon [a threat to sell Hampton], he said he could not be worsted, and was willing to go.[6]

Although slavery "worked" very well as an economic system, its fundamental conflict of interests created a highly unstable and violent society. The great sugar planters in southern Louisiana and cotton growers in the Delta country of Mississippi, often employing more than one hundred slaves on a productive unit, tried to merge Christian paternalism with a kind of welfare capitalism. Many provided professional medical care, offered monetary rewards for extra productivity, and granted a week or more of Christmas vacation. Several travelers noted that American masters wanted above all to be *"popular"* with their slaves—a characteristically American need that was probably rare in Brazil or the Caribbean.[7] (If slavery had persisted into the later twentieth century, as Abraham Lincoln predicted in 1858,[8] one can only

half-facetiously imagine large corporate planters passing out "overseer evalu-
ation forms" to the slaves.) The master's sense of his own popularity was
doubtless reinforced by the tendency of slaves "to think that the greatness of
their masters," as Frederick Douglass put it, "was transferable to themselves."
Hence, according to Douglass:

> Many [slaves] think their own masters are better than the masters of other
> slaves. . . . Indeed, it is not uncommon for slaves even to fall out and quarrel
> among themselves about the relative goodness of their masters, each con-
> tending for the superior goodness of his own over that of the others. . . .When
> Colonel Lloyd's slaves met the slaves of Jacob Jepson, they seldom parted
> without a quarrel about their masters; Colonel Lloyd's slaves contending
> that he was the richest, and Mr. Jepson's slaves that he was the smartest,
> and most of a man. . . . [T]o be a poor man's slave was deemed a disgrace
> indeed![9]

Like all humans, slaves were sensitive to privilege, status, and inequality.
As the historian Kenneth Stampp wrote long ago, "a thousand-dollar slave
felt superior to an eight-hundred-dollar slave," just as "domestics flaunted
their superiority over 'the less favored helots of the plough,' " and some Virginia field hands "could lavish their own contempt upon the 'coal pit niggers'
who were hired to work in the mines." More universal, perhaps, was the
disdain with which slaves regarded poor whites, "whom they scornfully called
'po' buckra' and 'white trash.' "[10]

Yet we must never forget that these same "welfare capitalist" plantations
in the Deep South were essentially ruled by terror. Even the most kindly and
humane masters knew that only the threat of violence could force gangs of
field hands to work from dawn to dusk "with the discipline," as one contemporary observer put it, "of a regular trained army." Frequent public floggings
reminded every slave of the penalty for inefficient labor, disorderly conduct,
or refusal to accept the authority of a superior.

Bennet H. Barrow, a particularly harsh Louisiana slaveowner, maintained
discipline by ordering occasional mass whippings of *all* his field hands. Barrow also had offenders chained or thrust under water, and on at least one
occasion he shot a black who was about to run away. But like other planters,
Barrow mainly relied on more minor punishments such as solitary confine-
ment, withdrawing visiting privileges, and forbidding a Saturday night dance.
As it happened, however, Barrow also gave frequent holidays, distributed
generous monetary bonuses to his slaves, and bought them much-desired
Christmas presents in New Orleans!

The South could point to far gentler masters who seldom if ever inflicted physical punishment, and who relied for incentives on prizes of various sorts and even large cash rewards for superior work. Slaves understood,

however, that even the mildest of whites could become cruel despots when faced with the deception or ingratitude of a people who, regardless of pretenses to the contrary, were kept down by force.[11]

Masters also uneasily sensed that circumstances might transform a truly loyal and devoted slave into a vengeful enemy. It is true that white Southerners could congratulate themselves on the infrequency of serious slave uprisings, especially when they compared the South with Brazil and most of the Caribbean (as we will see in Chapter Eleven). Yet the French colony of Saint-Domingue had enjoyed at least as secure a history as the American South before exploding with the greatest and most successful slave revolt in human history. To the outside world, Southerners presented a brave façade of self-confidence. Individual masters reassured themselves that their own slaves were happy and loyal, but rumors of arson, poisoning, and suppressed revolts continued to flourish. Alarmists frequently warned that outside agitators were secretly sowing discontent among the slaves. This widespread fantasy, which at times may not have been entirely fantasy, at least hinted at the truth: Not only did slavery have diminishing·approval in the outside world, but the institution ultimately depended on the sheer weight of superior force—perhaps, as the U.S. Constitution even recognized, on Northern and federal military aid in the event of a truly major crisis.[12]

As we have already noted with respect to the colonial period, the difficulties in generalizing about the slave's world are compounded by the extensive geographic, climatic, and cultural diversities of the "South"—now, in the pre–Civil War decades, a region extending from Maryland to Texas but also a region in which mountain highlands, pine forests, and swampy lowlands could all be encountered within a few hundred miles of one another.

Unlike the small and isolated West Indian islands, the sprawling South was in no way a united or uniform society. The sections most dependent on slave labor included the swampy lowcountry of South Carolina and the adjoining Sea Islands, the remarkably fertile Black Belt (named for the soil that extended from Georgia westward through Mississippi), the rich delta counties of Mississippi, and the sugar parishes (counties) of Louisiana.

In 1860, out of a white population of some eight million, roughly ten thousand families belonged to the planter "aristocracy." Fewer than three thousand families could be counted as owners of over one hundred slaves. Only one out of four white Southerners owned a slave or belonged to a family that did. There were extensive regions of eastern Tennessee and western Virginia where blacks, slave or free, were a rarity. By 1860 slavery had declined sharply in most of the Upper South—most dramatically of all in Delaware, where fewer than two thousand slaves remained. (Yet, as we will see in Chapter Fifteen, even Delaware's slaveowners turned down President Lincoln's appeal for compensated, gradual emancipation.) Nor could most of the nonslaveholding majority be classed as hillbillies or poor whites. In addition to artisans, factory workers, and professionals, there were millions of small farmers in the South who worked their own land or who grazed herds of cattle, pigs, and horses in the forests and open range of the public domain.[13]

During most of the antebellum years, almost half of the Southern slaveholders owned fewer than five slaves; 72 percent owned fewer than ten. The "typical" master would thus know a great deal about each of his or her slaves (a good many women, especially widows, did own slaves) and could thus devote close personal attention to this so-called human property. Some small farmers worked side by side with their slaves, an arrangement that might often have been far more uncomfortable and humiliating for the slaves than working in a field gang under black "drivers." Then again, there were clearly some sadistic black drivers, as well as some genial and kindly white farmers. From the slave's viewpoint, much depended on the accidents of sale, on an owner's character, on the size and nature of the slave community, on the norms of a given locality, and on the relative difficulty of harvesting cotton, rice, tobacco, or sugar.[14]

Slave experiences thus covered an immensely wide range—from a few cases of remarkable privilege and physical comfort, combined with a lack of restraint, to the most savage and unrelieved exploitation. As an example of extraordinary privilege, the Mississippi slave Simon Gray became the captain of a Mississippi River flatboat and actually paid wages to a crew including white men.[15] But to dwell on contrasting examples of physical treatment is to risk losing sight of the central horror of human bondage.

As the Quaker John Woolman pointed out in the mid-eighteenth century, no human is saintly enough to be entrusted with total power over another. The slave was an inviting target for the hidden anger, passion, frustration, and revenge from which no human is exempt. A slave's work, leisure, movement, and daily fate depended on the largely unrestrained will of another person. Moreover, despite the numerical predominance of small slaveholders, *most* Southern slaves were concentrated on large farms and plantations.

In other words, we find very different pictures if we look statistically at the typical masters and then at typical slaves. Over half the slaves in the American South belonged to owners who held twenty or more slaves; one-quarter belonged to productive units of more than fifty slaves. Throughout the South, slave ownership was the primary road to wealth, and the most successful masters cornered an increasing share of the growing but limited supply of human capital.

Let us consider, then, what life was like on a fairly large average plantation. Soon after sunrise, black drivers herded gangs of men and women into the fields. As described by Solomon Northup, a Northern free black who was kidnapped in Washington and then worked for twelve years as a slave in

Louisiana before being finally freed: "During all these hoeings the overseer or driver follows the slaves on horseback with a whip. . . .The fastest hoer takes the lead row. He is usually about a rod in advance of his companions. If one of them passes him, he is whipped. If one falls behind or is a moment idle, he is whipped. In fact, the lash is flying from morning until night."[16]

Slave women, including pregnant women and nursing mothers, were also subjected to heavy field labor. Even small children served as water carriers or began to learn the lighter tasks of field work, though many younger ones also played with the plantation's white children. We even have descriptions of slave children pretending to be drivers or overseers, whipping one another. That said, many slave children like Frederick Douglass did not fully realize that they were slaves until surprisingly late. But as Douglass and numerous other former slaves testified, the shock of coming to terms with a slave identity was then devastating, especially in a country that talked of liberty and equality and took such pride in disavowing hereditary titles and aristocratic status.[17]

Slaves who were too old for field work took care of small children and also worked in the stables, gardens, and kitchens. This full employment of all available hands was one of the economies of the system that increased the total output from a planter's capital investment. (In free-labor societies, a significant percentage of the total population performs little or no work at all.) Nevertheless, slaves often succeeded in maintaining their own work rhythm and in helping to define the amount of labor a planter could reasonably expect. Bursts of intense effort required during cotton picking, corn shucking, or the eighteen-hour-a-day sugar harvest were followed by periods of festivity and relaxation. Where the task system prevailed, as in coastal South Carolina, slaves were strongly motivated to complete specified tasks by working as hard as possible, thus freeing much of an afternoon for their own gardening or other pursuits. Elsewhere, even in relatively slack seasons, there were cattle to be tended, fences to be repaired, forests to be cleared, and food crops to be planted.

Black slaves were saved from becoming mere robots in the field by the strength of their own communities and evolving culture.[18] There has long been bitter controversy over the degree to which various African cultural patterns were able to survive in North America, to say nothing of the degree to which African American culture challenged the slave system or actually aided masters and slaves in negotiating a workable world. In contrast to Cuba and Brazil, where continuing slave importations sustained for blacks a living bond with African cultures, the vast majority of blacks in the nineteenth-century South were removed by several generations from an African-born ancestor.[19] In addition, America's slaves had far more diverse African tribal and ethnic origins than did the slaves in Brazil. Nevertheless, some archaeological and other forms of research have uncovered striking examples of African influence in the Southern slaves' oral traditions, folklore, songs, dances, language, sculpture, religion, and kinship patterns. The question at issue is not the purity or even the persistence of distinct African forms. In the New World *all* imported cultures, whether from Europe, Asia, or Africa, have undergone blending, adaptation, and combination with other elements. What matters is that Southern slaves, at least on the larger plantations, created their own African American culture, which helped to preserve some of the more crucial areas of life and thought from white control or domination without significantly reducing the productivity and profitability of slave labor.

Living within this African American culture, sustained by strong community ties, many slaves were able to maintain a certain sense of apartness, of pride, and of independent identity. Yet the brilliant former slave Frederick Douglass and some other black leaders pointed out that such apartness posed the seductive danger for freed blacks of perpetuating a slavelike subordination and of preventing blacks from mastering the skills and knowledge needed for eventual success and upward mobility in a nation like the United States. Every immigrant group faced this volatile question of acculturation, of modernization, and of acquiring the tools for a successful life in a competitive society.

At the present moment, when we see a global upsurge of nationalisms of all kinds, many Americans seem more conscious of the *costs* of adaptation and of the need for discovering distinctive ethnic, class, and cultural roots. As a result, some writers have exaggerated the autonomy and independence of the cultural forms embraced by African American slaves, when in actuality this African heritage not only intermixed with various European and Christian traditions but exerted a profound influence on Southern *white* patterns of speech, religion, and behavior.[20]

It is notable that plantations with more than fifty slaves contained on average 1.5 adult white males.[21] This fact dramatizes the relative weakness of white surveillance as well as the system's reliance on a hierarchy of black drivers, managers, artisans, and mechanics. And despite the hierarchies of power, these statistics show why African American culture could flourish in a largely black world—a world that did not undermine the white owners' overall goal of production. African kinship patterns seem to have been the main vehicle for the maintenance of cultural identity. As in West Africa, children were frequently named for grandparents, who were revered even in memory.

Kinship patterns survived even the breakup of families, although mother-headed families and family fragmentation were far commoner on plantations with fewer than fifteen slaves. On smaller plantations and farms, slaves found it far more difficult to find a spouse or keep families intact. On larger plantations, nonrelatives often took on the functions and responsibilities of grandparents, uncles, and aunts. Many younger slaves were cared for and protected by surrogate "aunts" and "uncles" who were not blood kin. Some of these older teachers and guardians passed on knowledge of the time when their ancestors had not been slaves, before the fateful crossing of the sea.[22]

Although slave marriages and slave families had no legal standing or protection, they were at least initially encouraged by most planters and provided a refuge from the dehumanizing effects of being treated as chattel property. The strength of family bonds is suggested by the thousands of slaves who ran away from their owners in search of family members separated through sale. The notion that blacks had weak family attachments is also countered by the swarms of freedmen who roamed the South at the end of the Civil War in search of their spouses, parents, or children and by the eager desire of freedpeople to legalize their marriages.[23]

Nevertheless, the slave family was a highly vulnerable institution, especially in long-settled regions like Virginia that became increasingly dependent on selling "surplus" slaves, especially young males, to the booming Deep South and Southwest. Although some slaveowners had moral scruples against separating husbands from wives or small children from their mothers, even the strongest scruples frequently gave way in times of economic need. The forced sale of individual slaves in order to pay a deceased owner's debts further increased the chances of family breakups. In many parts of the South it was common for a slave to be married to another slave on a neighboring or even distant plantation—a relationship called an "abroad marriage." Even though such arrangements left visitation to the discretion of the slaves' two owners, they resulted in high rates of fertility. At best, however, slave marriage represented a precarious bond. According to the former slave George Washington Albright, who at age eleven saw his father sold and shipped off, "plantation owner[s] thought no more of selling a man away from his wife, or a mother away from her children, than of sending a cow or a horse out of the state."[24]

Sexual relations revealed a similar gap between moral scruples and actual practice. White planter society officially condemned interracial sexual unions and tended to blame lower-class white males for fathering mulatto children. Yet there is abundant evidence that many slaveowners, sons of slaveowners, and overseers took black mistresses or in effect raped the wives and daughters of slave families. This abuse of power may not have been quite as universal as Northern abolitionists claimed, but we now know that offenders included such prestigious figures as James Henry Hammond and even Thomas Jefferson.[25] The ubiquity of such sexual exploitation was sufficient to deeply scar and humiliate black women, to instill rage in black men, and to arouse both shame and bitterness in white women. When a young slave named Celia finally struck and killed her owner and predator, a prosperous Missouri farmer named Robert Newsom, her action led to a major trial that opened a rare window on the nature of this forbidden subject.

As the historian Melton A. McLaurin has put it, "Celia's trial, its causes and consequences, confront us with the hard daily realities of slavery rather than with the abstract theories about the workings of that institution."[26] McLaurin vividly shows that these daily realities involved personal decisions by both blacks and whites "of a fundamental moral nature."

In 1850 Robert Newsom was a highly respected family man who lived with his two grown daughters and three grandchildren while his four male slaves[27] helped him profit from growing livestock as well as wheat, rye, and corn. But at age sixty Newsom had been a widower for nearly a year and longed for a sexual partner. Instead of courting one of the available white women in his own Callaway County, he slipped over to Audrain County and purchased Celia, who was approximately fourteen, and raped her as he took her home. While Celia was purportedly a housekeeper for Newsom's daughters, Newsom built her a brick cabin of her own and used it as the site for his sexual exploits. During the next five years Celia gave birth to two infants and exemplified as a concubine one of the less publicized uses of enslavement.

By 1855 Celia had become romantically attached to Newsom's slave George, who demanded that she cease all sexual contact with their master. Celia first appealed without success to Newsom's grown daughters, who clearly felt no bond of sisterhood. When Newsom refused to listen to Celia's pleas, she killed him and then burned and buried his remains. George, fearful for his own safety, then betrayed her and cooperated with those investigating the crime. After being repeatedly threatened by whites, Celia confessed. Most remarkable, perhaps, was the nature of the trial, in which Celia received a defense team of three court-appointed lawyers, one of them a respected three-term U.S. congressman. Even after conviction, Celia was in some way enabled to break out of jail in order to avoid execution before the Missouri Supreme Court could consider an appeal. Still, on December 21, 1855, Celia went to the gallows, following a series of decisions that underscored the ultimate powerlessness of slaves.

Although nothing is said of Celia's religion, the so-called Second Great Awakening, beginning in the first years of the nineteenth century, encouraged many Southern planters to promote the religious conversion of their slaves. In contrast to earlier planter hostility to missionaries, especially in the Caribbean, a growing number of Southern churchmen and planters argued that religious instruction would make slaves more obedient, industrious, and faithful. In conformity with numerous passages in the New Testament, the ideal Christian master would treat his slaves with charity and understanding. The ideal Christian slave would humbly accept his assigned position in *this* world, knowing that his patience and faithfulness would be rewarded in heaven.

Servitude, in short, could be softened, humanized, and perfected by Christianity. (The interests and behavior of masters like Robert Newsom were simply repressed.)[28]

Obviously, the reality of slavery fell far short of the ideal, but even fervent Christians would expect such shortcomings in a Fallen World, permeated with sin. Even those historians and economists who have tended to give a more benign picture of slave living standards have had to recognize that planter self-interest did not prevent a ghastly slave infant mortality rate or the serious malnutrition of slave children. Religion may well have induced some masters to take a sincere interest in their slaves' welfare. By the 1850s, at least, many religious leaders in the South were calling for the legalization and protection of slave marriages and for the repeal of laws against teaching slaves to read, especially reading the Bible. But religion could never eliminate the cruelty and injustice inherent in the system.[29]

That said, no white preachers could entirely purge the Judeo-Christian tradition, as embodied in the Bible, of some messages and values that tended to challenge slavery. One thinks, for example, of the frequently mentioned Hebrew Day of Jubilee, occurring every fifty years, when, according to many interpreters, *all* slaves were supposed to be freed.[30] Understandably, black spirituals became saturated with references to and faith in a coming Jubilee. Then there is the passage from the prophet Isaiah, which Jesus stood up to read in the synagogue at Nazareth, regarding his mission "to proclaim liberty to the captives, and the opening of the prison to them that are bound."[31] Above all, much of the Hebrew Bible turns on the fact that God responded not to the grandeur of kings exuding wealth and power but to the pleas and cries of lowly Hebrew slaves. Their deliverance from bondage in Egypt was clearly intended to teach the world some kind of lesson.

Nor could whites prevent black preachers from converting Christianity into a source of self-respect, dignity, and faith in eventual liberation—the longed-for Day of Jubilee. In both the North and the South, free blacks responded to growing racial discrimination by forming what they called African churches, usually Baptist or Methodist. And despite efforts by whites to control every aspect of their slaves' religion, the slaves created their own folk religion and shaped it to their needs and interests.

Especially on the larger plantations one could find conjurers whose alleged magic powers were thought to ward off sickness, soften a master's heart, or hasten the success of a courtship. Many black preachers mixed Christianity with elements of West African religions and folklore, including the famous "ring shout," a religious dance or shuffle:[32] Several slaves would beat time with their feet and sing in unison while others danced around a circle in single file, keeping their bodily movements in perfect time with the music. In the slave quarters particular prestige was attached to those who excelled at the traditional memorizing of songs, riddles, folktales, superstitions, and herb cures—who were carriers, in short, of African American culture, which especially in the twentieth century would be translated into forms that would thrill much of the world.

The slaves' oral communication allowed free play to the imagination, enabling African Americans to interpret and comment on the pathos, humor, absurdity, sorrow, and warmth of the scenes they experienced. Together with the ceremonial rituals, especially at slave weddings and funerals, the oral traditions preserved a sanctuary of human dignity that enabled most slaves to survive the humiliations, debasement, and self-contempt that were inseparable from human bondage.

A final word should be said concerning the status of free blacks. Before the American Revolution this status had been ambiguous, and the number of free blacks was insignificant. By 1810, however, as a result of the emancipations that had accompanied and followed the Revolution, there were approximately one hundred thousand free blacks and mulattoes in the Southern states. This group, for a time the fastest-growing element in the Southern population, was beginning to acquire property, to found "African" churches and schools, and to assert its independence, especially in the Upper South.

In response, white legislators tightened restrictions on private acts of freeing slaves in an effort to curb the growth of an unwanted population. A rash of new laws, similar to the later Black Codes of Reconstruction, reduced free blacks almost to the status of slaves without masters. The new laws regulated their freedom of movement, forbade them to associate with slaves, subjected them to surveillance and discipline by whites, denied them the legal right to testify in court against whites, required them to work at approved jobs, and threatened them with penal labor if not actual reenslavement. Paradoxically, in parts of the Deep South free blacks continued to benefit from a more flexible status because there were fewer of them than elsewhere in the South and they could serve as valued intermediaries between a white minority and a slave majority, as in the West Indies. Racial discrimination became harsher in the Upper South precisely because slavery was economically less secure in that region.[33] The intense and even worsening racism from Virginia to New England presented an ominous message with respect to a postemancipation America.

11

Some Nineteenth-Century
Slave Conspiracies and Revolts

SINCE THE 1960s most American historians have shown considerable sympathy and support for slave conspiracies and revolts as the most extreme form of legitimate resistance against racist dehumanization and oppression. In earlier decades most historians, who were overwhelmingly white, expressed horror over the slaughter of whites, especially women and children; paid little attention to the execution, often without a trial, of hundreds of blacks accused of conspiracy or rebellion; and looked upon such figures as Nat Turner as pathological killers.

Few writers noted that in 1777 the famous Samuel Johnson lifted his glass in Oxford and toasted: "Here's to the next insurrection of the negroes in the West Indies!"[1] And as early as 1760 a British writer who called himself "Philmore" set forth the moral justification for such slave violence:

> And so all the black men now in our plantations, who are by unjust force deprived of their liberty, and held in slavery, as they have none upon earth to appeal to, may lawfully repel that force with force, and to recover their liberty, destroy their oppressors: and not only so, but it is the duty of others, white as well as blacks, to assist those miserable creatures, if they can, in their attempts to deliver themselves out of slavery, and to rescue them out of the hands of their cruel tyrants.[2]

This form of argument resembled the "give me liberty or give me death" philosophy that undergirded the American Revolution. And for most African

Americans as well as for modern progressive white historians, evidence of resistance of all kinds has seemed extremely important in counteracting the older traditional white view that African American slaves passively accepted their plight and were even loyal and dutiful to their owners (as they were instructed to be by the epistles of Peter and Paul in the New Testament).[3]

When the famous escaped slave Frederick Douglass conducted lecture tours around the antebellum North, providing vivid testimony on the evils of Southern slavery, whites repeatedly asked him why the slaves did not rebel. Since whites in his audiences affirmed that *they* would overthrow such oppressors if they were enslaved, Douglass was forced to deal with the growing white consensus that the absence of revolts after 1831 proved that America's slaves were contented with their lot and were docile or cowardly by nature.

Though often referring to himself as a "peace man," Douglass pointed to the heroism of Nat Turner and Madison Washington, the slave who led the mutiny on the American slave ship *Creole*, which we will discuss in Chapter Fourteen. He then stressed the North's complicity and the constitutional commitment to protect slavery, and thus the hopelessness of a contest between "seventeen millions of armed, disciplined, and intelligent people, against three millions of unarmed and uninformed." He affirmed that millions of slaves longed to arise and strike for liberty, as they had in the Caribbean, but while admitting the joy he would feel at the news of an insurrection in the Southern states, Douglass also maintained, as human history has confirmed, that slave rebellions are almost always suicidal.[4]

As matters developed, the belief in American slave docility dominated popular and academic history in the long period from the turn of the twentieth century to the late 1950s, and inevitably gave support to white racist policies in the pre-civil-rights era. There were, of course, dissenting voices; among them was Herbert Aptheker's 1943 *American Negro Slave Revolts*, which uncovered countless rumors of slave conspiracies and defended figures like Nat Turner, but since Aptheker was a known Communist as well as a Marxist, his work had little influence on mainstream history at least until the 1960s. And because the subject of slave conspiracies and revolts has been so charged with high-voltage ideology, and because the actual evidence of conspiracies has been sparse, one-sided, and often repressed, today's readers need to be aware of conflicting interpretations and should not be sheltered from continuing professional controversies that may never be settled, such as the meaning of Nat Turner's bloody insurrection of 1831 and the reality of Denmark Vesey's much larger alleged conspiracy of 1822.

We have already examined some of the earlier slave uprisings, ranging from the Stono Rebellion in South Carolina to the most successful slave warfare in human history, the Haitian Revolution. In this chapter it is my hope to illuminate three of the controversial acts of resistance in the United States by comparing them to the three major slave revolts in the nineteenth-century British Caribbean.

At the outset we need to note the striking contrast between North America and the many other slave societies to the south with respect to the frequency and size of slave revolts as well as slave escapes to fairly durable maroon communities. Although the population of slaves in the United States eventually dwarfed the numbers in Brazil and the Caribbean, there were no significant revolts in the colonial Chesapeake from 1619 to 1775 or in the nation as a whole from 1831 to 1865.[5] In Brazil, by contrast, slave revolts were more common, and in the 1600s thousands of fugitives found refuge for nearly a century in the maroon community of Palmares, until the Brazilian army finally destroyed the refuge in 1694. Major slave insurrections continued to erupt in British Jamaica from the 1670s to 1831, and the island's maroon communities were so formidable that they negotiated treaties with the colonial government. Somewhat similar patterns appeared in Dutch Suriname, in Spanish Cuba, and in much but not all of the Caribbean.

As late as 1959, evidence of the American slaves' apparent passivity seemed so strong that the young historian Stanley Elkins flipped the message upside down, so to speak. He argued in a famous book that as a result of unmitigated capitalism, slavery in the United States became so uniquely severe and oppressive, especially in its affliction of psychological damage, that it could be compared to the Nazi concentration camps that supposedly reduced many victims to the absolute dependency of "the perpetual child." Elkins contrasted the bloody slave revolts and actual warfare between slaves and whites in Latin America with what seemed like pathetic gestures toward revolt in the United States.[6]

Although Elkins had wished to underscore the unprecedented harshness of American slavery, his portrait of the infantilized "Sambo" infuriated radicals of the 1960s and 1970s, both black and white. As a new generation of historians and novelists began to celebrate slave resistance, they searched for more detailed examples that went beyond what had been termed the "day-to-day resistance" of theft, sabotage, work slowdowns, poisoning the whites' food, and flight.[7] Some writers pointed with undisguised delight at a well-planned conspiracy led in 1800 by a slave named Gabriel (not Prosser, his owner's name, as some historians have assumed).

Gabriel and his fellow leaders, all privileged slaves familiar with the economics and culture of urban Virginia, hoped to take advantage of the increasing political warfare between Federalists and Republicans as the nation approached its most divisive presidential election prior to 1860 (Jefferson versus John Adams). Mobilizing large numbers of slave artisans and mechanics in towns from the coast to the piedmont, Gabriel's lieutenants might well have captured Richmond, Virginia, and taken Governor James Monroe hostage if a violent thunderstorm had not prevented a planned rendezvous and induced several house slaves to reveal the plot to the authorities. While this event traumatized Virginia's leaders and much of the slaveholding South, one should not minimize the fact that "loyal" slave informers prevented any whites from being killed or harmed, won freedom as their reward, and ensured that many other slaves (at least twenty-seven) would be hanged.[8]

Curiously, much less has been written about an actual revolt in January 1811 in the recently acquired territory of Louisiana. Led by a privileged slave driver named Charles Deslondes, as many as two hundred slaves marched toward New Orleans, burning three plantations and killing a number of whites before being checked and defeated by an official military force. As many as one hundred slaves were executed or killed in battle.[9]

Far more attention has been given to the Denmark Vesey conspiracy of 1822, which we will examine later on, and to Nat Turner's insurrection of 1831, which was primarily aimed at killing whites and has remained the central and highly contested symbol of American slave resistance. The Turner story exemplifies the problem of highly limited and unverifiable evidence, mostly records of slave testimony. Moreover, interpretations of the Vesey event from the era of abolitionists to modern histories, novels, and television documentaries have raised a controversial moral problem of means and ends: the attempt to justify the most extreme means of violence in order to raise the human cost of an oppressive system based on sheer violence.[10]

Historians seem to agree on the following bare narrative: Turner's revolt began in the dark early hours of August 22, 1831, in Southampton County, Virginia, a somewhat isolated rural region in which most whites owned only a few slaves and many owned none at all. Starting with Turner's "own" white family (he was legally owned by the nine-year-old Putnam Moore), Turner and his followers killed all the whites in one farmhouse after another as they moved by horse through the countryside. While there is no evidence of rape, plunder, or burning houses, the blacks—eventually but briefly including some fifty to sixty mounted insurgents—murdered nearly sixty whites, most of them women and children.[11]

By dawn the next morning the local militia had killed or captured all the rebels except Turner, who miraculously escaped and eluded searchers for sixty-eight days. Meanwhile, Virginia's governor mobilized over three thousand soldiers, the militia and vigilantes killed well over one hundred suspected insurrectionists, and whites gathered for possible racial war in Virginia and neighboring North Carolina. After a series of rapid trials, the authorities executed only nineteen of the thirty slaves who were convicted and sentenced to death. The others were transported outside the state, along with some three hundred Southampton County free blacks who agreed to be shipped to Liberia.[12]

One of the most telling and drastic responses to the Turner group's slaughter of whites was the rush by Southern states to pass laws making it a crime to teach slaves to read. Because Turner was literate and many whites suspected that he and his men had been influenced by such radical antislavery works as David Walker's *Appeal to the Coloured Citizens of the World*, published in 1829, this "legally mandated illiteracy," in the words of the historian James Oakes, became "an appallingly ironic indication of the degree to which Southern whites had imbibed the liberal enlightenment's conception of literacy as crucial for a free citizenry."[13]

While a writer like "Philmore" could say that Turner and his men had lawfully set out to "destroy their oppressors" and repel "force with force," we will never know if there was some plan for "recovering liberty" or even be sure that Turner was the main or only leader.[14]

Before Turner was hanged, on November 11, 1831, he provided a white lawyer, Thomas R. Gray, with a long interview. Gray then published his version of this interchange, *The Confessions of Nat Turner*, which is the uncorroborated source of most of what we "know" about Turner and the revolt. There is general agreement that Turner was literate, well versed in the Bible, and religious in a messianic way; he spoke of receiving divine revelations and before his death demanded, "Was not Christ crucified?" (The late Herbert Aptheker has called this "one of the great moments in human history.") But as a powerful PBS documentary film makes clear, Nat Turner has always been and remains "A Troublesome Property," a figure who has been portrayed as a murderous religious fanatic and, especially in African American folklore and oral traditions, as a much-needed hero, prophet, and even "legendary trickster."[15]

Despite this positive theme, many slaves must have learned that the number of blacks killed in summary executions far exceeded the number of Turner's rebels as well as the number of white victims. In contrast to various kinds of modern terrorism and attempts at random killings, including those by high school students who feel psychologically degraded and dehumanized, there were no imitations of "Turner" or so-called copycat killings. Indeed, Turner stands at the very end of a sequence of relatively small actual slave rebellions in North America.

Yet the Turner crisis coincided with the upsurge of "immediatist" abolitionism in the North and especially in Britain, where, as we shall soon see, the infinitely larger Jamaican slave insurrection of December 1831 greatly strengthened the hands of abolitionists while, at the same time, strengthening the conviction of slaveholders that abolitionism would incite insurrections. Even in Virginia the traumatic slaughter of so many white families underscored the risks and costs of an allegedly paternalistic institution, and in 1832 it enabled legislators from the largely nonslaveholding western counties to launch a unique and futile debate in the state legislature over the future of a labor system that greatly favored the tidewater regions.[16]

With respect to abolitionism in the Northeast, the bloodshed in Virginia, especially of women and children, no doubt reinforced the pacifistic bent of the Garrisonians. William Lloyd Garrison himself, "horror-struck at the late tidings" from Virginia, helped to ensure the "nonresistance" principles of the American antislavery movement, which began to crumble only in the 1850s and were finally buried by Nat Turner's white counterpart, the murderer and savior John Brown.[17]

Without endorsing the Garrisonians' extreme rejection of all violence, one should note that the defense of indiscriminate killing of people who are "part of" an oppressive system bears a disturbing resemblance to historical justifications for murdering infidels, alleged upholders of the *ancien régime*, Russian kulaks, or capitalists. And the psychology governing such massacres is little different from the mental state that leads to the genocide of Jews, Armenians, Tutsis, or Sudanese blacks.

Elkins had actually taken note of Gabriel, Vesey, and Turner but had stressed that they were not *plantation* laborers but rather "Negroes whose qualities of leadership were developed well outside the full coercions of the plantation authority-system." Thus Gabriel was a skilled blacksmith who lived near Richmond. Denmark Vesey was a freed carpenter who had earlier worked in Saint-Domingue and on board a ship that may have even sailed to Africa. Nat Turner was a literate preacher of recognized intelligence whose rebellion, in Elkins's words, "was characterized by little more than aimless butchery."[18]

Before turning to "model" insurrections in the British Caribbean, we should understand that the lack of such huge uprisings in North America by no means proves or indicates that slaves were happy, content, carefree, or infantilized Sambos. In the Caribbean, in contrast to the United States, slaves often constituted as much as 90 percent of a colony's population; the real mystery is how three or four whites could both manage and control a highly productive plantation on an isolated island.

Moreover, during the millennia for which we have records of human bondage—going back to ancient Greece and Mesopotamia—revolts appear to have been extremely rare, even though slaveholder societies from antiquity to colonial South Carolina often armed slaves to help fight formidable enemies.[19] Finally, when we look at the three major slave rebellions in the nineteenth-century British Caribbean, the outcome underscores the futility of *any* form of violent resistance in a modern slave society—unless that society, like Saint-Domingue in the 1790s, became embroiled in a revolution and civil war dividing the slaveowners themselves. The major revolts in British St. Vincent and Grenada in 1795–96, which were part of the Anglo-French struggle for the Caribbean following the French edict of emancipation in 1794, destroyed more British lives and property than any other slave uprisings in the history of British slavery. Yet, as the historian Seymour Drescher has written, these events "literally disappeared from metropolitan abolitionist consciousness."[20]

By 1816 Barbados was hardly typical of the Caribbean, since a slave rebellion had not occurred there in 115 years; in contrast to most other islands, the colony's slave population had achieved a natural rate of growth; and 93 percent of the 77,493 slaves were Creole, or New World born (compared with 56 percent in Trinidad, which had not been annexed by Britain until 1797). Most Barbadian planters had even favored Britain's ending of slave importations from Africa, a law that gave them a competitive advantage over colonies like Trinidad and Jamaica, whose declining slave populations made them more dependent on imported labor from Africa. Barbados also had an unusually high percentage of resident whites (some 16.6 percent, with only 80 percent of the population made up of slaves).[21]

The history of slave resistance highlights the importance of news or at least rumors of significant outside support. Frederick Douglass described the elation he felt as a youth when he first discovered the existence of Northern abolitionists. At the beginning of the Haitian Revolution many French slaves became convinced that planters had suppressed an order calling for slave emancipation from the king of France.[22] Some of Denmark Vesey's alleged rebels were said to be inspired by reports of the congressional debates over the admission of Missouri as a slave state, including Senator Rufus King's radical attack in 1820 on the very legality of slavery.

Similar wish-fulfilling rumors spread among the slaves of Barbados when planters received news of the angry debates in Parliament in 1815 over instituting a central Registration of all slaves in the British colonies.[23] Abolitionist M.P.s like William Wilberforce, prodded by his brother-in-law James Stephen, presented this measure as a way of detecting any illegal importation of African slaves but privately saw it as the entering wedge toward their goal of "ameliorating" the condition of slaves by assessing their mortality and regulating their diet, physical punishment, and other kinds of treatment in preparation for gradual emancipation.[24]

Though imperial registration was a seemingly moderate, even innocuous measure, the West Indian interests fought the proposal as if it demanded outright emancipation. Barbadian planters engaged in inflammatory talk against such government intervention, accused the abolitionists of sending agents and spies to the island (in the form of missionaries), and demonized Wilberforce, who quickly became a hero among slaves. (In Jamaica, a slave ditty began, "Oh me good friend, Mr Wilberforce, make we free!/ God Almighty thank ye! God Almighty thank ye!") By June 1816 even the London *Times* echoed the Barbadian planters' conviction that Wilberforce had inspired the literate "negroes of the worst dispositions" who had instigiated the insurrection.[25]

When Barbadian planters expressed relief in January 1816 over the defeat of registration in the Barbados House of Assembly, a few of the privileged slaves who could read local and even London newspapers concluded that the embattled colonial authorities were defying England's plan of emancipation. Nanny Grigg, a literate domestic slave woman living in a "great house," had argued that Britain intended to free all slaves on New Year's Day 1816; she then revised the prediction to Easter Monday. Convinced that the planters were obstructing the will of the British king, she told her fellow slaves that they must fight for their freedom as their fellow slaves had done "in Saint Domingo." Such beliefs radiated outward and downward through a hidden but well-constructed network of slave communication.[26]

Although some slaves favored a nonviolent strike, the evidence indicates careful planning for the start of a major uprising on the evening of Easter Sunday, April 14, 1816. Later named for Bussa, an African slave and chief ranger on the Bayley plantation, the rebellion quickly spread to the island's seventy largest estates, leaving great houses and many cane fields aflame. Rebels even seized an armory near St. Philip's Church before the militia could defend it.[27]

What the insurgents had not counted on was the bravery and the loyalty to the whites of the free colored militia and black regular troops. During the long wars with Revolutionary and Napoleonic France, the British had learned the indispensability of arming black West India regiments in the hotly contested Caribbean. They had also found that the free colored population would be mostly prowhite and proslavery, especially if they could expect to be rewarded with new civil liberties, as was the case in Barbados following the Bussa Rebellion. Thus while the rebellious slaves of 1816 could gut the houses of whites, burn some 20 percent of the sugarcane, and spread turmoil across the island, they could not face the firepower of the ranks of armed white and black Redcoats, let alone defeat them. It is significant that Colonel Edward Codd, one of the leaders of the white troops, let the black militia march ahead of his own and thus win the battle at Bayley's plantation.[28]

In the skirmishes on Easter Monday, the government's troops killed at least fifty of the rebels and then summarily executed seventy more in the field. Some three hundred captive insurgents were then carried to Bridgetown, the capital, for trial. The authorities executed 144 of these captives, exposed some of their bodies and decapitated heads in public places, and deported most of the survivors, many to Belize, in Central America. Reports reached other British colonies that about a thousand Barbadian slaves had been killed in battle or executed under martial law. The most startling statistic, however, was that despite much destruction of property and the certain death of hundreds of slaves, the rebellious blacks killed only one white civilian and one black British soldier![29]

Paradoxically, some white leaders, such as Colonel Codd, were convinced that the slaves wanted to kill all the Barbadian white men and then keep the white women for sexual pleasure. At least one slave conveyed a similar but secondhand report during interrogation.[30] This nightmare image of sexual conquest is important to note, since it had emerged in slave confessions following the 1741 conspiracy in New York City and would resurface in Demerara, in Jamaica, and in the confessions associated with at least two nineteenth-century American slave conspiracies. Yet in Barbados the rebel slaves must have exercised extraordinary self-discipline in order to protect the many whites barricaded in their great houses and to limit white casualties to a single death. One could dismiss this outcome as a totally freakish event if there were not similar surprises in the subsequent and even larger slave rebellions in Demerara and Jamaica.

Despite this sparing of white lives, the Barbadian revolt brought a setback to the British antislavery movement. Coming in the aftermath of the Napoleonic Wars and in a period of conservative reaction against the French Revolution and recent domestic unrest and turmoil, the news of thousands of slave insurgents in Barbados enabled Lord Liverpool's administration to persuade Wilberforce to withdraw his motion for imposing an imperial Registration and to simply encourage colonial legislatures to establish their own systems of slave registration. James Stephen, the true mastermind of the antislavery movement, became so disillusioned by this retreat that he resigned his seat in the House of Commons.[31]

When news of the 1816 Barbadian rebellion reached the British slave colony of Demerara, Governor John Murray proclaimed that the Barbadian slaves had been "misled" to believe that an emancipation edict had been sent out by the British king. According to Murray, such an act would be unthinkable since slavery had always been an accepted part of human life and "every history proves that slavery has existed since the world was made."[32]

Situated on the northeast coast of South America, Demerara (part of later British Guiana) was a narrow strip of fertile land backed by forests, to the west of Dutch Suriname and British Berbice (and to the east of Spanish Venezuela). Having been occupied several times by the Dutch, French, and British, the colony fell finally into British hands in 1803. Partly as a result of the destruction of French Saint-Domingue, the planters, many of them absentee owners in England, intensified their slaves' labor by shifting much production from cotton to sugar. By 1823, the year of one of the largest and most significant slave revolts in West Indian history, the colony's seventy-seven thousand slaves faced only twenty-five hundred whites and a roughly equal number of free blacks.[33]

The year 1823 happened to be a pivotal one in the regeneration of the antislavery movement in Britain as mostly religious forces continued to shape the complex cultural response to Britain's rapidly developing industrial society. While in Britain an evangelical revival spread from the dissenting sects to the so-called Saints within the Church of England (symbolized by Wilberforce), the West India colonists and newspapers denounced the religious trend toward abolitionism and pictured missionaries (all seen as "Methodists") as "democratic" subversives embodying the egalitarian ideas that had ignited the French and Haitian revolutions.[34]

Following the creation in 1822 and 1823 of the first societies dedicated to the actual if gradual emancipation of all colonial slaves, Thomas Fowell Buxton, who had succeeded Wilberforce as the abolitionists' leader in Parliament, presented a motion in the House of Commons affirming:

> That the state of slavery is repugnant to the principles of the British Constitution, and of the Christian religion; and that it ought to be abolished gradually throughout the British Colonies, with as much expedition as may be found consistent with a due regard to the well-being of the parties concerned.[35]

Since the government was caught between a flood of antislavery petitions and bitter opposition from the powerful Society of West India Planters and Merchants, George Canning, the skilled Tory foreign secretary, quickly seized the initiative and substituted for Buxton's gradual emancipation plan his own administration's program for slave *amelioration*.

Whereas Buxton and the abolitionists had called for the emancipation of all slave children born after a specific date (as had been done by four Northern states in America), Canning stressed the importance of religious instruction for slaves, prohibiting them from working or running their own markets on the Sabbath, and outlawing the flogging of slave women. Many of Demerara's wealthiest absentee planter-merchants, such as John Gladstone, who owned over two thousand slaves and was the father of the famous future prime minister, feared that the rhetoric of evangelical abolitionists would destroy some of the British elite's enormous investment in slaves and land by sparking Haitian-like revolutions. Yet living in England, far from the racism and daily brutalities of colonies like Demerara and Jamaica, many such slaveowners favored measures that would soften the public image of Caribbean labor. To the dismay of their on-site managers, overseers, and even governors, they therefore supported the reforms that Lord Bathurst, the colonial secretary, recommended to the colonies.[36]

Even most English opponents of the abolitionists approved the Christianization of slaves, and even the bishop of London thought that slaves should be taught how to read and thus gain access to the Bible. And as the London Missionary Society recruited young artisans like John Smith to spread the word of God among the "heathen" in Demerara and other forbidding colonies, the young evangelical missionaries were exhorted to teach all slaves to obey their masters and to never in any way endanger the public "peace" and "safety."[37]

But Smith and his wife, Jane, had already been exposed to the abolitionists' religious indictment of slavery and once in Demerara, where they faced increasing hostility from most planters as well as from Governor Murray and his officials, they discovered that the grim realities of slavery vividly confirmed the accusations of British abolitionists. Like other missionaries, mainly from the nonconformist sects, Smith expressed horror over the sounds of brutal, almost endless flogging, over the pervasive sexual exploitation of slave women by white males, and over the strong efforts to prevent slaves from learning to read or even attend religious services. As the historian Emilia Viotti da Costa has eloquently put it, Smith and another missionary "went to Demerara with the notion that slaves were savages to be civilized. But they soon discovered 'humanity' in the slaves and savagery in people of their own kind."[38]

While Smith would ultimately be tried for inciting the slaves to rebel but convicted only of complicity, he was still sentenced to be hanged, with a recommendation of mercy dependent on appeal to King George IV. From his arrival in Demerara in 1817, at age twenty-five, to his death in jail from consumption in early 1824, Smith remained loyal to the London Missionary Society's goal of baptizing and saving the souls of heathen. But as slaves swarmed to attend his daily and multiple Sunday services, often defying their masters' orders and risking severe punishment, Smith came to identify himself with their interests and constant ordeals.

This interaction depended in large measure on Smith's corps of slave teachers and on his slave deacons, especially Quamina, the head carpenter at the neighboring plantation *Success,* who helped Smith assemble at the *Le Resouvenir* plantation's chapel as many as six hundred "Exodus-seeking" slaves at a given time. (Slaves generally preferred the Old Testament, with its great exodus from Egypt.)

It was the pious deacon Quamina who kept track of which masters prevented their slaves from attending services at Smith's Bethel Chapel, which slaves had been flogged, which ones were in stocks, and which ones had committed adultery. In da Costa's words: "Smith always consulted Quamina when he wanted to know something about a member of the congregation. . . . He

was the most loyal, well-behaved, trustworthy and pious deacon." It was probably not coincidental that the great rebellion first erupted at Quamina's plantation, a plantation owned by the wealthy absentee John Gladstone, the estate
named *Success*.[39]

As da Costa emphasizes, the increasingly overworked slaves had their
own internal reasons for violent resistance, but news of the Canning recom-
mendations and parliamentary debates percolated in various form among the
more privileged household slaves and artisans. Quamina heard of a repressed
royal emancipation from his tall adult son, Jack Gladstone, a slave with "European features." Some slaves understood that the repressed "law" would
allow them three days of freedom each week; others believed that the king
and Wilberforce had abolished slavery. In any event, despite some dissent,
groups of Creoles as well as African Coromantees, Kongos, Mandingos, and
Popos joined the uprising launched on the evening of August 18, 1823.[40]

The ethnic diversity of these slave insurgents raises a question explored
more abstractly by the historian Walter Johnson with respect to the clash or
reconciliation of "temporalities," or different perceptions of one's place in
time. Noting that African and Creole slaves, to say nothing of their masters,
possessed different conceptions of the future and of their place in time,
Johnson warns against a simplistic interpretation of slave resistance as part of
the dominant "slavery-to-freedom narrative of American history." How did
rebellious slaves imagine the history they were making? Surely most African-
born slaves did not see themselves on a preordained path toward becoming
"African Americans."

In some eighteenth-century revolts, Johnson notes, Africans "drummed,
danced, swore oaths, assigned ranks, and made plans to enslave rival groups"
as an act of war. Yet in Demerara a slave named Daniel "advised conspirators
who approached him for help that they should wait for freedom rather than
trying to seize it: if it was 'a thing ordained by the Almighty,' it would come
in time." As Johnson concludes, "given the extraordinary complexity of the
layered temporalities evident in the objections of non-conspirators, it took
feats of extraordinary imagination (and sometimes intimidation) to synchro-
nize slaves into a shared account of what was happening and what was to be
done about it."[41]

Some slaves sought merely to force the government to guarantee a number of free days a week; others, when captured and interrogated, gave highly
questionable testimony, claiming, for example, that John Smith had taught
slaves to become dissatisfied with their lot and to demand freedom. At least
one slave told white interrogators that if the revolution had succeeded,
Quamina would have been made the king and Jack Gladstone the governor,
and all white men would have been put to work in the fields. According to
one account, the white women would have been allowed to leave the colony.

Other slaves reported that the white men would have been killed and the white women—some even specifically named—taken as "wives" by the blacks.[42]

In assessing this claimed sexual intent, we should note that at least three of the Demerara slaves confessed at the time of their execution that they had lied about Smith and other matters, and there is no evidence of a single rape of a white woman during the Demerara rebellion. Given our more recent knowledge of the false confessions of captives of many kinds, it is clear that black slaves often spoke the words their white interrogators were eager to hear. It is possible, of course, that sexual or even marital fantasies were part of the expectations or "temporalities" of certain slaves.

But what makes the three-day Demerara uprising so astounding is the way ten to twelve thousand slave rebels from some sixty plantations treated their white oppressors. When slaves in neighboring Berbice revolted in 1762–63 against their Dutch masters, they slaughtered large numbers of whites and won control of the colony for nearly a year before a very bloody Dutch repression. Though many of the Demerara slaves carried guns, cutlasses, or knives, they killed no more than two or three white men! One white woman was shot in the arm, and one proprietor suffered a broken nose as slaves seized his musket and locked him in the stocks, where some slave women could slap him in the face, as he had done to them.[43]

Clearly John Smith and his disciples had considerable influence on this amazing black slave self-discipline and determination not to kill whites. The 1823 rebellion was led and planned by a small group of slaves who now spoke of their "rights," who vowed to force the local government to recognize and carry out new laws transmitted from England, and who were surely aware—like rebel leaders in Barbados in 1816 and in Jamaica in 1831—that any widespread killing of whites would undermine their cause in antislavery Britain. To that end, slaves whipped and slapped some masters, managers, and overseers and placed many of them in stocks while stealing goods, destroying bridges, and torching some houses, but the ominous rallying sound of shell horns and drums on the evening of August 18 did not mean death to the masters.

The whites, unfortunately, had no such inhibitions. As with most conspiracies, a few "loyal" slaves tipped off their owners, but not soon enough to alert the government. Still, the colonial troops killed or wounded over 255 slaves during the three days in which slave leaders had hoped to build a foundation for negotiation. After Quamina was shot, whites hung his body in chains. Then a reign of terror, marked by random and summary executions, led on to the interrogations, the trials, much public flogging, and the display on roadside poles of ten of the thirty-three executed slaves' heads. In order to prevent Jack Gladstone from becoming a hallowed martyr (his testimony implicated Smith), the authorities wisely banished him to Saint Lucia. But the climax of these rituals of restoring order produced one of nineteenth-century Britain's most influential martyrs—John Smith.[44]

As the "Demerara Martyr," John Smith in some ways became a pacifist prototype for the American John Brown. (Even their names suggested an almost made-up commonality.) The London Missionary Society and evangelical press bombarded the British public with evidence of Smith's innocence and of the evils of colonies like Demerara, which treated hundreds of thousands of human beings, even Christian human beings, like beasts of burden. Hundreds of petitions descended on Parliament, providing Buxton and Henry Brougham with the occasion for sensational speeches attacking the colonial system and arousing the religious public. Meanwhile, in Barbados white mobs attacked a Methodist congregation, sacked a church, and threatened the life of a leading missionary, whose replacement had to travel under a military escort. Da Costa makes the excellent point that while the Demerara revolt may have briefly strengthened the British abolition movement, the stark depictions of the West Indian model of economic exploitation and oppression also provided British laborers with a rhetoric they could use to claim their own full rights of citizenship. It is against the background of the British workers' struggles (as well as evangelicals' and women's struggles) for an ampler concept of citizenship that reactions toward events in Demerara can best be understood.[45]

By the end of 1831 and the outbreak of Jamaica's greatest slave insurrection, the British antislavery movement had advanced to a stage unimaginable in 1816 or 1823. West Indian intransigence, coupled with the colonists' delay or refusal to implement the British government's ameliorative measures, converted younger reformers, in particular, to the doctrine of "immediate emancipation." Even Buxton and the more conservative wing of the Anti-Slavery Society supported for a time a new Agency Committee of paid lecturers who beginning in the summer of 1831 adopted the methods of religious revivalists as they circulated petitions and traveled from town to town preaching that slavery was an unmitigated sin. Though decisive parliamentary action would require the momentous electoral reform of 1832, which increased the number of liberal M.P.'s and greatly reduced the representation of West Indian interests, the European revolutions of 1830 helped to create even earlier the sense of a new era.[46]

On the night of December 27, 1831, fifty-six days after Nat Turner's execution in America, slaves in mountainous western Jamaica signaled the beginning of the revolt by igniting "beacon fires" on hilltops, especially a blaze at the Kensington estate high above Montego Bay. The Reverend Hope Waddell, a white Presbyterian missionary who had been alerted some hours earlier, described the clusters of fire as estates were consumed and "then the sky became a sheet of flame, as if the whole country had become a vast furnace." Yet despite the destruction of "these sugar estates, the causes and scenes of their [the slaves'] life-long trials and degradation, tears and blood," Waddell later recalled, "amid the wild excitement of the night, not one freeman's life was taken, not one freewoman molested by the insurgent slaves."[47]

Though some sixty thousand Jamaican slaves joined the month-long rebellion of 1831–32, it became known as "the Baptist War" as planters and Jamaican legislators blamed sectarian missionaries and their slave converts even more sweepingly than Demeraran authorities had done in 1823. And in fact the slave leaders who had given the cause months of secret planning were typified by the charismatic chief deacon of the Baptist missionary Thomas Burchell, Samuel "Daddy" Sharpe, a slave who enjoyed amazing freedom to travel and preach. Thanks to the missionaries' teaching, Sharpe could speak to the slaves of "the natural equality of man with regard to freedom," convey the news that England's king "had made them free, or resolved upon doing it," and urge his followers "to drive the whites off the estates but not to harm them except in self-defense."

By 1831 the British slave colonies had undergone years of turmoil, free blacks had won many civil rights (which helped to distance them from slaves), and the stream of news from Britain, while contradictory, was persuading knowledgeable slaves that an imperial emancipation decree was at least imminent. Ironically, household slaves were often better informed than white missionaries since the blacks overheard the ranting and swearing of the planters and managers who faced not only British demands to cease using the whip as an incentive for field work but also declining profits, bankruptcies, and increasing absenteeism. Some Jamaican planters and legislators vowed to resist any emancipation measures, which they claimed would lead to bloody uprisings and the rape of white women; they openly threatened secession and a possible annexation to the United States.[48]

Missionaries like the Reverend William Knibb apparently heard nothing of the impending revolt until a day or so before the nighttime explosion of beacon fires. Knibb, later seen by whites as the John Smith of Jamaica, had actually warned the slaves against any form of rebellion, discredited the rumors of a British emancipation edict, and assumed that he had pacified the restless slaves who had secretly used his dedication of a chapel on December 27 as the gathering place for launching the revolt.

Even if the missionaries opposed an actual insurrection, their influence can be seen in the number of rebel leaders who were Christian converts (mostly Baptist) and in the fact that the uprising occurred in Jamaica's western region, where most of the missionaries had preached. Though Africans constituted some 27 percent of Jamaica's slave population, 82 percent of the rebels were Creoles. Clearly Creolization, Christianization, and an amelioration of material living conditions nourished a conviction that collective protest could lead to freedom. As the historian Michael Craton has emphasized, of the rebels who were later indicted, "a disproportionately large number were members of the slave elite," including drivers, other headmen, carpenters, coopers, masons, and blacksmiths.[49]

This so-called Baptist War involved from five to six times as many rebels as the Demerara uprising (770 times the number in Nat Turner's revolt the same year). It also required over ten times the number of days to be repressed. After hundreds of plantation houses had been at least partly burned by arson, after hundreds of slaves had been killed in the fighting—and the whites were aided, contrary to modern assumptions, by the black Windward and Accompong maroons—the slave death toll, including executions, came to 540. Given these numbers, it is all the more remarkable that this enormous and prolonged Jamaican rebellion resulted in the death of only fourteen whites, or about one-quarter the number killed by Nat Turner's short revolt. (Indeed, Turner's men killed at least 3.5 times as many whites as the *combined* total who died in the infinitely larger Barbadian, Demeraran, and Jamaican insurrections.)[50]

These comparisons suggest three conclusions. First, Turner and other American rebels had no possibility of appealing to a strong, centralized government that showed increasing sensitivity to a burgeoning antislavery movement. In marked contrast to Protestant ministers in the South, British missionaries like Smith and Knibb empathized with the Caribbean slaves and favored their peaceful but not distant emancipation. Moreover, the rebel slave leaders were at least somewhat aware of British public opinion and the power of the British government, thanks to their remarkable networks of communication and the ranting of their masters against British attempts to interfere with a once-accepted system of colonial labor. In the nineteenth century, British slaves thus showed considerable wisdom and self-discipline when they focused their violence on property and took what must have been extraordinary measures to avoid the killing of whites.

This restraint greatly aided the abolition movement in Britain, which would surely have suffered a setback if Jamaican blacks had followed the example of Haiti and had massacred hundreds of whites. In 1832 and 1833 William Knibb and many other missionaries, now refugees from the Caribbean, preached abolitionism to thousands of Britons, testified before the Select Committee of the House of Commons, and played a critical part in underscoring the cruelty of planters, the white colonists' persecution of Christians, and the virtue and victimization of the slaves.[51]

The second conclusion is that slave insurrections, even with a sparing of white lives and even with a massive turnout of thousands of rebels, were suicidal. Although the Baptist War made an important contribution to the abolitionist movement, Britain would surely have freed its colonial slaves, no doubt a bit later, even without this sacrifice. And while the Reverend Knibb succeeded in the 1840s in having Samuel Sharpe's executed body moved from an unmarked grave in Jamaica to a rebuilt chapel in Montego Bay, it was the white missionaries, not the black rebels, who became celebrated as heroes. "Missionary Smith," the Demerara Martyr, had a far greater impact on British opinion and history than did the 540 Jamaican slaves who lost their lives eight years later.

I draw a third conclusion from a highly original doctoral dissertation just completed in 2005 at Boston College. Edward Bartlett Rugemer first documents the long and extremely close economic ties between North America and the West Indies and then shows in vivid detail how the massive slave revolts in Barbados, Demerara, and Jamaica jolted, dismayed, and alarmed planters in the American South, who were now able to blame the insurrections on British abolitionism and use this causal linkage to expose the momentous danger of tolerating any similar abolitionism in the Northern states. As early as 1827, for example, Robert J. Turnbull, a lowcountry planter, lawyer, and writer, proclaimed in some essays entitled *The Crisis* that *any* discussion of slavery in Congress would cause "DEATH and DESTRUCTION in the South," just as the debates in Parliament had sparked huge insurrectionary movements in the West Indies. Turnbull provided what I would term "paranoid" rhetoric for many Southern writers in the future, filling in a paradigm that first emerged when British and French writers accused the antislavery Amis des Noirs of precipitating the Haitian Revolution. In the year 1831 Turnbull's thesis seemed to be almost magically confirmed by the seeming convergence of William Lloyd Garrison's new radical abolitionist newspaper, the *Liberator*, Nat Turner's bloody insurrection in Virginia, the rising popularity of "immediatism" in Britain, and then the massive slave rebellion in Jamaica.[52] Yet despite all the extremist rhetoric of alarm, after the founding of the American Anti-Slavery Society (and British emancipation) in 1833, there were *no* genuine slave insurrections in the South (with the arguable exception of the much-neglected Second Seminole War in Florida[53]) in the 1830s, the 1840s, the 1850s, or even the 1860s, when Southerners like Turnbull would have expected a Haitian-like revolution ignited by the Civil War.

AT ALL EVENTS, South Carolina's Denmark Vesey conspiracy of 1822 was the largest and probably the most momentous symbol of slave resistance in North American history. As with Barbados in 1816, Demerara in 1823, and both the Jamaican and Nat Turner uprisings in 1831, there were interrogations, trials, executions, and deportations, but except for testimony and hearsay, nothing else really happened. As with the far less famous and more recently discovered slave conspiracy in Mississippi in 1861, black informers revealed the plots before they could be brought into action. The historian William

Freehling has written, "The surest way to free oneself, under domestic servitude, was not to join a revolution but to betray one to the patriarch."[54] And in the 1861 case, which we will examine after Vesey, the success of the white authorities in maintaining total secrecy suggests that there were in all probability a good many other slave conspiracies that we know little or nothing about.

Since 2001, the Vesey conspiracy has been the subject of a bitter and ongoing academic debate. The controversy began when Michael P. Johnson published in the highly respected *William and Mary Quarterly* a prizewinning sixty-one-page critical-essay review of three recently published books that upheld the traditional accounts of the magnitude and importance of the Vesey slave conspiracy. After exposing numerous and serious errors in one author's transcription of the limited surviving court records, as well as the wildly speculative character of some historians' claims, Johnson argued, on the basis of his own research, that the Vesey conspiracy was the artifact of white panic, political conniving, and tortured slaves telling white interrogators what they wanted to hear: "The court, for its own reasons, colluded with a handful of intimidated witnesses to collect testimony about an insurrection that, in fact, was not about to happen."[55] Professor Johnson, who is eager to overcome the oversimplified "resistance paradigm" and is now working on his own book intended to rectify generations of misinterpretation, also maintains that the dramatic Vesey story has served the interests and wishes of both slaveholding planters and later black and white historians eager to find examples of heroic slave resistance.[56]

The *William and Mary Quarterly* printed Johnson's challenging essay as the first part of a "Forum" and formalized the debate in 2002 by enabling the targeted authors and some other historians to reply. More recently I have had the privilege of reading some new and forthcoming works, especially by Robert L. Paquette and Douglas R. Egerton, attacking Johnson's thesis and introducing new evidence, especially the reports of many clergymen who talked with the convicted blacks up to the time they were executed, as well as specific oral accounts conveyed within the black community.

While I have neither the space nor research experience and expertise to become seriously involved in this controversy, and have already changed my mind at least once, I am now convinced that Denmark Vesey and a significant number of slaves were in all probability involved in a plot to rise in insurrection on the night of Sunday, July 14—Bastille Day—1822. No doubt some of the testimony about the size of the rebellion was grossly exaggerated. No doubt some of the slaves hanged were innocent: Only 23 of the 131 men arrested cooperated with the court; in Johnson's words, "nearly all the testimony about the conspiracy came from [six] witnesses who sought to protect themselves by implicating others."[57] Given the paucity of evidence and the failure of actual insurrections, we have no way of knowing how truly serious the threat to whites may have been. But even apart from empirical evidence and the outcome of the historians' debate, the Vesey story has for well over 180 years acquired a life of its own, which I will summarize below.

Like Nat Turner and the leaders of the British Caribbean slave revolts we have just discussed, Denmark Vesey was not a field hand or in any way a "typical" slave. He was, instead, a cosmopolitan *former* slave sailor and carpenter, in his mid-fifties. In 1799 he had bought a six-dollar ticket in a Charleston lottery and had won fifteen hundred dollars! He had then purchased his own freedom for six hundred dollars and had continued to work in Charleston as a carpenter, while his wife (or wives) and numerous children remained enslaved. As a free black, Vesey remained close to Charleston's independent and highly controversial African Methodist Episcopal Church, which the authorities temporarily closed in 1818. (The church had ties with the pioneering and antislavery black church in Philadelphia, a source of suspicion and alarm for some whites.)[58]

Vesey, a literate reader of the news, seems to have known that Haiti's President Jean-Pierre Boyer, who had recently conquered Spanish Santo Domingo, was inviting American free blacks to migrate to the poverty-stricken island and had agreed to pay (at least as a loan) the initial cost of their transportation. In the 1820s an estimated six thousand blacks from Philadelphia and other regions did accept this offer, but at least two thousand soon returned to the United States after discovering the realities of Haitian life.[59]

As a young teenager, Vesey, then known as Telemaque, had briefly worked in Haiti (then Saint-Domingue) as a slave, but his French owner had then returned Vesey to his seller, Captain Joseph Vesey, complaining that the boy was "unsound and subject to epileptic fits." While Denmark seemed to have no troubles serving on Captain Vesey's ship as a cabin boy, this brief Haitian connection proved to be relevant to the court in 1822, since Vesey had supposedly sent a letter to President Boyer and had told his insurgent followers that after killing Charleston's whites and setting the city ablaze, they would either be rescued by Haitian ships or could sail to the island safely. (Some testimony also referred to aid from Africa.)

Vesey's main lieutenants included "Gullah" Jack Prichard, a former East African priest and conjurer who in the eyes of the state's Governor Thomas Bennett was the true leader of the plot; Monday Gell, a harness maker of Egbo origin, at whose shop the conspirators often congregated; Rolla Bennett, a trusted house servant of Governor Bennett, who defended Rolla's innocence even though Rolla became a key witness in identifying Vesey as "the instigator and chief of this plot"; and Peter Poyas, who was called "a first-rate ship carpenter." Though free blacks in Charleston were more feared and

more distant to whites than in the British Caribbean, they generally separated themselves from slaves. Only three received sentences from the two
special courts that sent thirty-five men to the gallows and deported forty-two
others outside the country. As in many other New World conspiracies and
revolts, Vesey's insurgents included slave carters, draymen, sawyers, porters,
stevedores, mechanics, house servants—and, according to some testimony,
rural field workers who would rush into Charleston once the leaders had
seized the city's arsenals and had begun torching the buildings and killing
the whites.[60]

Some witnesses testified that Vesey had exhorted his followers "not to
spare one white skin alive, as this was the plan they pursued in Santo
Domingo." He had also supposedly read to slave followers from the Bible,
perhaps Deuteronomy 20:10–18, where, in the words of one witness, "God
commanded, that all should be cut off, both men, women, and children, and
said he believed it was no sin for us to do so, for the Lord had commanded us
to do it." In the actual biblical text, with respect to the more distant, non-
Canaanite towns, God *had* told the Israelites that after putting "all its males
to the sword," they could "take as your booty the women, the children, the
livestock . . . and enjoy the use of the spoil of your enemy which the Lord
your God gives you." Rolla Bennett may have had such generally repressed
biblical passages in mind when he supposedly told blacks that after they killed
the white men, "we know what to do with the wenches," and even boasted
that the governor's daughter would be his future "wench."[61]

Though even Douglas Egerton dismisses these lines as "nonsense served
up for the magistrates," they deserve to be coupled with the no less controversial words of the slave John Horry, quoted below, as symbols of the supposedly revealed "true mentality" of domestic servants who had previously
confirmed the planters' paternalistic ideology by acting like happy Sambos
when waiting on their masters and their masters' guests. The exposure of
Horry's "true feelings" appears in a letter written by Martha Proctor
Richardson, a wealthy widow living in Savannah, Georgia, who was in close
touch with the court proceedings in Charleston. Richardson told how Elias
Horry, a rice planter, had protested when the police had arrested his beloved
coachman, John. After hearing some troubling evidence, the master turned
to his slave: "Are you guilty?" he asked, incredulously. "What were your intentions?" John Horry then whirled on the patriarch: "I desired to kill you,
rip open your belly, and throw your guts in your face!"[62]

Disputes over the reality of this story, like the reality of the insurgents'
plans to poison individual wells and Charleston's water supply, miss two central points of the Vesey conspiracy: first, the total failure of whatever plot
there was;[63] second, the traumatic *shock*, in terms of feelings of vulnerability,
that the slaves' testimony delivered to Charleston, to South Carolina, and

even to the nation as a whole—a shock that threatened the most basic assumptions about human progress and where time is moving us. For readers today the only meaningful analogy would be September 11, 2001, and the prospect of future terrorist attacks with no end in sight, even though Charleston escaped from any massacre of whites or even physical damage.

Some white leaders hoped to minimize the sense of danger and prevent slaves from hearing about such possibilities as poisoning water, or from drawing dangerous conclusions about the weakness and vulnerability of the social system. Others, particularly the state's governor, Thomas Bennett, and his brother-in-law William Johnson, a justice of the U.S. Supreme Court, were so wedded to the growing paternalistic ideology that they rejected both the procedures and conclusions of the first special Court of Magistrates and Freeholders—though they never doubted the existence of a conspiracy, as some historians have claimed.

In a letter to Thomas Jefferson, Justice Johnson complained that the exaggerated "alarm of insurrection" would undermine "the confidence between us and our domestics" and described the plot as a "trifling cabal of a few ignorant penniless [*sic*] unarmed uncombined fanatics . . . which would certainly have blown over without an explosion had it never come to light."[64] Governor Bennett also had a deeply personal interest in the crisis: Four of his trusted domestic slaves were arrested and indicted, and three of them were hanged.

Despite all his doubts about the seriousness of the slave conspiracy, Governor Bennett secretly and successfully pleaded with Secretary of War John C. Calhoun to move federal troops from Savannah and St. Augustine to Charleston, to back up the local militia. The interrogators' attempt to get to the heart of the plot, to force slaves to reveal the very "worst" scenario, no doubt led to much fantasy. But this also meant that belief in the paternalistic ideology had to be balanced on a different level with new concerns about security—concerns based on the recognition that slavery in the American South was highly vulnerable.

Thus the South Carolina legislature soon passed a "Negro Seaman Act," requiring that all free black and slave sailors be held in custody while their ships were in port. The state also barred the admission of slaves from Latin America, the Caribbean, and Northern states. Many whites expressed a desire to get rid of slave artisans and other urban workers, making slavery an entirely rural institution. While Vesey's men had no chance of winning their own freedom, they did magnify and intensify South Carolina's suspicion and fear of antislavery in any form. We have already stressed the importance of rumors of outside support, especially in the British Caribbean. According to some theories, Vesey or other insurgents had been inspired by Senator Rufus King's attacks on slavery in the Missouri debates of 1820, and even by a

misunderstanding of local newspaper reports that used the word "emancipation" when describing the South Carolina legislature's discussion of a bill
regarding individual *manumissions*.[65]

It is surely noteworthy that Robert J. Turnbull was a member of the first
court that tried the insurgents. He became in the remaining eleven years of
his life a rabid nullifier and neo-secessionist who anxiously watched the
progress of the antislavery movement in Britain and helped to shape an ideology for eventual secession.[66]

IT WAS ONLY IN 1993 that students of slave resistance and general readers
interested in the Civil War learned of a hidden slave conspiracy that might
have had a considerable impact on the war's western theater if timed, as the
slaves had hoped, with the Union's capture of the lower Mississippi Valley. I
refer to the publication of Winthrop D. Jordan's widely praised book, *Tumult and Silence at Second Creek: An Inquiry Into a Civil War Conspiracy.*[67]
Since the planters and other authorities involved made no pretense of conducting a trial, there are far fewer sources than for Vesey's plot. Indeed, the
main document is a record kept by a Mississippi planter, Lemuel P. Conner,
of slave testimony given to a secret Examination Committee at an isolated
racetrack in Adams County, Mississippi, in September and October 1861,
five to six months after the war began. The interrogation of the slaves, conducted apparently with severe torture, led to the execution of more than
forty blacks, including several privileged drivers of family carriages.

Jordan's account of what I take to be a major slave conspiracy at the
beginning of the Civil War is a venture in historical therapy, an attempt to
overcome generations of denial and repression concerning the nature of racial interaction in America and the ultimate meaning of the Civil War. Jordan's
twenty-odd years of detective work represent an effort to master silence—
the curtain of silence that fell over the whites' discovery of and response to
the Mississippi plot. As we hear the aspirations, the pain, the rage of African
Americans—as opposed to "the-happy-go-lucky, lovable ol' darkies of mag-
nolia-blossom historic legend"—we come to realize that tyranny is a central
theme of American history, that racial exploitation and racial conflict have
been part of the DNA of American culture.[68]

As Jordan makes clear, however, the "lovable ol' darkies" were something more than legend. He quotes from a remarkable letter sent by the
daughter of a Mississippi planter-politician to her husband, a Confederate
officer then at the front in Virginia:

> [The servants] have all behaved extremely well, indeed I cannot utter the
> least complaint of them, they are deeply interested and very sympathizing
> with us all. They often speak to me about the war and there was great

rejoicing in the kitchen at the news of our recent glorious victory in Virginia [Battle of Bull Run]. What would those miserable abolitionists say to such manifestations of devotion and affection on the part of the poor maltreated slave, whose heart, according to them, is only the abode of hatred and revenge against their master—They know nothing of the bond that unites the master and servant[,] of its tenderness and care on the one side, and its pride[,] fidelity and attachment on the other.[69]

In the early twenty-first century we must guard against treating such words with mockery or contempt, since the author, Louisa Quitman Lovell, was surely being sincere and describing something real. Yet another reality was hidden from her as she wrote this letter in late July 1861, three months after a slave rebellion had begun to simmer in the vicinity of Natchez, where she lived, and two and a half months after some hitherto trusted carriage drivers had been hanged for suspected plotting. As Jordan notes, "Mrs. Lovell was not writing for any public but herself and her husband. She believed what she wrote."

One might add that she was also engaged in a private debate with the abolitionists and was eager to shape her experience in ways that would refute them. The "legend" of paternalism, in other words, could guide and order Southern behavior. Lemuel Parker Conner, the wealthy planter who left the priceless but puzzling transcript of the rebellious slaves' words when they were later interrogated near Natchez, had always remembered to add, in letters to his wife when he was away from home, "Howdy to the servants" (note the common Southern avoidance of the word "slaves").[70]

African Americans, like any human beings, were by no means invulnerable to such expressions of care. In 1937, when the WPA Federal Writers' Project sponsored the interviewing of large numbers of elderly former slaves throughout the South, a local historian in Natchez recorded the reminiscences of Charlie Davenport, a black who had once been owned by Gabriel B. Shields on a large plantation near the center of the conspiracy. Charlie's slave father William had somehow escaped, joined the Union army, and later fought in the Vicksburg campaign. Charlie Davenport was the only veteran of slavery whose recorded interview referred to the planned uprising along Second Creek, just south and east of Natchez. His testimony confirms and helps to explain Conner's important transcript of slave interrogation.

Jordan warns that the document must be treated with great caution. Mrs. Edith Wyatt Moore, who interviewed Davenport, was white (some of the WPA interviewers were black); Mrs. Moore thus represented the voice of authority in a rigidly segregated caste society based ultimately on terror. Certainly the elderly Davenport was aware that he was telling a white audience, in the midst of a long economic depression, about his memories of slavery. Still, Jordan's exhaustive research shows that many of Davenport's factual statements are confirmed by other sources.[71]

Insisting that "us didn't b'long to no white trash," Davenport, like many slaves and former slaves, expressed great pride in his master, "one ob de richest en highest quality gentlemen in de whole country," and took special delight in the character of the Surgets, the wealthy family of his owner's wife: "Dey wuz de out fightenist, out cussinest, fastest ridin, hardest drinkin, out spendinest folks I ebber seed. But Lawd, Lawd, dey wuz gentlemen eben in dey cups" (that is, when drunk).

Davenport clearly hated the overseer, "a big, hard fisted Dutchman" named Charles Sauter, who beat Charlie when he was a child until "I thought I'd die," proclaiming that "from now on you works in de field." But Davenport claimed that "our houses wuz clean en snug. We wuz bettah fed den I is now, en warmer too, kaize us had blankets en quilts filled wid home raised wool. I jist loved layin in de big fat feather bed a hearin de rain patter on de roof."[72]

Like many of the former slaves interviewed in the 1930s—most of whom had known slavery only as children—Davenport contrasted his own relatively benevolent plantation with others that were far less generous. After recalling the slaves' garden patches, their hunting and fishing, and his own support for Jefferson Davis, Davenport mused that "Marse Randolph Shields is a doctor way off in China. I b'leeves day would look aftah me now if day knowed I wuz on charity." Davenport then concluded with thoughts that confirmed the white racial mood in 1937 and that presumably brought a glow to the heart of Mrs. Moore:

> How I gwine to know 'bout de rights or wrongs ob slavery? Fur ez I is concerned I wuz bettah treated ez a slave den I is now. Folks says hit wuz wicked but fur all I kin see de colored folks aint made much use ob day freedom. Day is all in debt en chained down to somethin same ez us slaves wuz. . . . Day aint no sich thing ez freedom. Us is all tied down to somethin.[73]

Today it is highly unfashionable to discuss the effects of paternalism in either the antebellum or post-Reconstruction period. Jordan, who was primarily interested in Davenport's brief account of the planned slave uprising, did not really consider how the prevailing Southern white ideology, to which Charlie Davenport had been subjected during his long life as a "free Negro," might have shaped his recollections and final assessment of slavery. One way of dealing with this problem of submission can be found in the speeches and writings of black abolitionists. For example, a militant fugitive slave named J. Sella Martin assured audiences in Britain that American slaves were anything but "content." But let us suppose, Martin said in a speech at the Bristol Athenaeum, it were the fact that the black man was contented in bondage, suppose he was contented to see his wife sold on the auction-block or his daughter violated, or his children separated from him, or having his own manhood crushed out of him, I say that is the heaviest condemnation of the institution, that slavery should blot out a man's manhood so as to make him contented to accept this degradation, and such an institution ought to be swept from the face of the earth. [In a sense, this anticipates the Stanley Elkins argument, summarized at the beginning of this chapter.][74]

Of course, a slave's seeming contentment *could* be a way of making the best of a grisly situation in which ill humor or any sign of "surliness" became an excuse for whipping. Jordan has discovered that at Aventine Plantation, where Charlie Davenport was born and reared, the overseer called the roll of hands three times every Sunday, and some male and female slaves were put in the "stock" by the head or by the legs and then given lashes. In fact, in 1859 a slave named Davenport, probably Charlie's father, was put in the stock and given thirty-nine lashes for "being saucy and clinching his hands against the overseer." But many of the Second Creek rebels lived on plantations noted for lax or erratic discipline. Hence Jordan had good reason for suggesting "that the slaves on Aventine rejected joining [the rebels'] Plan because they were kept under unusually rigid and efficient discipline."[75]

In any event, Davenport recalled that one night when he was "a little boy" "a strange nigger come en he harangued de ole folks but dey wouldn't budge." This "powerful big black feller named Jupiter" reported that "de slaves had hit all worked out how dey wuz goin to march on Natchez aftah slayin all dare own white folks." In one of the two versions of Charlie's report, the rebels were determined to take the land after killing "dey white folks," but in contrast to the confessions of many of the rebel slaves who may have been forced to say what the white interrogators wanted to hear, Davenport said nothing (that we know of) about rape or sexual relations with white women.[76]

Many of the slaves interrogated at the racetrack were clearly filled with rage and resentment, and the examinations gave them a chance for self-assertion, for shocking some of the whites they had planned to murder. Knowing that they would soon be hauled to the gallows, they had little to lose. Yet we have seen that slaves in Demerara, when put in a somewhat similar position, made shocking statements that were contradicted by the actual behavior of the rebels and later confessed to be lies.

It is therefore difficult to judge the frequent report in Lemuel Parker Conner's record that specific slaves said they intended to "take," "ravish," and "ride" specific white women, often the wives or daughters of their owners. For them, apparently, nothing could exemplify the meaning of freedom better than inverting the slave/master relationship: kill the master, possess and rape the white wife or daughter, and seize the land. In recent times the systematic rape of women in Bosnia, Sudan, and other countries has added new meaning to the view of rape as a means of revenge, a weapon of war and dishonor—though going back to Homer or Genghis Khan, we can find multiple evidence that collective rape has been a part of military conquest through human history.

Yet another possibility can be seen when one finds that white women in the antebellum and Civil War South expressed little fear of black males, despite a long tradition in America—illuminated by Jordan in a famous previous book—of white males imagining and fantasizing that black slaves were oversexed, licentious, and secretly eager to rape the best-looking white women.[77] In view of these traditional white male preconceptions, why should we not expect the examiners to have asked the captured slaves: "What did you intend to do with the ladies?" "Who was Simon (or Albert or Peter) going to ravish?" "After you killed master and Mrs. Mosby, did you plan to ride Miss Anna?" And if the slaves were being savagely flogged or tortured in other ways, why wouldn't they have told the inquisitors what the inquisitors wanted to hear?

Davenport did not condemn the rebels' plan or express any judgment concerning the capture and hanging of Jupiter, except to say, "Dey didn't need no trial kaise he was kotch rilin de folks to murder." He had a simple explanation for the passivity of the blacks at Aventine: "Us folks wouldn't jine 'em kaise what we want to kill Ole Marse fur?"[78] Whatever its other shortcomings, this testimony from an allegedly loyal slave, combined with other evidence that Jordan has searched out in a remarkable feat of detective work, make it virtually certain that scores of slaves in Adams County, Mississippi, were prepared for a major uprising in the first months of the Civil War. But as I have already indicated, given the dire predictions of many rabid proslavery writers, it may be even more surprising that no such major rebellion occurred. Perhaps American slaves knew all too well that such actions were suicidal and that as the war progressed many of their brethren were being freed by Union armies. (See Chapter Fifteen, notes 69 and 70, for further thoughts on this question.)

12

Explanations of British Abolitionism

T HE SUBJECT OF BRITISH ABOLITIONISM has long been controversial, complex, and even baffling. It also raises the issue of moral progress in history—whether groups of reformers and even nations can succeed in eliminating deeply entrenched forms of human oppression, and if so, by what methods, misconceptions, and under what conditions?

We now know that with respect to economic self-interest, British humanitarianism, at least in its abolitionist form, did not pay. By 1857 many knowledgeable Britons agreed with the London *Times*:

> Confessedly, taking that grand summary view of the question which we cannot help taking after a quarter of a century, the process was a failure; it destroyed an immense property, ruined thousands of good families, degraded the Negroes still lower than they were, and, after all, increased the mass of Slavery in less scrupulous hands [i.e., Cuba, Brazil, and the United States].[1]

Even the antislavery *Economist* agreed that "with the example of West Indian emancipation before them, it could not be expected that Southern statesmen [in the United States] would ever risk the liberation of their slaves on such conditions."[2]

If Parliament had not outlawed the British slave trade in 1807, British West Indian plantations, especially in Jamaica and the recently conquered colonies of Trinidad and Demerara, would have produced much greater wealth, the kind of productivity and wealth later enjoyed for many decades by slave-importing Cuba and Brazil.[3] As the historian Seymour Drescher has recently shown, by the 1820s leading political economists had abandoned Adam Smith's famous arguments for the universal economic superiority of free labor. While many remained silent on the issue, Edward Gibbon Wakefield correctly predicted in 1830 that West Indian emancipation would lead to a sharp fall in sugar production if the freed slaves had any access to uncultivated land and thus to subsistence farming; Wakefield condemned slavery but saw emancipation leading to the substitution of "eight hundred thousand savages for the same number of slaves."[4] He would surely not have been surprised by the conditions of the 1840s that ultimately prompted Britain to assist West Indian planters in importing hundreds of thousands East Asian indentured servant "coolies," to replace slaves.

Yet in 1833 and especially in 1838, despite such warnings, Britain, hardly a champion of egalitarian democracy, took the leadership in peacefully emancipating its own nearly eight hundred thousand colonial slaves and also used its wealth and naval power to pressure other resisting and highly skeptical nations, such as France, Spain, and Portugal, to end their own oceanic slave trades. In 1843 Lord Aberdeen, the Tory foreign secretary, even risked serious damage to British-American relations by affirming that "Great Britain desires[,] and is constantly exerting herself to procure, the general abolition of slavery throughout the world."[5] Why would Britain have taken such gigantic steps that were clearly contrary to its national interests, as commonly defined?

Sad to say, in a present-day world that seems to be governed by clashing self-interests and material forces, where we have learned that idealistic rhetoric usually cloaks nationalistic purposes or even far more diabolical schemes, it has become increasingly difficult to explain *collective* actions that profess to be driven by virtuous ideals or a desire to make the world a better place. During the past century, various national leaders have ordered the slaughter of tens of millions of people as the supposedly necessary means to perfect the world. Today we are far more cynical, I fear, than the generations at the beginning of the past genocidal century, before the First World War and the Russian Revolution.

If we take a quick snapshot of Britain in the late eighteenth and early nineteenth centuries, it is not the first country we would choose in predicting the leader of a vast crusade to stamp out the slave trade and liberate hundreds of thousands or, through its influence, millions of slaves. Unlike the United States and France, England had no democratic revolution, and for British leaders the very ideal of equality was abhorrent. According to Edmund Burke and the anti-Jacobin coalition of Whigs and Tories, equality was synonymous with tyranny; aristocracy was synonymous with freedom in the sense of guarding against populist despotism and tyranny in the name of the majority.

Inequalities of power had shaped British society like a vast pyramid, with the nobility and great landlords at the top, in control of a highly decentralized government. Throughout the towns and countryside, a vast and deferential servant class waited on the privileged, including most people we would think of as "middle-class." If we accept the vivid portrayals by nineteenth-century English novelists, many of the servants acted and were treated like slaves.[6] Before 1832 suffrage was limited to a tiny minority, mostly owners of very substantial property. Catholics and Protestant Dissenters—that is, groups like the Quakers and Presbyterians, outside the Church of England—were barred from the professions, universities, and public office. In Ireland, a small Protestant minority exploited the country as if it were a plantation. In far-off India the British drew extraordinary wealth from systems of exploitive labor that were arguably as bad as slavery in the West Indies but that received far less publicity. (Indeed, it was not until 1860 that it became illegal in India to own a slave.) In England itself, young men of the lower orders were vulnerable to being kidnapped by press gangs and forcibly conscripted into the navy, where the punishment of flogging was as common as on a slave plantation. Lower-class women who were technically "free" worked long hours in mine shafts or mills; orphan children were transported northward by the thousands to work in the factories of Lancashire.

Despite some agitation in the 1780s and early 1790s for political reforms, especially the extension of suffrage, a powerful and prolonged reaction against the French Revolution, symbolized by its Reign of Terror, enabled a highly reactionary Tory government to block significant change. Even the modest enfranchisement of some of the more privileged middle class was not possible until 1832. Until 1875 some English workers were sent to prison for quitting a job. Antiquated "master-servant laws" often required and enforced yearlong or even longer contracts between employers and employees, and the latter were often jailed for violating a contract. It is easy to understand why by the 1840s working-class radicals attacked and broke up meetings of abolitionists, who were accused of ignoring and diverting attention from nearby oppression that was far worse than the treatment of distant Negroes.[7]

As it happened, despite reactionary politics and scenes of domestic oppression, Britain moved quickly from being the world's leading purchaser and transporter of African slaves to the total outlawing of its slave trade in 1807. Then, beginning in 1823, the nation took steps intended to protect and ameliorate the condition of slaves in its colonies in the West Indies, South Africa, and the Indian Ocean (but not India). And an act of Parliament in 1833 peacefully emancipated nearly eight hundred thousand slaves (who,

as we shall see, were not truly freed until 1838), providing the then staggering sum of twenty million pounds sterling as compensation to the slaves'
owners or the owners' creditors. In 1869 the great historian W.E.H. Lecky
famously concluded his *History of European Morals* with the statement: "The
unwearied, unostentatious, and inglorious crusade of England against slavery may probably be regarded as among the three or four perfectly virtuous
acts recorded in the history of nations."[8] Note that Lecky, no bleeding-heart
sentimentalist, cautiously included a "probably"; far more significant, he was
writing soon after the American Civil War had transformed much British
opinion by freeing the largest number of slaves in the Western Hemisphere.
Still, Lecky's phrase "perfectly virtuous acts" implies no hidden or ulterior
motives even if England did very little to widen the opportunities for emancipated slaves and their descendants.

When dealing with an enigmatic subject of this kind, a subject about
which we still have a great deal to learn, much can be initially learned by
telling the story of successive efforts of some key historians to diagnose
Britain's central interests and motives—what lay *behind* the abolitionists' success in "converting" the public and then the government of the most powerful and economically advanced nation in the world.

BEFORE WE TURN TO COMPETING EXPLANATIONS, it will be helpful to give a
fuller summary of the chronology of major events.[9] In 1772, as England's
conflict with its North American colonies advanced, Granville Sharp,
England's pioneering abolitionist, won in court the much-publicized *Somerset* case, which was popularly interpreted, in America as well as Britain, as
outlawing slavery in England.[10] Sharp also began corresponding with early
American abolitionists like the Quaker Anthony Benezet, who collected
and anthologized various antislavery documents. In 1783, with the end of
the American War of Independence, British Quakers formed two committees to work against the slave trade, to present a petition to Parliament, and
to begin distributing tracts among men of influence.[11] The loss of the dynamic slave society of the American South made the abolitionists' prospects
far better than if America had remained within the British empire. Sharp,
aided by the free Africans Ottobah Cugoano and Olaudah Equiano, helped
to publicize the facts of the 1781 *Zong* case, in which the owner of the slave
ship *Zong* attempted to collect insurance for 133 black slaves who had been
thrown overboard in accordance with the captain's orders after a viral epidemic had killed sixty Africans and seventeen crew members.[12]

A growing moral concern over the Atlantic Slave System and its creator
and sustainer, the slave trade from Africa, led in 1787 to the formation of
England's Society for Effecting the Abolition of the Slave Trade (SEAST),
11 percent of whose subscribers were women. This pioneer organization was

really an extension of the Quaker committees, now enlarged to include a few Anglicans like Sharp and Thomas Clarkson, who had won a prize for an essay he had written as a student at Cambridge University in 1785, published the next year as *An Essay on the Slavery and Commerce of the Human Species*. Clarkson, as a full-time agent for the SEAST, was the first paid and professional abolitionist, making the cause his long-lived career.[13]

He traveled to Liverpool, England's leading slave-trading port, and risked his life when he confronted hostile gangs on the docks, as he collected massive evidence on slave shipping that would later be presented to Parliament. Although Granville Sharp preferred a more general attack on the slave system, the reformers made a crucially important tactical decision to limit their focus to the slave trade. They assumed that if the trade were ended, planters would be forced to take far better care of their slaves and ultimately move toward emancipating their labor force.

As provincial abolitionist groups began to organize, the year 1788 marked the first national petition campaign to end the slave trade. In the booming industrial town of Manchester, in December 1787, 10,639 men, a significant proportion of Manchester's eligible males, signed a petition against the slave trade, and women constituted 10 percent of the subscribers or contributors to the national campaign. The next year the total petition signatures may have come close to one hundred thousand.[14] Emphasizing the range and diversity as well as the size of the petition campaigns, which reached from Northumberland to Cornwell, J. R. Oldfield observes that the estimated four hundred thousand who signed petitions in 1792 "would represent about thirteen per cent of the adult male population of England, Scotland, and Wales in 1791." In 1788 Prime Minister William Pitt overcame stiff resistance in the House of Lords to a bill introduced in the House of Commons by Sir William Dolben, who had been so horrified when he inspected a slave ship at dock that he succeeded in securing a law that restricted the number of slaves that could be carried on a slave ship (per ton) and that included other measures intended to reduce slave mortality.[15]

In 1789 William Wilberforce, a wealthy philanthropist and M.P. from Hull, and a close friend of Pitt—later esteemed, as we have seen, by literate West Indian slaves—introduced resolutions in the House of Commons against the slave trade, igniting the first heated Parliamentary debate on ending the trade. As Wilberforce continued to argue for the cause in 1790 and 1791, describing the inconceivable horrors of the traffic, a Select Committee of the House of Commons began examining witnesses and evidence.[16]

A Mr. Wilson told the committee that "it hurt his feelings much to be obliged to use the cat [whip] so frequently to force [the slaves] to take their food. In the very act of chastisement they have looked up at him with a smile, and in their own language have said, 'presently we shall be no more.'"

According to Mr. Claxton, another witness, some of the slaves on the same ship "had such an aversion to leaving their native places, that they threw themselves overboard, on an idea that they should get back to their own country. The captain, in order to obviate this idea, thought of an expedient, viz. to cut off the heads of those who died, intimating to them that if determined to go, they must return without their heads."[17]

In 1792 the government received 519 anti-slave-trade or antislavery petitions, containing some 390,000 signatures. The West Indian interests were stunned as the press began promoting the cause and a popular movement arose to boycott slave-grown sugar (much as the North American colonies had earlier boycotted British imports). In 1792 Wilberforce actually succeeded in persuading the House of Commons to outlaw the slave trade in four years, in 1796. However, the bill failed in the more conservative House of Lords, which adopted the tactic of delay. Then, beginning in 1793, abolitionists suffered an almost fatal setback from the ideological effects of the French Revolution, its Reign of Terror, and the outbreak of war with France. As we have seen in Chapter Eight, the British fought in the Caribbean to defend or restore black slavery, especially in revolutionary Guadeloupe, Martinique, and Saint-Domingue.[18]

Still, even in 1796 the conservatives and West India interests defeated Wilberforce's bill for the abolition of the slave trade by only four votes in the House of Commons. And by 1804 there was a strong revival of anti-slave-trade agitation; Napoleon's restoration of slavery and the slave trade suddenly made abolition compatible with patriotic hostility to the French. The House of Commons passed an abolition bill proposed by Wilberforce, but William Pitt's cabinet postponed debate in the House of Lords. (Pitt, for all his political pragmatism, remained a close friend of Wilberforce.)

Then the abolitionists, really led by James Stephen, shrewdly perceived that they could divide the West India interest by focusing first on the British slave trade to *foreign* colonies, which now constituted a large percentage of the total British commerce. In 1805 Prime Minister Pitt issued an Order-in-Council stopping the slave trade to foreign colonies, such as Trinidad, which the British had captured in 1797, and which speculators eagerly wished to develop into a major plantation society. In 1806 the abolitionists scored their first great triumph. Ironically, and brilliantly, as Roger Anstey pointed out long ago, they concealed all *humanitarian* motives and pushed hard for a Foreign Slave Trade Bill in terms of national and military self-interest. This ending of the major, and temporarily most profitable, branch of slave trading opened the way for the total abolition of the British slave trade in 1807. Significantly, the bill was now *introduced* in the House of Lords, where it passed 100 to 36, before moving on to a triumphal vote of 283 to 16 in the House of Commons. Thus it became unlawful for any British ship to participate in the Atlantic slave trade after January 1, 1808, the same date on which the United States took similar action.[19]

By 1812 Britain had taken the next step of issuing an Order-in-Council that required Trinidad, now a Crown colony without its own legislature, to set up a registry of slaves to help detect any illegal importations. Wilberforce, who as early as 1812 wrote privately about preventing any measures that might "totally obstruct our future reforms" regarding slavery, called in 1815 for a central Registry of all British colonial slaves, which would not only reveal illegal importations but also provide data on mortality rates and thus serve as an entering wedge for British reform legislation.[20] And in 1814, as the Napoleonic Wars came to a seeming end (followed by Napoleon's "one hundred days" and final defeat at the Battle of Waterloo in 1815), abolitionists claimed to have 750,000 names on eight hundred petitions demanding that England force France and other maritime nations to abolish their slave trades—in order to prevent them from simply purchasing and transporting the African slaves that England would otherwise have taken. The conservative international Congress of Vienna, in 1815, agreed to issue only an abstract and powerless condemnation of the trade, but Britain succeeded in bribing and negotiating treaties with France, Spain, Portugal, and other nations that were never rigorously enforced but that reduced, to some extent, with the help of the British navy, the number of African slaves transported to the New World.[21]

By 1822 some British abolitionists concluded that even ending the British slave trade had not had the predicted and desired effects on slavery in the British West Indies. It was therefore necessary to plan political action to secure the total though gradual emancipation of all British slaves. As the London abolitionists formed the Society for the Mitigation and Gradual Abolition of Slavery in 1823, Thomas Fowell Buxton emerged as its main parliamentary leader. In an attempt to head off and weaken the emancipationists' campaign, the administration of George Canning began to intervene in colonial affairs with "ameliorative measures," especially for the newer Crown colonies that were deprived of legislatures and more directly governed by England. Yet by 1830 it became clear that planter resistance was thwarting the step-by-step amelioration policy. A growing number of antislavery leaders adopted the principles put forth in 1824 by Elizabeth Heyrick's powerful and radical booklet, *Immediate, Not Gradual Abolition*.[22]

The central London Anti-Slavery Society reorganized and renamed itself in 1830, now calling for the immediate freedom of all slaves. Its Agency Committee disseminated a large amount of radical antislavery literature and sponsored lectures to stir up the public. Such activity alarmed conservatives, even antislavery conservatives, who thought they saw germs of democracy in such populist agitation. But in 1833 Parliament received more than five thousand antislavery petitions containing almost 1.5 million signatures, including a monstrous half-mile-long petition, sewn and pasted together by a team including Buxton's daughter Priscilla, and signed by 350,000 women.[23]

In the early 1830s, as in the late 1780s, early 1790s, and mid-1810s, there were far more petitions for the abolitionist causes than for any other issue. Toward the end of 1831, as we have seen in Chapter Eleven, this immense public pressure was reinforced by a massive slave rebellion in Jamaica, which signaled the hazards and costs of maintaining the slave system—as well as the moral discipline of the slaves, who, unlike the "savages" they were sometimes said to be, refrained from killing many whites.

In 1833 both Houses of Parliament passed a bill that emancipated nearly eight hundred thousand colonial slaves on August 1, 1834. In recognition of long-accepted legal property rights, the slaves' owners or their creditors received as compensation the immense sum of twenty million pounds sterling. Even many abolitionists who accepted this compensation as a pragmatic necessity strongly objected to the further provision that forced the "freed" slaves to undergo a period of uncompensated "apprenticeship," which in effect gave their former owners considerably more compensation in the form of unpaid, slavelike labor. Still, the abolitionists succeeded in reducing the period of apprenticeship from twelve to six and ultimately four years. Whatever compromises seemed necessary, Britons and many Americans hailed the emancipation act as one of the greatest humanitarian achievements in history. Significantly, American abolitionists would succeed in making August first, the anniversary of British slave emancipation, a day of great public celebration, especially in the 1840s and 1850s, when increasing numbers of prominent Britons came to view "the mighty experiment" as a dismal failure.[24]

THAT BLEAK VIEW tended to evaporate after Holland (1863), the United States (1865), Spain (1886), and Brazil (1888) emancipated all their colonial slaves, which helped make Britain appear as the pioneer and model for global liberation. And, of course, the model of economic failure or success took little account of the psychological, social, and cultural liberation of the freedpeople, who now took charge of their own lives, established families, and enlarged Afro-American cultures in various forms.

For at least eighty years after the American Civil War, the triumphant achievements of the British abolitionists were interpreted in Britain and then in much of the English-speaking world as irrefutable evidence to support the view, as phrased by the philosopher John Stuart Mill, that "the spread of moral convictions could sometimes take precedence over material interests." This conclusion, which I now think is basically correct when carefully qualified, meshed beautifully with so-called Whig history—that is, the view that all human history is the story of successive and inevitable triumphs of liberty, democracy, and progress over reaction (a belief I cannot, unfortunately, endorse). For numerous writers, the history of British antislavery served as a paradigm of how enlightened liberals and reformers struggled in one stage after another to overcome the forces of greed, tyranny, and the most *unambiguous* symbol of man's inhumanity to man.[25]

But as the twentieth century moved forward in ways that undermined many people's faith in irreversible moral progress, it became increasingly difficult to look back worshipfully at Wilberforce, Clarkson, Buxton, and the other so-called Saints, some of whom are buried in Westminster Abbey, and hail them as pure altruists who single-handedly (or with the aid of God) proved that the highest moral principles could progressively overcome the most deeply entrenched material interests.[26]

Yet if we have understandably become skeptics, we should recognize, even in purely pragmatic terms, some of the virtues of Whig history. Consider the psychological consequences of the abolitionists' deep faith that all human beings are created in the image of God, and that we therefore have a compelling duty to overcome institutions that dehumanize groups of people by treating them as exploitable animals. (There were also strong links between abolitionism and the movement to prevent cruelty to animals.) Such optimistic views can continue to encourage new efforts to achieve social justice, whereas cynicism and relativism can easily lead to apathy, resignation, and the sanction of egoism and individual self-interest as the only ends of life.

As it happened, even in the British abolitionists' own time, their supposedly underlying motives were attacked by the West Indian sugar and slave-trading interests, by white Americans in the slaveholding South, and by spokesmen for the French, Spanish, Portuguese, and other slave-trading nations. According to such opponents, the British slave colonies had been losing out to their competitors. Thus antislavery, as exemplified by the British and Foreign Anti-Slavery Society's World Convention in 1840, was a way of destroying all of the slave societies in the world in order to give an opening to the produce of cheap labor in British India. Antislavery, in short, was perceived as a tool of British imperialism, a Trojan Horse to enable "perfidious Albion" to gain control of Cuba, Texas, and even such other regions as Canton (as a result of the First Opium War in China).

Early critics also pointed out that abolitionist propaganda was a way of diverting Britons' attention from the much closer ravages of industrialism—from the "dark Satanic mills" where workers including women and small children were in effect imprisoned in factories and were far more oppressed than the slaves who worked in the open air and sunny fields. The historian E. P. Thompson quotes an anonymous Manchester cotton spinner who complained:

The negro slave in the West Indies, if he works under a scorching sun, has probably a little breeze of air sometimes to fan him: he has a space of ground, and a time allowed to cultivate it. The English spinner slave has no enjoyment of the open atmosphere and breezes of heaven. Locked up in factories eight stories high, he has no relaxation till the ponderous engine stops, and then he goes home to get refreshed for the next day; no time for sweet association with his family; they are all alike fatigued and exhausted.[27]

In the mid-twentieth century, the most influential challenge to the humanitarian thesis came from Eric Williams's *Capitalism and Slavery*, published in 1944. Williams, a brilliant black Trinidadian, wrote a doctoral dissertation at Oxford, taught at Howard University in Washington, and eventually became prime minister of Trinidad/Tobago.[28] His work is still widely accepted in the West Indies. During the 1984 sesquicentennial of British slave emancipation, his followers scorned any suggestion that Britain's slaves had been freed for humanitarian rather than for economic motives, despite the appearance of a growing body of scholarship that discredited Williams's economic arguments.[29]

Williams's principal arguments support two broad conclusions. First, he maintained that European merchant capitalism created the immensely lucrative New World plantation system, fueled by the Atlantic slave trade. According to Williams, profits from the slave trade or from the overseas slave system as a whole (it was sometimes difficult to tell which Williams meant) provided most of the capital that financed the English Industrial Revolution.

Williams's second conclusion stemmed from the assumption that the American War of Independence initiated a period of irreversible economic decline in the British Caribbean and also coincided with Britain's decisive shift from mercantilism toward the laissez-faire capitalism of Adam Smith. (Certainly believers in divine providence could conclude that Jamaica, Britain's wealthiest colony, had angered the Creator, since six devastating hurricanes struck the island in the first seven years of the 1780s.) Some earlier historians, especially Lowell Joseph Ragatz, in his *Fall of the Planter Class in the British West Indies*,[30] argued that the period of irreversible decline started earlier, in 1763. Both Ragatz and Williams presented a picture of inefficient slave labor, white population loss, chronic indebtedness, soil exhaustion, and plantation bankruptcies.

Thus for Williams, these former island cornucopias of wealth were increasingly sustained only by mercantilist duties or subsidies that led to chronic *overproduction* for the protected British market. While Williams acknowledged that a "brilliant band" of abolitionists won fame by conducting what he termed one of the "greatest propaganda movements of all time," he argued that in the broadest terms, slavery was doomed by the transition from mercantile to industrial capitalism and free trade. More specifically, the government's motives were determined by the fact that British planters could no longer compete with Cuban and Brazilian sugar in foreign markets and that their level of production for Britain must be brought down to the level of "home consumption." To that end, Williams insisted that sentimental history should not be allowed to obscure the essential truth: "Overproduction in 1807 demanded abolition [of the slave trade]; overproduction in 1833 demanded emancipation."[31] Such economic determinism easily leads to the ironic conclusion, surely not endorsed by Williams, that we cannot expect moral arguments to accomplish anything; we must either use force or passively wait for fundamental economic changes!

With respect to Williams's first thesis, no one can doubt that slave labor proved to be indispensable for the rapid European settlement and development of the New World. It seems no less certain that the expansion of the slave plantation system from fifteenth-century Sicily, Madeira, and São Tomé to nineteenth-century Cuba, Brazil, and North America contributed significantly to Europe's and also America's economic growth. But economic historians have wholly disproved the narrower proposition that the slave trade or even the plantation system as a whole created a major share of the capital that financed the Industrial Revolution.[32]

It is Williams's second thesis, the one regarding the end of the British slave trade, followed by slave emancipation, that has provoked the most heated controversy and that is most relevant here. A succession of deeply researched works by Roger Anstey, Seymour Drescher, and David Eltis, to say nothing of a somewhat separate debate in which I myself have been involved,[33] have reexamined the relationship between antislavery and capitalism.

In 1975 Anstey showed that by every canon of national economic interest, 1806–7 was the very worst time for Britain to abolish its slave trade. At that juncture in the Napoleonic Wars, Britain needed every export market outside of enemy control on which she could lay her hands. In the early nineteenth century, the British West Indies' share of Britain's total oceanic trade was *higher* than at any time in the eighteenth century.[34]

In 1977 Seymour Drescher's hard-hitting book *Econocide: British Slavery in the Era of Abolition* argued that abolition of the slave trade was comparable to committing suicide for a major part of Britain's economy. Loaded with statistical tables and organized like a lawyer's brief, *Econocide* totally destroyed the widely accepted belief that the British slave system had declined in value before Parliament outlawed the slave trade. Using statistics on overseas trade, Drescher showed that the value of British West Indian exports to England and of imports in the West Indies from England increased sharply from the early 1780s to the end of the eighteenth century. Drescher also demonstrated that the British West Indies' share of the total British overseas trade rose to high peaks in the early nineteenth century and did not begin a long-range decline until well *after* Parliament deprived the colonies of fresh supplies of African labor.[35]

After assessing the profitability of the slave trade, which brought rewards of around 10 percent on investment, and the increasing value of the British West Indies, Drescher contended that the British slave system was expanding, not declining, at the beginning of the nineteenth century. The 1807 abolition act came at a time when Britain not only led the world in plantation production but had the opportunity, thanks to naval power and the wartime conquests of Trinidad, Demerara, Berbice, and Essequibo, of nearly monopolizing the slave trade and gaining a preponderant share of the growing world market for sugar and coffee. Far from being "old" in some global sense—"old soil, old habits, old techniques," as Ragatz and Williams maintained—Drescher affirmed that "the British slave system was young . . . [and] it seemed so to contemporaries." As for the issue of soil exhaustion, complaints arose as early as the 1660s, and the erosion was never permanent. Plantation regions, like other farming regions, went through cycles of soil exhaustion and rejuvenation.[36]

Since it is easy to confuse symptoms of an *imbalanced* economy with economic decline, Drescher might have avoided some criticism if he had more clearly distinguished profitability and economic growth from the structural defects and *social* impoverishment of the British slave colonies. These were regions in which most English and Scottish planters and "bookkeepers" (managers) eagerly sought to make at least a small fortune and then return home across the Atlantic. As we have seen in Chapter Five, they gave little thought to schools, churches, urban centers, religious and social services, economic diversity, or even the production of food and other products that would have made them less dependent on imports. Still, *Econocide* undercut a vital part of the Williams thesis, and in 1987 it was reinforced by Drescher's *Capitalism and Antislavery* and by the massively researched work of David Eltis, *Economic Growth and the Ending of the Transatlantic Slave Trade.*[37]

Eltis's main arguments can be summarized as follows: Slave labor on the plantations of the New World and Indian Ocean (such as the British island, Mauritius) attained maximum economic importance *after* Britain and the United States had outlawed their overseas slave trades and during the half-century between 1816 and 1865. During this period Britain spent some twelve million pounds (a staggering sum) in its minimally successful effort to suppress the international slave traffic by patrolling African coasts, raiding African trading posts, bribing and coercing other nations to sign anti-slave-trade treaties, seizing suspected slave ships, and even sending cruisers to attack ships in Brazilian waters.[38]

According to Eltis, slavery became more valuable to the Atlantic economy because economic growth created a soaring demand for such consumer goods as sugar, coffee, tobacco, and cotton textiles, all of which could be produced much more cheaply by slaves. In Britain alone, from 1785 to 1805, sugar consumption rose 80 percent and cotton imports quadrupled despite rising prices. The supposedly glutted markets of slave-produced goods that caught the attention of Ragatz and Williams were artificial and temporary. Britain's preeminent textile industry could not have survived without an expanding supply of cotton, almost all of which was produced by slaves until 1865.[39]

At the beginning of the nineteenth century Britain possessed rich, uncultivated lands in Jamaica and especially in the newly acquired colonies of Trinidad and Demerara. Jamaica alone was exporting five times as much coffee as Cuba and Rio de Janeiro combined; even with a wholly inadequate supply of slaves, Demerara was emerging as a promising source of cotton for the British textile market. If British Guiana (which included Demerara) had been supplied with more slaves, Britain's dependence on U.S. cotton would have lessened. In the twenty-six years between Britain's abolition of its slave trade in 1808 and its emancipation of slaves in 1834, the slave population declined by 25.3 percent in the new sugar colonies and by 10.8 percent in Jamaica.[40]

The British government succeeded not only in stopping the flow of slave labor from Africa to the British colonies but also in restricting the sale or movement of slaves from the older, more densely populated islands like Barbados to the highly productive frontier zones. In the 1820s slaves in Demerara and Trinidad were producing three or four times as much as those in Barbados or Jamaica. This antislavery policy raised production costs and prevented British planters from exploiting the expanding world market. Hence British antislavery policy gave an enormous stimulus to entrepreneurs in Cuba and Brazil, who continued to import African slave labor, most often illegally.[41]

As Eltis convincingly argues, "for the Americas as well as for Britain at the onset of industrialization, there was a profound incompatibility between economic self-interest and antislavery policy."[42] After 1838 British leaders learned with dismay that free black laborers were unwilling to accept the harsh plantation discipline and working conditions that made sugar cultivation a highly profitable investment. To save the plantations of Jamaica, Trinidad, and British Guiana from complete ruin, after apprenticeship ended in 1838, Britain first resorted in 1840 to the device of making "contracts" with freed African slaves. After abolitionists put a stop to this subterfuge, Britain tried in 1843 to persuade the American government to participate in a plan for transporting American free blacks to the British West Indies. After that proposal failed, the British eventually turned to Asian immigrants as a solution to the labor shortage. The hundreds of thousands of East Indian "coolies" who arrived in Trinidad and British Guiana did eventually increase output, but they could not restore the British colonies to their earlier prosperity and competitive advantage.[43]

Despite the policing actions of the British navy, between 1811 and 1860 approximately 2.25 million African slaves were imported into the New World. Eltis estimates, after an analysis of demand and supply, that without British naval, diplomatic, and ideological pressure, approximately 213,000 more African slaves would have been shipped across the Atlantic after 1830, mainly to Brazil and Cuba.[44] Clearly the economic costs of such abolitionist policies were extremely high. During the first six decades of the nineteenth century, there was more than an ample supply of slaves on the African coasts. Since the "culture of enslavement" continued to operate in Africa long after the sharp drop in European demand, the number of slaves in West Africa soon surpassed the number in the New World. Hence the price of slaves remained relatively low and stable. Yet throughout the American plantation societies, slave prices continued to rise in response to labor shortages.[45]

If free-market conditions had prevailed (as increasing numbers of English leaders wished), if there had been no antislavery intervention by the British government, if the flow of African slaves to the New World had increased, labor costs on New World plantations would have fallen, and consumers would have paid much less for sugar, coffee, and cotton goods. British merchants could then have sold more manufactured goods in markets extending from Brazil and the West Indies to Africa itself. That said, we must conclude that capitalist self-interest, as a source of human exploitation and suffering in the early industrial era, *could* have been even worse than it proved to be! If Britain had not outlawed its slave trade, emancipated nearly eight hundred thousand slaves, and then promoted abolitionism throughout the world, the Western world's economic growth might well have increased at a faster rate—but with even more appalling human costs.

WHILE IT IS CLEAR that free-market policies would have led to even more horrendous social consequences as the price of economic growth (a lesson we should remember), how can we account for the fact that Britain *pursued* antislavery policies for so prolonged a period? Most British and American abolitionists would have agreed with Granville Sharp, who wrote that "no gains, however great, are to be put in competition with the essential rights of man" and that "no man can be truly *loyal* to God and his country, who is so totally devoid of *first principles* as to favour *slavery*."[46] But these were hardly principles that could long guide the leaders of the world's most powerful and economically expansive nation.

Clearly it is one thing to find various noneconomic motives among British abolitionists, the media, and the public they succeeded in mobilizing, and quite another to believe that majorities of hardheaded M.P.'s would vote for measures that they knew could lead to economic disaster, undermining the colonial plantation economy that by 1805 accounted for about one-fifth of Britain's total trade. In *The Mighty Experiment*, the most brilliant and imaginative analysis we have of this "mighty" subject, Seymour Drescher shows how the new allure of science—the belief in rational planning, social engineering, and controlled change—enabled the British government to launch optimistic "experiments," initially based on a commitment to extremely gradual progress and increasingly grounded in a faith in the ultimate economic superiority of free wage labor.

Ironically, Drescher has discovered that the major economists who succeeded Adam Smith acquired new doubts and failed to confirm or develop Smith's somewhat inconsistent thoughts on the inefficiency and high price of slave labor, even when they morally deplored it. Yet the years that immediately followed British emancipation, in 1834, conveyed the illusion of success, in part because the system of so-called apprenticeship still meant four years of unpaid, coerced labor. British consumers were also required to subsidize, by means of duties and high prices, the sugar and other commodities produced by former British slaves. And the news that Caribbean blacks had "accepted" apprenticeship by not resorting to violence, brought much relief and restored the confidence of many investors.

As we have seen, however, faith in the quasi-scientific experiment began to melt fairly soon after the abolition of apprenticeship enabled thousands of slaves in the larger colonies, such as Jamaica, Trinidad, and British Guiana, to leave the plantations and find land of their own. Drescher vividly chronicles this decline as West Indian planters, having lost a productive and dependable labor supply, faced invincible competition not only from Cuban and Brazilian slave-grown sugar but from European sugar beets. According to Benjamin Disraeli, the great Tory leader, the experiment was "the greatest blunder in the history of the English people." It "had simultaneously ruined the British colonies, encouraged the African slave trade, and revealed 'the quackery of economic science'!" By the later 1850s much of the English press agreed with the London *Times* that "the sum of slavery is not diminished, it has only been transferred from us to more grasping pitiless and unscrupulous hands. Never was the prospect of emancipation more distant than now that foreign slave-owners are establishing a monopoly of all he great staples of tropical produce." In 1855 one of Britain's "most venerable political economists predicted that "we do not venture to hope that we[,] or our sons or our grandsons, will see American slavery extirpated from the earth."[47]

IN HIS EARLIER WORK, having shattered the Williams tradition that antislavery succeeded because it advanced Britain's economic self-interest, Drescher addressed the quite different issue of explaining the power and immense public support of abolitionism. After rejecting economic interest as a motive, he emphasized the distinctive "political culture" that led a significant proportion of the British population to oppose slavery. By making informed comparisons with other countries, especially France, Drescher dramatized the remarkable uniqueness of the active British opposition to slavery, which cut across lines of class, party, and religion. This support, especially from the unenfranchised masses, cannot be explained by economic interest, at least in any conventional sense. Drescher argued that it depended on widespread literacy and a tradition of political consciousness and activism.

From the mid-eighteenth century on, publications like *Gentleman's Magazine* had attacked human slavery as a gross injustice; much English poetry conveyed the same message. The antislavery movement was itself a vehicle for political experience and training—for preparing men and women to form societies, to gather petitions, and to demand pledges from political candidates. By the late eighteenth century the British public not only refused to tolerate the intrusion into England of colonial institutions but began to insist that British standards of freedom be extended to the high seas and colonial plantations. From the colonial planters' viewpoint, this was "antislavery imperialism."[48]

Still, for all their brilliance and originality, Drescher's books never really tell us why antislavery, among dozens of competing reforms, won such overwhelming support that abolitionists were virtually unopposed in most regions of Great Britain, in striking contrast with the northern United States. By 1833 the ratio of British signatures calling for immediate emancipation, when compared to those in opposition, was more than 250 to 1. And while Drescher refers vaguely to "molders of public opinion," we still have more to learn about the local activists who organized meetings, disseminated tracts, and solicited petition signatures. Most historians have overlooked Thomas Clarkson's diary of his tours through England and Wales in 1823 and 1824,[49] which tells in great detail how he would visit local clergymen or town leaders, hand out antislavery tracts, and encourage them to set up local antislavery societies. At times, Drescher writes as if "mobilization of opinion" were a self-sufficient force. When discussing the initial mobilization in Manchester, for example, it is "Manchester" itself that launches the petition campaign, aims for a mass enrollment of its male inhabitants, and begins its long search for a "myth" that would elevate its citizens above the prosaic level of their daily working life.[50] In actuality, London's elite Committee for the Abolition of the Slave Trade established close ties from the start with the Manchester society; groups of ministers, manufacturers, and skilled artisans carefully planned tactics and programs to arouse the general public.[51]

But again, why was it England, a nation deeply transformed by the world's first industrialization and divided by class and religious struggles, that found a way of uniting a stable elite leadership with mass appeal—and in a cause that threatened specific property rights and social order, to say nothing of imperiling the economic benefits that David Eltis has so forcefully underscored? Whereas Drescher tends to idealize British traditions of liberty, Eltis says more about the continuing attempts in the seventeenth and much of the eighteenth century to ensure the industriousness of British workers by low wages and Draconian vagrancy laws. Such seemingly liberal notables as Bishop Berkeley, Francis Hutcheson, and Andrew Fletcher even advocated lifetime enslavement as the best means to discipline the beggars and idle rogues who roamed the eighteenth-century countryside.[52]

Like Edmund Morgan, Eltis connects this early acceptance of coerced labor with a preindustrial preoccupation with competitive exports and low labor costs. As Robert J. Steinfeld has graphically shown, even through much of the nineteenth century British employers made frequent use of coercive, nonpecuniary master-servant laws to discipline and exploit supposedly free workers.[53] By the late eighteenth century, however, an awareness of growing home or domestic markets was beginning to alert capitalists to the importance of "want creation" among consumers, as well as to such incentives as higher wages, as a way to increase both worker productivity and the number of consumers. Ironically, as Sidney W. Mintz points out in his insightful *Sweetness and Power: The Place of Sugar in Modern History*, it was slave-grown sugar that initially increased Britain's consumer-oriented market.[54]

"For owners of capital," Eltis observes, "a population responsive to market forces was a basic prerequisite to such a system [a free market with an optimum level of consumption], and if that population had no other means of supporting consumption than through wages, so much the better."[55] And as we have seen, it was precisely the products grown by slaves, such as sugar, coffee, tobacco, and cotton, that had stimulated so many new wants at every level of British society. Slave-grown commodities were the *precursors* to the endless number of products, many of them still produced by poverty-stricken, low-paid workers in the so-called developing world, that are now purchased in the shopping malls of modern high-income societies, in the expectation that they will satisfy what Eltis calls "nonsubsistence or psychological needs."[56]

The contradiction between the coerced labor used to produce plantation products and the consumer demand that eventually elevated British respect for wage labor sheds a wholly new light on Drescher's dichotomy between the metropolis in the British Isles and the colonial frontier in the Caribbean, Brazil, and the American South. It also brings us back to Eric Williams. In a statement that he unfortunately fails to develop, Eltis observes that

> the important aspects of the relationship between capitalism and abolition that Eric Williams was searching for were, first, that British employers had less need for coercion by the second half of the eighteenth century and

> that, second, both draconian vagrancy laws at home and predial [planta-
> tion] slavery in the colonies were examples of coercion. In the light of a
> system that relied on voluntary labor to satisfy individual wants going be-
> yond subsistence needs, forced labor appeared not only inappropriate but
> counterproductive [since it limited the global consumer markets].

This reformulation of Williams's linkage of capitalism and antislavery asserts the importance of ideology—specifically, an ideology of free labor that
would be understood in conflicting ways by workers and employers but that
would nevertheless unite many of them in condemning chattel slavery in
distant colonies.[57]

In other words, by the late eighteenth century there was a pressing need
felt by both skilled workers and employers to dignify and even ennoble wage
labor, which for ages had been regarded with contempt. And what could
better dignify and ennoble free labor, and even provide a sense of equality
between the man who pays wages and the man who receives them, than a
common crusade against chattel slavery? The very idea or image of chattel
slavery, as embodied in countless pictures of slave ships and of brutal masters, a whip in hand, lording it over semi-naked field hands, drew a boundary
line that marked off what was now unacceptable, indeed intolerable. In the
colonies and the American South, all labor, it was commonly said, was degraded by slavery.

Since Seymour Drescher's *Mighty Experiment* centers in part on "free
labor ideology," it is important to recognize the difference between his use
of the term and mine. He continually refers to the belief in the economic
superiority of free labor.[58] While I accept that meaning, I am more impressed
by a deeper transformation in British and then American culture in the North:
the desire to dignify and honor labor—a need and desire that made the British public in the early industrial era far more receptive to antislavery appeals.
And like other ideologies, the commitment to free wage labor could be felt
on a "gut level," apart from any explicit rational thinking. This kind of free-
labor ideology conveyed a sense of self-worth created by dutiful work—a
process that can cynically be seen as a way of disguising exploitation or can
be viewed as a way of genuinely recognizing elements of equality in people of
subordinate status.

I DOUBT that Williams's orthodox leftist followers would be satisfied by even
a well-developed theory relating British antislavery to free-labor ideology,
including the economic meaning conveyed by Drescher. Yet such a theory,
based on more empirical evidence, would confirm some of Williams's most
important insights: First, the slave system of the Americas contributed—both
by the effects of its products on consumerism and by the imagery of seminaked
laborers being driven by the whip—to *structural* transformations in British

life that made abolitionism acceptable to almost everyone not employed by the West India lobby. Second, British leaders became committed to colonial labor reform only when they became convinced that free labor would be less dangerous than slavery and more beneficial for the imperial economy as a whole. (As we have seen, there were important second thoughts after plantation production plummeted and after Britain became infected, beginning in the mid-nineteenth century, by much pseudo-scientific racist thought.)

In contrast to Williams's cynicism, however, a theory based on free-labor ideology does not diminish the moral vision and accomplishments of the abolitionists. There is a world of difference between abolition as a calculated response to "overproduction," and abolition as a means of promoting and dignifying free labor. The laws of 1807, 1833, and 1838 show that, given a fortunate convergence of economic, political, and ideological circumstances, the world's first industrial nation *could* transcend narrow self-interest and achieve genuine reform—a reform that greatly improved and uplifted the lives of millions of blacks (counting later generations), that curbed some of the worst effects of early global capitalism, and that can well stand, as Lecky said, "as among the three or four perfectly virtuous acts recorded in the history of nations."

13

Abolitionism in America

In the early nineteenth century, especially after the War of 1812–15, a "market revolution" and "transportation revolution" increasingly transformed American society. Improved roads and especially canals opened up markets and profits that were beyond the previous dreams of many enterprising farmers, skilled artisans, and manufacturers. But the rapid economic growth and urbanization of the 1820s devastated many other Americans who could no longer hold their own against more efficient and productive competitors. The owners of small, rock-strewn New England farms, for example, found it difficult to compete with Midwesterners who had the advantage of rich, loamy soil as well as the new Erie Canal that linked the Great Lakes to the Hudson River. In the eyes of many religious leaders, faced with geographic mobility and the breakup of traditional communities, it appeared that the United States had become increasingly dominated by materialism and greed.

For the clergy in New England and upstate New York, faced with the westward exodus of former parishioners and with the final disestablishment of Congregational churches in Connecticut (1818) and Massachusetts (1832), where there had still been no separation of church and state, it appeared that only a revival of Christianity could save America from a spirit of selfishness, materialism, and the pursuit of luxury. Only religious revivals could prevent society from unraveling into warring local interests and factions, degenerating into a Hobbesian-like state of nature where the life of man would be "solitary, poor, nasty, brutish, and short." Thus religious revivals were seen

as the essential instrument for creating a righteous society capable of fulfilling America's high ideals.[1]

As spectacular religious revivals established enclaves of piety in the midst
of a so-called unregenerate society, the question arose how to translate an
individual's momentary repentance and religious commitment into a just and
righteous society. While this "Second Great Awakening" was partly a reaction to the dramatic and unsettling economic and social changes of the 1820s,
the evangelical churches and revivalists were also addressing fundamental
questions about the meaning of human life, justice, and the human ability to
rise above sin.

This last issue of overcoming the inclination to sin acquired a special
urgency by 1830 because of a new American Protestant emphasis on human
ability and freedom. For many Congregationalists, Baptists, and Methodists,
it was not only within the power of the individual to achieve sanctification,
that is, a total transformation of moral character, but it was within the power
of the American nation to establish a new golden age, a new Eden or New
Jerusalem on earth. Here we see a striking amalgamation of secular and spiritual aspirations—a *sacralization* of time and of ethical questions like alcohol
abuse and slaveholding. The extremely high expectations of superstar revivalists like Charles Grandison Finney generated a new sensitivity to the fatal
discrepancies between American ideals and American practice.

Of course, it was in the very nature of evangelical Christianity to dwell
on collective shortcomings, usually for the purpose of dramatizing the living
possibilities for progress. America had a long tradition, going back to the
seventeenth century, of so-called jeremiad sermons—sermons cast in the
uncompromising language of the biblical prophet Jeremiah—designed to show
that the nation was going to hell, that the younger generation was betraying
the noble heritage of the founders, that the very tissues of society were rot-
ting from the spread of malignant sin.

By the early nineteenth century, however, one sees a tendency to portray
sin less as an abstract metaphysical evil, shared by all, and more as a particular mode of behavior. Thus Lyman Beecher, the son of a blacksmith and
the father of Harriet Beecher Stowe and Henry Ward Beecher, and for a
time the most prominent religious leader in America, denounced dueling
in 1806 as the great national sin: "With the exception of a small section of
the Union [New England], the whole land is defiled with blood. We are
murderers, a nation of murderers, while we tolerate and reward the perpe-
trators of the crime."[2]

By 1825 Beecher found sin exemplified in another kind of behavior:

> Intemperance is the sin of our land, and with our boundless prosperity, is
> coming in upon us like a flood; and if anything shall defeat the hopes of the

world which hang upon our experiment in civil liberty, it is that river of fire
[alcohol], which is rolling through the land, destroying the vital air and
extending around an atmosphere of death.[3]

The so-called temperance movement in reality demanded the end of
drinking all alcoholic beverages except wine (which Jesus had drunk) and
eventually condemned even that. It became the most popular of all pre–Civil
War reforms, in part because alcoholism had in fact become a major and
widespread national problem.[4]

The young abolitionists who began to emerge in the early 1830s had diverse backgrounds and temperaments, but almost all of them perceived Negro
slavery as *the* great national sin, in much the way that Beecher had perceived
dueling, intemperance, and Sabbath-breaking. Theodore Dwight Weld, the
passionate son of a Connecticut minister and a convert and close associate of
Charles Grandison Finney in upstate New York, personally symbolized the
fusion of American revivalism with the British antislavery movement.[5]

Weld's most intimate friend and religious model was the older Captain
Charles Stuart, a visiting British antislavery reformer who worked with
Finney's disciples in upstate New York and then in 1829 returned to England to throw himself into the final battle for slave emancipation. After being exhorted by Stuart to take up the cause in America, Weld shifted from
temperance and especially educational reform to abolitionism, becoming one
of the most fearless and powerful lecturers in the then vast region from Ohio
to Vermont. Weld's earlier passion for a movement combining education
with physical labor, so that even the elite would learn how to work and sweat
along with men from the lower classes, points to the kind of link between
antislavery and the desire to dignify labor that we examined in Chapter Twelve.

If Weld addressed Charles Grandison Finney, the great revivalist leader,
as "My dear father in Christ," Stuart addressed his letters to Weld as "My
dearly beloved Theodore" and spoke of being "one of your fathers, as well as
the younger brother of your soul."[6] While Weld was particularly interested
in combining education with manual labor and exercise, Stuart begged him
from England in 1831 to read some enclosed antislavery tracts and referred
to Toussaint Louverture as "the negro Christian Hero of St. Domingo."
Stuart also emphasized the "burning cause for gratitude to God, as in the fact
that while we continue guilty of [slavery], he can refrain from fairly breaking
up the world beneath our feet, and dashing us into sudden hell."[7]

Early in 1833 Weld declined a request by William Lloyd Garrison to
join the board of managers of the New England Anti-Slavery Society but
then went on to eloquently illuminate the meaning of slavery as sin:

That no condition of birth, no shade of color, no mere misfortune of circumstances, can annul the birth-right charter, which God has bequeathed

to every being upon whom he has stamped his own image, by making him *a free moral agent*, and that he who robs his fellow man of this tramples upon right, subverts justice, outrages humanity . . . and sacrilegiously assumes the prerogative of God; and further, though he who retains by force, and refuses to surrender that which was originally obtained by violence or fraud, is joint partner [*sic*] in the original sin, becomes its apologist and makes it the business of every moment to perpetuate it afresh, however he may lull his conscience by the vain plea of expedience or necessity.[8]

Weld's letter, in which he also declines to join the Garrisonians and tactfully intimates some doubts about Garrison's vilifying and off-putting rhetoric, sums up the ethical imperative that united abolitionists. This imperative undercut Southerners' excuses that they had simply inherited an institution that had been forced upon their ancestors.

The abolitionists' position conveyed three fundamental convictions: (1) that since all men *and women* have the ability to do that which is right and just, they are therefore morally accountable for their actions; (2) that the intolerable evils of society are those that degrade the image of God in man, stunting or corrupting the individual's capacities for dignity, self-control, and self-respect; (3) that the goal of all reform is to free individuals from being manipulated like animals, or, as one Garrisonian put it, that the goal of abolitionism was "*the redemption of man from the dominion of man.*" Since American slaveholders had long taken advantage of the moral privilege of dissociating themselves from the African slave trade (because of the natural increase of the American slave population), Weld skillfully linked the violent holding of a slave with the original violence of enslavement in Africa.

Weld emerged as a great abolitionist leader in 1834 as a result of what soon became known as "the Lane Debates." His activities in the Manual Labor Society, striving to dignify labor and eliminate the chasm between rich and poor, led him to select Lane Theological Seminary, near Cincinnati, as the training site where evangelical goals could be put into action. After persuading Lyman Beecher to accept the presidency of Lane, Weld led twenty-four converts from the Oneida region in New York to join sixteen other students, some from the Deep South. After struggling with a national cholera epidemic in 1832–33, Weld brought on eighteen days of intense debate over the issue of immediately emancipating all slaves. Since the arguments converted several Southerners, Henry R. Stanton concluded "that southern minds, trained and educated amidst all the prejudices of a slaveholding community, can, with the blessing of God, be reached and influenced by facts and arguments as easy as any other class of our citizens." Yet the executive committee of trustees, like many whites in Cincinnati, was infuriated by this development and also by the Lane students' interaction with free blacks in the city. When the trustees sought to suppress free speech and even dismissed Weld's only ally on the faculty, the Lane students left the seminary, some of them moving to the newly established Oberlin College, others joining Weld as abolitionist agents.[9]

AT TIMES one can see a strong self-interested though not selfish motive behind this structuring of reform goals. By the same token, even the most altruistic Christian would be self-interested enough to hope to end up in heaven.[10] Thus Wendell Phillips, a New England aristocrat who was converted by the revival and who became the most eloquent and powerful of white abolitionist orators, illuminated abolitionists' motives in two quite separate statements that become more meaningful when brought together:

> None know what it is to live, till they redeem life from its seeming monotony by laying it a sacrifice on the altar of some great cause. . . . Slavery, by the necessity of its abolition, has saved the freedom of the white race from being melted in luxury or buried beneath the gold of its own success.[11]

If these statements are taken out of their religious context and viewed cynically, Phillips is almost saying that white Americans were fortunate that hundreds of thousands of Africans were brought as slaves to North America since they then provided reformers with a glorious cause for overcoming materialism and redeeming their own white souls. But a similar statement could be made concerning any struggle against an evil that believers in a monotheistic and omnipotent God would interpret as being designed, like the bondage of the ancient Hebrews in Egypt, for a higher purpose. Clearly Phillips wanted to say that the existence of a hideous evil like racial slavery presented a spiritual and transcendent challenge to privileged whites.

It seems fairer to conclude that most abolitionists and other radical reformers yearned to merge themselves in a righteous crusade that they saw as a prerequisite to the liberty of both blacks and whites. Hence they felt that they must shock and awaken people, lifting a curtain to reveal that a concrete social evil had deluded them into a false sense of security when at any moment, as Charles Stuart put it, God's sense of justice should be "dashing us into sudden hell." This mentality stood in sharp contrast to the laissez-faire free-market ideology, which asserts that social progress is guaranteed by allowing each individual to pursue happiness in his or her own way. The laissez-faire ideology also assumes that self-fulfillment is ensured by the free exercise of individual self-interest, but many abolitionists came to recognize, quite accurately, that the slave system was a *product* of individual self-interest operating at a global level. Given the deeply rooted racism in the United States, along with the North's own heritage of black slavery and continuing vital ties with the South, American abolitionists faced far more daunting barriers than their brother and sister abolitionists in Britain. On the other hand, they drew on a far more radical, millenarian upsurge of reform.

Like the early Protestant Reformers of the sixteenth century, abolitionists were confident they had discovered and uncovered the fatal flaws of the entire social system; they were determined to clarify and reanimate an altogether different approach to self-fulfillment. It is significant that the main targets of radical reformers were precisely those forces that stunted or impeded the full development of an individual's moral capacities, as defined by the religious revivals: the violence and aggression of dueling and war; capital punishment and retributive punishment in general, which brings out the lowest, most un-Christian and bestial impulses of human nature; alcohol, which dulls or extinguishes a sense of social responsibility while stimulating aggression, self-assertion, and "animal passions"; laws and institutions that discriminate against women, depriving them of self-respect and subjecting them to male violence and sexual exploitation and degradation; above all, black slavery, the very epitome of institutionalized violence and debasement of the human spirit, treating humans as objects or animals, subject to unlimited coercion and manipulation.[12]

A common theme in these related reform movements, which were religious in inspiration but too radical to be accepted by existing churches, was the removal of obstacles to human perfectibility. All the same, as Wendell Phillips suggested, *participation* allowed the reformer to escape from a purely competitive or acquisitive life as he or she joined an ennobling yet deeply unpopular cause. As the letters of Weld and Stuart suggest, individual abolitionists enjoyed a profound bond of love, conviviality, and fellowship within even transatlantic reform groups as they redefined their own identity and faced common persecution, at least in America. Abolitionists acquired a shared language and outlook as they differentiated themselves from former friends and often even from family members.

FROM 1830 TO 1833, a growing number of young Northern whites, mostly converts of the Second Great Awakening, began to see Southern slavery in a wholly new perspective. There had already been a long history of American antislavery writing and organization, though the new generation of abolitionists rarely if ever acknowledged that racial slavery had long existed in the North—nor did they celebrate its abolition. (Recall that slavery was legal in New York until 1827 and in Connecticut until 1848.) This lack of any sense of continuity from the 1780s to the 1830s stands in sharp contrast to abolitionism in Britain.

Yet in both America and Britain most of the arguments against slavery had been formulated by the late eighteenth century, even if there was not yet an "immediatist" approach and mentality. The first phase of American anti-slavery agitation had been led by Quakers and Baptists, though by the 1780s American antislavery organizations also attracted an urban cadre of elite merchants and master craftsmen. In the early nineteenth century, antislavery groups appeared even in western North Carolina and eastern Tennessee. Since most of the radical abolitionists of the 1830s came from Federalist families, and since it was a surviving Federalist framer of the Constitution, Rufus King, who challenged the very legality of slavery in the U.S. Senate's Missouri debates of 1820, we still have much to learn about the political demise of Federalism and its influence on the decline of antislavery after 1800. (Significantly, the small number of free blacks who were entitled to vote voted overwhelmingly for Federalists and, after Federalism died, for Whigs.)

After the end of the war with England in 1815, American antislavery became increasingly absorbed and deflected by the so-called colonization movement. Some brave and outspoken early abolitionists, like the Reverend Samuel Hopkins of Newport, Rhode Island, had in the Revolutionary era stressed the need of supplying transportation for freed blacks who wanted return to Africa, where they had been born and brought up. The context had entirely changed by 1816, when the American Colonization Society (ACS) was formed. By then the vast majority of slaves had been born in the United States, and many had American ancestors stretching back for well over a century. Yet in the aftermath of the Haitian Revolution and the Gabriel slave conspiracy in Virginia, even whites who were genuinely abolitionist saw the colonization of freed slaves as "the safe and sane approach" to the problems of slavery and racial prejudice. The ACS immediately attracted a highly re-spectable leadership, including clergy, philanthropists, and young statesmen like Henry Clay. Indeed, from Jefferson to Lincoln most of the major politi-cal leaders, except for Southerners like John C. Calhoun who defended sla-very as a "positive good," supported the basic concept of colonization.[13]

"We must save the Negro," as one missionary put it, "or the Negro will ruin us." Here is the basic argument put forth by the colonizationists: Racial prejudice and racial differences were simply too strong in the United States for whites and blacks to live together as equals. Contrary to the utopian hopes of abolitionists like Garrison, colonizationists correctly predicted that racism would not quickly evaporate after the nation abolished slavery. Drawing on the dismal plight of free blacks in the North, who were mostly denied educa-tion and respectable jobs, colonizationists predicted that this castelike or even "untouchable" situation might last for well over a century, particularly in view of the new and rising tide of virulent racial prejudice among immigrants and the working classes of the North. Presumably because free blacks were deprived of educational and employment opportunities and were living in poverty and degradation, it was incorrectly assumed by many authorities, as we noted in Chapter Seven, that free blacks committed a highly dispropor-tionate number of violent crimes. In fact, while the black crime rate began to soar in the first decade of the 1800s, a larger percentage of black than white prisoners were jailed for minor theft or violation of minor city ordinances.[14]

Colonizationists repeated the argument again and again that the example of free black poverty and crime in the North was the main barrier to slave emancipation. In other words, they assumed that many Southern masters would free their slaves if they could be assured that the free blacks would not remain in their state and become a burden on society. There appeared to be no possibility of free blacks becoming self-supporting, productive citizens unless they were allowed high-quality education and were hired in nonmenial employments; yet this would mean social equality and integration, which white Americans were clearly unwilling to accept.

Therefore, since the ACS wanted to deny any accusation of forcible de-portation, the first step would be to found in Africa a highly attractive refuge for free American blacks. Once a beginning was made, so went the theory, emigration would prove to be as feasible and desirable as in the seventeenth-century planting of Plymouth and Massachusetts Bay colonies. Thousands of free blacks would eagerly join in the exodus, in order to escape the admit-tedly intolerable conditions in America as well as the hopeless future for their children and descendants.

Of course, it would make no sense to transport blacks to regions of Af-rica where they would likely be reenslaved and then sent to Cuba or Brazil, but according to the optimistic scenario of the ACS, settlers in Liberia, which was founded in 1822, would prove that blacks were capable of high civiliza-tion and self-government, once they were freed from America's racial dis-crimination. A flourishing Liberia would induce more slaveholders to manumit their slaves—or state governments to compensate slaveholders, since the ACS assumed there was a broad national consensus that both the institution of slavery and the presence of the Negro race were detrimental to the nation's long-term interest. The more religious backers also promoted the vision of America's "Christianized blacks" spreading the Gospel and Christian civili-zation throughout Africa. It is crucial to add that everything depended on one underlying premise: massive federal aid to the colonization cause from the profitable sale of the public's vast Western lands.

This was the official ACS line of argument, which repressed the crucial economic role of slavery in the nation's economy as well as the African Ameri-cans' contributions to the very meaning and existence of America. But like a political party, the ACS represented many diverse motives and interests. Many colonizationist leaders, especially in the North, were sincere opponents of slavery who abhorred the growing racism of the Northern masses and saw colonization as the only realistic means for preventing either civil war or racial war in the North and for inducing Southern planters to free their slaves.

In the South, however, the ACS was either advertised as a strong buttress *for* the slave system, as it removed the subversive population of free blacks, or attacked as a Yankee Trojan Horse, which would eventually lead to the end of the slave system. Though Paul Cuffe, a black sea captain and shipowner, had been an early pioneer in the colonization cause, most free blacks saw the scheme as an insult to their own identity as Americans and to the untold sacrifices of their ancestors, who had played a major part in building America.[15]

By the end of 1816, when the ACS was formed, the foundations of African American culture were well established in Philadelphia, New York, and even small cities like New Haven. We thus come to a crucial turning point in American antislavery history with the free-black initiative and organization exposing both the intended and unintended racism of the ACS and pointing out how such racism supported the entire slave regime. Black abolitionists in the 1810s and 1820s, culminating with David Walker's widely circulated *Appeal to the Colored Citizens of the World* (1829),[16] rejected the paternalism of ACS leaders and showed how the colonizationists' alleged concern for blacks actually accentuated and legitimated racism—particularly the bedrock assumption that the blacks' degradation in America was irremediable and permanent. The free African Americans also insisted that if their population were removed, slavery in the South would be greatly strengthened. Free blacks formed the basic structure of the Underground Railroad, helping fugitive slaves to escape into free states or find much greater security by entering Canada. In the South as well as the North, fugitive slaves found shelter and support among free blacks, who were sometimes even family members. Any movement for total colonization would remove such brethren as well as the only models of successful black freedom.[17]

Free blacks in Boston and Baltimore helped to persuade William Lloyd Garrison that the ACS was the main obstacle to slave emancipation. After reading *Freedom's Journal*, the first black newspaper, as well as Walker's *Appeal* and earlier radical works by such whites as George Bourne and Elizabeth Heyrick, Garrison became convinced by 1829 that any effective form of antislavery must accept the equal coexistence in America of blacks and whites and combat racial prejudice in the North as well as bondage in the South.[18] Blacks long made up a majority of subscribers to Garrison's *Liberator*. In effect, Garrison launched a new radical, populist movement based on a foundation built by black abolitionists.[19]

Though the point is often overlooked, the new, radical white abolitionism of the early 1830s was much indebted to the earlier militancy of anti-colonization blacks, eventually symbolized by Walker's *Appeal* of 1829 and Nat Turner's slave insurrection of 1831, which dramatized the national peril of an indefinite perpetuation of a labor system founded on violence. The ACS was also damaged far more decisively by vehement political opposition from the Deep South, which in the late 1820s ended the possibility of federal funding. Moreover, some black leaders who rejected the ACS continued to support the idea of black emigration. John B. Russwurm, a graduate of Bowdoin College and the co-editor of *Freedom's Journal*, underwent a transforming experience and emigrated to Liberia after earlier celebrating the Haitian Revolution and attacking the ACS.[20]

From the outset, however, black abolitionists worked closely with the new antislavery societies in New England and New York, including the American Anti-Slavery Society, formed in Philadelphia in late 1833, which included black members and pledged itself to work toward ending slavery immediately and gaining "rights and privileges" for free blacks. Then beginning with some highly publicized fugitive slaves, most famously Frederick Douglass's celebrated escape from slavery in 1838 and enlistment as a lecturer for Garrison's Massachusetts Anti-Slavery Society in 1841, black refugees performed the indispensable task of translating the abolitionists' abstract images into concrete human experience. The lectures and printed narratives of Douglass, William Wells Brown, Ellen Craft, Henry Bibb, Harriet A. Jacobs, Sojourner Truth, and Solomon Northup did much to undermine the widespread belief in the North that most slaves were kindly treated and contented with their lot.

The wit and articulate militancy of black abolitionists like Henry Highland Garnet, James McCune Smith, Sarah Parker Remond, and Charles Lenox Remond, coupled with the towering dignity of Douglass, also helped shake the confidence of some whites in the popular stereotypes of black inferiority. Moreover, as I have just noted, free blacks served as the main conductors on the Underground Railroad, as black vigilance committees helped a relatively small number of fugitives, mainly from the Upper South, find their way to security in Canada.

It would be hard to overemphasize another critical event that contributed to the emergence of immediatism around 1830 in America. I am thinking, of course, of the eruption in Britain of an "immediatist" antislavery movement based on mass *political* action. We have already discussed the unprecedented mobilization of English and Scottish public opinion, the hundreds of thousands and then nearly a million and a half of petition signers, including women, the interrogation of political candidates, and the vast outpouring of abolitionist literature. While American politicians exploited a continuing tradition of Anglophobia, American liberals, who prided themselves on their defense of freedom and human rights, were suddenly faced with the fact that the monarchic, aristocratic mother country, long blamed for "forcing" slavery on the South,[21] had taken the lead in liberating some eight hundred thousand colonial slaves.

However, in contrast to Britain, slave emancipation in America was inextricably tied to the explosive issue of racial equality after some two centuries of dehumanizing treatment of the descendants of Africans, who were legally prohibited, for example, from being taught to read and write. Even former slaves like Frederick Douglass, who happened to be extremely literate, carried the burden in the North of proving they were capable of freedom. The black abolitionist movement became almost obsessed with symbols of cultural uplift and elevation, presenting to whites examples of sober, genteel, self-disciplined, and "civilized Negroes."

Much has been written about the black reformers' growing tension and occasional rupture with white abolitionists who refused to hire or train black employees or accept African American co-workers in anything other than dependent, subordinate roles. Since this point has been so strongly emphasized in many studies, we should also take notice of the scores of black and white abolitionists who worked together, traveled together, and jointly shared the rage of white mobs and the infamy, stigma, and opprobrium heaped upon them by a self-righteously racist society. Garrison was by no means the only white reformer who even encouraged interracial marriage.[22] One poignant example of the abolitionists being far ahead of their time was their success in 1843 in repealing the Massachusetts ban on black/white intermarriages; it was 124 years later, in 1967, that the Supreme Court's decision in *Loving v. Virginia* finally negated the "antimiscegenation" laws of the sixteen remaining states.

DESPITE INCREASINGLY VIOLENT OPPOSITION, the American abolitionist movement grew with amazing rapidity in the mid-1830s. By 1838, following the financial panic and deep recession beginning in 1837, there were some 1,346 local antislavery associations with about 100,000 members. (In 1840 the population of the Northern states was around 9.7 million.) Compared with the British movement, which could support only six paid antislavery agents, Weld's vigorous band now included seventy paid agents. In 1834 the American Anti-Slavery Society distributed 122,000 pieces of literature; the next year, thanks to innovations in printing, that figure soared to 1.1 million, and it was 3 million by 1840, far exceeding anything done in the British campaign. And even more than in Britain, women played an absolutely central role in distributing antislavery literature and petitions; Garrison estimated that women outpetitioned men by "three to one."[23]

But President Andrew Jackson, like most antebellum presidents a Southern slaveholder, greatly valued the South's electoral advantage in counting three-fifths of its slaves for purposes of representation. He much looked forward to the annexation of Texas as a slave state, following the Texans' proclamation of independence from Mexico, and joined other national and local authorities in expressing alarm over the abolitionists' attempt to apply the methods of Bible and tract societies to a revolutionary purpose—a purpose that threatened the nation's most important capital investment as well as the national system for racial control.

The Northern and especially New England reformers learned to their dismay that American society was not only deeply permeated with racism but that the basic institutional structures from the judicial system to the interstate economy were connected with slavery: Most Americans wore or consumed slave-grown produce; many Northerners' jobs were tied in some way to Southern markets or to servicing the export of Southern products. To make matters worse, white workers, some of whom had seen black workers used as strikebreakers, expressed deep fears that even a partial emancipation would lead to the northward migration of freed blacks, who would then literally work for starvation wages. Further, to single out Southern slavery as the unique and paramount evil of American society raised fundamental issues regarding the meaning of the Bible and of the U.S. Constitution, both of which clearly sanctioned slavery.

Many Northerners who opposed slavery criticized the abolitionists for their extremism, or "ultraism," as it was often called in the nineteenth century. Along with their virulent denunciation of colonizationists and Southern slaveholders, the Garrisonians also became passionately involved with seemingly unrelated issues like women's rights and a form of pacifism that renounced all use of force and physical resistance or the support of a nation-state, even by voting, that ultimately relied on police or military violence.

Moreover, antislavery groups could hardly have been more querulous and divisive. Though differences regarding women's rights were the ostensible reason for the major split in the American Anti-Slavery Society in 1840, the testimony of the wealthy Tappan brothers and others who seceded when they were outnumbered by the Garrisonians shows that the divisions were far deeper and more complex. Historians have differed regarding the desirability after 1840 of a unified movement, yet the earlier British example points to the strengths of a relatively unified national organization. The British antislavery movement did not divide until 1843 (largely over free trade), five years after Britain's slaves had been truly freed. The Britons were also immensely fortunate in winning their national goals before the rise of scientific racism.

That said, it is important to recognize that by 1830 America had reached a dead end on the question of slavery. For decades, many cautious, rational plans had been proposed; calm appeals had been made for various kinds of gradual emancipation, but totally without effect. Even apart from central economic and ideological issues, the United States had no all-powerful parliament that could override the constitutional boundaries of slaveholding states. And even without significant importations, the number of slaves grew from 894,000 in 1800 to over 1.5 million in 1820, over 2 million in 1830, 3.2 million in 1850, and nearly 4 million in 1860, a period in which the institution also expanded rapidly into Kentucky, Tennessee, Florida, Alabama, Mississippi, Louisiana, Missouri, Arkansas, and Texas.

To account for the seemingly irrational behavior of many abolitionists, one must grasp the fundamental point that America's entire social and institutional structure prevented any effective approach to the question. By the time of the infamous *Dred Scott* decision in 1857, even a very moderate lawyer and former congressman like Abraham Lincoln became convinced there was a "Slave Power" conspiracy uniting proslavery presidents, the Supreme Court, and Southern Senators and congressmen, all intent on nationalizing the institution and overturning the Founders' dream of putting slavery on the path toward "ultimate extinction."[24]

After the explosive Missouri Crisis of 1819–21, national political parties and much of political life rested on the tacit premise that all discussion of slavery must be repressed. A bitter sectional conflict over tariffs, such as the dispute that led South Carolina to defy the federal government and threaten secession in 1832, could not disguise the fact that slavery lay sharply visible even in the shadows. As I have already suggested, any radical attack on slavery challenged the basic American premise that any institution is justified and in harmony with natural law if it is the result of a free market and the free competition of individual self-interest. Southern slavery appeared to be a "natural" labor system in the sense that it was the product of a free-market economy, cushioned by the "paternalism" of Southern planters whose "duties" to treat their slaves well were spelled out in state laws.[25]

On the other hand, the great religious revivals had been a powerful reaction against the primacy of self-interest, that is, against the doctrine that mankind is governed *only* by impulses to seek pleasure and avoid pain. Revivals nourished the desire to find and express an authentic self, mirroring the image of God. For abolitionists, like other Christian reformers, America's high mission could be fulfilled only by rejecting all compromises with sin. The abolitionists assumed, in a way that must have repelled small numbers of potential Jewish supporters,[26] that America was a genuinely "Christian nation," which, despite its sins and backsliding, could achieve a new and higher unity and brotherhood. Following the pattern of revivals, abolitionists believed that individual conversions to an "immediatist" antislavery perspective would bring a genuine and thoroughgoing change of heart. For Gerrit Smith, the extremely wealthy abolitionist leader who distributed many farms to free blacks in upstate New York, it was essential for whites to develop "a black heart," in the sense of seeing the world "through Negro eyes." Smith, who was eventually elected to Congress, also insisted that the same moral standards should be applied to government that applied to all human individuals. Smith forged extremely close bonds with black leaders and saw the abolition of slavery and the achievement of racial equality as the only way of regenerating American society and producing a unity based on something higher than self-interest and compromise.[27]

But when abolitionists violated the understood agreement of silence on slavery, their opponents built a virtual iron curtain around the South. The fruitless though remarkable debate over slavery in the Virginia legislature following Nat Turner's rebellion of 1831 would soon be inconceivable in any Southern state. Before long, generous bounties were being offered in the South for capturing and transporting Garrison, dead or alive. After Southern mobs burned antislavery mail taken from post offices in 1835, Postmaster General Amos Kendall began censoring such mail bound for the South. From 1836 to 1844, Congress also enforced a "gag rule" against receiving antislavery petitions.[28]

Such measures, justified as the only means for staving off slave revolts, undermined the basic assumptions of abolitionists, who had taken for granted the right of free speech and the legitimacy of transmitting information intended to "convert" large numbers of slaveholders. If that goal was hopelessly unrealistic, the gag rule also raised the issue of civil liberties, especially the right of every person to petition governments, a right that *then* seemed far more fundamental than freedom of speech. With respect to antislavery petitions, Northerners were acutely conscious of the successful British example. The gag rule thus helped to stimulate a great flood of petitions to Congress, demanding an end to slavery and to open slave marketing in the nation's capital, a restriction or prohibition of the vast interstate slave trade, authorized by the constitutional clause enabling Congress to regulate commerce "among the several states," and, after 1836, the denial of any move to annex the new slaveholding Republic of Texas.[29]

It was the elderly congressman and former president John Quincy Adams, aided by Theodore Weld, who fought a continuing war against the gag rule, using every parliamentary trick and tactic to read antislavery petitions and defend the petitioners' rights on the basis of the Declaration of Independence. Thanks to Adams's bold persistence, reinforced by Congressman Joshua Giddings of Ohio, Congress finally lifted the gag rule in December 1844.[30]

As abolitionists discovered how closely the social order was tied to slavery, a few of the extremists were driven to defiant gestures of disunion. William Lloyd Garrison, outraged by provisions in the Constitution protecting and sanctioning slavery, famously burned a copy of the document in

Boston Common, after terming it, in the words of the prophet Isaiah, "a covenant with Death and an agreement with Hell." Other more legalistic-minded abolitionists devised a whole body of doctrine arguing that the Constitution, which never used the term "slave" or "slavery," was in spirit and intent an antislavery document.

Meanwhile, in response to the conservatism of all Christian churches, many abolitionists withdrew or, as they often saw it, "excommunicated" churches that seemed to be in league with the devil. Even for more moderate Christians, slavery played a central part in the national division of the Presbyterian, Methodist, and Baptist churches, institutions that had served as the main cultural bridges between North and South. Thus, one's stand on slavery often became the crucial test of sincerity—a test of whether the United States was truly "a new hope for mankind," a more perfect society based on Christian brotherhood, or simply another nation-state ruled by power, coercion, and exploitation, gilded with the hypocritical coating of the Declaration of Independence.

Although the antislavery movement began as a movement for spiritual unity, it infuriated Southerners and brought an unraveling and disintegration even within its own organizations. To some extent this divisiveness can be seen in many radical movements for change, such as nineteenth- and twentieth-century feminism, but the heirs of the religious revivals faced a particular dilemma when they identified slavery with the very essence of sin. A need for individual doctrinal purity then took precedence over any concern for unity and effective strategy.

Nevertheless, in the 1840s and especially the 1850s, a more moderate and politically oriented form of antislavery emerged. Despite the division of churches and abolitionist organizations, one sees the paradox of a widened base of participation and increasing political involvement. The 1840s witnessed the rise of a new generation of antislavery politicians, men like Senators Thomas Morris of Ohio, John P. Hale of New Hampshire, and Salmon Chase of Ohio, who were especially attuned to the issue of civil liberties and to the preservation of "free soil," or a legal bar on slavery's expansion.

When Southern leaders defended their secession from the Union in 1860 and 1861, they pointed to two great issues of Northern betrayal: the attempt to bar slaveholding citizens from taking their legally approved slave property into the common territories, and the "personal liberty laws" and other measures that encouraged slaves to flee to the North and then blocked Southern efforts to reclaim such property. In the 1840s, when the first issue came to a climax with the annexation of Texas and the Mexican War, the issue of fugitive slaves evoked increasing outrage in both the South and the North. While the number of lost slaves was relatively small and never threatened the Southern economy, the mainly black Underground Railroad was remarkably successful in Maryland and the Ohio Valley, given the formidable obstacles, and the issue took on enormous *symbolic* importance—especially as Northern pride in laws guaranteeing personal liberty clashed with the Constitution's guarantee that any escaped slave ("person held to service or labor") shall be "delivered up on claim of the party to whom such service or labor may be due."[31]

After 1842, when the Supreme Court concluded in *Prigg v. Pennsylvania* that the Fugitive Slave Law of 1793 applied solely to the federal government's responsibility in helping to recover fugitives, and thus challenged the efforts of some Northern states to provide jury trials and protect free blacks from being kidnapped, several Northern states enacted new "personal liberty laws" prohibiting state officials from assisting in any way in the recapture of runaway slaves.[32]

Because Justice Joseph Story ruled in *Prigg* that slaveholders had a constitutional right to recapture fugitives in Northern free states, free blacks like Samuel Ringgold Ward, whose mother had only recently told his wife that his "being born free" was not "susceptible of *proof*," were thrown into panic. In April 1842 Ward wrote Gerrit Smith that he had decided to move to Canada immediately:

> The decision of the Supreme Court alarms me. I can see no kind of legal protection for any colored man's liberty. Every thing is made as easy as possible for the kidnapper. How easy it is to seize a man & under pretense of carrying him before a U.S. Judge to take him immediately south![33]

Though Massachusetts and Pennsylvania tried to blunt the effect of *Prigg* and allay the fears of free blacks like Ward, the South struck back with the Fugitive Slave Law of 1850, which not only required federal agents to recover fugitive slaves from sanctuaries in the North but permitted them to forcibly draft Northern citizens to aid them in seizing suspected blacks. The court-appointed federal commissioners who determined the fate of a captured Negro were paid twice as much for deciding that the black before them was a fugitive slave than for making the opposite ruling. The seized Negro was denied a jury trial and the law allowed a thousand-dollar fine and up to a year in jail for anyone who helped a fugitive escape.

The Fugitive Slave Law, which was part of the Compromise of 1850 that admitted California as a free state, directly challenged the North's integrity and its growing self-image as an asylum of liberty. The arrival of federal "kidnappers" and the spectacle of blacks like Anthony Burns being dragged through the streets of Boston invited demonstrations of defiance and civil disobedience; it probably cost as much as one hundred thousand dollars and took over fifteen thousand soldiers to escort Burns through an angry Boston mob of perhaps fifty thousand people to a U.S. revenue cutter that took him back to Virginia.[34]

The increasing Northern outrage over such events gave an enormous boost to abolitionists of all kinds. In 1854, for example, the Massachusetts Anti-Slavery Society held a huge Fourth of July rally at which Garrison, Sojourner Truth, Wendell Phillips, Lucy Stone, and even the great writer Henry David Thoreau addressed the crowd. Garrison, who attacked the church in the South as a "cage of unclean birds, and the synagogue of Satan," now burned a copy of the Fugitive Slave Law along with the U.S. Constitution. There were some hisses along with shouts of approval.[35] It was the issue of fugitives that Harriet Beecher Stowe was able to dramatize in the most influential and widely read of all antislavery works—and of all American novels— *Uncle Tom's Cabin*.

By the later 1850s a growing number of former pacifist "nonresistants" called for a slave uprising or predicted a prolonged conflict "that must end at last either in complete submission to the Slave Power, or in scenes of blood at the very mention of which we might tremble."[36] In 1859 Wendell Phillips could apparently place his hopes only in the long-term future, but he rejoiced "that every five minutes gives birth to a black baby; for in its infant wail I recognize the voice which shall yet shout the war-cry of insurrection; its baby hand will one day hold the dagger which shall reach the master's heart."[37]

Abolitionists increasingly accepted or advocated violence as they adopted a prophetic, biblical rhetoric, often predicting some kind of cataclysm that would be necessary to exterminate slavery and bring a oneness to mankind. As they demonized the slaveholder or cotton planter as a symbol of unlimited power and exploitation, a disciple of Mammon, Southern Slavery came to stand for all the accentuated evils of a commercial society—the undifferentiated units of labor in plantation gangs, the uprooting from native soil, the sexual exploitation and lascivious "breeding" of a labor force, the destruction of families through the separate sale of spouses and children. In many ways slavery symbolized an economy where individuals had become merely cogs in a dehumanizing machine, cut off from meaningful human relations, subjected to a rationale directed solely to the goals of profit, power, and sexual conquest.

Thus by condemning and fighting slavery, reformers affirmed the promise of America as something more than the triumph of collective self-interest. If abolitionists were always a small minority in the North, the slavery controversy took on the moral fervor and aspirations of the earlier revivals; as Julia Ward Howe phrased it, "as He died to make men holy, let us die to make men free." By the early years of the Civil War, many Northerners were coming to see the abolition of slavery as the only hope of purging the land of a deadly legacy of selfishness and injustice.

It was no revivalist who finally condensed the revivals' message on slavery into a few unforgettable words: "If we shall suppose," Lincoln said in his famous Second Inaugural Address,

> that American Slavery is one of those offences which, in the providence of God, must needs come, but which, having continued through His appointed time, He now wills to remove, and that He gives to both North and South, this terrible war, as the woe due to those by whom the offense came, shall we discern therein any departure from those divine attributes which the believers in a Living God always ascribe to Him? Fondly do we hope— fervently do we pray—that this mighty scourge of war may speedily pass away. Yet, if God wills that it continue, until all the wealth piled up by the bond-man's two hundred and fifty years of unrequited toil shall be sunk, and until every drop of blood drawn with the lash, shall be paid by another drawn with the sword, as was said three thousand years ago, so still it must be said, "the judgments of the Lord, are true and righteous altogether."[38]

14

The Politics of Slavery
in the United States

RACIAL SLAVERY was so central to American politics and foreign policy—
indeed, to all issues involving power in the period between the Revolution
and Civil War—that it would take a whole series of chapters or even a separate book to cover most of the ground.[1] In this chapter I will limit myself to
a brief discussion of American foreign policy, the Missouri Crisis of 1819–
21, the impact on America and especially the South of Britain's emancipation
of some eight hundred thousand slaves, and then, since we have already
touched on the Fugitive Slave Law of 1850, the issues dramatized by the
Lincoln-Douglas debates of 1858 and the road to Southern secession.

From the very start, America's foreign policy presupposed the national
government's commitment to protect and support the South's "peculiar institution," which was not yet peculiar or unusual when the United States
demanded either compensation or the return of the thousands of slaves who
had been freed and taken off by the British during the War of Independence
and then the War of 1812. Such actions actually ran counter to Britain's own
interests in maintaining and defending her own numerous slave colonies in the
Caribbean. However, in the 1830s, when Britain was moving toward the abolition of slavery in 1834 and then so-called apprenticeship in 1838, serious
ideological and legal conflicts exploded after British authorities in Bermuda
and the Bahamas liberated slaves brought there by American ships that had
run into heavy storms while sailing southward in the coastal slave trade.
Southern leaders like Senator John C. Calhoun complained that British

abolitionists had persuaded the government that "natural law" principles, as embodied in the *Somerset* case of 1772, could be extended across the sea, contrary to international law. The British refusal to pay compensation for escaped and seized slaves tied in with making Canada the destination of the Underground Railroad.[2]

A much more serious affair began on November 7, 1841, when a slave named Madison Washington led an armed rebellion on an American coastal ship, the *Creole*, en route from Virginia to America's leading slave market, New Orleans. The victorious blacks steered the ship into the British port of Nassau, where slavery had been abolished seven years earlier.

When the British authorities refused to return the blacks and validated their freedom, Secretary of State Daniel Webster sent an angry note to America's ambassador in England, even hinting war if the owners of the slaves were not compensated. In 1842 Southerners in the Senate expressed continuing fury. Even Webster, a Northerner, argued that Britain was bound to apply American law in determining the status of the persons on an American vessel under the U.S. flag.

The *Creole* blacks, unlike the *Amistad* captives, who had been shipped to Cuba in violation of Spanish law and Anglo-Spanish treaties, were lawfully enslaved (but had been taken into the open sea, where the laws of states might not apply). As tension rose, Britain and the United States finally agreed to submit the conflict to arbitration. In 1853 the umpire in an Anglo-American claims commission ruled in favor of Webster and the United States. Britain thus had to pay $110,330 to the American claimants. Aside from legal technicalities, this decision cast serious doubt on the later widespread assumption that by the 1850s justifications for slavery had been wholly repudiated in the nonslaveholding world.[3] As we have already seen, a growing consensus on the economic failure of slave emancipation in the British West Indies coincided with the emergence of scientific racism and a militant proslavery ideology in the American South.

America's overriding objective in the early nineteenth century, as in the post-Revolutionary period, was to prevent Britain or France from acquiring a foothold in the increasingly vulnerable Spanish territories of North America. But those territories, following Jefferson's momentous Louisiana Purchase of 1803, including Cuba, East and West Florida, and the Mexican province of Texas, were threats mainly to the slaveholding South. Many Southerners became so alarmed by the consequences of British emancipation in the Caribbean that they pictured a British seizure of Cuba as well as the British use of black troops in an invasion of Florida and the Gulf states—all part of an overarching plan to destroy the slave societies with which the impoverished British colonies could no longer compete.

The War of 1812 made it clear that the possession of Florida, which Jefferson as secretary of state had contemplated acquiring in the early 1790s, was essential for the security of the entire Lower South. From bases in supposedly neutral Spanish Florida, the British had in fact incited Indian raids, had encouraged slave desertions, and had originally planned to launch an invasion to cut off New Orleans and Mississippi navigation from the rest of the United States. As we have seen, the Haitian Revolution of 1791–1804 had also shown that war could ignite a massive slave uprising and totally destroy a slaveholding society. For nearly seventy years the image of Haiti hung over the South like a black cloud, a point of constant reference by proslavery leaders.[4]

One of the consequences of the Napoleonic Wars, which totally transformed Europe and ended in 1815, was the fatal weakening of slaveholding regimes in most parts of the New World. Not only did France lose Haiti, the most valuable sugar and coffee colony in the world, but this French defeat led Napoleon to sell what had been the Spanish Louisiana Territory, thus doubling the size of the United States. Moreover, Napoleon's seizure of Spain opened the way for independence movements in the immense Spanish territories from Mexico to Chile. The prolonged wars of liberation undermined the institution of slavery and either ended it within a few years, as in Mexico and Central America, or committed the future Spanish American republics to programs of very gradual and compensated emancipation, similar to those in the Northern states.[5]

As we have seen, after the British abolished their own slave trade in 1808, they embarked on a long-term policy of suppressing the slave trade of other nations. By 1823, when little remained of the former Spanish, Portuguese, and French New World empires, slavery was a declining institution except in Brazil (which became independent of Portugal in 1822), Cuba and Puerto Rico (still Spanish colonies), and, of course, the Southern United States.

This wider context of New World slavery dramatizes a momentous irony in American foreign policy from the time of Jefferson's presidency to the Civil War. The extension of what Jefferson called an "empire for liberty" was also the extension of an empire for slavery and thus a counterweight to the transatlantic forces that threatened to erode slavery throughout the hemisphere. In 1786 Jefferson claimed with some exaggeration that two years earlier he had sought in the Continental Congress to prevent the "abominable crime" of slavery "from spreading itself over the new country" of the Western territories, south as well as north of the Ohio River, and that "the fate of millions unborn" hung on the vote of one man, but that "heaven was silent in that awful moment."[6] But then, as president, except for urging Congress to outlaw the African slave trade, Jefferson gave no encouragement to the mildest antislavery measures, and instead initiated the policy of trying to isolate Haiti economically and diplomatically in order to end the spread of black revolution.

In 1820, in the midst of the Missouri Crisis and in response to Spain's delay in ratifying the Transcontinental Treaty of 1819, ceding East Florida to the United States, Jefferson, now retired and seventy-seven, privately assured President Monroe that with military force the United States could soon acquire not only East Florida but also Cuba and Texas.[7] Cuba was at that time becoming the world's greatest producer of slave-grown sugar, and Jefferson confidently but wrongly predicted that Texas would become the richest state in the Union, partly because it would produce more sugar than the country could consume.[8] It is difficult to imagine that the "Sage of Monticello," who vehemently opposed what he perceived as a Federalist conspiracy to convert Missouri into a free state, was thinking of free labor in an American Cuba and Texas. In fact, directly contradicting the principle of his 1784 ordinance excluding slavery from the West, Jefferson now argued that the slaves' "diffusion over a greater surface would make them individually happier, and proportionally facilitate the accomplishment of their emancipation, by dividing the burden on a greater number of coadjutors."[9]

From the annexation of Florida in 1821 to the actual annexation of Texas in 1845, the United States acquired no new territory that could upset the balance between free states and slave states achieved by the Missouri Compromise, to which we will turn in a moment. The Old Southwest, including Alabama, Mississippi, and Louisiana, still contained immense tracts of uncleared and uncultivated land, and some Southerners feared that reckless expansion would lead to excessive production, which would lower the price of cotton and other cash crops.

The connections between slavery and national expansion involved two basic and continuing assumptions that governed foreign policy. The first assumption was that territorial expansion was the only means of protecting and extending the principles of the American Revolution in a generally hostile world, a world devoted to monarchy. "The larger our association," Jefferson had predicted as president, "the less will it be shaken by local passions."[10] According to this nationalist view, Americans could deal with domestic imperfections once the nation had achieved sufficient power to be secure. Thus after the War of 1812, when Northern Federalists carried a fatal taint of treason because of their Anglophilia and secessionist Hartford Convention, ardent nationalists like the young John Quincy Adams felt that personal misgivings over slavery had to give way to the need for a united front against the monarchical despots of Europe. During the Missouri Crisis the antislavery forces could never overcome the unfair charge that they were serving Britain's interests by fomenting sectional discord and blocking the westward expansion of the United States.[11]

The second and related assumption, held with passionate conviction by all but one president from Jefferson to Buchanan, and especially by Tyler and Polk, was that Great Britain was America's "natural enemy."[12] These presidents saw Britain as a kingdom ruled by selfish interest, lusting for domination of the world, filled with a deep-rooted hatred for everything America represented, and committed to the humiliation and subjugation of its former colonies. Anglophobia had much to do with the swift death of the Federalist Party and the long delay in forming an organized antislavery movement, which was largely led in the 1830s by sons and daughters of Federalists, many of whom had strong ties with British reformers.

This hatred of England was nourished by contemptuous anti-American essays in British periodicals and by unflattering descriptions by English travelers that were widely reprinted in the United States. Even travelers who expressed admiration for many of America's accomplishments, such as religious toleration, continued to pounce upon the flagrant hypocrisy of defending slavery while celebrating the inalienable rights of man.[13] Many Americans blamed Britain for the economic depressions of 1819 and 1837. Irish immigrants regarded the English as their hereditary enemies, and defenders of slavery pointed to England's tyrannical treatment of Ireland as proof that a supposed concern for black slaves was a false humanitarian façade. No American politician could risk even the suspicion of being an unintentional agent of British interests. It was thus an unhappy coincidence that in the 1820s British interests veered increasingly toward antislavery—which many American leaders interpreted as a cloak for new forms of economic and ideological imperialism.

As WE HAVE SEEN, Southern white unity centered on race. Southern society, except for a growing aristocracy in seaboard South Carolina, was dedicated to the ideal of equality of opportunity as long as the ideal applied only to whites. The South also depended economically on a system of labor exploitation that was difficult to square with republican and liberty-loving principles. Racial doctrine—the supposed innate inferiority of blacks—became the primary instrument for justifying the persistence of slavery, for rallying the support of nonslaveholding whites, for underscoring the dangers of freeing a people allegedly "unprepared" for freedom, and for defining the limits of dissent. Ironically, the more outspoken Northern friends of blacks and critics of racism tended to be aristocratic Federalists like Rufus King and James Hillhouse, who defended what they saw as a natural hierarchy of social orders or classes, wholly apart from race. In 1813 the free black vote in New York State was decisive in winning a Federalist gubernatorial victory. It was the supposedly egalitarian Republicans, who often owed their national victories to the constitutional three-fifths representation for nonvoting Southern slaves, who pushed for the disenfranchisement of Northern free blacks.

From the time of the Continental Congress, American leaders had recognized that a serious dispute over slavery could jeopardize their bold experiment in self-government. Beginning with the Constitutional Convention, even leaders with clashing ideologies saw the need for compromise. The historian Don Fehrenbacher has presented strong arguments for the position that the Constitution of 1787 was basically "neutral" and open-ended with respect to slavery: For example, despite a number of important protections for slavery, when the framers substituted the words "such persons" for "slaves," they avoided official recognition of property rights in slaves; and at a time when British reformers assumed that abolition of the African slave trade would lead inevitably to the end of colonial slavery, the framers gave Congress the power to outlaw that slave trade in twenty years.[14]

Southern slaveholders would eventually express fury over the argument that slavery violated the constitutional guarantee "to every State in this Union [of] a republican form of government." And by the 1850s many Southerners deeply regretted that the Constitution made no mention of "slaves" or "slavery" and had apparently authorized Congress in 1820 to make engagement in the transatlantic slave trade a capital crime. Even though the American slave population increased at an unprecedented rate by natural means, in the 1850s there was a powerful movement in South Carolina and the Deep South to reopen the African trade.

Yet the entire structure of national politics had been designed to prevent any faction from directly threatening Southern slaveholders and thereby subverting common national interests. That is one reason why we still have an electoral college to choose presidents and a relatively weak central government compared with other democratic nations. It is therefore not surprising that before 1819 slavery never became a truly central issue in national politics, except for the brief but furious Southern response in the First Congress of 1790 to two moderate antislavery petitions. Slavery was thus an issue that sat like an inactivated bomb in the minds of the foremost political leaders.

The agreement to keep the bomb inactivated rested on two unwritten understandings: that the North would respect the *property* rights of Southern slaveholders, even though such property claims were not recognized in the Constitution; and that the South would recognize slavery as at least an abstract "evil," "stain," or "blight" that should be discouraged and eventually abolished whenever it became safe and practicable to do so.

Changing circumstances, including the shifting balance of sectional economic and political power, eventually forced repeated challenges to these understandings. The challenges took the form of clashes in Congress, during which representatives from the Lower South repeatedly threatened to dissolve the Union and even hinted at the possibility of civil war. On each occasion the resulting compromise strongly favored the South. This political process demonstrated the Americans' remarkable ability to make pragmatic adjustments in the interest of national stability. Yet these successful compromises depended on the dangerous assumption that Southern threats of disunion would always be met by Northern concessions and that most leaders of the Upper South, at least, remained committed to eventual abolition.

For a time the North could afford to make concessions, such as the acceptance of slavery in the Mississippi Territory, since slave states surrounded much of the region and this kind of expansion seemed to endanger no vital Northern interests.[15] But after the Napoleonic Wars ended in 1815, humanitarian causes had increasing appeal in the North, and a significant number of Northerners expressed moral, racist, or patriotic misgivings over the westward expansion of slavery. Sooner or later, as Southerners like John Randolph predicted, these Northern antislavery sentiments might become strong enough to create new sectional parties. Even by 1820, as a result of rapid population growth in the North, the major slaveholding states held only 40 percent of the seats in the House of Representatives, a drop from 48 percent in 1790. (Of course, in 1820 slavery was still in the process of being abolished in most Northern states.) Only the Senate could provide a firm and dependable defense against potential Northern encroachments regarding slavery, and the key to power in the Senate was new slave states, each appointing two new senators regardless of population size. In the Senate, following the admission of Mississippi in 1817 and Alabama in 1819, eleven slave states balanced eleven "free" states.

In addition to the desire to maintain Southern political power, Virginians in particular were concerned about racial demography when they increasingly advocated the "diffusion" of slavery into the broad and seemingly limitless West. In 1820 there were over 450,000 blacks in Virginia, or 7.6 blacks for every 10 whites. Even sincere opponents of slavery could not begin to tolerate the thought of such a high percentage of blacks in a free biracial society. Judge Spencer Roane no doubt expressed a nearly unanimous white fear when he told President Monroe that Virginians "are averse to be damned up in a land of Slaves, by the Eastern people. They believe that these people [i.e., Northerners] have no right to interfere in our concerns, nor to throw combustibles among us. They confide in you to resist the menaced restriction [on the westward expansion of slavery] in whatever form it may approach you."[16]

Thus when the Virginia congressman Charles Fenton Mercer secured the law in 1820 to make participation in the African slave trade a crime punishable with death, he was hailed as "the American Wilberforce"; but his major intent was to prohibit the further entry of a people whom most white Virginians hoped would be taken or sold into the vast Southwest, including Missouri.[17] And to a limited degree, diffusion worked. Despite the rapid natural increase of Virginia's black population, the ratio dropped from 7.65 per 10 whites in 1820 to 5.24 in 1860.[18]

The Missouri Crisis erupted unexpectedly in February 1819, when the House of Representatives was considering a bill that would enable the people of Missouri, which had been part of the Louisiana Purchase and lay west of the Mississippi, to draft a constitution and be admitted as a slave state. Slaves already constituted nearly one-sixth of the territory's population. James Tallmadge Jr., a New York Jeffersonian Republican who was deeply religious, offered an amendment that prohibited the *further* introduction of slaves into Missouri and provided for the emancipation, at age twenty-five, of all children of slaves born after Missouri's admission as a state. This moderate proposal was similar to the gradual emancipation measures that had been adopted earlier by states like New York and Connecticut;[19] in 1820 New York had about the same number of slaves as Missouri, but in 1817 Tallmadge had helped to secure a law that would terminate all New York slavery in ten years.

After a prolonged and often ferocious debate, the House approved Tallmadge's amendment by an ominously sectional vote. The Senate, after equally violent debates, passed a Missouri statehood bill without any restrictions on slavery.[20] The issue seemed hopelessly deadlocked. And while it took the press and Northern public many months to realize that the decision on Missouri really meant a referendum on the meaning of America, the congressional debates eventually sparked mass meetings and public demonstrations.[21]

Although Northern Republicans initiated and repeated the demand for restricting the spread of slavery, Virginia, the heart of Jeffersonian Republicanism, took the lead in militancy, trying to arouse a generally apathetic South to a common peril. Sanctified figures like Jefferson and Madison conveyed the alarm that any attempt to exclude slavery from Missouri was part of a Federalist conspiracy to create a sectional party and destroy the Union. The Missouri Crisis was aggravated by a sense that understandings had been broken, veils torn off, and true and threatening motives exposed. The congressional debates rekindled the most divisive issues that had supposedly been settled in the Constitutional Convention, and thus raised the hypothetical question of disunion.

In a sense, then, the House and Senate faced a reenactment of 1787, a ritual underscored by the prominence in the congressional debates of two of the Constitutional Convention's surviving antagonists: Representative Charles Pinckney of South Carolina, who openly defended slavery and now insisted that Congress had *no* power to exclude slaves, a form of legitimate property, from even the unsettled territories; and Senator Rufus King of New York, the alleged leader of the Federalist conspiracy, who "astonished" James Madison and many other Southern leaders when he announced in 1820 that any laws or compacts upholding slavery were "absolutely void, because [they are] contrary to the law of nature, which is the law of God, by which he makes his way known to man and is paramount to all human control."[22]

King, a foe of slavery even when he participated as an eloquent speaker at age twenty-two in the Constitutional Convention, had long denounced the three-fifths compromise (which had given the South the additional votes needed to elect Jefferson and defeat numbers of Federalists). King voted to exclude slaves from Arkansas and strongly opposed any discrimination against black voters in New York's 1821 constitutional convention, but as a conservative he inconsistently respected the rights of slaveholders in the existing states and would never have thought of proposing immediate slave emancipation. Nevertheless, no British abolitionist leader had at that time impeached the legality of all slaveholding in the light of a "higher law."[23] King's words, while anticipated by a few works like "Philmore's" *Two Dialogues on the Man-Trade* (London, 1760), pointed the way toward Garrison and the radical antislavery movements of the future.[24]

Apart from these polarized voices from surviving Founding Fathers, it was a new generation of Northerners who had to reaffirm or reject the kind of compromises over slavery that had created the original Union. Like the Founders, the Northern majority in Congress could do nothing about slavery in the existing states, but there had been an understood national policy, many Northerners believed, enshrined in the Northwest Ordinance and constitutional provision for ending slave imports, committing the government to restrict slavery in every feasible way. This understanding had seemingly been confirmed by repeated Southern statements that slavery was an evil imposed by Britain and inherited from the past. The North had accepted the original slave states' expectations that migrating slaveholders would not be barred from bringing their most valuable property—their slaves—into the territories south of the Ohio River and east of the Mississippi. But Missouri, part of the Louisiana Purchase and a gateway to the West, occupied the same latitudes as Illinois, Indiana, and Ohio (as well as Kentucky and Virginia). To allow slavery to become legally entrenched in Missouri might thus encourage its spread throughout the entire West, greatly harming both free labor and industry.

Despite many divisions in the North, the Pennsylvania legislature unanimously adopted a resolution instructing its senators and congressmen to vote against the admission of any territory as a state unless the region adopted the Tallmadge Amendment. The legislatures of New York, New Jersey, and even Delaware took similar action. Many Northern leaders warned that the South was intent on spreading the "evil" or "crime" of slavery from the banks of the Mississippi to the shores of the Pacific.[25] The sudden emergence of such unified demands for "free soil" anticipated the theme that finally mobilized the North in the 1850s and brought a new Republican Party to power. This gap in time of well over thirty years indicates the disastrous setback that resulted from the compromises reached in 1820 and 1821, and from the later rise of a two-party system based on North-South alliances. The strength of Northern opposition to admitting Missouri as a slave state might also raise questions about the off-putting rhetoric and ideological extremism of later Garrisonian abolitionism, which surely alienated many potential opponents of slavery.

Virginians and some other Southerners had increasingly argued, as we have seen, that if slavery were "diffused" over a large geographical area, it would weaken as an institution and the likelihood of slave uprisings would diminish (and, of course, the political power of slaveholding states would greatly increase). In 1820 Daniel Raymond, a prominent Northern political economist, gave the obvious reply: "Diffusion is about as effectual a remedy for slavery as it would be for the smallpox, or the plague."[26] We have already summarized a narrative that dramatically confirms this point with a vivid and appalling account of slavery in Missouri in the 1850s, as set forth in Melton A. McLaurin's *Celia, a Slave: A True Story*.[27]

Southerners were particularly outraged by the argument of Tallmadge and other Northern congressmen that the constitutional guarantee to every state of "a Republican Form of Government" meant that Missouri could not be admitted as a slave state. This argument not only ignored the fact that slavery had flourished in the Roman and other republics but implied that Virginia and the rest of the Southern states fell short of having "a Republican Form of Government" and therefore would not be admissible to a new Union. If this line of thinking prevailed, the Southern states would be reduced to a second-class status. If they accepted the Northern definition of a republican form of government, they had no choice but to take steps toward abolishing slavery, like the Northern states, or to face the punitive measures of an imperial authority.

Meanwhile, as tempers and threats rose in the halls of government, Tallmadge proclaimed:

> Sir, if a dissolution of the Union must take place, let it be so! If civil war, which [Southern] gentlemen so much threaten, must come, I can only say, let it come! . . . If blood is necessary to extinguish any fire which I have assisted to kindle, I can assure gentlemen, while I regret the necessity, I shall not forebear to contribute my mite. . . . If I am doomed to fall, I shall at least have the painful consolation to believe that I fall, as a fragment, in the ruins of my country.[28]

Henry Clay, the Speaker of the House of Representatives, spoke at one point of returning to Kentucky and enlisting troops. He also told John Quincy Adams that he was certain that within five years the Union would divide into three distinct confederacies.[29] But by finally exerting all the powers of his office and of his magnetic personality, Clay finally achieved a compromise.

After much political maneuvering, a small minority of Northern congressmen agreed to drop the antislavery provision as a prerequisite for Missouri's statehood. (Such "Northerners with Southern principles" would soon be known as "doughfaces" and would be indispensable in strengthening the unity of what Don Fehrenbacher aptly terms "the Slaveholding Republic.") For their part, a small minority of Southerners agreed that slavery should be excluded from the remaining and unsettled portions of the Louisiana Purchase north of latitude 36°30', the latitude of Missouri's southern border. In effect, this measure limited any further expansion of slavery within the Louisiana Purchase to Arkansas, directly south of Missouri, and what would later become Oklahoma (though one must remember Jefferson's musings about Texas becoming the richest state in the Union). Given the sectional balance of opposing majorities, the swing votes favoring these concessions were barely sufficient to carry the compromise. The way was now opened for admitting Maine as a free state, since Clay and the Senate had refused to accept Maine's statehood until the House had abandoned efforts to restrict slavery in Missouri.[30]

The press and legislatures of the North generally interpreted the Missouri Compromise as a crushing defeat for the North, a defeat made possible by the original three-fifths compromise. Much later, however, Northern antislavery forces would stalwartly defend the 36°30' line of division, and proslavery forces would fight to repeal this crucial part of the Missouri compromise, which was accomplished by the Kansas-Nebraska Act of 1854 and the *Dred Scott* decision of 1857, which denied Congress any power to restrict slavery in any of the national territories.

In 1820 a new and clearly misinformed hope arose in the North that public pressure could force Missouri to adopt a constitution providing for gradual emancipation. But the defiant Missourians drafted a constitution that prohibited the state legislature from emancipating slaves without the consent of their owners and that also barred free blacks and mulattoes from even entering the state. This measure seemed to undermine the ideology of diffusion, and since free blacks had been recognized as citizens by some of the Eastern states, this second provision, later adopted by such states as Iowa and Oregon, violated the constitutional guarantee that "the Citizens of each State shall be entitled to all Privileges and Immunities of Citizens in the several States."

Northern congressmen now stood firm in rejecting the Missouri constitution and in effect the entire compromise. Representatives from northern New England eloquently defended the rights and citizenship of free blacks and mulattoes, but Charles Pinckney, who claimed that he had drafted the relevant second section of the fourth article of the Constitution, asserted that it was impossible even to think of such a thing "as a black or colored citizen."[31] Eventually, in 1821, Clay's skillful manipulation of committees produced a vaguely worded compromise prohibiting Missouri from discriminating against the citizens of other states—an abstract and obscure resolution that still left citizenship undefined. The Missouri legislature accepted the promise "in such sarcastic and defiant language that the ire of the antislavery press was again aroused."[32] In general, however, the country applauded Clay for saving the Union.

But the Union would never be the same. In Southern eyes the uninhibited debates on slavery had opened a Pandora's box of dangers. Though the Federalist Party had mostly collapsed, thus removing what many Jeffersonians perceived as the major political threat, the free blacks of Washington had packed the galleries of the House and had listened intently to antislavery speeches. If Rufus King could be linked by his enemies to Anglophilic treason, his very name, King, combined with his seasoned eloquence, radiated power. In 1822, as we have seen in Chapter Eleven, during the trial of the alleged conspirators associated with Denmark Vesey, a Charleston slave testified that Vesey had shown him an antislavery speech delivered by Rufus King, "the black man's friend." The connection between the Missouri debates and a sizable slave conspiracy stunned South Carolina, confirming its worst fears.[33]

The cumulative effect was twofold: to unite most whites in the Deep South in the suppression of any dangerous discussion of slavery, wholly apart from their other political differences; and to strengthen the hand of both states' rights extremists and the defenders of slavery as a positive good.

Even more important, the entirely fortuitous outcome of the Missouri struggle contributed to the creation of a national two-party system intended to contain and neutralize the kind of sectional discord that erupted in 1819. From its very start, the Democratic Party of Martin Van Buren and Andrew Jackson sought to suppress criticism of slavery by blocking the delivery of abolitionist mail in the South, by enforcing the gag rule that tabled antislavery petitions in Congress, by challenging the judiciary when President Van Buren did everything he could to prevent a publicized trial of the *Amistad* captives, and by favoring the annexation of Texas as a slave state or cluster of slave states.[34] The Whig Party was no doubt less racist and far less committed to the westward or southward expansion of slavery, but since the political viability of the Whig Party depended on much support from wealthy Southern slaveholders, it provided few outlets for even moderate antislavery argument, even though many Northern Whigs began tilting in an antislavery direction. While Andrew Jackson, the founding Democratic president, defied the states' rights extremists in South Carolina in the Nullification Crisis of 1832–33, it was not until American slaveholding settlers in Texas proclaimed their independence from Mexico in 1836, seven years after Mexico had outlawed slavery, that the issues supposedly resolved by the Missouri Compromise began to thunder again on the southwestern horizon.

WE NOW COME TO A MOMENTOUS QUESTION that historians have seldom recognized. From 1789 to 1861 slaveholding Southerners dominated the federal government and played a central part in the nation's economic growth. Slaveholding Southern presidents governed the nation for roughly fifty of the seventy-two years between the inaugurations of Presidents Washington and Lincoln. Most of the Northern presidents eagerly catered to Southern proslavery policies, as did the U.S. Senate, the Supreme Court, and the two-party political system. Every Northern businessman knew that Southern slave-grown cotton was by far the largest American export, which paid for imports of everything from iron to textiles. The Southern "lords of the lash" forged close ties with Northern "lords of the loom," to say nothing of Northern banking, insurance, and shipping firms.[35] Moreover, these intersectional connections were reinforced by blatant antiblack racism in the North, and by the fear held by countless numbers of white workers that if slaves were emancipated, they would move north and drastically lower wages.

Largely because of this racism, coupled with Southern political domination and constitutional constraints, abolitionism in the 1830s and 1840s was pathetically weak and politically ineffective, especially when compared with the abolitionist mass movements in Britain. While the scathing, self-righteous rhetoric of men like Garrison may have deterred some potential supporters, there was really little that abolitionists could do in the way of changing solid realities. The gag rule long prevented Congress from even hearing their petitions; their naïve hopes of using "moral suasion" to transform the minds of Southerners led postal authorities to destroy their mail. In the North abolitionists often confronted hostile mobs; Southerners offered rewards for their bodies, dead or alive.

In view of these facts, the central question is why the South became so overwrought and increasingly hysterical over the supposed abolitionist menace. Why did Southern officials keep threatening disunion and escalate a series of counterproductive demands on the North, culminating with an unconditional federal sanction of slavery in the Western territories, when they had the continuing support of Northern doughface politicians and had long governed the nation?

The answer lies in large part in Great Britain, the monarchic "mother country," rejected and castigated from the time of Jefferson's list of indictments in the Declaration of Independence—and also the major market, in one of history's supreme ironies, for most of the South's slave-grown cotton. I hasten to add that it was the domestic American abolitionists and the common Anglo-American political and intellectual culture that made the British antislavery cause so threatening in Southern minds. The Portuguese historian João Pedro Marques reminds me that while the Brazilians and Portuguese expressed similar hostility to British antislavery "imperialism," there were no political responses like those in the Southern United States. But except in Brazil in the 1880s (as we will see in the Epilogue), there were no close ties between British abolitionists and a growing domestic antislavery movement. And as Steven Mitton has recently shown, by 1843 Southern leaders were beginning to suspect that as a result of the failure of Britain's "great experiment" of West Indian emancipation, Britain had strong economic motives to protect its own colonies by undermining slavery in the rest of the New World.

By 1861 one Southern woman could write to her cousin in England, arguing that the British West Indies had provided the South with a "window" for twenty-seven years—a window for viewing the total disaster of slave emancipation when British abolitionists won their way. By watching the British since 1834, she added, the South had learned that only resistance, even the resistance of war, could prevent a West Indian–like collapse into social and economic ruin.[36]

Even in the 1820s a few South Carolina planters or publicists like James Robert Turnbull, who had been educated in London and had served on the special court in 1822 for the trial of the Denmark Vesey conspirators, scrutinized the emerging British antislavery movement—a new phenomenon in the world. It appeared that the original efforts of Granville Sharp, Wilberforce, Clarkson, and their supporters, who seemed to call for nothing more than the outlawing of the African slave trade, had led to an irreversible concatenation of events that included imperialistic interference in the commerce of other nations, dictatorial treatment of Crown colonies, and then a massive and unprecedented popular outcry for the overthrow of colonial slavery itself. In other words, in the eyes of Turnbull and many others, once a small group of reformers succeeded in hammering in an "entering wedge" and in inflaming a public that had no knowledge of plantation life or of the capacity of Africans for freedom, nothing could prevent the destruction of millions of dollars' worth of property and of entire social systems.[37]

It was more than coincidental that a major American crisis of 1832–33, ignited by South Carolina's attempt to prove that a state could "nullify" a federal law (in this case a tariff), overlapped in time with the climax of the

British antislavery movement, which ended with an unprecedented assertion of parliamentary power. Jamaican planters and merchants, who did futilely threaten secession, would have given anything to be able to nullify the emancipation act of 1833. It is also worth noting that the Anglo-Texans' declaration of independence from Mexico, in 1836, occurred two years after the British emancipated some 800,000 slaves and two years before the British ended black "apprenticeship."

These events soon became closely related, since the British feared with some reason that a slaveholding Texas republic could quickly become a vast new market for slaves transported from Africa. When it became clear that the immediate annexation of Texas by the United States was not politically expedient, Britain secretly informed Texan leaders that slave-trade prohibition would be the price for any treaty with Texas or mediation with Mexico. Indeed, by 1843 Britain's foreign secretary, Lord Aberdeen, tried to sound out Mexico on a proposal linking recognition of Texan independence with slave emancipation. As we briefly noted in Chapter Twelve, Aberdeen went further in seeming to confirm the worst Southern fantasies when he privately acknowledged that "Great Britain desires[,] and is constantly exerting herself to procure, the general abolition of slavery throughout the world." As secretary of state, John C. Calhoun was able to publicize this statement as evidence of a British plot to destroy the Union. He also lectured the British on the blessings of black slavery as opposed to British factory labor.[38]

During the 1830s and 1840s Britain and America veered toward war a number of times as a result of disputes over the Canadian border, the slave ship *Caroline*, America's annexation of Texas, and conflicts over the boundaries of territory in the Pacific Northwest. After President John Tyler secured Texas annexation in 1845, his expansionist successor, James K. Polk, was careful to settle the Oregon boundary issue before provoking the Mexican War.

But this continuing tension enabled Southern leaders to keep alive memories of the Anglophilic and traitorous Hartford Convention of 1814–15, whose leaders had included such early radical abolitionists as Theodore Dwight. The fantasy that American abolitionists were in effect agents of a British conspiracy received some credence from Garrison's publicized trip to Britain in 1833 in search of funds and support, from the arrival in New England of British antislavery agitators like George Thompson, and from the attendance at the 1840 World's Anti-Slavery Convention in London of a handful of American male and female abolitionists. One should note that American abolitionists and literary figures like Ralph Waldo Emerson did their best to honor and celebrate the August 1 anniversaries of British slave emancipation. They also circulated positive accounts of the consequences of freeing West Indian slaves. But it was not until the 1850s that a more political brand of American antislavery began to pull free from the British stigma.

In late September 1833 South Carolinians received news that on August 29 the British Parliament had actually passed the monumental emancipation bill, to take effect on August 1, 1834. Many Southerners expected an almost immediate black revolution, as presaged by the great Jamaican slave revolt of 1831. Robert Monroe Harrison, America's consul in Kingston, Jamaica, had experienced this revolt and wrote to Secretary of State John Forsyth, a fellow proslavery Southerner, that Forsyth should imagine the feelings of the friends and relatives of murdered husbands who had had "their secret parts" cut off and placed in the mouths of their wives and daughters, who themselves were "afterward violated in the most cruel manner."[39]

When no news arrived of black insurrections, even as years passed, Southern leaders and commentators concentrated their attention on other negative results: the unwillingness of blacks to work on plantations, at least on the larger islands where enough land was available for subsistence agriculture; on the resulting plummet in sugar production and land values; on the alleged increase in crime and racial hostility; and on Britain's desperate efforts to find alternative plantation labor, first in Africa and the United States and then in India.

The historian Steven Heath Mitton has identified an important turning point in August 1843 when the British minister Edward Fox met in Washington with Secretary of State Abel P. Upshur to convey the conservative Peel ministry's startling proposal to pay the transportation costs for American free blacks to migrate to the British West Indies, where they would become free workers under contract. Fox admitted that the British colonies were "suffering severely in their productive industry from a dearth of agricultural laborers." Mitton argues that up to this point Upshur and even Calhoun, who following Upshur's death in February 1844 would succeed him as secretary of state, believed that British emancipation had been an economic success (as supposedly proved in 1840 by the testimony of the respected British Quaker abolitionist Joseph John Gurney.)[40]

As one would expect, Upshur, an ardently proslavery Virginian, rejected Fox's proposal on grounds of states' rights and also because he could not imagine allowing a British-directed recruiting effort, as Mitton puts it, "reaching deep into the South," especially at a time when British policy "had already given rise to the Underground Railroad" to Canada.

More important, given the context of Britain's intervention in Texas to prohibit the slave trade, this striking evidence of the failure of emancipation greatly alarmed Upshur and his colleagues with respect to Britain's future economic motives for undermining such competing slave societies as Cuba, Brazil, and the United States. Upshur ordered Robert Monroe Harrison to present a comprehensive report on the result of the great experiment in Jamaica. Harrison replied with detailed and surprisingly diverse conclusions from eight respondents, but his own—most memorably phrased—was that "England has ruined her own colonies, and like an unchaste female wishes to see *other* countries, where slavery exists, in a similar state." He also predicted that Jamaica "will therefore be ultimately abandoned, and become like San Domingo." Understandably, Upshur stepped up his own efforts to promote the annexation of Texas, confiding to Calhoun that Britain was "determined to abolish slavery throughout the American continent" and had formulated its plans for Texas with that purpose in mind.[41] The Southern leaders' mentality was not helped by the fact that since the late 1830s there had been a sharp decline in cotton prices, slave prices, and cotton exports (all wholly reversed in the 1850s).

As abolitionists tried to counter the depressing reports of economic failure, especially following the end of apprenticeship, Abel Upshur's State Department released Harrison's statistics claiming that by 1843 the price of freeholds in Jamaica had declined by half; coffee and sugar production had declined by as much as 50 percent, and some large plantations were worth less than 10 percent of their preemancipation value.[42] Since most Southern writers were convinced that this economic disaster was predictable—as well as being an enormous boon for competitive slaveholders in Cuba, in parts of the South, and in Brazil—the question of Britain's motives became central. As we have seen in Chapter Twelve, there was much disillusion in Britain itself.

Duff Green, the influential editor of the *U.S. Telegraph* and a close friend of John C. Calhoun, contended that British philanthropy was a mere screen for British industrialists and East India interests, groups convinced that free laborers would consume more British produce and that populous India would become Britain's major consumer market. If the British had any genuine humanitarian concerns, Green asked, why did they continue to brutalize and starve Ireland? *Niles' Weekly Register* also pointed to the British neglect of starving, naked whites in Ireland while great sums were being raised to free and teach religion to West India Negroes.

Writing at length to America's minister to France, Secretary of State Calhoun acknowledged that Britain had initially acted on humanitarian motives, assuming that tropical products could be produced more cheaply by free African and East Indian labor than by slaves. West Indian emancipation had been "calculated to combine philanthropy with profit and power, as is not unusual with fanaticism." But this experiment had proved to be catastrophic. British statesmen could read the statistics that showed how far Cuba, Brazil, and the United States had outstripped all the British tropical possessions in the production of coffee, cotton, and sugar.

In order to regain and keep her financial superiority, Calhoun affirmed, Britain was pursuing two simultaneous objectives. First, she aimed to restore her own capacity to produce tropical staples by exploiting only nominally free labor in the West Indies, East Africa, and her East India possessions. But this capital investment could never succeed unless Britain also *destroyed* the rival slave societies that "have refused to follow her suicidal policy" and that could therefore keep the prices of tropical staples "so low as to prevent their cultivation with profit, in the possessions of Great Britain, by what she is pleased to call free labor."[43]

Britain's increasing reliance on the importation of Indian "hill coolies," after an ocean passage of some 131 days to the West Indies, seemed to lend support to the arguments of people like Calhoun and Duff Green. The Southern press was especially elated when the London *Times* not only supported coolie labor in a series of editorials in 1857 but proclaimed that slave emancipation had been a colossal failure, destroying immense amounts of property and degrading Negroes still lower than they had been as slaves. Southern papers gleefully reprinted the *Times*'s demand that abolitionist fanatics go to the British West Indies and view the Negro in his "idleness, his pride, his ingratitude, contemptuously sneering at the industry of that race which made him free, and then come home and teach" other fanatics.[44]

While some British and Northern writers praised the peacefulness, Christianization, and desire for education exhibited by the former slaves, many previous advocates of emancipation had assumed that the freedpeople would continue to work with even higher productivity on plantations, and were thus unprepared for the reports of economic decline, subsistence agriculture, and local markets. For former slaves, however, nothing could be more important than freeing especially their women from constant heavy field labor under the threat of the lash.

The South's increasing fixation on British abolitionism and the declining economy of Haiti and the British Caribbean helps to explain the Southerners' paranoid, disproportionate response to critics in the North. For those convinced that abolitionism was a British-sponsored crusade to destroy American society and transform the South into another Haiti, it was only a short step to contemplate disunion and even to accept Leonidas Spratt's "global mission" of founding a "slave republic" based on the revival of the African slave trade. According to the Charleston editor Spratt, restrictions on the slave trade or on the further expansion of the Southern plantation system necessarily implied that slavery itself was wrong—and had historically served to isolate the South, sap its morale, and retard its economic and political growth.

Since Britain had made slave-trade abolition into a kind of totem symbolizing legitimate commercial power, there was a certain brilliance in throwing off all restraints and violating "civilization's" most pious taboo. Manisha Sinha has shown that the movement in the Deep South to legitimate and reopen the slave trade was much more powerful and widely accepted than most historians have assumed. For some Southerners who saw themselves besieged by an ideologically hostile world, defending the slave trade became a self-vindicating ritual that would test the integrity of their cause as well as the expected opportunism of capitalist nations that could not survive without cotton and whose tenderness for human rights, as Spratt put it, did not prevent them from crushing India, Algeria, and Poland or from tolerating the trade in white Circassian slaves to the markets of Constantinople.[45]

Despite this defiance of Britain, once the Southern states had seceded they had to face reality. The Confederacy's war for independence would depend in good part on gaining the recognition of Great Britain. It was surely for that reason that the Confederate Constitution nullified any possible reopening of the African slave trade while guaranteeing, unlike the Constitution of 1787, the permanent legality and security of racial slavery. Nevertheless, the overreaction of Southern extremists had made it much easier for moderate Northerners to rally in a political campaign against the so-called Slave Power, a home-grown tyranny that threatened the very survival of democracy in America.

BY THE MID-1850s a growing number of Northerners had become convinced that black slavery, by supporting "idle planters" and by associating work with servility, undermined the dignity of labor. As an alternative to the whips and chains of the South, the North offered an idealized vision of prosperity and progress without exploitation—a vision of industrious farmers and proud artisans, of schoolhouses, churches, town meetings, and self-made men. The vast territories of the West, unfenced and held in common by the American people, would thus become the critical testing ground for two competing versions of the American dream.

But as we have seen, for a growing number of Southern leaders and publicists, the Northeast was becoming a perfect replica of the British enemy. Britain, these Southerners believed, had first exploited its own slave colonies, then ruined them under the influence of misguided humanitarianism, and had finally used antislavery as a mask of righteousness in assuming commercial and ideological domination of the world. And the industrializing Northeast, like England, was now employing millions of wage earners, most of them immigrants, was developing vast and squalid urban centers, and was gaining mastery over what Southern "agrarians" saw as the corrupting sources of credit and investment capital. Unless Dixie made its stand, it would therefore share the fate of the exploited, debt-ridden, and ravaged West Indies. If the South were deprived of land and labor for expansion, if its boundaries were pushed back from the West and the Gulf of Mexico as well as from the North, it would then be subjected by a tyrannical government not only to slave emancipation but to "amalgamation" or the horror of race mixing (of course as abolitionists made clear, the large numbers of light-skinned mulattos in the South proved that slavery itself encouraged racial mixture through the sexual exploitation of slave women).

By the stormy 1850s the largest Protestant churches, which had been among the few national organizations that bridged North and South, had divided along sectional lines, in effect aggravating sectional discord. For a variety of reasons the Whig party suddenly collapsed, totally transforming the national two-party political system—and, unknown to Americans at the time, preparing the way for the new, sectional Republican party and thus for Southern secession. During the decade from 1841 to 1851 more immigrants entered the country than during the entire previous 234 years. This had a depressing effect on the wages of Northern nonfarm, native-born manual laborers, leading to what Robert W. Fogel has called a short "hidden depression" from 1853 to 1855. Since most of the newcomers were Irish and German Catholics, a volcanic eruption of anti-Catholic, anti-immigrant, anti-alcohol nativism gave rise to a so-called Know-Nothing Party, which in effect replaced the Whigs.[46] The national Democratic Party survived, but the struggle over the proslavery Lecompton constitution in Kansas, which the settlers rejected by a vote of nearly ten to one, then helped to split the Democrats fatally. Although the Democratic Party had always given the South disproportionate access to national power, this access depended on maintaining or winning the support of Northern allies. As the number of such doughface allies began to dwindle, they were partly replaced by the conversion of Southern Whigs to Southern Democrats. Thus as the Democratic Party became far more Southern in character, there were fewer restraints on attempts to test the party loyalty of Northern Democrats and to adopt an openly proslavery program. The Lecompton constitution and the *Dred Scott* decision were the critical tests imposed on Northern Democrats.[47]

In response to the *Dred Scott* decision of 1857, both the South and President Buchanan were jubilant. Despite vigorous dissenting opinions from Justices John McLean and Benjamin R. Curtis, the highest court in the land had ruled that excluding slavery from the territories—the issue that had divided the nation in the Missouri Crisis of 1819–21 and the goal that had brought the Republican Party into existence—was unconstitutional. Republican newspapers, among them the *New York Tribune*, scornfully replied that the decision was entitled to "just so much moral weight as . . . the judgment of a majority of those congregated in any Washington bar-room."[48] Stephen Douglas, the leading contender for the Democratic presidential nomination in 1860, remained silent for many weeks. He wholly agreed with the denial of black citizenship and took credit for the congressional repeal of the Missouri Compromise in his own Kansas-Nebraska Act of 1854. Yet his relations with Buchanan and the South were already strained, and he knew that his future career hinged on finding a way to reconcile the Southern version of *limited* popular sovereignty, embodied in the *Dred Scott* decision, with his own constituents' demand for genuine self-determination.

Douglas finally presented his response to the *Dred Scott* decision in an important speech at the Illinois statehouse in May 1857. He argued that the constitutional right to take slaves into a territory was a worthless right unless it was sustained, protected, and enforced by "police regulations and local legislation." By contrasting an empty legal right to bring slaves into a territory, as sustained by *Dred Scott*, with the necessary public support to enforce such a right, Douglas denied any meaningful contradiction between the *Dred Scott* decision and his own principle of popular sovereignty.[49]

Two weeks later Abraham Lincoln (a former Whig, now a Republican) gave his reply to Douglas from the same forum. Terming the *Dred Scott* decision erroneous, Lincoln reminded his audience that the Supreme Court had frequently reversed its own decisions, and he promised that "we shall do what we can to have it to over-rule this."[50]

Since 1854, when he had attacked the Kansas-Nebraska Act, Lincoln had been making a new career by pursuing Douglas. Lincoln was a self-educated Kentuckian, shaped by the Indiana and Illinois frontier. In moral and cultural outlook, however, he was not far from the stereotyped New Englander. He abstained from alcohol, revered the idea of self-improvement, dreamed of America's technological and moral progress, and condemned slavery as a moral and political evil. He told a Chicago audience in 1858:

> I have always hated slavery I think as much as any Abolitionist. . . . I have always hated it, but I have always been quiet about it until this new era of the introduction of the Nebraska Bill began. I always believed that everybody was against it, and that it was in course of ultimate extinction.[51]

The Kansas-Nebraska Act, which allowed voters to accept slavery in territories like Kansas, taught Lincoln that men like Douglas did not care whether slavery was "voted *down* or voted *up*." It also allowed him to exercise his magnificent talents as a debater and stump speaker—talents that had already distinguished him as a frontier lawyer, a state legislator, and an attorney and lobbyist for the Illinois Central Railroad and other corporations. Lincoln's humor, his homespun sayings, and his unaffected self-assurance all diverted attention from his extraordinary ability to grasp the central point of a controversy and to compress an argument into its clearest and most striking form. In 1856, after a period of watchful waiting, Lincoln played an important part in the belated organization of the Illinois Republican Party. Two years later the Republican state convention unanimously nominated him to run for Douglas's Senate seat.[52]

The Lincoln-Douglas contest was unprecedented in both form and substance. At the time, senators were elected by state legislatures (only after 1913, with the adoption of the Seventeenth Amendment, did the direct popular election of senators begin), and no party convention had ever nominated a candidate. In an acceptance speech on June 16, 1858, Lincoln concisely and eloquently stated the arguments he would present directly to the people, appealing for a Republican legislature that would then be committed to elect him to the Senate. Since Douglas had unexpectedly rejected the proslavery Lecompton constitution and had joined the Republicans in fighting it, Lincoln needed to persuade the electorate that Douglas's own crusade for popular sovereignty had rekindled the agitation over slavery and led directly to the *Dred Scott* decision and the Lecompton constitution. According to Lincoln, Douglas's moral indifference to slavery disqualified him as a leader who could stand firm against the Slave Power. For Lincoln was wholly convinced that the conflict over slavery would continue until a crisis had been reached and passed. As he said in his famous "House Divided" speech:

> "A house divided against itself cannot stand."
> I believe this government cannot endure, permanently half slave and half free.
> I do not expect the Union to be dissolved—I do not expect the house to fall—but I do expect it will cease to be divided.
> It will become all one thing, or all the other.
> Either the opponents of slavery, will arrest the further spread of it, and place it where the public mind shall rest in the belief that it is in course of ultimate extinction; or its advocates will push it forward, till it shall become alike lawful in all the States, old as well as new—North as well as South.
> Have we no tendency to the latter condition?[53]

The "House Divided" speech signified a turning point in American political history. Lincoln stated that expediency and an ethical neutrality toward slavery had undermined the Founders' expectation that slavery was "in course of ultimate extinction." If the North continued to make compromises and failed to defend a boundary of clear principle, the South was certain to dictate "a second *Dred Scott* decision," depriving every state of the power to discriminate against slave property. In Lincoln's view, Douglas's Kansas-Nebraska Act had been part of a master plan or conspiracy, which Lincoln compared to "a piece of *machinery*" that had been designed to legalize slavery, step by step, throughout the United States. In asserting that "the people were to be left 'perfectly free' subject only to the Constitution, Douglas had provided "an exactly fitted *niche*, for the *Dred Scott* decision to afterwards come in, and declare the perfect freedom of the people, to be just no freedom at all."

Lincoln was not an abolitionist or a radical of any kind. He was convinced that prohibiting the further spread of slavery would be sufficient to condemn it to "ultimate extinction," a belief shared by many Southern leaders. Yet Lincoln, who had been deeply troubled by reading George Fitzhugh's all-out defense of slavery, insisted on a public policy aimed at the goal of gradual abolition—a public policy similar to that of Great Britain in the early 1820s or, in Lincoln's eyes, to that of the Founders. For Lincoln, rejecting popular sovereignty in the territories was the same as rejecting the moral indifference exemplified by Douglas; and this was the first step toward national redemption.

Douglas seemed to be the nation's most likely choice for president in 1860. His struggle with Lincoln for reelection to the Senate in 1858 therefore commanded national attention. Making full use of newly constructed railroads, the two candidates traveled nearly ten thousand miles in four months. They crisscrossed Illinois, their tireless voices intermingling with the sound of bands, parades, fireworks, cannon, and cheering crowds. Each community tried to outdo its rivals in pageantry and in winning the greatest turnout from the countryside.

Lincoln and Douglas agreed to participate in seven face-to-face debates, which are rightly regarded as classics in the history of campaign oratory. Douglas tried to make the most of his experience as a seasoned national leader (at forty-five he was four years younger than Lincoln) and to portray his opponent as a dangerous radical. According to Douglas, Lincoln's "House Divided" speech showed a determination to impose the moral judgments of one section on the other. Lincoln's doctrines threatened to destroy the Union and to extinguish the world's last hope for freedom. Douglas repeatedly exploited his listeners' racial prejudice, drawing laughter from his sarcastic refusal to question "Mr. Lincoln's conscientious belief that the negro was made his equal, and hence his brother."[54]

Lincoln searched for ways to counteract the image of a revolutionary and "nigger lover." Always insisting on the moral and political wrong of slavery, he repeatedly acknowledged that the federal government could not interfere with slavery in the existing states. He opposed repeal of the Fugitive Slave Law. He wholly rejected the idea of "perfect social and political equality with the negro." He did maintain, however, that blacks were as much entitled as whites to "all the natural rights enumerated in the Declaration of Independence, the right to life, liberty, and the pursuit of happiness." If the black was "perhaps" not equal in moral or intellectual qualities, "in the right to eat the bread, without leave of anybody else, which his own hand earns, *he is my equal and the equal of judge Douglas, and the equal of every living man.* [Great applause.]"[55]

The election in Illinois was extremely close. The Republicans did not win enough seats in the legislature to send Lincoln to the Senate, but the campaign immediately elevated him to national prominence. Lincoln had expressed and defended a Republican antislavery ideology that combined fixed purpose with a respect for constitutional restraints. Southern Democrats were outraged by Douglas's response to Lincoln in the debate at Freeport, Illinois, where Douglas had maintained that regardless of what the Supreme Court might decide about the constitutionality of slavery in a territory, the people had the "lawful means to introduce it or exclude it" as they pleased. Repeating his familiar point that slavery could not exist "a day or an hour anywhere" unless it was supported by local police regulations, Douglas emphasized that the "unfriendly legislation" of a territorial government could effectively prevent slavery from being introduced. As Lincoln later quipped, this was to say, *"a thing may be lawfully driven from a place where it has a lawful right to be* [Cheers and laughter]."[56]

In 1859 the breach between Douglas and the South could no longer be contained. The people of Kansas ratified a new constitution prohibiting slavery, thereby giving bite to Douglas's so-called Freeport Doctrine. In the Senate, where Douglas had been ousted from his chairmanship of the Committee on Territories, he led the fight against the Southern demand for a federal slave code protecting slave property in all the territories. During a tour of the South, Douglas became alarmed by the growing movement, led by young proslavery "fire-eaters," to revive and legalize the African slave trade. Looking ahead to the Democratic convention of 1860, Douglas issued what amounted to an ultimatum about the party platform. Northern Democrats, he insisted, would not allow the party to be used as a means for reviving the African slave trade, securing a federal slave code, or pursuing any of the other new objectives of Southern extremists.[57] Douglas warned the South that Northerners would not retreat from defending genuine popular sovereignty, even though popular sovereignty was clearly running against the interests of the South.

By 1860 a multitude of previously separate fears, aspirations, and factional interests had become polarized into opposing visions of America's heritage and destiny. As many Southern leaders became increasingly obsessed with the British example and with the growth of Northern support for fugitive slaves and opposition to the expansion of slavery, traditional systems of trust and reciprocity had collapsed.

John Brown, who had warred against slavery in Kansas, was a key symbol in this polarization. Backed financially by a secret group of abolitionists, including the wealthy Gerrit Smith, Brown had also cultivated extremely close ties with free black communities in the North. On the night of October 16, 1859, he and twenty-one heavily armed white and black followers seized part of the federal arsenal at Harpers Ferry, Virginia (now West Virginia). Brown hoped to begin the destruction of slavery by igniting a slave revolt and creating in the South a free-soil refuge for fugitives. After resisting federal troops for two days, Brown surrendered; he was tried for conspiracy, treason, and murder and was hanged. For most Southerners he epitomized the nightmare of radical abolitionists igniting a Haitian-like slave revolution.[58]

During his trial Brown claimed to have acted under the "higher law" of the New Testament. He insisted that

> had I so interfered in behalf of the rich, the powerful, the intelligent, the so-called great, or in behalf of any of their friends . . . and suffered and sacrificed what I have in this interference, it would have been all right; and every man in this court would have deemed it an act worthy of reward rather than punishment.[59]

For Brown the higher law was not a philosophical abstraction but a moral command to shed blood and die in the cause of freedom. In the eyes of armchair reformers and intellectuals, Brown's courage to act on his principles made him not only a revered martyr but also a symbol of all that America lacked. Democratic editors and politicians, however, saw Brown's criminal violence as the direct result of the irresponsible preaching of William H. Seward and other so-called Black Republicans. The Democratic *New York Herald* reprinted Seward's speech on the "irrepressible conflict between slave and free states" alongside news accounts from Harpers Ferry. Many Southerners came to the stunned realization that Brown's raid could not be dismissed as the folly of a madman, since it had supposedly revealed the secret will of much of the North. Senator James M. Mason of Virginia told Congress that "John Brown's invasion was condemned [in the North] only because it failed." In the words of Jefferson Davis, a Mississippi senator who had been President Franklin Pierce's secretary of war, the Republican Party had been "organized on the basis of making war" against the South.[60]

Ironically, both the Republicans and the Southern extremists agreed that slavery must expand under national sanction if it were to survive for a longer period of time (though some modern economists have argued that in view of the amount of uncultivated land in the existing slave states, there was no pressing need for territorial expansion). They also agreed that if the *Dred Scott* decision was valid, the government had an obligation to protect slave *property*, like all other property, in all the territories. Above all, both the Republicans and the Southern extremists rejected popular sovereignty as Stephen Douglas had defined it. For Southerners the Constitution prohibited either Congress or a territorial legislature from depriving a settler of his slave property. For the Republicans the Constitution gave Congress both the duty and the power to prevent the spread of an institution that deprived human beings of their inalienable right to freedom.

Because these positions were irreconcilable, the Northern Democrats held the only keys to possible compromise in the presidential election of 1860. But like the Republicans, the Douglas Democrats had drawn their own firm limits against further concessions to Southern extremists. Early in 1860 Senator Jefferson Davis challenged those limits by persuading the Senate Democratic caucus to adopt a set of resolutions committing the federal government to protect slavery in the territories. For Davis and other leaders from the Deep South, a federal slave code was the logical extension of the *Dred Scott* decision. They also agreed that the forthcoming Democratic platform must uphold the principle of federal protection of slave property. The Douglas Democrats knew that such a principle of guaranteed protection would completely undercut their reliance on legislation unfriendly to slavery in a territory and that such a plank would guarantee their defeat in the North.

Beginning in April 1860, the Democratic Party became fatally divided and destroyed itself as a national force. During a series of complex events, delegates from the Lower South seceded from the party and adopted an extreme proslavery platform. They nominated Vice President John C. Breckinridge of Kentucky for the presidency. The surviving Northern Democrats remained loyal to popular sovereignty, however it might be modified in practice by the *Dred Scott* decision, and nominated Douglas.

Meanwhile, the division of the Democrats had given the Republicans greater flexibility in nominating a candidate. In 1858 Douglas had portrayed Lincoln as a flaming abolitionist, and the South had accepted this image. To the North, however, Lincoln appeared more moderate and less controversial than the better-known Senator William Seward of New York. Unlike Seward, Lincoln was not popularly associated with the "higher-law" doctrines that had led to Harpers Ferry.

Although Lincoln disapproved of Know-Nothing nativism, he was more discreet than Seward and thus stood less chance of losing the nativist vote in Pennsylvania and other critical states. If some Northerners regarded him as a crude buffoon from the prairies, he appealed to many other Northerners as the tall rail-splitter of humble origins, a man of the people, an egalitarian. Except for his general endorsement of the proposed Homestead Act, protective tariffs, and a transcontinental railroad—all programs that were popular in the North and West and that had been blocked in Congress by the South— Lincoln was associated with few political issues and had made few enemies. In May, at the Republicans' boisterous convention in Chicago, Lincoln finally overcame Seward's early lead and received the nomination.

The presidential campaign of 1860 was filled with the noisy hucksterism and carnival atmosphere that had been standard since 1840. The Republicans tended to discount the warnings of serious crisis, and they contemptuously dismissed Southern threats of secession as empty bluff, since South Carolinians in particular had been threatening secession for decades. The Breckinridge Democrats tried to play down these threats and to profess their loyalty to the Constitution and the Union. Yet various groups of moderates realized that both the Constitution and the Union were in jeopardy. This was the message of the new Constitutional Union Party, which was led largely by former Whigs and which won many supporters in the Upper South. And this was the message that Stephen Douglas repeated bravely and incessantly—in the South as well as in the North—in the first nationwide speaking campaign by a presidential candidate.

In November the national popular vote was divided among four candidates, and Lincoln received less than 40 percent of the national total. Yet he received 180 electoral votes—57 more than the combined total of his three opponents. He carried every free state except New Jersey, and he won 4 of New Jersey's 7 electoral votes. In ten of the slave states, however, he failed to get a single popular vote! Breckinridge, the Southern Democrat, captured all the states of the Lower South as well as Delaware, Maryland, Arkansas, and North Carolina. John Bell, the leader of the once powerful Whig Party in Tennessee and the candidate of the Constitutional Union party, carried Tennessee, Kentucky, and Virginia. Although Douglas received approximately 525,000 more popular votes than Breckinridge and trailed Lincoln by only 491,000, he won a mere 12 electoral votes (9 from Missouri and 3 from New Jersey). In many respects it was not really a national election. In the North it was essentially a contest between Lincoln and Douglas; in the South, between Breckinridge and Bell.

For the South the worst fears and predictions of forty years had come true. The United States had never had an administration that was even moderately hostile to black slavery. Although the South had dominated the federal government for most of its seventy-one years, slaveholding planters, especially in the Deep South, had always been alert to a central government's *potential* threat to slavery—a nightmare supposedly confirmed by Britain and in 1848 by France. (Yet the advocates of states' rights had had no qualms about the federal government's draconian enforcement of the Fugitive Slave Law of 1850.)

Lincoln's reassurances regarding the constitutional protection of slavery in the existing states could not mitigate the crucial new facts. The election had proved that the North was populous enough to bestow national power on a minority party that had no support in the South. The Republican Party was committed to free-labor ideology and to the proposition that slavery was morally wrong. Slaveholders would have to take Lincoln's professions of restraint on good faith. If he or his successors should become more militant, they could not be checked by a balance of political power. A dominant sectional party would control federal patronage, the postal service and military posts, and the appointment of federal judges and other officeholders.

Considerations of this kind strengthened the hand of secessionists. On December 20, 1860, South Carolina crossed the threshold that had been so closely approached during the nullification crisis of 1832. A special convention repealed the state's ratification of the Constitution and withdrew South Carolina from the Union. Unlike Jackson when faced with similar defiance, President Buchanan maintained that the federal government could do nothing to prevent the move.

Unionists mounted stiffer resistance to secession in other states of the Lower South. The chief controversies, however, involved timing—whether to follow the stampede of the fire-eating militants or to wait until Lincoln had shown his true colors after being inaugurated in March. By February 1, 1861, the militants had triumphed in Mississippi, Florida, Alabama, Georgia, Louisiana, and Texas. Inevitably the shock produced reflex actions toward the traditional "saving compromise." Although Senator John Crittenden's proposed amendments to the Constitution were defined as moderate, they matched the most extravagant Southern demands of a few years before. Even so, the leaders of the Lower South knew that no "compromise" would be secure unless the Republican Party miraculously cast off its antislavery principles. Most Republicans could not publicly approve Crittenden's "unamendable" amendment that would have guaranteed the *permanent* security of slavery. Nor could they return to the old Democratic proposal for extending the Missouri Compromise line to the Pacific. The 1850s had shown that any federal commitment to establishing and protecting slavery south of that line would only encourage the South's expansionist ambitions in the Caribbean and Latin America. As Lincoln confidentially warned William Kellogg, his spokesman in Congress: "Entertain no proposition for a compromise in regard to the *extension* of slavery. The instant you do, they have us under again; all our labor is lost, and sooner or later must be done over. Douglas is sure to be again trying to bring in his 'Pop.Sov.' [*sic*] Have none of it. The tug has to come & better now than later."[61]

By 1860 the North and South had moved beyond the reach of compromise. The United States had originally emerged from an act of secession— from a final rejection of compromise with Britain. Even after independence had been won, Americans continued to perceive Britain as a conspiratorial power that threatened to encircle the United States from Canada, Bermuda, the Bahamas, Florida, Cuba, Texas, and the Pacific Northwest, using antislavery ideology as the means of checking the nation's expansive energies.

Despite this peril, America had continued to prosper and expand. The period from 1820 to 1860 witnessed an extraordinary extension of limits, an overleaping of boundaries of every kind. History seemed to confirm the people's wish for total self-determination. The white American people, like the white American individual, seemed to be free from the burdens of their past and free to shape their own character. The one problem that their ingenuity could not resolve was black slavery, which the Founding Fathers had seen as an unwanted legacy of British greed. Ironically, the South increasingly came to regard black slavery as the necessary base on which freedom must rest. For many in the North a commitment to slavery's ultimate extinction became the test of freedom. Each section detected a fatal change in the other—a betrayal of the principles and mission of the Founding Fathers. Each section feared that the other had become transformed into a despotic and conspiratorial power, very similar to the original British enemy. And both sections shared a heritage of standing firm against despotic power.

15

The Civil War and Slave Emancipation

O<small>N</small> A<small>PRIL</small> 2, 1865, General Robert E. Lee sent a shocking telegram to Jefferson Davis, President of the Confederate States of America. Writing from Petersburg, Virginia, then twenty-five miles south of Richmond, where Davis still ruled from the Confederate capital, Lee warned that it was absolutely necessary to evacuate Richmond that night. Since Union troops were already forcing an abandonment of Petersburg, Lee had to choose between the loss of Richmond or the encirclement and loss of his dwindling and beleaguered army. President Davis turned pale when he received this news while attending Sunday services in St. Paul's Church. He would have been even more devastated if he had known that President Abraham Lincoln would enter Petersburg the next day and on April 4 would actually sit in Davis's own study, in the Confederate White House, only forty hours after Davis had left it.[1]

Even more shocking, from a Confederate point of view, was the large number of African American cavalry and infantry who took part in the Union army's capture of Richmond. As buildings burned and as looters searched for food and goods, huge crowds of black slaves sang and cheered as they greeted a black army of liberation made up mostly of former slaves. Soon troops of black Union soldiers joined a throng of Richmond blacks near "Lumpkin Alley," a site of public slave auctions and slave jails. As the crowd listened to the speech of a black army chaplain, who "proclaimed for the first time in that city freedom to all mankind," they began to hear the shouts and chanting of slaves who were still imprisoned behind the barred windows of Lumpkin's Jail.

Robert Lumpkin, a leading slave merchant, had recently acquired this shipment of slaves for future sale and had frantically tried to transport them outside the city on the same train that enabled Jefferson Davis and other Confederate leaders to escape. When this attempt failed, Lumpkin marched the slaves back to his two-story jail. Only hours later the black Union soldiers broke open the jail's cells, and many prisoners shouted out praise for God or "master Abe" as their liberators.[2]

As one might expect, Richmond's terrified whites locked and bolted their doors and windows as black soldiers patrolled the streets. Yet as the historian James M. McPherson describes it, Lincoln "the Emancipator," who had only days to live, was soon surrounded by an impenetrable cordon of black people shouting, "Glory to God! Glory! Glory! Glory! . . . The great Messiah! I knowed him as soon as I seed him. He's been in my heart four long years. Come to free his children from bondage. Glory, Hallelujah!" "I know I am free," shouted an old woman, "for I have seen Father Abraham and felt him." Overwhelmed by rare emotions, Lincoln said to one black man who fell on his knees in front of him: "Don't kneel to me. That is not right. You must kneel to God only, and thank Him for the liberty you will enjoy hereafter."[3]

While we will later examine the tortuous route that led Lincoln to this messianic position, it should now be stressed that no other images could underscore so dramatically the *revolutionary* meaning of the American Civil War—a revolutionary message that the South and then the nation would long struggle to repress. Few wars in human history have led to such a radical outcome as the liberation of some four million slaves—which meant the confiscation without compensation, which had been paid in some form in most slave emancipations, of a hitherto legally accepted form of property.[4] The slaves' value came to an estimated $3.5 billion in 1860 dollars. That would be about $68.4 billion in 2003 dollars. But a more revealing figure is the fact that the nation's gross national product in 1860 was only about 20 percent above the value of slaves, which means that as a share of today's gross national product, the slaves' value would come to an estimated $9.75 trillion.[5]

As investment capital, the value of the nation's slaves in 1860 had far exceeded (by perhaps a billion dollars) the cash value of all the farms in the South, including the border states of Delaware, Maryland, Kentucky, and Missouri. In 1860 the Southern slaves were also worth three times the cost of constructing all the nation's railroads or three times the combined capital invested nationally in business and industrial property. Moreover, despite the deeply rooted white racism in the North as well as the South (in the fall of 1865 Connecticut voted down Negro suffrage), the war led to the nation's first civil rights legislation and to constitutional amendments that extended to blacks full citizenship and equality before the law as well as the right to vote (for adult black males).

When hostilities began, in April 1861, such revolutionary change would have been unthinkable, except perhaps in the fantasies of a few radical abolitionists. A war to preserve the Union, it was widely believed, would be a short war, given the North's superiority in population and resources. Yet it became in many ways the modern world's first total war, finally fought by Generals Grant and Sherman with the goal of unconditional surrender. In this respect America's Civil War stood in marked contrast to the wars fought in Europe from 1648 to 1914 and in many ways, such as the transformation of some Southern cities into ruins and rubble, anticipated the two world wars of the twentieth century.[6]

Although the Civil War was an apocalyptic success in the sense that it brought an end to nearly a century of struggle and broken hopes regarding the ultimate extinction of African American slavery, it also combined new freedoms, as in other major revolutions, with shock, breakdown, trauma, and tragedy. Neither desired nor accurately anticipated by leaders in the North and South, the war dramatized the failure of the whole American system of political negotiation and compromise that had never weakened the institution of slavery but had supported democratic government for whites for over eighty years. By reducing national controversies to the test of military force, millions of Americans on one side or the other were bound to be defeated and burdened with a Lost Cause. And since slave emancipation came as an unexpected military decision, it precluded careful planning and preparation, including the kind that Lincoln himself desired. Moreover, the long-term outcome of this revolutionary decision would be determined within a context of sectional hate and bitterness, political revenge, and competing pressures for reconciliation, reunion, and forgiveness.

Given the economic growth and vitality of Southern slavery in 1860, it is difficult to imagine any other historical scenario that would have led to full and universal slave emancipation in the nineteenth or even early twentieth century.[7] This conclusion lends support to the argument that the Civil War was a necessary and "good war," a view originally endorsed by Frederick Douglass and most other black and white abolitionists, and seemingly by most American historians in recent decades, including me. This judgment would have arguably been more difficult if the North had unleashed full vengeance upon the defeated South, executing as traitors most of the Confederate leaders and officers; or if the freed blacks had fulfilled the Southern whites' worst fears, retaliating against their former masters and converting at least parts of the South into an American Haiti.[8]

As it happened, however, African Americans became the scapegoats of sectional hostility. Numerous Southern whites and some Northerners adopted the view that if it had not been for the presence of blacks, there would have been no devastating war. This conviction, as the historian David Blight argues, combined with Southern white rage over "the presence of assertive blacks wearing uniforms and carrying guns, organizing Union Leagues, or voting and serving in the legislature and on the judicial bench," helps to explain the eruption of antiblack mob violence and the dramatic increase and acceptance, by the 1890s, of the lynching of blacks as a form of "populist justice."[9]

Following the failure of Reconstruction, the political, psychological, and emotional reunion of North and South came to depend on the North's willingness to give Southern whites a free hand in defining and presiding over all racial policies—an understanding that prevailed from the late 1870s to at least the 1950s. The goal of reunion required the repression from memory of the revolutionary realities of the war, symbolized for us by the black Union troops freeing captive slaves in Richmond. Thus the ceremonial "Decoration Days" and "Memorial Days," honoring the war's fallen soldiers on each May 30, soon ignored the crucial racial aspects of the war; "emancipation" became unmentionable, as did the war's lethal and unlimited character.

As Americans slowly emerged from the deep fog of the war, and as younger generations queried their elders, both Northerners and Southerners faced an extremely puzzling question, a question that had also baffled many European observers throughout the conflict. Why was it that a democratic nation that prided itself on rational moderation, peace, common sense, expediency, and compromise became the scene of the world's first "modern" war, pursued by the North until its armies achieved unconditional victory, totally crushing the South?

This total war meant that the North alone, with an 1860 population of slightly less than 20 million, mobilized armed forces of about 2.1 million—equivalent today to over 31 million soldiers and sailors for the nation as a whole. While no such figures can be given with exactitude, the Civil War brought a total of approximately 620,000 military deaths, more than the 606,000 deaths in all the other American wars from the Revolution through the Korean War. The North lost some 360,000 military men, a number roughly equivalent to 5.4 million deaths today.[10] The war also led to a shocking 20 percent mortality for the nearly 200,000 African Americans in the Union army and navy.[11]

The 260,000 or more Confederate deaths (an even more approximate number) represented 18 to 20 percent of the Confederate states' white adult male population, about the same proportion as German military deaths in World War II. Some 26,000 to 31,000 Confederates died in Union prisons alone. Moreover, one-fifth of Mississippi's postwar state budget paid for the prosthetic limbs of surviving but maimed soldiers.[12]

Even apart from the Civil War's diseases, such as typhoid, dysentery, and pneumonia, which killed at least twice as many soldiers as the battles did, it was a war of virtual death camps, such as the infamous Andersonville camp for Union prisoners of war, almost 13,000 of whom died from disease, poor sanitation, malnutrition, overcrowding, or exposure to the elements. It was a war of deep-seated hatred, symbolized in its extreme by the Confederate women who wore necklaces made from teeth of dead Yankee soldiers; and a war ending in a will to destroy, as in General Sherman's "scorched earth policy" in the Deep South.

In the Civil War battles, which were more lethal than those in Europe's Napoleonic Wars, we see the first trench warfare and ultimately the first booby traps, the first rapid-firing Gatling guns and also self-igniting shells that showered soldiers with pieces of deadly shrapnel. Both sides became guilty at times of simply executing prisoners of war. The Confederate government called for the execution of all black Union soldiers taken prisoner, and on April 12, 1864, at Fort Pillow, Tennessee, General Nathan Bedford Forrest's Confederate forces massacred hundreds of captured black Union troops.[13]

If this massive death and suffering is seen as the necessary cost for slave emancipation, which was clearly the greatest social revolution in American history, one must consider the profound irony that Robert E. Lee's spectacular and continuing victories in Virginia *prolonged* the war until it finally destroyed slavery and the Southern plantation economy.[14] If the proslavery Union general George B. McClellan had achieved the Union's objectives and had captured Richmond in his Peninsular Campaign in the late spring and early summer of 1862, much of the Southern social system would probably have survived. President Lincoln would no doubt have rejoiced at an early Confederate defeat, while pinning his hopes on some long-term efforts at gradual emancipation and black colonization. But by war's end, Lincoln happily accepted the fact that there were more than twice the number of blacks in the Union army than the total number of soldiers in the Confederate army at the Battle of Gettysburg.[15]

Before we turn to Lincoln and the issue of slave emancipation, more should be said about the revolutionary character of the war—a sample of events and developments that were later forgotten in the ceremonial rituals of reconciliation. In both North and South the central governments assumed unprecedented powers, typified by the military draft, which was first inaugurated by the South (whose many loopholes included one white male exemption for each plantation containing twenty or more slaves).[16] Following the growth of a frightening deficit, the Union government desperately issued bonds, printed greenbacks or paper money, and adopted the first income tax in American history. Lincoln suspended habeas corpus in the North, leading to arbitrary arrests and court-martials for civilians. As thousands were jailed as security risks, Secretary of State William H. Seward was said to have boasted to the British minister, Lord Lyons, that at the touch of a telegraph, he could order the arrest of a citizen of Ohio or the imprisonment of a citizen of New York, and no power on earth except the president could obtain his release. To justify such measures, Seward and other authorities could point to the existence of actual conspiracies and spy networks, as well as to enemy infiltration and guerrilla raids.[17]

From the outset, however, Northerners repeatedly heard the argument that the war offered a transcendent opportunity for purification, a cleansing of self-centeredness related to past religious revivals and America's sense of mission. For Josephine Shaw Lowell, for example, the war finally provided the country with the means for overcoming materialism and greed. Josephine belonged to a New England upper-class abolitionist family now living in Staten Island and was not quite eighteen when the war began. As she wrote in her diary in August 1862:

> This war will purify the country of some of its extravagance and selfishness, even if we are stopped midway. It can't help doing us good; it has begun to do us good already. It will make us young ones much more thoughtful and earnest, and so improve the country. I suppose we need something every few years to teach us that riches, luxury and comfort are not the great end of life, and this will surely teach us that at least.

"War," she later wrote, is "exactly like a revival—a direct work of God, so wonderful are some of the conversions."[18] President Lincoln came to agree at least that the war was the direct work of God: "We must work earnestly in the best light He gives us," Lincoln wrote "trusting that so working still conduces to the great ends He ordains. Surely He intends some great good to follow this mighty convulsion, which no mortal could make, and no mortal could stay."[19]

In July 1863 Josephine's now famous brother, Robert Gould Shaw, was killed while leading the elite black troops of the Fifty-fourth Massachusetts Infantry in the attack on Fort Wagner. The battle killed nearly half of Robert's men. Later, Josephine's young husband was also killed in combat.

Northern intellectuals, especially in New England, seemed almost to welcome such sacrifice as they praised discipline and selflessness and repudiated "sickly sentimentality" and what Walt Whitman termed "miserable selfism." For Francis Parkman the war was "like a fresh breeze." According to Orestes Brownson, the Northerners, who had been "wholly engrossed in trade and speculation, selfish, and incapable of any disinterested, heroic or patriotic effort" were now responding "magnificently" to the call of self-sacrifice. In May 1862 Charles Eliot Norton wrote a friend, "I can hardly help wishing that the war might go on and on till it brought us suffering and sorrow enough to quicken our consciences and cleanse our hearts." And Ralph Waldo Emerson affirmed that now was a time when "one whole generation might well consent to perish" if that would bring "political liberty & clean & just life" for "the generations that follow." For such intellectuals and literary figures, the freeing of slaves was a concrete symbol of a much larger and deeper emancipation from the more corrupting *effects* of capitalism.[20] But in the later Gilded Age, with its triumphant materialism, these ideals quickly became for many idealists the North's Lost Cause, an ideological defeat that in time made many Northerners increasingly empathetic to the South's "culture of defeat," with its profound sense of loss and eloquent nostalgia for an irreplaceable paradise.[21]

Ironically, as the historians David Potter and Wolfgang Schivelbusch have pointed out, the South's persistent "agrarian tradition," which merged with the Lost Cause mythology, became "a way in which a man could renounce industrial capitalism and all its works without becoming a Marxist."[22] Schivelbusch compares the ideological power of "the culture of defeat" in the South following the American Civil War with that in both France following the surprising Prussian military victory in 1870 and Germany following World War I. Initially, he argues, the prewar Southern cotton planters were highly successful capitalist entrepreneurs who adopted a quasi-feudal cult of chivalry "to dress up and decorate what was actually an ongoing process of economic modernization and expansion." The Southern leaders' glorification of a knightly romanticism steeped in tales of seventeenth-century English cavaliers and the novels of Sir Walter Scott "played a role in the South similar to that of Richard Wagner's Teutonic mythology in Prussian-led Germany."[23]

Like France in 1870 and Germany in 1918, the defeated South temporarily became a "dreamland" of denial, emphasizing its own wartime triumphs and heroism as well as the unfairness and relative unimportance of the enemy's victory, which had depended on matériel and sheer numbers, not military superiority. Southerners reassured themselves that they "would resume their former place in the Union as equal partners," much as the French and Germans naïvely assumed in 1870 and 1918 that there would be no change in borders or territories. Though Southern leaders accepted the *necessity* of slave "emancipation," they quickly enacted Black Codes designed to keep former slaves under slavelike controls and supervision, as if no war had been lost. But in each of the three "dreamlands" the victor soon shattered these expectations of a happy return to national "freedom, innocence, and sovereignty."[24]

Former Confederates for a time felt helpless as Northern Radicals in Congress negated their Black Codes, dissolved their state governments, and divided their land into five military zones of occupation. As rebels organized

the Ku Klux Klan and other terrorist groups, they often thought of themselves as brave Scots resisting English tyranny (as in the egregiously inaccurate modern film *Braveheart*).[25]

As they looked back on the significance of the Civil War, former Confederate General Bradley T. Johnson and former president Jefferson Davis
expressed seemingly contradictory but widely held views. According to Davis,
voicing a belief that would become deeply nationalized in the first half of the
twentieth century, slavery was "in no wise the cause of the conflict, but only
an incident." Johnson gave a different verdict, which was seldom made explicit, but which lurked behind much Lost Cause culture, including the immensely popular film *Birth of a Nation*: "The great crime of the century was
the emancipation of the Negroes." (If this was true, slavery must have been
something more than "an incident.")[26]

The apparent contradiction between Davis and Johnson became from
the 1880s to the 1950s a profound but generally unrecognized contradiction
in American culture. On the one hand, a vast and increasingly popular literature, centered on memoirs and "the plantation novel," presented the antebellum South as an agrarian utopia or golden age in which devoted "mammies"
and other loyal slaves not only exemplified racial harmony but dramatized a
relationship between worker and "employer" that transcended all conflict.
As Jefferson Davis himself wrote, "Never was there a happier dependence of
labor and capital on each other." Authors of the Southern literature of nostalgia much preferred the word "servant" to "slave": so "sacred" was the "bond
between master and servant," Susan Dabney Smedes recalled, that it was as
"close as the tie of blood." Few if any writers from Thomas Nelson Page and
Susan Dabney Smedes to Margaret Mitchell *explicitly* defended slavery as an
institution (like harmonious communities, it was often said to be obsolete),
but black slavery was the very foundation of what Page termed "the purest,
sweetest life ever lived."[27] The literature and then films of nostalgia for the
antebellum South still conveyed and underscored the absolute necessity of retaining slavery's white supremacy. This conviction was greatly reinforced by
the growth of scientific racism in the Western world, and the books and films
more than implied that emancipation had been a colossal mistake if not a crime.

On the other hand, a contradictory current either erased slavery from
popular memory or marginalized it as an issue in the Civil War. This turning
away from slavery can be seen in the popular commemorations and reenact-
ments of the Civil War, which ignored the subject and in general excluded
blacks. A similar message appeared in the works of the most influential historians, such as William A. Dunning, Charles Francis Adams II, and even the
otherwise progressive Charles and Mary Beard, who essentially agreed with
the assertion of Jefferson Davis that slavery was "in no wise the cause" of the
Civil War (despite such evidence as President Lincoln's statement in his

message to Congress on December 1, 1862: "Without slavery the rebellion could never have existed; without slavery it could not continue").[28] David Blight's magisterial study of the Civil War in American memory shows that while African Americans and a few white writers struggled to preserve the revolutionary or "emancipationist" meaning of the Civil War, the compelling desire for reconciliation and healing, strengthened by white racism and disillusion over Reconstruction, led to a national consensus that made "everyone right, and no one truly wrong, in the remembered Civil War"—a vision that further divided whites from blacks and deprived emancipation of any substantial meaning.[29]

On one level, this consensus eliminated or at least smoothed over the contradiction of marginalizing the importance of slavery while maintaining or implying that emancipation had been the war's great mistake or crime. Many Northerners stressed that the war had been fought to preserve a now beloved Union but tacitly or unconsciously accepted the South's romantic depiction of prewar harmony and thus granted the "racially experienced" white Southerners full authority for dealing with the unfortunate consequences of emancipation (such as the supposedly widespread desire of freed black men to rape white women).

Identified for generations by the color of their old uniforms, Blue and Gray veterans led the way in focusing public attention on the minute details of each battle, a move that tended to distract attention from larger questions of meaning. Few if any other wars have created among the public such a strange fascination with the concrete details of military tactics and strategy, and thus pride in knowing where and when General Daniel Sickles lost his leg at Gettysburg, but not in knowing when slaves were freed in the District of Columbia. As the early twentieth century progressed, the Civil War came to resemble in many minds the nation's greatest athletic contest, a kind of mid-nineteenth-century Super Bowl between all-American heroes. Robert E. Lee and Abraham Lincoln could both become national saints. (Ulysses S. Grant surely became a great hero, at least in the North, but was somewhat demoted by his unfortunate presidency.)

The movement for national reconciliation and regeneration culminated with the fiftieth anniversary of the Battle of Gettysburg, held at Gettysburg, Pennsylvania, in the first days of July 1913. Union and Confederate veterans had met at earlier conciliatory commemorations, celebrating the values of manliness, valor, sacrifice, and honor, but in 1913 Woodrow Wilson had become the first Southern president since the Civil War, and the government spent lavishly in order to unite at Gettysburg 53,407 white veterans from every state except Nevada and Wyoming. Though the planners provided no space for black veterans, black laborers helped to build the enormous tent city with forty-seven miles of "avenues" spread out over the battlefield; blacks also delivered supplies and cleaned latrines. (The display of sensationally modern technology included forty modern latrines and five hundred electric arc lights.)[30]

President Wilson's speech to the veterans, whose average age was seventy-four, carried no echoes of Lincoln's magnificent Gettysburg Address, which, as Garry Wills has argued, "revolutionized the revolution" by enriching and extending the principle of equality.[31] Flanked by one Confederate and one American flag, held by veterans in gray and blue, Wilson proclaimed:

> We have found one another again as brothers and comrades, in arms, enemies no longer, generous friends rather, our battles long past, *the quarrel forgotten*—except that we shall not forget the splendid valor, the manly devotion of the men then arrayed against one another, now grasping hands and smiling into each others' eyes.

It is significant that Wilson, one of the most idealistic of all American presidents, made no mention of the Emancipation Proclamation. To do so, even if he had been so inclined, would have violated the spirit of the three-day event. An enthusiastic admirer of the highly racist film *Birth of a Nation*, with its sex-crazed blacks and romantic view of the Ku Klux Klan, Wilson would soon encourage the dismissal or segregation of African American workers in the federal government.[32]

While the Gettysburg reunion of 1913 symbolized the ultimate reconciliation of white Civil War veterans at a moment when virulent racism and the lynching of hundreds of blacks seemed to confirm the worst predictions of antebellum proponents of black colonization, the founding in 1910 of the National Association for the Advancement of Colored People and the voices of such figures as W.E.B. Du Bois, the black editor of the NAACP's *Crisis*, looked forward to an era when the Civil War's more revolutionary and emancipationist message would help to stimulate and nourish a new concern for universal civil rights.[33] The very possibility of such human change was intimated in some ways by Abraham Lincoln's own personal transformation, strongly influenced by more radical, antislavery Republicans, during the appalling and tumultuous years of war. If his assassination separated Lincoln from the alleged evils of Reconstruction, and thus assured his status as a martyr and kind of demigod, Lincoln's complexities have also enabled him to appeal to both the reconciliationist and emancipationist traditions.

As we turn now to Lincoln and the issue of slavery in wartime, it is interesting to note that in 1854, when Lincoln had no prospect of acquiring much political power, he confessed that he did not know how slavery could be abolished, given the almost universal white prejudice—including his own—against making black freedpeople, "politically and socially, our equals": "If all earthly power were given me," Lincoln told an audience in Peoria, Illinois, "I should not know what to do, as to the existing institution."[34] Little could Lincoln dream that a totally unpredictable series of fortuitous events would one day give him more power with respect to slavery than any other American had ever had. In fact, his Emancipation Proclamation (as even Karl Marx acknowledged at the time) was the most revolutionary pronouncement issued by any American president, before or since.[35]

From a young age Lincoln had deeply internalized as an article of faith the conviction that the Founding Fathers had intended to include African Americans when they declared to the world their belief that *all* men are created equal and endowed with such inalienable rights as life, liberty, and the pursuit of happiness. (In his 1854 political speeches he frequently misquoted the Declaration of Independence, affirming that all men are created "free and equal.") Though Lincoln was born in the slave state of Kentucky, grew up among Southerners in southern Indiana, and then married the daughter of a wealthy Kentucky slaveholding planter, he never wavered in his conviction that slavery was a great moral *and* political evil. He publicly attacked the institution as early as 1837, at age twenty-eight. In his addresses of 1854 he condemned "the monstrous injustice of slavery" and asserted that "no man is good enough to govern another man, *without that other's* consent. I say this is the leading principle—the sheet anchor of American republicanism." In a private letter of 1864 Lincoln declared: "I am naturally anti-slavery. If slavery is not wrong, nothing is wrong. I can not remember when I did not so think, and feel."[36]

Yet Lincoln was always a political moderate, committed to what he termed "the dictates of prudence" and attuned to the practical limitations and difficulties facing most of our attempts to achieve certain ends or goals.[37] He had little experience with African Americans except for some household servants and a Haitian barber in Springfield, Illinois. Since he immensely admired the famous Whig leader Henry Clay and insisted that Clay "ever was, on principle and in feeling, opposed to slavery," he long supported Clay's belief in the ideas of gradual emancipation and an eventual colonization of blacks outside the United States as the only effective way of undoing the evils of slavery.[38]

Like most Westerners, Lincoln took a dim view of abolitionists and said on occasion that he loathed their "self-righteousness." He did not become truly aroused on the slavery issue until the Kansas-Nebraska Act of 1854 struck many Northerners like a bombshell, since it appeared to betray the "sacred" compact between North and South regarding the future of the Western territories. No less shocking, the new militancy of the South, highlighted when Lincoln read George Fitzhugh's ardently proslavery book *Sociology for the South*,[39] challenged his faith in gradual progress, the faith that slavery would peacefully evaporate when it was geographically walled in and kept from expanding. As his biographer David Donald puts it, Lincoln now "identified slavery as the cause of the nation's problems" and wrongly concluded that even Northern Democrats like Illinois's Senator Stephen Douglas were beginning to accept Fitzhugh's argument that slavery was not only "a positive good for blacks but that it should be extended to white laborers as well."[40]

It would be a mistake to interpret Lincoln's pragmatic caution and seeming conservatism as he became more active in popular politics as a sign that slavery was somehow lower on his scale of ultimate priorities. If preserving the Union was the most urgent and immediate need in 1860–61, that was partly because Lincoln believed that slavery would thrive in an independent and expanding Confederacy but could be placed on the path to extinction in a Union that could not continue to be, as he famously put it, permanently "half slave and half free."

After being elected president, as at earlier times, Lincoln accepted the Fugitive Slave Law and promised that he would not interfere with slavery in the fifteen existing states where it was still legal. But that was because he was still confident, despite his fears of a conspiratorial Slave Power, that slavery could not survive for many decades if it was officially recognized as an evil that could not be allowed to expand. In the long period between Lincoln's election and inauguration (from November 1860 to March 1861), he was adamant only in his refusal even to *consider* any compromise with respect to the extension of slavery from the existing states. Still, the practical-minded William Henry Seward, whom Lincoln appointed secretary of state, assumed that Lincoln's election spelled the doom of slavery within the United States— a view clearly shared by most Southern secessionists. But abolitionists like Frederick Douglass bitterly attacked the Republican administration's early policy on returning fugitives as well as Lincoln's veto of General John C. Frémont's order emancipating slaves in Missouri. In time, Lincoln would become increasingly responsive to this pressure from the left.[41]

Looking backward, though, we must constantly guard against any sense of inevitability and suspend our knowledge that this would be a total war, dragging on until the end of May 1865. Both sides expected a short war, just as they had long expected some kind of compromise. At certain moments in 1862, 1863, and 1864 there was a widespread expectation that the war was about to end. Even after hostilities had begun, Lincoln kept counting on Unionist sentiment in the South. There was much debate over secession in parts of the South, and the pivotal state of Virginia did not secede until April 17, 1861, five days after South Carolina's attack on Fort Sumter and two days after Lincoln's call for troops. And in actuality, some one hundred thousand white Southerners from secessionist states ended up in the Union army.[42]

Lincoln was keenly aware, of course, that any radical policy against slavery would alienate not only Unionists in the secessionist South but also supporters of the Union in the absolutely crucial slaveholding border states of Maryland, Delaware, Kentucky, Missouri, and later West Virginia. James M. McPherson emphasizes that apart from their manpower, "the strategic importance of the rivers, railroads, and mountains of the border states (including West Virginia) can hardly be exaggerated."[43] Except for approaches by sea, Union troops had to cross slaveholding border states in order to invade the rebellious South from Virginia in the east to Arkansas in the west. It now seems appalling to remember that Union soldiers had to cross slaveholding and often hostile Maryland even to protect the national capital. As Lincoln himself put it very early in the war: "I think to lose Kentucky is nearly the same as to lose the whole game. Kentucky gone, we can not hold Missouri, nor, I think, Maryland. These all against us, and the job on our hands is too large for us. We would as well consent to separation at once, including the surrender of this capitol [*sic*]."[44]

When writing these words, Lincoln sought to picture the wider context that led him, apart from defending his own presidential authority, to overrule General Frémont's presumptuous proclamation of slave emancipation and martial law in Missouri, an act that had created a firestorm throughout the North. While abolitionists and some later historians have been sharply critical of Lincoln for overruling Frémont and then General David Hunter, who later issued a similar edict in South Carolina without consulting the president, wiser heads saw that in 1862 there was absolutely no chance of winning an abolitionist war, that is, a war run by antislavery Republicans who would alienate most moderates and probably lose the border states (to say nothing of not winning a war in which Union generals could decide on their own initiative to issue emancipation proclamations).[45]

As Lincoln found, it was extremely difficult even with a moderate, pragmatic policy to preserve some significant and indispensable support from Northern "War Democrats" (as distinct from the very hostile and disloyal "Peace Democrats" or "copperheads"), to say nothing of keeping the slaveholding border states within the Union. And even Lincoln tended to underestimate the virulent racism that thwarted his efforts to convince border-state legislatures to accept monetary compensation for very gradual slave emancipation.

Even in the nonslaveholding North, Democrats increasingly utilized racism as a means of attacking the "Black Republicans" as a "party of fanaticism," intent on freeing millions of "semi-savages" who would then infest the North, depriving whites of jobs and mixing with "their sons and daughters."[46] It was this Northern racism that in July 1863 finally dominated the notorious draft riots in New York City, where mobs, including many Irish immigrants, lynched eleven black men, mutilating some of their bodies, while also destroying a Colored Orphan Asylum, forcing a large exodus of blacks from the city, and carrying banners proclaiming, "We won't fight to free the nigger."[47]

Early in 1862 Lincoln quietly focused his antislavery efforts on tiny Delaware, which now contained fewer than eighteen hundred slaves and, if paid generous compensation by the federal government, could thus be the easiest first domino to start the consecutive fall of slavery in the other border states. "If I can get this plan started in Delaware I have no fear but that all the other border states will accept it," Lincoln wrote. This objective, the president fantasized, would not only keep the border states from joining the Confederacy but should have a discouraging influence on the Confederate South and thus shorten the war. As the war progressed, Lincoln stressed that three months of war expenditures would buy all the slaves in the four border states. He also warned that if the offer were refused, slaveholders might well lose their slave property *without* compensation, as a result of the "mere friction & abrasion of the war" as tens of thousands of soldiers moved through their states.[48]

From the outset, however, Lincoln received a series of negative responses from the border states, which were bitterly opposed to even gradual and well-compensated emancipation combined with intimations of some African American colonization. As the historian Allen C. Guelzo reports, Lincoln's agent in Delaware "was surprised to find, over and over again, that even Unionists 'who look upon slavery as a curse' were so deeply dyed by racial hatred that 'we also look upon freedom possessed by a negro, except in a very few cases, as a greater curse.' " Many border-state leaders pinned their hopes on an early Northern victory or some kind of truce, probably brokered by General George B. McClellan, a Democrat who was extremely popular with the Union troops and who adamantly opposed the slightest interference with slavery.[49]

Yet Lincoln persisted. On March 6, 1862, three weeks after Delaware's failure became clear, the president sent Congress a resolution affirming that the U.S. government should give pecuniary aid to any state that adopted "gradual abolishment of slavery." Although this measure evoked much hostility and was opposed by 85 percent of the Democrats and border-state Unionists, it passed both houses of the Republican-dominated Congress by wide margins. But despite a series of encouraging Union military victories in the spring of 1862, the border states stood frozen in their opposition to change. Lincoln finally became discouraged after July 12, following a conference with border-state congressmen who responded to his pleas by issuing a manifesto declaring that any step toward slave emancipation would be too "radical" and would have the effect of prolonging the war. As we shall see, Lincoln's thoughts now moved in a more radical direction.[50]

If financial incentives failed to free slaves in the border states, the presence of Union armies in slaveholding states provided the incentive for increasing numbers of slaves to "vote with their feet." From the outset of the war, as troops began to move through slaveholding regions, the appearance and behavior of soldiers became highly disruptive to labor regimes that depended on extracting labor by physical force. Union officers could not escape the increasingly explosive question of what to do with the growing number of slaves who took the initiative and risk of escaping behind Union lines and then stood in dire need of food and shelter. Confederate authorities demanded that Union generals obey the Fugitive Slave Law and return all runaways! When some Union officers did return fugitives to their owners in the early months of the war, critics understandably complained that the rebels quickly utilized the work of such slaves in their treasonous armed rebellion.

In March 1862 the Republican-dominated Congress prohibited under penalty of court-martial the return of any fugitives from army camps, even to masters who claimed to be loyal Unionists. The fugitive slaves who were given this protection were still officially defined as property, or as "contraband" confiscated from the rebels. After General Benjamin Butler's forces captured New Orleans in April 1862, he at first tried to please Unionist slaveholders by returning their slaves, but he soon saw the need to employ and pay small wages to "contraband" laborers, as did other Union officers. General Butler also used the earnings of contraband military laborers for the support of blacks who were not so employed.[51]

As with most armies throughout history, there were some Union soldiers who raped or tortured contrabands because they were so vulnerable; more generally, the blacks were put to work cooking, cleaning, carrying, and washing clothes. If very few Union soldiers were abolitionists, many no doubt agreed with one private who said, "I didn't come here to catch niggers for slaveholders." In Kentucky, a Union regiment from that state actually fought an Illinois regiment for concealing slaves![52]

Though few slaves were literate, some expressed in written words the feelings that led tens of thousands to flee, when they could, behind Union lines. One example, a proud letter to President Lincoln written by a female slave in Maryland in 1864, two months before the state finally adopted a constitution abolishing slavery, expresses widely held desires:

> Mr president   It is my Desire to be free. To go to see my people on the western shore. My mistress wont let me   you will please let me know if we are free. And what I can do. I write to you for advice. Please send me word this week. Or as soon as possible and oblidge.   Annie Davis[53]

The movement of hundreds of thousands of soldiers through a Southern region was inevitably disruptive, challenging the routine of work and the psychology of slaveholders' power, especially as officers commandeered food as well as slaves from planters. This was even true with respect to Confederate forces, since their soldiers sometimes took slaves as body servants and pressed planters to donate slaves for military work. As we have seen in Chapter Seven, however, slavery survived and then flourished after the American Revolution, despite similar disruptions and the successful escape of thousands of slaves behind British lines. Yet by 1862 antislavery thought and values had spread through much of the Western world in a way that was hardly imaginable in the 1770s and early 1780s. Lincoln, when making pleas to the border-state leaders to accept compensated emancipation, also accurately predicted that antislavery sentiment in the North was expanding and might well force his hand. (He did not predict that he would soon convert the Union army into an army of liberation.)

By the spring of 1862, Lincoln was acutely aware that abolitionism had won increasing support in parts of the North, especially New England (though Boston's conservative Mayor Joseph Wightman warned him that most of the citizens of Massachusetts opposed "the small sections or towns" that vocally called for emancipation and the arming of slaves). As they grasped the shockingly grim character of the war, even most moderate Republican senators and congressmen found themselves swinging toward a radical policy of universal slave emancipation as a means of undermining the Southern economy and thus winning the war. The political parties had become so polarized that on four critical roll-call votes on issues connected with slavery, 96 percent of the Democratic congressmen pitted their votes against 99 percent of the Republicans.

This growing hostility to slavery did not imply an acceptance of blacks and whites living together as equals. Illinois's Senator Lyman Trumbull, who designed a politically successful bill for confiscating and freeing Southern slaves made it clear that in Illinois "our people want nothing to do with the negro." In fact, in Lincoln's former home of Springfield, a proposal to deny free blacks the vote won by a margin of 2,500 to 20! And while the Republicans constituted a large majority in both the Senate and the House, Lincoln and other leaders knew that in such tumultuous times everything could be changed by the 1862 fall elections.[54]

The most dramatic early symbol of antislavery progress came on April 11, 1862, when Congress finally approved a bill abolishing slavery with compensation to the owners in the District of Columbia. This measure, which Lincoln signed into law five days later, freed more than three thousand slaves and was the first emancipation act of the U.S. government. On April 16 blacks enthusiastically celebrated the event. As George Templeton Strong noted in his now famous diary, "Only the damndest of 'damned abolitionists' dreamed of such a thing a year ago." Since Congress clearly had full constitutional authority over the nation's capital, abolitionists had unsuccessfully petitioned for this measure for many decades. Indeed, in 1849, when Lincoln was a one-term congressman from Illinois, he attempted to introduce such a bill. The Compromise of 1850 at least attempted to outlaw the *trade* in slaves within the District, which had offended many foreign diplomats and travelers.

Even so, after the withdrawal of all the Southern secessionist senators and representatives, the debate on abolition in Washington was long and bitter. A measure for the forcible deportation of the District's freedpeople lost in the Senate by one vote (cast by the vice president), and the emancipation law included some compensation for slaveowners and even an appropriation of six hundred thousand dollars for voluntary colonization (supported by two-thirds of the Republican congressmen). Further, the law failed to address the huge influx into the capital of fugitives from Maryland and northern Virginia or to improve the terrible plight of most of Washington's African Americans, who lived in squalor, jammed into shacks, wooden tenements, or contraband camps.[55]

Lincoln had apparently been convinced for some time of his *own* constitutional authority as commander in chief to emancipate all the rebels' slaves by decree. While Lincoln feared a judicial decision rejecting this principle, especially by Chief Justice Roger B. Taney's Supreme Court, the belief had been clearly affirmed by the now deceased John Quincy Adams and then conveyed to Lincoln by Senator Charles Sumner.[56] For Lincoln it really became a matter of timing—when the military situation and public opinion in the North might make such a decree effective and not self-defeating, or as Lincoln put it in September, at a gloomy moment five days before the Battle of Antietam changed everything: "What *good* would a proclamation from me do. . . . I don't want to issue a document the whole world will see must necessarily be inoperative, like the Pope's bull against a comet!" Whatever the risks, some two months earlier, on July 13, 1862, Lincoln shocked his cabinet secretaries William Seward and Gideon Welles by confiding that he "had about come to the conclusion that it was a military necessity absolutely essential to the salvation of the Union, that we must free the slaves or be ourselves subdued."[57]

On July 12, the day before Lincoln privately revealed this line of thought, a House-Senate conference committee brought forth for a vote what is known as the Second Confiscation Act, which Congress passed five days later. This radical measure defined rebels as traitors, ordered the confiscation of their property, including slaves, and declared that sixty days after passage of the bill, slaves of the rebels "shall be deemed captives of war and shall be forever free." Congress also passed a separate bill that empowered the president to free and enroll "persons of African descent" for "any war service," including service as soldiers, "for which they may be found competent." Lincoln was not yet ready to test public opinion by arming black soldiers, and he was deeply disturbed by the first law, since he remained convinced that *Congress* had no constitutional power to free slaves within a state. The Second Confiscation Act had also been very poorly drafted, especially with regard to enforcement, and was legally inconsistent on whether the government faced a genuine war or a domestic rebellion. After Congress accepted several of his modifications, Lincoln signed the Second Confiscation Act but also made clear in a statement that only the president, as commander in chief, had the power to free the rebels' slaves.[58]

Prodded now by this action of Congress, by General McClellan's defeats in his Peninsular Campaign in eastern Virginia, and by McClellan's increasing hostility to the government and rumors of military mutiny, Lincoln read to his cabinet on July 22 what he called his one "last card" to play— the first draft of his own Preliminary Emancipation Proclamation. In this draft, Lincoln still tried to blend his earlier proposals to border states of gradual, compensated emancipation (and even voluntary colonization in the September 22 draft) with his new acceptance of immediate freedom as a military necessity. But the key words constituted a new ultimatum to the Confederacy: The "Commander-in-Chief of the Army and Navy" declared that on the first day of January 1863 "all persons held as slaves within any state or states, wherein the constitutional authority of the United States shall not then be practically recognized, submitted to, and maintained, shall then, thenceforward, and forever, be free." As Professor Guelzo eloquently puts it, "in this single sentence of eighty-five words, Lincoln tersely identified the legal rationale for emancipation, the schedule by which he would do it, the people who were legally affected by it, and the new legal condition those same people would enjoy."[59]

While Secretary of State Seward and most of the other cabinet members supported the still-secret proclamation on July 22, Seward expressed fear that the edict would spark European intervention in order to protect the crucial supply of cotton. (Aside from the Union blockade, the South continued to hold up shipments of cotton in order to worsen the shortage in Europe and encourage the English and French to intervene.) Above all, Seward cautioned Lincoln to wait until the North had scored a major military success. Otherwise, given the recent series of bleak Union defeats, such a drastic proclamation would be viewed "as the last measure of an exhausted government, a cry for help . . . our last shriek, on the retreat."[60] Not immediately convinced, Lincoln brooded on the matter and finally accepted Seward's recommendation. He filed the proclamation in one of the pigeonholes of his desk, waiting anxiously for a major Union victory.

Since the future of slavery in America would now depend on a convergence of fortuitous military events, their effects on the election of 1862, and decision-makers in the governments of England and France, we must briefly turn to battlefields and military strategy. If we were considering the Civil War less selectively, I would emphasize the supreme importance of the Union victories in the West, beginning with the capture of New Orleans, the invasion southward along the rivers of Kentucky and Tennessee, and the capture of Vicksburg and thus control of the Mississippi Valley. But if the battles in the West had a greater impact on the lives of more slaves, the eyes of Europe focused on the East, and the Confederacy's greatest hopes lay with Anglo-French intervention.[61]

By late August 1862 a series of Confederate victories culminated in the extremely devastating, humiliating, and demoralizing Union defeat in the Battle of Second Manassas (also called the Second Bull Run), not far to the west of Washington. Without taking time for rest or refurbishing his ragged Army of Northern Virginia, many of whose men were still barefoot, General Robert E. Lee ordered his soldiers on September 4 to cross the Potomac, twenty-five miles northwest of Washington, into the state of Maryland. This could be, Lee reasoned, the winning stroke of the war as panic flooded such Northern cities as Harrisburg, Baltimore, and Philadelphia, as Maryland's slaveholders cheered and embraced the Confederacy,[62] and as Britain and France seized this display of power and independence as reasons for intervention and formal recognition. Lee also hoped that the invasion would be a godsend to the Northern Peace Democrats, in the coming fall election, who could now make a strong case for a negotiated settlement with a clearly independent Confederacy.

James M. McPherson, one of our foremost authorities on the Civil War, has noted the supreme irony of George B. McClellan's involvement in the first two "pivotal moments" of the war. McClellan was a general who detested his commander in chief, whom he termed "the gorilla" (and would run against him in the presidential election of 1864). As a commander, McClellan had a habit of greatly overestimating his opponents' numbers and was obsessed with never advancing on the enemy until he had, in his own words, "absolute assurance of success."[63] With respect to the first pivotal moment, McClellan found himself and his army of one hundred thousand in May 1862 on the outskirts of Richmond, the Confederate capital—actually within sound of its church bells. The Confederacy seemed nearly doomed, given its immense losses in the Mississippi Valley. So the "Little Napoleon" was in effect on the enemy's five-yard line, with the goalpost in sight, and was almost assured of victory (if I may use the conventional metaphors from team sports). But to Lincoln's utter and bitter astonishment, McClellan then failed to try either a run or a pass.[64]

In September, four months later, the fates of the Union and the Confederacy seemed to have been completely reversed, and the president again felt

compelled to entrust McClellan to handle an even more pivotal moment—
the attempt to check Lee at the *Union's* five-yard line—largely because there
seemed to be no better general for such a line of defense, and McClellan, a
man of great charisma, was so popular with his men. Given these circumstances, and Lincoln's knowledge that England and France could be on the
verge of recognizing the Confederacy, one can understand why a depressed
president directed his major plea to God. As a former deist and skeptic, Lincoln was keenly aware of the evil and contradictory claims of divine sanction
that had been made throughout history. He also believed that God's will was
inscrutable. But as he later told his cabinet, he had "made a vow, a covenant,
that if God gave us the victory in the approaching battle, he would consider
it an indication of Divine will, and that it was [then] his duty to move forward
in the cause of emancipation."[65]

Although Lincoln did not believe in miracles, something very close to a
miracle had a decisive effect on the Battle of Antietam, which repelled Lee's
invasion and probably prevented a kind of European intervention that would
have perpetuated American slavery for an indefinite period. I do not mean to
indulge in "chaos theory" (finding the underlying order in apparently random data), but sometimes we confront in history a small, extraordinary event
that has incredibly disproportionate consequences.

On September 13, as the Blue and Gray armies moved through western
Maryland, a Union corporal, Barton W. Mitchell, discovered as he rested in
some grass a bulky envelope that contained the detailed tactics of Lee's Army
of Northern Virginia. It was an amazing accident that a Union soldier would
find "Special Orders, No. 191," dropped by a Confederate officer, detailing
Lee's plan to split his army into four units and specifying their future movements. Even more fortuitous, perhaps, was the fact that the orders were then
passed on to a Union colonel who had once known Lee's assistant adjutant-
general and recognized his handwriting, thus confirming their authenticity.
Since it seems extremely unlikely that McClellan, given his past record, would
ever have had a chance of beating Lee, this was, in McPherson's words, "a
windfall such as few generals in history have enjoyed. It was a remarkable
example of the contingencies that change the course of history."[66]

If McClellan had moved more quickly and aggressively after he had seen
Lee's orders, he might well have destroyed the Army of Northern Virginia
before the lethal encounter on Antietam Creek, near Sharpsburg, Maryland.
The last and crucial day of battle, on September 17, 1862, remains "the bloodiest day in all American history." McPherson estimates that on that day between 6,300 and 6,500 Confederate and Union soldiers were killed or mortally
wounded. While the Union army won the battle and Lee ordered a retreat
back into Virginia, McClellan refused to take advantage of Lee's vulnerability or to pursue the defeated rebels across the Potomac. Indeed, he refused to

cross the river and move into Virginia for nearly six weeks. As one hard-fighting Union colonel wrote to his wife, "the whole Rebel Army could have been captured or destroyed easily before it could have crossed the Potomac—but indeed it seems to me that McClellan let them escape purposely."[67]

Yet five days after Lee's qualified defeat seemed to "answer" Lincoln's prayer, the president called a special cabinet meeting and announced that the time had come for him to issue a now revised Preliminary Emancipation Proclamation. Unlike the earlier version, the edict that was publicly released on September 22 was a military pronouncement, which in effect would convert the Union forces into an army of liberation. Lincoln first affirmed that on January 1, 1863, "all persons held as slaves within any state, or designated part of a state, the people whereof shall then be in rebellion against the United States shall be then, thenceforward, and forever free." But then, in the revolutionary heart of the message, Lincoln ordered "the military and naval authority" to "recognize and *maintain* the freedom of such persons, or any of them, in any efforts they may make for their actual freedom" (my emphasis).[68]

Though Lincoln still included sentences intended to encourage border states to accept compensated emancipation and also suggested that loyal slaveholders might later receive reparation for the loss of slaves occasioned by war, the last clauses quoted above could be interpreted as giving support for slave rebellions. Lincoln tried to soften this message with a plea to slaves for nonviolence in his final Emancipation Proclamation on January 1, 1863.[69]

Critics predictably seized upon the revolutionary implications of the presidential proclamation, implications that take us back to the revolutionary meaning of the war discussed at the beginning of this chapter. Horatio Seymour, a former Democratic governor of New York who was now successfully running for the same powerful office, condemned the Preliminary Proclamation as a "proposal for the butchery of women and children, for scenes of lust and rapine, and of arson and murder." Even the London *Times* interpreted the proclamation as an appeal "to the black blood of the African" and to the blacks' "gratification of yet fiercer instincts," while another British paper saw the edict as Lincoln's "last arm of vengeance . . . to carry the war of the knife to private homes where women and children are left undefended."[70]

Nevertheless, Prime Minister Palmerston now retreated from the idea of intervention in the American Civil War, an intervention that was strongly supported by France's Napoleon III and by Viscount Palmerston's own powerful cabinet members William Gladstone (the son of the rich absentee owner of thousands of West Indian slaves) and Lord John Russell. Before learning of Antietam, Palmerston had begun to agree that with another major Union defeat, Britain and France should propose an armistice ending the blockades and then recognize Confederate independence. It was the news of Antietam and other rebel defeats in the west, combined with Lincoln's commitment to slave emancipation, that led Palmerston to reject the possibility of successful mediation and that led the cabinet on November 12 to turn down a French proposal for joint intervention. Despite the cynicism of many British newspapers, the prospect of American slave emancipation evoked huge mass meetings of the British public, which drew on the country's long antislavery traditions.[71]

The response to Antietam and Lincoln's Preliminary Proclamation brought even sharper divisions in the American North. Before Lee's defeat, even most Republicans expected the Democrats to win control of the House of Representatives in the fall elections, since the party in power normally lost in off-year elections, and Confederate victories had given strength to many Democrats' insistence that the war had failed and should be replaced by negotiation. The Union victory of September 17 revivified faith in suppressing the rebellion, but then McClellan's weeks of inaction, which enabled the rebel Jeb Stuart to carry out a humiliating cavalry raid into Pennsylvania, diminished some of this optimism.

Meanwhile, the prospect of slave emancipation, vehemently attacked by Democratic candidates, failed to deprive the Republicans of their majority in the House of Representatives or their control of fifteen of the eighteen Northern state legislatures. If the Democrats could rejoice over winning the governorships of New York and New Jersey, Republicans retained the other sixteen top state offices and, more surprising and important, won five more seats in the U.S. Senate. While elections always involve many issues, it is clear that racist fears over emancipation, though deep-seated, could not overturn the more dominant desire to decimate the Confederate enemy.[72]

For the rest of his life, with the possible but unlikely exception of one controversial moment, Lincoln remained committed to his goal of immediate slave emancipation, even while flirting at times with various forms of voluntary black colonization.[73] Of course, the proclamation of January 1, 1863, did not apply to the border states and also exempted Tennessee and certain Union-occupied areas in Louisiana and Virginia. Slave emancipation could be celebrated that New Year's Day in parts of South Carolina's occupied Sea Islands and thenceforth in the wide paths left by Union invaders.[74] But Lincoln sought to use the vision of colonization as an incentive for the excluded slaveholding regions and, above all, as a way of preparing the racist white American public for universal emancipation—and of offering at least some free blacks an opportunity to escape a racist society.

On August 14, 1862, Lincoln became the first president to invite a "Committee" of African Americans to the White House, urging them to recruit black volunteers for a government-financed colonization project in Central America. While the president affirmed that "your race are suffering[,] in my judgment, the greatest wrong inflicted on any people," adding that "even when you cease to be slaves, you are yet far removed from being placed on an equality with the white race," he condescendingly implied that they bore some blame for racial conflicts and were at fault for not leading their less fortunate people to a more friendly settlement.

Again, in his Annual Message to Congress on December 1, 1862, Lincoln proposed three constitutional amendments, one of which would appropriate federal funds for the colonization outside the United States of blacks who were willing to move. Another proposed amendment provided compensation for any state that agreed to end slavery by the year 1900, and the third immediately guaranteed the freedom of all blacks who had achieved freedom "by the chances of the war" (such as escaping behind Union army lines).[75]

When Lincoln issued his Emancipation Proclamation of 1863, the Civil War had not even reached its halfway mark, and few Northern leaders could imagine that rumors of promised freedom were already spreading throughout slave communities of the South or that an extraordinary number of slaves would come to think of Lincoln as the Great Liberator. Especially for household slaves, it was only necessary to hear the rage and ranting of their masters and other Southern whites who perceived Lincoln as a radical Republican abolitionist. At the beginning of 1863 it would also have seemed highly improbable that Lincoln would abandon thoughts of colonization and assert, shortly before his death, that "the restoration of the Rebel States to the union must rest upon the principle of civil, and political equality of both races." Or that the president would ever seek the help and advice of the great black abolitionist Frederick Douglass, or confer with Sojourner Truth, the former slave and active abolitionist who provided help in the North for many black fugitives, who said she "never was treated by anyone with more kindness and cordiality."[76]

While the Emancipation Proclamation authorized the recruitment of black soldiers and sailors, they were originally assigned the limited role of maintaining "garrison forts, positions, stations, and other places, and to man vessels of all sorts in said service." By the spring of 1863, however, Lincoln had overcome his initial reservations about committing black soldiers to combat. Indeed, he now began urging the massive enlistment of African-American troops, and told Andrew Johnson, whom he had appointed wartime governor of Tennessee, that "the bare sight of fifty thousand armed and drilled black soldiers on the banks of the Mississippi would end the rebellion at once."[77]

Frederick Douglass, who like many radical abolitionists had been outraged by Lincoln's policies in the first year of the war, not only felt respected and at ease when he talked with the president but then wrote of Lincoln's "earnestness and fluency which I had not expected . . . to vindicate his policy respecting the whole slavery question and especially that in reference to employing colored troops."[78] Even apart from arming 150,000 former Southern slaves, Union officers had long discovered that slaves could be a crucial source of information. They knew the terrain, topography, and inland waterways that were foreign to Northern officers. Often they also knew how to navigate harbors and could reveal the locality of Confederate forces, especially when fugitive slaves had worked building Confederate forts or transporting supplies.

As a result of more virulent racism and proslavery ideology, most Confederate leaders apparently forgot that armed slaves had been indispensable in earlier wars, especially in the Caribbean, and had even helped to defend colonial South Carolina from attacks by Indians and the Spaniards. According to Howell Cobb, the famous Georgian political and military leader, "if slaves will make good soldiers our whole theory of slavery is wrong—but they won't make soldiers." (Yet in January 1865 a well-informed Georgian reminded Cobb that black soldiers "have done some very good fighting for the Yanks.")[79]

For a time Jefferson Davis tried to suppress all public discussion of freeing and arming slaves, but by November 1864 military matters had become so desperate, partly due to the desertion of many Confederate soldiers, that President Davis appealed to the Confederate Congress to at least purchase large numbers of slaves for military labor. Even so, despite Robert E. Lee's plea three months later for enlisting black soldiers, the Congress continued to stall. It was only in March 1865 that the legislature passed a clumsy and ineffective appeal to arm quotas of slaves, which led Lee to proclaim that he would only accept blacks whose incentives had been raised by freedom and the manumission of their families. This was, of course, far too late to have any effect on the decimated Confederate army, and despite many myths to the contrary, only a few dozen blacks donned Confederate uniforms in the last days of the war.[80]

Meanwhile, even after the Battle of Gettysburg, when Union forces once again and more decisively defeated and turned back an extremely threatening invasion of the North—and almost simultaneously, when General Ulysses S. Grant's forces captured Vicksburg, the last major rebel stronghold on the Mississippi River—the fate of slavery and the outcome of the war remained uncertain.

Apart from the endless battles and the incredibly costly victories and defeats, most knowledgeable Northerners came to see the presidential election of 1864 as an ultimate test. Lincoln was well aware that General McClellan, whom he had dismissed after the elections of 1862, had long been secretly courted by Northern Democrats as his most likely replacement as president. It was by no means certain, however, that Lincoln would even win the Republican nomination. In early 1863 the president was considered such a failure by many citizens that various factions of the Republican Party were ready to prosecute him in some way. There was a widespread assumption that McClellan, if elected, would quickly end the war and restore the Union *with* slavery, at least in the still rebellious states. Lincoln, in contrast, fearing that his Emancipation Proclamation might be overturned in court, became determined to fight for a constitutional amendment that would positively and permanently prohibit slavery in the United States. In his Annual Message to Congress in December 1863, Lincoln proclaimed that the South *must* accept emancipation as the basic condition for reunion. The 1864 Republican Convention—or what was now called the National Union Convention, in an attempt to attract War Democrats—endorsed this Thirteenth Amendment, but while the antislavery reformers won in the Senate, they failed to muster the necessary two-thirds majority in the House of Representatives.[81]

As we move into the summer of 1864, the scene becomes more ominous and discouraging. Though the Emancipation Proclamation initially sparked much jubilation in the North, a good bit of the enthusiasm arose from the expectation of a crippled Southern economy and thus a shorter war. Now the Union armies seemed to be permanently frozen in sieges of Atlanta, Georgia and Richmond, Virginia. The War Democrats and even conservative Republican leaders became deeply alienated when Lincoln made slave emancipation as much a war aim as the restoration of the Union—both minimal conditions for peace. As the summer progressed, Lincoln's chances for reelection grew so dim that even he discussed with Frederick Douglass a radical program to help more slaves escape the Confederacy during the expected lame-duck period after McClellan's election. During the election campaign, Democrats attacked Lincoln as "Abraham Africanus the First" and circulated "humorous" racist pamphlets featuring caricatured sketches of Lincoln with a black face.[82]

In retrospect, it appears that Lincoln and his commitment to slave emancipation were saved only by a stunning military victory combined with a massive soldier vote for the Republicans. In late August and early September, nearly two years after Antietam, General William Tecumseh Sherman's army finally won the long delayed Battle of Atlanta, which opened the way for his devastating "March to the Sea."[83] In his December Annual Message, following the November election, Lincoln could plead for universal emancipation as an inevitability. "The voice of the people now," he stated, "for the first time," has been "heard upon the question."

Using all the lobbying techniques of the executive to win votes, Lincoln and his men pressured the lame-duck session of the Thirty-eighth Congress to pass the Thirteenth Amendment, which on January 31 Congress barely did. Before submitting the amendment to the states for ratification, Lincoln, looking thin, and ten or twelve years older than his age of fifty-five, joyfully signed the document (though this was not required for constitutional amendments). Passionately confirming what would become "the emancipationist tradition," Lincoln remarked that this document rooted out "the original disturbing cause" of the great rebellion and civil war—a definitive response to all of those who later insisted that slavery was not the cause or major issue of the Civil War.[84]

As matters developed, emancipation, made possible by the bloodiest and most traumatic of all American wars, did not lead to the kind of freedom and equality before the law that abolitionists had envisioned and that Reconstructionists sought to achieve. From 1865 onward, there has been much speculation concerning the path Reconstruction might have taken if Lincoln had not been assassinated (and if Andrew Johnson, surely one of the worst of our presidents, had not tried to take command).

However one responds to this "counterfactual" question, it is clear that antiblack racism still predominated in the North and that Northern opinion, also affected by new issues of class and labor, was not ready to enforce the kind of fair and just policies advocated by Charles Sumner, Thaddeus Stevens, and other so-called Radical Reconstructionists. Even if a surviving Lincoln had succeeded in cooperating with Congress and in leading the way to a more moderate Reconstruction, it is hard to imagine that this exhausted and by then less popular president could have overcome the new conditions in the North as well as the defeated South's commitment to white supremacy. Even the relatively peaceful slave emancipations in the Caribbean and Latin America were followed by generations of destructive racial inequality that still persist in some forms to our own time.[85]

Nevertheless, we began this chapter with the images of slaveholder defeat and of armed black Union troops liberating slaves from a Richmond jail. That emancipationist meaning of the American Civil War, symbolized by the hundreds of thousands of Southern slaves who escaped to freedom, and permanently embodied in the Thirteenth Amendment, had a strong impact on both Cuba and Brazil, where slavery still flourished. Much later, by the 1960s, the "antislavery vanguard," as some writers called it, provided a crucial precedent for American reformers and activists in the civil rights movement. Since there has unfortunately been little continuity in American movements for reform—due in part to a long national tradition of forgetting history, of "present-mindedness"—it is crucially important to remind ourselves that some struggles for greater fairness and justice have succeeded; they are part of our past and thus open possibilities in our future.[86]

Epilogue

In 1880 José Ferreira de Menezes, the mulatto founder of the Brazilian abolitionist daily newspaper, *Gazeta da Tarde,* hailed the American Civil War as a decisive turning point in the world's struggle against slavery as well as in civilization's triumph over barbarism.[1] Obtaining from a resident American a list of immortal abolitionist names to be honored as promoters of human progress, Ferreira paid tribute to William Lloyd Garrison, Wendell Phillips, Lucretia Mott, Harriet Beecher Stowe, Charles Sumner, and the Christ-like martyr, Abraham Lincoln.[2]

Ferreira and his radical and fellow mulatto successor, José do Patrocinio, conveyed the image of a single, worldwide abolitionist movement, originally inspired by such Britons as Granville Sharp, Thomas Clarkson, and William Wilberforce, but including some Brazilians, such as the Pernambucan rebels of 1817. Even in Cuba, where there was much less abolitionist agitation in the 1880s, reformers made heroes of Wilberforce Garrison, and Lincoln, while uneasily merging the legend of humanitarian Catholic precedents with anticlerical rationalism. And it was reported that some Cuban slaves in the field sang,

> Avanza, Lincoln, avanza.
> Tu eres nuestra esperanza.
> (Advance, Lincoln, advance.
> You are our hope.)[3]

Yet the contexts within which emancipation took place could hardly have been more different in Cuba and Brazil than in the United States. In both Latin societies abolitionists would almost daily pass slaves and slaveholders on the streets; there were no free-soil states to the north and no mother country across the Atlantic dedicated to antislavery policies.

Because slave populations in both regions had strongly negative growth rates, both Cuban and Brazilian economies depended on a large and continuing importation of black slaves from Africa. The roughly 1.84 million Africans brought into Cuba and Brazil from 1820 to 1870 was nearly four times the total number of slaves imported into North America before the U.S. prohibition of 1808. This mainly illegal slave traffic was greatly encouraged by rising slave prices in both Cuba and Brazil. In Rio de Janeiro slave prices doubled from 1820 to 1850. The compelling need for slave labor put the Spanish and Brazilian governments in direct conflict with the British commitment to use naval power, even illegally, to suppress the oceanic slave trades (which, ironically, had the effect of increasing slave prices and profits from the slave trade). After some two decades of illegal importations, Brazil finally complied with British pressure in 1850, followed by Cuba seventeen years later. [4]

While British abolitionists had originally assumed that ending their own slave trade would lead to the gradual abolition of British colonial slavery (and had then changed their minds), it can surely be argued that this shutting off of supply impaired the institution's longer-term prospects in both Cuba and Brazil.

Both regions led the world in the production of slave-grown sugar after the destruction of French Saint-Domingue and especially after Britain and France emancipated their slaves in 1834 and 1848, though Brazil increasingly concentrated its coerced labor on the production of coffee. Of course, much of Brazil was still unsettled by whites and sparsely occupied by Indians, and Cuba was far more densely populated. In 1862 there were about 368,550 slaves in Cuba (27.1 percent of the total population), compared with 1,715,000 in Brazil in 1864 (16.7 percent of the population).

A far more critical difference pertained to political rule. Brazil gained its independence from Portugal in 1822 and crowned Dom Pedro I as its emperor. Cuba, along with Puerto Rico, remained the last fragment of Spain's once great New World empire. And despite some antislavery stirrings among Spain's liberals, a strong Cuban and Spanish consensus ruled that the protection and maintenance of Cuban slavery (including the illegal slave trade) was the best barrier against movements for Cuban independence. [5]

Although the governments of Spain, Cuba, and Brazil were generally conservative, the British model of slave emancipation seemed to some liberals by the 1840s and 1850s to have forecast a global pattern of inevitable "historical progress." If the European revolutions of 1848 brought catastrophic repression, they also brought permanent slave emancipation in the French and Danish colonies. Russia's abolition of serfdom in 1861 was followed two years later by Holland's gradual liberation of colonial slaves and by Lincoln's much-publicized Emancipation Proclamation.

In Spain, Julio Vizcarrondo and other resident Puerto Ricans launched a small but genuine abolitionist movement late in 1864. In 1868 a liberal revolution in Spain coincided with an armed rebellion in eastern Cuba, far from the major slave plantations in the west, which became known as the Ten Years' War against Spanish rule. If the rebellion initially failed, it involved the arming and freeing of many blacks on both the Spanish and rebel sides. Hoping to win the support of Afro-Cubans, the Spanish Cortes passed a gradual emancipation act in 1870, which freed all slaves at age sixty and older and all children (*patrocinados*) born since September 18, 1868, the date when "the Glorious Revolution" began.[6] Puerto Rico ended slavery in 1873 and a form of apprenticeship in 1876. Partly as a result of resistance by slaves and *patrocinados*, Spain abolished all colonial slavery in 1886.

We should note that planters in Cuba and Brazil were confident even in the 1860s and 1870s that slavery would last for many more decades. Slave prices reflected this optimism (as in the American South at the beginning of the Civil War). Moreover, some Hispanic liberals were highly critical of the way Britain and especially the United States had emancipated their slaves without forethought or careful preparation. For example, the liberal Spanish historian Josto Zaragoza asserted that British hypocrisy had led to the disastrous results of emancipation in the British Caribbean, uprooting an idle class of blacks while leaving the land under control of white proprietors. Zaragoza and others also pointed to the anarchy of Reconstruction in the American South and warned that Spain must avoid such social disruption by ensuring a slow transition from slavery to freedom—a carefully planned process in which blacks would be gradually replaced by white immigrant labor.[7]

Initially, Brazil followed the gradualist example of most of the Northern states in the United States, most of the independent Hispanic American nations (where slavery persisted into the 1850s and 1860s), and even the Dutch colonies, where ten years of apprenticeship (1863–73) were intended to "prepare" slaves for freedom while also reimbursing their owners. Even Brazil's Emperor Pedro II seemed to favor the 1871 Rio Branco Law of free birth, which liberated all newborn children of slaves after the date of the law, but required them to work for the mother's owner until age twenty-one. Yet slavery was so deeply entrenched in Brazil that proslavery legislators denounced the law as "a crime, robbery, theft, and a communist plot," and at least until the 1880s most planters and even middle-class slaveholders looked upon abolitionism as a treasonous scheme instigated by the English and other hostile foreigners. (Yet it was Britons who mainly financed Brazil's coffee boom; distributed its product; controlled major banks and insurance companies; and contributed to the building of railroads and even urban public utilities.)

Joaquim Nabuco, the elite parliamentary leader of abolitionism, who had been exiled in London and was a corresponding member of the British and Foreign Anti-Slavery Society, complained that any Brazilians who favored progress were branded as foreign agents. He also lamented that the free-birth law led to "another epoch of indifference for the fate of the slave, during which even the government could forget to comply with the law which it had passed."

But with the debatable exception of France, Brazil was the only non-English-speaking country in which abolitionism developed as a mass movement. That said, the movement differed markedly from those in Britain and the United States, especially with respect to individual liberations and slave initiative. First, individual manumissions and the opportunity for slaves to purchase their freedom were far more common than in Anglo-America. Brazil's long war with Paraguay, from 1864 to 1870, brought a new need for arming and freeing blacks as soldiers, which further reduced the size of the naturally declining slave population.

Then, in the far northeastern province of Ceará, a region of small farms, members of various social classes united to prevent slaves from being sold and transported southward. In 1883 and 1884 slaves were literally freed block by block and farm by farm as Cearense citizens raised funds to pay the slaves' owners. The sudden liberation of slaves in Ceará and then in Amazonas, to the northwest, where slaves were few, greatly inspired abolitionists throughout Brazil and helped legislators in 1886 to outlaw whipping as a punishment for slaves.

Nevertheless, the prospering coffee planters in São Paulo province seemed determined to resist all antislavery measures until 1887, when slaves themselves took the initiative and began to flee the great coffee *fazendas* (farms). Nothing in the history of slavery (except in the Hebrew Bible) approximates this mass exodus of thousands of bondspeople, who had no invading army, as in the American Civil War, to give them shelter. Antônio Bento, a radical pentecostal abolitionist—a Brazilian version of America's John Brown— encouraged slaves to escape and created a large secret network that provided shelter on trains and in shanty towns and in some cases even found jobs for the runaways. Most important, the Brazilian police and armed forces proved unwilling or powerless to pursue the fugitives.

Before long the Paulista planters, who had been enjoying a wave of prosperity, became desperate over the prospect of a lost harvest and economic ruin. They began to free large numbers of slaves in return for service contracts that would keep them in the fields. As most planters came to accept the necessity of free labor, the province of São Paulo took the next step and officially freed all slaves through legislative action. As matters developed, in 1888 more than ninety thousand European immigrants, most of them poor and many of them Italian, settled in the province. This meant that emancipation did not bring the expected decline in plantation labor.

When Brazil finally enacted immediate, uncompensated emancipation on May 13, 1888, there were days of public celebration of a kind not seen in the United States—music, parades, flowers, banners, pageants, and a solemn Catholic mass attended by Princess Regent Isabel (her father, the emperor, was away in Europe) and members of the government. Oddly enough, this royal sanction for slave emancipation enabled angry planters to join groups that had other reasons for staging a military coup d'état and overthrowing the monarchic government.

As in 1871, the reformers never seriously considered land redistribution and failed to provide any educational measures for the freedpeople. Like those in most of the Americas, former slaves were freed from the lash and other evils of inhuman bondage but sank to the lowest levels of a stratified society. As my colleague Emilia Viotti da Costa has put it:

> The ex-slave was left to his own devices. His difficulties in adjusting to new conditions were taken by the elites as proof of his racial inferiority. Many ex-slaveholders went as far as to say that the blacks had been happier as slaves than they were as free men since they were incapable of leading their own lives.[8]

Sadly, similar views became almost universal in postemancipation societies throughout the New World, and have by no means been limited to the New World.[9]

THE HISTORY OF POSTEMANCIPATION "reconstructions" is a vast subject that we cannot begin to explore in this book. In the first part of Chapter Fifteen I did argue that in the late nineteenth century and the first half of the twentieth the South won the "ideological Civil War" by repressing the issue of slavery and the war's revolutionary character, and by winning command over a policy of segregation based on the ardent belief in white supremacy. The tragic collapse of America's postwar Reconstruction, which the racist North never seriously supported, led in the South to a long era of Jim Crow discrimination that relied, like slavery, on the fear and terror of institutionalized physical violence.

This violence was not confined to vigilante groups like the Ku Klux Klan. First, as we saw in Chapter Two, with the lynching of Henry Smith in Paris, Texas, thousands of ordinary white men, women, and even children eagerly attended and endorsed the killing of wayward or designated blacks. These frequent mob executions seldom outraged the North, and as late as the 1930s Southern Democrats, on whom the New Deal depended, succeeded in blocking antilynching legislation. [10]

A second form of institutionalized terror can be seen in the Southern prison system, which one of the best historians on the subject has termed "worse than slavery." Many black males were incarcerated for very minor or trumped-up offenses, and Southern governors long rented out such convict labor to lumber companies, mining industries, and large-scale farms, where guards with shotguns, seated on mules or horses, gave orders to slavelike gangs of blacks in striped uniforms. [11]

That said, few slave emancipations in history have been followed by anything equivalent to America's first civil rights legislation and Fourteenth and Fifteenth Amendments, endowing former slaves with full citizenship and the right to vote. As a result of Reconstruction, a significant number of former slaves did vote, and many were elected to state legislatures. Between 1869 and 1901 two African Americans served in the U.S. Senate and twenty in the House of Representatives. Moreover, in contrast to much of the Caribbean, the South's sudden postemancipation drop in economic productivity was soon reversed and followed by rapid economic growth as white farmers began growing more cotton. Even more striking, many blacks succeeded in saving their earnings, and by the 1880s a surprising number became owners of small farms. Yet despite this moderate economic recovery during the late 1870s and the 1880s, real wages in the South at the end of the century were no higher than they had been in the late 1860s.

The small economic achievements with respect to land ownership were checked and partially reversed. By the early twentieth century most Southern white leaders would probably have agreed with a man in Tennessee who wrote, "As long as [the Negroes] are poor they are all right, but as soon as they get some money they get uppity." In 1900 an estimated 75.3 percent of black farmers in the South were sharecroppers or tenants, and twenty years later in the Mississippi Delta region blacks constituted 86 percent of the farm tenants and only 2 percent of the farm owners. [12]

Nevertheless, the United States had established important precedents that contributed to later levels of opportunity. Indeed, it is highly significant that many black West Indian immigrants were attracted by such opportunities and enjoyed in America a kind of success that would have been impossible in the supposedly less racist Caribbean. As one surveys the outcomes of the multiple emancipations in the New World, nothing is more tragic than the fate of Haiti, once the richest spot in the hemisphere and now for many generations the poorest, and yet the only slave society in human history in which the slaves bravely fought for and won their own liberation.

Looking back from the first decades of the twenty-first century on twentieth- and early twenty-first-century forms of slavery and coerced labor, we find grounds for some hope as well as discouragement. It is difficult in the wake of the past century to argue that human nature is perfectible, as many idealistic abolitionists believed, but major changes in moral perception have at least altered cultural norms, and some types of behavior have become almost universally unacceptable. Public whipping, for example, was an indispensable component of chattel slavery and long seemed necessary for the discipline of even white people, from sailors on the decks of ships to children in public schools. While whipping and flogging are now condemned in most of the world, we have a wealth of evidence to show that humans are no less eager than in the past to dominate, degrade, humiliate, and control—often in order to confirm their own sense of pride and superiority. (Adam Smith wrote in 1776 that this was the main motive for slavery.) But in most of the world, laws have at least removed *legal* sanctions for fulfilling such desires by becoming the owner and master of chattel slaves.

No doubt we will always have a small number of individual psychopathic torturers and serial killers. The worst evils arise when *institutions* encourage large numbers of "ordinary" people to adopt similar behavior and win approval and even admiration from, let us say, fellow guards at a Nazi death camp or even at an American-run Iraqi prison. We are seldom willing to recognize the truth that every war converts normal and ordinary citizen-soldiers into serial killers, often of so-called innocent civilians, as in the massive bombings of World War II. I say this having been rigorously trained to kill Japanese in the planned invasion in the autumn of 1945.

For over two decades the Garrisonian wing of the American abolitionist movement embraced radical pacifism and condemned slavery and war as the great twin evils (and we should recall that one classical defense of slavery found its origins in the humane sparing of life by the enslavement of a prisoner of war). But as the twentieth century dramatically showed, the progressive outlawing of slavery did not strengthen global pacifism or diminish the horrors of war.

In fact, in the last century's two world wars, the number of Europeans killed by other Europeans *far* exceeded the total number of Africans enslaved and shipped to the New World from the very beginning. The twentieth century also set wholly new records for the mass extermination or genocide of selected groups, epitomized but by no means ended with the unprecedented Nazi Holocaust.

The rise of such fascist and communist regimes, which used secular utopian "ends" to justify the most cruel and dehumanizing means, led to new forms of coerced labor that were often called "slavery," even though the workers were in effect "worthless" prisoners who were not defined as property that could be owned, purchased, or inherited. In the nineteenth century Frederick Douglass and some other former slaves and abolitionists understandably objected when people extended the term "slavery" to factory workers and other groups who, even if brutally exploited, were not deprived of membership in a family and did not pass on to their children an inherited status as private property. Scholars, reformers, and diplomats still debate the inclusiveness of the term "slave."[13] The issue has become more complex given the fact that the inmates of Soviet gulags or Nazi concentration camps were totally expendable in the eyes of the authorities. Chattel slaves at least represented a valuable investment, an investment of rising value in much of the New World, but that slightly protective aspect of chattel slavery was absent from twentieth-century "state slavery" and does not apply to the many millions of bonded and coerced workers in today's so-called developing world.

While traditional chattel slavery is still widespread in such Saharan nations as Niger, Mauritania, Chad, and Sudan, it is immensely overshadowed by what modern antislavery groups describe as "new forms" of slavery—the men, women and children who are physically forced to work, often under the guise of meaningless contracts, in sweatshops or in building roads and pipelines for multinational corporations. Along with the exploitive use of indebtedness as an excuse for forced labor, there is also an enormous international traffic, especially in eastern Europe and south Asia, in "sex slaves"—often girls or young women who have volunteered for decent-sounding jobs, only to find themselves being coerced into prostitution.[14]

I remember attending as a child the Chicago World's Fair of 1933, which celebrated "A Century of Progress." The title was, of course, chosen before the stock market crash of 1929, and it hardly required a cynic to note that 1933 was a year of deep economic depression and also the year when Hitler came to power. But as we have seen in this book, looking *backward* from 1933, only a century had elapsed since Britain's pioneering and peaceful emancipation of some eight hundred thousand slaves, which helped lead the way to the outlawing of chattel slavery in much of the world.

As I emphasized in the Prologue, by 1888, a century after the founding of the first feeble antislavery organizations in Philadelphia, London, Manchester, and New York, slavery had been outlawed throughout the entire New World—a hemisphere whose economies had long depended on the labor of millions of Africans or people of African descent. While some of this amazing emancipation can be attributed to slave resistance, especially the fleeing of hundreds of thousands of slaves behind Union lines in the American Civil War, and the mass exodus of thousands of slaves from farms and plantations in Brazil in the late 1880s, slave resistance was far more striking at *earlier* stages in the history of the New World—for example, in the creation of large maroon societies or in the Haitian Revolution. It is surely certain—as certain as one can be about any historical events—that the fall of New World slavery could not have occurred if there had been no abolitionist movements.

We can thus end on a positive note of *willed* achievement, a century's moral achievement that may have no parallel. It is an achievement, despite its many limitations, that should help inspire some confidence in other movements for social change, for not being condemned to fully accept the world into which we are born. But since we have devoted special attention to the origins and damage of antiblack racism, it is also crucial to add that we still face the heavy legacies of historical slavery throughout the Western Hemisphere, as well as in the still devastated continent of Africa.

Notes

PROLOGUE

1. The first such group, the Society for the Relief of Free Negroes Unlawfully Held in Bondage, appeared in Philadelphia in 1775. While their aims were far more limited and they met only four times, there was some continuity of personnel with the later 1787 Pennsylvania Abolition Society.

2. There were, to be sure, some isolated critiques of slavery before the mid-eighteenth century and, more frequently, attacks not on slavery itself but on the way that the European demand for coerced labor resulted in unjust forms of enslavement in Africa. For a detailed discussion of this subject, see David Brion Davis, *The Problem of Slavery in Western Culture* (New York, 1988), pp. 111–96, 291–445.

3. John T. Noonan Jr., *A Church That Can and Cannot Change* (Notre Dame, Ind., 2005), p. 123.

4. Frederick Douglass, *Narrative of the Life of Frederick Douglass, An American Slave. Written by Himself*, ed. Benjamin Quarles (Cambridge, Mass., 1960), pp. 94–95.

5. David Brion Davis, "At the Heart of Slavery," in Davis, *In the Image of God: Religion, Moral Values, and Our Heritage of Slavery* (New Haven, 2001), pp. 123–36.

6. This seminar for teachers was supported and organized by the Gilder Lehrman Institute for American History, in New York City. Beginning in 1995 I was assisted by the historian Steven Mintz. While my seminar on the origins and nature of New World slavery was the first to be sponsored by the Gilder Lehrman Institute, it now supports dozens of such courses for teachers, from coast to coast, and on a rich variety of historical subjects.

7. By 2005 historians, especially public historians, had become aware of a major upsurge of public interest in slavery that began in the late 1990s. African Americans, now more interested in and often proud of their heritage, have played a major role in this development, but there are also many "Neo-Confederates" who have been outraged by the consensus among most historians that slavery was the primary cause of the Civil War. On April 26, 2005, Yale's Gilder Lehrman Center for the Study of Slavery, Resistance, and Abolition held a Spring Forum on "The Problem of Slavery in Public History," at which a panel of leading public historians reviewed and discussed the public response to the ways that slavery is now presented at such sites as Civil War battlefields, Colonial Williamsburg, and Thomas Jefferson's Monticello. While this book can hardly resolve conflicts between "history" and what is sometimes called "family heritage," I hope it will encourage a broader and more multinational approach to what will long remain a highly sensitive and controversial subject.

CHAPTER 1

1. The standard work on the subject, on which I have heavily relied, is Howard Jones, *Mutiny on the* Amistad: *The Saga of a Slave Revolt and its Impact on American Abolition, Law, and Diplomacy* (New York, 1987; rev ed., 1988). I have also used court records, newspaper accounts, and other primary sources in Yale's Sterling Library, Manuscripts and Archives, especially *Supreme Court, January Term, 1841, The United States, Appellants v. The Libellants and Claimants of the Schooner* Amistad, *her Tackle, Apparel, and Furniture, together with her Cargo, and the Africans Mentioned and Described in the Several Libels and Claims, Appellees*; and *Argument of Roger S. Baldwin of New Haven before the Supreme Court of the United States, in the Case of the United States, Appellants, vs. Cinque, and Others, Africans of the* Amistad (New York: S. W. Benedict, 1841).

2. Nathan Huggins, quoted in Robin Blackburn, *The Making of New World Slavery: From the Baroque to the Modern, 1492–1800* (London, 1997), p. 1.

3. During the brief struggle, one black was killed and the two white sailors were probably either killed and thrown overboard or jumped into the sea and were drowned.

4. Leonard L. Richards, *"Gentlemen of Property and Standing": Anti-Abolition Mobs in Jacksonian America* (New York, 1970).

5. As early as October 24, 1823, Thomas Jefferson wrote to President James Monroe: "I candidly confess, that I have ever looked on Cuba as the most interesting addition which could ever be made to our system of States. The control which, with Florida Point, this island would give us over the Gulf of Mexico, and the countries and isthmus bordering on it . . . would fill up the measure of our political well-being." Jefferson added that he realized Cuba could be acquired only by war, and thus he favored the island's independence from Spain and especially England, which would leave acquisition by America "to future chances." *Thomas Jefferson: Writings*, Library of America (New York, 1984), pp. 1482–83.

6. Martin Van Buren to the U.S. Marshall for the District of Connecticut, January 7, 1840, Gilder Lehrman Collection 5636.01, on deposit at the New-York Historical Society; Jones, *Mutiny on the* Amistad, pp. 111–35.

7. *Argument of John Quincy Adams, before the Supreme Court of the United States, in the Case of the United States, Appellants, vs. Cinque and Others, Africans, Captured in the Schooner* Amistad, *by Lieutenant Gedney, Delivered on the 24th of February and 1st of March, 1841* (New York: S. W. Benedict, 1841), pp. 79–83.

8. The Spanish word *ladinos* was translated as "sound negroes," meaning that the Cubans only claimed that the Mendeans were sound and healthy when they boarded *La Amistad,* not, as the word actually meant, Spanish-speaking natives of Cuba whose parents or ancestors had arrived before 1820.

9. *Colored American,* September 28, October 5, 1839.

10. The Yale library possesses petitions from the Mendeans expressing their gratitude to Baldwin in particular.

11. *Argument of John Quincy Adams,* pp. 8–9.

12. John Quincy Adams to Roger S. Baldwin, November 11, 1840, Gilder Lehrman Collection 582. For a dramatic account of Adams's struggle against the gag law, see William Lee Miller, *Arguing About Slavery: The Great Battle in the United States Congress* (New York: Knopf, 1996).

13. For example, there seems to have been little if any coverage in *El Noticiosa y Lucero.*

14. *Herald of Freedom,* rpt. in *Colored American,* September 28, 1839.

15. *Argument of John Quincy Adams,* pp. 4, 6–7, 87.

16. Ibid., p. 44.

17. It is important to note that Garrison published in his *Liberator* material from the rival *Emancipator* and even praised his enemy Lewis Tappan for his "zeal and vigor" in helping the Africans. Henry Mayer, *All on Fire: William Lloyd Garrison and the Abolition of Slavery* (New York, 1998), pp. 208–9.

18. *Colored American,* October 12, November 23, 1839; *Commercial Advertiser,* rpt. in *Colored American,* November 23, 1839.

19. This account differs from that of Howard Jones, who writes that Cinqué was at first reluctant to speak but then, thanks to Gibbs, gave testimony covering his experiences from the time he was seized in Africa (*Mutiny on the* Amistad, p. 43).

20. *New Haven Record,* rpt. in *Colored American,* October 12, 1839.

21. John Pitkin Norton Papers, Group 367, Series II, Box 3, Diary, June 29, 1840, to September 15, 1841.

22. Norton, Diary, March 12, 16, 18, 1841. The trip to Farmington had to be postponed to Thursday the eighteenth because of a heavy snowstorm.

23. Yet on March 20, Norton also noted that Cinqué was capable of "a most savage expression."

24. On April 10 Norton noted that fifteen of the men had gone to New York to attend an antislavery meeting; he planned to accompany a delegation on May 18 to an antislavery meeting in Hartford.

25. Norton, Diary, September 4, 1841.

26. Norton, Diary, November 17, 1841.

27. *North Star,* August 4, 1848.

28. Jones, *Mutiny on the* Amistad, p. 205.

29. Ibid. (1988 ed.), p. 220. During the 1990s Professor Jones conducted further research showing that the myth of Cinqué becoming a slave trader originated in an American novel and then made its way into some respected textbooks.

30. *National Era,* March 4, 1847, p. 3; December 9, 1847; August 10, 1848, p. 127; *North Star,* January 7, February 4, 1848. For the moves to annex Cuba, see

North Star, June 8, 1849. When Martin Van Buren ran for president on the Free Soil ticket in 1848, he denied his role in sending the *Grampus* to New Haven and tried to blame Forsyth, his secretary of state. But Frederick Douglass and other abolitionists exposed his proslavery record at roughly the same time that President Polk attacked the Supreme Court's *Amistad* decision, claiming that American courts should have given "full faith and credit" to the ship's fraudulent papers. Some Southerners feared that if Cuba were annexed and if courts enforced the anti-slave-trade law, at least half of Cuba's slaves would be freed and would then send black senators and congressmen to Washington!

CHAPTER 2

1. Muhammad A. Dandamaev, *Slavery in Babylonia: From Nabopolassar to Alexander the Great (626–331 BC)*, trans. Victoria A. Powell, rev. ed. (DeKalb, Ill., 1984), pp. 345–68, 647–61.
2. For remarkable evidence of American slaves' ownership of property, see Dylan C. Penningroth, *The Claims of Kinfolk: African American Property and Community in the Nineteenth-Century South* (Chapel Hill, 2003); and Robert Olwell, *Masters, Slaves, and Subjects: The Culture of Power in the South Carolina Low Country, 1740–1790* (Ithaca, N.Y., 1998), pp. 141–80.
3. For the Tupinamba, see Orlando Patterson, *Freedom*, vol. 1, *Freedom in the Making of Western Culture* (New York, 1991), pp. 15–19, who draws especially on various works by Alfred Métraux and Florestan Fernandes. Patterson also discusses the Tupinamba in *Slavery and Social Death: A Comparative Study* (Cambridge, Mass., 1982), pp. 52, 81, 106–7, 402 n. 102.
4. In this chapter my discussion of slavery as a means of "animalization" draws heavily on my essay "At the Heart of Slavery," *New York Review of Books*, October 17, 1996, pp. 51–54, reprinted in my *In the Image of God: Religion, Moral Values, and Our Heritage of Slavery* (New Haven: Yale University Press, 2001), pp. 123–36, and in a slightly revised form as "Introduction: The Problem of Slavery," in *A Historical Guide to World Slavery*, ed. Seymour Drescher and Stanley L. Engerman (New York, 1998), pp. ix–xviii. My work on this subject is much indebted to Professor Karl Jacoby, once a Yale graduate student and now a professor of history at Brown University, whose original insights were incorporated in his article "Slaves by Nature? Domestic Animals and Human Slaves," *Slavery & Abolition* 15 (April 1994): 89–97.
5. For sickening descriptions of Southern lynching, which flourished from the 1880s to the 1930s, see Leon F. Litwack, *Trouble in Mind: Black Southerners in the Age of Jim Crow* (New York, 1998); and Orlando Patterson, *Rituals of Blood: Consequences of Slavery in Two American Centuries* (Washington, 1998), pp. 170–232.
6. We should note that some whites were also lynched, especially in the West. The Southern lynching of blacks peaked in the 1890s and rose to a total of about 3,200 from 1880 to 1930. See Paul Finkelman, ed., *Lynching, Racial Violence, and Law* (New York, 1992); *Lynching and Vigilantism in the United States: An Annotated Bibliography*, ed. Norton H. Moses (Westport, Conn., 1997); and Patterson, *Rituals of Blood*.
7. Of course the original Constitution included provisions supporting slavery and even the slave trade, but referred to slaves as "such persons" and "person held to service or labor."

8. See especially David M. Oshinsky, *"Worse Than Slavery": Parchman Farm and the Ordeal of Jim Crow Justice* (New York, 1996).

9. For the domestication of animals and plants, see Jared Diamond, *Guns, Germs, and Steel: The Fates of Human Societies* (New York, 1999), a brilliant book, which, unfortunately, says very little about slavery.

10. David M. Goldenberg, *The Curse of Ham: Race and Slavery in Early Judaism, Christianity, and Islam* (Princeton, 2003), p. 345 n. 44.

11. G.W.F. Hegel, *The Phenomenology of Mind*, trans. J. B. Baille, 2nd ed. (New York, 1964).

12. I discuss Hegel's paradigm in *The Problem of Slavery in the Age of Revolution, 1775–1823*, rev. ed. (New York, 1999), pp. 557–64.

13. See Walter Johnson, ed., *The Chattel Principle: Internal Slave Trades in the Americas* (New Haven, 2005). I think it is irrelevant to argue, as Patterson does, that prosperous modern athletes have been sold to a different team and that spouses have property rights in one another. Such spousal rights do not prevent an "I-Thou" relationship of equality. The "chattel principle" reduced the slave to a "thing" or commodity that could be sold and resold indefinitely. Moreover, as movable property the slave was subject not only to an individual owner's will but to claims of creditors, heirs, other family members, and the state. For Patterson's arguments, see *Slavery and Social Death*, pp. 21–27.

14. Frederick Law Olmsted, *The Cotton Kingdom: A Traveller's Observations on Cotton and Slavery in the American Slave States*, ed. Arthur Schlesinger Sr. (New York, 1984), p.452. When Olmsted asked the overseer if he had ever killed a Negro, he replied, "Not quite that," then described trying to shoot a slave who physically resisted him, "but the pistol missing fire, he rushed in and knocked him down with the butt of it" (p. 453). I am indebted to Margaret Abruzzo for tracking down this source, which I had forgotten.

15. Friedrich Nietzsche, *Der Antichrist: Fluch auf das Christentum*, p. 48 (http://homes.rhein-zeitung.de/~ahipler/kritik/antichr4.htm). The German text reads, "der Mensche fand die Tiere nicht unterhaltend,—er herrschte über sie, er wollte nicht einmal 'Tier' sein." Keith Bradley, probably the leading expert on Roman slavery, has drawn on the work of Karl Jacoby and myself to show in a brilliant article that "animalization" was a central feature of even nonracial slavery in antiquity: "Animalizing the Slave: The Truth of Fiction," *Journal of Roman Studies* 90 (2000): 110–25.

16. Stanley L. Engerman, "Labor Incentives and Manumission in Ancient Greek Slavery," in *Essays in Economic Theory, Growth, and Labour Markets: A Festschrift in Honor of E. Drandakis*, ed. George Bitros and Yannis Katsoulacos (Cheltenham, U.K., 2002), pp. 213–17.

17. Diamond, *Guns, Germs, and Steel*, pp. 157–75.

18. Aristotle, *Politics*, quoted in Thomas Wiedemann, *Greek and Roman Slavery* (London, 1981), pp. 18–19.

19. Bradley, "Animalizing the Slave," p. 110.

20. Keith Bradley, lecture at Yale's Gilder Lehrman Center for the Study of Slavery, Resistance, and Abolition, April 28, 2004; Robert W. Harms, *River of Wealth, River of Sorrow: The Central Zaire Basin in the Era of the Slave and Ivory Trade, 1500–1891* (New Haven, 1981), pp. 152–53, 185–86.

21. David Brion Davis, *The Problem of Slavery in Western Culture*, rev. ed. (New York: Oxford University Press, 1988), p. 74.

22. Peter Garnsey, *Ideas of Slavery From Aristotle to Augustine* (Cambridge, U.K., 1996), pp. 80–85.

23. Christopher Leslie Brown and Philip D. Morgan, eds., *Arming Slaves: From Classical Times to the Modern Age* (New Haven, 2006).

24. For an analysis of the awkward contradictions in Roman law, arising from continuing attempts to reconcile the notion of a "totally inferior" and "inhuman" being with the undeniable humanity of the slave, see Keith Bradley, "Roman Slavery and Roman Law," *Historical Reflections/Reflexions Historiques* 15, no. 3 (1988): 477–95.

25. These and related themes are richly developed in Orlando Patterson's *Freedom* and in my own *Slavery and Human Progress* (New York, 1984) and *Problem of Slavery* series.

26. Howard M. Sachar, *A History of the Jews in America* (New York, 1992), p. 35; Michael Walzer, *Exodus and Revolution* (New York, 1985).

27. See E. G. Pulleyblank, "The Origins and Nature of Chattel Slavery in China," *Journal of the Economic and Social History of the Orient* 1, pt. 2 (1958). This chapter also draws on the many sources I cite in *The Problem of Slavery in Western Culture*.

28. Yvon Garlan, *Slavery in Ancient Greece*, trans. Janet Lloyd, rev. ed. (Ithaca, N.Y., 1988), p. 46.

29. Gerda Lerner, *The Creation of Patriarchy* (New York, 1986), pp. 76–100. This theory is not inconsistent with my own theory regarding the model of domesticating animals, which may also have suggested a way of degrading women. Moreover, slaves were surely more dehumanized than were "free" wives and daughters in even the most patriarchal societies.

30. Still extremely useful are the pioneering works, Isaac Mendelsohn, *Slavery in the Ancient Near East: A Comparative Study of Slavery in Babylonia, Assyria, and Palestine, From the Middle of the Third Millennium to the End of the First Millennium* (New York, 1949), and William L. Westermann, *The Slave Systems of Greek and Roman Antiquity* (Philadelphia, 1955), to say nothing of the works of Moses I. Finley.

31. The Jubilee emancipation was clearly impractical for debt slaves, since no one would give credit if the emancipation year was approaching. Doubtless for this reason, Hillel removed the measure from rabbinical law. I am indebted to a paper by Raymond Westbrook, "Slavery in Ancient Near Eastern Law," for this point.

32. Leviticus 25:44–46. The King James Bible also avoids the word "slaves," using instead "bondmen" and "bondmaids" who will nevertheless remain "bondmen for ever." For the wider implications of such mistranslations, see Chapter Four, note 43.

33. In fact, Maimonides' Code did rule that heathen slaves could be worked "with rigor," though they should be treated with mercy and never abused or disgraced; moreover, a child born of a heathen female slave and sired by her Israelite master "has the status of a heathen in every respect and can be bought and sold and employed forever as other slaves are." Moses ben Maimonides, *The Code of Maimonides*, bk. 12, *The Book of Acquisition*, trans. Isaac Klein (New Haven, 1955), pp. 276–82.

34. Leviticus 19:18; Exodus 23:9.

35. Jean Barbot, a French slave-ship captain, claimed that he had observed the Golden Rule and that other traders should treat African slaves the way they would want to be treated if captured by Algerines. *A Description of the Coasts of*

North and South-Guinea . . . , in John Churchill, *A Collection of Voyages and Travels* (London, 1732), vol. 5, pp. 47, 100.

36. Exodus 21:6.

37. Not only was it a capital crime to murder a slave in nineteenth-century America but, as Eugene D. Genovese puts it, with supporting evidence, "a slave could kill a white man in self-defense and escape conviction, provided that his own life stood in clear and imminent danger." *Roll, Jordan, Roll: The World the Slaves Made* (New York, 1974), p. 34.

38. Victor Hanson, *The Other Greeks: The Family Farm and the Agrarian Roots of Western Civilization* (New York, 1995). I am indebted to my colleague Donald Kagan for calling my attention to this crucial book.

39. This distinction was originally made by Moses I. Finley, especially in his article "Was Greek Civilization Based on Slave Labour?" *Historia* 8 (1959): 145–64. See also Finley, ed., *Slavery in Classical Antiquity: Views and Controversies* (Cambridge, U.K., 1960). Though no certain statistics are available, there seems to be a consensus that slaves composed about 30 percent of the ancient Greek population, or about the same as in later Brazil and the United States.

40. Bernard Knox, "The Greek Way," *New York Review of Books*, November 18, 1993, p. 45. As we rightly condemn this enormous gap between the slave laborer and the gentleman of leisure, we should remember that no society has really escaped large inequalities even if they have become less extreme and the cleaners of latrines and other such workers have acquired certain legal symbols of freedom and human dignity. It is also true, as Stanley M. Engerman reminds me, that in the developed world the weekly hours of most workers have declined substantially since the early twentieth century, but the weekly hours of prosperous professionals, managers, and businesspeople have become much longer.

41. From an informal talk by my colleague Donald Kagan, the foremost authority on the Peloponnesian War.

42. Garlan, *Slavery in Ancient Greece*, p. 145.

43. Knox, "Greek Way," pp. 45–46.

44. Alan Watson, *Roman Slave Law* (Baltimore, 1987), pp. xviii–xix, 7. For Roman slavery in general, see Keith Hopkins, *Conquerors and Slaves: Sociological Studies in Roman History, vol. 1* (Cambridge, U.K., 1978); Keith Bradley, *Slavery and Society at Rome* (Cambridge, U.K., 1994); K. R. Bradley, "On the Roman Slave Supply and Slavebreeding," *Slavery & Abolition* 8 (May 1987): 42–59; Ramsay MacMullen, "Late Roman Slavery," *Historia* 36, no. 3 (1987), 359–82; and A.H.M. Jones, *The Later Roman Empire* (Oxford, 1964).

45. For the importance of classical education in the South, see Michael O'Brien, *Conjectures of Order: Intellectual Life in the American South, 1810–1860*, 2 vols. (Chapel Hill, 2004); and Eugene D. Genovese, *The Slaveholders' Dilemma: Freedom and Progress in Southern Conservative Thought, 1820–1860* (Columbia, S.C., 1992).

46. MacMullen, "Late Roman Slavery," pp. 359–82; Bradley, "Review Article: The Problem of Slavery in Classical Culture," *Classical Philology* 92 (1997): 273–82; Bradley, lecture at Yale, April 28, 2004.

47. MacMullen, "Late Roman Slavery," pp. 359–82; Hopkins, *Conquerors and Slaves*; Bradley, "On the Roman Slave Supply and Slavebreeding," in *Classical Slavery*, ed. M. I. Finley (London, 1887), pp. 42–64.

48. William D. Phillips Jr., *Slavery From Roman Times to the Early Transatlantic Trade* (Minneapolis, 1985), p. 18.
49. Watson, *Roman Slave Law*, p. 7.
50. *City of God* iv.iii, xix.xvi; Davis, *The Problem of Slavery in Western Culture*, pp. 87–88, 90, 93.
51. Bradley, lecture at Yale, April 28, 2004; Watson, *Roman Slave Law*, pp. 136–38.
52. Bradley, "Animalizing the Slave," pp. 112–24. I should note that Professor Bradley misinterprets my own work with respect to the ancient and universal contradiction of an institution that attempts to dehumanize humans—which he himself does much to illuminate—and the much later emergence of antislavery thought. From the outset, antislavery writers sought to *expose* this contradiction, but the rise of antislavery thought depended on fundamental religious, intellectual, and economic changes in the seventeenth- and eighteenth-century Anglo-American and French worlds. I have never suggested, as Bradley seems to think, that the kind of tensions and contradictions embodied in *The Golden Ass, or Metamorphoses* developed in some teleological way into modern abolitionism.
53. Keith Hopkins, "Novel Evidence for Roman Slavery," *Past and Present* 138 (February 1993): 3–27.
54. Ibid.
55. Guillaume-Thomas Raynal, *Histoire philosophique et politique des établissements et du commerce des Européens dans les deux Indes* (Geneva, 1781), vol. 6, pp. 171–72. There were several contributors to this work, and it was Jean de Pechméja who wrote some of the most radical pages on New World slavery and may well have been the author of the black Spartacus appeal.
56. C.L.R. James, *The Black Jacobins: Toussaint L'Ouverture and the San Domingo Revolution*, 2nd ed. (New York, 1963), p. 171; Robin Blackburn, *The Overthrow of Colonial Slavery, 1776–1848* (London, 1988), p. 233.

CHAPTER 3

1. C. Peter Ripley, ed., *The Black Abolitionist Papers*, vol. 3, *The United States, 1830–1846* (Chapel Hill, 1991), pp. 182–87. According to Imanuel Geiss, the neologism "racism" originated in Germany in the 1920s as a polemical term denouncing Nazi ideology. But "race," stemming from the Italian *razza* (noble breed or lineage), used in mid–sixteenth-century English for a group of people of common origin, may be traced back to the Arabic *ras*, meaning "head" in both the literal sense and as a leader of a clan or tribe. Geiss, *Geschichte des Rassismus* (Frankfurt am Main, 1988), pp. 16–17; Robert K. Barnhart, *The Barnhart Concise Dictionary of Etymology* (New York, 1995), p. 630.
2. Many definitions of racism are criticized for being too broad or too narrow. I think there is much to be said for George M. Fredrickson's choice of words: "My theory or conception of racism . . . has two components: *difference* and *power*. It originates from a mindset that regards 'them' as different from 'us' in ways that are permanent and unbridgeable. This sense of difference provides a motive or rationale for using our power advantage to treat the ethnoracial Other in ways that we would regard as cruel or unjust if applied to members of our own group. . . . In all manifestations of racism from the mildest to the most severe, what is being denied is the possibility that the racializers and

racialized can coexist in the same society, except perhaps on the basis of domination and subordination." *Racism: A Short History* (New York, 2002), p. 9.

Benjamin Isaac has enhanced our understanding of the subject by underscoring the importance of "proto-racism" in classical antiquity, but his definition of racism, while also useful in specifying the meaning of "difference," focuses only on ideas and attitudes and excludes behavior, practices, and consequences: "an attitude towards individuals and groups of peoples which posits a direct and linear connection between physical and mental qualities. It therefore attributes to those individuals and groups of people collective traits, physical, mental, and moral, which are constant and unalterable by human will, because they are caused by hereditary factors or external influences, such as climate or geography." Isaac, *Invention of Racism in Classical Antiquity* (Princeton, 2004), p. 23. As Isaac makes clear, until fairly recent times, characteristics supposedly acquired from climate or geography were considered to be hereditary and thus unalterable.

3. Charles Verlinden, "L'Origine de 'sclavus—esclave,'" *Archivum latinitatis medii aevi* 17 (1943): 97–128. The Slavic root for slave, *rab*, as in *rabotat*, "to work," made its way into "robot" (actually the old Czech word for serf). The likening of a slave to a robot or inhuman machine parallels the comparison of the slave to an animal or a permanent child. It should also be noted that from England and France to Spain, African slaves were often referred to simply as "Blackamoor," "Negro," "*nègre*," "*négresse*," etc.

4. Michael J. Guasco, "The Idea of Slavery in the Anglo–Atlantic World before 1619," Working Paper no. 00-28, International Seminar on the History of the Atlantic World, 1500–1800, Harvard University, August 17, 2000, p. 26. I am much indebted to Dr. Guasco for letting me cite his paper, which is related to his Ph.D. dissertation, "Encounters, Identities, and Human Bondage: The Foundations of Racial Slavery in the Anglo-Atlantic World" (College of William and Mary, 2000).

5. Isaac, *Invention of Racism*, pp. 50–168.

6. The Chinese also long equated slaves with criminals, since slavery often served as a punishment for certain crimes. The relatively small importation of foreign slaves included a few black Africans. Jared Diamond, *Guns, Germs, and Steel: The Fates of Human Societies* (New York, 1999), pp. 331–32; E. G. Pulleyblank, "The Origins and Nature of Chattel Slavery in China," *Journal of the Economic and Social History of the Orient* 1, pt. 2 (1958): pp. 205–6, 213, 215; Edward H. Schafer, *The Golden Peaches of Samarkand: A Study of T'ang Exotics* (Berkeley, 1963), pp. 15, 44–46.

7. Isaac, *Invention of Racism*, pp. 46–48, 169–224. Isaac notes a tendency in ancient literature to view those people living in the north as being brave while those in the south were dark-skinned and cowardly (p. 151).

8. Peter Kolchin, *Unfree Labor: American Slavery and Russian Serfdom* (Cambridge, Mass., 1987), pp. 170–73; Paul Freedman, *Images of the Medieval Peasant* (Stanford, 1999), pp. 133–73, 300–303.

9. Ruth Mazo Karras, *Slavery and Society in Medieval Scandinavia* (New Haven, 1988), pp. 56–68. In Iceland and Norway, Karras writes, "the slave's dark coloring in the literary sources may represent ugliness and lack of moral worth more than foreign origin" (p. 64).

10. David M. Goldenberg, *The Curse of Ham: Race and Slavery in Early Judaism, Christianity, and Islam* (Princeton, 2003), pp. 111–28.

11. Peter Garnsey, *Ideas of Slavery From Aristotle to Augustine* (Cambridge, U.K., 1996), pp. 41–43. Augustine, like Aristotle and much later defenders of black slavery, also believed that slavery was beneficial for some people.

      With respect to the widespread contempt for physical labor, we should add that even in medieval Europe many merchants and craftsmen took pride in their work, a pride one can find even among much later slave artisans in the New World. Nevertheless, the late eighteenth and early nineteenth centuries witnessed the beginnings of a fundamental cultural shift in moral perception with respect to the positive value of "free labor."

12. Orlando Patterson, *Slavery and Social Death: A Comparative Study* (Cambridge, Mass., 1982), pp. 96, 299–333; Stanley Elkins, *Slavery: A Problem in American Institutional and Intellectual Life* (Chicago, 1959), p. 82. It should be stressed that Patterson did not accept Elkins's thesis that American slavery was so severe and unchecked that slaves internalized, psychologically, many of these traits. But while Patterson proclaimed that "there is absolutely no evidence from the long and dismal annals of slavery to suggest that any group of slaves ever internalized the conception of degradation held by their masters" (p. 97), he quotes slaves expressing self-hatred and "psychological violence against [themselves]": "De Massa and Missus was good to me but sometime I was so bad they had to whip me. . . . I needed de whippin' " (p. 12); and in an endnote he takes a seemingly neutral stance toward "the thesis of Stanley Elkins regarding the personality of American slaves. . . . I can offer neither theoretical expertise nor relevant data" (p. 367, n. 41). John Hope Franklin and some other historians have argued, along lines similar to those taken by Keith Bradley's interpretation of Apuleius' *Golden Ass*, discussed in Chapter Two, that slaves adopted a Sambo-like pose in order to fool and manipulate their masters.

13. Frederick Douglass, *Narrative of the Life of Frederick Douglass, an American Slave. Written by Himself*, ed. Benjamin Quarles (Cambridge, Mass., 1960), pp. 94–95.

14. In Yiddish, for example, there are common phrases for "little deer," "little bear," "little wolf," and "little lion."

15. Alden T. Vaughan and Virginia Mason Vaughan, "Before Othello: Elizabethan Representations of Sub-Saharan Africans," in "Constructing Race," *William and Mary Quarterly*, 3rd ser., 54 (January 1997): 19–44; Diamond, *Guns, Germs, and Steel*, p. 297.

16. Keith Bradley, "Animalizing the Slave: The Truth of Fiction," *Journal of Roman Studies* 20 (2000): 110; Isaac, *Invention of Racism*, pp. 176, 201–15; David Brion Davis, "At the Heart of Slavery," in Davis, *In the Image of God: Religion, Moral Values, and Our Heritage of Slavery* (New Haven, 2001), pp. 123–36; Diamond, *Guns, Germs, and Steel*, p. 235.

17. It is worth recalling, with respect to the generally independent history of slavery and the persecution of Jews, that when Columbus sailed from the Spanish port of Palos in 1492, he observed the Spanish Jews being loaded into ships for deportation. Columbus later brought enslaved Indians back to Spain, and the New World would soon open up unprecedented markets for racial slaves, while in most parts of Europe the Jews would remain the largest population of non-Christian "aliens," a people who Cicero and many later Europeans said were "born to be slaves." Isaac, *Invention of Racism*, p. 316. More research needs to be done on why, given the virulence of medieval anti-Semitism, more Jews were not enslaved. The relation between Jews and colonial slaves would soon

become extraordinarily complex. See Jonathan Schorsch, *Jews and Blacks in the Early Modern World* (Cambridge, U.K., 2004); David Brion Davis, *Slavery and Human Progress* (New York, 1984), pp. 82–101.

18. Isaac, *Invention of Racism*, p. 51.

19. Ibid., pp. 5–8.

20. Our understanding of late ancient and early medieval slavery has been greatly enriched by my colleague Youval Rotman's *Les Esclaves et l'esclavage de la Méditerranée antique a la Méditerranée médiévale, VI–XI siècles* (Paris, 2004).

21. Hugh Thomas, *The Slave Trade: The Story of the Atlantic Slave Trade, 1440–1870* (New York, 1997), pp. 64–65.

22. Isaac, *Invention of Racism*, pp. 193–94.

23. *Sum. Theol.* 3rd Part, Supplement (London, 1922), Q. 52, Art. 1, 4; David Brion Davis, *The Problem of Slavery in Western Culture* (New York, 1988), pp. 95–97, 104; Garnsey, *Ideas of Slavery From Aristotle to Augustine*, pp. 191–219.

24. Schorsch, *Jews and Blacks*, pp. 17–22, 27, 36–49. Abravanel, who had been a wealthy servant of the Portuguese monarchy and of members of the nobility, finished this commentary in the Kingdom of Naples, having fled from Spain in 1492. Professor Schorsch shows that Abravanel's views on slavery, expressed at different times and places, were shared by many Muslims and Christians. We will turn to the biblical "Curse of Ham" in a few pages.

25. Joshua 9:16–24.

26. Though I am drawing here a bit from Alain de Botton's remarkable op-ed essay "Workers of the World Relax" (*New York Times*, Monday, September 6, 2004, p. A17), Botton makes no reference to the cultural prerequisites to anti-slavery. I lay the groundwork for this theme in my *Problem of Slavery in the Age of Revolution, 1775–1823* (New York, 1999), and will return to it in Chapter Twelve.

27. Frank Snowden Jr., *Blacks in Antiquity: Ethiopians in the Greco-Roman Experience* (Cambridge, Mass., 1970); Snowden, *Before Color Prejudice: The Ancient View of Blacks* (Cambridge, Mass., 1983).

28. Isaac, *Invention of Racism*, pp. 1–51, 492–516. Significantly, Professor Isaac says very little about Greco-Roman views and images of black Africans, "because they did not form much of an actual presence in the Greek and Roman worlds" (p. 49). On the other hand, Professor Snowden's work, supplemented by such works as Lloyd A. Thompson's *Romans and Blacks* (London, 1989) and various works on ancient art, shows a widespread interest in describing and depicting such people.

29. Goldenberg, *Curse of Ham*, pp. 1–4; Davis, *Problem of Slavery in Western Culture*, pp. 447–51.

30. Ibid., pp. 446–82.

31. Goldenberg, *Curse of Ham*, pp. 41–128; Ladislas Bugner et al., eds., *The Image of the Black in Western Art*, vol. 1, *From the Pharaohs to the Fall of the Roman Empire* (New York, 1976), passim; vol. 2, pts. 1 and 2, *From the Early Christian Era to the "Age of Discovery"* (New York, 1979), passim.

32. *Image of the Black in Western Art*, vol. 2, pt. 2, pp. 161–85; Paul Kaplan, *The Rise of the Black Magus in Western Art* (Ann Arbor, 1993), passim.

33. *Image of the Black in Western Art*, vol. 2, pt. 1, pp. 149–205. It appears that Saint Maurice had been depicted as white until 1240 or 1250, when a black African Maurice appeared as a sandstone statue at the Cathedral of Magdeburg, in Germany. While Saint Maurice was not universally portrayed as black, this

theme "was to enjoy an almost uninterrupted success for at least three centuries, and for this the archbishops of Magdeburg were largely responsible" (p. 166). Unlike most of the representations of the Black Madonna, Saint Maurice has striking African features.

34. Ibid., pp. 35–80; pt. 2, pp. 74–76, 204–9. Most earlier representations of this legend of the Greek saints Cosmos and Damian had the replaced leg taken from a dead or even buried black man.

35. Alexandre Popovic, *The Revolt of African Slaves in Iraq in the Third/Ninth Century*, trans. Léon King (Princeton, 1999). See also the many sources I cite in *Slavery and Human Progress* (New York, 1984), pp. 321–22. For a brief discussion of the tradition of romanticizing Islamic slaves, see Davis, "Slaves in Islam," in Davis, *In the Image of God*, pp. 137–41.

36. André Miquel, *La géographie humaine du monde musulman jusqu'au milieu du 11 siècle*, vol. 2 (Paris, 1975), pp. 3–11, 58, 90–133, 153–88. Miquel concludes that as late as the tenth and eleventh centuries, black Africa remained for the Arabs largely a continent of legend and mystery.

37. Leviticus 25:44–46.

38. Bernard Lewis, *Race and Slavery in the Middle East: An Historical Enquiry* (New York, 1990), pp. 57–61. In general, black slaves were forced to do the most menial and heavy work and very seldom enjoyed the opportunities available to a few privileged white slaves.

39. Raymond Mauny, *Les siècles obscurs de l'Afrique noir: Histoire et archéologie* (Paris, 1990), passim; Ralph A. Austen, "The Mediterranean Islamic Slave Trade out of Africa: A Tentative Census," in "The Human Commodity: Perspectives on the Trans-Saharan Slave Trade," ed. Elizabeth Savage, special issue, *Slavery & Abolition* 13 (April 1992): 214–48; Austen, "The Trans-Saharan Slave Trade: A Tentative Census," in *The Uncommon Market: Essays in the Economic History of the Atlantic Slave Trade*, ed. Henry A. Gemery and Jan S. Hogendorn (New York, 1979), pp. 23–76.

40. E-mail from Professor David Eltis, May 17, 2005, for the latest data on the percentage of African slaves who arrived in mainland British North America, as opposed to the total number imported into the New World. Professor Eltis is still working on the final estimate. I do not mean to imply that black Africans were the passive victims of Arab and Berber exploitation. As early as 720 the Nubians repelled an attempted Muslim invasion, agreeing to an armistice that provided for the annual delivery of several hundred slaves in exchange for wheat and other commodities. Bernard Lewis, ed. and trans., *Islam: From the Prophet Muhammad to the Capture of Constantinople*, vol. 1, *Politics and War* (London, 1976), pp. 232–34.

41. Robert C. Davis, *Christian Slaves, Muslim Masters: White Slavery in the Mediterranean, the Barbary Coast, and Italy, 1500–1800* (New York, 2003), pp. xiv–xix, 3–26. After much careful analysis of sources, Davis concludes "that between 1530 and 1780 there were almost certainly a million and quite possibly as many as a million and a quarter white, European Christians enslaved by the Muslims of the Barbary coast" (p. 23).

42. Bernard Lewis, *Race and Color in Islam* (New York, 1971), pp. 15–18; Lewis, *Race and Slavery*, pp. 59–61; Miquel, *La géographie* humaine, vol. 2, pp. 143–44. Lewis also notes that whereas the "emancipated white slave was free from any kind of restriction," the emancipated black slave "was at most times and places rarely able to rise above the lowest levels" (p. 60).

43. John Hunwick, "Arab Views of Black Africans and Slavery," paper given at Yale's Gilder Lehrman Center Conference on "Collective Degradation: Slavery and the Construction of Race," November 7, 2003, pp. 10–12. Ibn Khaldūn, who found similar defects in Slavs and other "northern Europeans," attributed this inferiority to zones of climate but also affirmed, like many ancient and medieval writers, that such traits were in effect hereditary. He did later admit that some West Africans were more civilized and could be redeemed by Islam (pp. 14–15).

44. Gernot Rotter, *Die Stellung des Negers in der islamisch-arabischen Gesellschaft bis zum XVI. Jahrhundert* (Bonn, 1967), pp. 162–63; Lewis, *Race and Color in Islam*, p. 38.

45. Lewis, *Race and Slavery in the Middle East*; Jean Fagan Yellin, *Harriet Jacobs, a Life: The Remarkable Adventures of the Woman Who Wrote* Incidents in the Life of a Slave Girl (New York, 2004).

46. A fascination with the black African's penis extended from ancient times to later European explorers and scientists. In 1799 the English geologist Charles White would write: "That the Penis of an African is larger than that of a European has I believe been shown in every anatomical school in London. Preparations of them are preserved in most anatomical museums, and I have one in mine." From White, *An Account of Regular Gradation in Man*, found on the Web at geocities.com/ruooruoo/racismhistory/18thcent.html. For a recent work on the continuing obsession with this subject, see Scott Poulson-Bryant, *Hung: A Meditation on the Measure of Black Men in America* (New York, 2005). Stereotypes are questioned and put in some perspective by Google: google.com/answers/threadview?id=366192. See also Winthrop D. Jordan, *White Over Black: American Attitudes Toward the Negro, 1550–1812* (Williamsburg, Va., 1968), pp. 30, 34–35, 158–59, 163, 464, 501.

47. It should be stressed that Christians and Jews living under Muslim rule were defined as "protected persons" (dhimmīs) who could not legally be enslaved unless they violated the terms of the contract that defined their status. Lewis, *Race and Slavery*, p. 7.

48. *Parliamentary Debates* (Lords), 5th ser., vol. 225 (1960), cols. 335, 341–43. For a typical account of the killing, raping, eviction, and humiliation of the black African majority in Dafur, see Marc Lacey and El Fasher, "Evicted From Camp, Sudan Refugees Suffer in Limbo," *New York Times*, August 2, 2004, p. A3.

49. Lewis, *Race and Slavery*, pp. 57–58. It should be noted that Ahmad Baba felt it necessary to make this eloquent point in order to contest an opposite view.

50. James H. Sweet, "The Iberian Roots of American Racist Thought," in "Constructing Race," *William and Mary Quarterly*, 3rd ser., 54 (January 1997): 159, 166. Imanuel Geiss makes essentially the same point (*Geschichte des Rassismus*, pp. 84–88), as does George Fredrickson, *Racism*, pp. 31–42.

51. A similar catastrophic flood appears in other diverse ancient Middle Eastern cultures, including the Babylonian-Akkadian epic of Atrahasis. But the Hebrew story is unique in picturing the flood as God's punishment for sin and evil and then in having God establish a moral covenant with Noah, who as "a righteous man . . . blameless in his age" represents future humanity (Genesis 6:9; 9:9–17).

52. Genesis 9:18–27, in *Tanakh: A New Translation of the Holy Scriptures According to the Traditional Hebrew Text* (Philadelphia, 1985), pp. 14–15. This Jewish Publication Society translation also appears in *The Torah: A Modern Commentary*,

ed. W. Gunther Plaut, whose commentary on Genesis I have also used. The J.P.S. translation differs little from that in *The HarperCollins Study Bible: New Revised Standard Version*, ed. Wayne A. Meeks (London, 1993), p. 16, except that the latter clearly states that Shem and Japheth "did not see their father's nakedness" and in a footnote observes that "the hostility toward Canaan is rooted in Israel's memory of Canaan's onetime hegemony in the land [later Israel] under protection of Egyptian might." According to the biblical scholar Gerhard Von Rad, the original narrative had nothing to do with Shem, Ham, and Japheth or the ecumenical "Table of Nations" that follows. Rather, there had been an older story, limited to Shem, Japheth, and Canaan, that was based on the horror felt by the newly arrived Israelites at the sexual depravity of the Canaanites. Later on, supposedly, an editor inserted the name "Ham" as father of Canaan, in an effort to harmonize the narrative with the later "Table of Nations." Such theories and speculations have not been included in the more recent scholarship and debates on the racist interpretations of "the Curse."

53. Augustine, *City of God*, bk. 19, chap. 15. Garnsey points out that for Augustine "it was God's intention for men to dominate animals, but not other men. The arrival of slavery following the Fall therefore represented a step down from the order of nature that God created. . . . The cause of slavery was not nature but sin." *Ideas of Slavery From Aristotle to Augustine*, pp. 217–18.

54. David Goldenberg, "What Did Ham Do to Noah?" in *"The Words of a Wise Mouth Are Gracious": Festschrift for Günter Stemberger on the Occasion of his Sixty-fifth Birthday, Studia Judaica*, ed. Mauro Perani (Berlin, 2005), pp. 265–74.

55. For various interpretations of Kush, see Goldenberg, *Curse of Ham*, 18, 100, 171–72.

56. Morris J. Raphall, *Bible View of Slavery: A Discourse Delivered at the Jewish Synagogue, "B'nai Jeshurum," New York, on the Day of the National Fast, January 4, 1861* (New York, 1861). Raphall was responding in part to Jewish abolitionists like Rabbi David Einhorn. Ironically, one of Raphall's sons served as an officer in the Union army.

57. Quoted in Goldenberg, *Curse of Ham*, pp. 175–76. As Goldenberg notes, Crummell had been educated at Cambridge and spent sixteen years in Liberia.

58. See especially Stephen R. Haynes, *Noah's Curse: The Biblical Justification of American Slavery* (New York, 2002), pp. 161–221.

59. Goldenberg, *Curse of Ham*, p.177.

60. Ibid., pp. 175–76.

61. Ibid., pp. 164–67.

62. Benjamin Braude, "The Sons of Noah and the Construction of Ethnic and Geographical Identities in the Medieval and Early Modern Periods," in "Constructing Race," *William and Mary Quarterly*, 3rd ser., 54 (January 1997): 111–42.

63. See especially the Nation of Islam's *The Secret Relationship Between Blacks and Jews* (Boston, 1991). The pioneering work in exposing racist myths and distortions concerning interpretations of "the sons of Ham" was Ephraim Isaac, "Genesis, Judaism, and 'Sons of Ham,'" *Slavery & Abolition* 1 (May 1980): 3–17.

64. Goldenberg, *Curse of Ham*, pp. 105, 141–56.

65. The Hebrew word for "Kushites" could also refer to dark-skinned Arabs. Ibid., pp. 124–25.

66. Frank Snowden Jr., the great African American ancient historian who carried out the most comprehensive studies of black Africans in antiquity, totally repudiated the popular Afrocentric theory that ancient Egyptians were mostly

black like their neighbors to the south. Of course there was some intermixture, but ancient Egyptian art, which often portrays Egyptians next to black African slaves, confirms Snowden's point.

67. As Goldenberg notes, many in the ancient world were aware that "in 701 B.C.E. Kush battled the Assyrian king Sennacherib to a standstill," that the Egyptians frequently made use of black mercenary troops, and that "there were Kushite contingents also in the Persian army of Xerxes." *Curse of Ham*, pp. 33–35.

68. Ibid., p. 190. Goldenberg adds that "it would appear that [this] passage transmitting an etiology of black African physiognomy derives from and is influenced by the Islamic cultural environment in which it was composed [Iraq, then part of Babylonia]" (pp. 102–5, 192).

69. Ibid., pp. 105–6; e-mail to me from David Goldenberg, August 3, 2005. In some Islamic versions, the fourth son was Yakhtoun or Yahtoun. I personally find it surprising that more emphasis was not given to having Canaan born on the ark, since that would help explain his being set apart from his brethren and being cursed for Ham's second act of disrespect for his father, Noah.

70. Goldenberg, *Curse of Ham*, pp. 158, 170.

71. Ibid., pp. 175, 356.

72. Ibid., pp. 178–82.

73. Quoted in Sweet, "Iberian Roots of American Racist Thought," p. 161.

74. Quoted in Schorsch, *Jews and Blacks*, pp. 146–47; Braude, "Sons of Noah," pp. 127–28. Some translations indicate that Zurara confused Ham with Cain; see Schorsch, p. 408 n. 62; Goldenberg, *Curse of Ham*, pp. 175, 355 n. 46. But the reference to the flood and to Noah clearly indicates the cursing of Ham.

75. Geiss, *Geschichte des Rassismus*, pp. 79–88, 121–22. For the ways in which purity of blood laws were applied to blacks in colonial Mexico, see María Elena Martínez, "The Black Blood of New Spain: *Limpieza de Sangre*, Racial Violence, and Gendered Power in Early Colonial Mexico," *William and Mary Quarterly*, 3rd ser., 51 (July 2004): 479–520.

76. Léon Poliakov, *The History of Anti-Semitism*, vol. 2, *From Mohammed to the Marranos*, trans. Natalie Gerardi (New York, 1973), pp. 117–25. Spanish Jews also played a critical role in transmitting knowledge of the ancient world and of the Near East to Christian Europe, largely by translating works on the arts and sciences into Castilian and other vernacular European languages (pp. 125–28).

77. Yosef Hayim Yerushalmi, "Assimilation and Racial Anti-Semitism: The Iberian and the German Models," *The Leo Baeck Memorial Lecture*, no. 26 (New York, 1982), pp. 8–11.

78. Yerushalmi points out that in 1637 one Spanish writer argued "that the foetus acquires the moral qualities of its parents at the moment of conception," and "even the milk of a Jewish wet nurse can engender perverse inclinations"— citing the case of a man burned at the stake as a judaizer, "verified to be of illustrious blood, but it was found that the nurse who suckled him was of infected blood," i.e., was a New Christian. Ibid., p. 16. A long Jewish tradition has understandably honored attempts by *Conversos* to secretly maintain and perpetuate their Jewishness, but historians have been divided regarding the number of New Christians who became assimilated to Christian culture, partly through intermarriage.

79. Henry Kamen, *The Spanish Inquisition: An Historical Revision* (London, 1997), pp. 231–50. Kamen argues that while "limpieza like other racial discriminations proved remarkably long-lived as a weapon in struggles for status, rank,

and promotion," the "deliberate use of limpieza to discredit enemies and rivals ended only in discrediting limpieza itself" (p. 253).

80. James Carroll, *Constantine's Sword: The Church and the Jews, a History* (Boston, 2001), pp. 333–62. Carroll shows that despite opposition from popes at Rome, Spain became the birthplace of "modern anti-Semitism" in the very years that Seville and Valencia were first importing black slaves from Portugal. The Inquisition also focused on Christian heretics, some of whom were burned at the stake. See also Henry Kamen, *Inquisition and Society in Spain: In the Sixteenth and Seventeenth Centuries* (Bloomington, Ind., 1985).

81. Fray Prudencio de Sandoval, *Historia de la vida y hechos del emperador Carlos V*, vol. 82, *Biblioeca de autores españoles* (Madrid, 1956), p. 319. I am much indebted to William Casey King for this reference, and for calling my attention to the related article by Jerome Friedman, "Jewish Conversion, the Spanish Pure Blood Laws, and Reformation: A Revisionist View of Racial and Religious Antisemitism," *Sixteenth Century Journal* 18 (1987): 3–29. Estimates of the number of converts in Spain by 1492 range from 250,000 to as many as one million.

82. For the later history of racial intermixture, see Werner Sollors, ed., *Interracialism: Black-White Intermarriage in American History, Literature, and Law* (New York, 2000).

83. Sweet, "Iberian Roots of American Racist Thought," p. 159; Geiss, *Geschichte des Rassismus*, passim.

84. David Eltis, *The Rise of African Slavery in the Americas* (Cambridge, U.K., 2000), pp. 15, 24–25. Eltis notes that "the Spanish forced relatively few African slaves to labor in the mines and the Amerindians they used instead were not slaves. . . . Some Amerindian enslavement occurred even after such slavery was banned in 1542, but the great bulk of the labor force in the silver mines of both New Spain and Peru was Indian and received remuneration" (pp. 24–25).

85. Sweet, "Iberian Roots of American Racist Thought," p. 144; Geiss, *Geschichte des Rassismus*, pp. 27–33. Like Benjamin Isaac, Geiss argues that the central elements and preconditions of racism—ethnocentrism, xenophobia, endogamy, and the myth of "purity of blood"—go back to antiquity. Modern scientific racism brought these dispositions together in one more or less coherent system of thought.

86. Jordan, *White Over Black*, pp. 216–65, 491–511.

87. Ibid., pp. 458–59, 492–93; Thomas Jefferson, *Notes on the State of Virginia* (New York, 1964), Query 14. For a comparison of the views on black slavery expressed by Jefferson and by two Caribbean "men of the Enlightenment," Bryan Edwards and Moreau de Saint-Méry, see David Brion Davis, *The Problem of Slavery in the Age of Revolution, 1775–1823* (Ithaca, N.Y., 1975), pp. 184–95.

88. See especially Seymour Drescher, *From Slavery to Freedom: Comparative Studies in the Rise and Fall of Atlantic Slavery* (Basingstoke, U.K., 1999), pp. 291–300; Fredrickson, *Racism*, pp. 67–69; and Davis, *Problem of Slavery in Western Culture*, pp. 454–59.

89. These and many similar antiblack and anti-Semitic quotations can be found on the Web, geocities.com/ru00ru00/racismhistory/18thcent.html. See also Davis, *Problem of Slavery in Western Culture*, pp. 454–59.

90. Fredrickson, *Racism*, p. 56.

91. Seymour Drescher, *The Mighty Experiment: Free Labor versus Slavery in British Emancipation* (New York, 2002), pp. 76–81, 219. In his first edition, in 1849, Carlyle had used the word "Negro" in the title; in 1853 he changed it to "Nigger."

92. *The Encyclopædia Britannica: A Dictionary of Arts, Sciences, Literature and General Information*, 11th ed., vol. 19 (New York, 1911), p. 344. The first long essay on "Negro" was written by Thomas Athol Joyce, M.A., an ethnographer at the British Museum; curiously, the second, non-racist, quantitative essay was written by a great American statistician and Census Bureau chief, Walter Francis Willcox, LL.B., Ph.D., who drew on the works of Booker T. Washington and W.E.B. Du Bois, and whom I interviewed at Cornell around 1963, when he was 102 years old.

CHAPTER 4

1. David Eltis, *The Rise of African Slavery in the Americas* (Cambridge, U.K., 2000), pp. 1–84. See also Stanley L. Engerman, ed., *Terms of Labor: Slavery, Serfdom, and Free Labor* (Stanford, 1999). Britain did deport many convicts and captive Irish people to the Caribbean and to such colonies as Maryland, but while salable, they were only required to work for a limited number of years and were not legally defined as chattel slaves for life, whose offspring would also be slaves.

2. For a carefully researched and eye-opening study of this neglected subject, see Robert C. Davis (no relation), *Christian Slaves, Muslim Masters: White Slavery in the Mediterranean, the Barbary Coast, and Italy, 1500–1800* (Basingstoke, Hampshire, U.K. and New York, 2003). See also Linda Colley, *Captives: Britain, Empire, and the World, 1600–1850* (New York, 2002), and Giles Milton, *White Gold: the Extraordinary Story of Thomas Pellow and Islam's One Million White Slaves* (New York, 2005).

3. Youval Rotman, *Les Esclaves et l'esclavage de la Méditerranée antique à la Méditerranée médiévale, VI–XI siècles* (Paris, 2004), pp. 171–84 and passim.

4. Colley, *Captives*, passim. My quotation is from the song "Rule Britannia," composed about 1740 and based on James Thompson's earlier poem with the same title.

    It is true, of course, that throughout these centuries Christians and Muslims traded with each other and that Muslims transmitted a rich intellectual legacy to European Christians, especially during the Islamic rule of Spain. But even though European Christians long supplied slaves to various Muslim states, the continuing struggle between the rival religious systems shaped western European conceptions of "just" and "unjust" forms of slavery and provided the initial moral framework for enslaving or purchasing enslaved African slaves. For a review of recent works on early Christian-Muslim relations, see William Dalrymple, "The Truth about Muslims," *New York Review of Books*, November 4, 2004, pp. 31–34.

5. For the development of antiblack prejudices in Britain, from the sixteenth through the eighteenth centuries, see Winthrop D. Jordan's classic work, *White Over Black: American Attitudes Toward the Negro, 1550–1812* (Chapel Hill, N.C., 1968), pp. 3–265.

6. This is a major theme in Benjamin Isaac's *Invention of Racism in Classical Antiquity* (Princeton, 2004).

7. The founders of Georgia merged philanthropic with economic and strategic motives, and for a time hoped that a slave-free buffer state between Carolina and Florida would check Spanish attempts to foment slaves' desertion or revolts in Carolina, while also making Georgia more attractive for white immigrants. See David Brion Davis, *The Problem of Slavery in Western Culture*, rev. ed. (New York, 1988), pp. 144–50.

8. David Eltis, "Free and Coerced Migrations From the Old World to the New," in *Coerced and Free Migration: Global Perspectives*, ed. D. Eltis (Stanford, 2002), pp. 33–74; updated by an e-mail from Professor Eltis, August 1, 2007. From 1820 to 1880 some 13.7 million Europeans departed for the Americas, greatly outnumbering the 2.3 million African slaves departing for the New World. As a result of high slave mortality and negative population growth rates (outside mainland North America, north of the Rio Grande), by 1825 blacks constituted only 18 to 19 percent of the New World population. Some 18 percent of this "black" population was mixed (including mixture with Indians.) Native Americans constituted 24 percent of the 1825 New World population. I am much indebted to Professors David Eltis and Stanley L. Engerman for providing me with these updated estimates, including the volume of the African slave trade.

9. [Malachy Postlethwayt], *The Natural and Private Advantages of the African Trade Considered: Being an Enquiry how far it Concerns the Trading Interest of Great Britain, Effectually to Support and Maintain the Forts and Settlements in Africa; Belonging to the Royal African Company of England . . .* (London, 1746), pp. 1–2. Later angered by Parliament's abandonment of the Royal African Company, Postlethwayt changed his mind regarding the benefits of the slave trade and argued that Britain's economic future did not lie in sugar and slaves but in beating France to the interior of Africa. Davis, *Problem of Slavery in Western Culture*, pp. 160–61.

10. Ibid., pp. 151–53.

11. Jean Barbot, *A Description of the Coasts of North and South-Guinea . . .* , in John Churchill, *A Collection of Voyages and Travels* (London, 1732), vol. 5, pp. 47, 110, 271–72, 547–48. Barbot was a French Protestant who fled to England in 1685.

12. William L. Sherman, *Forced Labor in Sixteenth-Century Central America* (Lincoln, Neb., 1979), pp. 39–67.

13. David Brion Davis, *Slavery and Human Progress* (New York, 1984), pp. 52–57; William D. Phillips Jr., *Slavery From Roman Times to the Early Transatlantic Trade* (Minneapolis, 1985), passim; Charles Verlinden, *The Beginnings of Modern Colonization: Eleven Essays with an Introduction*, trans. Yvonne Freccero (Ithaca, N.Y., 1970), pp. 35–40, 79–97 (and works by Verlinden cited in note 14).

14. Charles Verlinden, "L'esclavage en Sicile au bas moyen âge," *Institut historique belge de Rome* 35 (1963): 42–43, 68–79, 90–93; Verlinden, "L'esclavage noir en France méridionale et courants de traite en Afrique," *Annales du Midi* 78 (1966): 335–343; Verlinden, *L'esclavage dans l'Europe médiévale*, vol. 2, *Italie—Colonies italiennes du Levant—Levant latin—Empire byzantin* (Gent, 1977), pp. 208–20, 233–38, 329–30, 353–54.

15. Ibid., pp. 235, 377; Hugh Thomas, *The Slave Trade* (New York, 1997), pp. 10–11, 13–14, 84–86.

16. Felipe Fernández-Armesto, *The Canary Islands After Conquest: The Making of a Colonial Society in the Early Sixteenth Century* (Oxford, 1982), passim.

17. T. Bentley Duncan, *Atlantic Islands: Madeira, the Azores, and the Cape Verdes in Seventeenth-century Commerce and Navigation* (Chicago, 1972), pp. 9–11; Sidney M. Greenfield, "Madeira and the Beginnings of New World Sugar Cane Cultivation and Plantation Slavery: A Study in Institution Building," in *Comparative Perspectives on Slavery in New World Plantation Societies*, ed. Vera Rubin and Arthur Tuden (New York, 1977), pp. 536–52; Greenfield, "Plantations, Sugar Cane and Slavery," in Michael Craton, ed., *Roots and Branches: Current Directions in Slave Studies* (Toronto, 1979), pp. 85–88, 98–119.

18. John Thornton, *Africa and Africans in the Making of the Atlantic World, 1400–1680* (Cambridge, U.K., 1992), pp. 96–97; Stuart B. Schwartz, *Sugar Plantations in the Formation of Brazilian Society, Bahia, 1550–1835* (Cambridge, U.K., 1985), pp. 13–17; Schwartz, ed., *Tropical Babylons: Sugar and the Making of the Atlantic World, 1450–1680* (Chapel Hill, N.C., 2004), pp. 1–26, 42–84; Davis, *Slavery and Human Progress*, pp. 61, 63, 68, 71, 95–96.

19. For the African "agricultural revolution" occasioned by New World crops, see Joseph C. Miller, *Way of Death: Merchant Capitalism and the Angolan Slave Trade, 1730–1830* (Madison, Wisc., 1988), pp. 19–21.

20. In treating this early age of European expansion, I have especially benefited from J. H. Elliott, "The World After Columbus," *New York Review of Books*, October 10, 1991, and Kenneth Maxwell, "¡Adiós Columbus!," ibid., January 28, 1993.

21. J. H. Parry, *The Age of Reconnaissance* (London, 1963), chaps. 3–6; Felipe Fernández-Armesto, *Before Columbus: Exploration and Colonization From the Mediterranean to the Atlantic, 1229–1492* (London, 1987), passim.

22. Parry, *Age of Reconnaissance*, pp. 137–41. For Portuguese exploration and expansion in general, see C. R. Boxer, *The Portuguese Seaborne Empire, 1415–1825* (New York, 1969), pp. 16–17, 36–37. Years ago I saw a fascinating exhibition of sixteenth-century Japanese silk screen paintings at the Guimet Museum in Paris.

23. One should note that many centuries earlier the Polynesians, who had no nautical instruments, sailed across much of the Pacific and even founded settlements in such distant islands as Hawaii and Easter Island.

24. John Huxtable Elliott, *Imperial Spain, 1469–1716* (London, 1963), pp. 173–78, 188, 198–99; A.J.R. Russell-Wood, "Iberian Expansion and the Issue of Black Slavery: Changing Portuguese Attitudes, 1440–1770," *American Historical Review* 83 (February 1978), p. 18; Thomas, *Slave Trade*, pp. 76–77, 100–101, 300–301; Parry, *Age of Reconnaissance*, chap. 2; Ralph Davis, *The Rise of the Atlantic Economies* (Ithaca, N.Y., 1973), chap. 14; Richard Ehrenberg, *Capital and Finance in the Age of the Renaissance: A Study of the Fuggers and Their Connections* (New York, 1981), passim.

25. See especially Sidney W. Mintz, *Sweetness and Power: The Place of Sugar in Modern History* (New York, 1985), pp. 37–38, 74–150. For the effects of coffee, sugar, and other slave-grown products on European diets and consumer mentalities, see Ralph A. Austen and Woodruff D. Smith, "Private Tooth Decay as Public Economic Virtue: The Slave-Sugar Triangle, Consumerism, and European Industrialization," in *The Atlantic Slave Trade: Effects on Economies, Societies, and Peoples in Africa, the Americas, and Europe*, ed. Joseph E. Inikori and Stanley L. Engerman (Durham, N.C., 1992), pp. 183–203.

26. Thornton, *Africa and Africans*, pp. 1–9, 36–71.

27. Elizabeth Donnan, ed., *Documents Illustrative of the Slave Trade to America*, 4 vols. (Washington, 1935), vol. 2, p. 255; John Thornton, "Africa: The Source," in *Captive Passage: The Transatlantic Slave Trade and the Making of the Americas* (Washington, 2002), pp. 36–37. The Royal African Company also sought to find out the length of time it took for Africans to march their slaves down to the coast.

28. Thornton, *Africa and Africans*, pp. 72–97; Philip D. Curtin, *Economic Change in Precolonial Africa: Senegambia in the Era of the Slave Trade* (Madison, Wisc., 1974), table 8.10, p. 336 (copy sent to me with e-mails from Professor Robert Harms, October 5 and 6, 2004). On February 8, 2005, Professor Joseph C. Miller stressed the importance in early Africa of "immolating" and using slaves for public human sacrifice, in the second of his David Brion Davis Lectures at Yale, "History and Slavery as Problems in Africa." Almost all of the British travelers who wrote accounts of West Africa in the eighteenth and nineteenth centuries, including William Snelgrave, William Smith, Robert Norris, Archibald Dalzel, Andrew Battell, J. A. Skertchly, and Sir Richard Burton, claimed that human sacrifice was an important part of local religions. As late as the 1860s large numbers of slaves were being sacrificed upon the death of an African king.

29. Thornton, *Africa and Africans*, pp. 38–53, 66–71; Thomas, *Slave Trade*, pp. 315–31.

30. Thornton, *Africa and Africans*, pp. 60–62, 70–74, 94–97; A.C. de C.M. Saunders, *A Social History of Black Slaves and Freedmen in Portugal, 1441–1555* (Cambridge, U.K., 1982), pp. 11–12. David Eltis, e-mail, June 25, 2005. Slaves constituted at least one-third of the crew on 42 percent of the slave ships arriving in Rio de Janeiro from Africa between 1795 and 1811. Herbert S. Klein, *The Atlantic Slave Trade* (Cambridge, U.K., 1999), pp. 85–86.

31. Thornton, *Africa and Africans*, pp. 60–62, 70–74, 94–97. After the forced conversion of Jews, in 1497, the Portuguese government seized many Jewish children from their parents and sent them to São Tomé. Some of the survivors eventually became planters on the island.

32. Eltis, *Coerced and Free Migration*, p. 62, table 1; Thomas, *Slave Trade*, pp. 92–113, 117–27, 141–49, 235–36.

33. Thornton, *Africa and Africans*, pp. 39, 69, 108–9, 213–14, 258; Miller, *Way of Death*, pp. 106–26, 535–69). I also draw on an important Internet exchange: John Thornton's reply to Gloria Emeagwali's posting of an excerpt from King Afonso's (misdated) letter, SLAVERY@LISTSERV.UH.EDU, November 19, 1999.

34. Eltis, *Rise of African Slavery*, pp. 117–18; Saunders, *Social History of Black Slaves*, pp. 11, 13; Thomas, *Slave Trade*, pp. 304, 396, 411–16, 422–23; David Eltis, *Economic Growth and the Ending of the Transatlantic Slave Trade* (New York, 1987), p. 136.

35. *An Abstract of the Evidence Delivered Before a Select Committee of the House of Commons in the Years 1790 and 1791; on the Part of Petitioners for the Abolition of the Slave-Trade* (London, 1791), pp. 33–36, 39.

36. Eltis, *Rise of African Slavery*, pp. 156–57, 165. In the long period from 1662 to 1864, if one combines all the thousands of known slave-ship voyages, the average time is 74 days.

37. Ibid., pp. 157–60.

38. David Eltis and David Richardson, *Extending the Frontiers: Essays on the New Transatlantic Slave Trade Data Base* (New Haven, Forthcoming); Saunders, *Social History of Black Slaves and Freedmen*, pp. 54–55; Russell-Wood, "Iberian Expansion," 21–22.

39. Saunders, *Social History of Black Slaves and Freedmen*, pp. 15–17, 22–23, 28–31, 36–39, 108, 166–68; Russell-Wood, "Iberian Expansion," pp. 23–24, 26–28. For a detailed examination of the ways in which the Church condoned, justified, and participated in the Atlantic Slave System, see John T. Noonan Jr., *A Church That Can and Cannot Change: The Development of Catholic Moral Teaching* (Notre Dame, Ind., 2005), pp. 62–101.

40. Saunders, *Social History of Black Slaves and Freedmen*, pp. 40–41, 105–9, 121–22, 150–51; Debra Blumenthal, "Implements of Labor, Instruments of Honor: Muslim, Eastern and Black African Slaves in Fifteenth-Century Valencia" (Ph.D. dissertation, University of Toronto, 2000), passim; Blumenthal, "Defending Their Masters' Honour: Slaves as Violent Offenders in Fifteenth-Century Valencia," in *"A Great Effusion of Blood"? Interpreting Medieval Violence*, ed. Mark D. Meyerson et al. (Toronto, 2004), pp. 34–56.

41. I stress "nineteenth-century America" since, as we shall later see, black slaves and white indentured servants often had close ties in seventeenth-century Virginia and Maryland.

42. Saunders, *Social History of Black Slaves and Freedmen*, pp. 62–63, 102–5, 168, 174–75. While some Portuguese Jews did own slaves (before the forced conversion to Christianity in 1497), slaves could take advantage of their vulnerability to the Inquisition (pp. 62–63, 159).

43. Noonan, *A Church That Can and Cannot Change*, p. 25. Judge Noonan points out that the early Septuagint (Greek) and Vulgate (Roman Catholic) Bibles "faithfully translated" the Hebrew words for "slave" and "slavery" into their Greek and Latin equivalents. But Noonan stresses that in what he calls "a bowdlerization of the Bible," in the later translations—especially English ones, beginning with John Wyclif's, in 1382, and moving on to the Geneva and King James Bibles—"the rougher terms" disappeared. He is especially concerned about the latter long-enduring and extremely influential translation of 1611, since by 1600 "slave" was associated with blackness (p. 23). The word "slave" had clearly acquired very negative connotations.

    But we should note that the King James Bible's translation of Leviticus 25 makes it clear that the "bondmen" and "bondmaids" taken from "the heathen that are round about you" were meant to be slaves: "And ye shall take them as an inheritance for your children after you, to inherit *them for* a possession; they shall be your bondmen for ever: but over your brethren the children of Israel, ye shall not rule one over another with rigour" (Genesis 25: 45–46). If these biblical mistranslations of Hebrew and Greek "slave" tended to obscure the nearly universal acceptance of slavery in antiquity, they also made it easier for American Southerners to use the term "servants" for *their* slaves.

44. Thomas, *Slave Trade*, pp. 21–24; Russell-Wood, "Iberian Expansion," pp. 30–31.

45. For more detailed views of this "backward" Europe, see Henry Kamen, *Early Modern European Society* (London, 2000); Alison Rowlands, "The Condition of Life for the Masses," in *Early Modern Europe: An Oxford History*, ed. Euan Cameron (Oxford and New York, 1999), pp. 31–62; Mary Lindemann, *Medicine and Society in Early Modern Europe* (Cambridge, U.K., 1999). It is true that in terms of mass killings and torture, the past century has outdone even the worst excesses of the 1400s and 1500s. But most of the modern death camps

and gulags have been concealed, and most of the public, at least in "developed nations," has been insulated from mass killings and the use of torture.

46. Davis, *Problem of Slavery in Western Culture*, pp. 108, n. 35, 187–94; Tomás de Mercado, *Summa de tratos, y contratos* . . . (Seville, 1587), chap. 20; Bartolomé de Albornoz, "De la esclavitud," rpt. from *Arte de los contratos*, in *Biblioteca de autores españoles*, vol. 65, pp. 232–33. Judge Noonan notes that in 1517 the theologian Cajetan, who was master-general of the Dominican order, wrote that "on a living human being, so long as he is held in slavery, personal violence is continually inflicted." But Cajetan was explaining why "one may lawfully liberate Christians held in slavery by the enemy," and during "the Fifth Council of the Lateran, 1512–1518, no orator and no conciliar document touched on what was happening in the New World." Noonan, *A Church That Can and Cannot Change*, pp. 71–72.

47. For the *encomienda*, see Lesley Byrd Simpson, *The Encomienda in New Spain* (1950; rev. ed., Berkeley, 1966), and Robert Himmerich y Valencia, *The Encomenderos of New Spain* (Austin, Texas, 1991). According to the papal bull *sublimes Deus* of 1537, "Indians and all other people who may later be discovered by Christians are by no means to be deprived of their liberty . . . nor should they be in any way enslaved; should the contrary happen, it shall be null and of no effect." But as Noonan points out, the bull "avoided mention of the string of papal authorizations of enslavement" and "was not crafted clearly enough to revoke the earlier approvals." Noonan, *A Church That Can and Cannot Change* pp. 72–73.

48. It has been estimated that European and African diseases killed at least 90 percent of the New World's pre-Columbian inhabitants—at least thirty million and perhaps many more. The classic and now revised work on the effects of European conquest on the ecology and agriculture of the New World is Alfred W. Crosby Jr., *The Columbian Exchange: Biological and Cultural Consequences of 1492* (Westport, Conn., 1972), supplemented by Crosby, *Ecological Imperialism: The Biological Expansion of Europe, 900–1900* (Cambridge, U.K., 1986). For an introduction to some of the later literature, see Neal Salisbury, "The Indians' Old World: Native Americans and the Coming of the Europeans," *William and Mary Quarterly*, 3rd ser., 53 (July 1996): 435–58. For a reassessment of the role of disease in New World colonization, see Noble David Cook, *Born to Die: Disease and New World Conquest, 1492–1650* (Cambridge, U.K., 1998). In the most critical reevaluation of Crosby's thesis regarding "immunologic inadequacy" as the primary cause of Native American mortality, David S. Jones argues that malnutrition, drought, famine, and dislocations resulting from the European invasions increased the Indians' vulnerability to disease and chances of death. "Virgin Soils Revisited," *William and Mary Quarterly*, 3rd ser., 60 (October 2003): 703–42.

49. Las Casas later expressed regret and remorse for having advocated the larger supply of African slaves, but this confession was not completely published until 1951, and there is no indication that Las Casas publicly questioned the enslavement of blacks or advocated their emancipation. He apparently owned slaves himself as late as 1544. Lewis Hanke, *Aristotle and the American Indian: A Study in Race Prejudice in the Modern World* (Chicago, 1959), p. 9. For a more positive but also balanced view of Las Casas, see the case made by Judge John T. Noonan Jr., who points out that "the greatest foe of enslavement of the Indians ended judging himself an accomplice in the unjust enslavement of Africans." Noonan, *A Church That Can and Cannot Change*, pp. 70–77, 217–18.

It should be stressed that while Las Casas challenged the legality of enslaving Indians, and eventually of enslaving Africans, he never questioned the justice of slavery itself.

50. Davis, *Problem of Slavery in Western Culture*, pp. 192–93; Serafim Leite, *História da Companhia de Jesus no Brasil* (Rio de Janeiro and Lisbon, 1938–50), vol. 2, pp. 227, 346–47; VI, 350–51.

51. David Eltis, drawing on the recent work of historians of Africa as well as his own research, repeatedly stresses the theme of "bargaining as equals" as well as the power and influence of Africans on the Atlantic Slave System (*Rise of African Slavery*, pp. 148–92).

52. Michael A. Gomez, *Exchanging Our Country Marks: The Transformation of African Identities in the Colonial and Antebellum South* (Chapel Hill, 1998), p. 37. A surprisingly large percentage of Africans were preadolescent children at the time of their capture. There was also a more even sex ratio among slaves brought to North America, in part because those colonists found it hard to compete with regions to the south for highly prized young adult males.

53. I am greatly indebted to my colleague Professor Robert Harms, whose book *The Diligent: A Voyage Through the Worlds of the Slave Trade* (New York, 2002) is the most graphic and informative account we have of a slave-trading voyage, for his help on this subject. I have also drawn on Patrick Manning, *Slavery and African Life: Occidental, Oriental, and African Slave Trades* (Cambridge, U.K., 1990); Thornton, *Africa and Africans*; Klein, *Atlantic Slave Trade*; and Inikori and Engerman, *Atlantic Slave Trade*. For the historical changes in the European goods purchased by Angolans and others, in exchange for slaves, see Miller, *Way of Death*, pp. 78–94.

54. Paul E. Lovejoy, *Transformations in Slavery: A History of Slavery in Africa*, 2nd ed. (Cambridge, U.K., 2000), pp. 36–43, 49–61; Gomez, *Exchanging Our Country Marks*, pp. 29–33; David Richardson, MS tables based on forthcoming book, David Eltis, Stephen D. Behrendt, and David Richardson, *The Atlantic Slave Trade: A New Census*.

55. Gomez, *Exchanging Our Country Marks*, pp. 1–16, 38–153; John Thornton, *Africa and Africans in the Making of the Atlantic World*, 2nd ed. (Cambridge, U.K., 1998), pp. 320–34.

56. M. I. Finley drew this now widely accepted distinction between the few societies whose economies were in effect driven by slave labor, such as ancient Greece and the British West Indies, and societies in which slaves may have been common but not central to the economy. Finley, *The Ancient Economy*, Berkeley, 1973, pp. 70–83; Finley, "Was Greek Civilization Based on Slave Labor?" in Finley, ed., *Slavery in Classical Antiquity: Views and Controversies* (Cambridge, U.K., 1960), pp. 61–64.

CHAPTER 5

1. For the history of the westward migration of sugar cultivation, see Sidney W. Mintz, *Sweetness and Power: The Place of Sugar in Modern History* (New York, 1985). For the rise of the sugar plantation complex in northern Brazil, I have drawn heavily on Stuart B. Schwartz, "Colonial Brazil, c. 1580–1750: Plantations and Peripheries," in Leslie Bethell, ed., *The Cambridge History of Latin America* (Cambridge, U.K., 1984), vol. 2, pp. 423–30, and especially Schwartz, *Sugar Plantations in the Formation of Brazilian Society: Bahia, 1550–1835* (Cambridge, U.K., 1985).

2. Numbers updated by an e-mail from David Eltis, August 1, 2007, based on the next edition of David Eltis, Stephen D. Behrendt, and David Richardson, *The Atlantic Slave Trade: A New Census*. A large number of slaves were also reexported from the Caribbean to the Spanish mainland.

3. Joseph Ellis, *American Sphinx: The Character of Thomas Jefferson* (New York, 1997), p. 141; David Brion Davis, *In the Image of God: Religion, Moral Values, and Our Heritage of Slavery* (New Haven, 2001), pp. 156–57. Bill Cooke, senior lecturer in organizational analysis at the Manchester, U.K. School of Management, has written that since "ante-bellum slavery is demonstrated to have been managed according to classical management and Taylorian principles," the subject of slavery is "of intrinsic, but hitherto denied, relevance to [modern] management studies." Cooke, "The Denial of Slavery in Management Studies," *Journal of Management Studies* V. 40, no. 8 (December 2003): 1895–18. We might note that even Lenin was captivated by Frederick Winslow Taylor's ideal of scientific management.

4. See David Blight, *Race and Reunion: The Civil War in American Memory* (Cambridge, Mass., 2001) and David Brion Davis, "The Enduring Legacy of the South's Civil War Victory," *New York Times*, "Week in Review," August 26, 2001, sec. 4, pp. 1, 6. As we will see in Chapter Twelve, Seymour Drescher has recently shown that leading British and French political economists quickly retreated from the free-labor ideology associated with Adam Smith, which underscored the economic defects of slavery. Contrary to the hopes of abolitionists, economists in some ways anticipated the views of late twentieth-century "Econometricians" regarding the cheapness, efficiency, and profitability of New World slave labor, and thus warned of the economic costs of emancipation. Drescher, *The Mighty Experiment: Free Labor versus Slavery in British Emancipation* (New York, 2002), pp. 54–72, 202–37.

5. For the profitability of the Brazilian sugar trade, see C. R. Boxer, *The Portuguese Seaborne Empire, 1415–1825* (New York, 1969), pp. 104–5.

6. For views of such diversity, see Verene A. Shepherd, *Slavery Without Sugar: Diversity in Caribbean Economy and Society Since the Seventeenth Century* (Gainesville, Fla., 2002). Unlike the Caribbean economies, the sugar plantations of northeastern Brazil stimulated the growth of inland food production and even the export of animal hides and other commodities, which made the plantations far less dependent on imports than those in the West Indies.

7. J. R. Ward, *British West Indian Slavery, 1750–1834: The Process of Amelioration* (Oxford, 1988), pp. 14–17, 75–76; Richard S. Dunn, *Sugar and Slaves: The Rise of the Planter Class in the English West Indies, 1624–1713* (Chapel Hill, 1972), pp. 190–92; Elsa V. Goveia, *Slave Society in the British Leeward Islands at the End of the Eighteenth Century* (New Haven, 1965), pp. 118–20; Schwartz, "Colonial Brazil," pp. 431–35. Some of the sugar workers on the Canary Islands and other locations were indentured servants, not slaves.

8. Janet Schaw, *Journal of a Lady of Quality*, ed. E.W. and C.M. Andrews (New Haven, 1939), pp. 127–28; Ward, *British West Indian Slavery*, pp. 15, 75–76.

9. Ward, *British West Indian Slavery*, pp. 16–18, 99, 101–3; Goveia, *Slave Society in the British Leeward Islands*, pp. 130–32, Dunn, *Sugar and Slaves*, pp. 192–95; Goveia, *Slave Society in the British Leeward Islands*, pp. 130–32.

10. Schwartz, *Sugar Plantations in the Formation of Brazilian Society*, pp. 101, 105–6; Stuart B. Schwartz, *Slaves, Peasants, and Rebels: Reconsidering Brazilian Slavery*

(Urbana, Ill., 1996), pp. 41, 105; Sidney M. Greenfield, "Plantations, Sugar Cane and Slavery," in *Roots and Branches: Current Directions in Slave Studies,* ed. Michael Craton (Toronto, 1979), pp. 85–119.

11. Mintz, *Sweetness and Power,* pp. 46–60; Schwartz, *Sugar Plantations in the Formation of Brazilian Society,* pp. 142–45.

12. Mintz, *Sweetness and Power,* p. 50; Schwartz, *Sugar Plantations in the Formation of Brazilian Society,* p. 143.

13. Quoted in Mintz, *Sweetness and Power,* pp. 50, 48.

14. Hugh Thomas, *The Slave Trade: The Story of the Atlantic Slave Trade, 1440–1870* (New York, 1997), pp. 67–149.

15. Mintz, *Sweetness and Power,* p. 33. It was the western third of the island, the French colony of Saint-Domingue (later Haiti), that became the richest sugar-producing colony in the New World.

16. Ibid., pp. 32–35; Noel Deerr, *The History of Sugar,* 2 vols. (London, 1949), vol. I, pp. 132–34, 137, 139–40. Though the Spaniards had imported some African slaves in Seville and Valencia as well as the Canary Islands, the Portuguese had had far more experience with black slave labor in Lisbon and on plantations in their Atlantic islands.

17. Schwartz, *Sugar Plantations in the Formation of Brazilian Society,* pp. 91, 160–64, 169–72, 180; Dunn, *Sugar and Slaves,* pp. 10–11.

18. Quoted in Mintz, *Sweetness and Power,* p. 37. For English privateers' raids on Spanish and Portuguese trade routes, see Dunn, *Sugar and Slaves,* pp. 10–11; J. H. Parry, *The Age of Reconnaissance* (London, 1963), pp. 182–83.

19. Edmund S. Morgan, *American Slavery, American Freedom* (New York, 1975), pp. 9–14; Dunn, *Sugar and Slaves,* pp. 3–45. There was a general understanding that fighting or wars west of the prime meridian in the mid-Atlantic or south of the Tropic of Cancer would not impinge upon peace in Europe.

20. The city of Salvador, in Bahia, became the capital of all Brazil.

21. Dunn, *Sugar and Slaves,* p. 48; Mintz, *Sweetness and Power,* p. 36; Schwartz, *Sugar Plantations in the Formation of Brazilian Society,* pp. 91, 180.

22. Boxer, *Dutch Seaborne Empire,* pp. 23–26, 87–90, 94, 101, 242–44; Parry, *Age of Reconnaissance,* pp. 186–89, 260–63; Dunn, *Sugar and Slaves,* pp. 59–61; Mintz, *Sweetness and Power,* p. 36.

23. Dunn, *Sugar and Slaves,* pp. 8, 19–23, 119, 149–53, 161–63.

24. Seymour Drescher, *Econocide: British Slavery in the Era of Abolition* (Pittsburgh, 1977), pp. 21–23.

25. Gary B. Nash, *The Urban Crucible: Social Change, Political Consciousness, and the Origins of the American Revolution* (Cambridge, Mass., 1979), pp. 54–55, 77–78, 112–13, 123–24, 165, 176–79, 237–38, 271; Mintz, *Sweetness and Power,* pp. 180–81; Dunn, *Sugar and Slaves,* pp. 97, 188, 201–12; Goveia, *Slave Society in the British Leeward Islands,* pp. 1–5.

26. For the religious foundations of antislavery thought, especially in the English civil wars, see David Brion Davis, *The Problem of Slavery in Western Culture* (New York, 1988), pp. 291–316. I would now put even more emphasis on Britain's civil wars, the Putney debates, and the emergence of radical religious groups including the Quakers. It was chiefly this political and religious experience that differentiated Britain from Holland, which, despite its Protestantism and advanced market economy, later gave rise to no significant antislavery movements. For a comparison of Britain and Holland, against the backdrop of

capitalism and antislavery, see David Brion Davis, "The Perils of Doing History by Ahistorical Abstraction," in *The Antislavery Debate: Capitalism and Abolitionism as a Problem in Historical Interpretation*, ed. Thomas Bender (Berkeley, 1992), pp. 290–309.

27. Dunn, *Sugar and Slaves*, pp. 59–69. Unfortunately, Russell R. Menard's *Sweet Negotiations: Sugar, Slavery, and Plantation Agriculture in Early Barbados* (Charlottesville, 2006) was published too late to be of use in this book.

28. Dunn, *Sugar and Slaves*, p. 106. Though there were quite a few New Christians, or Portuguese of Jewish descent, among the Brazilian planters, some of whom were arrested and persecuted by the Inquisition, New Christian money helped finance the Portuguese reconquest and thus the expulsion of all unconverted Jews from Brazil. Suriname was the only New World colony in which a significant number of Jews became slaveholding planters.

29. Dunn, *Sugar and Slaves*, p. 67.

30. Ibid., pp. 87, 116.

31. Ibid. p. 116. One should add that after the British abolished slavery and apprenticeship in the 1830s, Barbados remained a highly productive colony. Unlike Jamaica and Trinidad, there was no unsettled land and former slaves had few if any alternatives to work on sugar plantations.

32. Ibid., pp. 64–65.

33. Ward, *British West Indian Slavery*, pp. 2–4, 18–22, 201–2.

34. B. W. Higman, *Slave Populations of the British Caribbean, 1807–1834* (Baltimore, 1984), passim; Philip D. Morgan, *Slave Counterpoint: Black Culture in the Eighteenth-Century Chesapeake and Lowcountry* (Chapel Hill, 1998), pp. 79–95, 101, 143, 163.

35. Davis, *Problem of Slavery in Western Culture*, p. 232; C. R. Boxer, *The Golden Age of Brazil, 1695–1750: Growing Pains of a Colonial Society* (Berkeley, 1962), p. 174.

36. Stuart B. Schwartz, *Slaves, Peasants, and Rebels*, p. 42.

37. Schwartz, *Sugar Plantations in the Formation of Brazilian Society*, p. 365; Schwartz, *Slaves, Peasants, and Rebels*, pp. 41–42; Dunn, *Sugar and Slaves*, p. 320.

38. Schwartz, *Slaves, Peasants, and Rebels*, p. 41; Schwartz, "Colonial Brazil," pp. 442–48; Richard B. Sheridan, *Doctors and Slaves: A Medical and Demographic History of Slavery in the British West Indies, 1680–1834* (Cambridge, U.K., 1985), passim; Kenneth F. Kiple, *The Caribbean Slave: A Biological History* (Cambridge, U.K., 1984), passim. In northeastern Brazil the annual rate of slave population decline seems to have increased from 3 percent or less to 5 percent and even 8 percent in the nineteenth century. Schwartz, *Sugar Plantations in the Formation of Brazilian Society*, p. 365. The rate of slave manumissions, at least before the 1880s, was far too low to have a significant effect on total population numbers.

39. For a discussion of the demographic "success" of North American slaves compared to those in the Caribbean and South America, see Michael Tadman, "The Demographic Cost of Sugar: Debates on Slave Societies and Natural Increase in the Americas," *American Historical Review* 105 (2000): 1534–75.

40. Stuart Schwartz explains that while *lavrador* could refer to anyone engaged in agriculture, "the term was usually modified by a description of the crop produced." In Bahia that meant that cane farmers "were a kind of farmer elite," who took pride "in their association with sugar," even though the group included people of "far humbler backgrounds and resources" than the *senhores de*

engenho, the wealthy planters. Schwartz, *Sugar Plantations in the Formation of Brazilian Society,* pp. 295–96.

41. Ibid., pp. 298–99.
42. Ibid., p. 99.
43. Ibid., p. 257.
44. Schwartz, *Slaves, Peasants, and Rebels,* pp. 42–43; Schwartz, *Sugar Plantations in the Formation of Brazilian Society,* pp. 133–34, 257. Readers were long misled by the claim, advanced by such historians as Gilberto Freyre and Frank Tannenbaum, that slavery in Brazil (and in Latin America in general) was far more humane and benign than slavery in North America. Numerous well-researched works have now undermined that myth, which, as Robert E. Conrad has observed, was based in part on the "inventions of former defenders and apologists of Brazilian slavery." Conrad, *Children of Fire: A Documentary History of Black Slavery in Brazil* (Princeton, 1983), pp. xx–xxiii.
45. Mary C. Karasch, *Slave Life in Rio de Janeiro, 1808–1850* (Princeton, 1987), passim.
46. See sources cited in Davis, *Problem of Slavery in Western Culture,* pp. 237–38, 283–84, 291; Schwartz, *Sugar Plantations in the Formation of Brazilian Society,* pp. 188–89; Emilia Viotti da Costa, *The Brazilian Empire: Myths and Histories* (Chicago, 1985), pp. 145–47.
47. Stanley J. Stein, *Vassouras: A Brazilian Coffee County, 1850–1900* (Cambridge, Mass., 1957), passim; Warren Dean, *Rio Claro: A Brazilian Plantation System, 1820–1920* (Stanford, 1976), pp. 24–87; Robert Conrad, *The Destruction of Brazilian Slavery, 1850–1888* (Berkeley, 1972), pp. 3–19, 58–59; Emilia Viotti da Costa, "The Political Emancipation of Brazil," in *From Colony to Nation,* ed. A.J.R. Russell-Wood (Baltimore, 1975), pp. 43–88; da Costa, *The Brazilian Empire,* pp. 145–47; Robert Slenes, "The Demography and Economics of Slavery, 1850–1888" (Ph.D. dissertation, Stanford University, 1976), p. 123; papers by Slenes and Richard Graham, conference on "Domestic Passages: Internal Slave Trades in the Americas, 1808–1888," at Yale's Gilder Lehrman Center for the Study of Slavery, Resistance, and Abolition, October 22–24, 1999.
48. Mintz, *Sweetness and Power,* pp. 143–44, 161, 196–97.
49. As Robert Brent Toplin points out, these young *ingenuos* were generally treated as slaves until they reached the age of twenty-one, and the first "maturity" date fell four and one-half years after the 1888 abolition law. In addition, "government agents had great difficulty conducting a census of slaves in the empire because of the problems involved in obtaining accurate information concerning isolated plantations and the reluctance of some slaveholders to cooperate." Accordingly, there was "no significant shift downward in the slave population [from the Rio Branco Law of 1871] until the mid-1880s. . . . In fact, by including the *ingenuos* in the slave totals of 1885, the sum shows, if anything, a slight increase in the slave population. Robert Brent Toplin, *The Abolition of Slavery in Brazil* (New York, 1972), pp. 20–21.
50. For some of the complex ties between Brazil and part of Africa, see "Rethinking the African Diaspora: The Making of a Black Atlantic World in the Bight of Benin and Brazil," ed. Kristin Mann and Edna G. Bay, special issue, *Slavery & Abolition* 22 (April 2001).
51. Carolyn E. Fick, *The Making of Haiti: The Saint Domingue Revolution From Below* (Knoxville, Tenn., 1990), p. 19. In striking contrast to other colonies,

the *affranchis*, or freed blacks and mainly mulattoes, "owned one-third of the plantation property, one-quarter of the slaves, and one-quarter of the real estate property in Saint-Domingue."

52. For more extended accounts of my experiences in a racially segregated army, see Davis, "World War II and Memory," *Journal of American History* 77 (September 1990: 380–87 and "The Americanized Mannheim of 1945–1946," in *American Places: Encounters With History: A Celebration of Sheldon Meyer*, ed. William E. Leuchtenburg (New York, 2000), pp. 79–91.

53. For samples of a vast literature on this subject, see Goveia, *Slave Society in the British Leeward Islands*, pp. 244–46; Dunn, *Sugar and Slaves*, pp. 250–51; Ira Berlin and Philip D. Morgan, eds., *Cultivation and Culture: Labor and the Shaping of Slave Life in the Americas* (Charlottesville, 1993); Thomas C. Holt, *The Problem of Freedom: Race, Labor, and Politics in Jamaica and Britain, 1832–1938* (Baltimore, 1992); Sidney W. Mintz and Richard Price, *The Birth of African-American Culture* (Boston, 1992).

54. See Chapter Eleven, and also Michael Craton, *Testing the Chains: Resistance to Slavery in the British West Indies* (Ithaca, N.Y., 1982).

CHAPTER 6

1. Leslie M. Harris, *In the Shadow of Slavery: African Americans in New York City, 1616–1863* (Chicago, 2003), pp. 15–16; Ira Berlin, *Many Thousands Gone: The First Two Centuries of Slavery in North America* (Cambridge, Mass., 1998), p. 369, table l. For a brief and excellent overview, see Betty Wood, *The Origins of American Slavery: Freedom and Bondage in the English Colonies* (New York, 1997).

2. John H. Moore, "Simon Gray, Riverman: A Slave Who Was Almost Free," *Mississippi Valley Historical Review* (now *Journal of American History*) 49 (December 1962), pp. 472–84; Philip D. Morgan, *Slave Counterpoint: Black Culture in the Eighteenth-Century Chesapeake and Lowcountry* (Chapel Hill, 1998), pp. 324–25. I should stress that there was also extraordinary diversity among slaves in other New World regions, especially Brazil. But this book must necessarily be limited in examples, and its ultimate focus is the land that became the United States.

3. P. Morgan, *Slave Counterpoint*, p. xxiv.

4. Ibid., pp. 659–60.

5. Elizabeth Donnan, ed., *Documents Illustrative of the History of the Slave Trade to America* (Washington, 1930–1935), vol. 3, pp. 6–9, 108–9; Winthrop D. Jordan, *White Over Black: American Attitudes Toward the Negro, 1550–1812* (Williamsburg, Va., 1968), pp. 69–71. Though the Hebrew Bible prescribes the penalty of death for "man-stealing," it was not inflicted on these Massachusetts sailors. (Exodus 21:16: "And he that stealeth a man, and selleth him, or if he be found in his hand, he shall surely be put to death." Of course, the Bible also positively sanctions slavery, and the passage on man-stealing clearly applied to a very limited and specific kind of kidnapping).

6. Quoted by Jean R. Soderland, in "Quakers," in *Macmillan Encyclopedia of World Slavery*, ed. Paul Finkelman and Joseph C. Miller, vol. 2 (New York, 1998), pp. 751–52.

7. David Brion Davis, *The Problem of Slavery in Western Culture*, rev. ed. (New York, 1988), pp. 307–9.

8. Ibid., pp. 342–48. By basing his tract on the biblical story of Joseph, who was physically assaulted and then sold to slave traders by his brothers, Sewall made excellent use of one of the few biblical narratives that could be read as containing an antislavery message.

9. My discussion of colonial New Amsterdam, New York, and East Jersey draws heavily on Graham Russell Hodges, *Root and Branch: African Americans in New York and East Jersey, 1613–1863* (Chapel Hill, 1999), and Harris, *In the Shadow of Slavery.*

10. Ira Berlin, in *Many Thousands Gone*, devotes much attention to these multilingual, multicultural slaves and free blacks, whom he terms "Atlantic creoles" (pp. 17–28, 39–45, 65, 90–91, 115, 183, 268). The term and concept are important and help to counteract the past tendency to think of slaves in the early periods as Africans who were wholly alien to Western culture and values. Yet there is a danger, which Berlin avoids, of envisioning most of the seventeenth-century slaves and none of the later ones as Atlantic Creoles.

11. Hodges, *Root and Branch*, pp. 18–23, 33.

12. Berlin, *Many Thousands Gone*, p. 54.

13. *Historical Statistics of the United States, Colonial Times to 1970*, bicentennial ed. (Washington, 1975), vol. 2, p. 1168, ser. Z 1–19.

14. Ibid., pp. 369–70, table 1.

15. Harris, *In the Shadow of Slavery*, pp. 11–14, 30–31; Hodges, *Root and Branch*, p. 41 and passim.

16. Ralph Foster Weld, *Slavery in Connecticut* (New Haven, 1935), pp. 8–9.

17. Hodges, *Root and Branch*, passim; Harris, *In the Shadow of Slavery*, passim.

18. Jill Lepore has noted that in contrast to the Salem witchcraft trials and executions, the story of the New York slave conspiracy has received very little attention in what we might call "American memory." *Proceedings of the American Antiquarian Society* 110, pt. 2 (2000): 272–76. Lepore's prizewinning book *New York Burning: Liberty, Slavery, and Conspiracy in Eighteenth-Century Manhattan* (New York, 2005) appeared too late for me to use.

19. Berlin, *Many Thousands Gone*, pp. 182–94.

20. T. H. Breen and Stephen Innes, *"Myne Owne Ground": Race and Freedom on Virginia's Eastern Shore, 1640–1676* (New York, 1980), pp. 9–17, 73–75, 83. As a freedman Payne had a white wife, but it is unclear whether she was the same wife that he liberated. Berlin, *Many Thousands Gone*, p. 44; Edmund S. Morgan, *American Slavery, American Freedom: The Ordeal of Colonial Virginia* (New York, 1975), p. 334.

21. Ira Berlin, "Time, Space, and the Evolution of Afro-American Society on British Mainland North America," *American Historical Review* 85 (1980): 69. There is a slightly different version of this statement in Berlin, *Many Thousands Gone*, p. 45.

22. Ibid.

23. E. Morgan, *American Slavery, American Freedom*, pp. 333–37; P. Morgan, *Slave Counterpoint*, pp. 14–16; Jordan, *White Over Black*, pp. 78–80.

24. P. Morgan, *Slave Counterpoint*, pp. 216–17.

25. Ibid., p. 267 and passim.

26. Ibid., p. 297.

27. Jordan, *White Over Black*, p. 143.

28. E. Morgan, *American Slavery, American Freedom*, p. 386.

29. Davis, *Problem of Slavery in Western Culture*, pp. 144–50.

30. P. Morgan, *Slave Counterpoint*, pp. 567–75.

31. For the much-neglected subject of property owned by slaves, see Dylan C. Penningroth, *The Claims of Kinfolk: African American Property and Community in the Nineteenth-Century South* (Chapel Hill, 2003), and also Robert Olwell, *Masters, Slaves, and Subjects: The Culture of Power in South Carolina* (Ithaca, N.Y., 1998).

32. Peter H. Wood, *Black Majority: Negroes in Colonial South Carolina From 1670 Through the Stono Rebellion* (New York, 1974), pp. 28–34, 59–62. See also Judith Ann Carney, *Black Rice: The African Origins of Rice Cultivation in America* (Cambridge, Mass., 2001).

33. Carney, *Black Rice*, pp. 124–30; Berlin, *Many Thousands Gone*, pp. 66–67; P. Morgan, *Slave Counterpoint*, pp. 17–18. For the military use of slaves throughout history, see Christopher Leslie Brown and Philip D. Morgan, eds., *Arming Slaves: From Classical Times to the Modern Age* (New Haven, 2006).

34. Berlin, *Many Thousands Gone*, p. 70.

35. Helen T. Catterall, ed., *Judicial Cases Concerning American Slavery and the Negro* (Washington, 1926–37), vol. 1, p. 330; vol. 2, pp. 269, 346–59, 385–86; vol. 3, pp. 392–93. The laws of American states differed considerably on the degree of black ancestry required for legal disabilities or slavery. In Virginia and Kentucky less than one-fourth part of "Negro blood" was *prima facie* evidence of freedom. As late as 1835 a South Carolina judge argued that "the condition [a colored person] . . . is not to be determined solely by . . . visible mixture . . . but by reputation . . . and it may be . . . proper, that a man of worth . . . should have the rank of a white man, while a vagabond of the same degree should be confined to the inferior caste."

36. Philip D. Morgan, "Black Life in Eighteenth-Century Charleston," *Perspectives in American History* 1 (1984): 187–232.

37. Morgan, *Slave Counterpoint*, pp. 358–67.

38. Ibid., pp. 373–76.

39. Ibid., pp. 455–56, 470.

CHAPTER 7

1. For a "counterfactual" analysis of the possible history of Anglo-American slavery if the British North American colonies had not won independence, see my essay "American Slavery and the American Revolution," in *Slavery and Freedom in the Age of the American Revolution*, ed. Ira Berlin and Ronald Hoffman (Charlottesville, Va., 1983), pp. 262–80.

2. East Florida, long a haven for fugitive American slaves, became a refuge for American Loyalists and their slaves as well as a region for guerrilla warfare during the American Revolution.

3. For general background, see Robert R. Palmer, *The Age of the Democratic Revolution*, 2 vols. (Princeton, 1959, 1964); Jonathan R. Dull, *A Diplomatic History of the American Revolution* (New Haven, 1985), pp. 66–72; Jacques Godechot, *France and the Atlantic Revolution of the Eighteenth-Century, 1770–1799*, trans. Herbert H. Rowen (New York, 1965); Peggy K. Liss, *Atlantic Empires: The Network of Trade and Revolution, 1713–1826* (Baltimore, 1983); Elise Marienstras, ed., *L'Amérique et la France: Deux révolutions* (Paris, 1990); Joseph

Klaits and Michael Haltzel, eds., *The Global Ramifications of the French Revolution* (Washington, 1994); David Brion Davis, *The Problem of Slavery in the Age of Revolution, 1770–1823* (New York, 1999).

4. David Eltis, *Economic Growth and the Ending of the Transatlantic Slave Trade* (New York, 1987), passim.

5. Department of Commerce, Bureau of the Census, *Negro Population in the United States, 1790–1915* (Washington, 1918), p. 57, table 6.

6. Davis, *Problem of Slavery in the Age of Revolution*, pp. 59–60.

7. Daniel Pipes, *Slave Soldiers and Islam: The Genesis of a Military System* (New Haven, 1981), passim. For a broad comparative view of the arming of slaves in various historical settings, see Christopher Leslie Brown and Philip D. Morgan, eds., *Arming Slaves: From Classical Times to the Modern Age* (New Haven, 2006).

8. Ira Berlin, *Many Thousands Gone: The First Two Centuries of Slavery in North America* (Cambridge, Mass., 1998), pp. 66–67.

9. Roger Norman Buckley, *Slaves in Red Coats: The British West India Regiments, 1795–1815* (New Haven, 1979), passim.

10. John V. Lombardi, *The Decline and Abolition of Negro Slavery in Venezuela, 1820* (Westport, Conn., 1971), pp. 35–78; Peter M. Voelz, *Slave and Soldier: The Military Impact of Blacks in the Colonial Americas* (New York, 1993), passim.

11. David Brion Davis, *The Problem of Slavery in Western Culture*, rev. ed. (New York, 1988), pp. 291–493; James G. Basker, *Amazing Grace: An Anthology of Poems About Slavery, 1660–1810* (New Haven, 2002), passim.

12. Sylvia R. Frey, *Water From the Rock: Black Resistance in a Revolutionary Age* (Princeton, 1991), p. 50.

13. Benjamin Quarles, "The Revolutionary War as a Black Declaration of Independence," in Berlin and Hoffman, *Slavery and Freedom in the Age of the American Revolution*, pp. 283–84.

14. James Boswell, *The Life of Samuel Johnson*, Modern Library ed. (New York, n.d.), pp. 747–48; Richard Dunn, "Black Society in the Chesapeake, 1776–1810," in Berlin and Hoffman, *Slavery and Freedom*, pp. 74–75; Philip D. Morgan, "Black Society in the Lowcountry, 1760–1810," in ibid., 115–17; Ira Berlin, *Many Thousands Gone: The First Two Centuries of Slavery in North America* (Cambridge, Mass., 1998), p. 259.

15. Edmund S. Morgan, *American Slavery, American Freedom: The Ordeal of Colonial Virginia* (New York, 1975). It should be added that Morgan's thesis does not account for the New Englanders' and other Northerners' dedication to freedom and equality for all whites. But as Morgan emphasizes, Virginians had a leading role in fighting for independence and founding the Republic. And antiblack racism surely played a role in the North—even in decisions to abolish slavery, often with the hope that the freed blacks could ultimately be "colonized" elsewhere.

16. Dunn, "Black Society," p. 52.

17. Winthrop D. Jordan, *White Over Black: American Attitudes Toward the Negro, 1550–1812* (Chapel Hill, 1968), p. 403.

18. Rush to Jacques Barbeu Dubourg, in *Ephémérides du citoyen* 9 (1769): 172–74.

19. *The Papers of Thomas Jefferson*, ed. Julian P. Boyd (Princeton, 1950–), vol. 1, p. 426. Jefferson also added that the king (meaning the British government and especially Virginia's royal governor, Lord Dunmore) "is now exciting those very people [the black slaves] to rise in arms among us, and to purchase that

liberty of which *he* has deprived them, by murdering the people upon whom *he* also obtruded them; thus paying off former crimes committed against the *liberties* of one people, with crimes which he urges them to commit against the *lives* of another." I disagree with some historians who see in this passage a flagrant contradiction of Jefferson's earlier moral condemnation of the African slave trade. One could be a sincere abolitionist and still protest attempts to incite a slave rebellion that would result in the killing of one's own people. In any event, representatives from the Deep South would never tolerate Jefferson's words that morally indicted the origins and foundation of the entire slave system.

20. Petition printed in Gary B. Nash, *Race and Revolution* (Madison, Wisc., 1990), pp. 171–73.

21. Frey, *Water From the Rock*, p. 51.

22. Eric Robert Papenfuse, "*The Evils of Necessity*: Robert Goodloe Harper and the Moral Dilemma of Slavery" (M.A. dissertation, Yale University, 1993), pp. 9–17.

23. Nash, *Race and Revolution*, pp. 173–74.

24. Frey, *Water From the Rock*, p. 77. For an overall view, see Philip D. Morgan and Andrew Jackson O'Shaughnessy, "Arming Slaves in the American Revolution," in P. Morgan and Brown, *Arming Slaves*, pp. 180–208.

25. A number of historians, drawing on Philip Foner's *Labor and the American Revolution* (Westport, Conn., 1976), p. 178, have quoted Washington proclaiming that the outcome of the war hinged "on which side can arm the Negroes the faster," but these words do not appear in the source that Foner cites, Washington's letter to Richard Henry Lee, December 26, 1775, nor in his letter to Joseph Reed, December 15, 1775. Philander D. Chase, ed., *The Papers of George Washington: Revolutionary War Series* (Charlottesville, Va., 1985), vol. 2, pp. 611, 553. Washington did change his mind and helped to persuade Congress to allow the enlistment of free blacks.

26. Frey, *Water From the Rock*, pp. 78–79; Sidney Kaplan, *The Black Presence in the Era of the American Revolution, 1770–1800* (Washington, 1973), pp. 55–59.

27. Alexander Hamilton to John Jay, March 14, 1779, in *The Papers of Alexander Hamilton*, ed. Harold C. Syrett (New York and London, 1961), vol. 2, pp. 17–19. I am much indebted to Philipp Ziesche for calling this letter to my attention. It is worth noting that both Hamilton and Jay combined a slaveholding background with a serious opposition to slavery. Though born and brought up in the Caribbean slave colonies, Hamilton could tell Jay that he favored future emancipation, "for the dictates of humanity and true policy equally interest me in favour of this unfortunate class of men." He later became an active member of the abolitionist society in New York City.

28. Donald L. Robinson, *Slavery in the Structure of American Politics, 1765–1820* (New York, 1971), pp. 118–22. George Washington, who had become close to young men like John Laurens and Alexander Hamilton, who favored the use of black soldiers, seems to have been sympathetic to the Laurens plan (p.121).

29. Frey, *Water From the Rock*, pp. 54–73. The American diplomat Silas Deane threatened at various times to play "their own game on them" by inciting slave insurrections in places like Jamaica, where in 1776 there was a massive uprising that resulted in more than thirty executions. Ibid., p. 71; Davis, *Problem of Slavery in the Age of Revolution*, p. 74.

30. Philip D. Morgan, *Slave Counterpoint: Black Culture in the Eighteenth-Century Chesapeake and Lowcountry* (Williamsburg, Va., 1998), p. 667.

31. Slavery persisted in Bolivia until 1861 and in Paraguay until 1869.

32. Frey, *Water From the Rock*, pp. 113–19. Frey adds: "In a practice reminiscent of the Romans, the British army claimed thousands of captive slaves as state property and used them on public works or as agricultural laborers, with the promise of manumission as an incentive for loyal work" (p. 123).

33. Ibid., pp. 86, 107.

34. Ibid., pp. 169–70; James Oliver Horton, *Free People of Color: Inside the African American Community* (Washington, 1993), p. 148.

35. For the fate of liberated blacks in Nova Scotia, see Mary Louise Clifford, *From Slavery to Freetown: Black Loyalists After the American Revolution* (Jefferson, N.C., 1999); Ellen G. Wilson, *The Loyal Blacks* (New York, 1976); James W. St. G. Walker, *The Black Loyalists: The Search for a Promised Land in Nova Scotia and Sierra Leone, 1783–1870* (London, 1976).

36. Granville Sharp to Dr. John Coakley Lettsom, October 13, 1788, Clarkson Papers, Henry E. Huntington Library; James Walvin, *Black and White: The Negro and English Society, 1555–1945* (London, 1973), p. 147.

37. For the importance of these negotiations in committing the United States to a defense of slavery, see Don E. Fehrenbacher, *The Slaveholding Republic: An Account of the United States Government's Relations to Slavery*, completed and ed. Ward M. McAfee (New York, 2001), pp. 15–47.

38. Robert William Fogel and Stanley L. Engerman, "Philanthropy at Bargain Prices: Notes on the Economics of Gradual Emancipation," *Journal of Legal Studies*, University of Chicago Law School, vol. 3, no. 2 (June 1974), 377–401.

39. Leonard P. Curry, *The Free Black in Urban America, 1800–1850: The Shadow of the Dream* (Chicago, 1981), p. 115. Curry also writes that "roughly the same proportion of white and black prisoners were committed for rape and arson, but black prisoners were much more likely than whites (by a margin of 7:4) to have been convicted of various kinds of theft" (or "jailed for violation of minor city ordinances").

40. For the subject of racism in the North, I have drawn on two outstanding works that illuminate the nature and depth of such prejudice: James Oliver Horton and Lois E. Horton, *In Hope of Liberty: Culture, Community, and Protest Among Northern Free Blacks, 1700–1860* (New York, 1997), and Joanne Pope Melish, *Disowning Slavery: Gradual Emancipation and "Race" in New England, 1780–1860* (Ithaca, N.Y., 1998).

41. Julie Winch, *Philadelphia's Black Elite: Activism, Accommodation, and the Struggle for Autonomy, 1787–1848* (Philadelphia, 1988); Winch, *A Gentleman of Color: The Life of James Forten* (New York, 2002).

42. Curry, *Free Black in Urban America*, p. 239.

43. Gary B. Nash and Jean Soderlund, *Freedom by Degrees: Emancipation in Pennsylvania and its Aftermath* (New York, 1991), p. 170.

44. For other works on blacks in the North, see James Oliver Horton, *Free People of Color: Inside the African American Community* (Washington, 1983); James Oliver Horton and Lois E. Horton, *Black Bostonians* (New York, 1979); and Gary B. Nash, *Forging Freedom: The Formation of Philadelphia's Black Community, 1720–1840* (Cambridge, Mass., 1988).

45. Davis, *Problem of Slavery in the Age of Revolution*, p. 306.

46. Ibid., pp. 174–77.

47. As in current efforts to avoid "politically incorrect" words, there is a particular irony in the Framers' abolition of a word that had no etymological connections with Africans or people of African descent. As we have seen, the western European words for "slave" derived from the Latin *sclavus,* meaning a Slav or Slavic person. Most slaves in the medieval Mediterranean were Slavs or considered Slavs. Like the Hebrew and Greek words for "slave," the Latin *servus* had no ethnic connotations. One should also note that many slaveholders, like the Framers of the Constitution tried to avoid the word "slave" and preferred "servant" or "Negro."

48. *Annals of Congress,* 1st Cong., 2nd Sess., 1224–30, 1239–42, 1244–48, 1501–23; Pennsylvania Abolition Society MSS, vol. 2, pp. 30–40, Historical Society of Pennsylvania; *Federal Gazette,* March 23, 1790.

49. See Peter P. Hinks, ed., *David Walker's Appeal to the Coloured Citizens of the World* (University Park, Pa., 2000).

CHAPTER 8

1. This is a revised, updated, and much expanded version of an essay that appeared in David P. Geggus, ed., *The Impact of the Haitian Revolution in the Atlantic World* (Columbia, S.C., 2001), pp. 3–14. Some of the other important secondary works on which I have drawn are Yves Bénot and Marcel Dorigny, eds., *Rétablissement de l'esclavage dan les colonies françaises, 1802: Aux origins d'Haiti* (Paris, 2003); Yves Bénot, *La révolution française et la fin des colonies: Essai* (Paris, 1987); David B. Gaspar and David P. Geggus, eds., *A Turbulent Time: The French Revolution and the Greater Caribbean* (Bloomington, Ind., 1997); Carolyn E. Fick, *The Making of Haiti: The Saint Domingue Revolution From Below* (Knoxville, Tenn., 1990); Robin Blackburn, *The Overthrow of Colonial Slavery, 1776–1848* (London, 1988); Laurent Dubois, *Avengers of the New World: The Story of the Haitian Revolution* (Cambridge, Mass., 2004); David Geggus, "The Arming of Slaves in the Haitian Revolution," in *Arming Slaves: From Classical Times to the Modern Age,* ed. Christopher Leslie Brown and Philip D. Morgan (New Haven, 2006), pp. 209–32); Alfred N. Hunt, *Haiti's Influence on Antebellum America: Slumbering Volcano in the Caribbean* (Baton Rouge, 1988; page numbers refer to Hunt's dissertation, "The Influence of Haiti on the Antebellum South, 1791–1865" [Ph.D. dissertation, University of Texas at Austin, 1975]).

2. *Chicago Tribune,* January 3, 1893; "Lecture on Haiti," in Frederick Douglass, *The Life and Writings of Frederick Douglass,* ed. Philip S. Foner, 5 vols. (New York, 1950–75), vol. 4, pp. 484–86. The speech recorded in the *Chicago Tribune* differs substantially from the text preserved in the Library of Congress and reprinted by Foner. I have drawn on both versions. The *Tribune* noted that the dedication ceremony, which was planned to commemorate the eighty-ninth anniversary of Haitian independence, had not been "advertised to any extent" and was apparently attended by only one Exposition official, who rushed to the scene just in time to make a speech. Douglass had been involved in an uphill struggle to win some recognition at the Exposition of black achievement. See Elliott M. Rudwick and August Meier, "Black Man in the 'White City': Negroes and the Columbian Exposition, 1893," *Phylon* 26 (Winter 1965): 354–61; and Robert W. Rydell, *All the World's a Fair: Visions of Empire at*

American International Expositions, 1876–1916 (Chicago, 1984), pp. 52–55. It was only with the achievement of independence, on January 1, 1804, that the former slaves replaced the name of the French colony, Saint-Domingue, with the local Amerindian name "Haiti."

3. Although Waldo E. Martin Jr. emphasizes the centrality of the Haitian Revolution in Douglass's mind, he relies on the 1893 Chicago speech and on some passages in a West Indian Emancipation Day address of August 2, 1858. Martin, *The Mind of Frederick Douglass* (Chapel Hill, 1984), pp. 50–52, 269, 271. But these passages do not appear in the text that was printed in *Frederick Douglass' Paper*, the *New York Times*, the *Rochester Democrat and American*, and other newspapers. John Blassingame's edition of Douglass's speeches and debates from 1841 to 1863 does not contain a single positive reference to the Haitian Revolution except for occasional praise of Toussaint Louverture. John W. Blassingame, ed., *The Frederick Douglass Papers. Series One: Speeches, Debates, and Interviews*, vol. 1 (New Haven, 1979); vol. 2 (New Haven, 1982); vol. 3 (New Haven, 1985). It seems probable that Douglass avoided the subject for tactical reasons, especially when addressing white audiences.

4. In contrast to Douglass, many other free black Americans, including the young John B. Russwurm, when he graduated from Bowdoin College, continued to praise and celebrate the Haitian Revolution (Russwurm Papers, Bowdoin College).

5. Douglass, "Lecture on Haiti," p. 486; *Chicago Tribune*, January 3, 1893. For colonial sources of North Atlantic sugar imports, see Seymour Drescher, *Econocide: British Slavery in the Era of Abolition* (Pittsburgh, 1977), p. 48, table 11.

6. Theodore Dwight, *An Oration Spoken Before "The Connecticut Society for the Promotion of Freedom and the Relief of Persons Unlawfully Holden in Bondage"* (Hartford, 1794), pp. 12, 18–21; Timothy M. Matthewson, "Abraham Bishop, 'The Rights of Black Men,' and the American Reaction to the Haitian Revolution," *Journal of Negro History* 67 (Summer 1982): 148–53; David Brion Davis, *Revolutions: Reflections on American Equality and Foreign Liberations* (Cambridge, Mass., 1990), pp. 50–52.

7. Timothy M. Matthewson, "George Washington's Policy Toward the Haitian Revolution," *Diplomatic History* 3 (Summer 1979): 321–36; Donald R. Hickey, "America's Response to the Slave Revolt in Haiti, 1791–1806," *Journal of the Early Republic* 2 (Winter 1982), 364–65. The Washington administration would probably have given much more aid to the French planters if it had not had to deal with the intrigue of the French ministers, Jean Baptiste de Ternant and Edmond Genet. The American army, as Matthewson points out, was preoccupied with hostile Indians on the Western frontier.

8. Bryan Edwards, *The History, Civil and Commercial, of the British Colonies in the West Indies*, 3 vols. (London, 1807), vol. 3, p. 99. See also Olwyn M. Blouet, "Bryan Edwards and the Haitian Revolution," in Geggus, *Impact of the Haitian Revolution*, pp. 44–56.

9. David Brion Davis, *The Problem of Slavery in the Age of Revolution, 1770–1823* (1975; New York, 1999), pp. 120–21; Jed Handelsman Shugarman, "The Louisiana Purchase and South Carolina's Reopening of the Slave Trade in 1803," *Journal of the Early Republic* 22 (Summer 2002): 263–90. On the banning of dangerous West India slaves from South Carolina, Cuba, and other regions, see Davis, *Problem of Slavery in the Age of Revolution*, p. 121; Juan R. González Mendoza, "Puerto Rico's Creole Patriots and the Slave Trade After the Haitian Revolution," in Geggus, *Impact of the Haitian Revolution*, pp. 58–71, and

passim. In 1798, when the outcome of the Haitian Revolution was still uncertain, Georgia became the last U.S. state to halt the import of African slaves. In
1803 even South Carolinians assumed that Congress would outlaw the slave
trade in 1807, as permitted by the Constitution. Hence South Carolina's leaders sought in the remaining four years to import as many African slaves as
possible. The Louisiana Purchase ensured American control of New Orleans
and thus the secure transport of cotton and other commodities throughout
the lower Mississippi Valley.

10. Katherine Plymley Diaries, 1066/1, bk.5, pp. 10–15, County Record Office,
Shire Hall, Abbey Fossgate, Shrewsbury, England. Clarkson was in close touch
with his coworkers Joseph and Katherine Plymley and kept them fully up-to-
date on abolitionist activities. In March 1792 Katherine noted that the abolitionists were being blamed for the bloodshed in Saint-Domingue; the West
Indians were complaining that their own slaves were aware of the abolitionist
agitation in England and were already showing signs of unrest, although
Joseph had obtained a letter from a planter who affirmed that "the Negroes
never were more peaceful & quiet, no disturbances of any kind nor the least
appearance of a revolt" (March 5–20, 1792, bk. 7, pp. 10–11). By November
1793 Clarkson was convinced that the upheavals in the French colonies had
persuaded even the British merchants that "nothing but ameliorating the condition of the slaves in the other West India islands can save the inhabitants
from revolts & insurrections, & the proportion of blacks to whites is now
greater than ever" (November 9–15, 1793, bk. 21, pp. 1–2). But Clarkson over-
estimated this fear and also underestimated the fear on the part of more conservative abolitionists that his sympathies with the French Revolution would
harm the cause. As we will see in Chapters Eleven and Fourteen, pre–Civil
War Southerners were much influenced by the belief that British and French
antislavery agitation had helped ignite the Haitian Revolution and then three
massive slave revolts in the nineteenth-century British West Indies.

11. Haiti's effects on British policy were more ambiguous. In 1795–96, when the
British colonies were most seriously threatened by racial warfare and by French
armies that included large numbers of emancipated slaves, Parliament deferred
to the British planters and merchants and failed to renew a 1792 resolution
calling for an end to the slave trade in four years. But it would be difficult to
show that fear of another Haitian Revolution had any appreciable effect on
Parliament's crucial votes in 1806 abolishing the slave trade to rival foreign
markets, which prepared the way in 1807 for abolishing the British slave trade
altogether. See Drescher, *Econocide*, pp. 167–70.

12. For the impact of the Haitian Revolution on Virginia slave conspiracies, see
Douglas R. Egerton, *Gabriel's Rebellion: The Virginia Slave Conspiracies of 1800
and 1802* (Chapel Hill, 1993), pp. 45–48.

13. Davis, *Problem of Slavery in the Age of Revolution*, pp. 138–39; Blackburn, *Over-
throw of Colonial Slavery*, p. 163; David Geggus, *Slavery, War, and Revolution:
The British Occupation of Saint-Domingue, 1793–1798* (New York, 1982), p. 6;
Robert I. Rotberg with Christopher K. Clague, *Haiti: The Politics of Squalor*
(Boston, 1971), p. 32; Robert Stein, *The French Sugar Business in the Eighteenth
Century* (Baton Rouge, 1988), passim.

14. *Patriote français*, no. 203 (February 27, 1790): 1; no. 204 (February 28, 1790): 2;
Journal des Etats Généraux, vol. 6, pp. 276–77; David Geggus, "Racial Equality,

Slavery and Colonial Secession During the Constituent Assembly," in Geggus, ed., *Haitian Revolutionary Studies* (Bloomington, Ind., 2002), pp. 157–70.

15. Dubois, *Avengers of the New World*, pp. 60–71.

16. Geggus, *Slavery, War, and Revolution*, pp. 18–23; Gwendolyn M. Hall, "Saint Domingue," in *Neither Slave nor Free: The Freedmen of African Descent in the Slave Societies of the New World*, ed. David W. Cohen and Jack P. Greene (Baltimore, 1972), pp. 183–92. John D. Garrigus points out that it was not until 1764 that racial codes were strictly applied in Saint-Domingue to wealthy families of mixed ancestry, a transformation that turned them into determined advocates of racial reform. Garrigus, " 'Sons of the Same Father': Gender, Race, and Citizenship in Saint-Domingue, 1760–1792," in *Visions and Revisions of Eighteenth-Century France*, ed. Christine Adams et al. (University Park, Pa., 1997), pp. 137–53; Garrigus, "Color, Class, and Identity on the Eve of the Haitian Revolution: Saint-Domingue's Free Colored Elite as Colons Américains," in "Against the Odds: Free Blacks in the Slave Societies of the Americas," ed. Jane G. Landers, special issue, *Slavery & Abolition* 17 (April 1996): 20–43; Dubois, *Avengers of the New World*, pp. 71–90. Dubois shows that there was far more anti-black prejudice in France than most historians have assumed.

17. Davis, *Problem of Slavery in the Age of Revolution*, pp. 95–100, 140–44; Geggus, "Racial Equality, Slavery, and Colonial Secession," pp. 159–61; Blackburn, *Overthrow of Colonial Slavery*, pp. 169–77; Daniel P. Resnick, "The Société des Amis des Noirs and the Abolition of Slavery," *French Historical Studies* 7 (1972), 558–69.

18. Thomas Clarkson, the English abolitionist, told the Plymleys that Ogé had returned to Saint-Domingue to report the National Assembly's actions "to his constituents" and that he had then been attacked by the whites and treacherously given up by the Spaniards after he had fled to the Spanish part of the island. Both Clarkson and the Abbé Grégoire, a leading French abolitionist, defended Ogé as a martyr who had fought for the freedmen's legitimate rights. Katherine Plymley Diaries, bk. 5, February 9–24, 1792, pp. 13–14; *Archives parlementaires* 25 (May 11, 1791): 737–41.

19. Dubois, *Avengers of the New World*, p. 89.

20. Davis, *Problem of Slavery in the Age of Revolution*, pp. 142–44; Yvan Debbasch, *Couleur et liberté: Le Jeu du critère ethnique dans un ordre juridique esclavagiste*, vol. 1, *L'Affranchi dans les possessions françaises de la Caraïbe, 1635–1833* (Paris, 1967), p. 80; Theodore Lothrop Stoddard, *The French Revolution in San Domingo* (Boston, 1914), pp. 119–127; Gabriel Debien, *Les Colons de Saint-Domingue et la révolution: Essai sur le club Massiac, Août 1789-Août 1792* (Paris, 1953), pp. 262–90.

21. Dubois, *Avengers of the New World*. pp. 94–95.

22. The origins of this great revolt are still a matter of controversy among historians. The objectives of the slaves were at first ambiguous, and it took years for them to unite in a struggle for freedom and independence. But it is clear that the thousands of slaves who suddenly began to kill whites and set fire to the estates and cane fields were a truly revolutionary force, capable of devastating guerrilla warfare even after the black and mulatto generals had capitulated. For a recent and innovative study that links the Haitian Revolution with the uprising in Guadeloupe and struggles in the French Caribbean in general, see

Laurent Dubois, *A Colony of Citizens: Revolution and Slave Emancipation in the French Caribbean, 1787–1804* (Chapel Hill, 2004).

23. Blackburn, *Overthrow of Colonial Slavery*, pp. 197–200, 221–22; David P. Geggus, "The 'Volte-Face' of Toussaint Louverture," in Geggus, *Haitian Revolutionary Studies*, pp. 125–28.

24. Geggus, *Slavery, War, and Revolution*, pp. 39–41, 68, 70, 84–85, 105, 114, 124–29; C.L.R. James, *The Black Jacobins: Toussaint L'Ouverture and the San Domingo Revolution*, rev. ed. (New York, 1963), pp. 164–66.

25. David Geggus, "The Cost of Pitt's Campaigns, 1793–1798," *Historical Journal* 26 (September 1983): 703–4. Only about one-third of these casualties occurred in Saint-Domingue; far more soldiers and sailors died in Saint Lucia, Grenada, and Martinique. See also Dubois, *Colony of Citizens*.

26. Geggus, *Slavery, War, and Revolution*, pp. 150–61, 182–84, 313–23, 388–90; Geggus, "Arming of Slaves," pp. 209–32. Many of the blacks who joined the British evacuation were over sixty, under fifteen, or disabled.

27. Gabriel Debien, Jean Fouchard, and Marie Antoinette Menier, "Toussaint Louverture avant 1789, légendes et réalités," *Conjonction, Revue Franco-Haitienne* 134 (June–July 1977): 67–77; Dubois, *Avengers of the New World*, pp. 171–72. According to one of Toussaint's sons, the great leader was the son of an African prince who had been captured and sent to Saint-Domingue as a slave.

28. Mats Lundahl, "Toussaint L'Ouverture and the War Economy of Saint-Domingue, 1796–1802," *Slavery & Abolition* 6 (September 1985): 130.

29. Constitution de la colonie française de Saint-Domingue, du 17 Août 1801 (29 Thermidor an 9), rpt. in *La révolution française et l'abolition de l'esclavage*, 12 vols. (Paris, n.d.), vol. 11, no. 18. Though Toussaint had conquered Spanish Santo Domingo and won complete power over the island, he refrained from proclaiming independence from France, partly because of waning British and American support. Ott, *Haitian Revolution*, pp. 119–20.

30. Bénot and Dorigny, *Rétablissement de l'esclavage*, pp. 13–93 and passim; Ott, *Haitian Revolution*, pp. 139–61. David Geggus estimates that the French sent a total of forty-four thousand troops to Saint-Domingue (private communication to me).

31. James, *Black Jacobins*, pp. 322–62; Stoddard, *French Revolution in San Domingo*, pp. 303–46; Ott, *Haitian Revolution*, pp. 170–82.

32. Quoted in Geggus, "British Opinion and the Haitian Revolution, 1791–1805," in *Slavery and British Society, 1776–1848*, ed. James Walvin (London, 1982), p. 136.

33. One should note, however, that in 1816 Alexandre Pétion furnished arms and supplies to Simón Bolívar on the secret condition that Bolívar would promote the cause of slave emancipation in South America. Although Bolívar offered freedom to slaves willing to fight the royalists, at the Panama congress of 1825, from which Haiti was excluded, he called for ruling-class unity in freeing Latin America from the fear of "this tremendous monster which has devoured the island of Santo Domingo." Quoted in David Nicholls, *From Dessalines to Duvalier: Race, Colour, and National Independence in Haiti* (New Brunswick, N.J., 1996), p. 63.

34. Geggus, *Slavery, War, and Revolution*, p. 90. For the repercussions of the Haitian Revolution, see Geggus, *Impact of the Haitian Revolution*, and Julius S. Scott III, "The Common Wind: Currents of Afro-American Communication in the Era of the Haitian Revolution" (Ph.D. dissertation, Duke University,

1986). Geggus presents convincing evidence that British slaves were aware of the strength of colonial military garrisons during the prolonged period of warfare with France and that insurrections were most likely when the garrisons were reduced. We will give more attention to specific slave revolts in Chapter Eleven.

35. Paul Lachance, "Repercussions of the Haitian Revolution in Louisiana," in Geggus, *Impact of the Haitian Revolution*, pp. 209–30 and passim; Michael Craton, *Testing the Chains: Resistance to Slavery in the British West Indies* (Ithaca, N.Y., 1982), pp. 260–61; Hunt, "Influence of Haiti," pp. 39, 41, 78, 114, 118, 123–29; Ira Berlin, *Slaves Without Masters: The Free Negro in the Antebellum South* (New York, 1974), pp. 124–25.

36. Egerton, *Gabriel's Rebellion*; Berlin, *Slaves Without Masters*, pp. 38–41; Hunt, "Influence of Haiti," pp. 128–30; Herbert Aptheker, *American Negro Slave Revolts* (New York, 1943; new ed. 1969). Hunt reports that in Virginia some advertisements for runaways said that the fugitives might try to head for the West Indies (p. 243, n. 49).

37. Gwendolyn Midlo Hall, *Social Control in Slave Plantation Societies: A Comparison of St. Domingue and Cuba* (Baltimore, 1971), pp. 55, 125–26; Matt D. Childs, " 'A Black French General Arrived to Conquer the Island': Images of the Haitian Revolution in Cuba's 1812 Aponte Rebellion," in Geggus, *Impact of the Haitian Revolution*, pp. 135–56; Edward Brathwaite, *The Development of Creole Society in Jamaica, 1770–1820* (Oxford, 1971), pp. 246–48, 251–59; Mavis Christine Campbell, *The Dynamics of Change in a Slave Society: A Sociopolitical History of the Free Coloreds of Jamaica, 1800–1865* (Cranbury, N.J., 1976), pp. 32–33; Gad J. Heuman, *Between Black and White: Race, Politics, and the Free Coloreds in Jamaica, 1792–1865* (Westport, Conn., 1981), pp. 33–41. In 1829 the British Colonial Office extended legal equality to all freedmen in the Crown colonies; hoping to unite the entire free population against slave emancipation, the Jamaican Assembly granted equal civil rights in 1830.

38. Douglas R. Egerton, *He Shall Go Out Free: The Lives of Denmark Vesey* (Madison, Wisc., 1999), p. 44. We will give more attention to this subject in Chapter Eleven. Egerton's book is by far the most thorough study of the Vesey conspiracy, but Michael P. Johnson has presented strong arguments for the case that there was no conspiracy and that South Carolina whites forced blacks to say what the whites wanted to hear. Johnson, "Denmark Vesey and His Co-Conspirators," *William and Mary Quarterly*, 58 (October 2001): 915–76. For the continuing controversy, see "Forum: The Making of a Slave Conspiracy, part II," *William and Mary Quarterly*, 3rd ser., 59 (January 2002).

39. Egerton, *He Shall Go Out Free*, passim; Robert S. Starobin, ed., *Denmark Vesey: The Slave Conspiracy of 1822* (Englewood Cliffs, N.J., 1970); Richard C. Wade, "The Vesey Plot: A Reconsideration," *Journal of Southern History* 30 (May 1964): 143–61; John Lofton, *Denmark Vesey's Revolt: The Slave Plot That Lit a Fuse to Fort Sumter* (Kent, Ohio, 1983).

40. Julie Winch, *Philadelphia's Black Elite: Activism, Accommodation, and the Struggle for Autonomy, 1787–1848* (Philadelphia, 1988), pp. 50, 72–73; Winch, *A Gentleman of Color: The Life of James Forten* (New York, 2002), pp. 134–35; Berlin, *Slaves Without Masters*, pp. 314–15; Peter P. Hinks, ed., *David Walker's Appeal to the Coloured Citizens of the World* (1829; University Park, Pa., 2000), pp. 22–23; Hinks, *To Awaken My Afflicted Brethren: David Walker and the Problem of Antebellum Slave Resistance* (University Park, Pa., 1997), pp. 39–40, 47, 58; Iain

McCalman, "Anti-Slavery and Ultra-Radicalism in Early Nineteenth-Century England: The Case of Robert Wedderburn," *Slavery & Abolition* 7 (September 1986):100–15. Walker associated Haiti with ancient Carthage and with "that mighty son of Africa, HANNIBAL," but the lesson he drew from both histories was that internal division led to the slaughter of blacks by their "natural enemies."

41. Geggus, "British Opinion," pp. 137–39. The romanticization of Toussaint Louverture as a "black Spartacus" and martyr stands in marked contrast to views of other leaders of the Haitian Revolution and subsequent rulers of Haiti.

42. Stanley Elkins and Eric McKitrick, *The Age of Federalism: The Early American Republic, 1788–1800* (New York, 1993), pp. 656–62.

43. Geggus, "British Opinion," pp. 140–49; Geggus, "Haiti and the Abolitionists: Opinion, Propaganda and International Politics in Britain and France, 1804–1838," in *Abolition and Its Aftermath: The Historical Context, 1790–1916*, ed. David Richardson (London, 1986), pp. 113–17. While I have drawn extensively from Geggus's masterly studies, I am skeptical about his conclusion that the British abolitionists won the argument regarding Haitian violence. They may have persuaded the public that emancipation in the British colonies would not lead to Haitian-like massacres, but they hardly overturned the dominant images of the Haitian Revolution. In the 1830s French officials, American observers, and even the leading British abolitionist Thomas Fowell Buxton expressed surprise that British emancipation proceeded *without* undue violence.

44. Nicholls, *From Dessalines to Duvalier*, p. 65.

45. See especially Geggus, "Haiti and the Abolitionists," pp. 117–37; Hunt, "Influence of Haiti," pp. 166–83. It is most depressing to imagine the profound shock Anglo-American abolitionists would experience if they could view Haiti and Sierra Leone, supposedly two future models of black independence and achievement, in the early twenty-first century.

46. See, for example, *Liberator*, April 25, 1845, p. 67.

47. Nicholls, *From Dessalines to Duvalier*, p. 45; Pompée Valentin de Vastey, *Réflexions sur une lettre de Mazères, ex-colon français* (Cap-Henri, Haiti, 1816), p. 14. Contrary to Nicholls, Vastey's text does not explicitly point to Haiti "as the first fruit of a great colonial revolution"; he rather quotes Rousseau and asserts that all Europe repudiates the racist aspersions of the former French colonists.

CHAPTER 9

1. Of course, ancient Greece had for a time been a democracy based on slave labor, as Southerners in the United States often reminded the world.

2. Morris Birkbeck, *Notes on a Journey in America From the Coast of Virginia to the Territory of Illinois* (London, 1818), p. 21.

3. Isaac Holmes, *An Account of the United States of America, Derived From Actual Observation, During a Residence of Four Years in that Republic* (London, 1823), pp. 325, 327.

4. Robert J. Steinfeld, *Coercion, Contract, and Free Labor in the Nineteenth Century* (Cambridge, U.K., 2001), passim.

5. Frances Trollope, *Domestic Manners of the Americans* (1832), ed. Donald Smalley (New York, 1949), pp. 221–22.

6. Ibid., p. 52. As we know, however, many Southerners called their slaves "servants," which further degraded the term when applied to whites.

7. Holmes, *Account of the United States of America*, pp. 144–45.

8. Charles Francis Adams, ed., *Memoirs of John Quincy Adams* (Philadelphia, 1874–1877), vol. 5 (March 3, 1820), pp. 10–11.

9. Dumas Malone, *The Public Life of Thomas Cooper, 1783–1839* (Columbia, S.C., 1961).

10. Britain did experiment briefly with a differential tariff on some slave-produced goods, in part because some abolitionists supported the interests of British West Indian planters following slave emancipation.

11. See my essay "At the Heart of Slavery," in David Brion Davis, *In the Image of God: Religion, Moral Values, and Our Heritage of Slavery* (New Haven, 2001), pp. 123–36; Keith Bradley, "Animalizing the Slave: The Truth of Fiction," *Journal of Roman Studies* 90 (2000): 110–25.

12. Keith R. Bradley, "Roman Slavery and Roman Law," *Historical Reflections/ Réflexions Historiques* 15, no. 3 (1988), pp. 487–95; David Brion Davis, *The Problem of Slavery in Western Culture* (New York, 1988), pp. 87–90.

13. Frederick Douglass, *Narrative of the Life of Frederick Douglass, an American Slave. Written by Himself*, ed. John W. Blassingame et al. (New Haven, 2001), pp. 35–36, 49.

14. Jean Fagan Yellin, *Harriet Jacobs, a Life: The Remarkable Adventures of the Woman Who Wrote* Incidents in the Life of a Slave Girl (New York, 2004), pp. 16, 30; Douglass, *Narrative*, p. 54.

15. Robert W. Harms, *River of Wealth, River of Sorrow: The Central Zaire Basin in the Era of the Slave and Ivory Trade, 1500–1891* (New Haven, 1981), pp. 152–53.

16. Amy Chua has recently described the importance of light pigmentation and claims to whiteness in present-day Latin America. Chua, *World on Fire: How Exporting Free Market Democracy Breeds Ethnic Hatred and Global Instability* (New York, 2003), pp. 54–57. There is a vast literature on this subject, beginning with such works as Thomas E. Skidmore, *Black Into White: Race and Nationality in Brazilian Thought* (New York, 1974); Magnus Mörner, ed., *Race and Class in Latin America* (New York, 1970); and Mörner, *Race Mixture in the History of Latin America* (Boston, 1967).

17. Michael P. Johnson and James L. Roark, *Black Masters: A Free Family of Color in the Old South* (New York, 1984), pp. 6, 14–15, 23, 50, 61–64, 76, 112–43. The authors stress that "everything suggests that Ellison held his slaves to exploit them, to profit from them, just as white slaveholders did" (p. 141). One should note that the great novelist Ralph Ellison was probably descended from one of William Ellison's slaves (p. 349, n. 13). While some free blacks simply purchased family members as a way of giving them de facto freedom, Loren Schweninger reports that there were overall about 3,700 "black masters" in the South; 1,500 of these free blacks owned 7,200 slaves, or an average of nearly 5 per owner. Schweninger, *Black Property Owners in the South, 1790–1915* (Urbana, Ill., 1990), p. 36. The best recent study shows that "slaveholding by African Americans was more common than has been supposed. In 1830 slaveholders made up 2 percent of the southern free black population." In 1830, at least, the majority of slaves owned by African Americans were owned for exploitive, profit-making reasons. David L. Lightner and

Alexander M. Ragan, "Were African American Slaveholders Benevolent or Exploitive? A Quantitative Approach," *Journal of Southern History* 71 (August 2005): 535–55.

18. It is often forgotten that the traditional view of slavery being a backward, inefficient, and unprofitable institution was challenged, along with other myths about the antebellum South, by Kenneth M. Stampp in *The Peculiar Institution: Slavery in the Ante-Bellum South* (New York, 1956), pp. 383–418. Robert W. Fogel and Stanley L. Engerman then broke crucial new ground with *Time on the Cross: The Economics of American Negro Slavery*, 2 vols. (Boston, 1974), which evoked such critiques as Paul A. David et al., eds., *Reckoning With Slavery: A Critical Study in the Quantitative History of American Negro Slavery* (New York, 1976), and Herbert G. Gutman, *Slavery and the Numbers Game: a Critique of Time on the Cross* (Urbana, Ill., 1975). Still aided by Stanley L. Engerman, Robert W. Fogel then produced *Without Consent or Contract: The Rise and Fall of American Slavery* (New York, 1989), a monumental work that revises some of the more marginal and extreme claims of *Time on the Cross* while underscoring the point that behavior that is economically successful can be combined with and consistent with criminal immorality.

19. Seymour Drescher, *The Mighty Experiment: Free Labor versus Slavery in British Emancipation* (New York, 2002), pp. 54–72.

20. For a comparison of the domestic or internal slave trades in the American South, Brazil, and the British West Indies, see Walter Johnson, ed., *The Chattel Principle: Internal Slave Trades in the Americas* (New Haven, 2004).

21. For the frequency and nature of slave sales and the immensity of America's domestic or internal slave trade, see Walter Johnson, *Soul by Soul: Life Inside the Antebellum Slave Market* (Cambridge, Mass., 1999), and Michael Tadman, *Speculators and Slaves: Masters, Traders, and Slaves in the Old South* (Madison, Wisc., 1989).

22. Brenda E. Stevenson, *Life in Black and White: Family and Community in the Slave South* (New York, 1996), p. 179.

23. David Brion Davis, ed., *Antebellum American Culture: An Interpretive Anthology* (University Park, Pa., 1997), pp. 324–25. It was not uncommon for a slave on one farm or plantation to be married to slave on another, in a so-called abroad marriage. Many examples are described in Stevenson, *Life in Black and White*.

24. Claudia Dale Goldin, *Urban Slavery in the American South, 1820–1860: A Quantitative History* (Chicago, 1976).

25. Lee Soltow, *Men of Wealth in the United States, 1850–1870* (New Haven, 1975), pp. 65–66; Fogel, *Without Consent or Contract*, p. 84.

26. Charles B. Dew, *Bond of Iron: Master and Slave at Buffalo Forge* (New York, 1994); Robert B. Starobin, *Industrial Slavery in the Old South* (New York, 1970).

27. Lee Soltow, *Men and Wealth in the United States, 1850–1870* (New Haven, 1975), passim. For the relationship between small farmers and slaveholding planters in the South, see Stephanie McCurry, *Masters of Small Worlds: Yeoman Households, Gender Relations, and the Political Culture of the Antebellum South Carolina Low Country* (New York, 1995).

28. In the 1810s and 1820s there were actually more antislavery societies in the Upper South than in the North. Despite Alice Dana Adams's *Neglected Period of Anti-Slavery in America*, published in 1908 by Radcliffe College, the period *remains* neglected. The antislavery societies in the Upper South, composed

mainly of Quakers, were generally small, ineffective, and gradualist in outlook. See H. Shelton Smith, *In His Image, but . . . : Racism in Southern Religion,
1780–1910* (Durham, N.C., 1972), pp. 69–73. For the distaste for slavery in
the Upper South, see William W. Freehling, *The Road to Disunion: Secessionists
at Bay, 1776–1854* (New York, 1990), pp. 121–43, 178–210, 564, and Merrill
D. Peterson, *The Jefferson Image in the American Mind* (New York, 1960), pp.
46–51.

29. Alison Goodyear Freehling, *Drift Toward Dissolution: The Virginia Slavery Debate of 1831–1832* (Baton Rouge, 1982).

30. Thomas R. Dew, *Review of the Debate in the Virginia Legislature of 1831 and
1832* (Richmond, 1832), reprinted in *The Pro-Slavery Argument; as Maintained
by the Most Distinguished Writers of the Southern States* (1852; New York, 1968),
p. 469.

31. William W. Freehling devotes much attention to the Southern hope for diffusion and what he terms the "conditional termination" of slavery in *Road to
Disunion*, pp. 119–210.

32. Bruce Levine, *Half Slave and Half Free: The Roots of Civil War* (New York,
1992), p. 167.

33. Leviticus 25:44–46. As we have seen, most English translations of the Bible
used words like "bondservants" until recent times. Yet the words "your property . . . for all time" clearly referred to slaves.

34. Genesis 9:25. Thomas Virgil Peterson, *Ham and Japheth: The Mystic World of
Whites in the Antebellum South* (Metuchen, N.J., 1978); Stephen R. Haynes,
Noah's Curse: The Biblical Justification of American Slavery (New York, 2002);
David M. Goldenberg, *The Curse of Ham: Race and Slavery in Early Judaism,
Christianity, and Islam* (Princeton, 2003); Benjamin Braude, "The Sons of Noah
and the Construction of Ethnic and Geographical Identities in the Medieval
and Early Modern Periods," *William and Mary Quarterly*, 3rd ser., 54 (January
1997): 103–42.

35. Peterson, *Ham and Japheth*, pp. 18–20, 24–26, 43, 48–56, 70, 74–84. 91–97,
103, 110, 117; Michael D. Pierson, " 'Slavery Cannot Be Covered Up With
Broadcloth or a Bandanna': The Evolution of White Abolitionist Attacks on
the 'Patriarchal Institution,' " *Journal of the Early Republic* 25 (Fall 2005): 383–
415; Haynes, *Noah's Curse*, pp. 103–4. In some of my previous works I myself
have underestimated the importance of "the Curse."

36. For an excellent and recent analysis of early Christian interpretations of slavery in the Bible, see John T. Noonan Jr., *A Church That Can and Cannot
Change: The Development of Catholic Moral Teaching* (Notre Dame, Ind., 2005),
pp. 17–67. It is crucial to note that while Jesus never criticized slavery, he
sometimes presented himself as a slave, and following Jewish tradition, true
believers were supposed to see themselves as the "slaves" of God (or Jesus). As
Noonan makes clear, these analogies served both to legitimate slavery and to
question at least some of the claims to power made by the human masters of
slaves.

37. For a discussion of the intellectual and cultural roots of proslavery and antislavery thought, see Davis, *Problem of Slavery in Western Culture*.

38. Drew Gilpin Faust, *A Sacred Circle: The Dilemma of the Intellectual in the Old
South, 1840–1860* (Baltimore, 1977), p. 8. I am indebted to Stanley L. Engerman
for helping me to slightly revise these figures.

39. I am indebted to Michael Sugrue for calling my attention to the remarkable centrality of South Carolina College in the development of proslavery ideology.

40. Faust, *Sacred Circle*, passim.

41. "Speech on the Admission of Kansas, U.S. Senate, March 4, 1858," in *Slavery Defended: The Views of the Old South*, ed. Eric McKitrick (Englewood Cliffs, N.J., 1963), p. 122.

42. Published in 1854, the first English translation of Gobineau was done in 1856 by Joseph C. Nott, in Philadelphia; a modern translation is entitled *The Inequality of Human Races*, trans. Adrian Collins (Los Angeles, 1966).

43. Faust, *Sacred Circle*, p. 124.

44. James Henry Hammond, *Two Letters on Slavery in the United States, Addressed to Thomas Clarkson, Esq.* (Columbia, S.C., 1845), rpt. in *Pro-Slavery Argument*, pp. 99–174.

45. Hammond, *Two Letters on Slavery*; Drew Gilpin Faust, *James Henry Hammond and the Old South: A Design for Mastery* (Baton Rouge, 1982), pp. 259, 267, 278–84.

46. Kevin Bales, *Disposable People: New Slavery in the Global Economy* (Berkeley, 1999). More work needs to be done on the historical use of and evasion of the word "slavery," a term that acquired highly negative connotations in western Europe even in late medieval times. Yet these negative associations did not necessarily mean opposition to de facto slavery. Bales and other writers have a justifiable wish to broaden the definition of "slavery." Yet in both the Caribbean and the American South, there were many attempts to avoid using the word "slaves" and to find more benign substitutes.

47. Hammond, "Speech on the Admission of Kansas," in McKitrick, *Slavery Defended*, p. 123.

48. George Fitzhugh, *Sociology for the South, or the Failure of Free Society* (1854; New York, 1965), pp. 10, 24.

49. Information supplied by John Stauffer, who has collected this correspondence and plans to write on it; see also Stauffer's *Black Hearts of Men: Radical Abolitionists and the Transformation of Race* (Cambridge, Mass., 2002), p. 92 and passim, which provides the most brilliant study of Gerrit Smith.

50. David Donald, *Lincoln* (New York, 1995), p. 187. Donald points out that Lincoln wrongly concluded that Fitzhugh was "a representative thinker" in the South, and that this fear contributed to Lincoln's famous "House Divided" speech, based on the conviction, shared by Fitzhugh, that the United States "must become all slave or all free" (pp. 191, 207).

51. See especially Manisha Sinha, *The Counterrevolution of Slavery: Politics and Ideology in Antebellum South Carolina* (Chapel Hill, 2000), pp. 125–52.

CHAPTER 10

1. Quoted in Walter Johnson, *Soul by Soul: Life Inside the Antebellum Slave Market* (Cambridge, Mass., 1999), p. 218. See also Johnson, ed., *The Chattel Principle: Internal Slave Trades in the Americas* (New Haven, 2004), a collection of essays based on the first international conference sponsored by Yale's Gilder Lehrman Center for the Study of Slavery, Resistance, and Abolition. Walter Johnson adopted the term "chattel principle" from Pennington.

2. For slave law and enforcement, see Thomas D. Morris, *Southern Slavery and the Law, 1629–1860* (Chapel Hill, 1996); Sally E. Hadden, *Slave Patrols: Law and Violence in Virginia and the Carolinas* (Cambridge, Mass., 2001); Ariela J. Gross, *Double Character: Slavery and Mastery in the Antebellum Southern Courtroom* (Princeton, 2000); Paul Finkelman, ed., "Symposium on the Law of Slavery," *Chicago Kent Law Review* 68, no. 3 (1993); Mark V. Tushnet, *Slave Law in the American South: State v. Mann in History and Literature* (Lawrence, Kans., 2003); and Tushnet, *The American Law of Slavery, 1810–1860* (Princeton, 1981). For a broad comparative approach, see Alan Watson, *Slave Law in the Americas* (Athens, Ga., 1989).

3. For runaway slaves, as a challenge to their masters' self-perception, and for advertisements for runaways, see John Hope Franklin and Loren Schweninger, *Runaway Slaves: Rebels on the Plantation* (New York, 1999), pp. 248–52, and Eugene D. Genovese, *Roll, Jordan, Roll: The World the Slaves Made* (New York, 1974), pp. 648–57. Genovese also presents the most insightful analysis of paternalism (pp. 3–7, passim). Walter Johnson shows that a culture of paternalism and the pursuit of commercial interests were not incompatible (*Soul by Soul*, p. 109 and passim).

4. For the complex relationships between planters, overseers, and slaves, see William Kauffman Scarborough, *The Overseer: Plantation Management in the Old South* (Baton Rouge, 1966), especially pp. 102–37.

5. Johnson, *Soul by Soul*, pp. 176–81; Gross, *Double Character*, passim.

6. Elizabeth Fox-Genovese, *Within the Plantation Household: Black and White Women in the Old South* (Chapel Hill, 1988), pp. 1–35 (Gayle is quoted on p. 23).

7. Genovese, *Roll, Jordan, Roll*, pp. 89–91. For the planters' use of labor incentives, see Kenneth M. Stampp, *The Peculiar Institution: Slavery in the Ante-Bellum South* (New York, 1956), pp. 162–70.

8. *The Collected Works of Abraham Lincoln*, ed. Roy P. Basler, 8 vols. (New Brunswick, N.J., 1953), vol. 3, p. 181.

9. Frederick Douglass, *Narrative of the Life of Frederick Douglass, an American Slave, Written by Himself* (1845), ed. David W. Blight (Boston, 1993), p. 50.

10. Stampp, *Peculiar Institution*, pp. 338–39. A concern for political correctness may have blinded some more recent historians to this kind of evidence.

11. Genovese, *Roll, Jordan, Roll*, pp. 64, 314; Edwin Adams Davis, ed., *Plantation Life in the Florida Parishes of Louisiana, 1836–1846* (New York, 1943).

12. Article IV, Section 4 of the Constitution states that the United States shall protect each state against invasion; "and on application of the legislature, or of the executive (when the legislature cannot be convened), against domestic violence." The framers definitely had slave uprisings in mind.

13. Stampp, *Peculiar Institution*, pp. 30–31 and passim. For demographic information regarding Southern slavery I have also relied heavily on Robert William Fogel, *Without Consent or Contract: The Rise and Fall of American Slavery* (New York, 1989). Despite the decline of slavery in the Upper South, Virginia still had more slaves than any other state.

14. Professor Stampp noted that relatively few slaves worked on the smaller farms, and that farmers who owned just a few slaves burdened them with an assortment of duties and tried as much as possible to assume a managerial role. Stampp, *Peculiar Institution*, pp. 34–42.

15. John H. Moore, "Simon Gray, Riverman: A Slave Who Was Almost Free," *Mississippi Valley Historical Review* (now *The Journal of American History*) 49 (December, 1962): 472–84.

16. Solomon Northup, *Twelve Years a Slave* (1853), ed. Sue Eakin and Joseph Logsdon (Baton Rouge, 1968), p. 124.

17. Genovese, *Roll, Jordan, Roll*, pp. 502–3, 506, 515–19; Brenda E. Stevenson, *Life in Black and White: Family and Community in the Slave South* (New York, 1996), pp. 187–88; Jacob Stroyer, "I Cannot Do Anything for You," in *African American Voices: The Life Cycle of Slavery*, ed. Steven Mintz, 2nd ed. (St. James, N.Y., 1999), pp. 105–7; Johnson, *Soul by Soul*, pp. 20–21; Wilma King, *Stolen Childhood: Slave Youth in Nineteenth-Century America* (Bloomington, Ind., 1995); Marie Jenkins Schwartz, *Born in Bondage: Growing Up Enslaved in the Antebellum South* (Cambridge, Mass., 2000).

18. My discussion of slave culture draws on some works already cited, especially Fogel, *Without Consent or Contract*, pp. 154–98, as well as on John W. Blassingame, *The Slave Community: Plantation Life in the Antebellum South* (New York, 1972); Herbert Gutman, *The Black Family in Slavery and Freedom, 1750–1925* (New York, 1976); Lawrence W. Levine, *Black Culture and Consciousness: Afro-American Folk Thought From Slavery to Freedom* (New York, 1977); Mechal Sobel, *The World They Made Together: Black and White Values in Eighteenth-Century Virginia* (Princeton, 1987); and Michael A. Gomez, *Exchanging Our Country Marks: The Transformation of African Identities in the Colonial and Antebellum South* (Chapel Hill, 1998). The complex historiography on this subject has moved from a denial of any continuing African influence or vibrant slave culture to the celebration of a rich autonomous culture that undermined and stood in opposition to the slaveholders' interests. I am inclined to agree with Christopher Morris, who has argued that "the aspects of slavery that could be most liberating and self-affirming for the slaves—family, economy, community—could become structures that made slavery profitable and enduring for the masters." Morris, "The Articulation of Two Worlds: The Master-Slave Relationship Reconsidered," *Journal of American History* 85 (December 1998): 987.

19. While this "generational distance" from Africa is important, one should remember that a "legally legitimate" slave trade brought some thirty-eight thousand Africans to South Carolina between the end of 1803 and the date of federal abolition, January 1, 1808. There is still disagreement over the number of slaves smuggled illegally into the country after 1808 (perhaps no more than the number of fugitive slaves who escaped from the South). Still, even a statistically small number of native Africans could have had some impact on reviving memories of African cultures in certain regions.

20. See, for example, Sobel, *World They Made Together*.

21. Fogel, *Without Consent or Contract*, pp. 58, 211–12.

22. Gutman, *Black Family*, pp. 197–99, 217–24. We should also remember that there were a great many slaves in West Africa, and while the nature of such bondage differed even within African regions, some slaves in the New World drew on family traditions of enslavement.

23. Stevenson, *Life in Black and White*, pp. 252–54; Franklin and Schweninger, *Runaway Slaves*, pp. 50–55, 57–63.

24. Quoted in George P. Rawick, ed., *The American Slave: A Composite Autobiography*, Vol. 6, *Mississippi Narratives*, pt. 1 (Westport, Conn., 1977), p. 10. For forced sales of slaves and the breakup of families to settle debts, see Stampp,

Peculiar Institution, pp. 199–200, 239–43; Genovese, *Roll, Jordan, Roll*, pp. 453–54. For "abroad marriages," see Stevenson, *Life in Black and White*, pp. 217, 230–33.

25. Hammond sexually exploited both a slave mother and her daughter before finally passing them on to his white son Harry. See Drew Gilpin Faust, *James Henry Hammond and the Old South: A Design for Mastery* (Baton Rouge, 1985). For Jefferson, see Jan Ellen Lewis and Peter S. Onuf, eds., *Sally Hemings and Thomas Jefferson: History, Memory, and Civic Culture* (Charlottesville, 1999) and Annette Gordon Reed, *Thomas Jefferson and Sally Hemings: An American Controversy* (Charlottesville, 1997).

26. Melton A. McLaurin, *Celia, a Slave: A True Story* (Athens, Ga., 1991), pp. ix–x.

27. Newsom also owned a five-year-old slave boy.

28. My discussion of slave religion draws on the works by Genovese, Levine, Sobel, and Blassingame already cited, as well as Albert J. Raboteau, *Slave Religion: The "Invisible Institution" in the Antebellum South* (New York, 1978); Anne C. Loveland, *Southern Evangelicals and the Social Order, 1800–1860* (Baton Rouge, 1980); John B. Boles, ed., *Masters and Slaves in the House of the Lord: Race and Religion in the Antebellum South, 1740–1870* (Lexington, Ky., 1988); Roger D. Abrahams, *Singing the Master: The Emergence of African-American Culture in the Plantation South* (New York, 1992); and Donald G. Mathews, *Religion in the Old South* (Chicago, 1977).

29. Eugene D. Genovese, *The Southern Front: History and Politics in the Cultural War* (Columbia, Mo., 1995), pp. 59–65.

30. As we have seen in Chapter Two, this liberation after fifty years was meant to apply only to Hebrew slaves. Other biblical passages, including Noah's "Curse of Ham," view slavery as perpetual.

31. Isaiah 61:1; Luke 4:18. This more radical translation is taken from the sermon of Ralph Wardlaw, a Scottish abolitionist, on emancipation day, August 1, 1834. Wardlaw, *The Jubilee: A Sermon Preached in West George-Street Chapel, Glasgow, on Friday, August 1st, 1834, the Memorable Day of Negro Emancipation in the British Colonies* (Glasgow, 1834), p. 4. In the King James translation, Luke 4:18, in which Jesus is quoting from Isaiah, reads "He hath sent me to heal the broken-hearted, to preach deliverance to the captives, and recovering of sight to the blind, to set at liberty them that are bruised." But the original passage from Isaiah, in the Jewish Publication Society translation, reads, "He has sent me as a herald of joy to the humble,/ To bind up the wounded of heart,/ To proclaim release to the captives,/ Liberation to the imprisoned."

32. Levine, *Black Culture and Black Consciousness*, pp. 37–38, 453 n. 27; Blassingame, *Slave Community*, pp. 134–35; Raboteau, *Slave Religion*, pp. 66–73.

33. Ira Berlin, *Slaves Without Masters: The Free Negro in the Antebellum South* (New York, 1974), pp. 15, 179–81, and passim; Stevenson, *Life in Black and White*, passim.

CHAPTER 11

1. James Boswell, *Life of Johnson* (New York, 1953), p. 876.

2. Philmore [pseud.], *Two Dialogues on the Man-Trade* (London, 1760), p. 21. Neither I nor my colleagues have been able to identify the author of this extremely rare pamphlet. The American Quaker Anthony Benezet, who quoted

      parts of the text, understandably omitted the justification for physical violence. See my "New Sidelights on Early Antislavery Radicalism," in *From Homicide to Slavery: Studies in American Culture* (New York, 1986), pp. 234–37.

3.   Peter even instructs slaves to "accept the authority of your masters with all deference, not only those who are kind and gentle but also those who are harsh." 1 Peter 2:18; Colossians 3:18, 22. As I have indicated, the King James and other early English Bibles translated the Hebrew, Greek, and Latin words for "slave" as "servant," even in contexts that clearly referred to slaves, an error corrected in most modern translations.

4.   *The Frederick Douglass Papers*, ser. 1, *Speeches, Debates, and Interviews*, vol. 2, *1847–54*, ed. John W. Blassingame (New Haven, 1982), pp. 46–47, 103–5, 130–31, 153–58, 171–72.

5.   In Chapter Eight we have already discussed the massive desertion of slaves during the American Revolution, and in Chapter Fifteen we will see even much larger desertions of slaves in America's Civil War. It is noteworthy, however, that neither the Revolution, the War of 1812, nor the Civil War ignited a genuine slave revolt. See note 53 for the issue of black slaves who participated in Florida's Second Seminole War of 1835–43.

6.   Stanley Elkins, *Slavery: A Problem in American Institutional and Intellectual Life* (Chicago, 1959).

7.   For a discussion of such resistance in French Martinique, see Dale W. Tomich, *Slavery in the Circuit of Sugar: Martinique and the World Economy, 1830–1848* (Baltimore, 1990), pp. 250–58. Kenneth M. Stampp, drawing on the pioneering work of Raymond A. Bauer and Alice H. Bauer, was one of the first historians to draw attention to the slaves' day-to-day resistance. Stampp, *The Peculiar Institution: Slavery in the Ante-Bellum South* (New York, 1956), pp. 97–109, 124–32.

8.   Douglas R. Egerton, "Gabriel's Conspiracy and the Election of 1800," *The Journal of Southern History* 56 (May 1990): 191–214; Egerton, *Gabriel's Rebellion: The Virginia Slave Conspiracies of 1800 and 1802* (Chapel Hill, 1993). It is highly probable that the Gabriel plot also involved some white Frenchmen. The conspiracy gave a new and substantial stimulus to the century-old idea of "colonizing" free blacks in the unsettled West or especially Africa, following the British example of Sierra Leone. Egerton, "'Its Origin Is Not a Little Curious': A New Look at the American Colonization Society," *Journal of the Early Republic* 5 (Winter 1985): 643–80. There has been some dispute concerning the connection between Gabriel's conspiracy and the presidential election, and especially any connection between national politics and a supposed slave plot in 1802. See Thomas C. Parramore, "Aborted Takeoff: A Critique of `Fly Across the River,'" *North Carolina Historical Review* 68 (April 1991): 111–21, and Egerton's "Rejoinder," pp. 122–24.

9.   Robert L. Paquette, "Revolutionary St. Domingue in the Making of Territorial Louisiana," in *A Turbulent Time: The French Revolution in the Greater Caribbean*, ed. David Barry Gaspar and David P. Geggus (Bloomington, Ind., 1997), pp. 218–20; Junius P. Rodriguez, "Always 'en garde'": The Effects of Slave Insurrection upon the Louisiana Mentality, 1811–1815," *Louisiana History* 33, no. 4 (1992): 399–416; Thomas M. Thompson, "National Newspaper and Legislative Reactions to Louisiana's Deslondes Slave Revolt of 1811," *Louisiana History* 33, no. 1 (1992): 5–29.

10. In his work on the Haitian Revolution, Laurent Dubois emphasizes and empathizes with the slaves' and free coloreds' desire for *"vengeance"*: "We can only imagine the exuberance and exhilaration the rebels must have felt as they took vengeance, turned the tables on their masters, and saw, perhaps for the first time, the extent of their power." Dubois, *Avengers of the New World* (Cambridge, Mass., 2004), pp. 113, 122, 176.

11. Stephen B. Oates, *The Fires of Jubilee: Nat Turner's Fierce Rebellion* (New York, 1975); Eugene D. Genovese, *From Rebellion to Revolution: Afro-American Slave Revolts in the Making of the Modern World* (New York, 1979), pp. 105–10; Kenneth S. Greenberg, ed., *The Confessions of Nat Turner and Related Documents* (Boston, 1996).

12. Kenneth Greenberg argues that the trials and commuted sentences should be seen as an attempt by white political leaders to recover from the indiscriminate violence in the immediate aftermath of the rebellion, which had suddenly exposed slavery's vulnerability as well as its foundation in power and oppression rather than in paternalism: "Masters were most powerful and most dangerous not when they cut off heads, but when they commuted the death sentences of fifteen-year-old children; not when their power was displayed in its most brutal form, but when their 'decency' was displayed in its most benevolent form." Greenberg, *Confessions of Nat Turner*, p. 22.

13. James Oakes, letter to H-NET List for the History of Slavery H-SLAVERY@H-NET.MSU.EDU, April 28, 2004. David Walker was a free black in Boston; we will discuss his *Appeal* in Chapter Thirteen.

14. Scot French, *The Rebellious Slave: Nat Turner in American Memory* (New York, 2004); Mary Kemp Davis, *Nat Turner Before the Bar of Judgment: Fictional Treatments of the Southampton Insurrection* (Baton Rouge, 1999), chap. 2. It is possible that Turner sought to protect other blacks by taking the blame for the revolt.

15. First shown in 2002, this outstanding hour-long documentary is now available as a VCR from California Newsreel, "Nat Turner: A Troublesome Property." (Director/Writer: Charles Burnett; Producer/Writer: Frank Christopher; Co-Producer/Writer/Historian: Kenneth S. Greenberg). As a sign of continuing public interest in the story, after the film had appeared several times on television, Felicia R. Lee gave it a prominent review in the *New York Times*, "Nat Turner in History's Multiple Mirrors," February 7, 2004, pp. B7, 9. Herbert Aptheker, who appears along with many other notable historians, makes this statement in the film.

16. Alison Goodyear Freehling, *Drift Toward Dissolution: The Virginia Slave Debate of 1831–1832* (Baton Rouge, 1982); William W. Freehling, *The Road to Disunion: Secessionists at Bay, 1776–1854* (New York, 1990). William Freehling maintains that "Virginia's legislative showdown over slavery . . . stemmed far more from white egalitarians' fury at elitist republicanism than from slaveholders' fear of black insurrection" (p. 178).

17. *Liberator*, September 3, 1831, quoted in Greenberg, *Confessions of Nat Turner*, pp. 69–72. Both Turner and Brown were born in 1800, were tried and hanged, and, however unfair their trials, had no compunctions about killing unarmed civilians — in Turner's case, women and children. A belief in the insanity or "monomania" of both men emerged in their own time and then became widely accepted by twentieth-century historians. Yet both men have long been celebrated as major heroes by a radical minority and especially by African Americans. Brown, who saw slavery itself as a form of war and whose martyrdom

brought enthusiastic comparisons with Christ, on the eve of the Civil War, fulfilled the frustrated abolitionists' late move toward an acceptance of violence and hope for a massive slave insurrection. Pieces of the rope from Brown's hanging became treasured and sacred relics, and the New England abolitionist Wendell Phillips made speeches with pistols in his belt and one of Brown's "pikes" in his hand. For this information I am indebted to Paul Finkelman and John Stauffer, who spoke on Turner and Brown at a panel sponsored by Yale's Gilder Lehrman Center for the Study of Slavery, Resistance, and Abolition on October 2, 2000.

18. Elkins, *Slavery*, pp. 138, 136 note 112.

19. Christopher Leslie Brown and Philip D. Morgan, eds., *Arming Slaves: From Classical Times to the Modern Age* (New Haven, 2006), passim.

20. Seymour Drescher, *Capitalism and Antislavery: British Mobilization in Comparative Perspective* (New York, 1987), p. 105.

21. Michael Craton, *Testing the Chains: Resistance to Slavery in the British West Indies* (Ithaca, N.Y., 1982), pp. 257, 259–60; Hilary McD. Beckles, *Black Rebellion in Barbados: The Struggle Against Slavery, 1627–1838* (Bridgetown, Barbados, 1987), p. 99, table 18.

22. Dubois, *Avengers of the New World*, pp. 106–8, 158–60. As in many of his previously published articles, Dubois emphasizes the importance for slaves of "news" from the outside world.

23. Like most historians who have dealt with slave conspiracies and revolts, I have learned much about the circulation of news and rumors among New World slaves, beginning especially with the Haitian Revolution, from Julius Scott, "The Common Wind: Currents of Afro-American Communication in the Era of the Haitian Revolution" (Ph.D. dissertation, Duke University, 1986), and also from a 2001 draft of a paper by Laurent Dubois, "Calling Down the Law: Prophetic Rumor and Politics of Slave Insurrection in the Atlantic Empires, 1730–1848." Ironically, similar rumors, usually much exaggerated, and concerning a transatlantic antislavery cabal, circulated among nineteenth-century Southern slaveholders and political leaders. See my book *Challenging the Boundaries of Slavery* (Cambridge, Mass., 2003), pp. 80–89.

24. John Pollock, *Wilberforce* (New York, 1977), pp. 249–53; David Brion Davis, *The Problem of Slavery in the Age of Revolution, 1775–1823* (Ithaca, N.Y., 1975), pp. 159–62.

25. Craton, *Testing the Chains*, pp. 241, 259–61; Beckles, *Black Rebellion*, pp. 106–7. The Jamaican slave ditty did not end on a passive note: "What negro for to do? What negro for to do?/ Take force with force! Take force with force!" The historian Emilia Viotti da Costa notes that whites in Demerara blamed the Barbadian revolt on Wilberforce and the parliamentary debates on the "Registry Bill," after first claiming that "Methodists" had been responsible—"until it was proven that there had been no missionaries in Barbados for more than seventeen months." Da Costa, *Crowns of Glory, Tears of Blood: The Demerara Slave Rebellion of 1823* (New York, 1994), pp. 78, 134. Trinidad, as a Crown colony with no legislature, had been forced to have a registry much earlier, and in 1817 the Barbados legislature actually passed its own registration bill to mollify Britain and to retain local autonomy. Craton, *Testing the Chains*, p. 265.

26. Ibid., pp. 259–61; Beckles, *Black Rebellion*, pp. 86–110; Hilary McD. Beckles, "Emancipation by Law or War? Wilberforce and the 1816 Barbados Slave

Rebellion," in *Abolition and its Aftermath: The Historical Context, 1790–1916,*
ed. David Richardson (London, 1985), pp. 80–103; Karl Watson, *The Civilised
Island: Barbados, a Social History, 1750–1816* (Barbados, 1979).

27. Hilary McD. Beckles, "Inside Bussa's Rebellion: Letters of Colonel John
Rycroft Best," *Journal of the Barbados Museum and Historical Society* 37, no. 2
(1984): 1–110; Beckles, *Black Rebellion,* p. 96. Beckles lists Bussa as the only
African involved in the leadership of the rebellion.

28. Roger Normal Buckley, *Slaves in Red Coats: The British West India Regiments,
1795–1815* (New Haven, 1979); Jerome Handler, *The Unappropriated People:
Freedmen in the Slave Society of Barbados* (Baltimore, 1974), p. 204; Beckles,
Black Rebellion, p. 113.

29. Craton, *Testing the Chains,* pp. 262–85; Watson, *Civilised Island,* p. 131; da Costa,
Crowns of Glory, p. 134. It has been argued that the low mortality of whites in the
three nineteenth-century British West Indian rebellions can be explained by the
slaves' inability to use firearms. Yet slaves did have some access to guns, and
many slaves had been armed during the Napoleonic Wars; they had often observed the loading and firing of weapons; and they could certainly have stabbed
or slit the throats of the many whites under their control. Further, some of the
slaves from Africa would have learned how to use guns in African wars and
campaigns to obtain slaves. Large numbers of whites had been killed in previous
Caribbean insurrections when firearms (such as wheelocks) would have been
more difficult to use. Insurgent slaves often talked of capturing arsenals of guns
or using hoes, axes, and machetes to kill the whites. It is true, of course, that in
Barbados few slaves would have been marksmen, and that crowds of poorly armed
rebels were demoralized when well-organized black and white troops greeted
them with volleys of fire. Still, the incredibly low white mortality was clearly the
result of the rebel leaders' intention and discipline.

30. Craton, *Testing the Chains,* p. 261.
31. David Brion Davis, *Slavery and Human Progress* (New York, 1986), pp. 176–77.
32. Da Costa, *Crowns of Glory,* pp. 78, 134.
33. Ibid., pp. xiii–xix, 4, 19, 28; Craton, *Testing the Chains,* pp. 69. Da Costa's
brilliant book is probably the best single study we have of a slave revolt. Having seen myself the chaotic and daunting records and source material in
Georgetown, once the capital of Demerara and now the capital of Guyana, I
could not be more impressed by the exhaustive detail of da Costa's research.
34. Da Costa, *Crowns of Glory,* p. 12. Seymour Drescher has emphasized the important connections between pivotal moments in the domestic British antislavery movement and the British West Indian slave revolts of 1816, 1823, and
1831. Drescher, *Capitalism and Antislavery,* pp. 102–10.
35. *Substance of the debate in the House of Commons, on the 15th May, 1823: on a
motion for the mitigation and gradual abolition of slavery throughout the British
dominions: with a preface and appendixes, containing the facts and reasonings illustrative of colonial bondage* (London, 1823), p. xxvi.
36. Davis, *Slavery and Human Progress,* pp. 192–93; da Costa, *Crowns of Glory,* pp.
48, 112, 177–78, 310–11, n. 115 and 116.
37. Da Costa, *Crowns of Glory,* pp. 12, 14, 17–19, 37, 131–32; Davis, *Slavery and
Human Progress,* p. 195.
38. Da Costa, *Crowns of Glory,* pp. xvii, 18, 102–3, 126, 134, 146, 152, 154.
39. Ibid., pp. 142–45, 180–83; Craton, *Testing the Chains,* pp. 274, 288. Craton
writes that Smith's average Sunday congregation rose to more than eight hundred slaves.

40. Da Costa, *Crowns of Glory*, pp. 145–46, 184, 195.

41. Walter Johnson, "Time and Revolution in African America: Temporality and the History of Atlantic Slavery," in *Rethinking American History in a Global Age*, ed. Thomas Bender (Berkeley, 2002), pp. 148–67. I am indebted to Professor Johnson for sending me a copy of this thought-provoking essay. It is important to add that for some New World slaveholders, the Haitian Revolution, including the emancipation decree of the French Convention, created the polar opposite of a laudable "slavery-to-freedom" linear scenario: that is, a black revolution leading to permanent economic disaster and total destruction, accompanied by the mass murder and rape of white people. This imagery, evident in most of the revolts and conspiracies we are examining, was frequently used to support the argument that whites and blacks could never live together as equals in a free society.

42. Da Costa, *Crowns of Glory*, pp. 170–72, 184, 240–41; Craton, *Testing the Chains*, p. 277.

43. Da Costa, *Crowns of Glory*, pp. 80, 198–202; Craton, *Testing the Chains*, p. 280–88. One white bugler was shot and killed accidentally by his own men.

44. Da Costa, *Crowns of Glory*, pp. 197–202, 219–20, 222–26, 243–44. The rebellion could very easily have spread into Berbice, Essequibo (both parts of the future British Guiana, along with Demerara), and even to maroons in the interior, which would have brought total disaster for the white colonists (p. 217).

45. Ibid., pp. 274–92. The British antislavery movement lapsed in the later 1820s, partly as a result of Buxton's health problems. For Smith's trial, see ibid., 251–74. In his own defense, Smith reminded the court that "in former revolts in the colony, as in Jamaica, Grenada, and Barbados—there had been bloodshed and massacres. But in this one 'a mildness and forbearance, worthy of the [Christian] faith they professed (however wrong their conduct may have been) were the characteristics.' The few attempts at bloodshed had been confined to Africans who had not yet been baptized" (p. 267); Smith also insisted "that at the time he had no idea that the slaves intended to revolt" (p. 266).

46. William A. Green, *British Slave Emancipation: The Sugar Colonies and the Great Experiment, 1830–1865* (Oxford, 1976), pp. 111–27; David Turley, *The Culture of English Antislavery, 1780–1860* (London, 1991), pp. 39–46; Adam Hochschild, *Bury the Chains: Prophets and Rebels in the Fight to Free an Empire's Slaves* (Boston, 2005), pp. 309–54.

47. Craton, *Testing the Chains*, pp. 293, 302–3.

48. Ibid., pp. 291, 294–95, 300–302.

49. Ibid., pp. 293, 297–98, 315.

50. Ibid., pp. 291, 311, 313–15.

51. Ibid., pp. 316–21; Mary Turner, *Slaves and Missionaries: The Disintegration of Jamaican Society, 1787–1834* (Chicago, 1982), pp. 20–21, 171–73.

52. Edward Bartlett Rugemer, "The Problem of Emancipation: The United States and Britain's Abolition of Slavery" (Ph.D. dissertation, Boston College, 2005), pp. 48, 81–138. I am most indebted to Dr. Rugemer for sending me a copy of his dissertation. See also David Brion Davis, *Challenging the Boundaries of Slavery* (Cambridge, Mass., 2003), pp. 80–91; Davis, *The Slave Power Conspiracy and the Paranoid Style* (Baton Rouge, 1969), pp. 32–61; Joe Bassette Wilkins Jr., "Window on Freedom: The South's Response to the Emancipation of the Slaves in the British West Indies, 1833–1861" (Ph.D. dissertation, University of South Carolina, 1977).

53. The H-NET List for the History of Slavery (H-SLAVERY@H-NET.MSU.EDU) has very recently contained an argument that the Second Seminole War (1835–43) in Florida involved "the largest slave rebellion in U.S. history." This conflict with the Seminole leader Osceola became the most costly of all wars with American Indians and took thousands of lives. Many plantation slaves did participate in the fighting, in addition to the fugitive Black Seminole maroons. But the issue of the conflict was the determination of the U.S. government to deport the Seminoles, like other Indians, to Oklahoma Territory. Therefore, the involvement of many slaves presents a very different context from other slave rebellions, but the subject clearly needs much more attention from historians, especially since some other Indians who were deported westward owned black slaves and took them to Oklahoma.

54. Freehling, *Road to Disunion*, p. 79.

55. Michael P. Johnson, "Denmark Vesey and His Co-Conspirators," *William and Mary Quarterly*, 3rd ser., 58 (October 2001): 913–76 (quotation on pp. 915–16). Of the books reviewed, the most useful is Douglas R. Egerton, *He Shall Go Out Free: The Lives of Denmark Vesey* (Madison, Wisc., 1999). Johnson shows that Edward A. Pearson, ed., *Designs Against Charleston: The Trial Record of the Denmark Vesey Slave Conspiracy of 1822* (Chapel Hill, 1999), is so filled with errors that it is wholly unreliable (pp. 925–35). In 1964 the historian Richard C. Wade advanced a thesis similar to Johnson's, also based on discrepancies between the court's *Official Report* and manuscript renditions of slave testimony. Wade, *Slavery in the Cities: The South, 1820–1860* (New York, 1964), pp. 228–41. In 1970 my former student Robert S. Starobin edited a very useful collection of primary and secondary sources that reveals much about ideology and history: *Denmark Vesey: The Slave Conspiracy of 1822* (Englewood Cliffs, N.J., 1970). While including an excerpt from Richard Wade's much criticized article, which appeared before his book, "The Vesey Plot: A Reconsideration," *Journal of Southern History* 30 (May 1964), Starobin exemplified the radicalism of the time by dedicating his book "to Bobby Seale and in memory of Fred Hampton," by contributing his book's royalties to Seale's Black Panther Party, and by using as his epigraph a quotation from Sterling Stucky, which reads in part: "Vesey's example must be regarded as one of the most courageous ever to threaten the racist foundation of America. . . . He stands today, as he stood yesterday . . . as an awesome projection of the possibilities for militant action on the part of a people who have—for centuries—been made to bow down in fear." The current debate over Vesey cannot be wholly separated from this historical context.

56. I am much indebted to personal correspondence with Michael Johnson, Douglas R. Egerton, Robert L. Paquette, and John Stauffer with regard to the Vesey debate. I am also much indebted to my research assistant, Philipp Ziesche, for his extensive notes and summaries of much of the literature on the controversy. My thinking at this point has been especially influenced by Paquette, "From Rebellion to Revisionism: The Continuing Debate about the Denmark Vesey Affair," *Journal of the Historical Society* 4 (Fall 2004); Paquette and Egerton, "Of Facts and Fables: New Light on the Denmark Vesey Affair," *South Carolina Historical Magazine* 105 (January 2004): 8–48; Paquette, "Jacobins of the Lowcountry: The Vesey Plot on Trial," in "Forum: The Making of a Slave Conspiracy, Part II," *William and Mary Quarterly*, 3rd ser., 59 (January 2002): 185–92; William H. Freehling, "Denmark Vesey's Antipaternalistic

Reality," in Freehling, ed., *The Reintegration of American History: Slavery and the Civil War* (New York, 1994), pp. 34–58; Walter Johnson, "Time and Revolution in African America," pp. 148–67.

57. M. Johnson, "Vesey and his Co-Conspirators," p. 948.

58. Egerton, *He Shall Go Out Free*, pp. 21–28, 78–83, 83–90, 110–18.

59. Julie Winch, *Philadelphia's Black Elite: Activism, Accommodation, and the Struggle for Autonomy, 1787–1848* (Philadelphia, 1988), pp. 50–61. While Boyer hoped to end Haiti's manpower shortage by attracting skilled workers as well as plantation laborers, he was especially eager to find ways of winning recognition from the U.S. government and preventing France from making any attempt to conquer its former colony. Though many migrants who had belonged to the American black elite enjoyed success in Haiti, the former urban workers had no taste for plantation labor. By 1825 even Boyer was becoming convinced, in Professor Winch's words, that "the entire undertaking had been a dismal failure" (p. 60). Some of the blacks who left Philadelphia for Haiti were recent migrants from Charleston, who had been forced out of South Carolina as a result of the Vesey conspiracy, and some were originally refugees from the Haitian Revolution. In 1821 Santo Domingo had declared its independence from Spain, but Boyer, fearing a Spanish reprisal, seized and annexed the entire eastern part of the island. This news apparently led Vesey or some Charleston blacks to hope for military aid from the much-enlarged Haiti.

60. Witnesses differed considerably in estimating the number of rural slaves who had or would join the conspiracy, with rumors ranging from five hundred to nine thousand. Michael Johnson points out that the total absence of plantation slaves in Charleston on the night of June 16 or any other night was, for Governor Bennett, "the strongest evidence of their having no participation, with the disaffected Metropolis," a conviction that allowed Bennett to conclude "it is scarcely possible to imagine [a plot] more crude or imperfect." M. Johnson, "Denmark Vesey and His Co-Conspirators," pp. 958–59. On the other hand, James Ferguson, "a big slaveholder with multiple estates near Charleston, recounted particulars of a visit he paid to Bennett on June 28 to inform him that on at least one of the Ferguson plantations, insurrectionary contagion was afflicting his slaves." Paquette and Egerton, "Of Facts and Fables," p. 19.

61. John Oliver Killens, ed., *The Trial Record of Denmark Vesey* (Boston, 1970), pp. 42–46, 59; Egerton, *He Shall Go Out Free*, p. 168; Freehling, "Denmark Vesey's Antipaternalistic Reality," p. 47. According to one white businessman, "the females were to be reserved *for worse than death*," while a newsweekly reported that a slave of Governor Bennett "was to have had his daughter, a beautiful young lady, as part of the spoils," a belief actually shared by the daughter, Anna Johnson. Starobin, *Denmark Vesey*, p. 6. As the historian Martha Hodes has shown, there is a danger in projecting the South's post–Civil War obsession with the African American rape of white women back into the antebellum and colonial eras. Before the war and the rise of the Ku Klux Klan, the Southern views of sexual liaisons between black men and white women were surprisingly flexible and complicated, and Hodes's examples of even alleged rape are a far cry from the imagery we have encountered in the aftermath of slave rebellions. Still, Hodes fails to consider the continuing Southern invocations of the Haitian Revolution, which various writers associated with the mass rape of

white women. Hodes, *White Women, Black Men: Illicit Sex in the Nineteenth-Century South* (New Haven, 1997).

62. Egerton, *He Shall Go Out Free*, p. 168; Michael Johnson, "Reading Evidence," *William and Mary Quarterly*, 3rd ser., 59 (January 2002): 196.

63. I am indebted to Stanley L. Engerman for pointing out that this lack of success has been largely overlooked in the prolonged debate.

64. William Johnson to Thomas Jefferson, December 10, 1822, quoted in Paquette, "From Rebellion to Revisionism," pp. 11–12. Paquette shows that both Justice Jackson and Governor Bennett had complex relationships with the court. Bennett believed that a "formidable conspiracy" simply could not "be matured in this State" but still termed the plot "the nefarious project." As we have seen, Johnson's grown daughter not only accepted the court's interpretation of a sophisticated plot but wrote that the slaves had marked her as one of their first victims (pp. 12–13, 15).

65. Robert Ernst, *Rufus King: American Federalist* (Chapel Hill, 1968), p. 372; M. Johnson, "Vesey and His Co-Conspirators," pp. 960–61. Johnson points out that the words "Congress" and "Missouri" "appear only twice in the transcript, both times in testimony about Monday Gell, not Vesey," and that the court substituted the word "Congress" for a reference to the state "Legislature" (pp. 961–62).

66. William W. Freehling, *Prelude to Civil War: The Nullification Controversy in South Carolina, 1816–1836* (New York, 1966); Michael O'Brien, *Conjectures of Order: Intellectual Life and the American South, 1810–1860*, 2 vols. (Chapel Hill, 2004), vol. 2, pp. 796, 818, 824–26; Wilkins, "Window on Freedom," pp. 57–62.

67. Winthrop D. Jordan, *Tumult and Silence at Second Creek: An Inquiry Into a Civil War Slave Conspiracy* (Baton Rouge, 1993). I draw in this section on parts of my own essay review of Jordan's book: "Terror in Mississippi," *New York Review of Books*, November 4, 1993, pp. 6–11, rpt. in Davis, *In the Image of God: Religion, Moral Values, and Our Heritage of Slavery* (New Haven, 2001), pp. 290–304. Like Richard Wade and Michael Johnson, with respect to the Vesey case, some reviewers of *Tumult* expressed doubts over much of the slave testimony.

68. Jordan, *Tumult and Silence*, p. 100.

69. Louisa Quitman Lovell to Joseph Lovell, July 28, 1861, quoted in ibid., p. 18.

70. Ibid., pp. 19, 86.

71. Ibid., pp. 128–35. In Documents Y and Z, in the book's appendix, Jordan provides two versions of the interview (pp. 341–45).

72. Ibid., pp. 341–46.

73. Ibid., pp. 344–48.

74. "Speech of J. Sella Martin, Delivered at the Athenaeum, Bristol, England, 27 October 1865," in *The Black Abolitionist Papers*, vol. 1, *The British Isles, 1830–1865*, ed. C. Peter Ripley (Chapel Hill, 1985), pp. 565–66.

75. Jordan, *Tumult and Silence*, pp. 41–44, 134–35.

76. Ibid., pp. 344–48.

77. Winthrop D. Jordan, *White Over Black: American Attitudes Toward the Negro, 1550–1812* (Chapel Hill, 1968), pp. 32–35, 38–40, 150–54, 398, 458–60. Despite this long tradition, which even ties in with medieval Arab stereotypes of black sexuality, Jordan notes in *Tumult and Silence* that white women in the South never seemed to share this phobia, at least in the pre–Civil War period, and they seldom if ever made allusion to black rapists in their letters and diaries. This point receives additional support from Professor Martha Hodes,

who makes the following observation about Southern white women during the Civil War: "Although white Southerners lived in fear of slave uprisings during the war, white women were not necessarily engulfed by sexual alarm when white men went off to war and left them alone with slave men." Hodes even quotes a white Virginia woman who as late as 1864 makes no overt mention of rape when describing hundreds of Negroes moving through the countryside, robbing and looting every house and committing "every crime that can be imagined." Hodes, *White Women, Black Men*, p. 140.

78. Jordan, *Tumult and Silence*, pp. 134–35.

CHAPTER 12

1. *Times*, July 18, 1857, quoted in Seymour Drescher, *The Mighty Experiment: Free Labor versus Slavery in British Emancipation* (New York, 2002), pp. 202–3. This editorial was a response to a parliamentary speech by the veteran abolitionist Lord Brougham.
2. Ibid., p. 201.
3. In 1803 Britain conquered Demerara, Berbice, and Essequibo, on the northeastern coast of South America, and they were formally ceded in 1814–15. It was not until 1831, however, that the three colonies were consolidated into British Guiana.
4. Ibid., pp. 54–72.
5. David Brion Davis, *Slavery and Human Progress* (New York, 1984), p. 236.
6. Aside from Charles Dickens, I am especially thinking of such outstanding novels as William Makepeace Thackeray's *Vanity Fair*.
7. Robert J. Steinfeld, *Coercion, Contract, and Free Labor in the Nineteenth Century* (Cambridge, U.K., 2001), passim; Drescher, *Mighty Experiment*, p. 161. For the complex historical relations between free and slave labor, see Stanley L. Engerman, ed., *Terms of Labor: Slavery, Serfdom, and Free Labor* (Stanford, 1999).
8. W.E.H. Lecky, *A History of European Morals: From Augustus to Charlemagne*, 2 vols. (1869; New York, 1876), vol. 1, p. 161.
9. For a recent, lively account of the British struggle for abolition, which focuses on such central characters as John Newton (the reformed slave trader), Olaudah Equiano (a former slave and abolitionist), and the abolitionists Granville Sharp, Thomas Clarkson, and William Wilberforce, see Adam Hochschild, *Bury the Chains: Prophets and Rebels in the Fight to Free an Empire's Slaves* (Boston, 2005). For the importance and complexity of the British antislavery tradition, see Howard Temperley's unequaled *British Antislavery, 1833–1870* (Columbia, S.C., 1972) and *White Dreams, Black Africa: The British Antislavery Expedition to the River Niger, 1841–1842* (New Haven, 1991).
10. The decision by Chief Justice Mansfield was actually much narrower. Mansfield freed the slave James Somerset, who had been placed in manacles on a ship about to sail for Jamaica, holding that no British law supported the use of such coercion or the forcible export of a slave for sale abroad. Planters continued to bring slaves to Britain for some decades, and as late as 1827 the Admiralty Court ruled that Grace Jones, a black woman who had been taken to England and had lived there for a year before returning to the Caribbean, remained a slave under West Indian laws. See David Brion Davis, *The Problem of Slavery in the Age of Revolution, 1770–1823* (New York, 1999), pp. 499–500). For a thor-

ough recent account of the Somerset case, the title of which overemphasizes its importance in leading "to the end of human slavery," see Steven M. Wise, *Though the Heavens May Fall: The Landmark Trial That Led to the End of Human Slavery* (Cambridge, Mass., 2005); see also Davis, *Problem of Slavery in the Age of Revolution*, pp. 471–522.

11. Benezet and the Philadelphia Quakers reprinted their English brethren's *Case of our Fellow-Creatures, the Oppressed Africans, Respectfully Recommended to the Serious Consideration of the Legislature of Great Britain, by the People Called Quakers* (Philadelphia, 1784), with the hope that it would influence American legislators. Davis, *Problem of Slavery in the Age of Revolution*, pp. 213–54.

12. It now seems quite possible that the famous Olaudah Equiano had not come from Africa, as he claimed in his best-selling and often reprinted book of 1789, *The Interesting Narrative of the Life of Olaudah Equiano, or Gustavus Vassa, The African*. See Vincent Carretta, *Equiano the African: Biography of a Self-Made Man* (Augusta, Ga., 2005). Carretta presents strong evidence that Equiano was born a slave in South Carolina before becoming a sailor and "inventing himself" as a spokesman for Africa and the British antislavery cause.

13. Davis, *Problem of Slavery in the Age of Revolution*, pp. 219–42, 403–36. The classic and highly detailed work on Britain's movement to abolish the slave trade is still Roger Anstey, *The Atlantic Slave Trade and British Abolition, 1760–1810* (London, 1975).

14. Seymour Drescher, *Capitalism and Antislavery: British Mobilization in Comparative Perspective* (New York, 1987), pp. 67–88; J. R. Oldfield, *Popular Politics and British Anti-Slavery: The Mobilization of Public Opinion Against the Slave Trade, 1787–1807* (Manchester, U.K., 1995), pp. 46–54, 113–19, 130, 137. For the crucial role of women in the antislavery campaign, see Clare Midgley, *Women Against Slavery: The British Campaigns, 1780–1870* (London, 1992), and Clare Taylor, *Women in the Anti-Slavery Movement: The Weston Sisters* (London, 1995). While Seymour Drescher and some other historians argued that the provincial antislavery societies took the leadership and became independent of the more conservative London Committee, Oldfield supports my own research, which indicates that abolitionists in Manchester and other towns kept in close touch with Thomas Clarkson and the London Committee.

15. Oldfield, *Popular Politics*, pp. 96–119; Anstey, *Atlantic Slave Trade and British Abolition*, pp. 269–70.

16. For important works on the economic context of abolition, see Seymour Drescher, *Econocide: British Slavery in the Era of Abolition* (Pittsburgh, 1977); Drescher, *Capitalism and Antislavery*; and Davis, *Problem of Slavery in the Age of Revolution*.

17. *An Abstract of the Evidence Delivered Before a Select Committee of the House of Commons in the Years 1790 and 1791; on the Part of the Petitioners for the Abolition of the Slave Trade* (London, 1791), pp. 41–42. As we have seen, for centuries many of the African slaves who boarded the slave ships believed they were being taken to a place where they would be killed and eaten by the white men. Slave-ship captains tried repeatedly to overcome this fear.

18. For the combination of war and revolution in the French Caribbean, see Laurent Dubois, *A Colony of Citizens: Revolution and Slave Emancipation in the French Caribbean, 1787–1804* (Chapel Hill, 2004). Despite the radicalism of the French Revolution, as we have seen, the French government continued to subsidize its slave trade until after the execution of Louis XVI and did not

abolish slavery until 1794, by which time the slaves of Saint-Domingue had gone far toward emancipating themselves. Napoleon then reinstituted slavery and the slave trade in 1802.

19. Anstey, *Atlantic Slave Trade and British Abolition*, pp. 343–413. We should recall that the U.S. Constitution prohibited Congress from interfering with the slave trade *until* 1807. However, in the United States it was becoming increasingly clear that, in contrast to the West Indies and Brazil, the slave population was growing rapidly by natural means. In both the North and the Upper South, this growth nourished fears of a future "overpopulation" of blacks. Thus when President Jefferson called on Congress to end the trade at the earliest permissible date, all the individual states, except for South Carolina, had already banned slave imports from abroad.

20. Davis, *Problem of Slavery in the Age of Revolution*, p. 412; Davis, *Slavery and Human Progress*, pp. 176–77. In Chapter Eleven we noted the connection between the parliamentary debates over the Registration bill and the great insurrection in Barbados. Wilberforce was persuaded to withdraw his motion and rely on local colonial slave registrations, a move that greatly upset James Stephen, the political architect of British abolitionism and a close friend and relative of Wilberforce.

21. For an excellent study of the last decades of the slave trade, see David Eltis, *Economic Growth and the Ending of the Transatlantic Slave Trade* (New York, 1987).

22. For a comparative study of the rise of immediatism, see David Brion Davis, "The Emergence of Immediatism in British and American Antislavery Thought," in Davis, *From Homicide to Slavery: Studies in American Culture* (New York, 1986), pp. 238–57. For new and important information on Elizabeth Heyrick, who affirmed, "Let compensation be first made to the *slave*," see Hochschild, *Bury the Chains*, pp. 324–28, 347; but Hochschild fails to note that the American Quaker abolitionist Benjamin Lundy quickly reprinted her radical treatise in his *Genius of Universal Emancipation*, where it was later read by Garrison and other American abolitionists.

23. For the details regarding negotiations that led to the emancipation act, see Davis, *Slavery and Human Progress*, pp. 198–219.

24. Edward Bartlett Rugemer, "The Problem of Emancipation: The United States and Britain's Abolition of Slavery" (Ph.D. dissertation, Boston College, 2005), pp. 372–448. By far the best analysis of the changing British perception of the emancipation act is Drescher, *Mighty Experiment*, pp. 158–237. Rugemer shows how American abolitionists and journalists overcame this interpretation. On the other hand, Dr. Steven Heath Mitton, in another new and important dissertation, shows that the British government acknowledged at least some economic failure in 1843 when it submitted a proposal to the American government for transporting American free blacks to the British West Indies. As Mitton shows, this recognition of the failure of Britain's "great experiment" had a decisive influence on Southern leaders. Mitton, "The Free World Confronted: The Problem of Slavery and Progress in American Foreign Relations, 1833–1844" (Ph.D. dissertation, Louisiana State University, 2005). I am much indebted to Dr. Mitton for sending me a copy of his dissertation.

25. A classic example of what became standard and almost official history (the British author was knighted) is Reginald Coupland, *The British Anti-Slavery Movement* (London, 1933).

26. Technically, Clarkson and Buxton were not "Saints," a term originally applied to Wilberforce and other Evangelicals within the Church of England but then often extended to other abolitionists.

27. E. P. Thompson, *The Making of the English Working Class* (New York, 1963), p. 201.

28. As prime minister, he expanded his economically based arguments in a radical book, *From Columbus to Castro: The History of the Caribbean* (London, 1970).

29. In 1984 I attended the conference in Bellagio, Italy, where an international group of historians discussed and debated the book that Williams had written at age thirty-three; some of the papers from this conference were published in Barbara L. Solow and Stanley L. Engerman, eds., *British Capitalism and Caribbean Slavery: The Legacy of Eric Williams* (New York, 1987).

30. Lowell Joseph Ragatz, *The Fall of the Planter Class in the British Caribbean, 1763–1833* (New York, 1928). Williams dedicated *Capitalism and Slavery* to Ragatz and drew heavily on his economic arguments. But Williams's Oxford dissertation was much more deferential to his Oxford teacher, Reginald Coupland, whose history Williams later attacked.

31. Eric Williams, *Capitalism and Slavery* (with a new introduction by Colin A. Palmer; Chapel Hill, 1994), pp. 149–53. Williams adds: "In justification of emancipation, it was argued that the restriction of production would give the planters a 'real' monopoly of the home market by equating production with home consumption. This was parliamentary strategy. Every effort was being made to make West Indian cultivation as expensive as possible." Williams then observes that this policy was reversed by the free-trade movement, which in 1846 succeeded in equalizing sugar duties and devastating the West Indian colonies: "The British West Indian colonies were thereafter forgotten" (p. 153). In some ways the emphasis that recent historians like Drescher and Mitton place on the economic failure of British West Indian emancipation ties in with the Williams thesis, even though they totally differ with Williams on the economic "success" of slavery. If the British colonies were blighted with failure—either the failure of slavery of the failure of emancipation—they would not be able to compete with other plantation systems. The difference would emerge with respect to periods of time, but it is clear that the abolitionists' success in cutting off African slave imports began to put most of the British colonies at a competitive disadvantage after 1808 or 1815.

32. Seymour Drescher, *From Slavery to Freedom: Comparative Studies in the Rise and Fall of Atlantic Slavery* (Houndmills, U.K., and London, 1999), p. 365, and sources cited on p. 376 in n. 33.

33. See Thomas Bender, ed., *The Antislavery Debate: Capitalism and Abolitionism as a Problem in Historical Interpretation* (Berkeley, 1992). While I still support most of the arguments I made in this interesting debate with Thomas Haskell, the debate is too extended and technical for a book of this kind.

34. Anstey, *Atlantic Slave Trade and British Abolition*, pp. 38–57; 321–425.

35. Drescher, *Econocide*, passim.

36. Ibid., pp. 162–63.

37. Drescher, *Capitalism and Antislavery*; Eltis, *Economic Growth and the Ending of the Transatlantic Slave Trade*.

38. Eltis, *Economic Growth and the Ending of the Transatlantic Slave Trade*, pp. 7–8, 138–41, and passim.

39. Ibid., pp. 3–61.
40. I have taken the figures on slave population decline from B. W. Higman, *Slave Populations of the British Caribbean, 1807–1834* (Baltimore and London, 1984), p. 72.
41. Eltis, *Economic Growth and the Ending of the Transatlantic Slave Trade*, pp. 8–9, 295.
42. Ibid., p. 15.
43. By 1904 the census for British Guiana listed 124,000 East Indians, 120,000 Negroes, 4,300 Europeans excluding about 11,600 Portuguese, 30,000 of "mixed race," and 6,500 aborigines. *Encyclopædia Britannica*, 11th ed (London, 1910), vol. 11, p. 676.
44. Eltis, *Economic Growth and the Ending of the Transatlantic Slave Trade*, p. 139. As Eltis notes, this is not "a very large figure [i.e., from 10 to 15 percent of the slave trade's total volume] relative to the perceptions of contemporary defenders of naval intervention."
45. Ibid., pp. 45–46, 185–204, 234–40. Seymour Drescher has more recently pointed out that by 1856–60 "the price of slaves being loaded in Africa had dropped by over 40 percent, but it had risen by 75 percent when they were landed in Cuba." While Cuban planters increasingly relied on indentured Chinese servants, who were treated like the slaves, "yet Cubans preferred the African slaves for as long as they could purchase them" and until 1860 "purchased two Africans for every indentured laborer from Asia." Drescher, *Mighty Experiment*, p. 193.
46. Granville Sharp, *Letter from Granville Sharp, Esq. of London, to The Maryland Society for Promoting the Abolition of Slavery, and the Relief of Free Negroes and Others, Unlawfully Held in Bondage* (Baltimore, 1793), pp. 3–11; Sharp, "Granville Sharp to the Honorable President and the Honorable Vice President and Committee of the Pennsylvania Society for Promoting the Abolition of Slavery and the Relief of Free Negroes Unlawfully Held in Bondage," July 30, 1788, Manuscript Collection Belonging to the Pennsylvania Society for Promoting the Abolition of Slavery, and for the Relief of Free Negroes Unlawfully Held in Bondage and for Improving the Condition of the African Race, vol. I (Philadelphia, 1876), document 165 (Microfilm Collection, Pennsylvania Abolitionist Society, Reel 2).
47. Drescher, *Mighty Experiment*, pp. 183, 200–201. Ironically, while some people may see this widespread British verdict of "failure" as the final death blow to the Eric Williams thesis, since it indicates that moral values must have been the driving force behind abolition, Williams himself took delight in quoting Disraeli and in presenting the shift in public opinion as evidence of the superficiality of earlier antislavery rhetoric and as a step toward the antiblack racism epitomized by Carlyle's essay "The Nigger Question." Williams, *Capitalism and Slavery*, pp. 194–96.
48. Drescher, *Econocide*, pp. 162–86; Drescher, *Capitalism and Antislavery*, pp. 20–24, 67–110, 162–66.
49. Thomas Clarkson, MS Diary, National Library of Wales, in Aberystwyth, Wales.
50. Drescher, *Capitalism and Antislavery*, p. 73.
51. Oldfield, *Popular Politics and British Anti-Slavery*, pp. 96–119 (my statement also draws on my own research in British primary sources).
52. For the surprising calls for slavelike social controls in eighteenth-century Britain, as well as for the religious and cultural foundations for *antislavery* in the

seventeenth-century English civil wars (including Quakerism), see Davis, *Problem of Slavery in Western Culture*, pp. 291–445.

53. Steinfeld, *Coercion, Contract, and Free Labor*. See also Jonathan A. Glickstein, *Concepts of Free Labor in Antebellum America* (New Haven, 1991).

54. Sidney W. Mintz, *Sweetness and Power: The Place of Sugar in Modern History* (New York, 1985), pp. 74–150.

55. Eltis, *Economic Growth and the Ending of the Transatlantic Slave Trade*, p. 20.

56. Ibid.

57. Ibid. For a collection of superb essays that help to illuminate this huge issue, see Stanley L. Engerman, ed., *Terms of Labor: Slavery, Serfdom, and Free Labor* (Stanford, 1999). The collection includes Seymour Drescher's "Free Labor vs. Slave Labor: The British and Caribbean Cases," pp. 50–86.

58. Drescher does briefly note that labor was degraded by slavery, but never develops the point (*Mighty Experiment*, p. 35).

CHAPTER 13

1. For excellent studies of the Second Great Awakening (the first occurred in the mid-eighteenth century) and its ties with social reform, see Whitney Cross, *The Burned-Over District: The Social and Intellectual History of Enthusiastic Religion in Western New York, 1800–1850* (New York, 1965); Steven Mintz, *Moralists and Modernizers: America's Pre–Civil War Reformers* (Baltimore, 1995); Mary Ryan, *Cradle of the Middle Class: The Family in Oneida County, New York, 1790–1865* (New York, 1981); Robert Abzug, *Cosmos Crumbling: American Reform and the Religious Imagination* (New York, 1994); Jon Butler, *Awash in the Sea of Faith: Christianizing the American People* (Cambridge, Mass., 1990); William Gerald McLoughlin, *Revivals, Awakening and Reform: an Essay on Religion and Social Change in America, 1607–1977* (Chicago, 1978).

2. Lyman Beecher, *The Remedy for Dueling: A Sermon, delivered before the Presbytery of Long-Island, at the opening of their session at Aquebogue, April 16, 1806* (Sag-Harbor, N.Y., 1807), pp. 37–38. Beecher's crusade against dueling was prompted in large part by the death in 1804 of the Federalist Alexander Hamilton at the hands of Aaron Burr. Ironically, Burr was the grandson of Jonathan Edwards, the most famous and influential of eighteenth-century New England divines.

   The Second Great Awakening is often described as originating in Kentucky and other frontier regions in the first years of the nineteenth century, but the revivals considered here began in New England and upstate New York in the 1820s.

3. Lyman Beecher, *Six Sermons on the Nature, Occasions, Signs, Evils, and Remedy of Intemperance* (Boston, 1827), p. 7.

4. By the 1820s average male alcoholic consumption had risen to an extraordinary level; see W. J. Rorabaugh, *The Alcoholic Republic: An American Tradition* (New York, 1979).

5. For an outstanding biographical study of Weld and his times, see Robert H. Abzug, *Passionate Liberator: Theodore Dwight Weld and the Dilemma of Reform* (New York, 1980).

6. Charles Stuart to Theodore Weld, New York, April 30, 1829, *Letters of Theodore Dwight Weld, Angelina Grimké Weld, and Sarah Grimké, 1822–1844*, ed. Gilbert H. Barnes and Dwight L. Dumond, 2 vols. (1934; Gloucester, Mass. 1965), vol. 1, p. 25. It is difficult today to recapture the close religious bond between men like Stuart and Weld: "Pray for me, my beloved Theodore. I am traversing the country, holding meetings wherever I can, and endeavouring to awaken the conscience of the Nation, that Negro Slavery may be put off. Wrestle for your brother, that in nothing he may presume, and that by nothing he may be daunted; but may prove a faithful minister of the God, who commands that the oppressed shall be let go free. . . .Tell me much about the progress and state of your own mind, and ever believe me Your faithfully and ardently affectionate C. Stuart" (p. 44).

7. Ibid., Charles Stuart to Weld [London, England], March 26, 1831, p. 43.

8. Ibid., Weld to William Lloyd Garrison, Hartford [Conn.], January 2, 1833, pp. 97–98. When considering the central importance of the biblical message that all men and women are created in the image of God (Genesis 2:27), we should recall that Gregory of Nyssa used this concept in his unique, late fourth-century attack on slavery (discussed in Chapter Two); many centuries later, when the French king Philippe the Fair freed the serfs in Valois, he affirmed: "Attendu que toute creature humaine qui est formée á l'image de Notre-Seigneur doit généralement être franche par droit naturel" ("since all human beings are created in the image of God, they must be free by natural right").

9. Abzug, *Passionate Liberator*, pp. 76–127. Before the debates, Beecher had hailed Weld as a "genius," adding that the students considered him "a god" (p. 80).

10. This dilemma led a few theologians, like the early abolitionist Samuel Hopkins, to argue that one must be willing to be damned to hell for the glory of God in order to be "saved."

11. Wendell Phillips to William Lloyd Garrison, from Naples, Italy, April 12, 1841, in Phillips, *Speeches, Lectures, and Letters*, 2nd ser. (Boston, 1905), p. 223; Phillips, "Public Opinion," address before the Massachusetts Anti-Slavery Society, January 18, 1852, in Phillips, *Speeches, Lectures, and Letters* (Boston, 1863), p. 52. For a fine biography, see James Brewer Stewart, *Wendell Phillips: Liberty's Hero* (Baton Rouge, 1986).

12. See especially Lewis Perry, *Radical Abolitionism: Anarchy and the Government of God in Antislavery Thought* (Ithaca, N.Y., 1973), and John Stauffer, *The Black Hearts of Men: Radical Abolitionists and the Transformation of Race* (Cambridge, Mass., 2002).

13. P. J. Staudenraus, *The African Colonization Movement, 1816–1865* (New York, 1961).

14. Leonard P. Curry, *The Free Black in Urban America, 1800–1850: The Shadow of the Dream* (Chicago, 1981), p. 115; Gary B. Nash, *Forging Freedom: The Formation of Philadelphia's Black Community, 1720–1840* (Cambridge, Mass., 1988), pp. 157–58. For the best survey of Northern free black history, see James Oliver Horton and Lois E. Horton, *In Hope of Liberty: Culture, Community, and Protest Among Northern Free Blacks, 1700–1860* (New York, 1997).

15. Horton and Horton, *In Hope of Liberty*, pp. 186–93.

16. See especially Peter P. Hinks, *To Awaken My Afflicted Brethren: David Walker and the Problem of Antebellum Slave Resistance* (University Park, Pennsylvania, 1997). For a superb edition of Walker's key work, see Peter P. Hinks, ed.,

David Walker's Appeal to the Coloured Citizens of the World (University Park, Pa., 2000).

17. Keith P. Griffler, *Front Line of Freedom: African Americans and the Forging of the Underground Railroad in the Ohio Valley* (Lexington, Ky., 2004); Horton and Horton, *In Hope of Liberty;* John Hope Franklin and Loren Schweninger, *Runaway Slaves: Rebels on the Plantation* (New York, 1999), pp. 116, 119, and passim; Larry Gara, *The Liberty Line: The Legend of the Underground Railroad* (1961; Lexington, Ky., 1996); William J. Switala, *Underground Railroad in Delaware, Maryland, and West Virginia* (Mechanicsburg, Pa., 2004).

18. Henry Mayer, *All on Fire: William Lloyd Garrison and the Abolition of Slavery* (New York, 1998), pp. 54–94; John L. Thomas, *The Liberator: William Lloyd Garrison, A Biography* (Boston, 1963), pp. 94–113.

19. Richard S. Newman, *The Transformation of American Abolitionism: Fighting Slavery in the Early Republic* (Chapel Hill, 2002), p. 138.

20. William M. Brewer, "John B. Russwurm," *Journal of Negro History* 13 (October 1928): 417–21. Russwurm, one of the first two black college graduates in America, wrote: "We have always said that when convinced of our error we would hasten to acknowledge it. That time has now arrived. The change which has taken place has not been the hasty conclusion of a moment. . . . [W]e have carefully examined the different plans now in operation for our benefit, and none, we believe, can reach half so efficiently the masses as the plan of colonization of on the West coast of Africa" (p. 417).

21. In Chapter Seven we took note of a section of the original Declaration of Independence that Congress deleted, which deserves to be quoted again in this new context. Jefferson accused King George III of "[waging] cruel war against human nature itself, violating its most sacred rights of life & liberty in the persons of a distant people who never offended him, captivating & carrying them into slavery in another hemisphere, or to incur miserable death in their transportation thither. This piratical warfare, the opprobrium of *infidel* powers, is the warfare of the CHRISTIAN king of Great Britain. Determined to keep open a market where MEN should be bought & sold, he has prostituted his negative [veto] for suppressing every legislative attempt to prohibit or to restrain this execrable commerce." Jefferson, "Original Rough Draught," *The Papers of Thomas Jefferson,* ed. Julian P. Boyd (Princeton, 1950–), vol. 1, p. 426.

22. For the most brilliant study of white abolitionists and the issue of race, see Stauffer, *Black Hearts of Men.*

23. Robert William Fogel, *Without Consent or Contract: The Rise and Fall of American Slavery* (New York, 1989), pp. 271, 328; Newman, *Transformation of American Abolitionism,* pp. 146–47. A few of the other important works on American abolitionism on which I have drawn are John R. McKivigan and Mitchell Snay, eds., *Religion and the Antebellum Debate Over Slavery* (Athens, Ga., 1997); Lewis Perry and Michael Fellman, eds., *Antislavery Reconsidered: New Perspectives on the Abolitionists* (Baton Rouge, 1979); Ronald G. Walters, *The Antislavery Appeal: American Abolitionism After 1830* (Baltimore, 1970); James Brewer Stewart, *Holy Warriors: The Abolitionists and American Slavery,* rev. ed. (New York, 1996); and John R. McKivigan, ed., *Abolitionism and American Religion* (New York, 1999).

24. See Leonard L. Richards, *The Slave Power: The Free North and Southern Domination, 1780–1860* (Baton Rouge, 2000), and David Brion Davis, *The Slave Power Conspiracy and the Paranoid Style* (Baton Rouge, 1969).

25. For the Mississippi laws on the "Duties of Masters towards Slaves," see Michael Wayne, *Death of an Overseer: Reopening a Murder Investigation From the Plantation South* (New York, 2001), pp. 79–80. Since slaves and free blacks could not testify in court, such laws were very difficult to enforce. Still, Wayne concludes that "slaveholders were occasionally brought to trial under these articles, occasionally even convicted."

26. There were some important Jewish abolitionists, such as August Bondi, Theodore Wiener, and Jacob Benjamin, all associates of John Brown. Leon Hühner, "Some Jewish Associates of John Brown," *Magazine of History*, September 1908, pp. 1–19; Jayme A. Sokolow, "Revolution and Reform: The Antebellum Jewish Abolitionists," *Journal of Ethnic Studies* 9 (Spring 1981): 27–41; Louis Ruchames, "The Abolitionists and the Jews," *Publications of the American Jewish Historical Society* 42 (September 1952–June 1953): 131–35. But except for some Reform Jews and secular radicals, the extremely small number of American Jews in the 1830–60 period would have been repelled by the Christian missionary mentality of many abolitionists. On the other hand, Garrison and a few other radical reformers spoke out against the discrimination that Jews had suffered along with blacks and condemned religious intolerance.

27. Stauffer, *Black Hearts of Men*, passim.

28. William W. Freehling, *The Road to Disunion*, vol. 1, *Secessionists at Bay, 1776–1854* (New York, 1990), pp. 291–92, 337–52; Mayer, *All on Fire*, pp. 196–206; William Lee Miller, *Arguing About Slavery: The Great Battle in the United States Congress* (New York, 1996), pp. 225–26, 279, 283, 346, 352, 360–81.

29. Although Mexico had outlawed all slavery in 1829, Americans in the northern province of Texas had brought in many black "servants" who were openly acknowledged as slaves only after Texas revolted and won its independence from Mexico in 1836. Because many Northerners opposed the prospect of adding such an enormous slaveholding province (which might have been split into several slaveholding states), Congress did not annex Texas until 1845, shortly before the expansionist James K. Polk took office.

30. Miller's *Arguing About Slavery* gives the fullest and most fascinating account of Adams's battle in Congress.

31. Keith P. Griffler, *Front Line of Freedom: African Americans and the Forging of the Underground Railroad in the Ohio Valley* (Lexington, Ky., 2004); Horton and Horton, *In Hope of Liberty: Culture, Community, and Protest among Northern Free Blacks, 1700–1860* (New York, 1997); Thomas D. Morris, *Free Men All: The Personal Liberty Laws of the North, 1780–1861* (Baltimore, 1974), pp. 1–4, 71–106.

32. Morris, *Free Men All*, pp. 107–29. Since seven of the justices wrote separate opinions, *Prigg* is a very difficult case to summarize. See especially Robert M. Cover, *Justice Accused: Antislavery and the Judicial Process* (New Haven, 1975), pp. 166–74.

33. Samuel Ringgold Ward to Gerrit Smith, April 18, 1842, in *The Black Abolitionist Papers*, vol. 3, *The United States, 1830–1846*, ed. C. Peter Ripley (Chapel Hill, 1991), pp. 383–84.

34. Albert J. Von Frank, *The Trials of Anthony Burns: Freedom and Slavery in Emerson's Boston* (Cambridge, Mass., 1998).

35. Donald Yacovone, "A Covenant With Death and an Agreement With Hell," http://www.masshist.org/objects/, pp. 1–3.

36. Speech of Parker Pillsbury, *Liberator*, November 4, 1859, vol. 29, issue 44, p. 176.

37. Speech of Wendell Phillips, ibid. I am much indebted to William Casey King for tracking down the Phillips quotation, which has long been erroneously cited.

38. Abraham Lincoln, "Second Inaugural Address," March 4, 1865, *The Collected Works of Abraham Lincoln*, ed. Roy P. Basler, 8 vols. (New Brunswick, N.J., 1953), vol. 8, p. 333.

CHAPTER 14

1. The best overall coverage of this subject is Don E. Fehrenbacher, *The Slaveholding Republic: An Account of the United States Government's Relations to Slavery*, completed and ed. Ward M. McAfee (New York, 2001), which should be supplemented by an important work that Fehrenbacher somehow missed, Joe Bassette Wilkins Jr., "Window on Freedom: The South's Response to the Emancipation of the Slaves in the British West Indies, 1833–1861" (Ph.D. dissertation, University of South Carolina, 1977), and Manisha Sinha, *The Counterrevolution of Slavery: Politics and Ideology in Antebellum South Carolina* (Chapel Hill, 2000).

2. Wilkins, "Window on Freedom," pp. 168–96; Steven Heath Mitton, "The Free World Confronted: The Problem of Slavery and Progress in American Foreign Relations, 1833–1844" (Ph.D. dissertation, Louisiana State University, 2005), pp. 23–28.

3. Robert M. Cover, *Justice Accused: Antislavery and the Judicial Process* (New Haven, 1975), pp. 109–16. For William Jay, Joshua Giddings, and other abolitionist legal theorists, this loss pointed to a mistake in the Supreme Court's decision in *Amistad*—a decision, according to Jay, "not wrong in its effect, but in the principle on which it was founded. That [inadequate] principle was, that by the law of Spain the Amistad Negroes were not properly slaves. But out of the jurisdiction of Spain the law of Spain had nothing to do with them. They were entitled to their liberty by the law of Nature." That is, according to the abolitionists, positive law on slavery could only be local and limited, ending at the border of territorial waters (pp. 113–14).

4. Robert Monroe Harrison, America's consul in Jamaica following slave emancipation, kept telling secretaries of state and southern governors that Jamaica was becoming a second Haiti. Wilkins, "Window on Freedom," pp. 116, 128, 140.

5. For the struggle to free slaves in Latin America, see Robin Blackburn, *The Overthrow of Colonial Slavery, 1776–1848* (London, 1988), pp. 331–415; Herbert S. Klein, *African Slavery in Latin America and the Caribbean* (New York, 1986); Rolando Mellafe, *Negro Slavery in Latin America* (Berkeley, 1975); John V. Lombardi, *The Decline and Abolition of Negro Slavery in Venezuela, 1820–1854* (Westport, Conn., 1971); Peter Blanchard, *Slavery and Abolition in Early Republican Peru* (Wilmington, N.C., 1992); Robert Conrad, *The Destruction of Brazilian Slavery, 1856–1888* (Berkeley, California, 1972); Rebecca J. Scott, *Slave Emancipation in Cuba: The Transition to Free Labor, 1860–1899* (Princeton, 1985). In the Epilogue we will examine the abolition of slavery in Cuba and Brazil, where the institution was far more central to the economy than in the rest of Latin America, and where it was not ended until the 1880s.

6. Jefferson, "Observations on Démeunier's Manuscript," in *The Papers of Thomas Jefferson*, ed. Julian P. Boyd (Princeton, 1950–), vol. 10, p. 58. Although Jefferson's clause in the Ordinance of 1784 excluding slavery from the Western territories after 1800 lost by one vote, the Continental Congress had no authority to enforce such a measure and virtually all Southern Congressmen were opposed to this restriction. Even with regard to territories north of the Ohio River, Illinois and Indiana came close to becoming slave states, despite the prohibition in the Northwest Ordinance of 1787.

7. Thomas Jefferson to James Monroe, May 14, 1820, in *The Writings of Thomas Jefferson*, ed. Paul Leicester Ford, 10 vols. (New York, 1892–99), vol. 10, pp. 158–59. Jefferson spelled Texas "Techas."

8. Ibid. For the influence of the Haitian Revolution on Jefferson, see Tim Matthewson "Jefferson and Haiti," *Journal of Southern History* 61 (May 2005): 209–48.

9. Jefferson to John Holmes, April 22, 1820, in *The Life and Selected Writings of Thomas Jefferson*, ed. Adrienne Koch and William Peden (New York, 1944), p. 698. It was in this famous letter to Holmes that Jefferson likened the Missouri Crisis to "a fire-bell in the night, [which] awakened and filled me with terror," and then moved on to say that "we have the wolf by the ears, and we can neither hold him, nor safely let him go. Justice is in one scale, and self-preservation in the other." His letters of this time are dramatically inconsistent, ranging from despair over the supposed betrayal of the heroism of "the generation of 1776" to his exuberant vision of acquiring vast new slave territories. Despite his linkage of antislavery with Federalist conspiratorial treason, he could reaffirm to Albert Gallatin his hopes for "some plan of general emancipation & deportation," which would place under state guardianship all children of slaves born after a certain date, who would then "at a proper age" be sent to "S. Domingo." Jefferson to Gallatin, December 26, 1820, in *Thomas Jefferson: Writings*, Library of America, ed. Merrill D. Peterson (New York, 1984), pp. 1447–50.

10. Jefferson's Second Inaugural Address, March 4, 1805, in ibid., p. 519.

11. For much crucial information on the political background, context, and substance of the Missouri Crisis I am deeply indebted to the work of my colleague Robert Forbes, "Slavery and the Meaning of America, 1819–1833," 2 vols. (Ph.D. dissertation, Yale University, 1994). When published, this should become the standard work on the Missouri controversy, which was the most important sectional crisis from the adoption of the Constitution to the Civil War.

12. I am exempting John Quincy Adams, despite his ardent nationalism when in Monroe's cabinet.

13. Forbes, "Slavery and the Meaning of America," vol. 1, pp. 137–39. Particularly after a widely reprinted pair of reviews of books on America in the *Edinburgh Review* in 1818, Forbes concludes, "neither patriotic Virginia Republicans nor anglophilic New England Federalists could any longer avoid seeing slavery through a British lens" (p.139). One should add that by 1818 the British antislavery movement was nearly dead and that none of the numerous British slave colonies had taken decisive steps, like the American states north of Maryland, to end slavery within that generation's lifetime.

14. Fehrenbacher, *Slaveholding Republic*, pp. ix–47. Especially since the time of the abolitionist William Lloyd Garrison, who as we have seen condemned the

Constitution as a proslavery "covenant with Death and an agreement with hell" (the words are the biblical prophet Isaiah's, not Garrison's), there has been sharp disagreement over the proslavery and antislavery aspects of the document. Fehrenbacher is in particular challenging such "Neo-Garrisonians" as the historian Paul Finkelman: "Slavery and the Constitutional Convention: Making a Covenant With Death," in *Beyond Confederation: Origins of the Constitution and American National Identity*, ed. Richard Beeman, Stephen Botein, and Edward C. Carter II (Chapel Hill, 1987), pp. 190–225. It should be stressed that Fehrenbacher's main thesis is that the United States became a "slaveholding republic" almost immediately after the Constitution was adopted.

15. Nevertheless, in 1798 Congress did debate a motion to exclude slavery from the Mississippi Territory.

16. Spencer Roane to James Monroe, February 16, 1820, "Letters of Spencer Roane, 1788–1822," *Bulletin of the New York Public Library* 10 (1906),: 175.

17. *Annals of Congress*, 15th Congress, 2nd Session (House), pp. 442–43, 540, 1430–33, 1436–38; 16th Congress, 1st Session (House), pp. 2210–11; Douglas R. Egerton, *Charles Fenton Mercer and the Trial of National Conservatism* (Jackson, Miss., 1989), pp. 164–68.

18. The most informed discussion of diffusion and what he terms "conditional termination" is William W. Freehling's *Road to Disunion: Secessionists at Bay, 1776–1854* (New York, 1990), though in trying to rehabilitate Jefferson's antislavery credentials as a diffusionist and colonizationist, Freehling overlooks Jefferson's thoughts about Cuba and Texas. For the massive export of slaves from northern Virginia in the 1840s and 1850s, as well as the virtual reenslavement of free blacks, see Brenda E. Stevenson, *Life in Black and White: Family and Community in the Slave South* (New York, 1996).

19. For the slow workings of Connecticut's law, see David Menschel, "Abolition Without Deliverance: The Law of Connecticut Slavery, 1784–1848," *Yale Law Journal* 111 (October 2001): 183–222.

20. For a breakdown of the voting in both the House and the Senate, see Glover Moore, *The Missouri Controversy, 1819–1821* (Lexington, Ky., 1953), pp. 53, 55, 61.

21. As Robert Forbes shows, even leading Federalists like Harrison Gray Otis and Rufus King were amazingly slow in recognizing the seriousness of the Missouri issue. One exception was the *New York Daily Advertiser*, which was edited by Theodore Dwight, a grandson of Jonathan Edwards and brother of Yale's president, Timothy Dwight. Having defended the Haitian Revolution in the mid-1790s, Theodore Dwight affirmed as early as March 1819 that if the sin of slavery were allowed to spread beyond the Mississippi, the political standing and influence of the Northern free states would be irrevocably sealed. Forbes, "Slavery and the Meaning of America," vol. 1, pp. 167–69.

22. Robert Ernst, *Rufus King: American Federalist* (Chapel Hill, 1968), p. 372; *Annals of Congress*, 16th Congress, 1st Session (Senate), pp. 380–81. Though King's speeches were not recorded, Senator William Smith reported that these were King's words on February 11, 1820, and Ernst notes that King's incomplete drafts and notes, coupled with Smith's and Pinkney's rebuttals and other correspondence, give credence to these reported words.

23. Ernst, *Rufus King*, passim. King, a large man with rugged features, came from a prosperous family on the Maine frontier. His father owned a few slaves, and in 1812 King freed his one known slave house servant. With respect to the

Western territories, he proposed in the Continental Congress a measure very similar to the one adopted in 1787 excluding slavery in the Northwest Ordinance, at a time when King was actively participating in the Constitutional Convention.

24. For "Philmore" and other radical statements in the eighteenth century, see my "New Sidelights on Early Antislavery Radicalism," in *From Homicide to Slavery: Studies in American Culture* (New York, 1986), pp. 228–37. Like Rufus King, abolitionist groups like the French Amis des Noirs could issue a ringing statement attacking the illegality and injustice of every moment of slaveholding, and then present a qualifying paragraph claiming that it would take much time and care to prepare both slaves and the rest of the world for their emancipation. For an analysis of this combination of an "immediatist" vision and cautious, fearful gradualism, see David Brion Davis, "The Emancipation Moment," in *Lincoln the War President: The Gettysburg Lectures*, ed. Gabor S. Boritt, (New York, 1992), pp. 65–88.

25. Forbes, "Slavery and the Meaning of America," vol. 1, pp. 180–81.

26. Daniel Raymond, *Thoughts on Political Economy* (Baltimore, 1820), p. 456.

27. (Athens, Ga., 1991; paperback ed., New York, 1993).

28. *Annals of Congress*, 15th Congress, 2nd Session (House), pp. 1204–05.

29. Forbes, "Slavery and the Meaning of America," vol. 1, pp. 248, 247.

30. For both the debate and passage of the compromise in the House, see *Annals of Congress*, 16th Congress, 1st Session (House), pp. 1572–73, 1576–88.

31. Moore, *Missouri Controversy*, pp. 166–68.

32. Ibid., 168.

33. John Lofton, *Denmark Vesey's Revolt: The Slave Plot That Lit a Fuse to Fort Sumter* (Kent, Ohio, 1973), pp. 129–30, 135, 216; Robert S. Starobin, ed., *Denmark Vesey: The Slave Conspiracy of 1822* (Englewood Cliffs, N.J., 1970), pp. 5, 11, 48, 90, 161. As we have seen in Chapter Eleven, there is some controversy over the actual existence of Vesey's conspiracy, but this has no bearing on the importance of references to King's speeches in the slaves' testimony.

34. For a detailed and highly readable account of the battle in Congress over antislavery petitions and other issues, see William Lee Miller, *Arguing About Slavery: The Great Battle in the United States Congress* (New York, 1996).

35. For a detailed analysis of how Southern slaveholders dominated the ruling political parties and branches of government, see Leonard L. Richards, *The Slave Power: The Free North and Southern Domination, 1780–1860* (Baton Rouge, 2000)

36. Mitton, "Free World Confronted," pp. 123–45; Wilkins, "Window on Freedom," pp. 317–18. Wilkins's work has now been richly extended and reinforced by Edward Bartlett Rugemer's important dissertation, "The Problem of Emancipation: The United States and Britain's Abolition of Slavery" (Ph.D. dissertation, Boston College, 2005).

37. Sinha, *Counterrevolution of Slavery*, passim; Wilkins, "Window of Freedom," passim; Frederick Merk, *Slavery and the Annexation of Texas* (New York, 1972), passim; British Library, MSS Brit. Emp. E 1/19, 10–11, and passim.

38. Merk, *Slavery and the Annexation of Texas*, pp. 82, 187–92, 257–64, 281–88; David M. Pletcher, *The Diplomacy of Annexation: Texas, Oregon, and the Mexican War* (Columbia, Mo., 1973), pp. 122–27, 134, 142–53; David Brion Davis, *The Slave Power Conspiracy and the Paranoid Style* (Baton Rouge, 1969), pp. 43–47; Mitton, "Free World Confronted," pp. 180–81.

39. Harrison to Forsyth, November 14, 1834, as quoted in Wilkins, "Window on Freedom," p. 123. As we have seen in Chapter Eleven, only 14 whites were killed in this insurrection, as opposed to some 200 blacks who were killed in the fighting and at least 340 more by various forms of execution. Michael Craton, *Testing the Chains: Resistance to Slavery in the British West Indies* (Ithaca, N.Y., 1982), pp. 291, 315. But the kind of lurid details mentioned by Harrison had much earlier emerged in accounts of the Haitian Revolution.

40. Mitton, "Free World Confronted," pp. 133–45. Mitton has earlier noted that Duff Green reported to Upshur in April 1842 that "the experiment in West India [*sic*] has failed," but one should remember that news from Barbados and Jamaica differed enormously, and Mitton argues that Green's conclusions were "far different from those entertained in Washington" (p. 87). On the other hand, I have learned from Stanley L. Engerman that, as early signs of a labor shortage following emancipation, the British plantation colony of Mauritius, off the east African coast, began importing East Indian labor after 1834, and that from 1839 to 1845 Trinidad imported some 1,300 subsidized free blacks from the United States.

41. Ibid., pp. 13–68; Fehrenbacher, *Slaveholding Republic*, p. 121. Upshur concealed Fox's proposal, which is not mentioned by the standard histories of Texas annexation and seems to have been discovered by Dr. Mitton.

42. Wilkins, "Window on Freedom," pp. 143–45.

43. Ibid., pp. 44–49, 82; Calhoun to William R. King, August 12, 1844, rpt. in Merk, *Slavery*, pp. 281–88.

44. Wilkins, "Window on Freedom," pp. 254–55, 302–3.

45. L. W. Spratt, *The Foreign Slave Trade the Source of Political Power—of Material Progress, of Social Integrity, and of Social Emancipation to the South* (Charleston, 1858), pp. 3–31; Spratt, "The Philosophy of Secession," rpt. in John Elliott Cairnes, *The Slave Power: Its Character, Career and Probable Designs*, 2nd ed. (London, 1863), pp. 390–410; Sinha, *Counterrevolution of Slavery*, pp. 125–52; Ronald T. Takaki, *A Pro-Slavery Crusade: The Agitation to Reopen the African Slave Trade* (New York, 1971), passim.

46. Robert William Fogel, *Without Consent or Contract: The Rise and Fall of American Slavery* (New York, 1989), pp. 281–387; Michael F. Holt, *The Rise and Fall of the Whig Party: Jacksonian Politics and the Onset of the Civil War* (New York, 1999), passim; Holt, *Political Parties and America's Development From the Age of Jackson to the Age of Lincoln* (Baton Rouge, 1992), pp. 726–985.

47. William E. Gienapp, *The Origins of the Republican Party, 1852–1856* (New York, 1987), pp. 37–67, 69–108, 295–99, 348–73, 439–48.

48. *New York Tribune*, March 7, 1857, as quoted in Don E. Fehrenbacher, *The Dred Scott Decision: Its Significance in American Law and Politics* (New York, 1973), p. 3. Throughout this section I have also drawn on Fehrenbacher's *Slaveholding Republic*, Sinha's *Counterrevolution of Slavery*, and David M. Potter's *Impending Crisis, 1848–1861*, completed and ed. Don E. Fehrenbacher (New York, 1976).

49. Robert W. Johannsen, *Stephen A. Douglas* (New York, 1973), p. 569. The *Dred Scott* decision gave legal expression to the most unqualified form of racist discrimination, declaring that at the time the Constitution had been adopted, Negroes had "for more than a century been regarded as beings of an inferior order . . . so far inferior that they had no rights which the white man was bound to respect; and that the negro might justly and lawfully be reduced to

slavery for his benefit." For the full text, see http://library.wustl.edu/vlib/dredscott/.

50. *The Collected Works of Abraham Lincoln*, ed. Roy P. Basler, 8 vols. (New Brunswick, N.J., 1953), vol. 2, p. 401 (hereafter cited as *CW*).

51. Abraham Lincoln, "Speech at Chicago, Illinois," July 10, 1858, in *CW*, vol. 2, p. 492; David Herbert Donald, *Lincoln* (New York, 1995), passim.

52. Donald, *Lincoln*, passim.

53. *CW*, vol. 2, pp. 461–62, 465.

54. "First Debate With Stephen A. Douglas at Ottawa, Illinois," August 21, 1858, in *CW*, vol. 3, p. 10.

55. Ibid., p. 16.

56. Ibid, pp. 51–52. The last, sarcastic quotation is from Lincoln's "Speech at Columbus, Ohio," September 16, 1859, in ibid., pp. 417–18.

57. For the new militancy in the Deep South, see Sinha, *Counterrevolution of Slavery*.

58. For some of the best works on John Brown, see John Stauffer, *The Black Hearts of Men: Radical Abolitionists and the Transformation of Race* (Cambridge, Mass., 2001); David S. Reynolds, *John Brown, Abolitionist* (New York, 2005); Paul Finkelman, ed., *His Soul Goes Marching On: Responses to John Brown and the Harpers Ferry Raid* (Charlottesville, Va., 1995); and Seymour Drescher, "Servile Insurrection and John Brown's Body in Europe," in Drescher, ed., *From Slavery to Freedom: Comparative Studies in the Rise and Fall of Atlantic Slavery* (London, 1999), 235–74.

59. *New York Herald*, November 3, 1859, as quoted in Potter, *Impending Crisis*, p. 377.

60. Oswald Garrison Villard, *John Brown, 1800–1859* (Boston, 1910), p. 566; Potter, *Impending Crisis*, p. 383.

61. "To William Kellogg," December 11, 1960, in *CW*, vol. 4, p. 150.

CHAPTER 15

1. James M. McPherson, *Battle Cry of Freedom: The Civil War Era* (New York, 1988), pp. 844–47; Leon F. Litwack, *Been in the Storm So Long: The Aftermath of Slavery* (New York, 1979), pp. 167–68; David Herbert Donald, *Lincoln* (New York, 1995), pp. 576–77.

2. Litwack, *Been in the Storm*, pp. 168–70. Lumpkin had a black mistress and two mulatto children; after the war, he married her as his legal wife. As the quotation indicates, untold numbers of Confederate slaves had long looked upon Lincoln as their liberator.

3. McPherson, *Battle Cry of Freedom*, pp. 846–47.

4. As we will see, the federal government adopted a form of compensated emancipation for the District of Columbia, and Lincoln long supported the idea of gradual, compensated emancipation for the border states.

5. I am much indebted to Professor Stanley L. Engerman for verifying these numbers in personal correspondence. Of course, the nation's economic structure was much different in 1860, and by today's standards the GNP was very small.

6. For the argument that the Civil War was the first "modern" or "total" war, see Mark E. Neely Jr., "Was the Civil War a Total War?" *Civil War History* 37 (1991): 5–28.

7. This point is strongly confirmed by the evidence presented in Robert W. Fogel, *Without Consent or Contract: The Rise and Fall of American Slavery* (New York, 1989). Given the work of Fogel, Stanley L. Engerman, and other economic historians, it is clear that American slavery would not have declined or disappeared for economic reasons. As we have seen, the abolitionist movement was powered by religious values and commitment, and it was this antislavery ideology that strongly influenced leaders of the Republican Party, including Abraham Lincoln. As we shall see, there was nothing inevitable about the destruction of the South's deeply entrenched and highly profitable institution. As with the results of many major wars, American slavery ended in 1865 thanks to the convergence of many random and fortuitous events.

8. One knowledgeable friend, after reading this paragraph, points out that the execution of Nazi leaders has not kept us from viewing World War II as a "good war," and that any assessment of a more "retaliatory" Civil War must take account of the South's systematic killing of black prisoners of war and of blacks seeking their freedom in the aftermath of the war.

9. David W. Blight, *Race and Reunion: The Civil War in American Memory* (Cambridge, Mass., 2001), pp. 110–11, 117. I am much indebted to Professor Blight's book for many of the themes of this chapter. For an especially bitter and vivid account of the triumph of Southern white supremacy, see Stetson Kennedy, *After Appomattox: How the South Won the War* (Gainesville, Fla., 1995).

10. I am using the U.S. Census Bureau's estimate for the U.S. population on October 31, 2005, of 297,557,215 (http://www.census.gov).

11. Blight, *Race and Reunion*, p. 64; McPherson, *Battle Cry of Freedom*, pp. 306–7 n. 41, p. 619 n. 53, p. 854; Wolfgang Schivelbusch, *The Culture of Defeat: On National Trauma, Mourning, and Recovery*, trans. Jefferson Chase (New York, 2003), pp. 37–38. I am much indebted to Steven Mintz for presenting me with a copy of the remarkable book by Schivelbusch, which deserves to be much more widely known.

12. Blight, *Race and Reunion*, p. 64; McPherson, *Battle Cry of Freedom*, p. 854; Schivelbusch, *Culture of Defeat*, p. 38. McPherson adds 50,000 civilian deaths to the South's total (p. 619, n. 53), and notes that on both sides officers, even generals, were far more likely than enlisted men to be killed in battle (p. 830). To keep things in perspective, in terms of global suffering, the United States in the 1860s was roughly comparable in population to Poland in World War II, which suffered 6,000,000 deaths as opposed to America's 620,000 in the Civil War. And of course one can find still higher figures in various modern wars in Asia and Africa.

13. There is continuing debate over the number of black Union soldiers slaughtered at Fort Pillow. David Blight writes that "of the 557 Union troops engaged, 262 were black, and most were massacred by Forrest's men after they had surrendered" (*Race and Reunion*, p. 142). For the Union response to the Confederacy's policy, including Lincoln's initial wish to execute a Confederate prisoner for every black soldier captive the rebels killed, see McPherson, *Battle Cry of Freedom*, pp. 792–800.

14. With respect to "the greatest social revolution in American history," I concede that one could argue that given the limitations in the improvement of the freedpeople's material and social conditions, the twentieth-century movement toward gender equality was a greater "social revolution." But I am using the

term "revolution" in its traditional sense of radical change within a short period of time.

15. Allen G. Guelzo, *Lincoln's Emancipation Proclamation: The End of Slavery in America* (New York, 2004), pp. 99–109. Even as late as 1864, when McClellan ran against Lincoln as president, he made it clear that while he would not reenslave the blacks who had been freed and enlisted in the Union army, he would not enforce the Emancipation Proclamation or interfere with slavery in the states where it existed.

16. I am indebted to Professor Robert E. Bonner for the information that the Confederate draft could exempt a young overseer or other employee, not just an owner of slaves.

17. McPherson, *Battle Cry of Freedom*, pp. 428–53; Dean Sprague, *Freedom Under Lincoln* (Boston, 1965), p. 159. In a very real sense, the Civil War disseminated an acute sense of danger and peril that far exceeded that of the War of 1812 and that reappeared only after the attacks of September 11, 2001. And of course it was the South, crisscrossed by invading armies, where many of the worst fears became realities.

18. Josephine Shaw Lowell, "A Young Girl's Diary," in *The Philanthropic Work of Josephine Shaw Lowell*, ed. William Rhinelander Stewart (New York, 1911), pp. 16, 24. See also Joan Waugh, *Unsentimental Reformer: The Life of Josephine Shaw Lowell* (Cambridge, Mass., 1997), and for the reaction of Northern intellectuals to the violence of the war, George M. Fredrickson, *The Inner Civil War: Northern Intellectuals and the Crisis of the Union* (New York, 1965), especially chap. 6.

19. Donald, *Lincoln*, pp. 514–15, 566–68.

20. Fredrickson, *Inner Civil War*, pp. 67–68, 71, 75–82, 113; David Brion Davis, *Slavery and Human Progress* (New York, 1984), p. 105; Blight, *Race and Reunion*, pp. 199–201. I stress the effects of capitalism and a market-oriented world, not capitalism itself, since the focus remained, as in religious revivals, on individual behavior. As Fredrickson shows, praise for the therapeutic values of military life led to the postwar idealization of "the strenuous life" (pp. 166–80). As Blight puts it, "such a culture of individual honor set against the crassness of the materialistic Gilded Age conditioned veterans of one section to accept their former enemies as comrades" (p. 201).

21. Schivelbusch, *Culture of Defeat*, pp. 98–101; David Anderson, "Down Memory Lane: Nostalgia for the Old South in Post–Civil War Plantation Reminiscences," *Journal of Southern History* 71 (February 2005): 105–36. Anderson's footnotes provide a large and updated bibliography on this subject. Schivelbusch cites Ralph Waldo Emerson, Herman Melville, Henry Adams, and Henry James as "losers in the victors' camp" who, after years of deploring slavery, "used Southerners as mouthpieces for criticizing their [postwar] times and as representatives of the 'other' America." But he especially points to the Great Depression as a time when Americans devoured scores of Civil War novels, when William Faulkner, Robert Penn Warren, and Thomas Wolfe came into their own, and when Margaret Mitchell's *Gone With the Wind* "became a national parable for America's fall from the heights of the 1920s into the depths of the Depression." On a far more sophisticated level, many Northern intellectuals found the ideological means of questioning the North's naïve optimism and "industrial and commercial triumph" in the thesis of the great Southern histo-

rian C. Vann Woodward, who drew on such close Southern friends as Robert Penn Warren: "The experience of evil and the experience of tragedy are parts of the Southern heritage that are as difficult to reconcile with the American legend of innocence and social felicity as the experience of poverty and defeat are to reconcile with the legends of abundance and success." Schivelbusch, *Culture of Defeat*, pp. 98–100; for the profound context of this quotation, see Woodward, "The Search for Southern Identity," in *The Burden of Southern History*, rev. ed. (Baton Rouge, 1968), pp. 3–25.

22. Schivelbusch, *Culture of Defeat*, p. 90. Schivelbusch insightfully adds that the same tradition has enabled some scholars to move from Marxism to Southern Conservatism, maintaining all the while a trenchant critique of both liberalism and the excesses of capitalism (pp. 90–91).

23. Ibid., pp. 37, 53.

24. The word "dreamland," first applied by the great historian Ernst Troeltsch to the German state of mind following the nation's defeat in 1918, refers mainly to expectations regarding the military victor as well as to the sense of a total break in historical continuity. Schivelbusch fails to stress that unlike France and Germany (except for Germany in 1945), the South had become totally devastated by invading armies, and that according to many memoirs, "Eden had become Hell." Anderson, "Down Memory Lane," p. 116.

25. For the Southern obsession with the Scots, including Bonnie Prince Charlie, see Schivelbusch, *Culture of Defeat*, pp. 47–53.

26. Blight, *Race and Reunion*, pp. 256–60.

27. Anderson, "Down Memory Lane," pp. 120, 126; Schivelbusch, *Culture of Defeat*, pp. 98, 99. Anderson fails to stress this point about the centrality of slavery to the antebellum society being idealized.

28. Lincoln, "Annual Message to Congress," December 1, 1862, in *The Collected Works of Abraham Lincoln*, ed. Roy P. Basler (8 vols., New Brunswick, N.J., 1953), vol. 5, p. 530 (hereafter *CW*). Of course, one could argue that slavery had not been a cause of the war but that radicals had persuaded President Lincoln to make slave emancipation a goal of Union victory. For example, Charles and Mary Beard, the most famous American historians in the 1930s, even denied that slavery was "the fundamental issue" in the late 1850s that led to secession and war: "Since the abolition of slavery never appeared in the platform of any great political party, since the only appeal ever made to the electorate on that issue was scornfully repulsed, since the spokesman of the Republicans [Lincoln] emphatically declared that his party never intended to interfere with slavery in the states in any shape or form, it seems reasonable to assume that the institution of slavery was not the fundamental issue during the epoch preceding the bombardment of Fort Sumter." Charles A. Beard and Mary R. Beard, *The Rise of American Civilization*, new ed. (New York, 1940), vol. 2, pp. 39–40. In recent decades numerous historians have demolished the Beards' thesis.

29. Blight, *Race and Reunion*, p. 4. For a fascinating and highly revealing sampling of interpretations of the Civil War from the 1860s to 1950, see Thomas J. Pressly, *Americans Interpret Their Civil War* (New York, 1954).

30. Blight, *Race and Reunion*, pp. 199, 384–87. Blight points out there is no evidence of any black veterans at the reunion, though according to the Pennsylvania Commission's rules black members of the Grand Army of the Republic with honorable discharges "were eligible to participate" (p. 385).

31. Garry Wills, *Lincoln at Gettysburg: The Words That Remade America* (New York, 1992), pp. 121–89.
32. Blight, *Race and Reunion*, pp. 7–8, 11, 386–97.
33. Ibid., pp. 65, 106, 371–80.
34. Lincoln, "Speech at Peoria, Illinois," October 16, 1854, in *CW*, vol. 2, pp. 255–56. As an ambitious Whig lawyer, campaigning for a seat in the state legislature, Lincoln was bitterly attacking Stephen Douglas's Kansas-Nebraska Act and held that this repeal of the Missouri Compromise and permission for slavery to expand into the territories was equivalent to reopening the African slave trade. As we shall see, by the time he became president Lincoln had a very specific plan for gradual emancipation and colonization, beginning with the border state of Delaware.
35. I borrow "revolutionary pronouncement" from Allen G. Guelzo (*Lincoln's Emancipation Proclamation*, p. 1). On October 12, 1862, Marx wrote in the Vienna *Presse* about "the most important document of American history since the founding of the Union, a document that breaks away from the old American Constitution—Lincoln's manifesto on the abolition of slavery. . . . In the history of the United States and in the history of humanity, Lincoln occupies a place beside Washington! . . . Never yet has the New World scored a greater victory than in this instance, through the demonstration that, thanks to its political and social organization, ordinary people of good will can carry out tasks which the Old World would have to have a hero to accomplish!" Quoted in David Brion Davis, *Slavery and Human Progress* (New York, 1984), pp. 248–49.
36. Donald, *Lincoln*, pp. 23–24, 165–78; Guelzo, *Lincoln's Emancipation Proclamation*, pp. 4, 22; Lincoln to Albert G. Hodges, April 4, 1864, in *CW*, vol. 2, p. 281. After detailing his constitutionally restricted efforts to combat slavery, Lincoln concluded this now famous letter by saying, "If God now wills the removal of a great wrong, and wills also that we of the North as well as you of the South, shall pay fairly for our complicity in that wrong, impartial history will find therein new cause to attest and revere the justice and goodness of God" (p. 282).
37. Guelzo, *Lincoln's Emancipation Proclamation*, pp. 3–4. Professor Guelzo stresses the supreme importance for Lincoln of "prudence."
38. Donald, *Lincoln*, p. 165–67. In his eulogy on Clay, Lincoln said that Clay "did not perceive, that on a question of human right, the negroes were to be excepted from the human race." Lincoln's interest in the possibilities of voluntary colonization led to a number of ill-conceived blunders, including the government's sponsorship in 1863 of a colony of a few hundred African Americans on a small island near Haiti. After many of the settlers died of smallpox or starvation, a naval ship brought the survivors back to the United States. McPherson, *Battle Cry of Freedom*, p. 509. While Lincoln eventually abandoned the bad dream of colonization, one should remember that various black leaders took up the cause in the later nineteenth and twentieth centuries. Indeed, Marcus Garvey, who led the first mass movement of African Americans, had nothing but praise for the white advocates of colonization in the antebellum era.
39. Discussed in Chapter Nine.
40. Donald, *Lincoln*, pp. 187, 191–92.

41. Guelzo, *Lincoln's Emancipation Proclamation*, p. 122; William S. McFeely, *Frederick Douglass* (New York, 1991), pp. 211–14. Despite his earlier reputation for antislavery rhetoric, Seward initially felt that after Lincoln's election, no further action was necessary.

42. Richard Nelson Current, *Lincoln's Loyalists: Union Soldiers From the Confederacy* (Boston, 1992). As William H. Freehling has more recently argued, when one adds to this 100,000 Southern Union troops the 200,000 Union soldiers from the border states and the nearly 150,000 *Southern* blacks who ended up in the Union army or navy, the South appears to be amazingly divided: a "total of 450,000 Southerners who wore Union blue, half as many as the 900,000 Southerners who wore Confederate gray." But these statistics make it all the more remarkable that the Confederacy fought off the Union for four long years and at times came close to winning the war. Freehling, *The South vs. the South: How Anti-Confederate Southerners Shaped the Course of the Civil War* (New York, 2001), preface and passim.

43. McPherson, *Battle Cry of Freedom*, pp. 306–7.

44. Lincoln to Orville H. Browning, September 22, 1861, in *CW*, vol. 4, p. 532.

45. As we have seen in Chapter Eight, a French official in Saint-Domingue did feel compelled to issue a limited emancipation proclamation in 1793, at an early stage of the Haitian Revolution. The measure was then extended to all colonial slaves by the French Convention the following year. But the situations were wholly different. Though thousands of Southern slaves ran away, they never revolted during the American Civil War, a nonevent that was later misused to indicate their supposed contentedness and docility. See my speculations on this issue in note 70.

46. James M. McPherson, *Antietam* (New York, 2002), p. 147; McPherson, *Battle Cry of Freedom*, pp. 506–7.

47. Iver Bernstein, *The New York City Draft Riots: Their Significance for American Society and Politics in the Age of the Civil War* (New York, 1990), pp. 4–5, 26–36, 288–89, note 8; Leslie M. Harris, *In the Shadow of Slavery: African Americans in New York City, 1826–1863* (Chicago, 2003), pp. 148, 264, 280–86. Opponents of the draft understandably complained against the provision that allowed the well-off to purchase an exemption for three hundred dollars. As a sample of Northern racism, in October 1862 an Ohio newspaper editor proclaimed that "a large majority of the men will make very poor fighters for niggers. They . . . see no reason why *they* should be shot for the benefit of niggers and Abolitionists. Those are their sentiments and they will stand by them, and if the *despot* Lincoln had a few hundred thousand such men in the field he would meet with the fate he deserves: hung, shot or burned—no matter which." Quoted in Wood Gray, *The Hidden Civil War: The Story of the Copperheads* (New York, 1942), p. 112.

48. Lincoln, "Appeal to Border State Representatives to Favor Compensated Emancipation," July 12, 1862, in *CW*, vol. 5, p. 318; Guelzo, *Lincoln's Emancipation Proclamation*, pp. 92–94; McPherson, *Battle Cry of Freedom*, p. 503.

49. Guelzo, *Lincoln's Emancipation Proclamation*, pp. 92, 106–7.

50. Ibid., pp. 93–97; McPherson, *Battle Cry of Freedom*, p. 503.

51. *Freedom: A Documentary History of Emancipation, 1861–1867*, ser. 1, vol. 3, *The Wartime Genesis of Free Labor in the Lower South*, ed. Ira Berlin et al. (Cambridge, UK, 1990), pp. 11–13, 347–77.

52. McPherson, *Battle Cry of Freedom*, p. 497; Reid Mitchell, *Civil War Soldiers* (New York, 1989), p. 125.

53. *Free at Last: A Documentary History of Slavery, Freedom, and the Civil War*, ed. Ira Berlin et al. (New York, 1992), pp. 349–50. There is no evidence that Lincoln ever received the letter.

54. Guelzo, *Lincoln's Emancipation Proclamation*, pp. 124–25; McPherson, *Battle Cry of Freedom*, pp. 494–95, 507–8. With respect to the suddenly increased abolitionist influence, McPherson points out that Wendell Phillips, the radical New England abolitionist, received a rare formal introduction on the floor of the Senate, and President Lincoln sat in an audience to hear one of Phillips's lectures (p. 495).

55. Guelzo, *Lincoln's Emancipation Proclamation*, pp. 81–91; McPherson, *Battle Cry of Freedom*, p. 509. As Guelzo notes, Lincoln himself was troubled by a bill that "cut loose elderly blacks who could not support themselves, did nothing for slave orphans whose parents had been sold away who knows where, and could beggar a widow whose only income came from hiring out the slaves left by her husband" (p. 87).

56. Guelzo, *Lincoln's Emancipation Proclamation*, pp. 118, 120; David Donald, *Charles Sumner and the Coming of the Civil War* (New York, 1960), p. 388.

57. Donald, *Lincoln*, pp. 364–65; McPherson, *Antietam*, p. 138; Guelzo, *Lincoln's Emancipation Proclamation*, pp. 112–13.

58. *CW*, vol. 5, pp. 219, 222, 329–31; Guelzo, *Lincoln's Emancipation Proclamation*, pp. 64–65, 112–21; Donald, *Lincoln*, pp. 364–65

59. Guelzo, *Lincoln's Emancipation Proclamation*, pp. 119–20.

60. McPherson, *Antietam*, p. 71; Donald, *Lincoln*, pp. 366, 374–75.

61. For an excellent account of the slaves' response to the war, see Steven Hahn, *A Nation Under Our Feet: Black Political Struggles in the Rural South From Slavery to the Great Migration* (Cambridge, Mass., 2003), pp. 13–115.

62. To Lee's dismay, his army failed to receive much public welcome in western Maryland, where the people seemed quite "cool." McPherson, *Antietam*, p. 98.

63. Ibid., p. 130.

64. McPherson, *Battle Cry of Freedom*, p. 454; McPherson, *Antietam*, pp. 154–55.

65. McPherson, *Antietam*, pp. 154–55; Donald, *Lincoln*, p. 374. There is also a record that he confided to Salmon Chase, his secretary of the treasury, "*I made a solemn vow before God, that if General Lee was driven back . . . I would crown the result by the declaration of freedom to the slaves.*" Guelzo, *Lincoln's Emancipation Proclamation*, p. 151.

66. McPherson, *Antietam*, pp. 107–9. For the contingencies of the war and their significance, see McPherson, *Battle Cry of Freedom*, pp. 857–58 ; Edward L. Ayers, "Worrying About the Civil War," in *Moral Problems in American Life: New Perspectives on Cultural History*, ed. Karen Halttunen and Lewis Perry (Ithaca, N.Y., 1998), pp. 160–61; and Ayers, *What Caused the Civil War? Reflections on the South and Southern History* (New York, 2005), passim.

67. McPherson, *Antietam*, pp. 130–31, 149. McPherson rejects the theory that McClellan was disloyal to the Union cause, but the general's contempt for Lincoln and the Republicans, coupled with his hostility to any interference with slavery, surely contributed to his reluctance to wage an all-out, "total" war.

68. Guelzo, *Lincoln's Emancipation Proclamation*, pp. 155–56, 255. The word "maintain" had been suggested by Secretary of State Seward. Guelzo reproduces the

texts of the "Emancipation Proclamation: 1. First Draft: July 22, 1862; 2. Preliminary Emancipation Proclamation: September 22, 1862; 3. Final Draft: December 29–31, 1862; and 4. Emancipation Proclamation: January 1, 1863" (pp. 253–60).

69. Ibid., pp. 155–56. In one of his harshest statements, Lincoln said that once the proclamation took effect, "the character of the war will be changed. It will be one of subjugation and extermination" (p. 156). As Guelzo puts it, "even Lincoln was a little surprised by black quiescence," and according to Ohio congressman William Holman, Lincoln "frankly stated that he had been disappointed in the blacks, who had not rallied as he supposed they would when the proclamation was issued" (pp. 226–27). One explanation, endorsed by Guelzo, is that the slaves thought they had already been freed and could thus patiently wait without lethal risk.

70. McPherson, *Antietam*, pp. 144–48. As we have seen in Chapter Eleven, the slaves in Barbados, Demerara, and Jamaica showed extraordinary discipline and restraint in protecting the lives of British whites during the rebellions of 1816, 1823, and 1831. This policy greatly aided the British antislavery movement, but a generation later, when many Britons had been stunned by the massacres of whites in India, some feared that Lincoln's Preliminary Emancipation Proclamation would incite a Haitian-like bloodbath in the South. The fact that the millions of slaves in the Confederate South never arose in insurrection, despite the invasions by Union armies and the shortage of young white men of military age on the plantations, may signify a shrewd appreciation of the importance of white public opinion in the "antislavery regions" that even went beyond the wise self-discipline of the earlier British Caribbean slaves.

71. Davis, *Slavery and Human Progress*, pp. 245–50; McPherson, *Antietam*, pp. 93–94, 141–46; Brian Jenkins, *Britain and the War for the Union*, 2 vols. (Montreal, 1974), vol. 2, pp. 42–43, 152–54, and passim. William W. Freehling notes that Palmerston and others were also afraid that intervention could lead to a war with America and the possible loss of Canada. Freehling, *South vs. the South*, pp. 179–80. In early 1863 Napoleon III again pressured Britain to intervene, and British tensions with America later became acute over the issue of ironclad warships that were being privately built in Britain for sale to the Confederacy. But the North's commitment to slave emancipation ultimately gave the British antislavery public decisive influence over governmental policy.

72. McPherson, *Antietam*, pp. 153–54. McPherson persuasively counters a common view among some historians that the election of 1862 was mainly a Republican defeat.

73. The controversial moment refers to Lincoln's unrecorded statements at the Hampton Roads conference of February 3, 1865, when Lincoln suddenly decided to accompany Seward at a meeting with three Confederate representatives, including Vice President Alexander H. Stephens, whom Lincoln had known long before as a fellow Whig. David Herbert Donald and a few other historians accept the claims of Stephens and another source that Lincoln "had now changed his mind about eradicating slavery." Donald speculates that Lincoln believed that "slavery was already dead" and that in order to keep the war from dragging on "for at least another year" he sought to "undermine the Jefferson Davis administration" through a "campaign of misinformation." I am more persuaded by James M. McPherson's argument that we cannot rely

on Stephens's postwar memoirs and that "both Lincoln and Seward were [and remained] committed to the ratification of the 13th Amendment as soon as possible." Certainly the Confederate delegation "returned dejectedly to Richmond," and nothing came of the Hampton Roads conference. The one significant point was Lincoln's unexpected suggestion at the conference that the federal government might compensate owners of slaves "to the amount of $400 million." Lincoln actually raised this issue with his Cabinet, but abandoned it after the cabinet expressed strong and unanimous disapproval. Lincoln's proposal accords with his view that the entire nation was responsible for the evil of slavery. Donald, *Lincoln*, pp. 555–60; McPherson, *Battle Cry of Freedom*, pp. 823–24, 823 n. 30.

74.   Though it is sometimes said that Lincoln's Emancipation Proclamation freed no slaves on January 1, 1863, Willie Lee Rose long ago provided a vivid description of the great emancipation celebration at the Union-occupied island of Port Royal, South Carolina, where the freedpeople sang "My Country, 'Tis of Thee." Rose explains why the Second Confiscation Act and the Militia Act of July 17, 1862, still left most of the blacks at Port Royal in an ambiguous status until "the great day" of January 1, 1863 arrived. Rose, *Rehearsal for Reconstruction: The Port Royal Experiment* (Indianapolis, 1964), pp. 186–87, 194–98.

75.   "Address on Colonization to a Deputation of Negroes," in *CW*, vol. 5, pp. 370–75; Guelzo, *Lincoln's Emancipation Proclamation*, pp. 170–72.

76.   Guelzo, *Lincoln's Emancipation Proclamation*, p. 235; Donald, *Lincoln*, p. 541. For a brief but telling account of the way most blacks celebrated Lincoln as the Great Emancipator, until a few prominent twentieth-century leaders scathingly rejected this tradition, see Guelzo, *Lincoln's Emancipation Proclamation*, pp. 244–47.

77.   Lincoln to Andrew Johnson, March 26, 1863, in *CW*, vol. 6, pp. 149–50.

78.   McFeely, *Frederick Douglass*, p. 229. As a result of the ferocious opposition to arming slaves, Lincoln moved slowly to the position that so delighted Frederick Douglass. While one major concern was the growing military manpower shortage, worsened by desertions as well as fatalities, David Herbert Donald stresses that "an unstated corollary of the President's new position was that plans to colonize blacks outside the United States were abandoned. Henceforth Lincoln recognized that blacks were to make their future as citizens of the United States. Donald, *Lincoln*, pp. 430–31.

79.   Bruce Levine, *Confederate Emancipation: Southern Plans to Free and Arm Slaves During the Civil War* (New York, 2006), pp. 84–85.

80.   Ibid., passim; Freehling, *South vs. the South*, pp. 184–95. For a broad historical analysis of the arming of slaves throughout history, including Joseph P. Reidy's chapter on the debate over arming slaves in the Confederacy, see Christopher Leslie Brown and Philip D. Morgan, eds., *Arming Slaves: From Classical Times to the Modern Age* (New Haven, 2006). Significantly, Frederick Douglass, who knew slavery well from his own experience, expressed fear in January 1865 that a significant number of Southern slaves would fight to defend the Confederacy, and thus slavery, if they could be assured of their own liberty: "If Jeff. Davis earnestly goes about the work to raise a black army in the South, making them suitable promises they can be made very effective in a war for Southern independence." Douglass, "Black Freedom Is the Prerequisite of Victory: An Address Delivered in New York, New York, on January 13, 1865," in *The Frederick*

Douglas Papers, ser. 1, *Speeches, Debates, and Interviews*, vol. 4, 1864–80, ed. John W. Blassingame and John R. McKivigan (New Haven, 1991), pp. 55–56.

81. Guelzo, *Lincoln's Emancipation Proclamation*, pp. 230–39; Donald, *Lincoln*, pp. 474–83, 509; Alexander Tsesis, *The Thirteenth Amendment and American Freedom: A Legal History* (New York, 2004), pp. 34–57.

82. Donald, *Lincoln*, pp. 520–45. As an example of racist "campaign literature," Lincoln is caricatured with a black face on the cover of *The Lincoln Catechism, Wherein the Eccentricities & Beauties of Despotism are Fully Set Forth. A Guide to the Presidential Election of 1864* (New York, 1864). The first "lessons" include: "By whom hath the Constitution been made obsolete? By Abraham Africanus the First. To what end? That his days may be long in office—and that he may make himself and his people the equal of the negroes."

83. While I have in general avoided military history in this chapter, except for the Battle of Antietam, for an understanding of the vast importance and consequences of the Battle of Atlanta, I highly recommend Albert Castel, *Decision in the West: The Atlanta Campaign of 1864* (Lawrence, Kans., 1992).

84. Guelzo, *Lincoln's Emancipation Proclamation*, pp. 231–33; McPherson, *Battle Cry of Freedom*, pp. 706–16, 823, 838–42.

85. While there is, of course, an enormous historical literature on Reconstruction, I recommend, along with Eric Foner's classic *Reconstruction: America's Unfinished Revolution, 1863–1877* (New York, 1988), a highly original recent work which shows that apart from racism, economic issues and class ideology played a crucial role in the North's disenchantment with Reconstruction: Heather Cox Richardson, *The Death of Reconstruction* (Cambridge, Mass., 2001). It is worth noting that the descendants of emancipated Russian serfs were not physically distinguishable and could be easily assimilated into the general population. But the very somatic traits that made sub-Saharan Africans "ideally suited" for slavery in the New World, as discussed in Chapter Three, have perpetuated the "stigma" of being descended from slaves, even when, as the *New York Times* columnist Brent Staples notes, they "discover that the African ancestry is a minority portion of their DNA." Staples, who was shocked when genetic screening showed that one-fifth of his ancestry is Asian, along with "a little more than half" from sub-Saharan Africa and over a quarter from Europe, makes the crucial point that because of continuing intermixture, large numbers of "white" Americans share similar African genes and that "racial distinctions as applied in this country are social categories and not scientific concepts. In addition, those categories draw hard, sharp distinctions among groups of people who are more alike than they are different." Staples, "Why Race Isn't as 'Black' and 'White' as We Think," *New York Times*, October 31, 2005, p. A18.

86. I borrow this phrase from Martin Duberman's timely work of 1965, to which I contributed, and which linked the antislavery past with the then current civil rights movement: *The Antislavery Vanguard: New Essays on the Abolitionists* (Princeton, 1965).

EPILOGUE

1. Since I long ago did a good bit of research on the slave emancipations in Cuba and Brazil (including research in Brazil), I have here drawn various passages based on those sources from my *Slavery and Human Progress* (New York, 1984) and have used some of that book's citations. In drawing comparisons I have

benefited immensely from Stanley L. Engerman's forthcoming book, *Slavery, Emancipation, and Freedom: Comparative Perspectives*, a manuscript copy of which he generously sent me.

2. *Gazeta da Tarde*, September 11, 14, 17, 28, 1880.

3. Ibid., May 21, June 2, September 25, 1883; Rebecca J. Scott, *Slave Emancipation in Cuba: The Transition to Free Labor, 1860–1899* (Pittsburgh, 2000), p. 38. For a brilliant comparison of Cuba and American Louisiana, see Scott, *Degrees of Freedom: Louisiana and Cuba After Slavery* (Cambridge, Mass., 2005).

4. David Eltis, *Economic Growth and the Ending of the Transatlantic Slave Trade* (New York, 1987), pp. 195, 244–45, tables A.1 and A.2, updated by e-mail from David Eltis, August 31, 2005; David Richardson, MS tables based on forthcoming book, David Eltis, Stephen D. Behrendt, and David Richardson, *The Atlantic Slave Trade: A New Census*.

5. Scott, *Slave Emancipation in Cuba*, pp. 6–15; Rebecca J. Scott et al., eds., *The Abolition of Slavery and the Aftermath of Emancipation in Brazil* (Durham, N.C., 1988); Robert Edgar Conrad, *The Destruction of Brazilian Slavery, 1850–1888* (Berkeley, 1972), p. 283; Emilia Viotti da Costa, *The Brazilian Empire: Myths and Histories* (Chicago, 1985), passim.

6. José Antonio Saco, *La esclavitud en Cuba y la revolucion de España, in Colección póstuma de papeles científicos, históricos, políticos . . .* (Havana, 1888), pp. 443–45; Saco, *Paralelo entre la isla de Cuba y algunas colonias inglesas* (Madrid, 1837), p. 17; Arthur F. Corwin, *Spain and the Abolition of Slavery in Cuba, 1817–1886* (Austin, 1967), pp. 149, 153–71, 181, 233–34, 239, 246, 250, 280–81; Scott, *Slave Emancipation in Cuba*, pp. 45–83; Ada Ferrer, *Insurgent Cuba: Race, Nation, and Revolution, 1868–1898* (Chapel Hill, 1999), pp. 1–89.

7. Justo Zaragoza, *Las insurrecciones en Cuba: Apuntes para la historia política de esta isla en el presente siglo* (Madrid, 1872–73), vol. 2, pp. 274–88; Corwin, *Spain and the Abolition of Slavery in Cuba*, pp. 141–51; Pedro C. De Mello, "Expectation of Abolition and Sanguinity of Coffee Planters in Brazil, 1871–1888," in *Without Consent or Contract: The Rise and Fall of American Slavery, Technical Papers*, vol. 2, ed. Robert W. Fogel and Stanley L. Engerman (New York, 1992), pp. 629–46.

8. Da Costa, *Brazilian Empire*, p. 170.

9. Suzanne Miers, *Slavery in the Twentieth Century: The Evolution of a Global Problem* (Walnut Creek, Calif., 2003), pp. 155–56 and passim.

10. For a brilliant analysis of lynching and the larger legacy of American slavery, see Orlando Patterson, *Rituals of Blood: Consequences of Slavery in Two American Centuries* (Washington, 1998).

11. David M. Oshinsky, *"Worse Than Slavery": Parchman Farm and the Ordeal of Jim Crow Justice* (New York, 1996).

12. Leon F. Litwack, *Trouble in Mind: Black Southerners in the Age of Jim Crow* (New York, 1998), pp. 12, 122. In 1878 one observer noted that "white will not sell, thinking the possession of land a sort of patent of nobility, to which black should not be admitted" (p. 121).

13. For anyone familiar with the global history of slavery, it is extremely ironic but also understandable that many African Americans today strenuously object to the use of the words "slave" and "slaves" when describing their ancestors' people. As we have seen, many Southern slaveholders also wished to avoid those words and succeeded in finding euphemisms for "slaves" in the U.S.

Constitution. Fortunately, there is no need to adopt the clumsy phrase "enslaved persons" in order to show that inhuman bondage was never successful in dehumanizing a people. In their own rich testimony, American bondsmen described what it meant to be a slave while protecting and preserving a human soul.

14. See especially Kevin Bales, *Disposable People: New Slavery in the Global Economy* (Berkeley, 1999).

ACKNOWLEDGMENTS

1. Ira Berlin, *Many Thousands Gone: The First Two Centuries of Slavery in North America* (Cambridge, Mass., 1998), 487.

Acknowledgments

Since THIS BOOK BEGAN as a large pile of written lectures without citations, I could not be more indebted to Philipp Peter Ziesche, who during most of his career as a graduate student at Yale took the time to help me track down sources with extraordinary skill, speed, and imaginative grasp of the subjects. Without Philipp's aid on the endnotes (finding most of the sources I had used and ones that revised and enriched my thinking), I simply could not have written this book. For assistance with other research over the past years I also want to thank Peter Hinks, Tanya Hart, Michael Mulyar, R. Owen Williams, Wayne Hsieh, Jennifer C. Lawrence, and, especially, William Casey King, who, along with making other discoveries, saved me in the last moments from having to cut from the book some important quotations for which I had no references.

John Stauffer long ago helped me immeasurably as a teaching assistant for my new Yale lecture course on slavery and abolition, using his professional skills to furnish me with scores of brilliant slides for my classroom projector (before the days of Power Point). I then learned much from his own scholarship, especially his prizewinning book, *The Black Hearts of Men*. More recently he has provided copies of maps and illustrations and gave an invaluable and critical reading of my completed book manuscript.

Stanley L. Engerman, who is probably the world's leading expert on comparative slavery, not only read the manuscript but penned in corrections and suggestions on more than one hundred pages. I am much indebted to both Stan Engerman and David Eltis for providing me with most of the numbers and statistics I needed for the book. And I have learned from both of them that estimated numbers on the slave trade and other subjects are continually being revised as they draw on new sources and become increasingly accurate.

Steven Mintz, to whom this book is dedicated, helped me create and then co-teach for many years a class on slavery and abolition for high school and middle school teachers—the class that quickly gave birth to my Yale lecture course and that remained the seedbed for this book, as I indicate in Chapter One. As one of my closest friends and advisers, Steve Mintz also gave the full manuscript an extremely helpful reading (and as editor of the Internet's H-NET List for the History of Slavery, Steve kept providing me with much up-to-date information). At one critical point, Steve's son Sean, a computer expert, told me how to merge and compare two different versions of the manuscript.

Let me emphasize that I would never have had the honor of teaching such a class and would never have embraced the goal of conveying our scholarly knowledge to a more general public if it had not been for the response of Richard Gilder and Lewis E. Lehrman to a lecture I gave on New World slavery at the Pierpont Morgan Library in New York in March 1994. Thanks to their decision, made at dinner that evening, to create the Gilder Lehrman Institute for American History, I was privileged to teach the first teachers' seminar in 1994 and then in 1998 to found Yale's Gilder Lehrman Center for the Study of Slavery, Resistance, and Abolition. As director of the Center I learned a tremendous amount from our first six international conferences as well as from fellows and individual lectures, some of which I've cited in this book's endnotes. (Most of the papers from the conferences are being published in separate volumes by Yale University Press.)

Lois E. Horton read an early version of the manuscript and saved me from a number of errors and misconstructions. I am enormously grateful to Robert Harms, David Goldenberg, David Geggus, Robert P. Forbes, João Pedro Marques, and Philip D. Morgan for reading chapters or sections of the book and helping me benefit from their own extraordinary knowledge. Rob provided immense help as associate director of the Gilder Lehrman Center, and as I indicate in endnotes, I am much indebted to his research and forthcoming book on the Missouri Crisis of 1819–1821 and its political legacy. Seymour Drescher, whose scholarly work has long influenced and contributed to my own (partly in a lively, prolonged, and productive debate we've had on British abolitionism), gave me essential advice at various points along the way. And in general, I am enormously beholden to the hundreds of devoted historians and economists who have illuminated the subjects of slavery and abolition over the past half-century, beginning especially with Kenneth

M. Stampp, who had much to do, beginning in the late 1950s, with the trajectory of my own career. As the historian Ira Berlin has written, it was Stampp who "broke the back of the racist scholarship in which the history of slavery was entrapped."[1]

I'm extremely grateful to the librarians at Yale who gave indispensable help to Philipp Ziesche and my other graduate student research assistants. While I did no research in primary sources for this specific book, I still owe immense gratitude to the libraries and archives I have used and thanked in previous works, which helped shape my understanding of slavery and abolition, extending from the Huntington Library in San Marino, California, to the New-York Historical Society, and from libraries in England, Scotland, and Wales (where I found a little-known diary of Thomas Clarkson), to collections in France, Brazil, Jamaica, and Guyana.

The great and legendary editor Sheldon Meyer gave me continuing and much-needed encouragement as he read drafts of my chapters from the start, and, from what I have heard, made an eloquent presentation of the book to Oxford University Press. I owe great thanks to India Cooper, my superb copy editor, and to Laura Stickney, Joellyn Ausanka, and Peter Ginna at Oxford, all of whom gave me enormous support and flexibility during the difficult last months of the project. And with respect to motivation, morale, and a wise allotment of time and priorities, my life continues to depend, as it has for some thirty-seven years, on my marvelous and loving wife, Toni Hahn Davis. While writing the book, I have also had the immense pleasure of watching my son Adam receive a Ph.D. at Princeton and write his own first book as a historian of medieval Europe; and then watch my son Noah, for a time a mechanical engineer, receive an M.B.A. with honors from the University of Chicago School of Business and then launch his career in business at Cisco. Both Adam and Noah gave me enormous support on my own writing project. I am also immensely indebted to my daughter, Martha, a professional editor and writer, who helped me improve the Prologue.

A few chapters of this book contain material, sometimes only a few paragraphs, that I first developed in much briefer and preliminary form in other works. I wish to thank the following publishers for use of this material: Harvard University Press, for some material from chapter one of my book *Challenging the Boundaries of Slavery* (2003); The University of South Carolina Press, for some material from my essay "The Impact of the French and Haitian Revolutions," in *The Impact of the Haitian Revolution in the Atlantic World*, ed. David Geggus (2001), 3–9; *The New York Review of Books*, for some material from my essay "Terror in Mississippi," 4 November 1993, 6–11; and for some material from my essay "The Benefit of Slavery," 31 March 1998, 43–45; Maisonneuve et Larose, for some material from my essay, translated into French by Yves Bénot, "Comment expliquer l'abolitionnisme britannique," in *Rétablissement de l'esclavage dans les colonies françaises, 1802: Ruptures et continuitiés de la politique coloniale française (1800–1830)*, ed. Yves Bénot and Marcel Dorigny (2003), 403–20; and Houghton Mifflin, for some material from my chapter 14 of *The Great Republic: A History of the American People*, Vol. I (third ed., originally published by D.C. Heath, 1985).

Finally, it is always indispensable, especially in an ambitious, risk-taking attempt to reconstruct a "Big Picture," to exempt everyone named in the "Acknowledgments"—as I now do—from any blame for the inevitable errors, misconceptions, and omissions—the shortcomings for which I take full responsibility.

Index

Note: Page numbers in *italics* refer to illustrations.

Abel (biblical), 69
Aberdeen, George Hamilton Gordon,
    Earl of, 232, 282
abolitionism
    and *Amistad* trial, 16, 19, 20, 21, 22,
        26
    in Brazil, 323–24
    in Britain, 8–9
    contradictions in, 175, 178
    convictions of, 253
    criticism of, 188–91
    in Cuba, 323–24
    and defense of slavery, 178
    Drescher on, 245–46
    and economics, 240–44, 247–48
    enactment of, 15
    explanations of, 231–49
    and French Revolution, 236
    and Haitian Revolution, 159, 170,
        173
    Lincoln on, 307
    petition campaigns, 235–36, 237,
        238, 246, 259, 263
    and religion, 188, 264
    and Revolutionary period, 154, 156
    and slave revolts, 209, 221
    in Spain, 325
    in United States, 185, 250–67, 280–
        81
    and violence, 266
    and West Indies, 214, 281
Abraham (biblical), 65, 187
Abravanel, Isaac, 55
Adams, Charles Francis, II, 304
Adams, John, 7, 154
Adams, John Quincy
    and *Amistad* case, 15, 18, 19, 20, 21–
        22
    and Calhoun, 177
    and foreign policy, 271
    on gag rule, 263
    on president's constitutional author-
        ity, 313
Aesop, 5, 46
Afonso I, 91
Africa and Africans
    African enslavement of Africans, 12–
        13, 89–91, 100, 143, 180

Africa and Africans (*continued*)
    assumed inferiority of, 53, 73–76,
        94, 189
    Caribbean blacks compared to, 130
    culture surviving from, 199, 378*n*18
    and "curse of Ham," 55, 64–70
    descendents of, 61
    and disease, 117
    and economic determinism, 77
    enslavement of, 50, 54
    ethnic diversity, 60
    and European trade, 88–89
    and free blacks, 130
    illegal slave trade from, 190, 237, 244
    and Islam, 61
    and long-term effects of slave trade,
        100, 331
    origins of enslavement, 82, 84, *105*,
        106
    portrayed in art, 58–59. *See also illus-
        tration section*
    South Carolina's importation of,
        138, 140
    and stereotypes, 66
African American culture, 129–30,
        199–200, 203–4
African churches, 203–4
Agassiz, Louis, 189
aged slaves, 199
agriculture. *See also specific crops, includ-
        ing* sugar
    and labor shortages, 33, 181–82
    in the North, 128–29
    and physical appearance of slaves,
        50–51
    and premodern bondage, 44
    revolution in, 40–41
    and slave-driven economy, 106–7
    soil exhaustion, 240, 242
    in the South, 138
    task system, 139
    and U.S. expansionism, 271
Alabama, 125, 182, 262, 271, 274, 295
Albornoz, Bartolomé Frías de, 96
Albright, George Washington, 201
ambition of whites, 131
amelioration policies, 214, 219, 237
American Anti-Slavery Society, 16,
        221, 259, 260, 261
American Colonization Society (ACS),
        256, 257, 258

American Negro Slave Revolts
        (Aptheker), 206
American Revolution. *See* Revolution-
        ary War
American Slavery, American Freedom
        (Morgan), 135
Amis des Noirs, 161, 162–63, 221,
        400*n*24
Amistad, 12–26, 25, 89, 142, 333*n*3,
        397*n*3
anciens libres, 166–67
ancient societies, 37–38
Andersonville prison camp, 301
Angola, 91
animals. *See also* bestialization
    and agriculture, 37
    domestication of, 30, 32–35
    slaves equated with livestock, 52, 62
Anstey, Roger, 236, 241
Antigua, 112, 115
apes, 62, 74
Aponte, José Antonio, 170
*Appeal to the Coloured Citizens of the
        World* (Walker), 156, 171, 209,
        258, 259
apprenticeship system, 14, 15, 238,
        245, 325
Aptheker, Herbert, 206, 209
Apuleius, 45
Aquinas, Thomas, 55
Arabs, 60, 61, 62, 65, 79
Arawak/Taino Indians, 97, 98, 110
Argaiz, Chevalier, 22
Aristotle, 3, 33–34, 41, 54–56, 62, 179
Arkansas, 125, 182, 262
arming of slaves, 363*n*29
    and American Revolution, 147–50
    in Brazil, 326
    and Civil War, 313–14, 320,
        410*nn*78, 80
    prevalence of practice, 35, 94, 143
    in South Carolina, 210
art, blacks depicted in, 58–59. *See also
        illustration section*
artisan trades, 133
Asante, 100
Asia and Asians, 38, 87
asientos (contracts), 90–91
Assyrians, 65
Athens, 37

Atlantic Slave System, 2, 26, 81, 234
Atlantic Slave Trade, 80–81, 84–85, 88, 89–102, 104, 106
auctions, slave, 94, 95, 139, 183
Augustine, 44, 51, 64–65, 67, 346*n*53
Australians, 53
Avicenna, 55

Baba, Ahmad, 63
babies, abandoned and enslaved, 40, 41
Babylon and Babylonians, 27, 37, 40, 65
Bahamas, 151
Baldwin, Roger Sherman, 19, 21
Baptists, 185, 187, 203, 251, 256, 264
"Baptist War" (slave rebellion), 218–21
Barbados
    and British slave-trade policies, 243
    English in, 111–12
    slave productivity in, 116
    and slave revolts, 169, 211–13, 218, 221
    sugar industry, 110, 114–15
Barbot, Jean, 81
Barrow, Bennet H., 196
battles of the American Civil War
    Battle of Antietam, 316, 317–18
    Battle of Atlanta, 321
    Battle of Gettysburg, 305–6, 320
    Battle of Second Manassas, 315
Beard, Charles, 304
Beard, Mary, 304
Beecher, Henry Ward, 251
Beecher, Lyman, 251–52, 253, 393*n*2, 394*n*9
Bell, John, 294
Benezet, Anthony, 126, 234
Bennett, Rolla, 223, 224
Bennett, Thomas, 223, 225, 387*n*64
Bento, Antônio, 326
Berbers, 60, 61
Berbice, 217, 242
Berkeley (Bishop), 247
Berlin, Ira, 131
bestialization of blacks, 2–3, 32
    and African enslavement, 52
    and animal domestication, 30
    and Douglass's self-portrayal, 52, 179
    and Haitian Revolution, 160
    and premodern bondage, 29, 45
Bibb, Henry, 259

Bible. *See also* Christianity; religion
    "Curse of Ham," 55, 63, 64–65, 68, 70, 73, 79, 187
    and dark-skinned people, 57, 64–69
    on Hebrew slaves, 60
    and illiteracy, 203
    and insurrection of 1822, 224
    on Kushites, 68
    on labor and slavery, 56, 95, 353*n*43
    and original sin, 35–36
    protocols for treatment of slaves, 38–40, 338*nn*32, 33
    and reconciliation of scriptures, 39
    sanctions for slavery, 78, 155, 187–88, 261, 360*n*5
The Bible View of Slavery (Raphall), 66
Bight of Benin, 101
Birkbeck, Morris, 176
The Birth of a Nation (film), 304, 306
Bishop, Abraham, 159
black (color)
    anti-black prejudice, 62
    assumed inferiority of, 189, 259, 272
    biblical references to dark skin, 57, 64–69
    black bones, 50
    symbolism of, 57–58, 63, 79, 94
Black Belt, 197
Black Codes, 303
Black Sea, 82, 84
Blight, David, 10–11, 300, 305
Blumenbach, Johann Friedrich, 75–76
Blumenthal, Debra, 94
bondsmen, 37
Bourne, George, 258
Boyer, Jean-Pierre, 173, 223, 386*n*59
bozales, 14, 18
Bradley, Keith, 34, 43, 45
branding, 28, 33, 38
Braude, Benjamin, 67
Brazil
    and abolitionism, 323–26
    discovery of, 87
    and emancipation, 1, 238, 327
    importation of Africans, 93, 95, 160, 199
    maroon settlements, 133
    and mortality, 117
    and Paraguay, 326

Brazil (*continued*)
  and Portugal, 103, 142
  premodern bondage, 28–29
  prevalence of slavery in, 15, 143
  racism in, 119, 120
  and slave-based economy, 120–21
  and slave revolts, 197, 207
  and slave trade, 110
  sugar industry, 13, 104, 107–8, 109,
    111, 114, 117–18, 120
Breckinridge, John C., 293, 294
Britain. *See also* England
  abolitionism, 8–9, 160–61, 173, 186,
    190, 209, 218, 220, 221, 244, 281
  amelioration policy, 116, 214, 237
  and American colonies, 149
  and arming of slaves, 143, 147
  and Brazil, 103
  civil war (17th century), 114, 132
  and colonial slavery, 14, 15, 80,
    165–66, 233–34
  and consumerism, 247
  and cotton demand, 184, 243
  and Cuba, 17
  and economy, 241, 281, 284–85
  and emancipation, 221, 233–34,
    238, 244, 260, 282, 283
  Foreign Slave Trade Bill, 236–37
  and freed slaves, 151
  free soil regions, 152
  and imperialism, 239
  and industrialization, 112, 190, 239
  and John Smith, 218
  labor conditions in, 233, 239–40
  and liberty vs. slavery contradiction,
    176–77
  and New World slavery, 90–91
  petition campaigns, 235–36, 237,
    238, 246, 259
  and Registry of colonial slaves, 211–
    12, 213, 237
  slave-trade policies, 13, 142, 231,
    233, 244
  and sugar industry, 112, 115–16,
    243
  and trade, 81, 240–41, 284–85
  and U.S., 176–77, 272, 282–86,
    295–96, 317–18

British and Foreign Anti-Slavery
    Society's World Convention
    (1840), 239
British Royal African Company, 88–89
Brougham, Henry, 172, 218
Brown, John, 210, 218, 291–92, 381n17
Brown, William Wells, 259
Brownson, Orestes, 302
Buchanan, James, 287
Burchell, Thomas, 219
Burke, Edmund, 57–58, 166, 188, 232
Burnah, 15
Burns, Anthony, 265
Bussa Rebellion, 211–13
Butler, Benjamin, 311
Buxton, Thomas Fowell, 214, 218, 237
Byrd, William, 135
Byzantine Empire, 29, 54, 60

Cain (biblical), 69
Calhoun, John C.
  on abolitionists, 268–69
  and *Amistad* case, 22
  on Britain, 282
  defence of slavery, 177, 256
  and Vesey conspiracy, 225
California, 175
Campbell, Archibald, 149
Canaan, 35, 55, 64, 65, 69, 187,
    345n52, 347n69. *See also* "Curse
    of Ham"; Ham
Canada, 1, 125, 161
cannibalism, 28–29
Cannibals All! (Fitzhugh), 191
Canning, George, 214, 237
capitalism, 240, 244, 247
Capitalism and Antislavery (Drescher), 242
Capitalism and Slavery (Williams), 240
caravels, 86, 93
Caribbean, 113
  agriculture in, 107
  British occupation, 166
  color distinctions, 180
  economic development, 109
  and emancipation, 269, 325
  free colored class in, 135
  and Holland, 110–11
  maroon settlements, 133
  prevalence of slavery in, 1, 15

and slave-driven economy, 121, 122
and slave revolts, 130, 197, 207,
  210–11
and sugar production, 115–16
Carib Indians, 110, 112
Carlyle, Thomas, 76
Carolina lowcountry, 125
Carter, Robert "King," 133, 134
Casas, Bartolomé de las, 55, 73, 98,
  354*n*49
Cassius, Gaius, 45
Celia (slave), 201–2
Celia, a Slave: A True Story (McLaurin),
  277
Central America, 15, 81, 110, 318–19
Chad, 330
Charleston Jacobin Club, 146
Charlestown (Charleston), South Caro-
  lina, 136
Charles V, 109
Chase, Salmon, 264
chattel property, 30, 32, 193, 337*n*13
Child, Josiah, 80
child metaphors in slavery, 52
children in slavery, 40, 41, 116, 131,
  199, 355*n*52
Chile, 1, 15, 98
chimpanzees, 73–74
China, 29–30, 37, 50, 87
chocolate, 87
Christianity, 126–27, 250–53, 262, 264,
  266–67. *See also* Bible; religion
  and abolitionism
  acceptance of slavery, 127, 187,
    375*n*36
  African churches, 203–4
  and brutality of slavery, 106
  and conversion of slaves, 94, 106, 128
  Crusades, 82
  Inquisition, 71–72
  and Islam, 77–78, 349*n*4
  Pinkster, 130
  revivalism, 250–51
  Roman adoption of, 44
  and scriptures on slavery, 39
Christophe, Henri, 167, 168, 173
Cinqué, Joseph
  capture of, 12
  dignity of, 24
  insurrection of, 14–15

living conditions on ship, 18
and Othello comparison, 21
return to homeland, 26
trial, 23, 335*n*19
civil rights, 219, 263, 264, 298, 328
Civil War, American, 297–322,
  403*nn*7, 8, 12, 13, 404*nn*15, 17,
  405*n*28, 407*nn*42, 47. *See also*
  battles of the American Civil
  War; Lincoln, Abraham
  and arming of slaves, 313–14, 320
  and Britain, 317–18
  Emancipation Proclamation, 1, 306,
    307, 314, 317, 321
  military strategies, 315–17
  mortality in, 300–301, 316
  Reconstruction, 300, 305, 322, 327,
    328
  secession of South, 192, 264, 294–
    95, 308
  and slavery in the Western Hemi-
    sphere, 1
  Thirteenth Amendment, 30, 321–22
Claiborne, William, 169
Clarkson, John, 151
Clarkson, Thomas, 161, 188–91, 235,
  281, 323
class divisions, 131, 177, 232–33
classical learning, 78–79
classifications of people, 73–76
Clay, Henry, 256, 278, 307, 406*n*38
Clinton, Sir Henry, 150
Cobb, Howell, 320
Codd, Edward, 212, 213
coerced labor, 36, 330
coffee, 87, 119–20, 158, 326
Colombia, 15
colonies, 80–81, 86, 112
Colored American, 19, 21, 23
Columbus, Christopher, 80, 84, 86, 87,
  109, 342*n*17
Committee for the Abolition of the
  Slave Trade, 246
compasses, 86
Compromise of 1850, 265, 313
Condorcet, Jean-Antoine-Nicolas de
  Caritat, 75
Confederate States of America, 294–95,
  297–98. *See also* Civil War,
  American
The Confessions of Nat Turner (Gray), 209

Congregationalists, 250, 251
Congress of Vienna, 237
Connecticut, 15, 142, 147, 152, 275
Conner, Lemuel P., 226
conspiracies. *See* slave revolts and conspiracies
Constituent Assembly (French), 162–65
Constitutional Convention, 273
Constitutional Union Party, 294
Constitution of the United States, 398n14
  Framers of, 154–55
  and president's constitutional authority, 26, 313, 314
  sanctions for slavery, 261, 263–64
  "three-fifths" clause, 17, 273, 276, 278
consumerism, 87–88, 99, 247, 248
Continental Congress, 154
contract labor, 36, 243
contradictions of slavery, 3, 31, 175–81
Conversos, 71–72
Cooper, Thomas, 178
Cornwallis, Charles, 150
Cortés, Hernando, 99, 109
Costa, Emilia Viotti da, 215, 216, 218, 327
cotton, 114, 125, 178, 181, 184
Covey, Edward, 179
Covey, James, 23, 26
Craft, Ellen, 259
Craton, Michael, 220
Creole (slave ship), 269
creoles, 117, 133
crime, 153, 257
Crittenden, John, 295
Cromwell, Oliver, 112
Crummell, Alexander, 66
Crusades, 82
Cuba
  and abolitionism, 323–24
  and *Amistad* trial, 19, 20, 22, 23, 25, 26
  and Haitian Revolution, 170
  importation of Africans, 13–14, 160, 199
  indigenous people of, 97
  mortality rates in, 117
  population, 134–35
  prevalence of slavery in, 143

  and slave revolts, 207
  sugar industry, 13, 109, 120
  and U.S., 17, 175, 271, 334n5, 335n30
Cuffe, Paul, 153, 258
Cugoano, Ottobah, 234
Curaçao (colony), 111, 114
"Curse of Ham," 64–65, 345n52
  Abravanel on, 55
  and blacks' physical traits, 63
  as justification of slavery, 187
  Muslim references to, 70, 79
  and Native Americans, 73
  and sub-Saharan Africans, 68
Curtis, Benjamin R., 287
Cush, 65–66
Cynics. *See* Diogenes of Sinope

Dahomey, 100
Daniel (slave), 216
Darfur genocide, 63
Davenant, Charles, 80
Davenport, Charlie, 227–28, 229
Davis, Jefferson, 292–93, 297, 304–5, 320
Day, George E., 23
Day of Jubilee, 203
Deane, Silas, 364n29
debt slaves, 40
Declaration of Independence, 144–46, 156, 307
Declaration of the Rights of Man, 162
defenders of slavery, 178, 186–92
defining slavery, 29–32
degradation, 31
dehumanization of slaves, 31, 37, 179–80, 201, 255
Delaware, 156, 197, 276, 309, 310
Demerara colony
  British conquest of, 242
  insurrection of 1823, 213–14, 215–18, 221, 383nn33, 34, 384n44
  trade, 231–32, 243
Democratic Party, 17, 287, 293, 312, 318
Denmark, 15
De Re Rustica (Columella), 5, 45
Desaussure, Henry William, 171
Deslondes, Charles, 208
Dessalines, Jean-Jacques, 167, 168, 169
Dew, Thomas R., 186

Diamond, Jared, 33
Dias, Bartolomeu, 86
diet, 137
dignity of slaves, 195, 203, 253
Diodorus Siculus, 42
Diogenes of Sinope, 34
discipline. *See* punishment of slaves
disease, 117. *See also* mortality
dishonor, condition of, 31, 36
Disraeli, Benjamin, 245
District of Columbia, 312
Dolben, Sir William, 235
Domestic Manners of the Americans
    (Trollope), 177
Domestic slave trade, U.S., 83–83
Donald, David, 308
Douglas, Stephen, 287–91, 292, 294, 308
Douglass, Frederick
    on abolitionists, 211
    on attitudes toward blacks, 76
    escape, 259
    on Haiti, 157–58, 159, 174
    on life of slaves, 2, 3, 52, 199, 200
    and Lincoln, 319–20, 321, 410*n*80
    literacy, 260
    on slaveholders, 196
    on slave revolts, 206
    on use of term "slavery," 330
Drake, Sir Francis, 49, 110
Drax, James, 114
Dred Scott case (1857), 26, 262, 278,
    287–89, 292–93, 401*n*49
Drescher, Seymour
    on abolitionism, 245–46
    on attitudes toward blacks, 76
    on British policies, 245, 356*n*4
    on capitalism, 241–42
    on free labor, 181, 232
    on slave revolts, 211
drivers (of slaves), 198
Dubois, Laurent, 164
Du Bois, W.E.B., 11, 306
Dunmore (John Murray), 149–50
Dunn, Richard S., 115
Dunning, William, 304
Dutch East India Company, 111
Dutch West India Company, 127
Dwight, Theodore, 159, 282

*Econocide: British Slavery in the Era of
    Abolition* (Drescher), 241, 242
*Economic Growth and the Ending of the
    Transatlantic Slave Trade* (Eltis),
    242
economics
    and antislavery policies, 152–53,
        240–44, 247–48
    and capitalism, 240, 244, 247, 248
    and consumerism, 87–88, 99, 247,
        248
    economic determinism, 77, 241
    efficiency of slave labor, 181, 243
    and emancipation, 238
    and European trade, 100
    and families in slavery, 116
    flexibility of slave economy, 185
    gross national product, 298
    and immigration, 287
    and slave-driven economy, 95, 106–
        7, 120–21, 122, 175, 178, 184
    slaves' value, 298
Economist, 231
education, 188
Edwards, Bryan, 160
Egerton, Douglas R., 222, 224
Egypt and Egyptians, 37, 39, 40, 56,
    59, 65, 346*n*66, 347*n*67
elites, 51, 53
Elkins, Stanley, 51–52, 207, 210, 342*n*12
Ellison, William, 180–81
Eltis, David, 77, 92, 241, 242–43, 247–48
emancipation
    in Brazil, 327
    in Britain, 221, 233–34, 238, 283,
        390*n*24, 391*n*31
    in Caribbean, 269, 325
    debate on, 186, 192
    Lincoln on, 310, 318
    in Massachusetts, 152
    and postemancipation, 327–28
    in United States, 155, 261–62, 312
Emancipation Proclamation, 1, 306,
    307, 314, 317, 321, 409*n*69,
    410*nn*74, 76. *See also* Lincoln,
    Abraham
Emerson, Ralph Waldo, 282, 303
employment for freedmen, 153–54, 256
encomendero, 97
encomienda, 97, 98

engenhos, 118
Engerman, Stanley L., 153, 181
England. See also Britain
    and colonization, 81, 111–12
    and emancipation, 176
    and Haitian independence, 173
    population, 132
    prevalence of slave trade, 90
    and slavery in America, 154, 178
Enlightenment, 74–75, 144
entrepreneurship, 137
equality, 191, 232
Equiano, Olaudah, 234, 389n12
Escoffery, Edward, 170
Essequibo, 242
Ethiopians, 62
ethnicity, 47, 50, 56–57, 102
Europeans, enslavement of, 54, 77–78,
    81–82
Exodus theme (biblical), 36
Ezra, ibn (twelfth-century writer), 69

Fabanna, 18
Fall of the Planter Class in the British
    West Indies (Ragatz), 240
families of slaves, 116, 183, 200–201
Federal Gazette, 155
Federalists, 271, 272, 279
Fehrenbacher, Don, 273, 278
Felton, Rebecca, 29
female captives and slaves
    as archetypal slaves, 38
    fertility of slaves, 116, 117, 201
    and gender ratios, 61, 100, 117, 134,
        138, 200
    and premodern bondage, 33, 38
    sexual exploitation, 3, 93, 201–2,
        255, 287
    on slave ships, 91–92, 93
Ferdinand V, King of Spain, 98
Ferrer, Ramón, 14
fertility of slaves, 116, 117, 201
Finney, Charles Grandison, 251, 252
Fitzhugh, George, 191–92, 289–90,
    307
Fletcher, Andrew, 247
Florida
    and expansion of slavery, 262
    fugitive slaves in, 125, 133
    secession of, 295

and Spain, 142
U.S. acquisition of, 270, 271
Fogel, Robert William, 153, 181, 287
foreigners and outsiders, 39, 50, 53, 79
foreign policy of the United States, 268
Foreign Slave Trade Bill (Britain), 236–
    37
Forrest, Nathan Bedford, 301
Forsyth, John, 17, 18, 283
Forten, James, 153, 171
Fox, Edward, 283
Framers of the Constitution, 154–55
France
    and abolitionism, 326
    and Brazil, 103
    and colonization, 81
    and Constituent Assembly, 162–65
    emancipation of colonial slaves, 15
    free soil regions, 152
    French Revolution, 142, 159, 161–
        69, 236, 389n18
    and Haiti, 7, 173
    Napoleonic Wars, 270
    and Revolutionary War, 141
    and trade, 90
Franklin, Benjamin, 36, 154, 155
Fredrickson, George, 75
free blacks
    and abolitionism, 256–58
    civil rights of, 165–66, 219
    employment for, 153–54, 256
    and French Revolution, 162–63
    and racial distinctions, 180
    as slave owners, 95, 121
    and slave revolts, 171
    and use of word "African," 130
Freedman, Paul, 50
freedom, buying, 36, 131
Freedom's Journal, 258
Freehling, William, 221–22
free labor, 181, 232, 245, 248, 249
Freeport Doctrine, 291
free soil regions, 264, 277
free trade, 240
Frémont, John C., 308, 309
Frey, Sylvia, 150
Fugger family, 87
Fugitive Slave Law of 1850, 9, 265–66,
    290, 294, 308, 311

fugitive slaves
    capture of, 162
    and John Brown, 291–92
    lectures and printed narratives of,
        259
    and paternalism, 194
    settlements of, 120, 133–34
    and Underground Railroad, 258,
        264–65
Futa Jallon, 100

Gabriel slave conspiracy, 170, 207–8,
    210, 256, 380*n*8
Gama, Vasco da, 86–87
Garnet, Henry Highland, 259
Garnsey, Peter, 35
Garrison, William Lloyd
    and abolitionism, 9
    and Constitution, 263–64, 398*n*14
    and emancipation, 258
    and interracial marriage, 260
    Liberator, 153, 158, 221, 258, 335*n*17
    pacifism of, 210
    tribute paid to, 323
Gayle, Sarah, 195
Gedney, Thomas, 15
Geertz, Clifford, 187
Geggus, David, 166
Geiss, Imanuel, 73
Gell, Monday, 223
genetics, 33
Genoa, 81
gens de couleur, 166, 180
Georgia
    agriculture in, 125, 182
    fugitive slaves, lost in Revolutionary
        War, 150
    importation of Africans, 80, 152,
        154
    prevalence of slavery in, 136
    secession of, 295
    slave imports ended, 156
    slave troops in, 148
Gerais, Minas, 119
Gibbs, Josiah Willard, 23
Giddings, Joshua, 263, 397*n*3
Gladstone, Jack, 216, 217
Gladstone, John, 214, 216
Gladstone, William, 317
Gliddon, George, 189

Gobineau, Joseph de, 189
Gold Coast, 90, 101
The Golden Ass, or Metamorphoses
    (Apuleius), 45
Goldenberg, David, 66, 67, 68
Grabeau, 18, 24
Grant, Ulysses S., 305, 320
Grasser, Erasmus, 58
Gray, Simon, 198
Gray, Thomas R., 209
Great Awakenings, 102, 202–3, 250–51
Greater Antilles, 97
Greco-Roman world, 58
Greece, ancient, 34, 41–42, 50, 53, 56–57
Green, Duff, 284–85
Gregory of Nyssa, 34–35, 55
Grenada, 211, 166
Grigg, Nanny, 169
Guadeloupe, 165, 166, 168
Guanche natives, 84
Guelzo, Allen C., 310, 314
Gullah language, 136
Gurney, Joseph John, 283

Haiti, 328
Haitian Revolution (1791–1804), 157–
    74, 366*n*2, 367*nn*3, 4, 7, 9,
    368*nn*10, 11, 369*nn*16, 18, 22,
    370*nn*33, 34, 372*nn*43, 45, 47
    influence of, 13, 116, 120, 142, 152,
        158, 170, 256, 384*n*41
    leadership of, 147
    response of slaves to, 169, 211,
        381*n*10
    success of, 270
    support for, 7
    U.S. response to, 270–71
Hale, John P., 264
Ham (biblical), 64–65. *See also* Canaan;
    "Curse of Ham"; Noah
    Abravanel on, 55
    and blacks' physical traits, 63
    as justification of slavery, 187
    Muslim references to, 70, 79
    and Native Americans, 73
    and sub-Saharan Africans, 68
Hamilton, Alexander, 147–48, 154,
    155, 364*nn*27, 28
Hammond, James Henry, 188–91, 201,
    379*n*25
Hammurabi Code, 32, 38

Hanson, Victor, 40
Hapsburgs, 111
Harms, Robert, 100
Harper, Robert Goodloe, 146–47
Harpers Ferry, Virginia, 291–92
Harrison, Robert Monroe, 283–84
Hart, Henry, 24
Hartford Convention of 1814-15, 282
Hawkins, John, 110
Hebrews, 56, 68
Hegel, Georg, 31
Henry, Infante of Portugal, 88
Herald of Freedom, 21
Herodotus, 68
Heyrick, Elizabeth, 237, 258
Hillhouse, James, 272
Hispaniola, 97, 109
History of European Morals (Lecky), 234
Hiyya, 68
Holabird, William S., 18
Holland and the Dutch
    and emancipation, 238, 325
    and Portugal, 144
    prevalence of slave trade, 90, 127
    and Revolutionary War, 141
    struggle for independence, 110–11
    and sugar industry, 114
Holmes, George Frederick, 188, 189
Holmes, Isaac, 176
homosexuality, 65
Hopkins, Keith, 46
Hopkins, Samuel, 256
Horry, Elias, 224
Horry, John, 224
household servants, 129, 133, 219, 319
Howe, Julia Ward, 266
Huger, Isaac, 147
Huggins, Nathan, 13
Hume, David, 74–75, 76
Hunt, James, 76
Hunter, David, 309
hunting-and-gathering societies, 37
Hutcheson, Francis, 75, 247

Iberia and Iberians, 70, 79, 93, 120
iginu'du, 38
illegitimate children, 131. *See also* mis-
    cegenation; mulattoes
Illinois, 142, 154
illiteracy, 144, 188, 203, 209, 260

Immediate, Not Gradual Abolition
    (Heyrick), 237
immigrants, 184–85, 287
incentives for slaves, 116, 195, 196–97
Incidents in the Life of a Slave Girl
    (Jacobs), 179
indentured servants, 115, 127–28, 132
independence of black slaves, 137–39
India, 50, 61, 143, 233, 239
Indiana, 142, 154
indigenous slavery, 88–91
indigo, 109, 138
Indonesians, 37
Industrial Revolution, 181
infants, abandoned and enslaved, 40, 41
"inhuman" (term), 2–3
Inquisition, 71–72
Iowa, 278
Irish laborers, 185
Isaac, Benjamin, 57
Isabella I, Queen of Spain, 98
Isaiah (biblical), 203
Islam
    and Christianity, 77–78
    expansion of, 58, 60
    and Mâle revolt, 170
    Qur'an, 57, 62
    and racism, 62–63
    slavery in, 54, 60–64, 69, 79, 94, 143
Israelites, 65, 73, 187
Italy, 44

Jackson, Andrew, 260–61, 279, 280
Jackson, James, 155
Jacobs, Harriet, 63, 179, 259
Jamaica
    civil rights in, 170
    exports, 243
    importation of Africans, 160
    indigenous people of, 97
    Maroon War, 166
    quality of life in, 123
    and racial distinctions, 180
    and Saint-Domingue insurrection,
        165, 169
    and slave revolts, 207, 218–21, 238
    sugar industry, 109, 110
Jamestown, Virginia, 124, 132
Japheth (biblical), 187

Jay, John, 147–48, 154, 155, 364*n*27
Jay, William, 21, 397*n*3
Jefferson, Thomas, 363*n*19, 395*n*21
    and benefits of slave labor, 179
    on Haiti, 270–71
    prejudices of, 74
    and prevalence of slavery, 145–46
    on problem of slavery, 154, 155
    sexual relations with slaves, 201
    slaves of, 104, 150, 201
    and Vesey conspiracy, 225
Jeffersonian tradition, 185
Jesus (biblical), 187, 203
Jews and Judaism, 39, 67, 70–72, 79,
    114, 342*n*17, 346*n*56, 347*nn*76,
    78, 396*n*26
Jim Crow discrimination, 327
Jocelyn, Simeon, 19
John III of Portugal, 90
Johnson, Andrew, 319, 322
Johnson, Anthony, 131
Johnson, Bradley T., 304
Johnson, Michael P., 222
Johnson, Samuel, 144, 205
Johnson, Walter, 216
Johnson, William, 225
Jones, Howard, 26
Jordan, Winthrop D., 73, 226–29, 230
Joseph (biblical), 5, 50, 53
Joshua (biblical), 56
Judson, Andrew T., 16, 18–19, 20, 21,
    22, 23
Justinian Code, 21–22, 35, 42–43, 55

Kamen, Henry, 71
Kansas, 175
Kansas-Nebraska Act of 1854, 278,
    287, 288, 289, 307
Kant, Immanuel, 75
Kasanje, 100
Kellogg, William, 295
Kendall, Amos, 263
Kennah, 24
Kentucky, 134, 141, 156, 262, 294, 309
Khaldūn, 62
kidnapping victims, 38, 154
killing slaves, 40
King, Rufus, 399*nn*21, 23
    on legality of slavery, 211, 225, 256,
        400*n*24

and Pinckney, 275–76, 397*n*32
on problem of slavery, 154
and Vesey conspiracy, 279
kinship patterns among slaves, 200–201
Knibb, William, 219, 220, 221
Knight, Sarah Kemble, 129
Know-Nothing Party, 287, 293
Knox, Bernard, 42
Ku Klux Klan, 306
Kushites, 65–66, 69

laborers, European, 132, 233
labor shortages, 181–82, 243–44
ladinos, 14, 18, 23, 335*n*8
lançados, 90
Lane Theological Seminary, 253–54
language, 38
latifundia, 44
Laurens, John, 147–48
Laveaux, Etienne, 47
lavradores de cana (tenant farmers), 117–
    18
laws. *See also specific acts and laws*
    on manumission, 132, 154, 161,
        180, 193–94, 204
    on marriage of slaves, 36–37, 203,
        260
    master-servant laws, 233
    property rights, 27, 139, 273
    to protect slaves, 36–37
    state laws on slavery, 193–94
Lay, Benjamin, 127
Leavitt, Joshua, 19
Lecesne, Louis, 170
Lecky, W. E. H., 234, 249
Leclerc, Charles Victor Emmanuel,
    167–68
Lee, Robert E., 297, 301, 305, 315,
    316–17, 320
Leeward Islands, 110
Lerner, Gerda, 38
Lévi-Strauss, Claude, 52, 187
Liberator, 158, 221, 258
Liberia, 173, 257
licenses for slave trade, 90
life expectancies, 95, 116–17
Life of Aesop, 46
limpieza de sangre, 70–72

Lincoln, Abraham, 402*n*2, 405*n*28,
    406*nn*34, 38, 408*nn*54, 55, 67
  on basis of enslavement, 191
  and Civil War, 298, 301, 302, 305,
    306–14, 317–22
  and Douglas (Stephen), 288
  on *Dred Scott* decision, 288–91
  elections, 293, 294–95
  Emancipation Proclamation, 1, 306,
    307, 314, 317, 318, 321, 406*nn*35,
    36
  Gettysburg Address, 156
  "House Divided" speech, 289, 290
  and president's constitutional au-
    thority, 26, 313, 314
  and Reconstruction, 306
  Second Inaugural Address, 266–67
  on "Slave Power" conspiracy, 262
  and Thirteenth Amendment, 321–22
  tribute paid to, 323, 410*n*76
Linnaeus, Carl, 75, 76
Lisbon, 93
literacy, 144, 188, 203, 209, 260
literature, antebellum South in, 304–5
living standards, 36, 91–92, 95–96, 313
London, England, 151
London Anti-Slavery Society, 237
London Missionary Society, 215, 218
London *Times*, 169, 231, 285, 317
Long, Edward, 74
longevity of slaves, 116
Lost Cause, 299, 303, 304
Lost Tribes of Israel, 73
Louisiana
  dependency on slaves, 197
  and expansion of slavery, 262
  land of, 271
  plantations of, 125–26
  racial intermixture in, 180
  secession of, 295
  and slave revolts, 208
  sugar industry, 185
  textile industries in, 182
Louisiana Purchase of 1803, 156, 269
Louverture, Toussaint, 167–68, 370*n*27
  capitulation of, 172
  and Spanish invasion of Saint-
    Domingue, 165, 370*n*29
  Spartacus comparisons, 47, 372*n*41

Stuart on, 252
  support for, 7
Lovejoy, Elijah P., 16
Lovell, John, 110
Lovell, Louisa Quitman, 227
Loving v. Virginia, 260
Lowell, Josephine Shaw, 302
Lumpkin, Robert, 298, 402*n*2
Lunda Empire, 100
lynching, 29, 300, 309–10

MacMullen, Ramsay, 43, 44
Madanu-bel-usur, 27, 29
Madden, Richard, 18
Madeira Islands, 84
Madison, James, 144, 154, 276
Maine, 142, 278
male captives and slaves
  castration of, 61
  and gender ratios, 61, 100, 117, 134,
    138, 200
  and premodern bondage, 33, 38
  on slave ships, 91–92, 93
Mâle revolt, 170
Mamluks of Egypt, 29
management of slaves, 45
Manet, Edouard, 57–58
Manhattan African Burial Ground, 129
Manual Labor Society, 253
Manuel I, King of Portugal, 72, 91, 94
manumission
  and American Revolution, 144–45
  in ancient Rome, 44
  in Brazil, 326
  in Greek society, 42
  laws on, 132, 154, 161, 180, 193–94,
    204
  rates of, 36, 40, 195
Marchionni, Bartolomeo, 84
maroon settlements, 133, 207
Maroon War in Jamaica, 166
Marques, João Pedro, 281
marriage of slaves
  abroad marriages, 201
  attempts to protect, 192, 203
  encouragement of, 134, 201
  interracial marriages, 95
  laws on, 36–37, 203, 260
Marshall, John, 17

Martin, J. Sella, 228–29
Martinique, 165
Maryland, 125, 131, 132, 156, 265, 309
Mason, James M., 292
Massachusetts, 126, 142, 152, 156, 265, 312
Massachusetts Anti-Slavery Society, 259, 266
master-servant laws, 233
Maugham, W. Somerset, 2
Maurice, Saint, 59, 343*n*33. *See also illustration section*
Mauritania, 330
McClellan, George B.
    inaction of, 318, 408*n*67
    and Northern Democrats, 320–21
    Peninsular Campaign, 301, 314, 315–17
    pro-slavery stance of, 310
McGillivray, Alexander, 137
McLaurin, Melton A., 202, 277
McLean, John, 287
McPherson, James M., 309, 315, 316
Meade, Richard, 15
medical care for slaves, 195
Mediterranean, 40, 81–82, *83*
Melville, Herman, 57
Menezes, José Ferreira de, 323
Mercado, Tomás de, 96
Mercer, Charles Fenton, 274–75
Mesopotamia, 38, 39
Methodists, 185, 187, 203, 251, 264
Mexico, 15, 61, 98, 142, 280, 396*n*29
Middle East, 61
The Mighty Experiment (Drescher), 245, 248
military slaves, 29
Mill, John Stuart, 238
mining, 42, 61
Mintz, Sidney W., 247
Mintz, Steven, 4
"Miracle of the Black Leg" (painting), 59, 344*n*34
miscegenation. *See also* sexual relations
    African Americans and Native Americans, 138
    in the Bible, 68
    in Caribbean and Latin America, 180
    exploitation of slaves, 201–2, 286–87
    laws on, 131–32, 260
    and racial distinctions, 3, 180
Mississippi
    dependency on slaves, 197
    and expansion of slavery, 262
    land of, 271
    secession of, 295
    slave conspiracy in, 221, 226–30
    textile industries in, 125, 182
    U.S. acquisition of, 274
Mississippi Territory, 274
Missouri
    debates on annexation of, 176, 211, 225, 276–77
    and expansion of slavery, 262
    Frémont's emancipation order in, 308, 309
Missouri Compromise, 271, 276–80
Missouri Crisis of 1819-21, 262, 271, 275, 287, 398*nn*9, 11, 399*n*21
Mitchell, Margaret, 304
Mitton, Steven, 281, 283
Molina, Luis de, 96
Monroe, James, 271, 274
Monroe Doctrine, 142
Montabert, Jacques-Nicolas Paillot de, 57
Montes, Pedro, 14, 15, 16, 19
Montesquieu, Charles de Secondat, 75
Montserrat, 112
Moore, Edith Wyatt, 227–28
Moorish Dancer (Grasser), 58
Moors, 78, 94. *See also* Islam
The Moral and Intellectual Diversity of Races (Gobineau), 189
Morgan, Edmund S., 135, 145, 177
Morgan, Philip D., 124–25, 134, 139
Mormons, 69
Morris, Gouverneur, 154
Morris, Thomas, 264
mortality
    of Amerindians, 97–98, 354*n*48
    in Brazil, 116, 117
    in Civil War, 300–301, 316
    life expectancies, 95, 116–17
    and Registry of colonial slaves, 237
    in Sierra Leone, 151
    on slave ships, 93, 235–36
    in South Carolina, 138

Morton, Samuel, 189
Moses (biblical), 31, 187
mothers in slavery, 199
Mott, Lucretia, 323
"mud-sill" class, 189
Muhammad, Ali ibn, 60
mulattoes
    and blacks, 166, 167–68
    and Constituent Assembly (French),
        162–65
    interracial marriages, 95
    laws regarding, 131
    and miscegeny, 201
    and racial distinctions, 180
    in South Carolina, 138
    as sugar farmers, 118
Murray, John (Lord Dunmore), 149–
    50, 213, 215
music, 94, 203–4
mustees, 180

Nabuco, Joaquim, 326
Napoleon, 167
Napoleonic Wars, 270
Napoleon III, 317
National Association for the Advance-
    ment of Colored People
    (NAACP), 306
National Union Convention, 321
Native Americans
    and African enslavement, 49, 73,
        98–99
    and economic determinism, 77
    enslavement of, 54, 81, 97, 126
    mortality, 97–99
    relationship between blacks and,
        137–38
    warfare of, 137
natural rights, 149, 156
"natural slaves," 33–34, 53, 56, 62, 188
navios, 86, 93
Nazis, 53, 107, 329–30
Negro Election Day, 130–31
Negroes, people classified as, 49
Negro Seaman Act, 225
neoteny, 32, 33
Nevis, 112, 115
New Amsterdam, 127, 128
New England, 1, 112, 156, 279

New England Anti-Slavery Society, 252
New Hampshire, 152
New Haven Record, 23
New Jersey
    abolition in, 153, 156
    emancipation in, 142
    prevalence of slavery in, 128, 129,
        152
    and Tallmadge Amendment, 276
New Orleans, Louisiana, 169
Newsom, Robert, 202, 203
New York
    abolition in, 153, 156
    conspiracies of 1712 and 1741, 130
    elections, 272, 294
    emancipation in, 142, 275
    prevalence of slavery in, 129, 152
    and Tallmadge Amendment, 276
    and West Indies, 112
New York City, 184, 309–10
New York Herald, 20–21, 292
New York State Anti-Slavery Society,
    48
New York Times, 4
New York Tribune, 287
Nicaragua, 175
Nicias, 42
Nietzsche, Friedrich, 32
Niger, 330
Noah (biblical), 35, 55, 64–69, 187,
        345n51. *See also* Canaan; "Curse
        of Ham"; Ham
Nobrega, Manuel da, 98
North America, 221
Northampton County (Virginia), 131
North Carolina, 136, 185, 256
Northern Peace Democrats, 315
Northern United States, 126–31. *See
    also specific states*
    abolitionism, 209–10, 255, 261
    and Civil War, 300, 302, 305
    and emancipation, 152, 186
    and fugitive slaves, 264–66
    and industrialization, 184
    and labor shortages, 182
    racism in, 257–58
    and slave revolts, 171, 206
Northup, Solomon, 198–99, 259

Northwest Ordinance of 1787, 154, 276, 398*n*6
Norton, Charles Eliot, 302–3
Norton, John Pitkin, 24
Notes on the State of Virginia (Jefferson), 74
Nott, Josiah C., 189
nouveaux libres, 166–67
Nova Scotia, 151
Nubians, 62
Nullification Crisis of 1832–33, 280

Oakes, James, 209
Occasional Discourses on the Nigger Question (Carlyle), 76
Of Human Bondage (Maugham), 2
Ogé, Vincent, 163
Oglethorpe, James, 136
Ohio, 142
Ohio Valley, 265
Oldfield, J. R., 235
old slaves, 199
Olmsted, Frederick Law, 32
oral traditions, 8, 204
Oregon, 278
Organization of American Historians, 4
original sin, 35–36, 44
origins of enslavement, *105, 106*
    biblical origins, 69
    in Rome, 46–47
    and sugar trade, 82, 84
    violence associated with, 41
    white slaves, 49
owners of slaves. *See* slaveholders

Page, Thomas Nelson, 304
Palmares maroon community, 207
Palmerston, Henry John Temple, Viscount, 317–18
papacy, 79, 94
Paquette, Robert L., 222
Paris, Texas, 29
Parkman, Francis, 302
paternalism
    of ACS leaders, 258
    in Brazil, 118
    as duty, 262
    effects of, 228–29
    and fugitive slaves, 194–95, 377*n*3

no need in modern slavery, 107
and punishment of slaves, 134
Patrocinio, José do, 323
Patterson, Orlando
    on definitions of slavery, 30–32
    on natal alienation, 94
    research of, 36–37
    on "Sambo" stereotype, 51–52
    on "social death" of captives, 38
    on sources of slaves, 39
    on warfare practices, 28
Payne, Francis, 131
peasantry, 50–51, 53, 57
Pedro II, Emperor of Brazil, 325
Pennell, Charles, 116
Pennington, James W. C., 22, 193
Pennsylvania, 112, 142, 152, 156, 265
Pennsylvania Abolition Society, 155, 333*n*1
Persians, 38, 56, 62
Peru, 1, 15, 61, 98, 149
Peterson, Thomas Virgil, 187
Pétion, Alexandre, 168, 370*n*33
Philadelphia, Pennsylvania, 171
Philistines, 65
Phillips, Wendell, 254, 255, 266, 323
Philmore (writer), 205
Philo of Alexandria, 65
Phoenicians, 56
physical appearance of slaves
    branding, 33, 38, 53
    and "Curse of Ham," 63
    depicted in art, 58–59. *See also illustration section*
    and empathy, 53
    Greeks and Romans on, 56–57
    identification of slaves, 53
    as sign of inferiority, 56–57, 79
    skin colors, 50–51, 57–58, 189
    and stereotypes, 58, 66
    ugliness, 50
Pierce, Franklin, 292
Pinckney, Charles, 275–76, 279
Pinkster, 130
piracy victims, 38, 78
Pitt, William, 235, 236
plantations and planters
    and abolitionism, 325–26
    acquisition of slave labor, 183–84
    and capitalism, 240

plantations and planters (*continued*)
  and culture of African Americans,
    199–200
  decline in, following emancipation,
    245
  efficiency of slave labor, 181
  gender ratios in, 200
  and importation of Africans, 132–33
  scope of operations, 103
  and slave revolts, 170, 210
  task system, 199
  and working conditions, 198–99
Plato, 55
Plutarch, 40
Poliakov, Léon, 71
Polk, James, 26, 272, 282
polygenesis, 189
polygyny, 100
popes, 79, 94
Portugal and Portuguese
  and Afonso I, 91
  auctions in, 94
  and Brazil, 103, 142
  and colonization, 81
  and Dutch East India Company, 111
  and Holland, 144
  importation of Africans, 53–54
  and Jews, 70, 79
  trade, 84, 87, 90
  treatment of Africans, 33
Postlethwayt, Malachy, 80
Potter, David, 303
poverty, 196
Poyas, Peter, 223
Pratt, Charles, 23
pregnant slaves, 199
premodern bondage, 27–48
Presbyterians, 187, 264
Prichard, "Gullah" Jack, 223
Prichard, James Cowles, 76
Prigg v. Pennsylvania, 265
Prince (slave), 144
prison labor, 36, 328, 329, 330
prisoners of war, 38, 44, 52, 301
property rights, 27, 139, 273
Ptolemy of Lucca, 55
Puerto Rico, 15, 97, 324, 325
punishment of slaves
  extreme forms of, 118

owner/slave relations, 196
  and paternalism, 134
  and productivity, 116
  in Roman law, 43, 44–45
  separation of families, 183
  and working conditions, 198–99
purchase of freedom, 36, 131

quadroons, 180
Quakers, 126–27, 155, 185, 234–35,
    256, 374n28
Quamina (slave), 215–16, 217
quilombos, 120
Qur'an, 57, 62

Race and Reunion (Blight), 10–11
racism
  and *Amistad* trial, 20–21
  antiblack racism, 62–63, 72
  aspects of, 31
  in Brazil, 119
  and Civil War, 309–10
  definitions of, 49, 340nn1, 2, 348n85
  and emancipation, 153
  and laws of slavery, 42
  proto-racism, 57
  and religion, 62–63
  and slavery, 53
  in United States, 192, 254–55, 256,
    257–58, 261
  and white ambition, 131
Radical Reconstructionists, 322
Ragatz, Lowell Joseph, 240, 242, 243
Raimond, Julien, 162, 163–64
Raleigh, Sir Walter, 110
Randolph, John, 274
Raphall, Morris Jacob, 66
Raymond, Daniel, 277
Raynal, Abbé, 47
Reconstruction, 300, 305, 322, 327,
    328, 411n85
red-haired Thracians, 47
religion. *See also* Christianity; Islam;
    Jews and Judaism
  and abolitionism, 126–27, 188, 264,
    357n26
  and amelioration policies, 214–15
  and conversion of slaves, 94, 106, 128

"Curse of Ham," 55, 63, 64–65, 68, 70, 73, 187
  on emancipation, 185
  and evangelism, 54–55
  and Great Awakenings, 102, 202–3, 250–51
  influence of, 77–78
  and justifications of slavery, 55, 81, 94
  missionaries, 215, 219, 220, 221
  and Nativity depictions, 59
  and origins of human race, 54
  and popes, 79
  and racism, 62
  revivalism, 144, 250–51, 262
  and sin, 55, 251, 252
  and sugar harvests, 118
Remond, Charles Lenox, 259
Remond, Sarah Parker, 259
renting slave labor, 183
Republican Party, 277, 287, 294–95, 312, 318, 320–21
resistance of slaves, 207, 210–11, 216, 222. *See also* slave revolts and conspiracies
Revolutionary War, 141, 142, 144–52, 234, 240, 364n25
Rhode Island, 126, 142, 147, 152
rice, 138
Richardson, Martha Proctor, 224
Richmond, Virginia, 297
Rigaud, André, 167
Rio Branco Law, 325
Rio de Janeiro, Brazil, 119, 324
Rives, William C., 186
Roane, Spencer, 274
Robespierre, Maximilien, 163
Rochambeau, Jean-Baptiste-Donatien de Vimeur, comte de, 168
Rogers, Nathaniel P., 21
Roman law, 30, 42–47
Rome, 37, 44, 56, 79
Rotter, Gernot, 62
Royal African Company, 88–89
Rugemer, Edward Bartlett, 221
Ruiz, José, 14, 15, 16, 19, 23
rum, 87
runaway slaves. *See* fugitive slaves
Rush, Benjamin, 145

Russell, John, 317
Russia, 50, 325
Russwurm, John B., 259, 395n20

"Sacred Circle," 188
Saffin, John, 186
Saint Bartholomew Massacre of 1572, 96
Saint-Domingue, 112, 120, 121, 135, 180, 324. *See also* Haitian Revolution (1791-1804)
Saint Lucia, 165
Saint Vincent, 166
sambos, 180
Sambo stereotype, 33, 51–52, 207
Sandoval, Fray Prudencio de, 72
Santo Domingo, 109, 110, 112, 169, 223
São Jorge da Mina (Elmina), 89
São Paulo, 326, 327
São Tomé, 84, 86, 90
Sarah (biblical), 65
Saturnalia, 46
Sauter, Charles, 228
Schivelbusch, Wolfgang, 303
Schorsch, Jonathan, 70
Schwartz, Stuart B., 118
Scotch-Irish indentured servants, 115
Scott, Sir Walter, 303
Second Battle of Bull Run, 315
Second Confiscation Act, 313–14
Second Seminole War in Florida, 221, 385n53
segregation, 145, 187
self-purchase of slaves, 36, 131, 180, 223
self-respect of slaves, 63, 195, 203, 253
The Selling of Joseph (Sewall), 127
Seneca, 178–79
Senegambia, 100–101
Sepúlveda, Juan Ginés, 55
settlement of Americas, 2
Seven Years' War (1756-1763), 141
Sewall, Samuel, 127
Seward, William H., 292, 293, 302, 308, 313, 314, 407n41, 408n68
Sewell, Samuel, 186
sexual relations, 386n61, 387n77. *See also* miscegenation
  and Bussa Rebellion, 213
  and ethnicity, 3, 56–57, 138

sexual relations (*continued*)
  exploitation of slaves, 3, 93, 201–2, 255, 287
  gender ratios, 117
  homosexuality, 65
  and premodern bondage, 37, 46
  and slave revolts, 217, 229–30
  on slave ships, 91–92, 93
  stereotypes regarding, 63, 76, 305, 345*n*46
Seymour, Horatio, 317
Shackleton, Edward, 63
Sharp, Granville, 151, 234, 235, 244, 281, 323
Sharpe, Samuel "Daddy," 219, 221
Shaw, Robert Gould, 302
Shem (biblical), 187
Sherman, William Tecumseh, 321
Shields, Gabriel B., 227
ships, slave, 91–93, 100, 133, 235–36
Sicily, 44
Sickles, Daniel, 305
Sierra Leone, 12, 100, 101, 173
silver, 87
Sinha, Manisha, 285
skin color. *See* physical appearance of slaves
slave codes, 193–94
slaveholders
  blacks as slaveholders, 180–81, 373*n*17
  paternalism, 107, 118, 134, 194–95, 228, 258, 262
  and *Prigg v. Pennsylvania*, 265
  relationships between owners and slaves, 46, 55, 194–97, 226–27, 304
  and slave codes, 193–94
  statistics on slaves held, 197–98, 200
Slave Power, 266, 286, 289, 308
slave revolts and conspiracies, 205–30.
  See also specific events
  and abolitionism, 160–61, 238
  and black informants, 221–22
  danger of, 47, 122, 206, 220–21
  fear of, 93, 149
  and *gens de couleur*, 166
  historical sympathy for, 205–6
  and manumission, 161
  motivations for, 144
  and Native Americans, 137

in North America, 120, 197, 207
  prevalence of, 123
  and privileged slaves, 133
  and revolutionary ideology, 149–50
  violence associated with, 217, 220, 224, 229–30
Slavery and Social Death (Patterson), 30, 342*n*12
Smedes, Susan Dabney, 304
Smith, Adam, 181, 232, 240, 329
Smith, Gerrit, 191, 262, 265, 291
Smith, Henry, 29, 31, 327
Smith, James McCune, 259
Smith, John, 215, 216, 217, 218, 220, 384*n*45
Social Darwinism, 73
"social death," 38
socialization, 95
Société des Amis des Noirs, 161, 162–63, 221
Société des Colons Américains, 162
Society for Effecting the Abolition of the Slave Trade (SEAST), 234–35
Society for the Mitigation and Gradual Abolition of Slavery, 237
Sociology for the South (Fitzhugh), 191, 307
Solon, 40
Somerset case (1772), 20, 234, 269, 388*n*10
Sonthonax, Léger-Felicité, 165
sources of African slaves, 100–101, *101*
South America, 142. *See also specific countries*
South Carolina
  and abolition, 164
  agriculture in, 138, 182
  conservative culture in, 135–36
  cultural autonomy in, 139
  dependency on slaves, 81, 86, 197
  fugitive slaves, 150
  importation of Africans, 140, 154, 156, 160, 273, 378*n*19
  secession of, 262
  slave troops in, 148, 210
  textile industries in, 125
  and Vesey conspiracy, 221, 222–26
Southeast Asia, 87
Southern United States. *See also specific states*
  and abolitionism, 185, 280–81

and agriculture, 106–7, 181
antebellum South, nostalgia for, 304
and Civil War, 308, 309
and Confederate States of America, 297–98, 300
defenders of slavery, 186–92
equality in, 272
and fugitive slaves, 264
Hammond on, 190
importation of Africans, 152, 273
and labor shortages, 182
prevalence of slavery in, 197–98
and racial distinctions, 180
racism in, 192
Reconstruction, 300, 305, 322, 327, 328 (*see also* Civil War, American)
and Roman slave law, 43
secession of, 192, 264, 294–95, 308
and slave-driven economy, 178, 184
and slave revolts, 221
slave trade in, *182*, 183–84
and U.S. Constitution, 273
Spain and Spanish
and abolitionism, 325
and *Amistad* trial, 17–18, 20, 22, 26
and chattel slavery, 33, 70
and colonization, 81, 324
and Cuba, 14
and Dutch East India Company, 111
and emancipation, 238
importation of Africans, 53–54
and Jews, 79
and Native Americans, 97, 98
and Puerto Rico, 14
and Revolutionary War, 141, 142
and sugar production, 109, 110
Transcontinental Treaty of 1819, 271
and Treaty of Tordesillas, 90
and "virgin soil pandemic," 97–98
Spartacus, 5, 47, 51
Spence, Thomas, 171
Spiritans (French Catholic missionaries), 2
Spratt, Leonidas, 285–86
Stamp Act crisis of 1765, 146
Stampp, Kenneth, 196
Stanton, Henry R., 253

state laws on slavery, 193–94
status among slaves, 196
St. Christopher, 107, 111–12, 115
Steinfeld, Robert J., 247
Stephen, James, 211, 213, 236
stereotypes of slaves
of black inferiority, 259
ethnicity, 47
in Iberian societies, 73
and physical appearance, 58, 66
Sambo stereotype, 33, 51–52, 207
of savagery, 172
and trade, from Muslims to Christians, 63–64
of *Zanj*, 63
St. Eustace (colony), 111
Stevens, Thaddeus, 322
Stone, Lucy, 266
Stono Rebellion, 139–40
Story, Joseph, 22, 265
Stowe, Harriet Beecher, 251, 266, 323
Strong, George Templeton, 312
Stuart, Charles, 252, 254, 255
Stuart, Jeb, 318
Stuyvesant, Peter, 127
St. Vincent, 211
Sudan, 63, 330
sugar
and African slave trade, 82, *83*, 84
In Barbados, 114
boycott of slave-grown, 236
Brazilian exports, 120, 356n6
and British consumption, 112, 115–16
and consumerism, 247
Cuba's exports, 13
and emancipation, 232
harvests, 118
and Madeira Islands, 84
and merchant-bankers, 87
and plantation system, *85*, 103, 104
production and labor, 107–11
from Saint-Domingue, 158
and slave-driven economy, 95
and Texas, 271
and white slave trade, 49, 81–82
Sumeria, 32–33, 37, 52
Sumner, Charles, 26, 313, 322, 323
Suriname, 114, 207

Sweet, James H., 64, 73
Sweetness and Power (Mintz), 247
Syrians, 56

Tallmadge, James, Jr., 275
Tallmadge Amendment, 276–77
Taney, Roger B., 26, 313
tangomãos, 90
Tappan, Arthur, 16
Tappan, Lewis, 16, 19, 21, 22
task system, 199
tattoos, 37
Teçora, 13, 25
temperance movement, 252
tenant farmers (*lavradores de cana*), 117–
    18, 128
Tennessee, 141, 185, 197, 256, 262,
    294
tetanus, 117
Texas
    annexation of, 175, 271, 282, 396*n*29
    and expansion of slavery, 125, 182,
        262, 396*n*29
    secession of, 295
textiles, 125, 182, 184. *See also* cotton
Thirteenth Amendment, 30, 321–22
Thompson, E. P., 239–40
Thompson, George, 282
Thompson, James, 78
Thompson, Smith, 19
Thoreau, Henry David, 266
Thornton, John, 88, 89, 91
Thracians, 47
"three-fifths" clause in the Constitu-
    tion, 17, 273, 276, 278
tobacco, 87, 110, 114, 125, 133
Torah, 70
Torquemada, Fray Tomás de, 71
trans-Appalachian territory, 154
Transcontinental Treaty of 1819, 271
Treaty of Tordesillas, 90
Trinidad, 160, 231–32, 237, 242, 243
Trollope, Frances, 177
Trumbull, Lyman, 312
Truth, Sojourner, 128, 259, 266, 319
Tucker, Thomas, 155
Tumult and Silence at Second Creek (Jor-
    dan), 226
Tupinamba, 28–29, 37

Turks, 37, 82
Turnbull, Robert J., 221, 226, 281
Turner, Nat, 208–9, 381*nn*12, 14, 15, 17
    context of insurrection, 221
    Douglass on, 206
    governmental remedies available to,
        220
    influence of, 186, 259
    leadership of, 210
    popular fear of, 205
Tuscarora War of 1711-12, 137
Tyler, John, 272, 282

ugliness, 50
Ulpian, 45
"ultimate slaves," 29
Underground Railroad, 258, 259, 264–
    65, 269, 283
United States. *See also* Northern United
    States; Southern United States;
    specific states
    abolitionism, 160–61, 250–67
    American Revolution, 141, 142,
        144–52, 234, 240
    and Britain, 272, 282–86, 295–96
    economic development, 241
    and emancipation, 238, 261–62
    expansionism of, 271, 318–19
    foreign policy, 268
    liberty vs. slavery contradiction,
        175–76
    life expectancies in, 117
    prevalence of slavery in, 143
    racism in, 254–55, 256, 261
    slave-trade policies, 142
Upshur, Abel P., 283, 284
USS *Grampus*, 18
U.S. Supreme Court, 265. *See also spe-
    cific cases, including Amistad*

vacations for slaves, 195
Valencians, 94
Van Buren, Martin, 17–18, 19, 20, 21,
    23, 279
Vastey, Pompée Valentin, 174
Venezuela, 15, 143, 149
Venice, 81
Vermont, 152

Vesey, Denmark
 controversy surrounding, 222–23,
  371*n*38, 385*n*55, 386*n*60, 400*n*33
 influence of Haitian Revolution on,
  170–71
 insurrection of 1822, 222–26
 and King (Rufus), 279
 leadership of, 210
 modern awareness of, 206, 208
 motivations for rebellion, 211
 symbolic status of, 221
Vesey, Joseph, 223
violence. *See also* punishment of slaves
 and abolitionism, 266
 antiblack mob violence, 300
 in slave revolts and conspiracies,
  217, 220, 224, 229–30
Virginia
 and abolition, 156
 and arming of slaves, 148
 and Civil War, 297–98, 301
 elections, 294
 and manumission, 132, 154
 and miscegenation, 131–32
 and Nat Turner's revolt of 1831,
  186
 paternalism in, 134
 prevalence of slavery in, 125, 135,
  197
 and racial demography, 274
 racism in, 135, 204
 secession of, 308
 and slave revolts, 161, 170, 208–10,
  221, 256
"virgin soil pandemic," 97
Voltaire, 75
voting rights, 328
vulnerability of slaves, 37

Waddell, Hope, 218–19
wage-slavery, 191
Wakefield, Edward Gibbon, 232
Walker, David, 156, 171, 209, 258
Walzer, Michael, 36
Ward, Samuel Ringgold, 265
War Democrats, 321
warfare. *See also specific wars, including*
  Civil War
 and arming of slaves, 35, 94, 143,
  147–50, 210, 313–14, 320, 326

 and justifications of slavery, 65
 and premodern bondage, 28
 prisoners of war, 38, 44, 52, 301
War of 1812, 270
Washington, George, 147, 154, 179,
  364*nn*25, 28
Washington, Madison, 206, 269
Watkins, William, 171
Watson, Alan, 42, 43, 44
The Wealth of Nations (Smith), 181
Webster, Daniel, 269
Wedderburn, Robert, 171
Weld, Theodore Dwight, 252–53, 255,
  263, 394*nn*6, 8, 9
Welles, Gideon, 313
Welser family, 87
West Africans
 and African enslavement, 12–13, 89,
  244
 and Brazil, 110
 gender ratios in, 100
 as laborers, 99
West Central Africa, 101
West Indies
 and abolitionism, 214, 236, 281
 apprenticeship system, 15, 238
 defenders of slavery, 187
 and emancipation, 269
 and free blacks, 162, 165–66
 planters in, 104, 245
 productivity of slave labor, 143
 and Registration of colonial slaves,
  211–12
 and slave revolts, 211–21
 sugar industry, 109, 114, 232
 trade, 2, 112, 241
West Virginia, 309
Wheatley, Phillis, 69
Whig Party, 238–39, 279–80, 287
Whipple, William, 144
White Over Black (Jordan), 73
whites, poor, 196
white servants and laborers, 131, 132–
  33, 177, 233
white slaves, 54, 62, 81–82
Whitman, Walt, 302
Wightman, Joseph, 312
Wilberforce, William, 382*n*25
 abolitionism of, 216
 influence of, 281, 323

Wilberforce, William (*continued*)
 and Registry of colonial slaves, 211–12, 213, 237, 390*n*20
 and slave-trade resolutions, 235, 236
Williams, Eric, 240–41, 242, 243, 247–48
Williamson, Sir Adam, 165, 166
Wills, Garry, 306
Wilson, Woodrow, 305–6
wind systems of the Atlantic, 86
Winthrop, John, 157
witchcraft, 96
Wood, Peter H., 137
Woolman, John, 126, 198
Wordsworth, William, 172
working conditions, 42, 198–99
World's Anti-Slavery Convention in London, 282

WPA Federal Writers' Project, 227–28
Wright, Theodore S., 48, 58

xenophobia, 50, 58
Xenophon, 33

Yemasee War of 1715, 137
Yerushalmi, Yosef Hayim, 71
Yonton, 69
Young, Brigham, 69

Zanj, 60, 62, 63
Zaragoza, Josto, 325
Zong case (1781), 234
Zuazo, Licenciado, 98
Zurara, Gomes Eannes de, 70, 95